CONSTITUTIONAL LAW *in the* POLITICAL PROCESS

CONSTITUTIONAL LAW *in the* POLITICAL PROCESS

Edited by

John R. Schmidhauser

STATE UNIVERSITY OF IOWA

RAND McNALLY & COMPANY/Chicago

RAND M^CNALLY POLITICAL SCIENCE SERIES

Morton Grodzins, *Advisory Editor*

GOLDWIN,
Six Papers on United States Military Policy

GOLEMBIEWSKI,
Behavior and Organization; O & M and the Small Group

LONG,
The Polity

MILBRATH,
The Washington Lobbyists

SCHMIDHAUSER,
Constitutional Law in the Political Process

STRAUSS AND CROPSEY,
A History of Political Thought

ULMER,
Introductory Readings in Political Behavior

WILLIAMS AND PRESS,
Democracy in Urban America: Readings on Government and Politics

Preface

Constitutional Law and the Political Process is designed to combine the best features of the traditional casebook with the desirable features of the behavioral approach. Consequently, this textbook consists of selections from appropriate articles and essays, as well as from judicial decisions, legislative debates, and election campaign documents. The unifying theme is the exploration of the role of the federal Supreme Court in the American political process. In part such exploration necessarily consists of the utilization of the so-called "standard" leading cases, such as *Marbury* v. *Madison*. However, the introductory essays are designed to provide an appropriate setting for such cases. A major effort is made to distinguish clearly judicial from legislative or executive action (or inaction) in broad policymaking areas. Where possible the issues chosen for analysis are those that have created the most intense contemporary social and political antagonisms: labor-management relations, rural versus urban political ascendancy, race relations, and problems relating to the intellectual freedoms. The emphasis upon social and political conflict is employed to demonstrate the diversity of institutional and individual responses which are manifest in the judicial process.

The shift in emphasis in the textbook is not limited to substance but extends to questions of method as well. Without eschewing the very useful and necessary techniques of historical analysis and biographical interpretation that have influenced teaching and writing in constitutional law in the past three decades, the selections and essays are also designed to apply, where appropriate, the methods and findings of the behavioral sciences.

The intellectual debts incurred in the preparation of this work are many. Interest in the broad problems inherent in a process-oriented text was stimulated during my graduate student days at the University of Virginia. Of great benefit were two opportunities to consider problems of teaching and research in the company of scholars from diverse fields. The first of these was a Research Institute on the Judicial Process sponsored by the Social Science Research Council in 1958. The second was the program for research in law and the behavioral sciences conducted at the Law School of the University of Chicago (1959–1960). Carl Auerbach and William Beaney, co-directors of the Institute on the Judicial Process, were especially helpful. Michigan Supreme Court Justice Talbot Smith demonstrated in splendid fashion the highest qualities of the appellate judge during his visit to the Institute. At Chicago, Professors Hans Zeisel, Rita James, and Duncan MacRae were especially helpful with respect to the problems attending the application of behavioral techniques to analysis of the judicial process.

I also owe a great personal debt to Mr. Francis Winter and Mr. Dick Wells for invaluable assistance in gathering relevant materials and aiding in the editorial work entailed. Mrs. Maurine Wells rendered expert typing assistance of the highest order. Despite such excellent assistance, both editorial and substantive, errors may well remain. For these I am solely responsible.

John R. Schmidhauser

April, 1962
State University of Iowa
Iowa City, Iowa

Contents

3 Federal Judicial Authority: Federalism, Separation of Powers

4 The Supreme Court in the Hierarchy of American Courts

5 Traditions and Procedures of Judicial Institutions

6 The Selection of
Federal Judges

7 *The Crucial Role of the Bar*

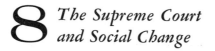

8 The Supreme Court and Social Change

9 The Roots of Judicial Behavior

10 Conclusion

CONSTITUTIONAL LAW *in the* POLITICAL PROCESS

1 Democratic Theory and the Administration of Justice

A. THE CITIZEN'S PERSPECTIVE: JUSTICE IN A REPRESENTATIVE DEMOCRACY

[Constitutional law studied in its political context comprises a tapestry of interwoven factors of infinite complexity. Lawyers, judges, lesser court officials, legislators, state and federal executives, to mention a few of the obvious actors, all play meaningful roles in its creation as *individuals*. The governmental bodies on which they serve or the groups of which they are members fulfill *institutional* roles of considerable importance.

In assessing the significance of these factors, it is of crucial importance to consider first the variety of standards by which individual or institutional performance in the political process may be evaluated. Is law primarily concerned with the achievement of ethical goals or is it essentially a manifestation of power relationships within American society? American political and legal thought has provided a number of answers to this question, some of them sharply contradictory.

Thus Bowen argues that "the fundamental security of all peoples lies, not in the *justice,* but in the *certainty,* of their laws."[1] Conversely, Edmond Cahn, in the article partially reproduced below, supports a different conception of law, one which stresses normative considerations. Cahn's essay on the relationship of democratic political theory to the administration of justice provides perspective for subsequent evaluation of the instrumentalities of justice in America.]

[1] William A. Bowen, "Dissenting Opinions," *Green Bag,* XVII (1905), 690.

1

1. Consumers of Injustice*

There was an incident in 1781 that symbolized the beginning of a new age for government and law. The Revolutionary War had been going on since 1775, and the final battle was fought at Yorktown on the coast of Virginia during the month of October, 1781. The British army, sent to subdue the colonists, found itself hopelessly wedged between a formidable French fleet on one side and the American forces under General Washington on the other. The British commander decided that capitulation was inevitable, and General Washington granted him generous and honorable terms. The last great body of imperial troops paraded on the Yorktown plain in surrender to a threadbare and despised collection of amateur soldiers, who had resolved to pursue their national destiny under a free, republican government. As the brilliant ranks of redcoated soldiers filed across the plateau, the British bandmaster signaled to his band and they began playing a popular English tune of the time. It was to this tune that the defeated army marched stiffly away from the scene of battle. Though no one knows even now whether the bandmaster selected the tune purposely or by chance, the name of the tune furnished an inspired commentary. It was "The World Turned Upside Down."

I. THE CONSUMER PERSPECTIVE

Ever since that time philosophers have been attempting either to ignore or to build upon the historic fact which the British band acknowledged so candidly. Some have perceived quite clearly, others have refused to perceive, that the world of political and legal relations had been turned upside down and the old systems and perspectives would never be adequate again. Henceforth, though a philosopher looking at the legal world would see all the established and familiar elements which his predecessors had been describing since ancient times, everything could look different to him, for he could see all the concepts and phenomena of the institution in a radically new perspective. Everything had turned 180 degrees. What had once looked trivial now became important, and what had previously dominated the stage shifted now to the deep background.

The new factor is the power and the responsibility of the citizen entitled to a free vote in a representative democracy. As the right to vote has expanded, group by group and class by class, it has revolutionized the functions of law in the democratic countries. In one form or another the scene at Yorktown has been reenacted again and again in other lands and on other shores all over the world, and we may safely predict that there will be other Yorktown surrenders until there is no further occasion for them. In the emancipated countries (including, of course, Britain itself, which was emancipated by Yorktown only slightly less than America), the right to vote spread slowly and tediously as parliaments gradually eroded the old barriers of religion, property, race, and sex. Though the process is incomplete, we know that

*Edmond Cahn, "The Consumers of Injustice," *Social Research*, XXVI (Summer, 1959), 175–94. [Footnotes omitted.] Reproduced with permission of the author and the publisher. Copyright © 1959 by *Social Research*.

every impulse and current in human affairs operates to favor it. More and more, men realize that there is no hope of genuine enfranchisement unless they have the franchise.

What then is this new perspective that is based on the vantagepoint of the voting citizen, and how does it differ from the old, pre-democratic perspective? The new perspective is the perspective of the democratic citizen in the role of consumer of the law. The old perspective, developed while observing an empire, a kingdom, a landed aristocracy, or an oligarchy, was essentially a ruler's or at best an official's perspective; what democratic legal theory has been trying to attain since 1781 is a consumer's perspective.

How does a person become a consumer of the law? The most obvious way consists in being safeguarded and regulated from day to day by official rules or becoming involved directly with the legal mechanism—for example, being charged with a crime or engaging in a law suit. A second way, which representative government makes available to its citizens, is to influence the shape and form of law, as by voting, by advocating reforms, by asserting group interests. Then there is the third way, which is perhaps the most characteristically democratic. It is the way of assuming and shouldering responsibility for those acts that our representatives do in our name and by force of our authority, the evil acts as well as the good, the oppressive and unjust and the foolish, too.

This is the way that is new. The philosophy that does not reckon with it is talking a pre-democratic language and addressing us in terms that are fit for powdered wigs and knee breeches. To cope with the problem of our democratic era we need to reassess all the familiar, accepted doctrines. We need to ascertain how suitable they are for the specific, homely experiences of individual human beings. This alone is the genuinely democratic perspective. And when we do adopt it and do concern ourselves with the individual human being as consumer of the law, what will we think about the traditional notions of law and justice? How adequate are they for the new age of representative government?

Let me put a concrete instance. Not long ago a couple of masked bandits entered a store in one of our largest cities, pointed their guns at the woman who owned the store, and demanded the contents of the cash register. It happened that a policeman was visiting her at the time. When the bandits saw the policeman, they shot and killed him, took the money and disappeared. Incensed by the murder of one of their comrades, the police rounded up a number of unemployed young men of the neighborhood. The woman identified two of them as the burglars. Although they protested their innocence and offered credible evidence that they were elsewhere at the time of the crime, the district attorney prosecuted them zealously, the jury believed the woman's testimony, and on their conviction for the robbery and killing, the judge sentenced them to ninety-nine years in the penitentiary.

One of the young men, whom I shall call only by his first name, Joe, had come from Poland to America as a baby in the arms of his mother, Tillie. After Joe's conviction was affirmed on appeal and all hope of legal redress had been abandoned, it was Tillie, a simple scrubwoman, who caused the truth to come to light. She posted a newspaper advertisement offering a reward of 5,000 dollars which represented eleven years of savings from scrubbing floors. The advertisement intrigued newspaper reporters, who began investigating and soon discovered that the entire prosecution had been baseless.

The prosecution's key witness, the woman who owned the store, had originally refused to identify the two defendants. She had changed her testimony and identified them only because the police, knowing that she had been selling liquor illegally, had threatened to send her to jail if she did not lie as they demanded. But the conspiracy was not confined to the police; at its apex stood the district attorney. Why had he been so eager for a conviction and so ruthless in securing one? Because, at the time of the crime, a great international exposition was about to open in the city and visitors and customers had to be reassured that the prosecutor and police were efficient and that the streets of the city were entirely safe.

After these facts were disclosed in the newspaper, public clamor brought it about that the two young men were pardoned and released. By then, of course, the exposition was long since over, and the district attorney had been honored at many community meetings and lawyers' banquets, had received the usual certificates, tributes, resolutions, and diplomas, had eaten and digested his meals, smoked and enjoyed his cigars, and delivered solemn speeches at his church.

II. THE NEW DEMOCRATIC INVOLVEMENT

What shall we say is new about this case in terms of the theory of justice? Surely men have been imprisoned, tortured, and executed for crimes they did not commit as far back as we can trace the history of law to the very dawn of politically organized society. In innumerable instances where a crime was actually committed, the wrong person has been punished; in innumerable other instances, a person has been punished though no crime at all was committed and the judicial authorities were either deceived or chose to be deceived in upholding a baseless accusation. Here is the testimony of Michel de Montaigne, who was an experienced lawyer and magistrate as well as a very great essayist:

> *How many innocent people we have known to be punished, I mean without the fault of the judges; and how many are there that we have not known of! This happened in my time: Certain men are condemned to death for murder; the sentence, if not pronounced, is at least decided and fixed. At that point the judges are informed, by the officers of an inferior court near by, that they hold several men in custody who openly confess to that murder, and are able to throw a light on the whole business that admits of no doubt. And yet they deliberate whether they shall interrupt and defer the execution of the sentence passed upon the first accused. They consider the novelty of the case, and its consequence for suspending judgments; that the sentence is juridically passed, and the judges have no reason to repent of it. To sum up, those poor devils are sacrificed to the forms of justice.*
>
> . . . .
>
> *How many condemnations I have witnessed more criminal than the crime!*

The disaster befell Joe and his mother Tillie because it was convenient for the city and its merchants that someone, almost anyone, be found, identified, and convicted. We must concede that most of the pattern is very old, older than the Bible. It is older that the death that came to Uriah the Hittite because a king desired to possess Uriah's wife, or the death that came to Naboth because another king desired to possess Naboth's vineyard, and there is no comforting reason to assert that any city or state is today immune from incidents of the kind.

Certainly, there was little novelty in Joe's position. In all probability, no one—not even the district attorney—hated Joe personally, at least at the start. True, Joe's catastrophe did have some special aspects, which he may have considered rather important. It happened that at the time when Joe was accused of the crime his wife was expecting a child, which was born during the course of the prosecution. After Joe had been convicted and the conviction affirmed by the highest court, and after a long period had passed during which he remained in the penitentiary, he and his wife had agreed that she should divorce him and marry a friend of theirs, so that the child might have a normal home and family. All this was carried out before Tillie had saved enough money to offer a reward. But though Joe may have attached special importance to the circumstances, it is improbable that they were in any sense unusual in the annals of legal systems.

Who will contend that there was anything novel about Tillie's behavior? Mothers have always defended their sons, on every continent in every age, and if the case is exceptional at all, it must be because Joe happened to be as innocent as Tillie believed him. In all probability, all she needed was his unsupported assertion that he was innocent. She could not have been influenced by mountains of evidence to the contrary. Moreover, being completely unacquainted with the shibboleths and slogans of popular psychology, she did not even have to fear that she was yielding to an Oedipus complex.

As all the factors in Joe's or Tillie's predicament were old and familiar, so are most of the factors in our own. It has always been possible for the members of a society to project themselves imaginatively—as we do now—into the place of a victim of legal oppression and share the impact of his experience. This capacity to identify ourselves with him has great survival value for all concerned. Our personal impulse for self-preservation becomes active the moment we realize that what happened to him might readily happen to us if we were caught in the toils of a similar mischance.

In some instances there is also a higher, more unselfish level that our identification may reach. On this level we become eager to save Joe not because of any collateral or contingent threat to our own safety but because any harm to Joe, as a specimen of the *genus homo* inflicts immediate harm on all mankind, and as our larger self encompasses Joe, his injury automatically becomes ours. On this level we are not so much preoccupied with the possibility that we may some day stand in the prisoner's dock. We are more preoccupied with the fact that we already stand there—in Joe's person.

Yet, all these things were true before 1781, and were known to the wise men of ancient times. The new factor is quite different. It is not that we find ourselves identified with either Joe or Tillie. It is that, progressively since the beginning of the modern period, we citizens find ourselves identified with the *district attorney*. This is the new factor. Representative government has implicated us. We are participants—accomplices, if you will—in the deeds that are done in our name and by our authority. We are the principals whom the district attorney represents as agent, and though no one contends that we are accountable as moral sureties for anything and everything he may do, we feel somehow and to some degree linked and tied to the consequences of his behavior. Without intending anything of the sort, we have wandered into the circle of responsibility. As human beings, it has always been possible to connect ourselves with the victim of wrong; as citizens, the new, democratic experience is that we find ourselves unexpectedly connected with the inflicter of wrong. What can this experience do but tighten and intensify our involvement in Joe's mistreatment at the hands of the law?

Though this new burden has become a feature of our citizenship, there is sadly little in the traditional theories of justice to assist in coping with it. The reason is all too evident. Like general philosophy, the philosophy of law had brilliant beginnings in ancient Greece. Aristotle clearly intimated that he sensed some of the significance of cases like Joe's. Even he did not go beyond the threshold of the problem, perhaps because he was primarily concerned with a pattern of distributive, hence political justice, perhaps because the ancients were unacquainted with our notions of representative government, or perhaps because he could not quite throw off the dream of an all-wise, benevolent despot. Be that as it may, the curtain of history fell immediately on the Athenian democratic experiment, and when in the course of time it rose again the new scene would be composed in the Latin language and would be played in the vicinity of the Roman forum. And while general philosophy may have remained more or less true to its Hellenic sources, the philosophy of government and law has for two thousand years carried the marks and reflected the values of the Roman empire. It has remained a view of law from the perspective of the emperor, or prince, or ruler, sometimes an ecclesiastical ruler but a ruler nonetheless. This is the perspective that has continued to dominate the philosophy of law even in modern England and America, though Jeremy Bentham, John Stuart Mill, Louis D. Brandeis, Benjamin N. Cardozo, and Jerome Frank attempted in divers ways to revise and democratize it.

What support or understanding can the traditions of legal philosophy offer to either Joe or Tillie, or for that matter to us in our modern democratic predicament? If we consult the principal currents of natural-law theory, whether derived from Thomas Aquinas on the one hand or John Locke on the other, we find no more than the political systems of their times would have led us to expect; that is, they assume that their utmost task is to declare, on some ground or other, at what final point and in what extreme circumstances the people of a country may be justified in disregarding a royal statute or in opposing and dethroning their prince. In the various traditions there are philosophic formulas for decapitating a statute, and other philosophic formulas for decapitating a monarch, but there are no formulas to meet the needs of Joe's case, where no one questioned the propriety or justness of the criminal statute. Joe would not think of overthrowing the government; for that matter, he would not even attempt to nullify the laws against holdups and murders. Approving completely of these laws, he desired only to be acquitted of violating them.

What John Locke said in the seventeenth century about the inalienable rights of the citizenry makes good doctrine for revolutionary purposes, and it may be needed on future occasions in one country or another. The difficulty is not its falseness but its inadequacy. It is something like the constitution of the Russian empire under the Romanovs, which was defined as consisting of "despotism tempered by assassination." In an ongoing democracy, solutions are not so simple, and the central problems of justice cannot be removed by assassinating or overthrowing the sovereign. There are times when they can be solved by assassinating or repealing a particular statute, such as one providing for racial segregation. Nevertheless, in the overwhelming majority of cases everything of human import depends on how the general, abstract rules are adapted and applied to the circumstances of the specific transaction. This is philosophy's greatest challenge in a modern democratic society. . . .

III. TRUSTING THE AVERAGES

The ugliest sign of our thralldom to the old outlook is that it tends to desensitize men of fine intellect and good will. Somehow they learn not to notice what happens to people like Joe, and even to suppress, though they cannot entirely forget, their own inevitable involvement. As it was customary for an emperor, king, or despot to think of the people in large quantitative terms, as raw material for programs or convenient fodder for cannon, a view of law conceived in the old imperial perspective will almost inevitably adopt the same wholesale approach. Fancying himself a ruler of the destinies of men, or perhaps a species of pagan god, the old-style philosopher assumed a post of lofty remoteness where he could look down on the scurryings of the populace as one might watch a swarm of interesting but not very important insects. If curiosity happened to draw him closer to the scene, they might appear somewhat larger to his eye and then, instead of assimilating them to a beehive or an anthill, he might call them "the herd." . . .

Once we examine law and government from the consumer perspective, we are less likely to be beguiled by averages. If one-half of the statutes passed at a legislative session are too lavish and extravagant with the people's money, and the other half too scant and niggardly, it is not probable that an intelligent electorate will be satisfied just because the averages come out well. If a foreign office is too aggressive and bellicose in certain affairs, can it gain public confidence by being too backward and diffident in others? And if an innocent man named Joe is wrongfully convicted of a crime, who will have the impudence to solace him by pointing out how many guilty men escape altogether from punishment? In the anthropocentric view, the quality of government and law is to be tested and approved or found wanting, case by case. While the particular case may involve a whole nation, a class or group within the nation, or a single individual, it is by what they do here—in this case— that the legislators, executives, or judges must vindicate themselves. In matters of political and administrative discretion it is reasonable to evaluate the whole record and set failures off against successes; but in a matter like Joe's, any such policy of indulgence is impossible, for there can be only one outcome—success or failure, right or wrong—in which we, the citizens, have been implicated.

Somehow the old imperial perspective still continues to sway men's thinking. Let us take an example that is directly pertinent to Joe's unjust conviction: the general problem of "police lawlessness" in the United States. Whenever popular protests are raised against police lawlessness or whenever the Supreme Court endeavors to require lawful methods of the police, some very conscientious lawyers will protest that efficiency in punishing crime is the more important consideration and that the "third degree" and like horrors are not used frequently—or, at least, are not exposed frequently. Here is a typical rationalization in a recent book: "The dangers of encouraging police lawlessness are not to be minimized; but surely there is a good deal of hyperbole, if not nonsense, in the current judicial apprehension. It leaves out of account the question of the scale of police lawlessness. The danger to civil liberties is not great so long as the misconduct of the police is no more than occasional." . . .

V. THE PUBLIC SENSE OF INJUSTICE

When do men experience the "sense of injustice"? Typically, when officials violate or threaten to violate their demands for equality, for recognition of desert, for respect of human dignity, for conscientious adjudication, for the confinement of government to its proper functions, and for the fulfillment of the common expectations of the society. These are the circumstances that arouse the sense of injustice and summon it into operation. For example, whenever officials misuse their power, or oppress the innocent and unoffending, they provoke our sense of injustice.

When we see or hear or read about this sort of conduct we feel that sympathetic reaction of outrage, resentment, and anger and those affections of the viscera and adrenal secretions that prepare human beings to resist attack, for our physiology has equipped us to regard an act of injustice to another as a personal aggression against ourselves. Empathy or imaginative interchange projects us into the place of the one who is wronged, not merely to pity or compassionate him but to resist and defend. The sense of injustice transmutes the wrong into an act of assault, and prepares our psychic organs for measures of self-defense.

This is the way justice can acquire a public meaning. Through mutual communication and discussion the men who live in a particular ethos may perceive the same threat and experience the same bodily reactions. The fact that they are roused individually and jointly gives us sufficient warrant to speak of "justice" without utter relativism or subjectivism or solipsism. Anyone who desires empirical proof can observe and verify this interchangeability for himself. It is real and demonstrable. It is also indispensable to the preservation of society. If man did not have the capacity to recognize oppression of another as a species of attack on himself he would be unprepared—in the glandular sense—for survival as a political being. In short, the human animal as we know him is equipped and predisposed to fight injustice.

This predisposition, like other natural capacities, being designed to end in action, is finite and limited. Each of us is bound by the perspective predicament to his own brief time and narrow place, and though the sense of injustice gives him a lengthening tether to enable him to wander some distance away from self and its immediate setting, he does remain tethered. Since he lives a finite existence in a finite world, his survival does not require that the sense of injustice encompass infinitude; nor need he wait for assurance that what it admonishes him to do would be universally right and valid, for when he faces any particular crisis of his own he does not feel compelled to legislate for the universe. If we were to ask him whether the voice of his sense of injustice is right in all times and all places he would reply—quite reasonably —that the injustices he needs to subdue arise invariably in particular times and particular places. Injustice does not threaten him *semper et ubique* but here and now. He can safely assume that he will never be called to combat it in all times and all places.

Nevertheless, the tether that holds us is a rather elastic one. If the circumstances of the specific case permit us to engage in imaginative interchange we can respond to an injustice despite great disparities of time, place, culture, law, and ethical tradition. For example, the trial and condemnation of Socrates will stir men's sense of injustice as long as they can conceive the danger of corrupt judges and mob passions.

Here, then, is the sense of injustice at work within men and the law. Is it nothing more than a reasonless compound of glandular secretions and angry emotions, a mere syndrome of outraged feelings, a "sense," as it were, that is completely without sense? Clearly not. While the sense of injustice uses empathy, projection, and emotion, it simultaneously summons perception, reasoning, intelligence, and judgment—all the capacities that make for understanding and the application of sense. In the experience of the sense of injustice, thinking and feeling suffuse each other reciprocally, reason and empathy blend together indissociably, and the rational directs the emotional while the emotional impels the rational. The combined process enables men to develop and communities to advance. Without reason the sense of injustice could not serve the purposes of social utility, which only observation, analysis, and science can discern, while without empathy it would lose its warm sensibility and cogent drive. Compounded indissolubly of both reason and impulsion, it is an active, spontaneous source of law. It makes a practical, working difference in courts, legislatures, and administrative tribunals.

In this compound the democratic citizen and the democratic state find their best, eventual hope of cohesion and survival. The public experience of the sense of injustice can work the greatest of social transformations, because it incites men to join one another and participate—first in recognizing a jeopardy, then in resisting it, and finally in exulting side by side whenever they have practiced justice successfully. All of these are public acts of solidarity, which weld a people together and fill them with a patriotism of irresistible power. There is no established interest, no sinister influence, no outworn institution or superstition that can stand against it. If, by way of metaphor, we imagine the ancient stronghold of Jericho as a citadel of injustice, then no wonder its walls collapsed—not, however, as some have thought, when the priests blew their trumpets but, as the Scripture makes clear, when the people shouted in unison with a great and mighty voice. In less dramatic circumstances the public sense of injustice is equally solidary. Though like any other human capacity it is finite and fallible, it can create its own cumulative rewards by addressing the weak, the insecure, and the deviant ones of the community with a promise of mutual support and confidence.

In public life or private, the sense of injustice offers us no categorical warranty; how amid the ways of this world should we ever come to expect one? What it does offer should supply hope and certainty enough for the responsible citizens of a free land. It promises men that, if they only will, they can close ranks in mutual defense, collaborate with their neighbors in the enterprises of justice, and from day to day become increasingly secure. It promises that persuasion and free assent can triumph over brute force and build the foundations of a happier commonwealth.

2 The Constitution and the Status of Individuals and Groups

A. DOES AMERICAN JUSTICE DEPEND UPON FINANCIAL MEANS?

[The literature of political science is replete with frequent references to the power and influence of the Supreme Court of the United States. The Supreme Court's classic assertions of interpretative authority have been the standard fare in generations of constitutional law classrooms. Most assuredly, such assertions of authority are highly significant to the understanding of American constitutional law, but when presented without the leaven of more prosaic materials, they sometimes create an unrealistic impression. For the ordinary citizen, the more dramatic constitutional controversies are indeed often remote because the opportunities to invoke fundamental constitutional rights and remedies are curtailed by a variety of seemingly picayune factors. Yet it is clear that any meaningful evaluation of the conditions of freedom in the United States must be based upon an understanding of the social realities. In a word, certain economic and social pre-conditions have effectively governed the prospects for successful judicial invocation of fundamental constitutional rights.

Some individuals and certain groups in American society have, on occasions, been implicitly denied the basic protections of the Constitution because they lacked the elementary economic resources to assert their just claims or because the ethnic, religious or ideological group to which they belonged was discriminated against in some fashion. A classic statement of the problem as it relates to poverty was made by Reginald Heber Smith many years ago in his *Justice and the Poor*.]

11

1. Justice and the Poor*

FREEDOM, EQUALITY AND JUSTICE—THE IDEAL

> To no one will we sell, to no one will
> we refuse or delay, right or justice.
> *Magna Carta.*

Freedom and equality of justice are twin fundamental conceptions of American jurisprudence. Together they form the basic principle on which our entire plan for the administration of justice is built. They are so deep-rooted in the body and spirit of our laws that the very meaning which we ascribe to the word justice embraces them. A system which created class distinctions, having one law for the rich and another for the poor, which was a respecter of persons, granting its protection to one citizen and denying it to his fellow, we would unhesitatingly condemn as unjust, as devoid of those essentials without which there can be no justice.

From the dawn of Anglo-Saxon legal history, this idea has been manifest. The earliest laws continually directed that justice be done alike to rich and poor. The equal right to law was asserted in the Charter of Liberties of Henry II. The idea received its classic embodiment and statement in the fortieth paragraph of *Magna Carta,* where was inscribed *"nulli vendemus, nulli negabimus, aut differemus, rectum aut justiciam."* As a purely historical fact this did not signify, or inaugurate, an era of absolute freedom of justice, but it was a first step in that direction. Its supreme importance, however, lies in the tradition which gradually attached to it, and which glorified the idea into an ideal—an ideal which steadily persisted in men's minds throughout five centuries, and which was brought by the colonists to the New World.

In the constitutional conventions which followed the American Revolution the ideal was given concrete expression in the various state Bills and Declarations of Rights. The Massachusetts Constitution, adopted in 1780, declared:

> *Every subject of the Commonwealth ought to find a certain remedy, by having recourse to the laws, for all injuries or wrongs which he may receive in his person, property, or character. He ought to obtain right and justice freely, and without being obliged to purchase it; completely, and without any denial; promptly, and without delay; conformably to the laws.*

As state after state has been added to the Union, its people, in constitutional assembly, have written the same declaration into their fundamental law. In New York the declaration is contained in a statute, but this is exceptional. Today, the constitution of nearly every state, by express provision of the Bill of Rights, guarantees the freedom and equality of justice. The Fourteenth Amendment to the Con-

*Reginald Heber Smith, *Justice and the Poor,* Bulletin 13 of the Carnegie Foundation for the Advancement of Teaching (3rd ed.; 1924), pp. 3–5. [Footnotes omitted.] Reproduced with permission of the publisher. Copyright (1924) by the Carnegie Foundation for the Advancement of Teaching.

stitution of the United States adds to the state guaranty the authority of the supreme law of the land.

As a matter of law, the right stands inviolable. It is recognized and established by the highest possible authority. But that is not all. Its incorporation into the Bills of Rights transformed the principle from merely a legal or juristic conception to a political consideration of supreme importance. Not only was the right to freedom and equality of justice set apart with those other cardinal rights of liberty and of conscience which were deemed sacred and inalienable, but it was made the most important of all because on it all the other rights, even the rights to life, liberty, and the pursuit of happiness, were made to depend. In a word, it became the corner-stone of the Republic.

Ours was designed to be, and is, a government of laws and not of men. Under a government so constituted the right of the individual to life, to freedom of motion, of thought, of conscience, to his children, to his home, and the social interest in securing these things to human beings all depend, in last resort, entirely and abso-lutely on law. This is recognized by our constitutions, and has been repeatedly emphasized by decisions of courts, in the speeches of statesmen, and in treatises on government. The New Hampshire constitution, which is typical, thus expresses it:

It is essential to the preservation of the rights of every individual, his life, liberty, property, and character, that there be an impartial interpretation of the laws and administration of justice.

To secure impartial laws and an equal administration of justice, and thereby to make possible the enjoyment of the rights and opportunities contemplated by a democracy, the State itself exists. The best welfare and the greatest possible happi-ness of the men, women, and children of the nation is the ultimate goal. The State is their servant and its government the means by which the desired end can best be obtained.

Concerning these fundamentals there is no dispute, at least within America. Their extended statement here would be superfluous but for the fact that, although the dependency of every right and interest on law is recognized, the consequences which inevitably flow from such a form of government seem not to be generally appreciated.

These consequences, summarily stated, are:—First, there can be no political, social, or economic equality, no democracy, unless the substantive law by fair and equitable rules gives reality to equality by making it a living thing. Second, the substantive law, however fair and equitable itself, is impotent to provide the necessary safeguards unless the administration of justice, which alone gives effect and force to substantive law, is in the highest sense impartial. It must be possible for the humblest to invoke the protection of law, through proper proceedings in the courts, for any invasion of his rights by whomsoever attempted, or freedom and equality vanish into nothingness.

To withhold the equal protection of the laws, or to fail to carry out their intent by reason of inadequate machinery, is to undermine the entire structure and threaten it with collapse. For the State to erect an uneven, partial administration of justice is to abnegate the very responsibility for which it exists, and is to accomplish by indirection an abridgment of the fundamental rights which the State is directly forbidden to infringe. To deny law or justice to any persons is, in actual effect, to outlaw them by stripping them of their only protection.

It is for such reasons that freedom and equality of justice are essential to a democracy and that denial of justice is the short cut to anarchy.

[Although Reginald Heber Smith made his contribution as early as 1919, it was not until 1932 that the federal Supreme Court, in *Powell* v. *Alabama,*[1] began to concern itself seriously with the social realities which preclude meaningful invocation of basic constitutional rights. In the Powell case, the Court addressed itself to the problem created by the state court's failure to provide adequate defense counsel rather than to the broader problem of the impact of poverty upon the administration of justice. Indeed it was not until 1956 that the Supreme Court faced the latter problem directly. To the extent that an awakened American conscience may influence the judicial process, such change often comes slowly. The Griffin case, presented below, illustrates the situation admirably. By a narrow margin, the Supreme Court extended federal judicial authority to procedural areas traditionally left to state control. The reluctance of the minority of four justices to so extend that authority suggests at least a partial explanation for the time lag noted above.]

2. For Aggressive Federal Supervision of the Administration of Justice*

Illinois law provides that "Writs of error in all criminal cases are writs of right and shall be issued of course." The question here is whether Illinois may, consistent with the due process and equal protection clauses of the Fourteenth Amendment, administer this statute so as to deny adequate appellate review to the poor while granting such review to all others.

The petitioners Griffin and Crenshaw were tried together and convicted of armed robbery in the Criminal Court of Cook County, Illinois. Immediately after their conviction they filed a motion in the trial court asking that a certified copy of the entire record, including a stenographic transcript of the proceedings, be furnished them without cost. They alleged they were "poor persons with no means of paying the necessary fees to acquire the Transcript and Court Records needed to prosecute an appeal. . . ." These allegations were not denied. Under Illinois law in order to get full direct appellate review of alleged errors by a writ of error it is necessary for the defendant to furnish the appellate court with a bill of exceptions or report

* Mr. Justice Black in *Griffin* v. *Illinois,* 351 U.S. 12 (1956).
[1] 287 U.S. 45 (1932).

14

of proceedings at the trial certified by the trial judge. As Illinois concedes, it is some-times impossible to prepare such bills of exceptions or reports without a stenographic transcript of the trial proceedings. Indigent defendants sentenced to death are pro-vided with a free transcript at the expense of the county where convicted. In all other criminal cases defendants needing a transcript, whether indigent or not, must themselves buy it. The petitioners contended in their motion before the trial court that failure to provide them with the needed transcript, would violate the due process and equal protection clauses of the Fourteenth Amendment. The trial court denied the motion without a hearing.

Griffin and Crenshaw then filed a petition under the Illinois Post-Conviction Hearing Act. Only questions arising under the Illinois or Federal Constitution may be raised in proceedings under this Act. A companion state act provides that indigent petitioners under the Post-Conviction Act may, under some circumstances, obtain a free transcript. The effect is that indigents may obtain a free transcript to obtain appellate review of constitutional questions but not of other alleged trial errors such as admissibility and sufficiency of evidence. In their Post-Conviction proceeding petitioners alleged that there were manifest non-constitutional errors in the trial which entitled them to have their convictions set aside on appeal and that the only impediment to full appellate review was their lack of funds to buy a transcript. These allegations have not been denied. Petitioners repeated their charge that refusal to afford full appellate review solely because of poverty was a denial of due process and equal protection. This petition like the first was dismissed without hearing any evidence. The Illinois Supreme Court affirmed the dismissal solely on the ground that the charges raised no substantial state or federal constitutional questions—the only kind of questions which may be raised in Post-Conviction proceedings. We granted certiorari. . . .

Counsel for Illinois concedes that these petitioners needed a transcript in order to get adequate appellate review of their alleged trial errors. There is no contention that petitioners were dilatory in their efforts to get appellate review, or that the Illinois Supreme Court denied review on the ground that the allegations of trial error were insufficient. We must therefore assume for purposes of this decision that errors were committed in the trial which would merit reversal, but the petitioners could not get appellate review of those errors solely because they were too poor to buy a stenographic transcript. Counsel for Illinois denies that this violates either the due process or the equal protection clause, but states that if it does, the Illinois Post-Conviction statute entitles petitioners to a free transcript. The sole question for us to decide, therefore, is whether due process or equal protection has been violated.

Providing equal justice for poor and rich, weak and powerful alike is an age-old problem. People have never ceased to hope and strive to move closer to that goal. This hope, at least in part, brought about in 1215 the royal concessions of *Magna Charta*: "To no one will we sell, to no one will we refuse, or delay, right or justice. . . . No free man shall be taken or imprisoned, or disseised, or outlawed, or exiled, or anywise destroyed; nor shall we go upon him nor send upon him, but by the lawful judgment of his peers or by the law of the land." These pledges were unquestionably steps toward a fairer and more nearly equal application of criminal justice. In this tradition, our own constitutional guaranties of due process and equal protection both call for procedures in criminal trials which allow no invidious discriminations between persons and different groups of persons. Both equal protection and due process emphasize the central aim of our entire judicial system—all people charged with crime must, so far as the law is concerned, "stand on an equality before the bar of justice in every American court." *Chambers* v. *Florida*. . . See also *Yick Wo* v. *Hopkins*. . .

Surely no one would contend that either a State or the Federal Government could constitutionally provide that defendants unable to pay court costs in advance should be denied the right to plead not guilty or to defend themselves in court. Such a law would make the constitutional promise of a fair trial a worthless thing. Notice, the right to be heard, and the right to counsel would under such circumstances be meaningless promises to the poor. In criminal trials a State can no more discriminate on account of poverty than on account of religion, race or color. Plainly the ability to pay costs in advance bears no rational relationship to a defendant's guilt or innocence and could not be used as an excuse to deprive a defendant of a fair trial. Indeed, a provision in the Constitution of Illinois of 1818 provided that every person in Illinois "ought to obtain right and justice freely, and without being obliged to purchase it, completely and without denial, promptly and without delay, conformably to the laws."

There is no meaningful distinction between a rule which would deny the poor the right to defend themselves in a trial court and one which effectively denies the poor an adequate appellate review accorded to all who have money enough to pay the costs in advance. It is true that a State is not required by the Federal Constitution to provide appellate courts or a right to appellate review at all. But that is not to say that a State that does grant appellate review can do so in a way that discriminates against some convicted defendants on account of their poverty. Appellate review has now become an integral part of the Illinois trial system for finally adjudicating the guilt or innocence of a defendant. Consequently at all stages of the proceedings the due process and equal protection clauses protect persons like petitioners from invidious discriminations.

All of the States now provide some method of appeal from criminal convictions, recognizing the importance of appellate review to a correct adjudication of guilt or innocence. Statistics show that a substantial proportion of criminal convictions are reversed by state appellate courts. Thus to deny adequate review to the poor means that many of them may lose their life, liberty or property because of unjust convictions which appellate courts would set aside. Many States have recognized this and provided aid for convicted defendants who have a right to appeal and need a transcript but are unable to pay for it. A few have not. Such a denial is a misfit in a country dedicated to affording equal justice to all and special privileges to none in the administration of its criminal law. There can be no equal justice where the kind of trial a man gets depends on the amount of money he has. Destitute defendants must be afforded as adequate appellate review as defendants who have money enough to buy transcripts.

The Illinois Supreme Court denied these petitioners relief under the Post-

Conviction Act because of its holding that no constitutional rights were violated. In view of our holding to the contrary the State Supreme Court may decide that petitioners are now entitled to a transcript, as the State's brief suggests. We do not hold, however, that Illinois must purchase a stenographer's transcript in every case where a defendant cannot buy it. The Supreme Court may find other means of affording adequate and effective appellate review to indigent defendants. For example, it may be that bystanders' bills of exceptions or other methods of reporting trial proceedings could be used in some cases. The Illinois Supreme Court appears to have broad power to promulgate rules of procedure and appellate practice. We are confident that the State will provide corrective rules to meet the problem which this case lays bare.

The judgment of the Supreme Court of Illinois is vacated and the cause is remanded to that court for further action not inconsistent with the foregoing paragraph. Mr. Justice Frankfurter joins in this disposition of the case.

Vacated and remanded.

[The concurring opinion of Justice Frankfurter and the dissenting opinions of Justices Burton, Minton, Reed and Harlan are omitted.]

3. The Effect of the Griffin Case upon Assignment of Counsel*

There is a probability that the *Griffin* decision will eventually be construed to require a state to furnish reasonably competent counsel to all indigent persons accused of serious crimes.

Realistically this should be inevitable. There is no protection against wrongful conviction like a good criminal lawyer. As Justice Sutherland said in *Powell* v. *Alabama*:

> *The right to be heard would be, in many cases, of little avail if it did not comprehend the right to be heard by counsel. Even the intelligent and educated layman has small and sometimes no skill in the science of law. If charged with crime, he is incapable, generally, of determining for himself whether the indictment is good or bad. He is unfamiliar with the rules of evidence. Left without the aid of counsel he may be put on trial without a proper charge, and convicted upon incompetent evidence, or evidence irrelevant to the issue or otherwise inadmissible. He lacks both the skill and knowledge adequately to prepare his defense, even though he have a perfect one. He requires the guiding hand of counsel at every step in the proceedings against him. Without it, though he be not guilty, he faces the danger of conviction because he does not know how to establish his innocence. If that be true of men of intelligence, how much more true is it of the ignorant and illiterate, or those of feeble intellect.*

*Bertram F. Willcox and Edward J. Bloustein, "The Griffin Case—Poverty and the Fourteenth Amendment," *Cornell Law Quarterly*, XLIII (Fall, 1957), 23–25. [Footnotes omitted.] Reproduced with permission of the authors and the publisher. Copyright © 1957 by Cornell University.

A system of justice which undertakes, as a part of its fundamental philosophy, to protect all individuals from the risks of false conviction, simply must provide counsel to all those in need. Otherwise no meaningful trial is offered.

Since the classic discussion in *Powell* v. *Alabama*, the right to counsel has been looked upon solely in terms of the requirements of due process. The "fair trial standard" which the court has applied in right to counsel cases is a due process standard. The *Griffin* case suggests a new departure. By that same legal alchemy by which the failure to provide a transcript has been held to violate *both* the due process and equal protection clauses, failure to provide counsel may likewise be seen in the double perspective of due process and equal protection. A person accused of a serious crime who is without counsel to defend him on account of poverty is not receiving that protection of the law which those who can afford counsel receive. Thus, even though, of itself, the failure to provide counsel may not be violative of the due process clause, in conjunction with the violation of equal protection, there is a constitutional wrong of sufficient moment to fall afoul of the fourteenth amendment.

Mr. Robert C. Casad, in the Michigan Law Review, suggests that the *Griffin* decision extends only to unjust discriminations which completely shut the court's door in the face of the poor person. Only when counsel are a *sine qua non* of getting into court at all, he says, should the appointment of counsel become a requirement of due process. But could there be a more sophistical legal fiction? "Law addresses itself to actualities," said Justice Frankfurter in the *Griffin* case, and this theme runs through Black's and Frankfurter's opinions. Can it be supposed that these devoted and clear-sighted Justices, and those who concurred with them, will now say that there is a difference in kind between giving a convict no hearing at all and giving him a hearing under a killing handicap? Will not the failure to provide an adequate hearing, like the failure to provide an adequate appeal, run afoul of both the equal protection and due process clauses?

A small fraction of criminal convictions are appealed. Therefore the number of cases in which injustice can be done by denying or restricting appeal is relatively small. The number of cases in which injustice is done by failing to provide counsel at trial is very much greater.

To condone the second but condemn the first would be a retrogression to the sort of legal fiction for which modern and realistic judges would blush in shame. It would be a sort of judicial recidivism. It would be to take shelter from the inconvenient realities by a comfortable reliance on the fiction that so long as the accused can be brought to the court, due process is not concerned with the condition in which he may be brought there.

As students of the administration of criminal justice, the authors must, in honesty, urge a further point which they know will seem radical to many. Counsel must not only be appointed; counsel must be paid. And counsel must have funds for the preparation of the defendant's case. The bland assumption that counsel, from sheer sense of duty, from pleasure in being chosen, from desire to make a reputation, will do their utmost for their "shotgun" clients, is often no more than a pious hope. In many instances they will; and will dig into their own pockets to do what

urgently needs doing to win a client's case. Lawyers are professional people; therefore many of them will do these things. But lawyers are also businessmen; therefore many will not do these things. Many who sincerely intend to do their utmost for assigned clients will in actuality do something less than their utmost, because of the competing demands of regular clients upon their limited supply of time. This is human nature. Who denies its effects is living in a dream world.

Thus in 1943 the late Judge Augustus Hand, in a report to the Judicial Conference of Senior Circuit Court Judges, made the statement which is now a classic in this field.

> *It is clear that when cases of poor persons needing defense become numerous and occur repeatedly, the voluntary and uncompensated services of counsel are not an adequate means of providing representation. To call on lawyers constantly for unpaid service is unfair to them and any attempt to do so is almost bound to break down after a time. To distribute such assignments among a large number of attorneys in order to reduce the burden upon anyone, is to entrust the representation of the defendant to attorneys who in many cases are not proficient in criminal trials, whatever their general ability, and who for one reason or another cannot be depended upon for an adequate defense. Too often under such circumstances the representation becomes little more than a form.*

[The setting of the Griffin case was the Criminal Court of Cook County, Illinois. Does poverty operate to prevent invocation of fundamental constitutional rights only in the heavily populated metropolitan areas of the United States? Willcox and Bloustein provide compelling evidence concerning both the scope and nature of the problem in relation to the system of court-assigned lawyers in an essentially rural setting.]

4. Representation of Rural Indigents Accused of Crime*

The effective defense of poor persons accused of crime is a major social problem. Most of the discussion of it has been focused upon the great metropolitan areas, with their crowded courts and overworked officials. In the present article, by contrast, we report on the same problem in a more rural setting: Tompkins County, a farm community of central New York, and Ithaca, the small city which is the seat of Tompkins County. . . .

*   *   *

In the United States, at present, the availability of counsel to an indigent criminal defendant tends to vary with the court he is in and the crime with which he is

*Bertram F. Willcox and Edward J. Bloustein, "Account of a Field Study in a Rural Area of Indigents Accused of Crime," *Columbia Law Review,* LIX (April, 1959), 551–53. [Footnotes omitted.] Reproduced with permission of the authors and the publisher. Copyright © 1959 by the Directors of the Columbia Law Review Association, Inc.

charged. Some jurisdictions do not go beyond the precise holding in *Powell* v. *Alabama*; these make assignment of counsel mandatory only when a death penalty is at issue. Other jurisdictions provide for counsel in prosecutions for a felony only. Still others provide for them in prosecutions for a misdemeanor or for even a lesser criminal offense.

Powell v. *Alabama* makes it clear that a merely formal appointment of counsel must be distinguished from effective representation by counsel. Due process is not satisfied by a bare legal right to retain counsel if exercise of the right is impossible because of poverty. Similarly, due process is not satisfied by any formal appearance of counsel who are unable or unwilling, for any reason, to conduct an effective defense. It is the legal reality, not the legal appearance, that counts.

Thus, it is not enough in evaluating the defense of indigents to say, for example, that a jurisdiction makes the appearance of counsel mandatory in felony cases. The realistic test, and in some cases the legal test, is whether the appearance is effective. Was counsel able and willing to fulfill the minimum requirements of representation of a criminal defendant? The answer depends to a large extent on the system by which counsel is provided.

In American courts poor persons charged with crime may be represented by attorneys in private practice or by attorneys who are paid a salary for such representation. The latter are called defenders, public defenders when their salary is paid by a governmental body, private defenders when it comes from some private source such as a legal aid society. The attorneys in private practice who serve occasionally are assigned by the courts, either haphazardly or from a rotating roster. In some jurisdictions their services will in the ordinary case be compensated out of public funds; in most jurisdictions, however, they will be so compensated only in an unusually serious case.

The assigned counsel system is used in all but a few jurisdictions. The system varies somewhat from state to state on such matters as whether the assignment is mandatory or discretionary, at whose instance it is made, the type of case in which it will be made, the time at which it will be made, the use of a rotating roster of attorneys, and the compensation and expenses provided. One major similarity in the various methods of assignment, however, enables us to make some generalizations about the system of assignment as a whole. This similarity lies in the nature of the basic relation between the indigent defendant, his counsel, and the court. The assigned counsel serves his client as an officer of the court at the court's request, and usually without adequate remuneration. He is motivated by a sense of obligation to the court, to the indigent client, and to society in general. The adequacy of the assignment system must therefore depend, fundamentally, on the strength of the assigned lawyer's sense of social responsibility as measured against the demands on his time and effort which the assignment makes.

A number of students of legal aid have evaluated the system of assigned counsel. From the classic treatment of Reginald Heber Smith to the recent study of Emery A. Brownell, the uncontradicted judgment is that the system, on the whole, usually fails in several ways to do what it is intended to do. And yet the system of assigned counsel persists, and there seems to be little impetus for drastic change.

It is hard to understand this persistence of a legal procedure which has been disapproved over so long a time by so many competent critics. It will hardly do to cite social inertia as the reason, for social inertia does not always succeed in blocking change. The question always is why such inertia is or is not effective in the given instance.

We suggest that an important reason why the system of assigned counsel has not been improved is that most of the adverse criticism focuses on its failures in metropolitan areas. The accepted view is that it works well in rural areas. This statement has, in fact, come to be taken as a truism. And when it is coupled with the tendency of many Americans, even well educated ones, to think of the United States as still mainly rural, it may help to explain the lack of general concern over the system of assigned counsel and the feeling that its failure is essentially a problem for a few metropolitan areas rather than for the nation as a whole. If this diagnosis is correct, a study of the operation of the assignment system in a rural area should serve as a critical test, since all agree that rural areas see the system at its best. If it works poorly there, it must work poorly everywhere.

A study of the assignment system in a rural area also serves another purpose. It directs attention to that segment of American society to which Americans are traditionally responsive. Our cities are rather new arrivals, as contrasted with our towns. When something is wrong with the cities "somebody ought to do something about it," but when something goes wrong in the towns "something has to be done."

I. THE STUDY

Our survey was designed, as we have said, to describe and evaluate the system of assigned counsel as it operates in Tompkins County and in Ithaca, the county seat.

Our investigation was carried out by means of conferences, observation, study of court records, and questionnaires. It was conducted mostly in the last three months of 1956 and the first three months of 1957. We talked with judges and justices, lawyers, prosecutors, and other officials whose work had given them knowledge of how the system of assigned counsel actually functioned. (These persons will sometimes be referred to as "our consultants.") We did not talk with police officers, either state or local. The statements about the role of police officers in criminal enforcement, therefore, like other evidence coming from our consultants, are set forth as our consultants' opinions and not as established fact. They are relevant because they bear upon what the local practicing lawyers deem to be the difficulties confronting an indigent accused of crime. From time to time we observed the proceedings of the city court.

After we thought we had learned what questions to ask, we sent out our questionnaire to 57 members of the local bar. We asked for anonymous answers. Many of our consultants, of course, were members of this group of 57, although the judges, the probation officer, and some other officials were not.

Of the 57 lawyers, 44, or 77 per cent, responded. These responses were received and tabulated in April and May 1957. The following Fall we decided to send similar questionnaires to the bars of two nearby counties, where the conditions might be expected to be similar, to try to get some light on whether Tompkins County was fairly typical. These counties were Cortland County, adjoining Tompkins on the east, and Tioga County, adjoining it on the south. Of 30 lawyers in Tioga County to whom questionnaires were sent, 21, or 70 per cent sent answers. Of 34 lawyers in Cortland County receiving questionnaires, 22, or 65 per cent, sent answers. Thus, of all 121 questionnaires sent out, 87, or 72 per cent, were answered. While the numbers are not large, because these are small communities, the percentage of answers returned and the interest thus shown in the problem were gratifying. We owe much to the lawyers and bar associations of these three counties.

There is no record, in the courts or elsewhere, of the number or proportion of the persons accused of crime in Tompkins County who cannot afford to pay for counsel. Estimates vary from 50 per cent to 80 per cent. The highest estimate was given by the County Probation Officer, who has recently retired after many years of service. These estimates, or guesses, refer to the persons appearing before all the courts in the county. Considering all of them, we believe that it is reasonable to assume that more than half of the persons accused of crime are too poor to hire a lawyer. If so, the importance of the problem needs no underscoring.

A. THE "LOWER COURTS"

"Lower courts" is the term usually applied to the Ithaca City Court and to the justice courts presided over by the justices of the peace of the towns and by the police justices of the villages. The judge of one of these lower courts is normally the first judicial officer to see a person accused of a crime. (For brevity the justices of the peace and the police justices will be called "justices.")

If the charge is of an indictable offense, the function of the city judge, or the justice, before whom the accused is first brought, is to decide whether there is enough evidence to hold him for the grand jury. For the making of this decision the city judge or the justice must hold a preliminary hearing on the People's case, unless that hearing is waived by the accused. If it is decided—as it is in most cases— that there is enough evidence to hold the accused, the judge or the justice will commit him to the county jail and will set bail.

If the charge is not of an indictable offense, but is instead a charge of one of many misdemeanors specified by statute, a charge of an offense against an ordinance, or a charge of a violation of any one of several statutes specified by statute, the city judge or the justice has jurisdiction not merely to hold, but to hear and decide. He thereupon tries the case, either with or without a jury.

1. *Proceedings Prior to and Including the Preliminary Hearing in an Indictable Offense.* A person suspected of having committed an indictable offense appears first before a magistrate. As already indicated, in Tompkins County this magistrate is almost always either the city judge or one of the justices. The appearance results from the service of a summons, the execution of a warrant of arrest, or an arrest made by a peace officer or other person without a warrant. The chief functions of this proceeding are to tell the accused what he is charged with, to advise him of his right to the aid of counsel in every stage of the case, and thereafter to examine into the existence of probable cause to hold him for the grand jury.

Our consultants suggest that in the usual case, once an arrest has been made, the arresting officer does not attempt to protect the constitutional rights of his prisoner, such as the right to avoid self-incrimination and the right to obtain the help of counsel. Instead, the officer will question his prisoner about what he did and why he did it, and will suggest that if the prisoner confesses to the magistrate he will "get off" lightly, but that if he does not "come clean" he will be punished harshly. In addition, we are told, it is quite usual for the officer to advise the prisoner to waive his legal right to a preliminary hearing.

Opinions differ concerning the frequency, and the severity, of the use of intimidation short of threats and violence to obtain from the prisoner a statement which may incriminate. A few of our consultants believed they had reliable evidence even of violence or threats of violence. We believe that such abuse is quite infrequent in Tompkins County, if it occurs at all. But far more frequent, we fear, is the use of strong pressure, short of violence or threats thereof, to induce a confession. And even where no such pressure is used, the prisoner is rarely, if ever, told of his right to remain silent. Usually he is urged to give a statement, sometimes as the price of a promised favor. In some cases, no copy of this statement ever becomes available to him or to his counsel.

The committing magistrate does not ordinarily impress upon the prisoner the importance of the preliminary examination; instead he usually advises him to save time by either waiving it or "getting it over with." This amounts to suggesting that the prisoner either waive the examination altogether or else allow the People to examine their witnesses before he has a chance to get counsel. The committing magistrate looks upon the preliminary hearing as an unimportant detail, a mere formal step toward the finding of probable cause. The indigent person, who has no counsel at this stage nor any offer of assigned counsel, is most unlikely to withstand the combined pressures from police and magistrate for his waiver of hearing or for a "quick hearing" without counsel.

Here another difference of opinion has to be reported. All but one of our consultants with extensive criminal practice repeatedly stressed the crucial importance to the defense of the preliminary hearing. The People's case appears on this examination. Its weaknesses can then be probed and exploited before the trial. The witnesses are more likely to tell the truth at the hearing than at the trial, because the events are fresher in their memories; hence their later wishful recollections, coached or spontaneous, can more easily be exposed at the trial for what they are. One consultant, on the other hand, thought that defense counsel should usually waive the preliminary hearing, largely on the ground that it facilitates the People's proof of their case if, later on, some witness who has testified at the hearing should become unavailable for the trial. In that event, the transcript of the hearing can be read at the trial, to "plug the gap." He further believed that the record of the hearing is often used unfairly to confuse honest witnesses at the trial.

We submit that the majority view is the more reasonable one. Even allowing that some of the enthusiasm for the hearing stems from that adversary spirit which does so much to pervert our criminal law, still there are important advantages, of a legitimate kind, which inhere in this examination and which make it unfair for an accused to be talked out of it without the advice of counsel. But even if the minority view, that the preliminary hearing is disadvantageous to the defense in most cases, is correct, it would still be vitally important that defense counsel, rather than the accused, decide in the particular case whether the hearing should be waived.

2. *The Courts of Special Sessions.* The trial of a nonindictable offense is conducted by the city judge or by a justice sitting as a court of special sessions. (For convenience we shall sometimes refer to the judge or justice, when he is acting in this capacity, as a "special sessions judge.") A special sessions judge has a statutory duty to inform the accused of his right to have counsel, of his right to have an adjournment for the purpose of getting counsel, and of his right to send a free message to counsel. Our consultants say that the special sessions judges perform this duty more or less by rote, expecting that the defendant will not avail himself of any of the proffered rights. Many of the defendants hear what the judge has to say without understanding him at all. It is our impression, based on the views of a number of our consultants, that some of these judges do not really want counsel interposed between the court and the defendant. They are said to be apprehensive lest "learned counsel" make them look ignorant.

Here, just as when a judge or justice sits as a committing magistrate, there is no express statutory duty to assign counsel. In practice, the assignment of counsel in the courts of special sessions is limited almost entirely to the city court. Of the 44 lawyers who answered our questionnaire in Tompkins County, 13 reported having received a total of 91 assigned cases during the three years 1954 to 1956. Of these, 57 were assignments in the county court, 33 in the city court, and only 1 in a justice court. These figures must be read in the light of the fact that there are more than twice as many criminal cases before the courts of special sessions as before the county court.

Courts of special sessions are held by the judge of the city court and by some ten to a dozen active justices throughout the county. There is no doubt that some of these special sessions judges operate in a more judicial manner than others. Widely differing opinions were expressed by many consultants about how well these courts function. Our impression, based on everything we heard, leads to the following observations about the workings of these courts.

Before a hearing, the arresting officer frequently will talk privately with the special sessions judge about what has happened, stressing the bad record of the accused—if he has a prior record—and his clear and obvious guilt, and urging the need for a conviction. The officer also "fills in" the special sessions judge on the law. One consultant told us that on one occasion, when he was counsel for a defendant, he had heard that a police officer was to reach the house of the special sessions judge thirty minutes before the time for the hearing. Our consultant reached the house forty minutes before that time. Thus, law practice in the justice courts sometimes becomes a simple "race to reach the judge's kitchen" first.

The special sessions judges differ, of course, in the extent to which they allow or encourage these tactics. The city judge is a practicing lawyer who understands and respects the rights of the accused. One of the police justices is also a lawyer. These two, and at least one other justice who handles many cases, may have acquired the difficult judicial art of avoiding prejudgment. But many have not.

Some show such deference to the police officers as to be impatient with anyone who disputes what these officers say. The powerful influence exercised by the police over many of the special sessions judges was a matter of general comment by those with whom we talked. Several noted also that many of these judges rely heavily on the district attorney or his assistant for advice; they telephone or call on them in person to discuss troublesome questions. This undoubtedly upsets the adversary balance when the district attorney or his assistant prosecutes a case. It is perhaps even more prejudicial when—as often happens—the case is tried without the prosecutor's presence but his advice controls the court's determinations nevertheless.

It is the general view that the city judge is an able lawyer who tries to protect constitutional rights and privileges. We observed many sessions of his court and were impressed by his fairness. This court is conducted in a regular courtroom, informally but with dignity and firmness. These observations confirmed the impressions we had already received from our consultants that the city judge handles his court well.

He does not usually take the affirmative step of asking whether a defendant wants counsel assigned. His practice here contrasts with that of the county judge, who makes statutory assignments of counsel to any accused person who, after inquiry, indicates that he wants an attorney but cannot afford to retain one. If any defendant in the city court takes the initiative, however, and says that he wants counsel but cannot afford to pay, the city judge will assign one.

Opinions differ on the adequacy of the assignment system in the city court. There are those who believe that the judge makes assignments whenever there is a real need. Others, however, think that he does not; some suggest that he feels that his strong sympathy for a poor person obviates the need for counsel and provides sufficient protection. Finally, many consultants stress the fact that where the city judge does not himself take the initiative, many of the indigent accused are too ignorant to know that the judge would assign counsel if they asked him to do so.

Outside the city, the problem is worse. The justices make no attempt to assign counsel. They say that they have no power to assign. Furthermore, great practical difficulties would be involved. There are few attorneys in the towns and villages. Moreover, the justices, who in all but one instance are not themselves lawyers, would feel hesitant to call on a lawyer to render free professional services. And many lawyers doubt that the justices have authority to assign them.

One of the most conscientious of the justices, by general repute, makes informal assignments from time to time; he will ask a nearby lawyer to consult with someone who is before his court and whom he knows to be in need of legal help. But he does not ask such a lawyer to appear in court for such a person. These cases usually involve matrimonial disputes, abandonment, or nonsupport. This justice, furthermore, told us that he had on occasion asked the county judge to assign counsel for an accused person whom he, the justice, thought to be in urgent need of counsel. He also pointed out that he does his best to protect persons who are accused in his court, preventing them if possible from pleading guilty to a charge where he feels any serious doubt about the guilt. Strong confirmation of this justice's practices was volunteered to us by several of our consultants. But some other consultants volunteered doubts about the efficacy of these admittedly good intentions of this particular justice.

The work of this justice is discussed in some detail because the varying opinions about it are rather typical. He is, by all the reports, one of the two or three best of the non-lawyer justices. All agree that he makes a devoted and conscientious effort to do a good job. But some believe that his lack of legal training makes it impossible for him to protect accused persons adequately against the pressures that are brought to bear on them and on him by the police and the prosecutors.

The reports of convictions which the justices are required to file monthly with the county clerk contain blanks to be checked to indicate that the convicted person was notified of his constitutional and statutory rights. A sampling of these reports indicates that they are filed with no regularity. During the year prior to March 1957, for example, only one such report was found filed in each month—and not all these twelve from the same justice. Such reports as are filed do indicate that the accused were duly advised of their constitutional and statutory rights. But the number of reports is so small that they offer no indication of the general practice of the justices. It seems clear that these forms are filled and filed only when the justices think of it and have nothing better to do.

Likewise, inspection of the city court docket indicates that it leaves much to be desired concerning the record of assignment of counsel. The clerk recognized that the fact of assignment of counsel probably ought to appear, but said that it usually does not. The standard docket page provides a space to be checked to indicate that the defendant was informed that he was entitled to counsel and to an adjournment to obtain counsel. This space is checked on the record of every criminal case heard.

B. COUNTY COURT

The grand jury is impanelled by one of the justices of the supreme court, who sit in Ithaca from time to time on circuit. After indictment, all cases, with one rare exception, are transferred to the county court for trial. The exception is first-degree murder cases, which are tried in the supreme court itself. But there has been only one of these in Tompkins County during the last decade. In such cases, the problem of obtaining experienced and skillful legal assistance is not acute because of the statutory compensation allowed and also because of the public's interest in murder cases.

In all other cases the county court arraigns persons charged with indictable offenses, takes pleas from them, and tries them. It also deals, similarly, with any lesser crimes which may be transferred to the county court pursuant to certificate, but such transfers are rare. In addition, the county court hears any appeal from a conviction in a court of special sessions or from a denial of an application for a writ of error in a coram nobis proceeding in such a court.

The county judge, as already noted, is expressly charged by statute with the duty of assigning counsel for any person arraigned before him who, in answer to the judge's inquiry, requests such assistance. All our consultants agree that the county judge is careful and conscientious in his assignment practice. In this court, as distinguished from the justice courts, and to a lesser degree from the city court, assignments are normal and expected.

Although there is good evidence that assignments in county court are made when needed, there is also substantial evidence that they do not entirely fulfill their purpose. The indictable offenses normally carry heavy penalties. And, it would seem, adequate preparation and investigation of many of these cases may require considerable amounts of time and money. The county judge tends to discount this need, saying that most of these cases are comparatively simple, involving local events and persons. But our talks with lawyers and the responses to our questionnaire presented rather impressive evidence to the contrary. On the Tompkins County questionnaire 28 of the 35 respondents who answered the question about funds for preparation thought that the lack of such funds was an inadequacy of the system. Fifteen of them thought this inadequacy serious; only 7 were satisfied.

Sharp disagreement was found among our consultants concerning the helpfulness of the prosecutor in protecting an accused indigent against the possibility of a mistaken conviction. The county judge and the two district attorneys who served in succession during the period of our study told us that the district attorney's office was always willing to open its files and to give all the information and assistance possible, without discrimination between counsel assigned and counsel retained. Some consultants agreed, but a slight majority disagreed. The comments of this majority are in no sense a reflection on the fairness or conscientiousness of any individual district attorney. The criticism goes rather to the nature of the office and to the tendency, inherent in the adversary system, for any district attorney to try to get as many convictions as he can. Those consultants who have been successful in their dealings with the district attorney incline, no doubt, to feel that the prosecutor has been fair; whereas those who have not been so successful incline to be censorious.

Our own conclusion is that the district attorney's claim that he protects the rights of the accused as diligently as the rights of the People is somewhat exaggerated. Some attorneys, particularly in cases where trial seemed inevitable, found it impossible to avail themselves of the district attorney's asserted willingness to open his files to counsel for all defendants. In general, we believe that the district attorney does feel a real responsibility to protect indigent persons against unjust convictions, within the limits allowed by his attitude toward the duties of his office. But we doubt whether his conception of his own function is adequate for the protection of the rights of the indigent—more than half of all those indicted. Under the existing assignment system, the indigent defendant is represented by counsel without pay and without funds, and he is pitted against the county's resources of men and money. It takes little imagination to see his terrifying disadvantage. To compensate, he needs more than a mere passive fairness on the part of the district attorney; he needs his active solicitude to avoid the danger of an unjust conviction.

Another matter of great importance concerning county court assignments is the time at which counsel is assigned. Although assignment is sometimes made by a communication from the county judge to the lawyer either before or after the arraignment, the usual procedure is to make the assignment in open court at the arraignment. But there is some evidence, as already noted, that police officers usually question a suspect before they take him to a committing magistrate for his first hearing, and that they may continue to question him thereafter. This questioning often results in a confession or, at the least, in a statement which will gravely prejudice the defendant's case. We believe that such practices occur frequently enough to be a serious hazard to the fair determination of guilt or innocence. It is a hazard which earlier assignments might alleviate. A few consultants, at least, held strong opinions to the effect that assignment comes too late when it comes after the arrest, hearing, and indictment. It should be made at the first hearing, at the latest, so that counsel can advise about waiving the preliminary examination and can participate in it if it is held. One attorney with much criminal experience insisted that assignments should be made immediately after an arrest.

In view of these expressions of opinion it was surprising that of the 44 respondents to our Tompkins County questionnaire only 3 answered that the usual time of assigning counsel is "very much too late." But it is to be noted that these three respondents handled half of the criminal cases in the county from 1954 through 1956.

The county judge does not maintain any formal roster of assignments. Only 12 of the 44 practitioners who answered the questionnaire had had county court assignments in the years 1954 through 1956. Of the 57 cases assigned to these 12 lawyers during that period, 31 were assigned to two young lawyers with less than five years of practice. In 1956 there were 26 cases assigned. Of these, one lawyer with one and a half years of experience had 15 cases.

The county judge told us that it is his policy to give assignments mainly to young lawyers. In a serious case, however, he assigns a lawyer of greater experience. He gave as a reason for not assigning experienced trial lawyers in most cases the fact that he did not want to impose upon them. It is interesting to note, on the other hand, that some trial lawyers when asked why they never had assignments answered that the judges do not like trials and that if experienced counsel were assigned the judges could be sure there would be trials.

Handling cases without fee is thought by most of our consultants and by 8 of our 44 respondents to be "a serious hardship" on the lawyer. Six of the 8 so answering are among the 9 having extensive criminal experience. Another 19 think it "a hardship but not a serious one." The remaining 9, of the 36 who replied to this question, think it "no hardship at all." It has been reported to us that some years ago resentment against the assignment system induced some of the younger lawyers to meet to plan a protest against the hardships it imposes. But nothing further was done about it.

The county judge told us that it is his practice to ask the accused in open court whether he can afford counsel. At the same time he advises the accused that it will be to his benefit to retain private counsel if he can. But if the accused convinces the judge that he cannot, an assignment is made without further investigation. Knowing the community and its people as he does, the judge feels that he is rarely mistaken about the indigency of a person appearing before him.

Assigned counsel differ as to the way in which they treat the question of the indigency of a client. About half will assume without investigation that the defendant cannot pay. The other half make investigations of their own. If substantial assets or a likelihood of future earnings appear, the attorney may ask the court to relieve him of the assignment or may arrange to receive remuneration without informing the court. There were doubts and differences of opinion as to the correct course to follow.

We have not heard of any case of assigned counsel's "bleeding" the family of an indigent person. This is in striking contrast with what we are told occurs in some large metropolitan areas; there, many assigned lawyers make a business of "squeezing" fees out of defendants and their families and friends.

The county judge told us that in cases where he thinks the accused has enough to pay a modest fee to a lawyer, but not enough to pay a normal fee, he will ask a lawyer to take the case charging a specified fee, possibly from a half to a third of what the lawyer would ordinarily bill. Six of our respondents indicated that they had received cases from the county judge on this "partial assignment" basis.

There are some kinds of indirect compensation for counsel who take assigned cases. One such form arises out of the fact that the county judge in Tompkins is also the surrogate. He is able to reward those young lawyers who take assignments by conferring remunerative appointments as special guardians. He does this as a matter of policy. Opinion is unanimous that he handles this with great fairness and that he does not allow political considerations to enter into his treatment of counsel.

Some of our consultants mentioned another form of indirect compensation for the assignments. This is the publicity that results from appearances in county court to defend indigents in cases that command the public interest and are reported in the local press.

The duties undertaken by assigned counsel without remuneration are not, by and large, as heavy as the above discussion might suggest. It is rare for assigned counsel actually to conduct a trial; not one tenth of his assignments result in trials. It is unheard of for him to conduct an appeal.

II. EVALUATION

We have noted that most authorites treat it as a truism that the lot of the indigent defendant in a community such as Tompkins County is less hard than in a metropolis. The usual reasons given are that in a small community people take a friendly interest in one another's affairs; they are more apt to know one another and to know a lawyer.

There is doubtless some validity in this general view. It is a fact, for instance, that the courts of this county are less hurried than those of most urban centers. There is no great pressure, as there is in those centers, to keep up with the case load. The assigning judge can look at the indigent persons before him as individuals, rather than as a mass, because their number is small.

On the other hand, it is our belief that the much vaunted "neighborliness" of the small-town lawyer is overemphasized. The pressure of economic circumstance plays as great a part in the life of the small-town lawyer as it does in the life of his big-town brother. He, like his big-town brother, must weigh every part of his practice from the point of view of its economic reward. He has no more time for "neighborliness" than he would have if he were practicing in Manhattan. Nor is there any evidence that the small-town lawyer has a more compelling sense of duty than his big-city counterpart. The picture of the small-town lawyer as a public spirited benefactor is a popular myth, but we have found no reason to credit it. Our consultants have seemed to us to display about the same level of professional responsibility one would expect from lawyers in a big city. Each has a living to make from practice. Each responds to many motives—only one of which is his professional duty as an officer of the court.

A major reason why the system works as well as it does in this county is the fairness of the judiciary and of the prosecuting officials. This virtue has its drawback, however, in that it depends on the accident of the incumbency of particular individuals.

Major defects of the system are, first, the fact that the prosecutors and the police —often because of an eager and tough devotion to their job as they see it—are not sufficiently solicitous of the rights of accused persons or sufficiently awake to the ever-present danger of an erroneous charge; and, secondly, that most of the justices are without legal training and, partly for that reason, are subject to some degree of domination.

Some consultants expressed the view that Tompkins County is approaching the critical population at which some system other than the assignment system will be needed. We talked with the recently retired county judge in Chemung County, which has nearly half again the population of Tompkins. He told us that the assignment system, in his opinion, is utterly inadequate in his county.

There is a sharp difference of opinion among our consultants and respondents about the competence of the young lawyers who take the bulk of the assigned cases from the county and city judges. These judges, the recently retired district attorney, and a number of lawyers, consider these men quite able to do all that is needed to assure justice for their clients. On the other hand, a large minority of the Tompkins respondents with most criminal experience are skeptical of the ability of raw young attorneys to handle adequately any but the easiest cases. They agree on the zeal and devotion with which these young attorneys carry out their allotted tasks. But they emphasize the recognized fact that criminal practice cannot be learned from books, and that long experience alone can guide the criminal lawyer in the delicate decisions which he must make with wisdom if he is to serve his client well. As one of our respondents wrote on his questionnaire, "if an attorney who is experienced and is successful in his assignments, at times feels himself inadequate, how good can the inexperienced attorney be in his assignment outside of 'seeming' to defend his assigned client?" Of the 44 respondents to our questionnaire, 8 thought assigned lawyers too inexperienced. Three of the 7 experienced criminal practitioners (those who had had 10 or more criminal cases apiece in three years) indicated that they thought this; the other 4 said that assigned counsel were competent.

In addition to the handicap to the indigent which may result from young counsel's lack of skill, there is the handicap that often results from counsel's inability (in most cases) to spend a single cent for defense unless he takes it out of his own pocket. In a case of any difficulty there may be witnesses and expert witnesses to be secured, scientific tests to be made, records to be checked, and a host of other matters to be attended to. The injustice to the defendant and the frustration to the lawyer of having no money to do any of these things, when and if they become important, is easy to imagine for any lawyer who has ever taken part in litigation.

30

This is the sort of handicap which the assignment system, as it operates in Tompkins County, imposes on defendants. We must also consider the burden that it places on the lawyers, and the inequitable way in which this burden is distributed among them. To be sure, the young lawyers, who do the great bulk of the work, appreciate that they are learning a great deal. They are conscious as well of the fact that they are performing a major social service. But they are also uncomfortably aware of their own limitations and of the misfortunes that these limitations may occasionally impose upon their clients. Furthermore, after one or two years of practice they begin to feel the competition between their growing private practice and their charitable work. What was in most respects a boon becomes in most respects a burden.

The lawyers who take assignments also resent the fact that the great majority do not. Thirty-one of our 44 respondents reported no assignments in any court in 1954 through 1956. Lawyers, young and old, who engage mainly in office practice seem never to shoulder any part of the burden that the defense of indigent criminal defendants imposes on the bar. Nor do they contribute any part of their earnings to help with that burden. Resentment of this immunity may account, in part, for the abortive "rebellion," already mentioned, of a few years ago.

Another comparison which causes much dissatisfaction is the contrasting treatment of the medical profession in this county. The doctors receive almost their full fee out of county public welfare funds for services rendered to "welfare" patients. Why should not lawyers receive similar treatment? It is true that the analogy may not be quite perfect, but it is close enough to cause a general sense of grievance among the young lawyers who bear the burden of the unpaid assignments.

One defense of the assignment system advanced by several judges and lawyers got short shrift from most of our consultants. This is the argument that assigned work affords an excellent education for young and inexperienced lawyers—an education which they could receive in no other way. The answer is obvious, but overwhelming. Why should the needed education be gained at the expense of impoverished defendants? If education is an objective of the assignment system, fairness, not only to the indigent client, but even to the young lawyer himself, requires that such a lawyer work under the supervision of more experienced counsel.

As we have seen, some experienced criminal lawyers say that one of the reasons, conscious or unconscious, why judges assign so many cases to young lawyers is that the judges want pleas rather than trials. This explanation is probably extreme. To meet the criticism thus voiced, however, the judges might well try assigning more cases to the most experienced criminal lawyers in the county, perhaps with younger counsel as associates.

B. IS SUPERVISION THE ANSWER?

[What effect, if any, has federal Supreme Court supervision of state administration of criminal law actually had? Is such supervision necessary and desirable? Professor Francis A. Allen provides the following appraisal.]

5. For Intervention by the Supreme Court*

No precise measure of the impact of the Court's decisions on local law-enforcement practices is available. Obviously, the lines of communication between the courts and the police are dangerously imperfect. There are no data upon which to base an estimate of the Court's influence, if any, on general public attitudes toward the issues litigated in the state criminal cases or in the development of what appears to be a quickening public interest in the administration of criminal justice. Nevertheless, the Court's influence on state criminal justice has been substantial. This influence has not been of equal significance in all states or with reference to all issues. But it can fairly be said that the Court has been one of the most important factors in recent efforts at reform of various aspects of American criminal-law administration. It is important to note how this influence has operated. By identifying and dramatizing aspects of the criminal process in a particular state, the Court has often succeeded in opening the way for local legislative action. This is no mere conjecture. The experience in Illinois provides a concrete example. In the course of a decade and a half, these changes, among others, have been produced: Practices relating to the appointment of counsel have been liberalized. Time for filing of exceptions in the review process has been extended by rule of the Illinois supreme court. A new statute to meet a critical problem of post-conviction remedies was enacted by the legislature. A rule of the Illinois prison system that barred state prisoners from direct access to the courts was withdrawn. The state supreme court eliminated barriers that blocked impoverished defendants from appellate review of their convictions. It is perfectly clear that all these measures were the direct or indirect product of judicial supervision of Illinois criminal procedures by the United States Supreme Court. It may also be asserted that these alterations in the existing law were necessary and desirable.

[The favorable reaction in the articles by Illinois Supreme Court Justice Walter V. Schaeffer and Professor Francis Allen was not reflected in all professional and judicial circles. In August of 1958, the Conference of State Chief Justices adopted a report severely critical of the Supreme Court of the United States. Of the Griffin decision, the chief justices made the following comments.]

6. The State Chief Justices in Rebuttal*

We shall not comment in this report upon the broad sweep which the Supreme Court now gives to habeas corpus proceedings. . . .

*Francis A. Allen, "The Supreme Court, Federalism, and State Systems of Criminal Justice," *University of Chicago Law School Record*, VIII (Autumn, 1958), 18–19. [Footnotes omitted.] Reproduced with permission of the author and the publisher. Copyright © 1958 by the University of Chicago.
*Report by the 1958 Conference of State Chief Justices. See *Harvard Law Record*, Special ed., October 23, 1958. Thirty-six of the chief justices supported the report, eight opposed it, and six did not vote on the issue.

We cannot, however, completely avoid any reference at all to habeas corpus matters because what is probably the most far reaching decision of recent years on state criminal procedure which has been rendered by the Supreme Court is itself very close to a habeas corpus case. That is the case of *Griffin* v. *Illinois, . . .* which arose under the Illinois Post Conviction Procedure Act. The substance of the holding in that case may perhaps be briefly and accurately stated in this way: If a transcript of the record, or its equivalent, is essential to an effective appeal, and if a state permits an appeal by those able to pay for the cost of the record or its equivalent, then the state must furnish without expense to an indigent defendant either a transcript of the record at his trial, or an equivalent thereof, in order that the indigent defendant may have an equally effective right of appeal. Otherwise, the inference seems clear, the indigent defendant must be released upon habeas corpus or similar proceedings. Probably no one would dispute the proposition that the poor man should not be deprived of the opportunity for a meritorious appeal simply because of his poverty. The practical problems which flow from the decision in *Griffin* v. *Illinois* are, however, almost unlimited and are now only in course of development and possible solution. This was extensively discussed at the 1957 meeting of this Conference of Chief Justices in New York.

We may say at this point that in order to give full effect to the doctrine of *Griffin* v. *Illinois,* we see no basis for distinction between the cost of the record and other expenses to which the defendant will necessarily be put in the prosecution of an appeal. These include filing fees, the cost of printing the brief and of such part of the record as may be necessary, and counsel fees.

The *Griffin* case was very recently given retroactive effect by the Supreme Court in a per curiam opinion in *Eskridge* v. *Washington State Board of Prison Terms and Paroles. . . .* In that case the defendant, who was convicted in 1935, gave timely notice of an appeal. His application then made for a copy of the transcript of the trial proceedings to be furnished at public expense was denied by the trial judge. A statute provided for so furnishing a transcript if "in his [the trial judge's] opinion justice will thereby be promoted." The trial judge found that justice would not be promoted, in that the defendant had had a fair and impartial trial, and that, in his opinion, no grave or prejudicial errors had occurred in the trial. The defendant then sought a writ of mandate from the Supreme Court of the state, ordering the trial judge to have the transcript furnished for the prosecution of his appeal. This was denied and his appeal was dismissed. In 1956 he instituted habeas corpus proceedings which on June 16, 1958, resulted in a reversal of the Washington Court's decision and a remand "for further proceedings not inconsistent with this opinion." It was conceded that the "reporter's transcript" from the trial was still available. In what form it exists does not appear from the Supreme Court's opinion. As in *Griffin,* it was held that an adequate substitute for the transcript might be furnished in lieu of the transcript itself. Justices Harlan and Whittaker dissented briefly on the ground that "on this record the Griffin case decided in 1956 should not be applied to this conviction occurring in 1935." This accords with the view expressed by Mr. Justice Frankfurter in his concurring opinion in *Griffin* that it should not be retroactive. He did not participate in the *Eskridge* case.

Just where *Griffin* v. *Illinois* may lead us is rather hard to say. That it will mean a vast increase in criminal appeals and a huge case load for appellate courts seems almost to go without saying.

* * *

The danger of swamping some state appellate courts under the flood of appeals which may be loosed by *Griffin* and *Eskridge* is not a reassuring prospect. How far *Eskridge* may lead and whether it will be extended beyond its facts remain to be seen.

[The strong opposition of the 1958 Conference of State Chief Justices serves to underscore the fact that throughout the history of the American federal system the ultimate success of the Supreme Court has been heavily dependent upon its ability to gain acceptance of its decisions. This has, in the past, been dependent upon the clear exercise of constitutional authority and upon whatever prestige and influence the Court could muster. These factors have been crucial in the relationship of the federal Supreme Court to other branches of government, whether state or federal. The section which follows consists primarily of materials which illustrate salient developments in the historical growth of federal judicial power.]

3

Federal Judicial Authority: Federalism, Separation of Powers

A. INTRODUCTION

[Essential to the effective exercise of national judicial power in the American constitutional system is the cooperation of the coordinate branches of the federal government and the often grudging acceptance of national constitutional authority by the instrumentalities of the states. Throughout its history, the Supreme Court of the United States has, in the process of constitutional interpretation, played a crucial role with respect to the two principles governing power relationships between functional and regional organs of government. The Court's most controversial decisions in the first half of the nineteenth century were related primarily to problems of federalism. The great conflicts involving the coordinate branches of the national government (the principle of separation of powers) generally arose later. But the early decision in *Marbury v. Madison* was seminal.

A basic ingredient in the early nineteenth century growth of Supreme Court doctrinal influence was the Court's ability either to gain vital political support at critical junctures or to avoid head-on clashes when the stakes appeared to be too great. As Hamilton had indicated, power proved to be an essential factor in the development of federal judicial authority. In Hamilton's view, the federal Supreme Court was "the weakest of the three departments of power." In making this observation, Hamilton recognized that the effectiveness of the Supreme Court as protector of private rights depended ultimately upon the support accorded the Court by other branches of the national government.]

1. Federalist *No. 78**

Whoever attentively considers the different departments of power must perceive, that, in a government in which they are separated from each other, the judiciary, from the nature of its functions, will always be the least dangerous to the political rights of the Constitution; because it will be least in a capacity to annoy or injure them. The Executive not only dispenses the honors, but holds the sword of the community. The legislature not only commands the purse, but prescribes the rules by which the duties and rights of every citizen are to be regulated. The judiciary, on the contrary, has no influence over either the sword or the purse; no direction either of the strength or of the wealth of the society; and can take no active resolution whatever. It may truly be said to have neither FORCE nor WILL, but merely judgment; and must ultimately depend upon the aid of the executive arm even for the efficacy of its judgments.

[The prophetic quality of Hamilton's analysis was established with astonishing accuracy in the head-on clash of authority which occurred in connection with the Revolutionary War prize claim brought by Gideon Olmstead against the state of Pennsylvania. Only the cool and firm support of President Madison finally tipped the scales in favor of federal judicial authority.]

B. THE SUPREME COURT AND FEDERALISM

1. *The Tensions of Federalism: The Case of Judge Peters**

In 1809, the Marshall Court faced its first great challenge from a state. In order to describe accurately the sentiments of Jeffersonian Republicans in Pennsylvania in 1809, some consideration of the attitudes of that state toward the exercise of paramount determinative authority by the Confederation Congress, and later by the Supreme Court in the past is necessary.

In 1778 Gideon Olmstead and three other citizens of Connecticut were captured by the British, carried to Jamaica, and there were put on board the sloop *Active* in order to assist as mariners in navigating the sloop to New York, which at that time was in the possession of the British. During the voyage, Olmstead and the others overcame the British members of the crew and attempted to reach Egg Harbor, New Jersey. However, they were overtaken and captured by the brig *Convention,* a ship

---

* Alexander Hamilton in Edward Mead Earle (ed.), *The Federalist* (New York: Random House, 1937), pp. 503–4. [Footnotes omitted.] Reproduced with permission of the publisher. Copyright (1937) by Random House, Inc.

*John R. Schmidhauser, "The Role of the Federal Judiciary in Establishing the Supremacy of the National Government" (Charlottesville, Va.: Master's Thesis, University of Virginia, 1952), pp. 123–34. [Footnotes omitted.]

belonging to the state of Pennsylvania. The *Convention's* captain libelled the sloop *Active* as a prize in Philadelphia. Olmstead and his companions, on the other hand, claimed the *Active* as their exclusive prize. A state court of admiralty awarded Olmstead and his fellow claiments only one fourth of the prize, dividing the rest between the state of Pennsylvania and the privateers. Olmstead appealed to the court of commissioners for appeals in prize cases. This prize court of the Confederation Congress awarded the proceeds of the sale of the sloop to Olmstead, but Judge Ross of the state court refused to carry out this decree. He placed the disputed prize money in the care of the state treasurer, David Rittenhouse.

The Confederation Congress investigated the affair. Its committee reported that the Congressional prize court had the authority to review the state court's decision, and resolved that "no act of any state can, or ought to, destroy the right of appeal to Congress . . ." The legislature of Pennsylvania thereupon ordered the state admiralty court to ignore the Congressional committee resolution. The Confederation Congress did not take any further action, and Olmstead again resorted to the state courts. This time he obtained a judgment by default in a county court, but lost again when the case was taken on appeal to the Supreme Court of Pennsylvania. Chief Justice McKean declared that "the decree of the Committee of appeals [is] contrary to the provisions of the act of Congress, and of the general assembly, extra-judicial, erroneous and void." After this judicial defeat, Olmstead made no attempt to contest the validity of the state court decision until 1803.

Pennsylvania's propensity to defy central authority was not curbed when the shaky Confederation was discarded for the stronger Federal Government. It was in Pennsylvania that the Whisky Rebellion occurred. And in 1798, Chief Justice McKean defied the Federal Judiciary in a conflict over jurisdiction. This early challenge, which was never brought before the Federal Supreme Court for review, arose from an attempt by Federalist newspaper editor William Cobbett to remove a libel suit from a Pennsylvania court to a Federal Circuit Court on the ground of diversity of citizenship. McKean denied the right to remove, holding that,

> . . . *if a state should differ with the United States about the construction [of the powers granted by the Constitution], there is no common umpire but the people who should adjust the affair by making amendments in the constitutional way, or suffer from the defect . . . There is no provision in the Constitution that in such a case the judges of the Supreme Court of the United States shall control and be conclusive.*

This direct challenge was followed by another outburst of state indignation by the Pennsylvania legislature in 1807. The occasion for this display of independence was Chief Justice John Marshall's opinion in *Huidekoper's Lessees* v. *Douglass*. And again in 1809 the state legislature defied a Supreme Court citation notifying the state to appear, if she thought fit, to become a party to a suit involving conflicting Federal and state claims. In 1805, the Supreme Court of Pennsylvania had decided against a claim of the United States for priority in payment from the property of a debtor. This precise question had been decided by Chief Justice Marshall in 1804 in *United*

States v. *Fisher,* but the Pennsylvania judges were not aware of that decision. State Court Judge Yeates had taken the following extreme states-rights stand on the question:

> *Congress have the concurrent right of passing laws to protect the interests of the Union as to debts due to the Government of the United States arising from the revenue, but in so doing they cannot detract from the uncontrollable power of individual States to raise their own revenue, nor infringe or derogate from the sovereignty of any independent state.*

When, in 1809, the United States Supreme Court invited the state to become a party to a suit to settle the conflicting claims, the Pennsylvania legislature reacted violently, denying that the state had "surrendered to the General Government a power to defeat or destroy her right to enforce the collection of her own revenues." This act of defiance prompted Republican United States Attorney Dallas to write to Attorney-General Caesar A. Rodney that "the conduct of our Legislature at Lancaster is very strange and may be very mischievous. They have prostrated the constitutional barrier between the Judicial and Legislative departments. The Legislature at Boston will probably attempt to prostrate the barrier between the State and Federal Governments . . . The times are bad."

Dallas' reference to "the Legislature at Boston" indicated the very real anxiety of the Republican Administration concerning the strong states-rights tendencies in Federalist New England. For during this period, New England resentment to the Jeffersonian Embargo Acts had converted the formerly nationalistic Federalists into staunch advocates of state sovereignty. Jefferson's Louisiana Purchase had earlier infuriated the New England Federalists, and by 1809 separation from the Union and formation of a northern confederacy were being widely discussed by many embittered Federalist leaders. Fortunately, Federalist Circuit Judge John Davis, in *United States* v. *Brigantine William,* upheld the Administration's Embargo Act as a valid regulation of commerce, as a preparation for war under the congressional war powers, and as appropriate under the necessary and proper clause. However, successful defiance of the Supreme Court by any state would undoubtedly have encouraged the New England separatist movement, and would probably have destroyed the authority of the Federal Government in the states outside New England as well. It was in this critical period that the sovereignty-conscious legislature of Pennsylvania sought to assert its version of the states-rights constitutional doctrine of state sentinelship.

The issue was joined over the long dormant Olmstead prize claims. Gideon Olmstead had resurrected his claim for the Sloop *Active* prize money in 1803 when he filed suit in a Federal District Court. By the decision in *Penhallow* v. *Doane,* Federal District Courts were held to have authority to execute the decrees of the old Confederation courts of appeals in cases of capture. In January, 1803, District Judge Peters upheld Olmstead's claims and, under the Penhallow doctrine, decreed that the prize money be paid to Olmstead. The Pennsylvania legislature immediately passed a law defying the District Court's ruling as a usurpation of jurisdiction. The statute directed the Governor "to protect the just rights of the state from any process issued out of any Federal Court." Finally, after five years, this direct challenge to the Federal Judiciary was reviewed by the Supreme Court. In 1808, Olmstead, now eighty-two years old, applied to the highest national tribunal for issuance of a *mandamus* to Judge Peters to compel him to enforce obedience to his district court decision of 1803. Such a *mandamus* was issued directing Peters to exercise the sentence pronounced by him in *Gideon Olmstead and others* v. *Rittenhouse's Executrices* or show cause for not so doing. Judge Peters answered that "from prudential, more than other motives, I deemed it best to avoid embroiling the government of the United States and that of Pennsylvania (if the latter government should choose to do so), on a question which has rested on my single opinion."

In 1809, the *United States* v. *Judge Peters,* Chief Justice John Marshall pointed out that it was with "great attention, and with serious concern" that the Supreme Court had considered "the return of Judge Peters to the *mandamus*."

> If [stated Marshall] the legislatures of the several states may, at will, annul the judgments of the courts of the United States, and destroy the rights acquired under those judgments, the constitution itself becomes a solemn mockery; and the nation is deprived of the means of enforcing its laws by the instrumentality of its own tribunals. So fatal a result must be deprecated by all; and the people of Pennsylvania, not less than the citizens of every other state, must feel a deep interest in resisting principles so destructive of the Union, and in averting consequences so fatal to themselves.

Marshall held that "the ultimate right to determine the jurisdiction of the courts of the Union" necessarily resides in "the supreme judicial tribunal of the nation," not the state legislatures. After briefly reviewing and upholding the lower Federal Court decision, Marshall "with extreme regret" awarded a peremptory *mandamus*.

Republican Governor Snyder immediately sent a message to the state legislature informing the representatives that he intended to call out the militia to prevent enforcement of the decree. On March 24, Judge Peters issued process against the holders of the contested prize money, Mrs. Sergeant and Mrs. Waters, executrices of the deceased state treasurer, David Rittenhouse. When the United States Marshal attempted to serve process, he met with the resistance of a body of state militia commanded by General Bright. He then summoned a *posse comitatus* of two thousand men. For a time bloodshed seemed imminent. On April 3, the Pennsylvania legislature adopted resolutions denying that the Supreme Court had the power "to decide on State rights." But by April 6th, the Pennsylvania authorities began to weaken.

As one discerning newspaper correspondent had observed, "It had been supposed that the marshall, [a] good, easy man, would make but a faint attempt to enforce the service of the process. The active attempt made by him has awakened the most serious apprehensions . . . it is understood that measures will be taken to compromise matters with the much injured, old veteran." On April 6, Governor Snyder wrote to the President, James Madison, expressing the hope that the latter would "justly discriminate between opposition to the Constitution and laws of the United States

and that of resisting the decree of a Judge founded . . . on a usurpation of power."
The newly-elected President, although a staunch Republican, replied as follows:

> *The Executive is not only unauthorized to prevent the execution of a decree sanctioned by the Supreme Court of the United States, but is expressly enjoined, by statute, to carry into effect any such decree, where opposition may be made to it.*

The Pennsylvania legislature ordered removal of the state militia from the Rittenhouse residence and began consideration of a bill to appropriate enough money to restore the contested prize fund. Mrs. Sergeant, now under arrest for refusal to obey the Federal Court order, applied for a writ of *habeas corpus* to Chief Justice Tilghman of the Pennsylvania Supreme Court. He dismissed her petition, holding that she was properly in Federal custody. By April 26, the state made the payment required by the Federal Court. Relieved, President Madison wrote to Attorney-General Rodney: "The affair of Olmstead has passed off without the threatened collision of force."

The final humiliation for the state of Pennsylvania came when General Bright was tried and convicted before Justice Bushrod Washington in Federal Circuit Court. For forcibly resisting a federal marshal, Bright and his associates were sentenced to fine and imprisonment. However, President Madison pardoned them on the ground that "they had acted under a mistaken sense of duty." As Professor Johnson expressed it, "The paramount authority of the National Government was thus sustained at every point in the controversy."

At the very height of the controversy, the Pennsylvania legislature had stated, in resolutions which were submitted to the legislatures of the other states, its own version of the doctrine of state sentinelship. It acknowledged the supremacy of "the General Government," but while it submitted to the latter's authority when such authority was:

> . . . *exercised within Constitutional limits, they [the state legislatures] trust they will not be considered as acting hostile to the General Government, when, as guardians of the State rights, they cannot permit an infringement of those rights, by an unconstitutional exercise of power in the United States Courts. . . . To suffer the United States' courts to decide on State rights will, from a bias in favor of power, necessarily destroy the Federal part of our government.*

The Pennsylvania resolutions were answered by resolutions of disapproval by the legislatures of Tennessee, Kentucky, New Jersey, Maryland, Ohio, Georgia, North Carolina, Virginia, New Hampshire, and Vermont. In reply to the Pennsylvania proposal that the "sister states" support it in endeavoring to get a constitutional amendment establishing an "impartial tribunal to determine disputes between the General and State Governments," the Virginia legislature resolved that,

> . . . *a tribunal is already provided by the Constitution of the United States; to wit: the Supreme Court, more eminently qualified from their habits and duties,*

from the mode of their selection, and from the tenure of their offices, to decide the disputes aforesaid in an enlightened and impartial manner, than any other tribunal that could be erected.

[Bitter and direct conflicts of authority between the federal judiciary and the governments of the states have, of course, occurred from time to time since 1809. Governor Orval Faubus of Arkansas provided the most striking example in his defiance of a federal judicial desegregation program for the public schools of Little Rock. Again as in 1809, the President of the United States had to support the federal courts. However, unlike the situation in Pennsylvania, President Eisenhower had to send federal troops to Little Rock to gain state compliance. *Cooper* v. *Aaron,* reproduced in part below, contains not only a full account of the episode, but a pointed example of the contemporary Court's attitude toward modern invocation of the states' rights doctrine.]

2. The Little Rock Case*

As this case reaches us it raises questions of the highest importance to the maintenance of our Federal system of government. It necessarily involves a claim by the Governor and Legislature of a state that there is no duty on state officials to obey Federal court orders resting on this Court's considered interpretation of the United States Constitution.

Specifically it involves actions by the Governor and Legislature of Arkansas upon the premise that they are not bound by our holding in Brown v. Board of Education . . . That holding was that the Fourteenth Amendment forbids states to use their governmental powers to bar children on racial grounds from attending schools where there is state participation through any arrangement, management, funds or property.

We are urged to uphold a suspension of the Little Rock School Board's plan to do away with segregated public schools in Little Rock until state laws and efforts to upset and nullify our holding in Brown v. Board of Education have been further challenged and tested in the courts. We reject these contentions.

The case was argued before us on September 11, 1958. On the following day we unanimously affirmed the judgment of the Court of Appeals for the Eighth Circuit . . . which had reversed a judgment of the District Court for the Eastern District of Arkansas . . .

The District Court had granted the application of the petitioners, the Little Rock School Board and School Superintendent, to suspend for two and one-half years the operation of the School Board's court-approved desegregation program. In order

---

* *Cooper* v. *Aaron,* delivered *per curiam* on September 30, 1958, and reported in full on that day in the *Washington Post and Times Herald*, p. B 3. [All citations omitted.] This newspaper account has been utilized because it retains more of the dramatic political overtones of the opinion than has been preserved in the formal version in the United States Reports.

that the School Board might know, without doubt, its duty in this regard before the opening of school, which had been set for the following Monday, Sept. 15, 1958, we immediately issued the judgment, reserving the expression of our supporting views to a later date. This opinion of all of the members of the Court embodies those views.

The Court, having fully deliberated upon the oral arguments had on August 28, 1958, as supplemented by the arguments presented on September 11, 1958, and all the briefs on file, is unanimously of the opinion that the judgment of the Court of Appeals for the Eighth Circuit of August 18, 1958, must be affirmed. In view of the imminent commencement of the new school year at the Central High School of Little Rock, Arkansas, we deem it important to make prompt announcement of our judgment affirming the Court of Appeals. The expression of the views supporting our judgment will be prepared and announced in due course.

It is accordingly ordered that the judgment of the Court of Appeals for the Eighth Circuit, dated August 18, 1958, reversing the judgment of the District Court for the Eastern District of Arkansas, dated June 20, 1958, be affirmed, and that the judgments of the District Court for the Eastern District of Arkansas, dated August 28, 1956, and September 3, 1957, enforcing the School Board's plan for desegregation in compliance with the decision of this Court in Brown v. Broad of Education . . . be reinstated. It follows that the order of the Court of Appeals dated August 21, 1958, staying its own mandate is of no further effect.

(The judgment of this Court shall be effective immediately, and shall be communicated forthwith to the District Court for the Eastern District of Arkansas.)

SEGREGATION DECIDED DENIAL OF PROTECTION

The following are the facts and circumstances so far as necessary to show how the legal questions are presented.

On May 17, 1954, this Court decided that enforced racial segregation in the public schools of a state is a denial of the equal protection of the laws enjoined by the Fourteenth Amendment. . . . The Court postponed, pending further argument, formulation of a decree to effectuate this decision. That decree was rendered May 31, 1955. . . .

In the formulation of that decree the Court recognized that good faith compliance with the principles declared in Brown might in some situations "call for elimination of a variety of obstacles in making the transition to school systems operated in accordance with the constitutional principles set forth in our May 17, 1954, decision." The Court went on to state:

"Courts of equity may properly take into account the public interest in the elimination of such obstacles in a systematic and effective manner. But it should go without saying that the vitality of these constitutional principles cannot be allowed to yield simply because of disagreement with them.

"While giving weight to these public and private considerations, the courts will require that the defendants make a prompt and reasonable start toward full compliance with our May 17, 1954, ruling. Once such a start has been made, the courts may find that additional time is necessary to carry out the ruling in an effective manner. The burden rests upon the defendants to establish that such time is necessary in the public interest and is consistent with good faith compliance at the earliest practicable date.

"To that end, the courts may consider problems related to administration, arising from the physical condition of the school plant, the school transportation system, personnel, revision of school districts and attendance areas into compact units to achieve a system of determining admission to the public schools on a nonracial basis, and revision of local laws and regulations which may be necessary in solving the foregoing problems." . . .

Under such circumstances, the District Courts were directed to require "a prompt and reasonable start toward full compliance," and to take such action as was necessary to bring about the end of racial segregation in the public schools "with all deliberate speed.". . . Of course, in many locations, obedience to the duty of desegregation would require the immediate general admission of Negro children, otherwise qualified as students for their appropriate classes, at particular schools.

On the other hand, a District Court, after analysis of the relevant factors (which, of course, excludes hostility to racial desegregation), might conclude that justification existed for not requiring the present nonsegregated admission of all qualified Negro children. In such circumstances, however, the Court should scrutinize the program of the school authorities to make sure that they had developed arrangements pointed toward the earliest practicable completion of desegregation, and had taken appropriate steps to put their program into effective operation.

It was made plain that delay in any guise in order to deny the constitutional rights of Negro children could not be countenanced, and that only a prompt start, diligently and earnestly pursued, to eliminate racial segregation from the public schools could constitute good faith compliance. State authorities were thus duty bound to devote every effort toward initiating desegregation and bringing about the elimination of racial discrimination in the public school system.

STATEMENT OF POLICY ISSUED BY BOARD

On May 20, 1954, three days after the first Brown opinion, the Little Rock District School Board adopted, and on May 23, 1954, made public, a statement of policy entitled "Supreme Court Decision—Segregation in Public Schools." In this statement the Board recognized that:

"It is our responsibility to comply with Federal constitutional requirements and we intend to do so when the Supreme Court of the United States outlines the method to be followed."

Thereafter the Board undertook studies of the administrative problems confronting the transition to a desegregated public school system at Little Rock. It instructed the Superintendent of Schools to prepare a plan for desegregation, and approved such a plan on May 24, 1955, seven days before the second Brown opinion.

The plan provided for desegregation at the senior high school level (grades 10 through 12) as the first stage. Desegregation at the junior high and elementary levels was to follow. It was contemplated that desegregation at the high school level would commence in the fall of 1957, and the expectation was that complete desegregation of the school system would be accomplished by 1963.

Following the adoption of this plan, the Superintendent of Schools discussed it with a large number of citizen groups in the city. As a result of these discussions, the Board reached the conclusion that "a large majority of the residents" of Little Rock were of "the belief . . . that the plan, although objectionable in principle," from the point of view of those supporting segregated schools, "was still the best for the interests of all pupils in the District."

Upon challenge by a group of Negro plaintiffs desiring more rapid completion of the desegregation process, the District Court upheld the School Board's plan, Aaron v. Cooper . . . The Court of Appeals affirmed. . . . Review of that judgment was not sought here.

While the School Board was thus going forward with its preparation for desegregating the Little Rock school system, other State authorities, in contrast, were actively pursuing a program designed to perpetuate in Arkansas the system of racial segregation which this Court had held violated the Fourteenth Amendment

First came, in November, 1956, an amendment to the State Constitution flatly commanding the Arkansas General Assembly to oppose "in every constitutional manner the unconstitutional desegregation decisions of May 17, 1954, and May 31, 1955, of the United States Supreme Court,". . . and, through the initiative, a pupil assignment law . . .

Pursuant to the constitutional command, a law relieving school children from compulsory attendance at racially mixed schools, . . . and a law establishing a State Sovereignty Commission. . . were enacted by the General Assembly in February 1957.

WORK CONTINUED ON PROGRAM START

The School Board and the Superintendent of Schools nevertheless continued with preparations to carry out the first stage of the desegregation program. Nine Negro children were scheduled for admission in September, 1957, to Central High School, which has more than 2000 students. Various administrative measures, designed to assure the smooth transition of this state of desegregation, were undertaken.

On September 2, 1957, the day before these Negro students were to enter Central High, the school authorities were met with drastic opposing action on the part of the Governor of Arkansas, who dispatched units of the Arkansas National Guard to the Central High School grounds, and placed the school "off limits" to colored students. As found by the District Court in subsequent proceedings, the Governor's action had not been requested by the school authorities, and was entirely unheralded. The findings were these:

"Up to this time (Sept. 2), no crowds had gathered about Central High School and no acts of violence or threats of violence in connection with the carrying out of the plan had occurred. Nevertheless, out of an abundance of caution, the school authorities had frequently conferred with the Mayor and Chief of Police of Little Rock about taking appropriate steps by the Little Rock police to prevent any possible disturbances or acts of violence in connection with the attendance of the nine colored students at Central High School. The Mayor considered that the Little Rock police force could adequately cope with any incidents which might arise at the opening of school.

"The Mayor, the Chief of Police, and the school authorities made no request to the Governor or any representative of his for State assistance in maintaining peace and order at Central High School. Neither the Governor nor any other official of the State government consulted with the Little Rock authorities about whether the Little Rock police were prepared to cope with any incidents which might arise at the school, about any need for State assistance in maintaining peace and order, or about stationing the Arkansas National Guard at Central High School.". . .

The Board's petition for postponement in this proceeding states: "The effect of that action (of the Governor) was to harden the core of opposition to the plan and cause many persons who theretofore had reluctantly accepted the plan to believe that there was some power in the state of Arkansas which, when exerted, could nullify the Federal law and permit disobedience of the decree of this (District) Court, and from that date hostility to the plan was increased and criticism of the officials of the (School) District has become more bitter and unrestrained."

The Governor's action caused the School Board to request the Negro students on September 2 not to attend the high school "until the legal dilemma was solved." The next day, September 3, 1957, the Board petitioned the District Court for instructions, and the Court, after a hearing, found that the Board's request of the Negro students to stay away from the high school had been made because of the stationing of the military guards by the state authorities.

The Court determined that this was not a reason for departing from the approved plan, and ordered the School Board and Superintendent to proceed with it.

CHILDREN BARRED BY NATIONAL GUARD

On the morning of the next day, September 4, 1957, the Negro children attempted to enter the high school but, as the District Court later found, units of the Arkansas National Guard "acting pursuant to the Governor's order, stood shoulder to shoulder at the school grounds and thereby forcibly prevented the 9 Negro students . . . from entering," as they continued to do every school day during the following three weeks. . . .

That same day, September 4, 1957, the United States Attorney for the Eastern District of Arkansas was requested by the District Court to begin an immediate investigation in order to fix responsibility for the interference with the orderly implementation of the District Court's direction to carry out the desegregation program. Three days later, September 7, the District Court denied a petition of the School Board and the Superintendent of Schools for an order temporarily suspending continuance of the program.

Upon completion of the United States Attorney's investigation, he and the Attorney General of the United States, at the District Court's request, entered the proceedings and filed a petition on behalf of the United States, as amicus curiae, to enjoin the Governor of Arkansas and officers of the Arkansas National Guard from further attempts to prevent obedience to the Court's order.

After hearings on the petition, the District Court found that the School Board's plan had been obstructed by the Governor through the use of National Guard troops, and granted a preliminary injunction on Sept. 20, 1957, enjoining the Governor and the officers of the Guard from preventing the attendance of Negro children at Central High School, and from otherwise obstructing or interfering with the orders of the court in connection with the plan. . . . The National Guard was then withdrawn from the school.

The next school day was Monday, Sept. 23, 1957. The Negro children entered the high school that morning under the protection of the Little Rock Police Department and members of the Arkansas State Police. But the officers caused the children to be removed from the school during the morning because they had difficulty controlling a large and demonstrating crowd which had gathered at the high school. . .

On Sept. 25, however, the President of the United States dispatched Federal troops to Central High School and admission of the Negro students to the school was thereby effected. Regular Army troops continued at the high school until Nov. 27, 1957. They were then replaced by federalized National Guardsmen who remained throughout the balance of the school year. Eight of the Negro students remained in attendance at the school throughout the school year.

NEGROES' WITHDRAWAL PROPOSED BY BOARD

We come now to the aspect of the proceedings presently before us. On Feb. 20, 1958, the School Board and the Superintendent of Schools filed a petition in the District Court seeking a postponement of their program for desegregation. Their position in essence was that because of extreme public hostility, which they stated had been engendered largely by the official attitudes and actions of the Governor and the Legislature, the maintenance of a sound educational program at Central High School, with the Negro students in attendance, would be impossible.

The Board therefore proposed that the Negro students already admitted to the school be withdrawn and sent to segregated schools and that all further steps to carry out the Board's desegregation program be postponed for a period later suggested by the Board to be two-and-one-half years.

After a hearing the District Court granted the relief request by the Board. Among other things, the Court found that the past year at Central High School had been attended by conditions of "chaos, bedlam, and turmoil"; that there were "repeated incidents of more or less serious violence directed against the Negro students and their property"; that there was "tension and unrest among the school administrators, the class-room teachers, the pupils, and the latter's parents, which inevitably had an adverse effect upon the educational program"; that a school official was threatened with violence; that a "serious financial burden" had been cast on the School District; that the education of the students had suffered "and under existing conditions will continue to suffer"; that the Board would continue to need "military assistance or its equivalent"; that the local police department would not be able "to tail enough men to afford the necessary protection"; and that the "situation was intolerable." . . .

The District Court's judgment was dated June 20, 1958. The Negro respondents appealed to the Court of Appeals for the Eighth Circuit and also sought there a stay of the District Court's judgment. At the same time, they filed a petition for certiorari in this Court asking us to review the District Court's judgment without awaiting the disposition of their appeal to the Court of Appeals, or of their petition to that court for a stay. That we declined to do. . . .

The Court of Appeals did not act on the petition for a stay, but on August 18, 1958, after convening in special session on August 4 and hearing the appeal, reversed the District Court . . . On August 21, 1958, the Court of Appeals stayed its mandate to permit the School Board to petition this Court for certiorari.

Pending the filing of the School Board's petition for certiorari, the Negro respondents, on August 23, 1958, applied to Mr. Justice Whittaker, as Circuit Justice for the Eighth Circuit, to stay the order of the Court of Appeals withholding its own mandate and also to stay the District Court's judgment. In view of the nature of the motions, he referred them to the entire Court.

COURT IS CONVENED IN SPECIAL TERM

Recognizing the vital importance of a decision of the issues in time to permit arrangements to be made for the 1958–1959 school year, . . . we convened in special term on August 28, 1958, and heard oral argument on the respondent's motions, and also argument of the Solicitor General who, by invitation, appeared for the United States as amicus curiae, and asserted that the Court of Appeals' judgment was clearly correct on the merits, and urged that we vacate its stay forthwith.

Finding that respondent's application necessarily involved consideration of the merits of the litigation, we entered an order which deferred decision upon the motions pending the disposition of the School Board's petition for certiorari, and fixed September 8, 1958, as the day on or before which such petition might be filed, and September 11, 1958, for oral argument upon the petition. The petition for certiorari, duly filed, was granted in open Court on September 11, 1958, . . . and further arguments were had, the Solicitor General again urging the correctness of the judgment of the Court of Appeals.

On September 12, 1958, as already mentioned, we unanimously affirmed the judgment of the Court of Appeals in the per curiam opinion set forth in the margin at the outset of this opinion.

In affirming the judgment of the Court of Appeals which reversed the District Court we have accepted without reservation the position of the School Board, the Superintendent of Schools, and their counsel that they displayed entire good faith in the conduct of these proceedings and in dealing with the unfortunate and distressing sequence of events which has been outlined.

We likewise have accepted the findings of the District Court as to the conditions at Central High School during the 1957–58 school year, and also the findings that the educational progress of all the students, white and colored, of that school has suffered and will continue to suffer if the conditions which prevailed last year are permitted to continue.

The significance of these findings, however, is to be considered in light of the fact, indisputably revealed by the record before us, that the conditions they depict are directly traceable to the actions of legislators and executive officials of the state of Arkansas, taken in their official capacities, which reflect their own determination to resist this Court's decision in the Brown case and which have brought about violent resistance to that decision in Arkansas.

In its petition for certiorari filed in this Court, the School Board itself describes the situation in this language: "The legislative, executive, and judicial departments of the state government opposed the desegregation of Little Rock schools by enacting laws calling out troops, making statements vilifying Federal law and Federal courts, and failing to utilize state law enforcement agencies and judicial processes to maintain public peace."

ACTIONS OF STATE AGENCIES CITED

One may well sympathize with the position of the Board in the face of the frustrating conditions which have confronted it, but regardless of the Board's good faith, the actions of the other state agencies responsible for those conditions compel us to reject the Board's legal position.

Had Central High School been under the direct management of the State itself, it could hardly be suggested that those immediately in charge of the school should be heard to assert their own good faith as a legal excuse for delay in implementing the constitutional rights of these respondents, when vindication of those rights was rendered difficult or impossible by the actions of other state officials.

The situation here is in no different posture because the members of the School Board and the Superintendent of Schools are local officials; from the point of view of the Fourteenth Amendment, they stand in this litigation as the agents of the State.

The Constitutional rights of respondents are not to be sacrificed or yielded to the violence and disorder which have followed upon the actions of the Governor and Legislature.

As this Court said some 41 years ago in a unanimous opinion in a case involving another aspect of racial segregation: "It is urged that this proposed segregation will promote the public peace by preventing race conflicts. Desirable as this is, and important as is the preservation of the public peace, this aim cannot be accomplished by laws or ordinances which deny rights created or protected by the Federal Constitution."

Thus law and order are not here to be preserved by depriving the Negro children of their Constitutional rights. The record before us clearly establishes that the growth of the Board's difficulties to a magnitude beyond its unaided power to control is the product of State action. Those difficulties, as counsel for the Board forthrightly conceded on the oral argument in this Court, can also be brought under control by state action.

SEES CONTROLLING PRINCIPLES PLAIN

The controlling legal principles are plain. The command of the Fourteenth Amendment is that no "State" shall deny to any person within its jurisdiction the equal protection of the laws.

"A State acts by its legislative, its executive, or its judicial authorities. It can act in no other way. The constitutional provision, therefore, must mean that no agency of the State, or of the officers or agents by whom its powers are exerted, shall deny to any person within its jurisdiction the equal protection of the laws. Whoever, by virtue of public position under a State government . . . denies or takes away the equal protection of the laws, violates the constitutional inhibition; and he acts in the name and for the State, and is clothed with the State's power his act is that of the State. This must be so, or the constitutional prohibition has no meaning." . . .

Thus the prohibitions of the Fourteenth Amendment extend to all action of the state denying equal protection of the laws; whatever the agency of the state taking the action . . . or whatever the guise in which it is taken . . .

In short, the Constitutional rights of children not to be discriminated against in school admission on grounds of race or color declared by this Court in the Brown case can neither be nullified openly and directly by state legislators or state executive or judicial officers, nor nullified indirectly by them through evasive schemes for segregation . . . attempted "ingenuously" . . .

What has been said, in the light of the facts developed, is enough to dispose of the case. However, we should answer the premise of the actions of the Governor and Legislature that they are not bound by our holding in the Brown case. It is necessary only to recall some basic Constitutional propositions which are settled doctrine.

"Article VI of the Constitution makes the Constitution the 'supreme Law of the Land.' In 1803, Chief Justice Marshall, speaking for a unanimous Court, referring to the Constitution as 'the fundamental and paramount law of the nation,' declared in the notable case of *Marbury* v. *Madison,* . . . that 'It is emphatically the province and duty of the judicial department to say what the law is'."

The decision declared the basic principle that the Federal judiciary is supreme in the exposition of the law of the Constitution, and that principle has ever since been respected by this Court and the country as a permanent and indispensable feature of our Constitutional system.

It follows that the interpretation of the Fourteenth Amendment enunciated by this Court in the Brown case is the supreme law of the land, and Art. VI of the Constitution makes it of binding effect on the States "anything in the Constitution or Laws of any State to the Contrary notwithstanding."

Every state legislator and executive and judicial officer is solemnly committed by oath taken pursuant to Art. VI, Par. 3 "to support this Constitution." Chief Justice Taney, speaking for a unanimous Court in 1859, said that this requirement "reflected the framers' anxiety to preserve it [the Constitution] in full force, in all its powers, and to guard against resistance to or evasion of its authority, on the part of a State . . ."

RIGHT OF STUDENT HELD 'FUNDAMENTAL'

No state legislator or executive or judicial officer can war against the Constitution without violating his undertaking to support it.

Chief Justice Marshall spoke for a unanimous Court in saying that: "If the legislatures of the several states may, at will, annul the judgments of the Courts of the United States, and destroy the rights acquired under those judgments, the Constitution itself becomes a solemn mockery . . ."

A Governor who asserts a power to nullify a Federal court order is similarly restrained. If he had such a power, said Chief Justice Hughes, in 1932, also for a unanimous Court, "it is manifest that the fiat of a state Governor, and not the Constitution of the United States, would be the supreme law of the land; that the restrictions of the Federal Constitution upon the exercise of state power would be but impotent phrases . . ."

It is, of course, quite true that the responsibility for public education is primarily the concern of the states, but it is equally true that such responsibilities, like all other state activity, must be exercised consistently with Federal Constitutional requirements as they apply to state action.

The Constitution created a Government dedicated to equal justice under law. The Fourteenth Amendment embodied and emphasized that ideal. State support of segregated schools through any arrangement, management, funds, or property cannot be squared with the Amendment's command that no state shall deny to any person within its jurisdiction the equal protection of the laws.

The right of a student not to be segregated on racial grounds in schools so maintained is indeed so fundamental and pervasive that it is embraced in the concept of due process of law. . . .

The basic decision in Brown was unanimously reached by this Court only after the case had been briefed and twice argued and the issues had been given the most serious consideration. Since the first Brown opinion, three new Justices have come to the Court. They are at one with the Justices still on the Court who participated in that basic decision as to its correctness, and that decision is now unanimously reaffirmed.

The principles announced in that decision and obedience of the states to them, according to the command of the Constitution, are indispensable for the protection of the freedoms guaranteed by our fundamental charter for all of us. Our Constitutional ideal of equal justice under law is thus made a living truth.

C. THE SUPREME COURT AND THE
SEPARATION OF POWERS

[Conflicts of authority between the three functional branches of the federal government have recurred throughout American history. The resolution of such conflicts by the Supreme Court was not spelled out explicitly in the Constitution although some of the delegates to the Philadelphia Convention of 1787 had supported the concept. The application of the doctrine of judicial review to the relationship of the federal executive, legislature, and judiciary came many years after the Court had begun developing the doctrine with respect to the relationship of the states to the nation. The political circumstances attending this application are perceptively discussed by Mr. Justice Harold Burton below.]

1. The Cornerstone of Constitutional Law: The Extraordinary Case of Marbury v. Madison, Part I*

One hundred and fifty years ago, the feud between the Federalists, led by President Adams, and the Anti-Federalists, led by Vice President Jefferson, was at fever heat. Until the adjournment of Congress in May, General John Marshall of Virginia had been serving his first and only term as a Federalist member of the House of Representatives. In June, he became Secretary of State and supported President Adams throughout his bitter and unsuccessful campaign for reelection.

The Anti-Federalists carried enough states to elect Jefferson in the electoral college. However, that cumbersome institution was still operating under the original provision whereby each elector must vote for two candidates for President. The candidate receiving the highest vote was to become President and the next highest Vice President. The Anti-Federalists had expected to elect Jefferson President and Aaron Burr Vice President. Nevertheless, their electors all voted for both, with the result that Jefferson received seventy-three votes, Burr seventy-three, Adams sixty-five, Pinckney sixty-four and Jay one. This threw the election into the House of Representatives where a majority of the sixteen states, each casting one vote, was necessary for a choice. Finally, on February 17, 1801, two weeks before his inauguration, Jefferson was chosen President on the thirty-sixth ballot. This was after Federalist Hamilton, who disapproved of both candidates, threw his influence to Jefferson as the less dangerous of the two. Marshall declined to express a preference.

ADAMS APPOINTS MARSHALL TO SUPREME BENCH

In the meantime the Federalists had concentrated their hopes for the survival of the Republic upon the federal judiciary. The Supreme Court consisted of six Federalists. Four had been appointed by Washington. They were Chief Justice Ellsworth of Connecticut and Associate Justices Cushing of Massachusetts, Paterson of New Jersey and Chase of Maryland. Two had been appointed by Adams. They were Bushrod Washington of Virginia and Moore of North Carolina. Chief Justice Ellsworth was in France, doubling as Minister to France. Being in ill health, he resigned as Chief Justice in time to give President Adams a chance to appoint a

---

* Mr. Justice Harold Burton, "The Cornerstone of Constitutional Law: the Extraordinary Case of *Marbury* v. *Madison*," *American Bar Association Journal*, XXXVI (October, 1950), 805–8. [Footnotes omitted.] Reproduced with permission of the author and the publisher. Copyright (1950) by the American Bar Association.

Federalist successor. The President promptly named former Chief Justice Jay to the vacancy. With equal promptness, Jay declined the appointment. On January 20, the President made a surprise appointment of his Secretary of State, John Marshall, to the Chief Justiceship. He was confirmed January 27 and, on February 4, 1801, entered upon his duties. He continued to serve also, without salary however, as Secretary of State to the end of President Adams' term on March 3, 1801. He was succeeded by James Madison on March 5. Almost the first official duty performed by John Marshall, as Chief Justice, was his administration of the oath of office to Thomas Jefferson, on March 4, 1801.

"MIDNIGHT JUDGES" APPOINTED AS ONE OF ADAMS' LAST PRESIDENTIAL ACTS

In the midst of this embroilment the Federalists in Congress, on February 13, 1801, had passed a new Circuit Court Bill. On its merits this seems to have been a well-considered bill intended to do away with the need for circuit duty by the Justices of the Supreme Court and to provide circuit judges to assume those duties. This would speed up the delayed litigation in the circuits. It also would do away with the embarrassment of the constant presence on the Supreme Court of Justices who had heard the same cases on circuit. To accomplish this, it authorized the appointment of sixteen additional federal judges and President Adams at once filled all those vacancies with Federalists. The nominees were confirmed by the Senate on March 2. Their commissions were signed by President Adams and sealed by his Secretary of State, John Marshall, on March 3. These were nicknamed the "midnight judges." Occasionally it is erroneously thought that their commissions were the ones that became the subject of the *Marbury* v. *Madison* litigation.

The fact is that the case of *Marbury* v. *Madison* arose out of a distinct but somewhat comparable situation. It arose from the passage, on February 27, 1801, of the District of Columbia Organic Act and appointments under it. That Act provided for the appointment by the President of justices of the peace, for five-year terms, for the respective counties of Washington and Alexandria within the District. The President did not overlook this opportunity. On March 2, he nominated forty-two such justices of the peace—twenty-three for Washington and nineteen for Alexandria. They were confirmed by the Senate and their commissions were signed by the President and sealed by Secretary Marshall before midnight, March 3. They were the "midnight justices of the peace." Some of these commissions were delivered to the appointees on the night of March 3 by Marshall's brother, James, but not all were delivered. Among those not delivered was that of William Marbury of the County of Washington. It was his claim to that commission, together with the claims of three other similarly situated appointees, that became the subjects of the famous litigation.

In the midst of these extraordinary circumstances, the Supreme Court, on February 2, 1801, met for its first time in Washington. It met in the single section of the Capitol which had been built. That section consisted of a square building immediately north of the future dome. It now stands between the dome and the Senate wing. The Senate met in the East front room, the House met at the rear. The Court occupied a committee room twenty-four feet wide and thirty feet long.

That room later became the office of the Marshal of the Court. There Chief Justice Marshall, on February 4, 1801, at the age of 44, assumed his duties. The Court passed on several motions, handed down no reported opinions and adjourned on February 10. At its next Term in August, 1801, the Court handed down one opinion. Instead of the several Justices rendering separate opinions, *seriatim,* as had been the custom, the new Chief Justice spoke for the Court as a unit. Thereafter, until 1805, each opinion was delivered in that manner, except in two instances where the Chief Justice had participated in the case on the circuit.

MARBURY CASE EXPECTED TO LEAD TO IMPEACHMENT OF JUDGES

The Court met again in December, 1801. It was then that the Marbury litigation was started. The attorney for Marbury was Charles Lee. Until recently Lee had been Attorney General under President Adams. The Marbury proceeding was instituted by a motion for a rule to show cause why a writ of mandamus should not issue to direct James Madison, as Secretary of State, to deliver to Marbury a commission as a justice of the peace. The Court ordered Madison to show such cause on the fourth day of the next Term. It was expected that the next Term would be held in June under the new Circuit Court Act. This expectation was not fulfilled, because Congress, with the obvious purpose of preventing the Court from passing so soon on this and other highly controversial issues, abolished the June Term and prescribed Annual Terms meeting in February. Accordingly, Marbury's case was heard in February, 1803, after an extraordinary interval of about fourteen months between succeeding Terms of Court.

The Jefferson Administration regarded the Marbury suit as a brazen attempt to induce the Supreme Court to interfere unlawfully with the conduct of the Executive Branch of the Government. While the Administration believed the judiciary to be without constitutional right to issue a mandamus against the Secretary of State, nevertheless it feared that the Federalist Justices on the Supreme Court would attempt to assert that right. If the Justices did so, some Anti-Federalists indicated that those Justices would render themselves subject to impeachment.

At the same time that this situation existed as to the midnight justices of the peace, an even more serious situation arose as to the sixteen new circuit judges. The Anti-Federalists, outraged by the appointment of these Federalist judges, determined to repeal the entire new Circuit Court Act. While not removing the new judges from their offices, Congress would thus abolish the offices and eliminate the judgeships. Their plan was to restore, in large measure, the terms of the Judiciary Act of 1789. The plan also would return the Justices of the Supreme Court to their circuit duties.

On January 6, 1802, Senator Breckenridge of Kentucky accordingly sought the repeal of the Circuit Court Act which had been passed less than a year before. The repeal bill was fully and ably debated in both Houses. It passed the Senate sixteen to fifteen and the House fifty-nine to thirty-two, becoming law March 31, 1802. The midnight judges protested to Congress but did not litigate their claims. The arguments on the bill, however, had dealt with those claims at length. Those discussions explored fully the constitutional right of Congress to abolish courts to which judges already had been appointed.

The debate also had reviewed the fundamental issue of the right to a judicial review of the constitutional validity of any Act of Congress. The latter issue was the great issue to which the Court subsequently addressed itself in deciding *Marbury* v. *Madison*. The Anti-Federalists insisted that Congress was the equal of the courts and that the Constitution gave no power of judicial review over the constitutional validity of Acts of Congress. The Federalists insisted, with equal vigor, that such a power was vested in the courts by the Constitution. The Anti-Federalists confidently expected that the six Federalist members of the Supreme Court would take the latter view. They expected also that the Court would attempt to apply that power of review to the repealer that Congress had passed and would find some ground upon which to declare that repealer to be constitutionally invalid. The Anti-Federalists expected also that the Court would challenge the power of the Executive to withhold a commission from Marbury. Furthermore, it was suggested that, if the Court asserted such power over the Legislative and Executive Branches of the Government, this assertion would provide Congress with the necessary basis for the impeachment of the offending Justices and for their removal from office. The extraordinary thing is that Chief Justice Marshall found a way to announce and establish the principle of judicial review in both of these fields without making an immediate application of it hostile to the Administration and without providing the expected basis for impeachment proceedings.

Although the circuit judges declined to press, on their own account, the issue of the constitutionality of the repeal of the Circuit Court Act, the Supreme Court could not avoid the issue. Even before the Court assembled for its new February Term in 1803, the Justices were obliged to decide whether to resume their duties on circuit or to refuse to do so. By a majority conclusion, ascertained by correspondence, the Justices determined to resume, without controversy, the circuit duties which had been terminated by the Act of 1801 but had been reimposed by the Act of 1802.

UNUSUAL FEATURES OF TRIAL OF MARBURY *V.* MADISON

Such was the extraordinary background for the trial of *Marbury* v. *Madison* in February, 1803. There were further unusual features connected with the trial itself. The first such feature, judged by the practice today, was the unhesitating and apparently unquestioned participation of Chief Justice Marshall in the trial. Assuming that the Court had jurisdiction of the case and had a right to issue a writ of mandamus to the Secretary of State, the issue between the parties turned upon the right of Marbury to secure possession of the very commission which the Chief Justice, as Secretary of State, had sealed on March 3, 1801, but which the Chief Justice's brother had not delivered when he delivered others on that night. It also appears from John Marshall's correspondence with his brother that, as Secretary of State, John Marshall believed that these appointments were complete with the affixation to them of the Seal of the United States and that the subsequent recordings and deliveries of the commissions were not essential to the appointments. As Chief Justice, he later stated that conclusion in the opinion of the Court.

Furthermore, while the report of this case at 1 Cranch 137 shows no absence of Justices from the Court at this trial, the minutes of the Court do not record Justice Cushing as present at any trial session or on the date of handing down the decision. Apparently, he did not participate in the case. The minutes also show that Justice Moore was present on February 24 when the decision was announced but they do not record his presence on February 10 or 11 when they show that the case was before the Court for hearing and argument. Accordingly, on those two days, if the Chief Justice had disqualified himself, there would not have been the required quorum of four present.

Jefferson's Attorney General, Levi Lincoln, participated only as a witness. He answered some but not all the questions submitted to him. Those questions were reduced to writing at his request and the Court allowed him until the next day to determine what response, if any, he should make to them. The Court heard at least three other witnesses and read a material affidavit from James Marshall, the brother of the Chief Justice. All this testimony related to the signing, sealing and failure to deliver the commissions. The Court then heard an argument by Mr. Lee for the petitioners, both on the question of jurisdiction and on the merits. No argument was made in opposition and no one officially represented the Secretary of State in the proceeding.

Finally, and quite in keeping with the extraordinary circumstances surrounding this leading case in American constitutional law, it now appears that, although this proceeding was entered on the Court docket and notations were made showing that certain hearings were held, the Court today has no file on the case and no papers relating to it.[1] The rule to show cause was marked "discharged the Court not having jurisdiction to issue a Mandamus in this case." If it were not for the careful reporting of the case by William Cranch and the informal newspaper reports of the opinion rendered, we, today, would have no reliable record of the fundamental legal principles then announced by the Court and which have become of primary significance in American constitutional law.

[The excerpts from Chief Justice John Marshall's opinion reproduced below contain the essential elements of the doctrine of judicial review.]

2. Marbury *v.* Madison, *Chief Justice Marshall for the Court**

The question whether an act repugnant to the Constitution can become the law of the land, is a question deeply interesting to the United States; but, happily, not of an intricacy proportioned to its interest. It seems only necessary to recognize certain principles, supposed to have been long and well established to decide it.

---

[1] Mr. Justice Burton subsequently modified this statement, writing that "when the early records of the Supreme Court were being transmitted to the Archives there was found among some of the partially burned papers some affidavits in this case. While the affidavits do not contribute anything of particular value, they do at least evidence the presence of the case in this court." Letter to John R. Schmidhauser, February 17, 1961.
*1 Cranch 137 (1803).

That the people have an original right to establish, for their future government, such principles as, in their opinion, shall most conduce to their own happiness, is the basis on which the whole American fabric has been erected. The exercise of this original right is a very great exertion; nor can it nor ought it to be frequently repeated. The principles, therefore, so established, are deemed fundamental. And as the authority from which they proceed is supreme, and can seldom act, they are designed to be permanent.

This original and supreme will organizes the government, and assigns to different departments their respective powers. It may either stop here, or establish certain limits not to be transcended by those departments.

The government of the United States is of the latter description. The powers of the legislature are defined and limited; and that those limits may not be mistaken, or forgotten, the Constitution is written. To what purpose are powers limited, and to what purpose is that limitation committed to writing, if these limits may, at any time, be passed by those intended to be restrained? The distinction between a government with limited and unlimited powers is abolished, if those limits do not confine the persons on whom they are imposed, and if acts prohibited and acts allowed are of equal obligation. It is a proposition too plain to be contested, that the Constitution controls any legislative act repugnant to it; or, that the legislature may alter the Constitution by an ordinary act.

Between these alternatives there is no middle ground. The Constitution is either a superior paramount law, unchangeable by ordinary means, or it is on a level with ordinary legislative acts, and, like other acts, is alterable when the legislature shall please to alter it.

If the former part of the alternative be true, then a legislative act contrary to the Constitution is not law; if the latter part be true, then written constitutions are absurd attempts, on the part of the people, to limit a power in its own nature illimitable.

Certainly all those who have framed written constitutions contemplate them as forming the fundamental and paramount law of the nation, and, consequently, the theory of every such government must be, that an act of the legislature, repugnant to the constitution, is void.

This theory is essentially attached to a written constitution, and is consequently to be considered, by this Court, as one of the fundamental principles of our society. It is not, therefore, to be lost sight of in the further consideration of this subject.

If an act of the legislature, repugnant to the Constitution, is void, does it, notwithstanding its invalidity, bind the courts, and oblige them to give it effect? Or, in other words, though it be not law, does it constitute a rule as operative as if it was a law? This would be to overthrow in fact what was established in theory; and would seem, at first view, an absurdity too gross to be insisted on. It shall, however, receive a more attentive consideration.

It is emphatically the province and duty of the judicial department to say what the law is. Those who apply the rule to particular cases, must of necessity expound and interpret that rule. If two laws conflict with each other, the courts must decide on the operation of each.

So if a law be in opposition to the Constitution; if both the law and the Constitution apply to a particular case, so that the court must either decide that case conformably to the law, disregarding the Constitution, or conformably to the Constitution, disregarding the law, the court must determine which of these conflicting rules governs the case. This is of the very essence of judicial duty.

If, then, the courts are to regard the Constitution, and the Constitution is superior to any ordinary act of the legislature, the Constitution, and not such ordinary act, must govern the case to which they both apply.

Those, then, who controvert the principle that the Constitution is to be considered, in court, as a paramount law, are reduced to the necessity of maintaining that courts must close their eyes on the Constitution, and see only the law.

This doctrine would subvert the very foundation of all written constitutions. It would declare that an act which, according to the principles and theory of our government, is entirely void, is yet, in practice, completely obligatory. It would declare that if the legislature shall do what is expressly forbidden, such act, notwithstanding the express prohibition, is in reality effectual. It would be giving to the legislature a practical and real omnipotence, with the same breath which professes to restrict their powers within narrow limits. It is prescribing limits, and declaring that those limits may be passed at pleasure.

That it thus reduces to nothing what we have deemed the greatest improvement on political institutions, a written constitution, would of itself be sufficient, in America, where written constitutions have been viewed with so much reverence, for rejecting the construction. But the peculiar expressions of the Constitution of the United States furnish additional arguments in favor of its rejection.

The judicial power of the United States is extended to all cases arising under the Constitution.

Could it be the intention of those who gave this power, to say that in using it the Constitution should not be looked into? That a case arising under the Constitution should be decided without examining the instrument under which it arises?

This is too extravagant to be maintained.

In some cases, then, the Constitution must be looked into by the judges. And if they can open it at all, what part of it are they forbidden to read or to obey?

There are many other parts of the Constitution which serve to illustrate this subject.

It is declared that "no tax or duty shall be laid on articles exported from any State." Suppose a duty on the export of cotton, of tobacco, or of flour; and a suit instituted to recover it. Ought judgment to be rendered in such a case? Ought the judges to close their eyes on the Constitution, and only see the law?

The Constitution declares "that no bill of attainder or ex post facto law shall be passed."

If, however, such a bill should be passed, and a person should be prosecuted under it, must the court condemn to death those victims whom the Constitution endeavors to preserve?

"No person," says the Constitution, "shall be convicted of treason unless on the testimony of two witnesses to the same overt act, or on confession in open court."

Here the language of the Constitution is addressed especially to the courts. It prescribes, directly for them, a rule of evidence not to be departed from. If the legislature should change that rule, and declare one witness, or a confession out of court, sufficient for conviction, must the constitutional principle yield to the legislative act?

From these, and many other selections which might be made, it is apparent that the framers of the Constitution contemplated that instrument as a rule for the government of courts, as well as of the legislature.

Why otherwise does it direct the judges to take an oath to support it? This oath certainly applies in an especial manner to their conduct in their official character. How immoral to impose it on them, if they were to be used as the instruments, and the knowing instruments, for violating what they swear to support!

The oath of office, too, imposed by the legislature, is completely demonstrative of the legislative opinion on this subject. It is in these words: "I do solemnly swear that I will administer justice without respect to persons, and do equal right to the poor and to the rich; and that I will faithfully and impartially discharge all the duties incumbent on me as _____, according to the best of my abilities and understanding, agreeably to the Constitution and laws of the United States."

Why does a judge swear to discharge his duties agreeably to the Constitution of the United States, if that Constitution forms no rule for his government? if it is closed upon him, and cannot be inspected by him?

If such be the real state of things, this is worse than solemn mockery. To prescribe, or to take this oath, becomes equally a crime.

It is also not entirely unworthy of observation, that in declaring what shall be the supreme law of the land, the Constitution itself is first mentioned; and not the laws of the United States generally, but those only which shall be made in pursuance of the Constitution, have that rank.

Thus, the particular phraseology of the Constitution of the United States confirms and strengthens the principle, supposed to be essential to all written constitutions, that a law repugnant to the Constitution is void; and that courts, as well as other departments, are bound by that instrument.

The rule must be discharged.

3. The Cornerstone of Constitutional Law: The Extraordinary Case of Marbury v. Madison, Part II*

. . . it is important to note the reasoning by which the Court brought the doctrine of judicial review into this case. To do this, it was necessary for the Court to establish two points.

Neither of these points had been presented on argument. It must have been a substantial surprise to many when the Court based its decision squarely upon them. These two points were:

* Mr. Justice Harold Burton, "The Cornerstone of Constitutional Law: the Extraordinary Case of *Marbury* v. *Madison,*" *American Bar Association Journal*, XXXVI (October, 1950), 881–83. [Footnotes omitted.] Reproduced with permission of the author and the publisher. Copyright (1950) by the American Bar Association.

(1) That *Section 13 of the Judiciary Act of 1789* attempted to give the Supreme Court power to issue a writ of mandamus *in an original proceeding* against an officer of the United States, including the Secretary of State.

(2) That *Article III of the Constitution* prohibited the grant of such a power by Congress to the Supreme Court.

We are not concerned here whether, as a new question, either or both of these conclusions would be supportable. It is enough for our present purposes that the Court expressly upheld them. Without them, the principle of the judicial review of the constitutional validity of a statute would not have been material to this case. With them, that principle became material.

It is an appropriate part, however, of any study of the extraordinary features of this case to note how bold each of these propositions was and how the Court might have found a way to discharge the rule to show cause on statutory grounds without relying on, or raising, the great constitutional issue.

The fact is that Section 13 of the Judicature Act of 1789, which purported to define the original jurisdiction of the Supreme Court, could have been interpreted as not attempting to extend the jurisdiction of the Supreme Court to the issuance of a writ of mandamus in an original proceeding. It has been suggested that this clause merely extended the remedy of mandamus to the cases over which the Court already had jurisdiction, and that the clause accordingly did not enlarge the Court's jurisdiction. . . . In the face of the subsequently demonstrated constitutional objections to the broad interpretation of this clause which was adopted by the Court, there is much to be said for the narrower interpretation suggested. If the narrower interpretation were adopted, the rule would have been discharged for lack of jurisdiction. The ground for discharge would have been the simple absence of statutory, as well as constitutional, provision for it. There thus would have been no issue in the case as to the constitutionality of any statute and there would have been no opportunity to expound the doctrine of judicial review of that constitutionality.

The success of the Chief Justice in discovering and announcing the Court's broad construction of Section 13, which was in conflict with the Constitution, is all the more extraordinary when the sponsorship of Section 13 is recalled. That section was a part of the Judicial Code of 1789. Its authorship is attributed to Senator Oliver Ellsworth, who had been a delegate to the Constitutional Convention of 1787, and who was the Chief Justice of the Supreme Court who immediately preceded Marshall. It was a bold step to assert that, in spite of such sponsorship, this section was an attempt by Congress to enlarge the original jurisdiction of the Supreme Court beyond its constitutional limits. Equally striking is the conversion of Justice Paterson to the interpretation of Section 13 adopted by the Chief Justice. Justice Paterson, as a Senator from New Jersey, had been associated with Senator Ellsworth on the Judiciary Committee which had sponsored this Act. He also had been a delegate to the Constitutional Convention of 1787, not to mention the New Jersey Convention that ratified the Federal Constitution. Obviously, neither of these men knowingly would have sought, by statute, to enlarge the Court's jurisdiction beyond the constitutional limit of that jurisdiction.

Finally, assuming that the statute was an attempted enlargement of the Court's original jurisdiction, the Chief Justice's constitutional argument to establish its invalidity was also a bold one. Under the leadership of the Chief Justice, the Court found in the *limited affirmative statement* of the Court's original jurisdiction an *implied negative that all other original jurisdiction was denied* to the Court. The Court admitted that, standing alone, the limited affirmative scope of the Court's jurisdiction covering its original proceedings did not necessarily exclude all other original jurisdiction. The Court stated, however, that it was convinced, by the next clause, that it did so. That clause added the statement that in *"all the other Cases* before mentioned, the Supreme Court shall have *appellate Jurisdiction,* both as to Law and Fact, *with such Exceptions,* and under such Regulations *as the Congress shall make."* (Italics supplied.) The Court said that this meant that in all those other cases the Court's jurisdiction was to be *solely appellate and not original.* The exceptions which could be made by Congress might omit some of this appellate jurisdiction of the Supreme Court but apparently Congress could not, by way of an exception, convert any of that appellate jurisdiction into original jurisdiction. This point is not mentioned here to discuss its strength or weakness. It is mentioned only to show how resolutely the Court pushed away another possible disposition of the case and faced, with readiness, the issue of the unconstitutionality of the jurisdictional statute.

In the week following that in which the opinion in *Marbury* v. *Madison* was announced, the Court again disarmed its opposition by its decision in *Stuart* v. *Laird,* 1 Cranch 299. The Court there applied the doctrine of judicial review to the statute which had repealed the Circuit Court Act of 1801 and had terminated the existence of courts on which the midnight judges had been appointed to serve. The Supreme Court upheld the constitutional validity of that repealer. This decision made it still more difficult for the Anti-Federalists to claim that there was great danger in the doctrine of judicial review.

The battle, however, was resumed later along another front. On February 4, 1805, nearly two years after the decision in *Marbury* v. *Madison,* the House of Representatives impeached Justice Chase of the Supreme Court. The charges related primarily to his conduct on the circuit. The arguments made against him also reflected a view that impeachment was not merely a punitive process but an inquest of office. After extended debate, a majority of the Senate, on March 1, acquitted Justice Chase on five of the eight counts. On the other three, an actual majority, but not the required two-thirds, voted for his conviction. This failure to convict disposed of impeachment as a ready means of legislative recall of federal judges. The right of the Court to be independent in its judgments, as well as its right to review the constitutional validity of the Acts of Congress, was thus sustained.

D. WHAT IS THE NATURE OF THE SUPREME COURT'S POLITICAL ROLE?

[Classic assertions of judicial authority such as Judge Peter's case and *Marbury* v. *Madison* provided definitive interpretations of the Supreme Court's role in connection with the constitutional principles of federalism and separation of powers. But it should be noted that too great an emphasis upon topical lines of doctrinal development tends to obscure the fact that the evolution of the Supreme Court's power in American society was predicated perhaps as much upon what was done (or omitted) by other political institutions as it was upon the decision-making tendencies of the justices. This may be seen by viewing the complex of political and economic issues that divided the nation in a particular era, rather than the seemingly disparate threads of doctrinal developments. Alan F. Westin's study provides an excellent example.]

1. The Supreme Court, The Populist Movement and the Campaign of 1896*

De Tocqueville observed as early as 1835 that "scarcely any political question arises in the United States that is not resolved, sooner or later, into a judicial question." Even though we have long recognized that our Supreme Court exercises a directing hand over American political and economic development in a manner unparalleled by other federal systems, the extensiveness of this directional force is still being traced and recorded by constitutional historians. This paper is a report on one neglected chapter in our constitutional history: the relationship between the Supreme Court and the People's Party. For although most writers on the Populist movement allude to the Court's 1895 decisions as a factor which increased the strength of Populism, the full scope of Supreme Court opinions from 1876 to 1896 and their effect upon Populist thought have never been systematically treated. Neither has there been a statement of the tremendous impact of this relationship between the Court and the Populists upon the issues and conduct of the Presidential campaign of 1896.

Yet it was in this period that the Supreme Court created a wide disenchantment with constitutional processes, a disenchantment which rendered millions of Americans more willing to break away from traditional political patterns, to strike out at a governmental system which seemed in all its parts to be insensitive to the needs of the farmers and workers in the new industrial age. James Baird Weaver, Populist candidate for President in 1892, wrote that ". . . it is not alone essential that our courts shall be pure in fact. The people must have an abiding faith in their integrity. Society becomes insecure in proportion as popular confidence is shaken in this respect.". . .

[Professor Westin stressed the impact of Supreme Court decision-making in the following problem areas: (a) the farmer's debt crises of the 1870's, 1880's and 1890's, (b) the resolution of public land disputes, (c) state control of grain ele-

*Alan F. Westin, "The Supreme Court, The Populist Movement and the Campaign of 1896," *Journal of Politics*, XV (February, 1953), 3, 30–41. [Footnotes omitted.] Reproduced with permission of the author and the publisher. Copyright (1953) by the Southern Political Science Association.

vators, (d) state power to regulate railroad rates, (e) federal jurisdictional and receivership questions, (f) the income tax question, (g) the Pullman strike, and (h) the scope of the Sherman Anti-Trust Act of 1890.]

THE SUPREME COURT AS A CAMPAIGN ISSUE IN 1896

When the Democratic Convention convened in Chicago in July 7, 1896, the vast hall was drenched with heat, but every convention rumor predicted that things would get even hotter once the proceedings got under way. This was to be a rough-and-tumble fight between the silver and radical Democrats on the one hand and the old line Cleveland men on the other. Everyone was ready for a barrage of oratory on the "money question," "bunco dollars," and the "pernicious machinations of Wall Street and Lombard Street." But few observers were ready for the attack on the sheet-anchor, the august tribunes, the injection of a shout, "No government by judges" to accompany the cry of "No cross of gold."

The Convention's opening address was delivered by Temporary Chairman John W. Daniel, Senator from Virginia, on the morning of July 7. Daniel wasted no time in raising the Court Issue.

> So far as a revenue to support the Government is concerned, the Democratic Party, with but a slender majority in the Senate, was not long in providing it, and had not the Supreme Court of the United States reversed its settled doctrines of a hundred years, the income tax incorporated in their tariff bill would long since have supplied the deficit.

This was a warming up process. At the morning session on the eighth, Governor J. S. Hogg of Texas let loose a full-scale blast, branding the Supreme Court an instrument of Republican corporate power and threat to the working man. Said Hogg:

> This protected class of Republicans proposes now to destroy labor organizations . . . proposes through Federal courts, in the exercise of their unconstitutional powers by issuance of extraordinary, unconventional writs, to strike down, to suppress, and to overawe those organizations.

Already an undercurrent of astonishment was felt in the hall at the introduction of the federal judiciary and the Supreme Court into the convention oratory. When the first draft of the platform was read by Senator James K. Jones (Arkansas) for the Committee on Resolutions and Platform, the battle began in earnest, for under its section on the income tax appeared the following:

> But for this decision of the Supreme Court, there would be no deficit in revenue under the law passed by a Democratic Congress in strict pursuance of the uniform decisions of that Court for nearly one hundred years, that Court having in that decision sustained constitutional objections to its enactment which

had previously been overruled by the ablest judges who have ever sat on the bench.

Furthermore, asserted the plank:

We declare that it is the duty of Congress to use all the constitutional power which remains after that decision, or which may come from its reversal by the Court as it may hereafter be constituted, so that the burdens of taxation may be equally and impartially laid, to the end that wealth may bear its due proportion of the expense of the government.

In a later section, the platform added:

We especially object to government by injunction as a new and highly dangerous form of oppression by which Federal judges, in contempt of the laws of the states and rights of citizens, becomes at once legislators, judges and executioners. . . .

When the platform advocated jury trials in all contempt cases and a final plank opposed life tenure for all federal officials, the full force of the Resolutions Committee work could be felt. Senator David Hill rose in anger to attack the Court planks, demanding:

Why was it wise to assail the Supreme Court of your country? . . . That provision [a "reversal by the Court as it may hereafter be constituted"] if it means anything, means that it is the duty of Congress to reconstruct the Supreme Court of the country. It means, and such purpose was openly avowed, it means the adding of additional members to the Court, or the turning out of office and reconstructing the whole court.

The conservative press were horrified by the platform, by the suggestion that constitutional verities might change with shifts in the Court's personnel. The *Tribune* considered the Democratic Platform as an "anarchistic attack on the federal judiciary" and *Harper's Weekly* wrote that "It is because their programme is one of spoliation that Mr. Bryan and his mentor Governor Altgeld want free riots and a Supreme Court that will obey the passions of the multitude." Everyone recognized the mark of the Populists on the phrasing of the issues, and could recall the authorship by Trumbull, Lloyd, and Altgeld of the "government by injunction" charge. The Richmond (Virginia) *Times* (Democrat) stated it would not support these men "who avow a purpose to overturn the courts—the palladium of an orderly government," and the Leavenworth (Kansas) *Times* (Republican) concluded that "There is more in the Chicago platform than the clamor for unlimited silver coinage. There is the old spirit of secession and rebellion against the Constitution."

When the silver-tongued orator rose the next day to make his famous speech to the assembled delegates, he concentrated heavily on this issue of the Supreme Court and the income tax. Bryan declared to the convention:

They say we passed an unconstitutional law. I deny it. The income tax was not unconstitutional when it was passed. It was not unconstitutional when it went before the Supreme Court for the first time. It did not become unconstitutional until one judge changed this [sic] mind, and we cannot be expected to know when a judge will change his mind. (Applause, and cries, "Hit 'em again") . . .

As to the press attack on the anti-Court planks, Bryan made it clear that the Court was not above criticism, and that the doctrines of the Court would be an integral part of the Democratic campaign.

Following this Democratic onslaught, the People's Party Convention in St. Louis, on July 24, was almost an anticlimax. The two sections of the Populist platform dealing with the Supreme Court were almost identical with the statements of the Democrats. These read:

Seventh: We demand a graduated income tax, to the end that aggregated wealth shall bear its just proportion of taxation, and we regard the recent decision of the Supreme Court relative to the income tax as a misinterpretation of the Constitution and an invasion of the rightful powers of Congress over the subject of taxation.

Under their "Miscellaneous" section, the People's Party declared:

The arbitrary course of the courts in assuming to imprison citizens for indirect contempt and ruling by injunction should be prevented by proper legislation.

Within a few days, people were singing the newest "Populist and Silver Songs for 1896" including one stanza of:

The masses of the people want more freedom,
No trials by injunction if you please,
No soldiers at the back of corporations,
But Jury and the law instead of these.

The *Railway Times*, organ of the American Railway Union, stated that they were "going into politics" with the People's Party to beat the "corporation courts," since "with the election of such a man as Bryan, a Caldwell will find his way to the Supreme Bench and in due time labor will cease to crawl in the dirt, and stand erect."

When Bryan delivered his speech of acceptance for the Democratic nomination in New York City on August 12, 1896, he dealt again with the Court issue, since it had been seized upon by Mark Hanna as "warfare against the courts," a blow at the "integrity and independence of the judiciary," and a "Covert Threat to Pack the Supreme Court of the United States." Bryan answered in defense of the Democrats' Chicago platform:

> *Our critics even go so far as to apply the name Anarchists to those who stand upon that plank of the platform. . . . Not only shall I refuse to apologize for the advocacy of an income tax law by the National Convention, but I shall also refuse to apologize for the exercise by it of the right to dissent from a decision of the Supreme Court.*

Two weeks later, former President Benjamin Harrison delivered a major Republican campaign address before a mass meeting in Carnegie Hall. Harrison declared:

> *In my opinion there is no issue presented by the Chicago convention more important or vital than the question they have raised of prostituting the power and duty of the national courts and national Executive. Tariff and coinage will be of little moment if our constitutional government is overthrown.*

Harrison went on for the remainder of his speech to lash the Chicago "frenzy" under which "government by the mob was given preference over government by the law enforced by the court decrees. . . ."

Warned Harrison:

> *I cannot exaggerate the gravity and the importance and the danger of this assault upon our constitutional form of government; [upon] the high-minded, independent judiciary that will hold to the line on questions between wealth and labor, between the rich and poor. . . .*

The Philadelphia *Press* (Republican) applauded vigorously, stating it was useless for Bryan to deny he is an anarchist when the platform he proudly endorses proposes "to pollute the stream of Federal law at its source by making partisan changes in the Supreme Court." The New York *Evening Post* (Independent) said Harrison "showed that the intention of the Chicago convention was to make judicial decisions on purely legal and Constitutional questions matters of party determination, and that the inevitable end and finish of such a course must be the overturning of liberty."

Bryan's reply to Harrison in a Tammany Hall address adopted a rather conciliatory tone: "There is nothing in that platform that assails the integrity or questions the honesty of the Supreme Court of the United States. I challenge you to read that platform and find in it a single sentiment that justifies the language used by the former President." With this reservation, Bryan went on to explain that the real fear of the Republicans was not his lawlessness but that he would actually *enforce* the law against corporations, against trusts, and against government defrauders, and he observed that the Republicans were using the court issue as a smear tactic.

Meanwhile the Democratic Old Guard had realized that the new Democracy stood committed to a rejection of Grover Cleveland, free silver, a "responsible" federal judiciary, and William Jennings Bryan. Meeting in a rump convention in Indianapolis, September 3, 1896, the conservatives formed the National Democratic Party, in protest against the currency plank and also because the "declarations of the

Chicago Convention attack individual freedom, the right of private contract, the independence of the judiciary, and the authority of the President to enforce Federal laws." In their platform, the National Democrats stated:

> *The Supreme Court of the United States was wisely established by the framers of our constitution as one of the coordinate branches of the government. Its independence and authority to interpret the law of the land without fear or favor must be maintained. We condemn all efforts to degrade that tribunal or impair the confidence and respect which it has deservedly held.*

Senator Caffrey (Louisiana) told the delegates that "The declarations of the Chicago platform . . . attack the integrity of a coordinate branch of government . . ." and General Simon Buckner, Vice Presidential candidate of the rump convention, thundered that ". . . the Chicago convention would wipe virtually out of existence that Supreme Court which interprets the law. . . ." In response to the Chicago plank denouncing the injunction doctrines of the Supreme Court in the Debs case, the National Democrats issued a special pamphlet entitled "The Question of Law and Order." There they maintained that:

> *. . . the party which makes this kind of authoritative exposition of the law the subject of rancorous denunciation, ranges itself on the side of disorder and proclaims itself the propagandist of revolution.*

The Supreme Court had by this time become a major concern at the Democratic Convention in Chicago, had been mentioned prominently as a cause of defection by the rump Democrats, and was developing into a constant stump-issue as the campaign of 1896 wore on. A keen observer suggested in a letter to the Tribune that the attack on the Supreme Court probably stemmed from a fear on the part of free silver-men as well as Populists that the Supreme Court would declare a silver law to be unconstitutional. The August issue of *Bankers' Magazine* reassured their subscribers that the silver cause could not be won at the polls "as long as special gold contracts are upheld by the Supreme Court of the United States," and the editors stated that the court "as now constituted" would certainly declare a Congressional silver act unconstitutional.

As the campaign heat grew in intensity, the Supreme Court plank of the Democrats and Populists received increasing attention. *Harper's Weekly* on September 12 published a front page cartoon of "A Forecast of the Consequence of a Popocratic Victory to the Supreme Court of the United States." Amid the smoking skull and daggers of Anarchy, a big "50 cent Bunco Dollar," a torn, falling Constitution, and the scowling busts of Guiteau, Spies, Fisher, and Lingg sat the fierce justices: a diabolic Altgeld, Tillman with his pitchfork in hand, "King Debs," General Coxey, "Bloody Bridle Waite," and a fist-clenching Pennoyer. "Gold Clause Stewart" was pictured with his feet upon the bar, and in the extreme right-hand corner of the cartoon, draped over the court desk, was a long black beard representing General Weaver.

On September 21, Attorney-General Harman issued a statement to the press criticizing Bryan's support of the Chicago platform in its denunciation of the *Debs* case. The issue of "government by injunction" was taken up in hundreds of newspapers, articles, speeches, and pamphlets, and the editors of the *Literary Digest,* in collecting samples of these opinions declared that "No plank of the Chicago platform seems to have aroused more radical differences of opinion . . ." than the injunction plank. When Chauncey Depew delivered a major address before an immense "sound-money" audience in the Chicago Coliseum on October 9, he said the monetary issue was fundamentally linked with the Supreme Court question. Depew thundered against the "wild career of constitutional and economic changes" being advocated and stated that

> *There are two places in this country where all men are absolutely equal: One is the ballot-box and the other is the Supreme Court. Bryan proposes to abolish the Supreme Court and make it the creature of the party caucus whenever a new Congress comes in, because it decided the income tax to be unconstitutional.*

Replies from the anti-Court spokesmen were not lacking. Horace L. Traubel wrote in the *Conservator* (Philadelphia) that "Even supreme courts may be summoned to the tests of the higher courts of conscience. The court of final resort is not this court of august judges but that court of the personal soul which passes upon the court at Washington. If the Washington court stands between man and his liberties, between any man and the justice that belongs to him . . . it is all folly to pretend that it is the buttress of law and order."

Governor Altgeld devoted his Cooper Union speech in New York City on October 17 to defending the Court plank, stating the "The Supreme Court cannot by mere decision upon a constitutional question rob the people of the powers of self-government . . . ," and he was quickly answered by the fiery new Republican orator Theodore Roosevelt who roundly condemned these denunciations of the Court by Altgeld to a delighted audience in Chicago. In Pennsylvania, the state People's Party resolved:

> *We disapprove of the way in which our courts have in recent years too frequently taken sides in favor of capital and corporations and against the laboring and producing classes. All citizens and all legal interests should be absolutely impartial in the dispensing of justice, regardless of the wealth or poverty of those applying for justice.*

Perhaps the most spectacular single campaign event was a letter suddenly issued by Archbishop Ireland of St. Paul, Minnesota. Circulated profusely by the Republicans, and setting off violent reactions in the press, the letter attacked Bryan and his program, stating that "The monetary question is, indeed, a secondary issue in this campaign; the primary issue being the spirit of socialism that permeates the whole movement. Specifically, the Catholic prelate highlighted the Court stand of the Democrats, warning that

> *The personification of law and of social order in America is our courts, and the promise of safety to our free institutions is the prompt obedience of the people to those courts. . . . And now, the courts are to be shorn of their power . . . [by a program] bourne in hands of reckless men, [who] may light up in the country the lurid fires of a "commune"!*

November finally arrived, the polls were opened, the votes were counted and the results of the election made public. The press comment on the day after the election reveals even further how important a part of the campaign the Court had been. The Rochester (New York) *Post-Express* declared that "The continental verdict means that the Supreme Court is to continue to be one of the very bulwarks of our institutions, safeguarded against any and all attempts to soil its ermine." The Indianapolis (Indiana) *News* termed the election "a determination on the part of the people everywhere to maintain the dignity and supremacy of the courts. The Seattle (Washington) *Post-Intelligencer* applauded the defeat of the movement to debase our currency and "the really more dangerous threat to the perpetuity of our national institutions involved in the proposals to subvert the courts and to withdraw from the national government the power to enforce its own laws." The New York *Press* exulted, "Never again in our time or in our children's children's time will the right of the Federal Judiciary to interpret or of the Federal Executive to enforce Federal laws be questioned," and a similar breath of relief appeared in the New York *Herald* (I).

The campaign of 1896 was thus the second in the great "anti-Supreme Court" campaigns of American party politics, matched only by the furor in 1860 over the Dred Scott decision, and to be equalled again only by the struggle for "recall" in 1912. By 1896, the discontent with the Court which had been reserved to the Populist forces had been transferred to the "Popocratic" coalition, and the conservative elements of the Democratic Party had been forced to bolt the Democracy. The Supreme Court had fallen from its position as a venerated, inviolate tribunal and had emerged as a personal villain in the minds of millions of citizens.

THE FRUITS OF SUPREME COURT POLICY

The fact that the Supreme Court became a major issue of the People's Party and, through its agitation, of the Democratic Party, is itself highly significant. The intensity with which a large segment of the population resists Supreme Court opinions is a useful standard for testing the conceptions of judicial review and constitutional limitation being used by the Court. Beyond this index of workability, however, the record of the Supreme Court in the Populist era provides many insights into the impact of a Supreme Court on our political and economic processes.

First, the development by the Supreme Court of constitutional interpretations denying state power to control corporations, through legislation, helped to turn the focus of progressive forces from local or state-based organizations to the national arena and the People's Party. As Granger and Farmer's Alliance groups saw their hard-won regulatory statutes invalidated by an agency far off in Washington, and as these groups were told by the Supreme Court that their problems were matters for national legislation, it was a natural reaction for the progressive elements to move toward nationally focused efforts. At the same time, much of the breakdown of "non-partisan" farmer and labor organizations can be traced from the same development, since the influence which a non-political organization could exert at the state level was difficult to apply nationally.

Second, the legally defensible but insensitive decisions of the Supreme Court in the municipal bond cases revived in the most direct way the anti-legal tradition which had been a farmer-debtor heritage since Shay's Rebellion, the Whiskey Rebellion, and the Jacksonian period. As in the earlier cases, this disenchantment with "law" and courts and lawyers forced the farmer to seek redress through political activity. In this way, by breaking into farmer patterns of group action and imposing upon farmer communities debt burdens which could not be endured, the Supreme Court assisted the impulsion of the farmer into politics, and, ultimately, radical politics.

Third, the Supreme Court stimulated the strength of the Populist movement by convincing large segments of the nation that the entire government was in the hands of the "plutocrats," that they had no voice in their government, and that only a fundamental change in the relations of property to people could remedy the situation. Traditionally, faith in the ballot and the legislative process have been a deterrent to radical activity in the United States. Thus, when progressive forces were told by the Supreme Court that they could not enact an income tax law, that their Sherman Act did not apply to the sugar trust, that guardianship of property rights permitted federal courts and the Supreme Court to intervene in labor disputes in favor of corporations, and as these forces foresaw that their basic currency reform of free silver was likely to meet a similar fate, the foundations were laid for a violent break with traditional social protest. In 1895, the most respectable agency of American government, an agency beyond the reach of ordinary political processes, was dedicated to private property, "due process" of law, and Herbert Spencer's *Social Statics*. In this position as Seneschal of the Status Quo, the Supreme Court strengthened the radical character of the People's Party, weakened the influence of its moderate leadership, and aided it immeasurably in capturing the Democratic Party.

Fourth, by severely limiting the possibility of social ond economic reform at the popularly accessible legislative level, the Supreme Court gave capitalist forces in the United States a vital period of protected incubation. This cutting off of popular control of corporations and monopoly at the state level in the 1880's and at the national level in the 1890's, sheltered corporate development in its most vulnerable moments— the years of expansion and consolidation. Through this protection, the Supreme Court affected the distribution of wealth in the nation, the class stratification of the population, and the developing relationships between individuals and government in a rapidly centralizing social system. It would be an error to assign too great a causative function to the Supreme Court alone, but the Court's contribution as a master sculptor of American society is too often minimized. Since the Populist movement was an attempt to resist the development of a monopoly-capitalist society in which the farmer and the worker could neither compete successfully nor retain their former status, the Supreme Court by sheltering corporations was in fact as much a midwife to the Populist revolt as the sugar trust, the railroads, or the debt crisis.

Lastly, the Supreme Court effectively smothered the newly-developed willingness of the Populist movement to use legislative and administrative government for social control. Under its "due process" omnipotence, the Court repudiated the creative possibilities of legislation, and rejected the national government as an instrument by which an essentially Jacksonian movement could make the balancing adjustments necessary to keep the race for survival "fair" in the era of industrial consolidation. Not only did the Court deny regulation and planning in the specific cases before it, but it implied that all such attempts were alien to the genius of our constitutional system, and embedded this concept so deeply into constitutional doctrine that it influenced judicial review for forty years to come. Thus the nine quiet men of the public land cases, of the railroad and bond decisions, of the income tax, Sherman Act, and *Debs* case lived on beyond their own age. They fashioned the tools with which the Sutherlands, McReynolds, and Van Devanters were to deal with social progress in the twentieth century, until progressive forces were produced strong enough to overthrow the basic assumptions of the Supreme Court of the Populist Era.

[The experiences of the era of the Fuller Court stimulated thoughtful reappraisal of the role of the Supreme Court not only by the antagonistic Populists but also by students of American institutions who were basically supporters of judicial review. Perhaps the most perceptive of the latter was James Bradley Thayer, whose views on judicial review strongly influenced modern jurists.]

2. For Judicial Self-Restraint as a Function of Democratic Trust in the People*

When one reflects upon the multitude, variety, and complexity of the questions relating to the regulation of interstate commerce, upon the portentous and ever increasing flood of litigation to which the Fourteenth Amendment has given rise; upon the new problems in business, government, and police which have come in with steam and electricity, and their ten thousand applications; upon the growth of corporations and of wealth, the changes of opinion on social questions, such as the relation of capital and labor, and upon the recent expansions of our control over great and distant islands,—we seem to be living in a different world from Marshall's.

Under these new circumstances, what is happening in the region of constitutional law? Very serious things, indeed.

The people of the states, when making new constitutions, have long been adding more and more prohibitions and restraints upon their legislatures. The courts, mean-

* James Bradley Thayer, *John Marshall* (Boston: Houghton Mifflin, 1901), pp. 102–10. [Footnotes omitted.] Reproduced with permission of the publisher. Copyright (1901) by Houghton Mifflin Co.

time, in many places, enter into the harvest thus provided for them with a light heart, and too promptly and easily proceed to this distrust, and more and more readily incline to justify it, and to shed the consideration of constitutional restraints, —certainly as concerning the exact extent of these restrictions,—turning that subject over to the courts; and, what is worse, they insensibly fall into a habit of assuming that whatever they can constitutionally do they may do,—as if honor and fair dealing and common honesty were not relevant to their inquiries.

The people, all this while, become careless as to whom they send to the legislature; too often they cheerfully vote for men whom they would not trust with an important private affair, and when these unfit persons are found to pass foolish and bad laws, and the courts step in and disregard them, the people are glad that these few wiser gentlemen on the bench are so ready to protect them against their more immediate representatives.

From these causes there has developed a vast and growing increase of judicial interference with legislation. This is a very different state of things from what our fathers contemplated, a century and more ago, in framing the new system. Seldom, indeed, as they imagined, under our system, would this great, novel, tremendous power of the courts be exerted,—would this sacred ark of the covenant be taken from within the veil. Marshall himself expressed truly one aspect of the matter, when he said in one of the later years of his life: "No questions can be brought before a judicial tribunal of greater delicacy than those which involve the constitutionality of legislative acts. If they become indispensably necessary to the case, the court must meet and decide them; but if the case may be determined on other grounds, a just respect for the legislature requires that the obligation of its laws should not be unnecessarily and wantonly assailed." And again, a little earlier than this, he laid down the one true rule of duty for the courts. When he went to Philadelphia at the end of September, in 1831, on that painful errand of which I have spoken, in answering a cordial tribute from the bar of that city he remarked that if he might be permitted to claim for himself and his associates any part of the kind things they had said, it would be this, that they had "never sought to enlarge the judicial power beyond its proper bounds, nor feared to carry it to the fullest extent that duty required."

That is the safe twofold rule; nor is the first part of it any whit less important than the second; nay, more; to-day it is the part which most requires to be emphasized. For just here comes in a consideration of very great weight. Great and, indeed, inestimable as are the advantages in a popular government of this conservative influence,—the power of the judiciary to disregard unconstitutional legislation,—it should be remembered that the exercise of it, even when unavoidable, is always attended with a serious evil, namely, that the correction of legislative mistakes comes from the outside, and the people thus lose the political experience, and the moral education and stimulus that come from fighting the question out in the ordinary way, and correcting their own errors. If the decision in Munn v. Illinois and the "Granger Cases," twenty-five years ago, and in the "Legal Tender Cases," nearly thirty years ago, had been different; and the legislation there in question, thought by many to be unconstitutional and by many more to be ill-advised, had been set aside, we should

71

have been saved some trouble and some harm. But I venture to think that the good which came to the country and its people from the vigorous thinking that had to be done in the political debates that followed, from the infiltration through every part of the population of sound ideas and sentiments, from the rousing into activity of opposite elements, the enlargement of ideas, the strengthening of moral fibre, and the growth of political experience that came out of it all,—that all this far more than outweighed any evil which every flowed from the refusal of the court to interfere with the work of the legislature.

The tendency of a common and easy resort to this great function, now lamentably too common, is to dwarf the political capacity of the people, and to deaden the sense of moral responsibility. It is no light thing to do that.

What can be done? It is the courts that can do most to cure the evil; and the opportunity is a very great one. Let them resolutely adhere to first principles. Let them consider how narrow is the function which the constitutions have conferred on them,—the office merely of deciding litigated cases; how large, therefore, is the duty intrusted to others, and above all to the legislature. It is that body which is charged, primarily, with the duty of judging of the constitutionality of its work. The constitutions generally give them no authority to call upon a court for advice; they must decide for themselves, and the courts may never be able to say a word. Such a body, charged, in every State, with almost all the legislative power of the people, is entitled to the most entire and real respect; is entitled, as among all rationally permissible opinions as to what the constitution allows, to its own choice. Courts, as has often been said, are not to think of the legislators, but of the legislature,—the great, continuous body itself, abstracted from all the transitory individuals who may happen to hold its power. It is this majestic representative of the people whose action is in question, a coordinate department of the government, charged with the greatest functions, and invested, in contemplation of law, with whatsoever wisdom, virtue, and knowledge the exercise of such functions requires.

To set aside the acts of such a body, representing in its own field, which is the very highest of all, the ultimate sovereign, should be a solemn, unusual, and painful act. Something is wrong when it can ever be other than that. And if it be true that the holders of legislative power are careless or evil, yet the constitutional duty of the court remains untouched; it cannot rightly attempt to protect the people, by undertaking a function not its own. On the other hand, by adhering rigidly to its own duty, the court will help, as nothing else can, to fix the spot where responsibility lies, and to bring down on that precise locality the thunderbolt of popular condemnation. The judiciary, to-day, in dealing with the acts of their coordinate legislators, owe to the country no greater or clearer duty than that of keeping their hands off these acts wherever it is possible to do it. For that course—the true course of judicial duty always—will powerfully help to bring the people and their representatives to a sense of their own responsibility. There will still remain to the judiciary an ample field for the determinations of this remarkable jurisdiction, of which our American law has so much reason to be proud; a jurisdiction which has had some of its chief illustrations and its greatest triumphs, as in Marshall's time, so in ours, while the courts were refusing to exercise it.

[It would be misleading, of course, to evaluate the significance of Supreme Court decision-making only in terms of the dramatic constitutional decisions. The Supreme Court's role in statutory interpretation has, in the twentieth century, often assumed more importance in institutional development than constitutional interpretation. As is often the case, the evolution of institutional relationships may, in the long run, be influenced more fundamentally by gradual transitions indicated only slightly by year-to-year shifts in interpretative emphasis. The relatively undramatic developments in Congressional–Supreme Court relations in the period 1945–1957 provide important insights with respect to contemporary trends.]

3. Congressional Reversal of Supreme Court Decisions, 1945–1957*

As significant as the decisions of the Supreme Court may sometimes be, its determinations have not always been final. The judicial mandates of one generation have been undone by those of the next. In some cases the Court's constitutional interpretations have been "reversed" by constitutional amendment. In many more instances Congress has intervened and, by passing new legislation, has reversed decisions of the Court interpreting statutes and otherwise administering the federal system. The interplay of legislative and judicial power since the end of the Second World War is of especial interest. By that time the New Deal had run its course, leaving behind a general acceptance of the relatively new and expanded role of the federal government. The post-1945 congressional response to judicial action may best be seen in those cases that were a focus of public or academic controversy.

A tabulation of the situations in which the Court and Congress have disagreed shows that the Court was twice "reversed" by Congress after it had upheld individual rights against the imposition of federal power; no decision restricting individual liberty was overturned. In at least five cases the Court was reversed after sustaining federal jurisdiction against claims that state power should prevail; in only one case did Congress modify a judicial decision refusing to extend federal power at the expense of state jurisdiction. In at least ten instances Congress reversed decisions of the Court which favored government regulation of economic activity over self-regulation by the parties concerned; in only one case did Congress act to modify a Court decision denying federal authority to regulate an industry, and this case is of doubtful significance.

Though this sampling of cases is small, the consistent position taken by the Court implies that more than chance has been at work. Analysis of the individual cases will show, however, that any alleged political predisposition of the Court represents far too simple an account of the phenomenon. The results also cannot be explained on the apparently plausible hypothesis that the postwar Congresses have merely been

*Note, "Congressional Reversal of Supreme Court Decisions, 1945–1957," *Harvard Law Review*, LXXI (May, 1958), 1324–37. [Footnotes omitted.] Reproduced with permission of the publisher. Copyright © 1958 by the Harvard Law Review Association.

undoing proper judicial interpretations of earlier statutes the federal legislature no longer favors. Although much of the congressional activity reported in this Note did modify the effects of decisions construing New Deal social-welfare legislation, the decisions of the Court in these cases were not compelled by the statutes construed, for in most instances their meanings were uncertain and their legislative histories silent. The interaction between Congress and the Court was, in fact, the product of many causes, and cannot be explained by any single operative principle or simple political preference.

I. INSTITUTIONAL DIFFERENCES BETWEEN CONGRESS AND THE COURT

Out of the total of twenty-one instances of congressional reversal discovered, six cannot be viewed primarily as a conflict between the two branches of government. Rather, Congress was able to take into account policy factors that the Court could not properly have considered in ruling on property disputes or in applying a clear statutory directive. For example, in *United States* v. *South-Eastern Underwriters Ass'n,* the Court held, for the first time, that the insurance industry operated in interstate commerce and was therefore subject to the antitrust laws. Rather than enforce competition in the industry with these laws, Congress decided to prohibit certain specific restrictive practices and return to the industry its immunity from the antitrust laws to the extent that the industry was regulated by the states—a move which had the calculated effect of inducing forty-one states to enact some type of regulatory statute. . . .

II. DOMINANT PURPOSE AS A GUIDE TO STATUTORY CONSTRUCTION

The scope and standards of legislative programs are, of necessity, frequently described in general terms. Only with the guidance of an ascertained legislative purpose can the courts interpret a statute properly in the numerous and varied situations to which the statute may apply. However, seven of the instances in which the Court's construction of statutes was modified by Congress suggest that the Court placed too great an emphasis on a single dominant purpose and failed to limit this purpose when it clashed with other national policies or with reasonable and well-established private institutional arrangements. Particularly was this true in a series of cases arising under the Fair Labor Standards Act of 1938. . . . [Examples omitted.]

Analysis of the instances of congressional reversal of Supreme Court decisions since the Second World War demonstrates that nearly all these reversals involved a return to a "common understanding" which had been disrupted by the Court's decision, and that nearly all enjoyed the almost unanimous support of the politically articulate groups affected by the Court's decision. The few exceptions to this generalization occurred either at the time of a major legislative reassessment in the area of the decision, or through the efforts of a political group powerful enough to maintain an intense, nationwide lobbying campaign. Since judicial decisions, if they have political significance at all, will ordinarily please some groups and displease others, it must be a rare ruling that arouses the opposition of almost all the politically powerful groups concerned. The fact that almost all the instances found involved decisions that met with nearly unanimous disapproval shows that those decisions that provoke a mixed reaction—and they must be far more numerous—are very rarely overruled by Congress. The few exceptions to this conclusion serve only to emphasize the difficulties encountered in attempting to change the Court's statement of the law. General legislative reassessments of a broad area may be very infrequent: the long intervals between periods of congressional action in the civil-rights and labor-relations areas exemplify this fact. If more immediate action is desired, the losing party must maintain a lobbying effort sufficient to arouse a favorable response from both Congress and the executive despite opposition from other powerful interests.

Judicial reluctance to overrule past decisions or to correct an imperfection in the drafting of a statute is often based on the easy assumption that the legislature will act to change an unsatisfactory result. Some authorities in the field even go so far as to place the duty to correct errors in statutory interpretation exclusively with the legislature. But a recognition of the unusual unanimity of interest and opinion which is generally required to bring about a congressional reversal of a Supreme Court decision indicates that reliance on legislative correction is rarely warranted.

[If one keeps in mind the important distinction between the dramatic, but infrequently invoked power of the Supreme Court to interpret the Constitution, and the subtler process of statutory interpretation, the broader problem of intelligently describing the *over-all* role of the Court in the American political system may be put in proper perspective. One of the most compelling attempts at over-all appraisal was undertaken by Professor Wallace Mendelson. In 1959, he contributed the analysis of the historical interplay of judicial activism and undisciplined political parties reproduced below.]

4. *Judicial Review and Party Politics**

It has been suggested that intrusion upon legislative policy by judicial review "is a consequence of that fragmentation of political power which is normal in the United States. No cohesive majority, such as normally exists in Britain, would permit a politically irresponsible judiciary to usurp decision-making [policy] functions, but, for complex social and institutional reasons, there are few issues in the United States on which cohesive majorities exist." When they do exist, as in the recent tidal wave of anti-communism, the Supreme Court is not apt to test its strength against them. Rather it practices a judicious self-restraint.

*Wallace Mendelson, "Judicial Review and Party Politics," *Vanderbilt Law Review*, XII (1959), 447–57. [Footnotes omitted.] Reproduced with permission of the author and the publisher. Copyright © 1959 by Vanderbilt University Press.

Distinguishing between parliamentary and popular majorities, another commentator finds support in Australian experience for this view of the relation between judicial and political policy-making. Australian courts have been able to override their national legislature, it is said, because they have had the support of cohesive popular majorities. Conversely, we are told, judicial review does not exist in Britain, because there, in contrast to Australia, monolithic legislative majorities reflect solid popular majorities.

No doubt, as these comments suggest, judges like the rest of us are sensitive to public opinion. A more adequate explanation of policy-making via judicial review in the United States and Australia (and its absence in Britain) may lie in the special character of their respective political party systems. Could it be that "judicial supremacy" and irresponsible political parties are related phenomena? This at least seems clear: court intrusion upon national policy has thrived in the United States only in periods of unusual weakness in our party system. To explore this thought is the purpose of the present essay.

Our classic age of judicial legislation on a national scale came between the Civil War and 1937. It arose with the decline of sectional politics and ended with the advent of what Arthur Holcombe calls "the new" urban politics. In short, judicial supremacy *vis-à-vis* national policy seems to have prospered only in a transitional interlude between two dynamic political party systems. That this is not mere coincidence is indicated by the fate of judicial pretension before and after the period in question. Thus the checkmating of incursions upon national policy by the Marshall and Taney Courts while sectionalism reigned is matched only by the humiliation of the "nine old men" who challenged the vigorous new urban politics of our day.

Frederick Turner and his followers have shown how in the early days shifting alignments of Northeast, West and South, each with a distinctive economy and culture, provided the key to national policy. As Turner put it:

> *We in America are in reality a federation of sections rather than of states. State sovereignty never was influential except as a constitutional shield for the section. In political matters the states act in groups rather than as individual members of the Union. They act in sections and are responsive to the respective interests and ideals of the sections. They have their sectional leaders, who, in Congress and party conventions, voice the attitude of the section and confer and compromise their differences, or form sectional combinations to achieve a national policy and position.*

Between the Constitutional Convention and the Civil War four major sectional combinations successively came into being. Then, indeed, brokerage in regional interests was the nub of American statesmanship. An alliance of the agrarian West and South under Jefferson's leadership in 1800 replaced the Federalist combination of commercial Northeast and planter South. Revitalized in 1828 by the Jacksonians, this Democratic coalition dominated politics until slavery made such an alignment untenable. Then the West turned to the Northeast to form the modern Republican Party—a most tenacious alliance as Professor MacMahon has suggested, because its cold economic bargains were cemented with the sentimentality of brotherhood in arms.

But no sooner had Northeast and West accomplished their immediate purpose (defeat of the "slave power") than economic tension threatened to tear them apart. The Granger, Greenback, Alliance, Populist and Free Silver movements, were an open manifestation of a long and persistent agrarian rebellion largely within the reigning Republican coalition. When before the Civil War the major elements in a political bloc fell out, sectional realignment was promptly accomplished. Discordant tensions were neutralized and mounting pressures were relieved in a series of shifting sectional accommodations. The end result was national policy. Resort to the judiciary for the solution of national policy problems was superfluous and, when attempted, was immediately suppressed by violent political reaction. But the Civil War and its aftermath destroyed the vitality of sectional politics. The accord which the Republicans effected at Chicago in 1860 was the last of the great sectional realignments. This may be a clue to the peculiar success of judicial supremacy *vis-à-vis* Congress in the years that followed.

Plainly the rigidity of post-bellum, sectionalism springs from the Civil War itself. Even the churches, despite protestations of brotherly love, remained divided regional bodies. The agrarian South and West had formerly supported each other in national politics. After the war each had its grievances against the "money power" of the Northeast.

If the South were readmitted to the Union, Southern and Western men would inevitably unite their strength and arrange a national policy which would serve their [agrarian] interests. Andrew Johnson, in spite of his loud talk during the early months of his presidency, represented the promise and guarantee of such a combination. Hence the bitter struggle to impeach him. Industrial men succeeded by a campaign of hatred both in defeating Johnson and in holding the South out of the Union for a decade. Meanwhile, industrialism made its position secure.

Thaddeus Stevens saw the problem quite plainly in economic terms. As he put it in the House of Representatives in January, 1876,

I am now confining my argument to Negro suffrage in the rebel states. . . . The white Union [i.e., Republican] men are in a great minority in each of those states. With them the blacks would act in a body . . . the two united would form a majority. . . . It would assure the ascendency of the Union Party. . . . If impartial suffrage is excluded in the rebel states then everyone of them is sure to send a solid rebel representative delegation to Congress, and to cast a solid rebel electoral vote. They with their kindred Copperheads of the North would always elect the President and control Congress. . . . Now you must divide them between loyalists, without regard to color, and disloyalists, or you will be perpetual vassals of the free-trade, irritated, revengeful South. (Emphasis added.)

Unlike those who had actually done the fighting, General Sherman observed, politicians were ready to "prolong the war ad infinitum." Commenting upon the Greenback "heresy," Hayes wrote Blaine in 1876 that the Republican Party's "strong ground is the dread of the Solid South, rebel rule, etc., etc. I hope you will make these topics prominent in your speeches. It leads the people away from 'hard times' which is our deadliest foe." Garfield approved this advice as "sound strategy." As late as 1884 a wit supposed that the Republicans "might wring one more president from the folds of that battle-stained garment," the bloody shirt. Significantly every successful Republican candidate for the presidency from Appomattox to Manila Bay was both a westerner and a former "hero" of the Union Army. The GOP had won a lasting hold on the affections of the North because for many it seemed to have been the instrument of Providence in preserving the nation in a time of crisis.

In short, extraneous sentiments blocked the free play of geo-economic forces and, by impairing the resilience of sectional politics, crippled it as the effective arbiter of national policy. The South had been neutralized politically by an emotional barrier that defied economic expediency. Western agriculture was wedded incompatibly to Northeastern business in a union which neither could dominate by mere political devices. Their differences, *i.e.,* national policy, had to be settled at another level. Here was an entree for judicial mediation on a grand scale. The judges simply filled a political vacuum that resulted from the ossification of sectional politics.

In the seventy-two years preceding the Civil War only two acts of Congress suffered judicial veto. There can be no doubt that just as the "rich and well-born" Federalists disliked democracy, they also shunned popular political parties (factions) and plainly contemplated judicial review to protect their special interests from popular legislation. Apparently they anticipated the present thesis as to the relation between popular government, political parties and judicial review. In any case when the Federalists lost political control of the nation and sought to make good that loss through a carefully packed Supreme Court, they encountered capable political opposition, particularly the Chase Impeachment. As J. Q. Adams observed:

> [T]he [Jeffersonian] assault upon Judge Chase . . . was unquestionably intended to pave the way for another prosecution, which would have swept the Supreme Judicial Bench clean at a stroke.

Plainly moved by this response to *Marbury* v. *Madison* "the great Chief Justice" wrote a strange and doubtless tongue-in-cheek apologia:

> I think the modern doctrine of impeachment should yield to an appellate jurisdiction in the legislature. A reversal of those legal opinions deemed unsound by the legislature would certainly better comport with the mildness of our character than [would] a removal of the Judge who has rendered them unknowing of his fault.

Never thereafter, though he was to be on the bench for another thirty years, did Marshall, or any member of his Court, ever challenge another act of Congress.

Marbury v. *Madison* was born before its proper day; a sport doomed to languish until new political conditions generations later offered a more congenial environment. The Jeffersonian combine of South and West was too potent to be defeated from the bench by the old-guard Federalists. Significantly the latter resorted after the Chase affair not to judicial review, but to the Hartford Convention which by its resolutions confirmed J. Q. Adams' observation that "the alarm and disgust of the New England Federalists at Mr. Jefferson's anti-judiciary doctrines and measures . . . were one of the efficient causes which led to the project of separation and a Northern Confederacy."

Not until the *Dred Scott* case in 1857 did the Supreme Court again venture to assert its supremacy over the national political processes. The repercussions of that fiasco again indicate that relationship between a vigorous political system and judicial review. The Democratic Party had dominated national policy since 1800 and "slavocracy" had come to control the Democratic Party. Their latest victories had been the Fugitive Slave Law, the Kansas-Nebraska Act and the tariff reform of 1857. But in *Dred Scott* they overreached themselves. Abraham Lincoln exploited that blunder in the famous debates with Douglas. At Freeport he forced from his opponent the fatal doctrine that tore the South from the West and broke the Democratic Party. Promptly thereafter a realignment of sectional forces brought Northeast and West together in a winning combination that carried Lincoln to the White House and overrode the *Dred Scott* decision. Once again resilient sectionalism had frustrated a judicial venture into the national policy preserve.

In contrast to its two thwarted assertions of supremacy in the seventy-two years before the Civil War, the Court struck down seventy-six congressional measures and emasculated others in a like period (1865–1937) thereafter. But cold statistics hardly tell the story. After its first coup the Court had not seen fit to strike again for more than fifty years. Its second coup brought ugly repercussions which few thought the Court could ever out-live. Yet in a decade beginning only eight years after the *Dred Scott* catastrophe the Justices vetoed not less than eight acts of Congress. Significantly the principal issues that came before the high Court after 1865 involved clashes of interest between major partners in the dominant political alliance—businessman, grain farmer and laborer. As Wilfred Binkley demonstrates, Lincoln's Republican Party had been an agrarian-labor alliance, but the adoption of it in Grant's day by powerful Eastern capitalist interests gave it incongruous economic-sectional wings. Because of the bloody shirt this incongruity was resolved not by sectional realignment as in 1800, 1828 and 1860, but by intra-party litigation. Judicial review replaced sectional politics as the prime arbiter of national policy.

> *In spite of the Court's condemnation of the theory that "parties have an appeal from the legislature to the courts," powerful interests from the time of the Civil War were encouraged by the trend of decisions to carry to the Supreme Court all cases lost in Congress, and the power of judicial review came more and more to resemble a political veto. But there was opposition within the Court itself to being cast in the role of censor. Led by the brilliant and forceful [Mr. Justice] Miller, it resisted for a few years the ceaseless pressure of creditors, bond-*

holders, railroads, and coupon-clippers. The first ominous rumble of what lay in the future was heard in the famous Legal Tender Cases.

For a time it was touch and go. If business interests prevailed via judicial supremacy in the first round of the paper money controversy, agrarianism as reflected in congressional policy won in the second. But by the mid-nineties the Court, and through it "business," had achieved a dominant position. The Interstate Commerce Act of 1887, the Sherman Act of 1890 and the Income Tax Act of 1894 had all germinated on the western plains. They were the produce of a long agrarian political struggle against the excesses of the American industrial revolution. What had taken years to achieve the Court destroyed in a matter of months. The income tax was invalidated. The anti-trust act and the railroad legislation were emasculated. Simultaneously "government by injunction" sprang up to keep labor "in its place." In short, carefully exploited emotions of the Civil War and Reconstruction went far to sustain an uneasy alliance between agrarian West and industrial Northeast, while judicial review insured the supremacy of business interests within that "dominant" combination.

That the Supreme Court had achieved a new role in American government was not unnoticed by astute contemporary observers. As President Hadley of Yale saw it in 1908,

> *the fundamental division of powers in the Constitution of the United States is between the voters on the one hand and property owners on the other. The forces of democracy [sic] on the one side, divided between the executive and the legislature, are set over against the forces of property on the other side with the judiciary as arbiter between them.*

To make good its new role the Court needed new tools. Thus the interregnum between our two political party systems was perhaps the most "creative" era in the development of American constitutional law. Due process acquired a substantive economic content. Liberty of contract and laissez faire became the law of the land. The labor injunction was invented. The concept of property was expanded by the myth of "fair value." New meaning for an antiquarian constitutional phrase gutted hopes for fiscal reform. What Holmes called an "invisible radiation" (dual federalism) was discovered in the tenth amendment: a radiation which somehow restricted even expressly delegated national powers. But these new vehicles of policy—to be used or ignored in the Court's discretion—were the creatures of their age. Not one of them survived the political vacuum in which they were born!

Meanwhile, endless agricultural depression aggravated the difficulty of the tenuous Republican coalition. Plainly a new sectional alliance was struggling to be born. Hamlin Garland pointed out that "As ten cent corn and ten percent interest were troubling Kansas, so six cent cotton was inflaming Georgia." Mrs. Lease, exhorting farmers to "raise less corn and more hell," declared that "the West and South are prostrate before the manufacturing East." In a great sectional upheaval "the Gracchus of the West," William Jennings Bryan, sought to rally the forces of discontent under the delusively simple emblem of Free Silver. He would use the *Debs* and the *Income Tax* cases, as Lincoln had used *Dred Scott*. The silver issue struck at the very jugular of the "money power" and exposed the deep fissures that divided the awkward Republican sectional coalition. Obviously if Bryan's assault upon judicial supremacy should succeed as had those of Jefferson, Jackson and Lincoln, the special immunities that business had won at the bar against income taxes, anti-trust laws, railroad regulation and labor unions would be jeopardized. But unlike its predecessors in 1800, 1828 and 1860, the revolt of 1896 failed. For the first time in American history the embattled western farmer suffered political defeat. Against him Mark Hanna had deployed the "money power" in the most expensive campaign the nation had ever seen. Bryanism, according to Governor Altgeld of Illinois, was "confronted by all the banks, all the trusts, all the syndicates, all the corporations, all the great papers— by everything that money could buy. . . ." But this and a capricious rise in the price of wheat just prior to the election (thanks to crop failures abroad) did not solve the problems that confronted the American people. Some day the embarrassing issues that Bryan had forced into national politics would have to be faced.

A few weeks after the election, Theodore Roosevelt observed that Bryanism was still a "real and ugly danger and our hold upon the forces that won the victory for us [is] by no means too well assured." The bloody shirt had lost its political efficacy. Could new distractions be found lest South and West see their common interest and unite? By chance or design the decrepit position of the Republicans was bolstered by what Secretary of State Hay called "the splendid little war with Spain." After that Imperialism, World War I and "back to normalcy" helped postpone the evil day.

Having reached a high plateau of power in 1895, the Supreme Court fought for the most part a consolidating action until the mid-1930's. Only in the destruction of labor legislation perhaps did it extend its position.

> By 1933 Attorney General (later Mr. Justice) Jackson observed, the Court was no longer regarded as one of three equal departments among which the powers of government were distributed. Instead, [it was said to be] invested with acknowledged and supreme authority, and the whole conservative and property philosophy became oriented around "judicial supremacy."

A premonition of things to come appeared in the Senate's 1930 refusal to confirm the appointment of Judge John Parker to the Supreme Court. His offense had been a faithful adherence as lower court magistrate to the "anti-labor" doctrines of the highest court of the land!

The difficulty was that industrialization had transformed America into a nation of city dwellers and thereby laid the foundation for "new party politics." Labor had replaced the farmer in the nightmares of businessmen. Industry, throttled by the institutions of a pre-industrial economy of scarcity, could not distribute the plentiful products of an "affluent society." Bewildered old-guard observers called it "overproduction." "The Common Man" faced starvation in the midst of plenty. These new horizontal fissures in American life were replacing the old vertical tensions of sectionalism as the nub of national politics. Only the catalyzing magic of an effective political leader was wanting.

When the national economy collapsed Franklin Roosevelt succeeded where Bryan had failed. As Samuel Lubell explained,

> *The really revolutionary surge behind the New Deal lay in this coupling of the depression with the rise of a new generation, which had been malnourished on the congestion of our cities and the abuses of industrialism. Roosevelt did not start this revolt of the city. What he did do was to awaken the climbing urban masses to a consciousness of the power in their numbers. . . . In turn, the big-city masses furnished the votes which re-elected Roosevelt again and again—and, in the process, ended the traditional Republican [sectional] majority in this country. . . . In the past American political realignments have always followed sectional lines. The Revolt of the City, however, has drawn the same class-conscious line of economic interest across the entire country, overriding not only regional distinctions but equally strong cultural differences.*

Mr. Hoover was not the first chief executive to lose office via economic depression. But surely no one before F.D.R. had attained the presidency through an election in which functional (as distinct from geographic) cleavage was as clear as it was in 1936 when 61 per cent of the white-collar, 67 per cent of the skilled, 74 per cent of the semi-skilled, and 80 per cent of all organized, workers supported him as did 60 per cent of the middle, and 76 per cent of the lower, income groups.

Could judicial review continue to dominate national policy? With boldness reminiscent of its counter-revolution in the 1890's the Supreme Court struck down virtually the entire New Deal recovery program. Indeed, it went so far that Mr. Justice Cardozo is said to have remarked, "We are no longer a Court." But what judges had achieved under petrified sectionalism, they could not maintain in the face of a vigorous urban politics. Like the great statesman of the old politics of sections (Jefferson, Jackson and Lincoln), the first master of urbanism had his way with the Court. The "Packing Plan" of 1937, like the Chase Impeachment of 1805, failed only in its immediate aspects. The Supreme Court began at once a long and extended retreat from which it has not yet rallied.

If it be urged that six acts of Congress have been struck down since 1936, one answer is that this in itself is something of a post-bellum record. In a corresponding twenty-two year period prior to 1937, for example, thirty national measures had been invalidated. But a mere count of cases does not reveal the extent of the Court's new self-restraint. Pre-1937 judicial vetoes cover the whole broad spectrum of national economic and social policy. The half-dozen post-1936 vetoes are confined to one specialized field—where legislation jeopardizes the right to a fair trial. Surely here courts may be deemed to have some special competence *vis-à-vis* Congress. What meaning is there in the separation of powers, if that principle does not justify judicial review for the protection of the judicial process itself?

In perspective then, American experience suggests that the success of judicial review of national policy varies in close inverse relation to the efficacy of the political party system. Or to put it differently, judicial "legislation" apparently feeds on defects in the political structure. If, as some insist, public opinion is important in the judicial process, it seems even more important when implemented by dynamic and responsive party machinery. The Supreme Court's only power is its power to persuade. Purse and sword are in other hands. But judicial persuasiveness multiplies when political opposition is lacking or disorganized. On the surface at least, Australian experience with judicial review seems to teach the same lesson and by contrast so does that of Great Britain.

[Just as it is true that realistic assessment of the role of the Supreme Court depends upon an appraisal of its function in the context of a tripartite national government, it is equally important to evaluate its role with respect to the variety of judicial systems which have developed in the framework of American federalism. On a day-to-day and year-to-year basis, the federal Supreme Court is more intimately concerned with the operation of the inferior federal courts and the judicial systems of the fifty states than with the executive and legislative branches of the national government. It is with the highest tribunal's relationship with other courts that Part 4 is concerned.]

4 *The Supreme Court in the Hierarchy of American Courts*

[This portion of *Constitutional Law in the Political Process* incorporates materials illustrative of several facets of judicial relations. One important dimension is the scope of the legal authority of the federal Supreme Court over the inferior federal courts and the highest appellate courts of the states. A second involves the historical analysis of the circumstances under which such authority was established. Third, ideology similarly has a bearing on the influence of one court upon others. Litigatory strategy by contending lawyers may on occasion be fashioned to fit ideological necessities. And fourth, the over-all reputation of a judge as a judicial craftsman may enhance considerably the prestige of the court on which he serves.

A. FEDERALISM AND THE COURTS

The effectiveness of the federal Supreme Court as a defender of individual rights is predicated in large part upon its ability to supervise the other courts which comprise the American system. The essence of the *legal* relationship of the Supreme Court to the inferior federal tribunals and the separate judicial systems of the fifty states is incorporated in the Constitution. Sections 1 and 2 of Article III and Section 2 of Article VI are of crucial importance.]

1. Article III of the Constitution

Section 1. The judicial power of the United States, shall be vested in one Supreme Court, and in such inferior courts as the Congress may from time to time ordain and establish. The judges, both of the Supreme and inferior courts, shall hold their offices during good behavior, and shall, at stated times, receive for their services, a compensation, which shall not be diminished during their continuance in office.

Section 2. (1). The judicial power shall extend to all cases, in law and equity, arising under this Constitution, the laws of the United States, and treaties made, or which shall be made, under their authority;—to all cases affecting ambassadors, other public ministers and consuls;—to all cases of admiralty and maritime jurisdiction;—to controversies to which the United States shall be a party;—to controversies between two or more States;—between a State and citizens of another State;—between citizens of different States;—between citizens of the same State claiming lands under grants of different States, and between a State, or the citizens thereof, and foreign States, citizens or subjects.

(2). In all cases affecting ambassadors, other public ministers and consuls, and those in which a State shall be party, the Supreme Court shall have original jurisdiction. In all the other cases before mentioned, the Supreme Court shall have appellate jurisdiction, both as to law and fact, with such exceptions, and under such regulations as the Congress shall make.

(3). The trial of all crimes, except in cases of impeachment, shall be by jury; and such trial shall be held in the State where the said crimes shall have been committed; but when not committed within any State, the trial shall be at such place or places as the Congress may by law have directed.

2. Article VI of the Constitution

Section 2. This Constitution, and the laws of the United States which shall be made in pursuance thereof; and all treaties made, or which shall be made, under the authority of the United States, shall be the supreme law of the land; and the judges in every State shall be bound thereby, anything in the constitution or laws of any State to the contrary notwithstanding.

[When the Philadelphia Convention was completed, its product, the new Constitution, did not expressly establish inferior federal courts, but permitted Congress to do so if it so desired. During the First Congress, a complete system of inferior federal courts was indeed established and, perhaps more importantly, the Supreme Court was made the effective arbiter of federal-state relations through the provisions of Section 25 of the Judiciary Act. Because these twin developments were crucial to the future development of federal judicial power, the ideological assumptions basic to the establishment of the federal court system are of considerable importance.]

3. The Origin of the Supreme Court's Power as Arbiter In Federal-State Relations*

The ideological content of states' rights doctrine has, over the past century and one-half, undergone so fundamental a transformation that a resurrected John Taylor of Caroline probably would cheerfully embrace the nationalistic welfare state. For the modern states' rights philosophy, with its primary objective the protection of vested interests, could hardly be acceptable to a political theorist who sought to defend the rights of the many against political and economic power in the hands of the few.

Despite the remarkable changes affecting the purposes of states' rights doctrine in American history, the methods of achieving these purposes have remained essentially the same. Political argument based upon alleged constitutional scruples has been for over sixteen decades the big gun in the states' rights polemical arsenal.

One of the most important of the states' rights constitutional arguments concerns the legitimacy of the Supreme Court's power to render definitive decisions in conflicts between the federal government and the states, or between individuals and states which denied them rights guaranteed by the Federal Constitution. Whether the decisions were those in the notable *McCulloch* or *Cohens* cases in the early nineteenth century or those of the "Tidelands Oil" or racial segregation cases in the middle of the twentieth century, the consistent states' rights reaction has been to deny that the Supreme Court had constitutional authority to render such decisions, The continued vitality of this old constitutional argument was strikingly illustrated on March 12, 1956, when Senator Walter George introduced a manifesto signed by nineteen Senators and seventy-seven Representatives from the Southern states. The manifesto referred to the Supreme Court's decision in *Brown* v. *Board of Education* as "judicial usurpation," a substitution of "naked power for established law" and an "unwarranted exercise of power . . . contrary to the Constitution."

Although the supporters of this manifesto made no attempt to formulate serious theoretical or historical arguments to buttress their charge of judicial usurpation, they may properly be considered the intellectual heirs of the constitutional argument of John C. Calhoun. For in advocating the repeal of the twenty-fifth section of the Judiciary Act of 1789, Calhoun unequivocally denied that the framers of the Constitution had chosen the Supreme Court as federal umpire.

The challenges of judicial usurpation of the power to arbitrate in federal-state relations, whether made by a Calhoun or one of his modern successors such as Byrnes or Talmadge, are susceptible to historical examination. The record of history unequivocally demolishes these challenges.

The conception of a powerful judicial body maintaining a division of powers between a government of a whole nation and governments of its parts or sections did not appear miraculously to the Justices of the Supreme Court after the adoption of the Constitution. It was clearly understood and partially applied during the

* John R. Schmidhauser, " 'States' Rights' and the Origin of the Supreme Court's Power as Arbiter in Federal-State Relations," *Wayne Law Review,* IV (Spring, 1958), 101–14. [Footnotes omitted.] Reproduced with permission of the publisher. Copyright © 1958 by the *Wayne Law Review.*

period when America was a colony of Great Britain and under the old Articles of Confederation.

The British Empire maintained the fiction that it was a unitary system until after the American Revolution, but the Empire's relationships with the thirteen colonies had, in reality, become essentially federal. The government of the whole Empire, that of Great Britain, had been forced by the pressure of European wars and great distances to leave most problems of domestic legislation and administration to the governments of the "parts" of the Empire, notably the American colonial governments. Naturally enough, the development of local autonomy in the colonies led to conflicts of authority between the mother country and the colonies as well as among the colonies themselves. It was a quasi-judicial institution of the British Empire, the Committee on Trade and Plantations of the British Privy Council, which resolved such conflicts.

After the American colonies broke with Great Britain a new problem arose, that of balancing the powers of the states and the new central government in North America. A temporary solution was found in the creation of a confederate system. The old Articles of Confederation established a very limited form of judicial arbitration in two narrow fields: the settlement of disputes between the states and the settlement of disputes between the Confederation Congress and the states concerning cases of capture at sea.

The first category of disputes was to be settled in accordance with the ninth article of the Articles of Confederation. This provided that "the united states in Congress assembled shall also be the last resort on appeal in all disputes and differences now subsisting or that hereafter may arise between two or more states concerning boundary, jurisdiction or any other cause whatever. . . ." The parties to a dispute could be directed by Congress "to appoint by joint consent, commissioners or judges to constitute a court for hearing and determining the matter in question." Or if the disputing parties could not agree, Congress could itself make the appointments. The article further provided that "the judgment and sentence of the court . . . shall be final and conclusive. . . ." A serious land dispute was peacefully resolved under this article in 1782. Yet such a court of arbitration lacked permanence. Consequently, it was probably the second judicial institution created under the Confederation which was more influential in the evolution of the judicial arbiter concept in American federalism. For the Court of Appeals in cases of capture was a permanent judicial body which heard 118 cases before the Articles of Confederation were replaced by the new Federal Constitution. A member of this court, Judge John Lowell, made the experiences of this judicial body available to the constitutional framers in 1787 and to the Senate in 1789, sketching a plan for a federal judiciary in a letter to some of the framers and later, in 1789, giving his counsel and advice to the Senate Judiciary Committee.

During the waning years of the Confederation itself, serious attention was given to various proposals to establish a more powerful central judiciary capable of putting an end to state encroachments on or defiance of the authority of the Confederation government. Although these proposals never were adopted by the Confederation, they do provide unmistakable evidence that political leaders of this era were fully aware of the potentialities of a judicial arbiter in confederate or federal governmental systems. A confederation congress committee report, submitted in 1786 by Charles Pinckney, contained, in essence, a complete arrangement for creation of a federal court capable of umpiring federal-state disputes. Pinckney's committee suggested that the Confederation Congress be authorized:

> . . . *to institute a federal judicial court for trying and punishing all officers appointed by congress for all crimes, offenses, and misbehavior in their offices, and to which court an appeal shall be allowed from the judicial courts of the several states in all causes wherein any question shall arise on the meaning and construction of treaties entered into by the United States with any foreign power, or on any law of nations, or wherein any question shall arise respecting any regulations that may hereafter be made by congress relative to trade and commerce, or the collection of federal revenues pursuant to powers that shall be vested in that body, or wherein questions of importance may arise, and the United States shall be a party* . . .

Similar ideas for strengthening the confederation government through creation of some sort of federal judicial arbiter were formulated or discussed by Rufus King, James Madison, and Nathan Dane. Just prior to the Philadelphia Convention of 1787, however, a significantly different argument was discussed widely. Instead of viewing a federal judicial arbiter as primarily a defender of the central government, a broadly circulated pamphlet proposed:

> *In order to prevent an oppressive exercise of powers deposited with Congress, a jurisdiction should be established to interpose and determine between the individual States and the Federal body upon all disputed points, and being stiled The Equalizing Court, should be constituted and conducted in the following manner* . . .

This proposal appeared in the *Pennsylvania Gazette* in Philadelphia on June 6, 1787 and was republished in the leading newspapers during the early days of the Convention. Thus, while supporters of the idea of a strong national government had begun to favor the judicial arbiter concept as a means of restraining the states, those who feared the encroachments of a strong national government had begun to look upon a strong judicial system as a protector of individual and states' rights. Recognition of this development makes more understandable the absence of states' rights or anti-Federalist opposition to most of the proposals made in the Convention which strengthened the federal judiciary.

One of the major reasons for holding the Philadelphia Convention had been the necessity to find a remedy for the evils arising from state legislation which hurt or interfered with the interests of other states, infringed treaties made by the Confederation Congress, oppressed individuals, or invaded the sphere of authority of the confederation government. The convention delegates were faced with the task of finding suitable means of restraining such state legislation or action. Despite the fact that the idea of a judicial arbiter was understood and widely discussed before the opening of the Convention, the creation of a high federal court to solve this problem was by no means a foregone conclusion. Years after the close of the Convention, James Madison referred to the situation in the following manner: ". . . [T]he obvious necessity of a control on the laws of the States so far as they might violate the Constitution and laws of the United States left no option, but as to mode . . . ," noting as the three possible choices "a veto [executive] on the passage of the State laws, a Congressional repeal of them, a judicial annulment of them."

Analysis of the record of the Philadelphia Convention underscores the fact that the granting of power to the Federal Supreme Court to arbitrate finally in federal-state relations came about through a complex series of developments. Basically they represented a compromise between the strong nationalists who originally wanted a veto over the states vested in the new national legislature or executive and the states' righters who either opposed such supervision of the states or preferred that such power be vested in what they considered a weaker and more impartial agency, notably the supreme federal court suggested in the original Paterson Plan.

Among the more important of these developments were (a) the repudiation of coercion of the states by force and the adoption of coercion of individuals by law, (b) the readiness of every major bloc in the Convention to set up a federal judiciary, (c) the demands of one powerful group for a system of inferior federal tribunals, (d) the defeat of the congressional negative proposals and the substitution by Luther Martin of a supremacy clause, and (e) the tendency to look upon a federal judiciary as a protector of individual and states' rights which was reflected in the proposals for a Council of Revision. Very often these developments seemed totally unrelated, but their cumulative effect was the granting of final interpretive powers in federal-state relations to a supreme federal tribunal.

A provision for a congressional veto of state laws was prominent among the resolutions for the Union presented by Edmund Randolph at the opening session of the Convention. It provided "That the national legislature ought to be empowered . . . to negative all laws, passed by the several States, contravening, in the opinion of the national legislature, the articles of union." Later, on May 31, the Convention, in committee of the whole house, amended it by addition of the phrase "or any treaties subsisting under the authority of the Union." The entire resolution was agreed to by the committee without debate or dissent. However, when this resolution was reported from the committee to the Convention on July 17, it met with violent opposition. Gouverneur Morris thought such power "likely to be terrible to the States"; Luther Martin considered it improper; and Sherman believed that since the state courts would hold invalid any laws contravening the authority of the Union, such a veto would be unnecessary. Madison and Charles Pinckney did not share Sherman's confidence in the state courts, however, and held that the congressional negative was necessary as, in the words of Madison, "the most mild and certain means of preserving the harmony of the system." In spite of Madison's appeal, the Convention defeated the proposal for a congressional negative on state laws by a vote of seven to three.

Even before the rejection of the congressional negative by the Convention on

July 17, there was clear-cut evidence that the advocates of a strong central government were prepared to limit the congressional negative by providing for final appeal to a national judiciary. As early as July 10, Randolph had sent Madison a list of concessions to be used "as an accommodating proposition to small states" which then were bitterly opposed to the principle of representation based upon population. In terms of the judicial arbiter concept, the fourth and fifth of Randolph's proposals were particularly significant, because they clearly anticipated the Supreme Court's modern role as both a federal umpire and as a defender of individual rights against state infringement. His suggestions provided:

IV. *That although every negative given to the law of a particular state shall prevent its operation, any state may appeal to the national judiciary against a negative, and that such negative if adjudged to be contrary to the powers granted by the articles of the Union, shall be void.*

V. *That any individual, conceiving himself injured or oppressed by the partiality or injustice of a law of any particular state, may resort to the national judiciary, who may adjudge such a law to be void, if found contrary to the principles of equity and justice.*

Randolph was prepared to offer these conciliatory proposals to the Convention on July 16, but did not do so because of the victory of the small states, on that day, in securing equal voting rights in the Senate.

Throughout the course of the Philadelphia Convention the major discussions of the federal judicial arbiter were generally related to the nationalists' attempts to gain approval for the congressional negative of state laws. However, other discussions in the Convention also contributed to the evolution of the supreme federal tribunal. The proposals for a council of revision, composed of the chief executive and judges of the highest national court, while eventually defeated, stimulated discussion of the power of judicial review. Rejection by the Convention of the proposals to coerce the states by force, contained in both the Randolph and Paterson Plans, were followed by adoption of the principle of direct coercion of individuals by the national government itself. This solution reflected the recognition by Convention leaders of the need to discover a peaceful mode of limiting state interference with national authority. The initiative in finding such a solution was now taken by the leaders of the small states bloc in the Convention, many of whom were of states' rights persuasion.

Using as their starting point a clause from the Paterson Plan guaranteeing the supremacy of the national government within the sphere of its legitimate authority, states' rights supporters attempted to placate the nationalists who were bitterly disappointed by the defeat of the congressional negative proposal on July 17. Luther Martin submitted what he undoubtedly considered a mild substitute for such a negative. His original proposal stated:

. . . [T]*hat the Legislative acts of the United States made by virtue and in pursuance of the Articles of Union, and all treaties made and ratified under the authority of the United States shall be the supreme law of the respective States, as far as those acts or treaties shall relate to the said states, or their citizens and inhabitants—and that the Judiciaries of the several States shall be bound thereby in their decision, anything in the respective laws of the individual States to the contrary notwithstanding.*

Later, the nationalists in the Convention changed this relatively mild resolution in several important respects. These amendments were made in the closing days of the Convention in August and September. On August 5, 1787, the Convention's committee on detail had compressed Martin's resolution and made two significant changes—federal laws were declared supreme over state constitutions as well as state laws, and the duty to uphold the supreme law was imposed on "the Judges in the several States" instead of on "the Judiciaries of the respective states." On August 23, John Rutledge proposed the following important addition: "This Constitution and the laws of the United States made in pursuance thereof . . . shall be the supreme law of the several states." Thus the Constitution was made judicially enforceable law. The Convention adopted his proposal without debate. Finally, on September 12, the committee on style completed the final draft of the Constitution. Luther Martin's resolution had become a part of Article VI. From the point of view of federal-state relations this was the crucial provision in the fundamental document. Section three of that article read:

This Constitution, and the laws of the United States which shall be made in pursuance thereof; and all treaties made, or which shall be made, under the authority of the United States, shall be the supreme law of the land; and the judges in every state shall be bound thereby, anything in the Constitution or laws of any state to the contrary notwithstanding.

Defeat of the congressional negative plan left the Convention with two institutional alternatives for the enforcement of national supremacy. The first was an ultranationalistic suggestion put forth by Alexander Hamilton in his plan for union. Section ten of the plan provided that "all laws of the particular States contrary to the Constitution or laws of the United States to be utterly void; and the better to prevent such laws being passed, the Governour or president of each state shall be appointed by the General Government and shall have a negative upon the laws about to be passed in the state of which he is Governour or President." Hamilton's alternative was not even seriously considered by the Convention. The second was the judicial arbiter which had been an integral part of the original Paterson Plan. Section five had provided "that a federal judiciary be established to consist of a supreme tribunal the judges of which to be appointed by the Executive. . . ." Section two of the same plan proposed that violations of acts of the federal congress be tried in the first instance in "the superior Common Law Judiciary" of the state concerned, "subject . . . for the correction of all errors, both in law and fact . . . , to an appeal to the Judiciary of the United States."

Actually, every major plan for union—Randolph's, Hamilton's and Paterson's—had provided for a national judicial system. The essential difference between the nationalistic plans of Randolph and Hamilton and the states' rights plan of Paterson is that the latter failed to provide a system of inferior federal courts. The nationalists did not actually oppose the adoption of a judicial arbiter, but merely felt, as James Wilson later indicated, that a judicial check on the states would not be sufficient to maintain a strong central government. On August 10, 1787, Charles Pinckney grudgingly admitted that the federal judges "will even be the Umpires between the United States and individual states as well as between one State and another." However, a few days later, on August 23, he tenaciously sought to reinstate the congressional negative, but was defeated by a six to five vote. In urging support for Pinckney's motion, Wilson recognized impliedly that in the absence of a congressional negative, the national judiciary would seek to maintain the supremacy of the national government. This he felt was not enough because "the firmness of Judges is not of itself sufficient. Something further is requisite—it will be better to prevent the passage of an improper law, than to declare it void when passed."

A letter exchange between Thomas Jefferson and James Madison concerning the relative merits of the congressional negative and the judicial arbiter illustrates clearly the contrasting positions of the states' righters and the nationalists. Although he did not attend the Convention, Jefferson was representative of those who, while they feared establishment of a national government in which all authority would be centralized, realized quite clearly that some degree of centralized control was necessary to bring stability to the then chaotic thirteen states. In his reply to Madison's inquiry concerning a congressional negative on state laws, Jefferson presented a viewpoint which might be taken as indicative of the attitude of other advocates of strictly limited government. He wrote:

> *The negative proposed to be given them on all the acts of the several Legislatures is now for the first time suggested to my mind. Prima Facie I do not like it. It fails in an essential character, that the hole and the patch should be commensurate; but this proposes to mend a small hole by covering the whole garment. . . . Would not an appeal from the state judicatures to a federal court in all cases where the act of Confederation controlled the question, be as effectual a remedy, and exactly commensurate to the defect?*

On the other hand, the advocates of a strong central government, while favoring the granting of broad judicial powers, had realized that judicial nullification of state laws was possible only when federal questions arose in bona fide cases before the new Supreme Court. Madison's letter to Jefferson after the close of the Convention indicated the lack of assurance he shared with other strong government advocates. He wrote:

> *It may be said that the Judicial authority under our new system will keep the states within their proper limits and supply the place of a negative on their laws. The answer is that it is more convenient to prevent the passage of a law than to declare it void, after it is passed; that this will be particularly the case, where the law aggrieves individuals who may be unable to support an appeal*

against a state to the Supreme Judiciary, that a state which would violate the legislative rights of the Union would not be very ready to obey a Judicial decree in support of them, and that a recurrence to force, which in the event of disobedience would be necessary, is an evil which the new Constitution meant to exclude as far as possible. A Constitutional negative on the laws of the states seems equally necessary to secure individuals against encroachments on their rights. The mutability of the laws of the States is found to be a serious evil.

After the final defeat of the congressional negative in the Convention on August 23, the nationalists determined to make the best of an unhappy situation by strengthening the federal arbiter by means of grants of broad constitutional jurisdiction and through institution of a complete system of inferior federal courts. The extension of the Supreme Court's jurisdiction to all cases, state and federal, arising under the Constitution was made without states' rights argument. But the attempt at creation of a system of inferior federal courts aroused such fierce opposition that the nationalists were compelled to accept a compromise by which the establishment of such courts was left to the discretion of the new Congress.

Nationalist bitterness at the substitution of a judicial arbiter for their cherished congressional negative persisted to the end of the Convention. For example, on September 12, James Madison supported a motion by Mason which provided that the clause relating to export duties be amended to allow the states to lay such duties for "the sole purpose of defraying the charges of inspecting, packing, storing and indemnifying the loses in keeping the commodities in the care of public officers before exportation." Gorham and Langdon had asked: "How was redress to be obtained in case duties should be laid beyond the purpose expressed?" Madison coldly replied that "[t]here will be the same security as in other cases—The jurisdiction of the Supreme Court must be the source of redress. So far only had provision been made by the plan against injurious acts of the States. His own opinion was, that this was insufficient,—A negative on the State laws alone could meet all the shapes which these could assume. But this had been overruled."

The Philadelphia Convention record indicates unmistakably that the new Supreme Court had been clearly designated the final judicial arbiter in federal-state relations and that it was primarily the states' righters in the Convention who had brought this to pass. The nationalists had not opposed the creation of the judicial arbiter, but had felt strongly that a national judiciary would not, by itself, be strong enough to cope with state encroachments on national authority.

In spite of their misgivings, the advocates of strong central government did not let lack of confidence in a federal judiciary weaken their efforts to secure ratification of the Constitution. Two of the contributions to the *Federalist* by Madison and Hamilton were devoted to an examination of the proposed judicial arbiter, its purposes and its impartial character. Within the state ratifying conventions, the nationalists frequently found themselves the staunchest defenders of the same judicial arbiter for which they had indicated only luke-warm enthusiasm during the Philadelphia Convention; for serious states' rights objections were raised to certain provisions of the judicial clauses in the new Constitution, notably those concerning the possible establishment of a system of inferior federal courts and those extending federal jurisdiction to suits between a state and individuals. In five of the more important of the state ratifying conventions—Connecticut, North Carolina, Virginia, Pennsylvania, and South Carolina—the new Supreme Court's function of resolving state and federal conflicts was discussed clearly and ultimately was accepted. In virtually all of the ratifying conventions some jurisdictional grants to the new federal court system were subjected to severe criticism. Out-and-out opponents of the Constitution, such as Robert Yates of New York, recognized the scope of the Supreme Court's power and made the judicial grants a major point for attack on the proposed new system of government. Under the pseudonym of "Brutus," Yates wrote that "the opinions of the Supreme Court . . . will have the force of law; because there is no power provided in the Constitution that can correct their errors or control their jurisdiction. From this court there is no appeal." But in the end, the nationalists managed to secure early ratification in all of the most important states.

These facts stand out as a result of this analysis of the Philadelphia Convention and the state ratifying conventions. Both the nationalists and the states' righters were in substantial agreement on the need for a supreme judicial arbiter in federal-state relations. By 1789 it was clearly understood that the Supreme Court of the United States was to fulfill that role. Naturally enough, the nationalists tended to emphasize the aspect of judicial arbitership concerned with the protection of national supremacy against state encroachments. However, both nationalists and states' righters explicitly recognized that the Supreme Court's role was that of an *impartial* arbiter. Thus, it was also anticipated that federal laws violative of states' rights were to be declared unconstitutional. The prevailing contemporary conception of the new Supreme Court's role is best illustrated by Oliver Ellsworth's description in the Connecticut Ratifying Convention of January, 1788:

> *This Constitution defines the extent of the powers of the general government. If the general legislature should at any time overleap their limits, the judicial department is a constitutional check. If the United States go beyond their powers, if they make a law which the Constitution does not authorize, it is void; and the judicial power, the national judges, who, to secure their impartiality, are to be made independent, will declare it to be void. On the other hand, if the states go beyond their limits, if they make a law which is a usurpation upon the general government, the law is void; and upright, independent judges will declare it so.*

On March 4, 1789, the wheels of the new central government began to turn; but for eleven months after the United States came into existence, it lacked a judicial branch of government. Although the first judiciary bill was introduced the very next day after the new Senate was organized, it was six months before the bill became law and before President Washington could appoint members to the first Supreme Court.

While the constitutional framers had drawn the broad outlines of the judicial power, they had left to congressional discretion the composition of the federal courts, the extent of the appellate jurisdiction of the Supreme Court, the existence or non-existence of any inferior federal courts and the extent of their jurisdiction. Conse-quently, the manner in which the first Congress dealt with these problems in the Judiciary Act of September 24, 1789, set the pattern for subsequent development of the federal judicial system. This act was especially important because without broad grants of appellate jurisdiction to the Supreme Court by Congress, the entire judicial arbiter plan would have fallen into abeyance for lack of implementation.

The first judiciary act was largely the product of the Senate Judiciary Committee, and within the committee, Oliver Ellsworth and William Paterson took leading roles in drafting the bill. In the early stages of this drafting, Ellsworth sought to establish a complete network of inferior federal courts and to extend their jurisdiction to the limits set by the Constitution. However, to secure the concurrence of Richard Henry Lee, Ellsworth apparently had to accept a more limited inferior federal court system. This setback was mitigated by inclusion of a provision which allowed a defendant sued in a state court in a case involving a federal question to remove the case to a federal circuit court, or to appeal to the Supreme Court, by writ of error, after trial in the highest court of law or equity in a state in which a decision in the suit could be had.

When debate on the draft bill began in the Senate in committee of the whole, on June 22, the issue centered around the question whether there should be any district courts at all or whether the functions of executing federal laws should be left in the first instance to the state courts. Ellsworth had been opposed to giving the state courts such power on the grounds discussed in a letter he wrote later on the subject. He felt that "to annex to State Courts jurisdiction which they had not before, as of admiralty cases, and perhaps, of offenses against the United States, would be constituting the Judges of them, *pro tanto*, Federal Judges, and of course they would continue such during good behavior, and on fixed salaries, which in many cases, would illy comport with their present tenure of office. Besides, if the State Courts, as such, could take cognizance of those offenses, it might not be safe for the General Government to put the trial and punishment of them entirely out of its own hands."

Debate over the various proposals in the bill raged for three months in the Senate and the House. The crucial issues were whether there should be any inferior federal courts, and, if there were to be any such courts, whether the Constitution required that they be vested with the full jurisdiction which the Constitution per-mitted. In its final form the bill was a compromise. The nationalists were forced to abandon their contention that the federal courts be granted the broadest jurisdiction possible under the Constitution, while the states' righters were unable to confine federal cases to state courts, subject only to final appeal to the new federal Supreme Court. Section twenty-five, which became the very cornerstone of federal judicial supremacy, established the appellate jurisdiction of the Supreme Court over state courts where such courts decided against a claimed federal right. Significantly, the states' righters in Congress actually advocated this crucial grant of jurisdiction in 1789.

In sum, the modern states' rights charges of federal "judicial usurpation" of power to arbitrate in federal-state relations may be viewed as a particularly persistent bit of political mythology. For examination of the Philadelphia Convention, the state ratifying conventions, and the legislative history of the first judiciary act indicates unmistakably that the framers clearly intended that the Supreme Court be given responsibility for umpiring the federal system, that the federal judicial arbiter was understood and accepted by the more important of the state ratifying conventions, and that appellate jurisdiction necessary for the fulfillment of its responsibilities was granted the Supreme Court by the first Congress.

Ironically, it was the states' righters of that era—the anti-Federalists—who were largely responsible for the acceptance of the judicial arbiter in the Philadelphia Convention. Similarly, they strongly supported its implementation in the first Congress. Later their basic assumption, gloomily shared by many nationalists, that the federal judicial arbiter would be a rather mild check on state authority proved to be false. And later, the confidence of the states' righters in the impartiality of the Supreme Court was shaken, particularly during the tenure of Chief Justice John Marshall. But during the formative period, 1786–1789, both the states' righters and the nationalists, the former with confidence, the latter with grave misgivings, had accepted the new Supreme Court as the arbiter in federal-state relations.

[It was not until nearly two decades after the adoption of the federal Constitution that the role of the Supreme Court as federal umpire was subjected to truly searching attack. The Court's definitive answer to these attacks in *Martin v. Hunter's Lessee* is one of the great landmarks in the establishment of federal judicial power.]

4. Martin v. Hunter's Lessee: *A Classic Conflict of State and Federal Judicial Authority**

The twenty-fifth section of the Judiciary Act of 1789 provided that final judgment in any suit in the highest court of law or equity of a state,

> . . . *where is drawn in question the validity of a treaty or statute of, or an authority exercised under the United States, and the decision is against their validity, or where is drawn in question the validity of a statute of, or an authority exercised under any state, on the ground of their being repugnant to the Constitution, treaties or laws of the United States, and decision is in favor of their validity, or where is drawn in question the construction of any clause of the Constitution, or of a treaty, or statute of, or commission held under the United States, and the decision is against the title, right, privilege or exemption specially set up or claimed by either party, under such clause of the said Con-*

* John R. Schmidhauser, "The Role of the Federal Judiciary in Establishing the Supremacy of the National Government" (Charlottesville, Va.: Master's Thesis, University of Virginia, 1952), pp. 155–62. [Footnotes omitted.]

stitution, treaty, statute or commission may be re-examined and reversed or affirmed in the Supreme Court of the United States upon writ of error.

In 1789 both the nationalists and the anti-Federalists had approved the granting of such jurisdiction to the Supreme Court. The first major challenge to the exercise of final determinative authority by the Court had come in the form of the statement of the doctrine of state interposition in the Virginia and Kentucky Resolutions of 1798–1799. However, these Resolutions had been drawn up to protest the failure of the Supreme Court to declare unconstitutional the Alien and Sedition Acts. Thus, this early challenge to the Court's power to arbitrate finally in conflicts involving Federal-state relations was not aimed specifically at the Court's exercise of power under the twenty-fifth section of the Judiciary Act. Moreover, it appears that with the exception of the two attacks of Pennsylvania, the Supreme Court was not seriously challenged in the exercise of such power for twenty-six years. By 1815, the Supreme Court had taken jurisdiction, without arousing serious opposition, of writs of error to state courts in sixteen cases. However, in that year the Court of Appeals of Virginia challenged for the first time the right of the Supreme Court to exercise that power. Virginia's attack marked the beginning of a new period in the Supreme Court's history—the advent of bitter attacks by a number of states upon the Court and the advent of a decade in which that tribunal was destined to make its greatest contributions toward the establishment of the supremacy of the national government.

When Justice Story reversed the judgment of the Virginia Court of Appeals in *Fairfax's Devisee* v. *Hunter's Lessee* in 1813, a mandate was sent to the Virginia court ordering it to execute the Supreme Court reversal decision. In 1814 the state court considered this mandate from the highest national tribunal. The Virginia Court of Appeals was not simply the highest judicial body in the state, but was "the controlling center of a dominant and self-perpetuating political party." And in this period the president or chief justice of that state court was the most powerful politician in Virginia, Spencer Roane. Roane dominated the Virginia Legislature, was founder of the *Richmond Enquirer,* and was the political heir to the Virginia Republican party machine created by Jefferson and Madison. With *Richmond Enquirer* editor Thomas Ritchie and John Taylor of Caroline, Spencer Roane managed that state political machine. It was reported in 1800 that Spencer Roane had been "slated" for the appointment as Chief Justice of the United States, but Ellsworth's timely resignation enabled John Adams to appoint John Marshall. Whether because of personal animosity or constitutional scruples (or both), the members of the Virginia Court of Appeals refused to obey the Supreme Court's mandate.

Before rendering a decision, the Virginia tribunal consulted Jefferson, Monroe, and the leading members of the Virginia bar. The crucial question for the state court was stated by Judge Cabell: Can Congress "confer on the Supreme Court of the United States, a power to re-examine, by way of appeal or writ of error, the decision of the state court," (when that decision involves the construction of a treaty), and affirm or reverse that decision, and "command the state court to enter and execute a judgment different from that which it had previously rendered?"

The Virginia judges delivered *seriatim* opinions. Every judge denied that Congress had been empowered to grant the Supreme Court such jurisdiction. The opinions of Judges Cabell and Roane contained the best statements of the states' rights view. Judge Cabell held that,

> . . . *neither [Federal or state] government . . . can act compulsively, on the other or on any of its organs in their political or official capacities . . . The Constitution of the United States contemplates the independence of both governments, and regards the residuary sovereignty of the states, as not less inviolable, than the delegated sovereignty of the United States. It must have been foreseen that controversies would sometimes arise as to the boundaries of the two jurisdictions.* Yet the Constitution has provided no umpire . . . *to give the general government or any of its departments a direct and controlling operation upon the state departments, as such, would be to change at once the whole character of our system.*

Similarly, Judge Roane denied that the Supreme Court had the authority to review and reverse the decision of the highest Virginia court. After an opinion which was perhaps more political in character than judicial, Roane concluded with the warning that "no calamity would be more to be deplored by the American people, than a vortex in the General Government, which should ingulph and sweep away every vestige in the State Constitutions."

The Virginia judges then joined, in a unanimous opinion, in declaring that,

> . . . *the appellate power of the Supreme Court of the United States does not extend to this court, under a sound construction of the Constitution of the United States;—that so much of the 25th section of the act of Congress to establish the judicial courts of the United States, as extends the appellate jurisdiction of the Supreme Court to this Court, is not in pursuance of the Constitution of the United States; that the writ of error in this case was improvidently allowed under the authority of that act; that the proceedings hereon in the Supreme Court were* coram non judice *in relation to this court; and that obedience to its mandate be declined by this court.*

In *Martin* v. *Hunter's Lessee,* the Supreme Court, in an opinion by Justice Story, met this challenge to Federal judicial power.

Interpreting the Constitution's preamble in a manner that was destined to be utilized approvingly by Webster and fiercely challenged by Calhoun in subsequent decades, Justice Story started with the premise that "the constitution of the United States was ordained and established, not by the states in their sovereign capacities, but emphatically, as the preamble of the constitution declares, by 'the people of the United States.'" Thus the sections of the Constitution defining the jurisdiction of the Federal courts are "the voice of the whole American people, solemnly declared, in establishing one great department of the government which was, in many respects, national, and in all, supreme. It is a part of the same instrument which was to act not merely upon individuals, but upon states; and to deprive them altogether of some powers of sovereignty, and to restrain and regulate them in the exercise of others." In order to accomplish this, the jurisdiction of Federal courts was extended to all cases arising under the Constitution, laws, and treaties of the United States. It was the case, not the court, that determined jurisdiction.

In answer to the argument that "the Constitution was not designed to operate upon the states in their corporate capacities," Story pointed out that,

> [The Constitution] is crowded with provisions which restrain or annul the sovereignty of the states in some of the highest branches of their prerogatives. . . . The language of the constitution is also imperative upon the states, as to the performance of many duties. . . . When, therefore, the states are stripped of some of the highest attributes of sovereignty, and the same are given to the United States; when the legislatures of the states are, in some respects, under the control of congress, and in every case are, under the constitution, bound by the paramount authority of the United States; it is certainly difficult to support the argument, that the appellate power over the decisions of state courts is contrary to the genius of our institutions. The courts of the United States can, without question, revise the proceedings of the executive and legislative authorities of the states, and if they are found to be contrary to the constitution, may declare them to be of no legal validity. Surely, the exercise of the same right over judicial tribunals is not a higher or more dangerous act of sovereign power.

Story then reversed the decision of the Virginia court of appeals, stating,

> That the appellate power of the United States does extend to cases pending in the state courts; and that the 25th section of the Judiciary Act, which authorizes the exercise of this jurisdiction, in the specified cases, by a writ of error, is supported by the letter and spirit of the Constitution.

[State court evasions of Supreme Court mandates are not merely a matter for the distant past. The highest appellate courts of the states are often ideologically out of step with the federal Supreme Court. On many occasions, the state justices comply with the mandates of the highest federal court with utmost reluctance as did Chief Justice Duckworth of the Georgia Supreme Court in the selection below. Occasionally, lawyers successfully maneuver to avoid raising a federal question in a manner consistent with the advice of American Bar Association President Walter Armstrong reproduced below. And finally, state courts may deliberately evade a federal Supreme Court mandate.]

5. Reluctant Compliance with the Federal Supreme Court*

It strikes us as being a futile gesture to solemnly declare the sacred and indestructible constitutional right of one to freedom of speech and freedom of worship, and

*Chief Justice Duckworth of Georgia in Nancy M. Looper v. Georgia, Southern and Florida Railway Company, Southeastern Reporter 2nd, 101, 104–105 (1957).

then sanction a denial of that same one's right to work which is the indispensable economic support without which neither freedom could endure. One could not for long enjoy speaking and worshipping freely if he was hungry and was denied bread or the means of obtaining it.

(3) Anyone familiar with the experiences of the thirteen original colonies under the dictatorial powers of the King as expressed in the Declaration of Independence, the reluctance of the States to surrender or delegate any powers to a general government as evidenced by the Articles of Confederation, and the demonstrated need for more powers in the area where jurisdiction was given the general government, will have no difficulty in clearly understanding the meaning of the Constitution when it defines those powers and by the Ninth and Tenth Amendment removes all doubt but that powers not expressly conferred were retained by the States. Even the school children in these original States know that solely because of the erection by individual States of trade barriers inimical to other States, and the inability to remove this evil by State action, the commerce clause, art. 1, sec. 8, clause 3 (Code # 1–125), invested the general government with exclusive jurisdiction of interstate commerce to insure the free flow of commerce across State lines. But claiming authority under this clause the Congress, with the sanction of the Supreme Court, has projected the jurisdiction of the general government into every precinct of the States and assumed Federal jurisdiction over countless matters, including the right to work, which are remotely, if at all, related to interstate commerce. By this unilateral determination of its own powers the general government has at the same time and in the same manner deprived its creators, the States, of powers they thought and now believe they retained. But State courts, irrespective of contrary opinions held by their own judges which by law are required to have had experience as practicing attorneys before they can become judges of the law, must obey and accept the decisions of the Supreme Court of the United States pertaining to interstate commerce. We believe that a single person armed with right—*the right to work,* should in all courts of justice be able to defeat the selfish demands of multitudes though they be members of a labor union who seek to deprive him of that right. We would so rule in any case where we are allowed jurisdiction. When the Supreme Court has, as seen above, held the closed shop labor contract act valid we must likewise hold, not upon our own judgment, but solely because we are required to follow the Supreme Court ruling. We have made these observations to indicate our deep distress over the utter helplessness of a free American under this law, and our inability to judge his cause according to our understanding of the Constitution.

(4) We go now to the single point raised which the Supreme Court has, we believe, clearly indicated is still open for decision. The petition of these non-union employees alleges that they have been notified in accordance with the law and the contract of employment that unless they become members of a union within 60 days their employment will be terminated. It is alleged that the union dues and other payments they will be required to make to the union will be used to "support ideological and political doctrines and candidates" which they are unwilling to support and in which they do not believe, and that this will violate the First, Fifth and Ninth Amendments of the Constitution. While *Railway Emp. Dept.* v. *Hanson, . . .* up-

held the validity of a closed shop contract executed under # 2, Eleventh, that opinion clearly indicates that that court would not approve a requirement that one join the union if his contributions thereto were used as this petition alleges. It is there said, "Judgment is *reserved* [italics ours] as to the validity or enforceability of a union or closed shop agreement if other conditions of union membership are imposed or if the exaction of dues, initiation fees or assessments is used as a cover for forcing ideological conformity or other action in contravention of the First or the Fifth Amendment." We must render judgment now upon this precise question. We do not believe one can constitutionally be compelled to contribute money to support ideas, politics and candidates which he opposes. We believe his right to immunity from such exactions is superior to any claim the union can make upon him.

Accordingly, the trial court erred in dismissing the amended petition which alleges that such uses will be made of dues and other money which as a member of the union petitioners would be required to contribute to the union.

Judgment reversed.
All the Justices concur.

6. *Avoidance of Federal Questions for Ideological Reasons**

. . . a great state supreme court, construing the Federal Constitution, in a case where there is no binding precedent, will not merely engage in a guessing contest as to the view that the Supreme Court of the United States will take, but will arrive at its independent conclusion and assert its own views. If this feeling of independence comes to pervade the state courts to as full an extent as I believe it will, we have a right to expect from them great opinions expounding the Federal Constitution— opinions that will challenge the attention of the nation and materially influence the development of constitutional law.

The effect will by no means stop there. The construction of its own constitution by a state supreme court is, of course, conclusive in the Supreme Court of the United States. None the less, even here, the Supreme Court of the United States has wielded great influence. Many provisions of state constitutions are identical with those of the Constitution of the United States. When such provisions have in the past been construed, state supreme courts have usually followed the construction placed by the Supreme Court of the United States on similar provisions of the Federal Constitution. Many have gone further and—sometimes contrary to their own inclination— adopted constructions of their own constitutions which they consider in line with the current tendency of the Supreme Court of the United States, even though that court has not passed on the question. *Here, too, in the future we may expect a greater independence on the part of the state supreme courts.*

*Walter P. Armstrong (President, American Bar Association), "The Increasing Importance of State Supreme Courts," *American Bar Association Journal*, XXVIII (1942), 2–3. [Footnotes omitted.] Reproduced with permission of the author and the publisher. Copyright (1942) by the American Bar Association. Italics the editor's.

Already cases are arising where rights are asserted under provisions of state constitutions similar to clauses of the Fourteenth Amendment and where counsel are careful not to make any claim under the Federal Constitution.

7. State Court Evasion of United States Supreme Court Mandates*

State court independence has been frequently asserted by an evasion of United States Supreme Court mandates. A recent instance of the apparent disregard of such a mandate is found in a Nebraska case, *Hawk* v. *Olson*. There petitioner, sentenced to life imprisonment after a murder conviction, sought a writ of habeas corpus on grounds of perjured testimony, deprivation of opportunity to consult counsel and prepare a defense, and subsequent curtailment of the right to appeal. During six years of persistent attempts in five different courts to obtain a hearing on these allegations, ten former applications had been denied, all for technical or jurisdictional reasons, without affording him a chance to prove the merits of his claims. The Nebraska Court rejected his eleventh request, stating that habeas corpus was a collateral attack available only against a judgment void on its face, and that the application stated mere conclusions rather than facts. The United States Supreme Court, although accepting the Nebraska decisions that sufficiency of evidence could not be raised by habeas corpus, and that Hawk's petition did not establish any interference with his right to appeal, reversed and remanded, declaring that the allegations included facts showing a deprivation of the effective assistance of counsel, in violation of the due process clause of the 14th Amendment, sufficient to entitle the petitioner to a hearing.

Nevertheless, Hawk's motion for compliance with the resulting mandate was denied by the Nebraska Court. In the explanatory opinion the majority stated that the Supreme Court must not have recognized the real basis of the previous Nebraska decision, namely, that the applicant had mistaken his remedy, and that under state procedure the issue of denial of counsel was not justifiable in a habeas corpus proceeding. The Court further asserted that although the Supreme Court might declare the petitioner's right to some remedy under the 14th Amendment, it could not dictate within the state the choice of one particular remedy.

The legal pattern of such attack on an appellate order was set by the early case of *Davis* v. *Packard*. There, with approval by affirmance, the United States Supreme Court permitted the effect of its own opinion and mandate to the dernier court of New York to be avoided, the latter court having declared that under state law the appellate court's jurisdiction did not permit a reversal of the trial court for a factual error not appearing on the face of the record. The Supreme Court affirmance was hinged on the New York court's recognition that a coram nobis writ was still available.

*Note, "State Court Evasion of United States Supreme Court Mandates," *Yale Law Journal*, XXXVI (1947), 574–83. [Footnotes omitted.] Reproduced with permission of the publisher. Copyright (1947) by the Yale Law Journal Co., Inc.

Variations on this method of avoidance, similarly founded on the autonomy of state courts within the realm of state law, were subsequently authorized by the Supreme Court. Among the devices used were a revised construction of a state statute, the discovery of a hitherto unconsidered alternative ground for judgment under state law, and the development of a "factual" approach.

Two further rationales as grounds for evasion, at present untested by the Supreme Court, were recently advanced by this same Nebraska Court in *Johnson* v. *Radio Station WOW*. In reviewing the original state decision, the Supreme Court had conceded the absolute jurisdiction of the state over the issue of fraud in the lease of a radio station, but, in the interest of effectuating the overriding policies of the Federal Communications Act, had ordered certain changes to be made in the timing of the retransfer decree. The Nebraska Court, however, relying on Mr. Justice Frankfurter's concession of state jurisdiction, held the situation to be within the principle of *Davis* v. *Packard* and refused to comply. It was further asserted that a Supreme Court mandate impinging on that jurisdiction violated Section 265 of the Judicial Code and might be treated as advisory.

Neither of the new rationales thus advanced seems tenable. It is true that the Judicial Code's long-standing prohibition of federal injunctions against state courts has been sometimes construed to include orders not directly restraining the court but necessarily having that effect. But it has never been applied to successive decisions or orders in the identical action. To do so would invalidate the entire theory and practice of appellate jurisdiction. Second, extension of the *Davis* v. *Packard* doctrine through reliance on conceded jurisdiction appears to overlook completely the Supreme Court resolution of intertwining state and federal questions. Thus to interpret that doctrine as meaning that the state court may determine the dividing line conflicts directly with the supremacy clause and its natural corollary that the Supreme Court must be final arbiter of the extent of its own power.

The evasion in the *Hawk* case, in contrast, falls more directly into the *Davis* v. *Packard* principle, but only if the assumption be made that Hawk will in fact be granted a hearing on application for a writ of coram nobis or on a statutory motion for a new trial, the only remaining possible remedies. Until such an attempt is made, actual disobedience is not yet real. It is, however, significant that in its first denial of this application the court stated that a writ of coram nobis was the correct procedure for the introduction of new evidence, while its opinion after reversal contained no finding that coram nobis would be allowed for a showing of denial of counsel; nor did it include what course the applicant should properly have pursued. Instead, the later opinion justified its result by pointing to the unused remedies which had been available to petitioner after original conviction and cited the legal principle that a constitutional right may be forfeited by the failure to make timely assertion of that right. If from these statements it may be deduced that the court now deems the forfeited remedies the only ones allowable, and so intends to deny a possible future request for a hearing, there is substantial conflict with and disobedience of the Supreme Court mandate, which was patently issued with full knowledge of the loss of some rights by petitioner.

As the extent of disobedience in the *Hawk* case is thus not yet definitely ascertainable, and as the validity of the grounds of disobedience in the *Johnson* case will not now be tested in the Supreme Court, these two Nebraska opinions have significance and effect only in the contribution of their iota of discredit to the country's judicial system. The layman expects that an adjudication of a party's rights by the United States Supreme Court is determinative; and loss of respect follows naturally if its mandates are evaded or if litigation is again prolonged.

In the past, little has been done to prevent this type of discredit by taking action against state courts after evasion has occurred. At times a reappeal by the aggrieved party has forced the Supreme Court into action in affirmance of its former decree. Yet, with theoretical methods of enforcement possibly available, including mandamus, and even prosecution of the disobedient state judges, no remedy more severe than a directly issued award of final execution or a mandate ordering a specific judgment has yet been invoked.

To preclude evasion in the first instance the two most sweeping solutions presently available would be a direct award of execution whenever feasible, or enforced waiver of alternative grounds for the state judgment not brought in issue in the earlier litigation. The latter method might be further modified by Supreme Court recognition of its own ability to adjudicate undetermined state law. Although none of these possible remedies would seem to conflict with the Constitution, nor with the present Judicial Code, they would entail an important change from present practices, perhaps disproportionate to the magnitude of the ill. An additional objection lies in the possibility of decisions inconsonant with the normal policies and substantive law of a state.

A less thorough remedy not open to the above objections could be achieved by an overruling of *Davis* v. *Packard* with respect to jurisdictional and procedural issues alone. Although occasional decisions deviating from normal state procedure might thereby result, verdicts under substantive law of the state would be consistent. Such a limitation would considerably narrow the field for state technical evasion without prolonging litigation, and the unlikely event of state non-evasive defiance could then justifiedly be met by one of the aforementioned modes of enforcement.

[In actuality the effectiveness of the federal Supreme Court as supervisor of the courts of the nation and the states may well depend more upon its long-term *influence* than upon bare invocation of its *authority*. The influence of court systems has been a matter of controversy for some years; Chancellor Kent, for example, stated in his *Commentaries on American Law,* that

> *The judiciary of the United States has an advantage over many of the State Courts, in the tenure of office of the Judges, and the liberal and stable provision for their support. The United States are, by these means, fairly entitled to command better talents, and to look for more firmness of purpose, greater independence of action, and brighter displays of learning. The federal administration of justice has a manifest superiority over that of the individual states, in conse-*

quence of the uniformity of its decisions, and the universality of its application. Every state court will naturally be disposed to borrow light and aid from the national courts, rather than from the courts of other individual states, which will probably never be so generally respected and understood.[1]

In the early 1930's Rodney Mott devised an ingenious scheme to evaluate systematically the influence of the highest appellate courts of the states. Unlike Kent, Mott stressed creative decision-making and the quality of the judicial product rather than factors associated with the judicial selection process.]

8. Judicial Influence*

It is axiomatic that some supreme courts are more influential than others. A dictum by one judge may carry more weight than a decision by another. Anyone who has studied the opinions of our highest courts is constantly assigning values to them, and the combination of these impressions may determine the relative standing of these tribunals for that individual. That this process of appreciation or depreciation is usually unconscious, and frequently irrational, does not make the prestige which results from it any less real or less potent a factor.

No one would claim that reputation is the only standard by which a court should be judged. A thoroughly satisfactory tribunal must have many qualities, but certainly the esteem accorded it is one of its most valuable assets. The finality of the decisions of a court of last resort and the importance of the conflicts of interests which it must settle demand a high degree of confidence in its intelligence and integrity. Furthermore, the duties of a court to develop the unwritten law and to interpret the statutes render its prestige a matter of prime concern. Lawyers look to it for statements of the law, teachers of jurisprudence require their students to study its opinions, and tribunals in other states as well as its own may accord weight to its views. The extent to which a court is able to mold the law depends to a considerable degree on the esteem in which it is held.

This article reports an attempt to secure comparable data with respect to the professional reputations of the various supreme courts—data which will be more complete and accurate, more capable of measurement, than casual remarks.

ESTEEM BY LAW PROFESSORS

The initial investigation secured data concerning the attitudes of law school professors toward the various courts. Two methods were used. During the spring of 1931, a form was sent to each of the 600 law professors in schools which were mem-

[1] James Kent, *Commentaries on American Law*, I (5th ed.; New York: James Kent, 1844), 443–44.

*Rodney Q. Mott, "Judicial Influence," *American Political Science Review*, XXX (1936), 295–315. Reproduced with permission of the author and the publisher. Copyright (1936) by the American Political Science Association.

bers of the Association of American Law Schools. This form requested the professor to classify each supreme court, if he was familiar with its work, in one of seven categories ranging from lowest esteem to highest esteem. He was asked to base his judgment on the work of the court since 1900, and merely to indicate his reaction to the various courts without attempting to analyze the bases for his opinion. It was not necessary for each professor to give a rating to the highest court in every one of the 48 states. He was requested to rate only those courts concerning which he had a reasonable basis of judgment.

Returns were received from 259 professors located in 37 states and the District of Columbia. All sections of the country were represented, although, of course, not in proportion to their population, or even to the enrollment of the law schools located in them.

* * *

The esteem in which a court is held is, of course, purely subjective with the rater. It may be based on snap-judgment, prejudice, impressions, or even a flip of a coin. The number of chance factors that may influence a rater's opinion are infinite, and for this reason one modest consultee declared that his ratings were "of no value except perhaps to show how little worthy my esteem is."

The significance of the ratings lies largely in the story they tell of the impressions which members of law school faculties have of the courts. Whether or not these impressions are justified is another matter. An index of esteem is intended to be a gauge of opinion—not an objective criterion of worth. At the same time, few would say that the quality of work of a court has no effect on the esteem in which it is held. If the composite rating of a court faithfully represents its prestige among law teachers, it must be presumed that there is some basis for that prestige. It is obvious that the basis was not merely the whim of the rater. Had this been so, the distribution of ratings would have shown no differentials between the various states.

Certainly the professors in American law schools might be expected to have a better basis for judging the work of the state supreme courts than any other group. Most of these institutions pride themselves on the fact that their outlook is national rather than local or only state-wide. Their faculties are composed of men who are as impartial and as informed as any group in the United States. Teachers of law spend their lives studying the cases in their fields, and frequently go over an entire branch of the law when preparing a case-book for student use, or when writing a treatise for the benefit of practitioners. It is true that very few of these professors have a complete grasp of the work of the courts in all of the fields of law. But, taken as a body, it seems reasonable to assume that all of the fields are covered.

* * *

The average esteem for each court ranged all the way from 1.3 in the case of New Mexico to 6.6 for the United States Supreme Court. It will be observed that the state courts with the highest standing are those in New York, Massachusetts, New Jersey, and Connecticut, in that order. Furthermore, the New York court of appeals not only ranked first in esteem among the state courts, but was substantially ahead

TABLE IV. *Esteem of Supreme Courts by Law Professors*

State	Average Esteem Rating*	State	Average Esteem Rating*
Alabama	3.4	Nevada	2.1
Arizona	1.7	New Hampshire	4.7
Arkansas	1.5	New Jersey	5.4
California	4.3	New Mexico	1.3
Colorado	3.4	New York	6.5
Connecticut	5.1	North Carolina	4.1
Delaware	3.7	North Dakota	2.3
Florida	1.6	Ohio	4.1
Georgia	2.3	Oklahoma	2.0
Idaho	2.1	Oregon	3.0
Illinois	4.3	Pennsylvania	4.7
Indiana	2.9	Rhode Island	4.4
Iowa	3.9	South Carolina	2.3
Kansas	4.1	South Dakota	1.8
Kentucky	3.2	Tennessee	2.7
Louisiana	2.8	Texas	2.5
Maine	4.8	Utah	2.6
Maryland	4.6	Vermont	4.6
Massachusetts	5.8	Virginia	4.0
Michigan	4.9	Washington	3.5
Minnesota	4.6	West Virginia	3.4
Mississippi	1.6	Wisconsin	4.7
Missouri	3.5	Wyoming	2.4
Montana	2.6	U.S. Supreme Court	6.6
Nebraska	3.3		

*Highest possible rating, 7; lowest possible rating, 1.

of its nearest rival, the Massachusetts supreme court, and was only one-tenth of a point below the United States Supreme Court.

It will be seen that there is a distinct relationship between the average esteem in which a court is held and the number of times it was rated. Those courts which were most frequently rated were, on the whole, the courts which were most highly regarded. It can hardly be considered accidental that more law professors are familiar with the work of the New York and Massachusetts courts than with those of other states. Either the prestige of the court is closely related to the extent to which its opinions are known, or else professors of law charitably follow the injunction to say nothing if they can say nothing good. It may very well be that both of these elements enter into the picture. Certain it is that the remark of Tacitus, "It is common to esteem most what is most unknown," does not apply here.

LAW SCHOOL CASE-BOOKS

Another estimate of the esteem in which the state courts of last resort are held may be obtained by inspecting the case-books which are used in the various law schools. These volumes are important for two reasons: (1) the opinions which are included in them are selected because they appeal to the editors, and therefore they reflect the attitude of leading law teachers toward the courts; (2) the case-books furnish almost the sole study material for law students, and consequently the opinions which are included in them exert an important influence on the next generation of lawyers. The number of opinions from each court which are reprinted in these case-books can be used, accordingly, as a measure of the attitude of a selected group of law teachers toward the court and as a rough index of the influence of the court on legal instruction.

A case-book is usually prepared by a professor who has made a special study of the particular field of law covered by it, and who is, therefore, especially familiar with its literature. In selecting opinions for inclusion in the case-book, he may take into consideration numerous factors. An effort is generally made to secure a series of problems illustrating the points of law which have arisen in the subject. Preference is frequently given to cases with interesting or unique facts rather than to those of a more prosaic character. Simple cases are often preferred to complicated ones involving several subjects. Some editors seek opinions which summarize the law in a succinct fashion, which contain vigorous dissenting opinions, or which discuss problems recently presented to the courts. If these were all of the considerations which were taken into account in compiling a case-book, the number of cases from each state should be roughly in proportion to the volume of opinions prepared by the court of last resort. Thus the number of opinions by the Supreme Court of the state of Washington which could qualify should be about the same as the number of opinions by the New York court of appeals.

It was found, however, that the distribution of opinions in the case-books bore little or no relation to the volume of litigation in the state courts of last resort. There were naturally only a few opinions from Delaware, where there is very little litigation in the highest court, or from Louisiana, where a different system of law prevails. But the difference in the extent to which other courts were drawn on for case material indicates that the editors of the case-books were influenced by still other factors in considering cases for inclusion.

An opinion which is cogently written is better instructional material than one which is poorly prepared. A vigorous discussion of even an uninteresting case may make better case-book material than a dull discussion of an exciting one. Furthermore, an editor's view concerning the correctness of the decision undoubtedly entered into consideration. Some editors have a reputation for including cases which they believe to be clearly wrong in order to develop the critical faculties of the student. But, in general, the opinions included in the case-books may be presumed to represent the weight of authority on the particular point decided. Thus the number of cases from each jurisdiction should bear some relation to the attitude of the editors toward the court in that state, with respect either to the correctness of its decisions or to the cogency of its discussion of the points involved.

In any event, it is clear that those courts which are drawn on most frequently for opinions in the case-books are more likely to influence the legal thinking of the next

TABLE V. *Opinions Reprinted In Law School Case-Books*

State	Opinions Reprinted	State	Opinions Reprinted
Alabama	120	Nebraska	74
Arizona	21	Nevada	6
Arkansas	66	New Hampshire	81
California	148	New Jersey	259
Colorado	62	New Mexico	14
Connecticut	181	New York	747
Delaware	43	North Carolina	141
Florida	28	North Dakota	38
Georgia	91	Ohio	79
Idaho	26	Oklahoma	114
Illinois	256	Oregon	83
Indiana	53	Pennsylvania	178
Iowa	173	Rhode Island	68
Kansas	180	South Carolina	51
Kentucky	132	South Dakota	42
Louisiana	21	Tennessee	66
Maine	91	Texas	57
Maryland	66	Utah	32
Massachusetts	572	Vermont	88
Michigan	151	Virginia	52
Minnesota	255	Washington	143
Mississippi	49	West Virginia	94
Missouri	87	Wisconsin	193
Montana	42	Wyoming	12
		Total	5626

generation of lawyers than those which are ignored. Whatever other functions a court of last resort may have, two are certainly of prime importance: the development of the law of the state; and the instruction of the legal profession in the law as developed. If the opinions which a court renders are not good instructional material, it is clearly missing one of its most important sources of influence.

An analysis was made, accordingly, of practically all of the case-books widely used in American law schools. These fifty-nine case-books embraced sixty-one volumes and covered all of the more commonly studied law school subjects, and most of the others. Only books published since 1915 were included, and in the list there are a considerable number which have been prepared for the newer types of law courses now being developed in some schools. It is believed that this list was a fair sample of the case-books most widely used in law schools.

The number of times each court had an opinion reprinted in these books is shown in Table V. It will be observed that the New York court of appeals and the supreme judicial court of Massachusetts were much more frequently drawn on for case material than were any of the other courts of last resort. Almost a quarter of all the opinions included in the case-books now used in our law schools were handed down in one of these two courts. Only three other courts—those of New Jersey, Illinois, and

Minnesota—furnished more than 250 cases each for these volumes, while nearly two-thirds of the states furnished less than 100 opinions each.

A comparison between the number of cases from each state which were included in the various case-books and the average esteem reported by the law professors shows that there is a distinct relationship between these two indexes. The same three courts head each of the lists, and in the same order.

It is interesting to note, likewise, that there is an even closer correlation between the number of cases cited in case-books and the number of raters who were willing to express an opinion of the court on the rating form. Perhaps law professors draw their impressions of the standing of a court, in part at least, from the frequency with which the opinions of that court are found in the case-books they teach. Certainly there is a distinct increment of prestige to any tribunal of last resort whose opinions are frequently used in the classroom.

ESTEEM BY OTHER COURTS

The opinions of other tribunals concerning the esteem of a court of last resort is in some respects more important than the opinion of either law teachers or the editors of case-books. A court's fellow-judges are directly in contact with the problems which an appellate tribunal must face. In deciding cases, the judges frequently consult, compare, and choose between the opinions of the courts of other states. There is probably no body of persons better qualified to estimate the work of the various courts than the members of those courts themselves. Furthermore, the extent to which the decisions of a court are followed by its fellows is more than a mark of its prestige; it is evidence of its influence on the general development of the law in the United States. A court whose views are highly regarded in other jurisdictions is in an enviable position of leadership.

It was obviously impracticable to secure a direct expression of the views of judges regarding one another. Accordingly, it was found necessary to turn to indirect indexes. Three such were constructed: (1) the number of times each court was cited in the opinions of the courts of other states; (2) the number of times each state court was cited in the opinions of the United States Supreme Court; (3) the number of times each state court was cited *with approval* in the opinions of the United States Supreme Court. 　　　　* * *

. . . there is a close relationship between the total number of citations in state courts and the number of citations approved by the United States Supreme Court.

It seems fair to assume that the opinion of the United States Supreme Court concerning the state tribunals is more important than that of the state courts themselves, but when these two indexes compare closely, it must be concluded that ratings given in them have a high degree of reliability. And when the opinion of the United States Supreme Court agrees closely with that of law professors in the principal law schools—and with that of the editors of the case-books—it is clear that there is a general consensus of opinion among those in a position to judge the standing of the state supreme courts.

It has been shown that these various indexes of judicial standing and influence all bear a distinct relationship to each other. No one of them can be conceived of as a perfect criterion of judicial prestige. In each case, outside factors, chance considerations, and possible inaccuracies may have crept in to cast doubt on the validity of the index. It is very significant, however, that a high degree of relationship exists between any two of them. It is clear, moreover, that the standing of the court is an important factor in each of them.

There is a possibility that some common factor besides the prestige of the court, common to each of these indexes, might account for the high correlation between them. It will be observed that the older, more populous, and wealthy states tend to rank higher than their newer, poorer, more rural sisters. As an eastern professor shrewdly wrote on his rating form, "Some courts may be noteworthy because they necessarily deal with great problems; others are obscure, largely for geographical reasons." The factors producing a court with a high prestige might well be analyzed. But whatever those factors may be, a court's prestige as an index of its standing would still be significant. An opinion from a court of high prestige may be no better law than an opinion from one of low esteem, but it certainly has a better chance of being accepted as authoritative.

A study of the tables will show, moreover, that some states rank surprisingly high in view of their small populations and wealth, while other courts which might be expected to be near the top of the list rate below them. These deviations from the expected order are perhaps more significant than the ratings themselves.

COMBINED PRESTIGE RATING

If the prestige of the court is an important element in each of these indexes, it should be feasible to combine them into a composite index. In such a combination, the chance elements of one index might tend to neutralize the chance elements in another, and hence the resulting index would be more reliable than any of the single ones. Accordingly, a composite table has been constructed using the following factors: (1) the esteem in which the law professors held the courts; (2) the extent to which opinions from each court were used in law school case-books; (3) the number of prestige ratings given each court; (4) the number of citations of opinions of the court by other state courts; (5) the number of cases cited with approval by the United States Supreme Court.

This composite rating of prestige is given in Table VIII. . . .

. . . A comparison of these composite ratings of prestige with the composite rating of personnel of the courts which was prepared in another connection shows that there is a fair degree of relationship between the prestige of a court of last resort and the personnel of the court. This is, of course, what would be expected, and the fact that it is shown by the data tends to strengthen the presumption of the validity of each index.

A study of the relation between the standing of a state's tribunal and its position in other respects may disclose important conditions which will promote or decrease the influence of a court of last resort. Will a higher salary, longer term, broader jurisdiction, or a more professional bar enhance the standing of the judiciary? Or is it dependent upon such uncontrollable factors as the antiquity of the tribunal, the natural resources of the state, the wealth of its inhabitants, or the development of its industries? . . .

TABLE VIII. *Combined Prestige Rating in Order of Rank*

State	Prestige Rating	State	Prestige Rating
New York	25.18	West Virginia	6.30
Massachusetts	23.09	Nebraska	6.08
Illinois	15.77	Texas	6.04
New Jersey	14.08	Virginia	6.04
California	12.26	Georgia	5.85
Pennsylvania	11.79	Colorado	5.78
Michigan	11.75	Oregon	5.48
Minnesota	11.59	Tennessee	5.45
Wisconsin	11.44	Oklahoma	5.35
Iowa	9.87	Louisiana	4.58
Kansas	9.32	Delaware	4.52
Connecticut	9.23	South Carolina	4.43
Ohio	8.89	North Dakota	4.39
Missouri	8.64	Mississippi	4.36
Indiana	8.17	Montana	4.32
North Carolina	7.98	Arkansas	4.28
Vermont	7.90	Utah	3.96
Washington	7.81	South Dakota	3.43
Maine	7.35	Idaho	3.33
Alabama	7.12	Wyoming	3.32
Kentucky	7.01	Florida	3.27
Rhode Island	6.99	Nevada	2.94
New Hampshire	6.85	Arizona	2.58
Maryland	6.77	New Mexico	2.12

B. COURT ORGANIZATION: ITS RELATIONSHIP TO JUDICIAL INFLUENCE

[Rodney Mott's study of judicial influence accurately gauged the relative positions of higher state appellate courts on the basis of professional assessment and acceptance of the decisions of these courts. But the administration of justice is not carried out primarily at the lofty level of appellate decision-making. For the average citizen, contact with a court may never involve appellate court action. Rather, it may mean involvement in a judicial world in which clerks, bailiffs and inferior court judges predominate. Perhaps no single work has captured the realistic sense in which judicial organization may affect the public's expectations with respect to the attainability of justice to the degree achieved by Albert Lepawsky in his work on the Chicago area courts.]

1. The Organization of the Courts in Metropolitan Chicago*

A description of metropolitan judicial work illustrates the gulf which separates the fictions from the realities of government. The popular conception of a judicial proceeding is a trial of a notorious criminal, a dispute over fabulous riches, or at least a breach of promise suit with testimony exposing wayward affections and broken hearts. But actually, the courts of the Chicago Area are mainly concerned with traffic violations, minor business claims, and family problems. A court is conceived as the sanctum of the law where the judge weighs the pleas of two contenders for public justice. Yet many cases are disposed of merely by the payment of a fine before the cashier's cage, by a proceeding which does not even require parties to appear in court, or by a probation officer's visit at the home of a delinquent youth. The orthodox conception of judicial organization is an orderly system of lesser powers and appellate authorities. But in the Chicago Region we find, instead, a confusing array of overlapping courts.

In order to understand the metropolitan court system it is necessary to probe behind these judicial fictions and forms, to explore the background and analyze the nature of metropolitan judicial work. This is the function of the present chapter.

Volume, variety, and expansion are the outstanding features of metropolitan judicial work. These underlying characteristics may be observed, first, in the number of cases, second, in the types of cases, and, third, in the territorial extension of judicial functions.

I. THE GROWING VOLUME OF JUDICIAL WORK

Almost three-quarters of a million cases are commenced in the courts of the Chicago area each year. The average number of cases filed annually during the three-year period 1929–31 was approximately 731,000, in spite of a decided decline after the slump period commencing in 1929. The volume and concentration of work can be better appreciated if we consider the figures for the nucleus of the Region, that is Cook County, which includes Chicago. Here over 85 per cent of the Regional cases are heard. For the three-year period 1929–31 the average for the courts in Cook County was approximately 633,000 cases per year. The Municipal Court alone dealt with an average of 473,426 cases per year during the same period.

A glance at this court, which deals with almost two-thirds of all the cases filed in the Region, illustrates the incessant flow of work confronting the metropolitan judicial system. Over a wide expanse of city area, three thousand patrolmen are unearthing offenses and complaints which are poured upon the dockets of the specialized criminal branches and the branch police courts in various sections of the city. In the congested Loop in the heart of the metropolis, traffic policemen with their staccato whistles serve "tickets" on careless auto drivers. Motorcycle cops wearing the insignia of their

*Reprinted from *The Judicial Systems of Metropolitan Chicago* by Alfred Lepawsky by permission of the author and the University of Chicago Press. [Footnotes omitted.] Copyright (1932) by the University of Chicago. Note that the Lepawsky study was published in 1932. It contains, in addition, material on the judicial council movement which helps to balance this phase of the study.

respective governments—the city, West Park, South Park, Lincoln Park—perform similar duties over the boulevard systems radiating from the Loop.

But one fails to appreciate fully the volume of work confronting the Municipal Court of Chicago unless one visits the office of the court clerk on the eighth floor of the City Hall. There he beholds the vortex of all kinds of civil disputes which arise in the swollen hub of the metropolitan region. Before a dozen windows and cages, queues of law clerks and lawyers are restlessly awaiting their turn to have the seal of the clerk of the municipal court imprinted on the papers that are to be filed—as though the ten or fifteen minutes spent in line will add much time to the months or years that are likely to elapse before the case is disposed of. Searching cash baskets overhead dart back and forth from cashier's cage to filing windows. Attending at these windows are busy filing clerks whose moods shift from familiarity to brusqueness as an antidote to the monotony of their duties. Behind them, scores of other clerks with pens and rubber stamps are working over stacks of "half sheets," or records of the cases, which are classified and assigned to the various branch courts on the floors above. Similar scenes are enacted in the bailiff's office a block distant across the hall on the same floor, where arrangements are made for the service of writs. And in the courtrooms, as the cases are being forced through the mill, the routine is only occasionally tempered by an inexperienced attorney who makes a ridiculous plea.

Almost a half million cases a year, seventeen hundred cases each working day, enter this central court of the metropolitan area. So far as volume is concerned, the Municipal Court of Chicago is a veritable adjudicating giant, colossal enough to consume the personalities of lawyers, clerks, bailiffs, social service experts, medical attaches, and judges who serve it. Its mass of work alone threatens to dwarf the pleas of the poor tenant, the merchant, and the landlord who come to secure justice, of the taxicab driver who insists under oath that he stopped for only a second in the middle of Randolph Street to take on a fare, of the public that wishes to punish a notorious gangster, and of the self-educated 'bo from Bughouse Square who cites the bill of rights as he is flung into a cell after leading a demonstration on unemployment to the City Hall.

To be sure, the great volume of work in the Municipal Court of Chicago places it on one extreme of the scale of the metropolitan judiciary. Omitting the various degrees of court activity, we find at the other extreme of the judicial scale, courts which have only a small amount of judicial business. If you are a lawyer and you have a case to file in the Circuit Court of Kendall County, you drive up to the red-brick, two-story courthouse on top of the hill in Yorkville, and walk up a flight of stone steps through a short, deserted hallway to the office of the clerk of the circuit court, who is also the recorder of deeds. On entering, you greet Mrs. Davis, the incumbent of this dual office, and her deputy, Marguerite. Jiggs, Mrs. Davis' dog, backs out from under the table wagging his tail gleefully and turns around to be petted by the newcomer. The case is filed, plans are discussed for an evening drive to the theater in Chicago, and after more chat with Marguerite, you are off to Aurora. When the case comes up for hearing, the procedure is as calm and as leisurely as the original filing of the suit. But there are only about 150 cases filed annually in the

Circuit Court of Kendall County. For the courts conducting the bulk of the Region's judicial work, the scenes enacted in the Municipal Court of Chicago are more characteristic of the metropolitan judicial system.

Not only is this volume of cases overwhelming at any given time, but it tends to increase from year to year. Though there are some alternate declines, the figures for the most important courts in the Chicago Area show a decided upward swing. In the Municipal Court of Chicago alone, which deals with two-thirds of the cases in the Region, the number of judicial proceedings has increased about five times as fast as the population of the city since 1910.

* * *

II. THE INCREASING VARIETY OF CASES

This growth of judicial work reveals more than an increase in the volume of cases. It also discloses a growing variety in the types of cases coming before the courts. Judicial business, it appears, increases not merely with the growth of metropolitan population but also with changes in metropolitan life. Greater business activity, increased mobility of metropolitan inhabitants, extended definitions of crimes and misdemeanors, and new economic methods like installment buying open up new sources for social and economic conflicts which are presented to the courts as judicial proceedings.

In analyzing these proceedings it is necessary to appreciate the hazards of quantitative measurement in judicial work. Dissimilar cases are combined as though they were units of equal measure, when actually they differ widely. The time element, for example, varies from case to case. A traffic violation may be disposed of in a few minutes, while a chancery proceeding on a partnership matter may run along for months or years. Default divorce cases may be ground out at the rate of two dozen an hour; a guardianship, on the other hand, may remain alive on the dockets for decades. Even cases that are classed in the same category may vary widely. A larceny case with a plea of not guilty and a request for a jury trial is not the equivalent, from the administrative viewpoint, of another larceny case where the plea is guilty and no jury is requested. Furthermore, the dearth of statistical information makes it impossible to give complete and comparable data for the various groups of cases. With this understanding of the limitations of the available judicial information, we may briefly analyze the types of proceedings coming before the courts of the Chicago Area.

The first fact to reckon with is the predominance of cases which are regarded as relatively insignificant. This is true of both criminal proceedings, which constitute about 60 per cent of the total, and of civil suits which make up the remainder. Only a small proportion of criminal cases are the more serious crimes or felonies like burglary, murder, and forgery. Misdemeanors and derelictions of minor regulations such as traffic violations, disorderly conduct cases, offenses in regard to gambling and prostitution, and violations of liquor laws predominate. In Chicago, where three-fourths of the Region's criminal cases arise, traffic or automobile cases alone account for approximately 50 per cent of the criminal proceedings disposed of, while felonies account for only 4 per cent. Among civil cases, too, minor disputes hold the balance in metropolitan adjudication. Actions for unpaid accounts, notes, or contracts, suits between landlord and tenant in regard to payment of rent, and damage suits usually over automobile accidents are the chief types of common-law actions.

Novelty is another characteristic of metropolitan judicial proceedings. The legal classification which employs such categories as common law, criminal, chancery, and their various subheads of tort, contract, felony, and misdemeanor are inadequate for a description of the actual types of conflicts with which the courts are burdened. There are arising newer distinctions between cases, based upon the problem to be adjusted or the status of the person involved. We are confronted with auto collisions, rent disputes, garnishments, morals cases, divorce cases, domestic relations cases, juvenile delinquencies, and boys' cases.

Associated with the rise of the newer types of cases is the tendency for metropolitan judicial functions to extend into newer phases of social life. It is true that some restrictions in the scope of court activity are apparent in the work of quasi-judicial commissions like workmen's compensation boards or in the arbitral or punitive functions of the employers' association, the tong, the Verein, the synagogue, the union. But despite these tendencies toward administrative and unofficial adjudication, the recognized judicial functions of the state are not appreciably curtailed. On the contrary, the metropolitan courts seem to be embracing a wider and wider field of social life.

Referring again to the predominant types of cases in the metropolitan area, we find that the duties of the courts are no longer restricted to the unusual: trivial violations of a traffic code enforced upon scurrying citizens at congested crossings by flashing stop-and-go lights and on the open highways of the metropolitan area by eager constables or highway officers; infractions of regulations governing the daily habits and behavior of myriads of individuals; unpaid debts so easily incurred in an age of high-pressure salesmanship, commercial display, instalment buying, misjudged business ventures, and insecure incomes; conflicts between landlord and tenant so frequent in a civilization in which the typical habitat is coming to be the apartment rented for short terms by mobile families; damage claims for crushed fenders and for personal injuries, resulting from slippery roads, confusing traffic, blinding lights, and preoccupied thoughts of a weary driver; family disruptions and juvenile delinquencies nourished by the conflicting associations of urban centers.

These are the problems which consume most of the efforts of the judiciary in the Metropolitan Area of Chicago. In such a district, where human contacts and potential conflicts are innumerable and incessant, there is little immediate likelihood that the range of judicial functions will be narrowed.

* * *

[Lepawsky indicated that the character of the litigatory problems confronted in metropolitan Chicago has influenced the position of judicial officials other than judges.]

II. THE EXERCISE OF JUDICIAL DISCRETION

The most striking evidence of the growing importance of judicial specialists and routine employees is the fact that their work is beginning to involve more discretion and to influence judicial decisions even more than the duties performed by the judge himself in certain types of cases.

When we think of the work of the courts, we conceive of a series of legal and technical steps in which the degree of judgment rises from a purely ministerial duty to a function requiring a high degree of discretion. The judge we place at the apex of the hierarchy, with the greatest degree of discretion, and the rest of the judicial officers we regard as mere adjuncts to the judge, who makes the ultimate decision. Legally, this view is no doubt correct. In operation, judicial work is different. A comprehensive view of the daily work of the courts will show that much of what is regarded as the "judicial process" consists of preliminaries to the final judgment with which the judge does not deal.

These steps in the process often bear a greater relation to the outcome of the case than the final hearing before the judge. They include the filing of papers which must be correct in minute details, the service of writs and notices at stipulated time, the recording of necessary motions and orders, and now, in certain types of juvenile, criminal, and family cases, the determination of facts upon which the decision of the court is based. Technical preliminaries, which in part were originally designed to serve as the method of getting the dispute heard, have become in the rush of metropolitan business the essence of the legal game. The officials intrusted with technical and fact-finding duties are the pawns of the judicial chessboard, and without proper provisions for them the courts are in danger of becoming clogged and stalemated.

As the young lawyer learns to his dismay, the center of judicial business is the clerk's office, not the courtroom. There, cases are commenced; there, papers, answers, replications, and demurrers are filed, writs are issued, record entries made. Even erudite arguments on points of law will there be heard between experienced clerks and lawyers. An attorney insists that the clerk has no power to issue a writ. "The clerk must issue the writ," argues an obscure record writer, with all the trappings of legal logic one would expect to hear only at the bar. "The Supreme Court fought the thing out a dozen times. See 243 Ill. 541. We've got to issue the execution. How can we go into the case to find out whether malice is the gist of the action?"

Even in the court, where the judge is presumed to be the foremost official, justice is, in effect, frequently meted out by others. In the Municipal Court of Chicago, where for practical and political reasons judges are shifted from one specialized branch to another, the period of the judges' service is brief as compared with that of clerks assigned to the branch courts. In other courts as well, it frequently happens that the elective system brings to office a judge who is raw and untrained compared with the so-called minute clerk. Recurring cases furnish the clerks with a knowledge of technical detail and substantive law which the judges can acquire only through long experience. As a result of the difference in specialization and experience, we sometimes observe the paradox of a dignified judge looking down from his tribune upon the lowly clerk beside him, hoping to catch a glimmer of confirmation for the ruling he is about to enter. In the specialized courts in the center of the Region, the wise novice on the bench depends upon his clerks and learns much from them.

III. SOCIAL AND LEGAL EXPERTS

Expert judicial officers are especially essential in courts dealing with family, juvenile, and certain criminal cases. These officers make the investigations of fact. They compile the records of social data. They are acquainted with the people involved, their family situation, their customary explanations and alibis. In Chicago and Cook County, they investigate in certain criminal, divorce, adoption, and non-support cases, and in all domestic relations and juvenile cases. Since the "rent riots" in 1931, even the orthodox civil proceedings of landlord and tenant (rent cases) are brought under the purview of social service officers in the Municipal Court of Chicago.

These judicial officers are frequently in the courtroom, where they aid and sometimes advise the judge. In the morals branch of the Municipal Court of Chicago the judge cautions the girl before him to see that she is never "caught" in court again. After a short lecture, he hesitates and looks toward his social service clerk, an experienced woman with a photographic eye for some 8,000 girls who are brought before the court under a new alias at each arrest. She blinks significantly behind her huge spectacles. Thereupon the judge turns to the girl again and eyes her knowingly. "You've been here before. How many times do you think you can get away with this?"

In several of the Regional courts, the judge's decision and the outcome of the case are thus shaped by the functions of expert socio-legal officers.

* * *

IV. NON-GOVERNMENTAL SUPERVISION

While there are no official authorities which may be regarded as effective agencies of general supervision, there are certain non-governmental authorities which have an important bearing upon judicial control in the Chicago Area. Eliminating a number of agencies ranging from the urban press to civic clubs, with exercise some degree of control and discipline on occasions, we are left with three fairly effective and significant unofficial supervisory agencies in metropolitan Chicago. These are the Chicago Bar Association, the Chicago Crime Commission, and the Chicago Motor Club.

In addition to their advisory services in recommending candidates for judicial election, bar associations exercise some supervisory functions over the judiciary. The most active of these agencies in the Region is the Chicago Bar Association. Its work takes a variety of forms. It investigates problems of court organization and practice, and it recommends the necessary modifications. Joint conferences with judges are sometimes held, at which the suggested changes are discussed. The Association frequently embodies its suggestions in bills, or ordinances, or court orders, and it submits these to the proper authorities for adoption. Thus, after an extended inquiry into the work of the Second District of the Municipal Court of Chicago, covering South Chicago, the Bar Association prepared its report, recommended the abolition of the separate judicial district, and drew up the necessary order of court and resolution of the city council to make the change effective. In cases where judges are charged with injudicious conduct, the Chicago Bar Association through its grievance committee criticizes the judges' behavior after investigating the circumstances of the case. In some instances, the judge himself appears before the investigating committee to defend his conduct. While the Bar Organization does not function as a regular controlling authority, the fact remains that in many important respects it acts as a substitute for an official supervisor.

The Chicago Crime Commission, another unofficial supervisory agency, is a logical outgrowth of a judicial system which lacks its own devices for administrative cohesion. This body, organized with the help of the Chicago Association of Commerce in 1919, restricts its work largely to the cases which come before the Criminal Court of Cook County. It cannot, therefore, be regarded as a controlling authority of extensive scope. And yet, the Chicago Crime Commission has more of the earmarks of a centralized power in the administration of justice than any of the other managing agencies, official or unofficial.

In the Commission's headquarters will be found a complete record of every felony case in Cook County, a record which includes information that could otherwise be compiled only after a tour through the offices of the Chicago Police Department, of the clerk of the criminal court, the sheriff, the state's attorney, and the coroner of Cook County. In addition to its comprehensive docket, the Commission also has a filing card system with detailed social data about thousands of criminals, professional bondsmen, and witnesses—information that is available through no official source. The records and dockets are kept up to date through detailed daily reports from the Commission's observers who are stationed in each of the branches of the criminal court. Special crime investigators are continually adding to the Commission's recorded information about suspected individuals.

In specific cases where the lack of co-ordination among judicial authorities causes the proceeding to be bungled, the Commission's integrated record system supplements the official facilities. A murder charge against three holdup men is on the daily court call in one of the branches of the criminal court. The judge asks why the defendants are not before the bar. The bailiff, the minute clerk, and the assistant state's attorney exchange fruitless glances. The bailiff announces that the prisoners are not in the county jail, and the minute clerk reports they are not out on bail. The assistant state's attorney therefore assumes that the men have not been arrested and that the case has been prematurely filed. Following the usual practice in cases where defendants are not apprehended, he moves for the state that the case be stricken with leave to reinstate. The order is entered. But the records of the Crime Commission show that the three defendants are in the Pontiac Reformatory serving sentences for robbing the person they are accused of murdering. When the state's attorney's staff hears of the Commission's findings, it recognizes its error of disposing of the robbery charge before the murder charge, and it takes steps to correct the proceeding.

The Commission's discovery in this case was a comparatively simple one, because the unit of reference in its record system is the name of the accused rather than the separate case or charge which is the unit of reference in the official records. With a superior record system at its disposal, the Commission is in a strategic position to supplement the official proceeding when errors of this sort occur.

Besides acting as a clearing house of information on criminals and on the progress of the proceedings against them, the Commission frequently serves as an unofficial prosecuting authority. Many specific complaints by victims and witnesses are made in the first instance to the Commission rather than to the state's attorney. Even where the case is instituted through official channels, the detailed daily reports on the progress of all felony cases serve as a basis for advisement and recommendation. There seems to be no attempt to dictate to the state's attorney or judge in specific cases. But the constant check of the Commission's representative and the promptness with which errors and omissions are called to the attention of the authorities constitute an effective day-by-day supervision. Cases are watched at all stages. Before trial begins, one of the representatives of the Commission observes and reports on bail bond proceedings. After imprisonment, the Commission submits its report and recommendation in requests for parole along with the reports required by law from the state's attorney and the judge.

In addition to its direct influence in individual prosecutions, the Commission performs some of the functions of a typical administrative superior. It recommends and frequently secures the adoption of changes in routine and the assignment of more judges to the criminal court. It stimulates and takes part in joint conferences of judicial and police authorities. It prepares and lobbies for specific legislation on judicial procedure. The Commission's reports go into detail on the work performed by the individual judges on the number of cases each judge disposes, on the felony waivers approved by him, on the number of defendants he convicts, and on the hours he spends on the bench.

The newspaper publicity which the Commission secures for its reports mentions specifically the names of judges who are doing commendable or unsatisfactory work according to standards set up by the Commission's reporting system. The Commission's influence upon the public is sometimes driven home by recommendations to defeat or elect certain judges of the Municipal Court of Chicago. As a supervisor of personnel, the Commission has gone so far as to accuse judges of the Criminal Court of Cook County of malfeasance and to secure a public trial of these judges before the executive committees of the Circuit and Superior courts of Cook County.

In short, the Commission combines the characteristics of a daily inspector, a bureau of criminal information, an unofficial state's attorney, an adviser on judicial policy, and a board of personnel discipline.

The Chicago Motor Club extends its functions over a wider territorial area than the Chicago Crime Commission. While the Commission restricts itself to Cook County, the Club is active over the whole Chicago Area and sometimes beyond the metropolitan district. Unlike the Commission, the Club is a profit-making institution. Its services are mechanical aid, insurance, distribution of road information, and legal aid to the motoring public.

In furnishing legal aid, the Club exercises a wide range of functions, from the defense of Club members arrested for speeding to the prosecution of appeals in which it attacks the fee system in justice courts of metropolitan Indiana. In arrests for speeding, Club members are usually released after they deposit their Club bond with the arresting officer. They then notify the Club and do not trouble to appear for trial, especially when they have been summoned before a justice court outside the metropolis. Officers of the Club settle with the justice usually over the phone. Generally the case is disposed of when the Club forwards a check for the fine and costs and the justice returns the bond. If a motorist insists that his arrest was not justified, the Club assigns one of its attorneys to represent the defendant at the trial. If repeated complaints of unfair arrests and undeserved fines are made against certain arresting officers and justices, the particular town or crossroad is branded as a speed trap at the Club's headquarters. Then the investigations begin.

Every spring, with varying degrees of intensity, the Chicago Motor Club goes on the warpath against speed traps. In his daily newspaper, the Chicagoan reads of raids on justice court speed traps, of the seizure of justice court records, and of threatened indictments of justices and constables. In its newspaper reports, the Motor Club warns him about particularly dangerous traps nestling around the metropolis in much the same way as it notifiies him of highway detours for his holiday motoring program.

In the Club's headquarters, the investigation takes on a definite form. For weeks, the Club's famous questionnaires and affidavits from members have been accumulating. These are to constitute the evidence against officers and justices who were either too eager or too careless in selecting their prey. The Club's files begin to bulge with harmless-looking questionnaires entitled "Automobile Arrest Questionnaire" for ordinary arrests, more imposing sheets entitled "Questionnaire Investigation of Motor Vehicle Law Arrests" for doubtful cases, and yellow "Speed Trap Investigation Questionnaire" for suspected speed traps.

With this evidence, the state's attorneys of the respective Regional counties are confronted. Then follow the grand jury "investigations," the raids on justice courts, and the seizure of records. The records are not really seized except in rare cases. It is not necessary to do so, since facsimiles and figures are generally obtained by the Club's photostatic force and by its tabulators and investigators who are members of the raiding squad. Photostatic copies of docket sheets and arrest records and neat tabulations of speeding charges and of fines begin to supplement the Club's questionnaires. This new accretion to the Club's files constitutes the direct evidence to be used when the Club decides to indict culpable officers and justices.

To be sure, this is the public's evidence. It belongs to the state's attorney's office. But he has delegated the matter to the Chicago Motor Club, and the documents are securely filed at its headquarters. The whole investigation is at law an official one, but, in fact, it is the work of the Club. The personnel of the investigating squad and its motor cars are even furnished by the Club, though a few deputy state's attorneys are taken along on the raiding expeditions. But as one of the officers of the Club explained, "The state's attorney merely gives his time." It is not strange, therefore, that the state's attorneys of the Regional counties know little about the progress and outcome of the investigations. "See so-and-so of the Chicago Motor Club," they advised.

How shall we evaluate these unique forms of judicial supervision by unofficial agencies like the Chicago Bar Association, Chicago Crime Commission, and Chicago Motor Club? Needless to say, judges and justices are generally opposed to these self-appointed guardians of the metropolitan courts. After a recent case in which the Bar Association reprimanded a judge for improper conduct during a murder trial, any disciplinary effect the bar might have secured from the publicity given the investigation was counteracted by a complimentary banquet at which fellow-judges and political leaders extolled the virtues of the misjudged jurist. Many justices insist that the true purpose of the Motor Club's investigations is to present its activities to the public in dramatic form through the press, for the purpose of fostering its membership campaigns. Similarly, Cook County judges, though they publicly truckle to the Crime Commission's recommendations, entertain an intense private dislike for its stringent supervision. Occasionally, the conflict between the judges and the Commission flares out in the open, over conferences called by the Commission, over the interpretation of statistics on the subject of jury waivers, and over charges made by the Commission that certain judges are "paltering with crime." Generally, the opposition of the judges resolves itself into a quiet undercurrent of discontent, psychologically aggravated by the constant presence in the courtroom of the Commission's observers.

It is, no doubt, true that non-governmental supervision is a negative form of discipline which does little to awaken a sense of self-responsibility among the judicial personnel; and except for the work of the Chicago Crime Commission, it is a sporadic rather than a continuous form of judicial control. Despite its defects, however, it results in some degree of judicial integration and effective supervision. In specific cases, the Chicago Crime Commission integrates the work of police, courts, and other judicial officers by extra-legal means that no official authority in Cook County has the power to adopt. In the work of the Chicago Motor Club we notice that the official supervisor, the state's attorney, goes through the motions of judicial management while the unofficial body performs the actual work and contributes the drive. While the cumbersome system of official impeachment is never resorted to, the Chicago Bar Association, Crime Commission, and Motor Club make charges of misconduct and secure the trial of individual judges and justices. In its territorial scope, the Chicago Motor Club disregards county and state lines and brings the minor courts of the whole metropolitan area under a common form of scrutiny. In fact, geographically, the Club is the only judicial supervisor that is active in the whole Chicago Area.

[The system which Lepawsky described comprised the courts of one metropolitan region. This system was in itself a segment of the judicial systems of two states, Illinois and Indiana. But side by side with these state systems are the separate courts of the federal government. From the moment of the creation of the inferior federal courts in the great organic act of 1789, the district and circuit (now courts of appeal) courts provided greater flexibility to those litigants who recognized that the instrumentalities of federalism afforded countless opportunities for interest group maneuvering. The political consequences of such maneuvering are examined in the subsequent section.

C. THE SIGNIFICANCE OF THE DISTRICT COURTS

Because the federal district courts perform the vital function of trial courts in the hierarchy of federal courts, they represent the first line of contact in situations in which the validity of new legislation is being tested. Perhaps one of the most dramatic and politically combustible of such situations occurred in the mid-1930's when many New Deal measures were engulfed in a veritable tidal wave of litigatory challenges.]

1. Roosevelt's Autumn of 1935*

Roosevelt's promulgation of a breathing spell in the autumn of 1935 reduced political pressure against the New Deal for a moment. What reduced it even more was the apparent approach of recovery—the marked and seemingly steady upswing in business activity in late 1935, with increases in jobs, output, stock prices, and corporate dividends. But this momentary lull did not solve Roosevelt's problems. At this point the most insistent challenge to the New Deal was coming from another direction. The Supreme Court's evident readiness to throw out enactments of the New Deal Congress was creating a stampede of litigation and judgment beyond the power of benign presidential letters to halt. There was to be no breathing spell in the federal courts.

II

Under the laws of 1935, a single district judge could issue an injunction suspending the application of a federal statute. This would seem a power for a prudent judiciary to employ with utmost discretion. But in 1935–36, federal judges issued some sixteen hundred injunctions preventing federal officials from carrying out federal laws. "At no time in the country's history," observed the annual appraisal of the Court's work in the *Harvard Law Review,* "was there a more voluminous outpouring of judicial rulings in restraint of acts of Congress than the body of decisions in which the lower courts, in varying degree, invalidated every measure deemed appropriate by Congress for grappling with the great depression." The administration, noting (as Homer Cummings had informed Roosevelt in 1933) that only 28 per cent of the 266 federal judges were Democrats, regarded this explosion of judicial nullification as almost a political counteroffensive.

Unhappily, there was just enough in the tone of the campaign to lend plausibility to such suspicions. In Kentucky, for example, Judge Charles I. Dawson, finding for a coal company against the National Industrial Recovery Act, blasted the Coal Code as "the boldest kind of usurpation—dared by the authorities and tolerated by the

*The selection from Arthur Schlesinger, Jr., *The Politics of Upheaval,* Vol. III of *The Age of Roosevelt* (Boston: Houghton Mifflin, 1960), pp. 447–49 is reprinted by permission of and arrangement with Houghton Mifflin Company, the authorized publishers. [Footnotes omitted.]

public only because of the bewilderment of the people in the present emergency." (Judge Dawson resigned shortly thereafter to represent other coal companies in their suits against the government and to re-enter Republican politics). Enough other judges delivered stump speeches as they struck down New Deal laws to remind historians of the "political harangues by early Federalist judges" in the young republic.

Given this predisposition on the bench—and over a hundred federal judges, well over a third of the entire corps, issued injunctions in this singular period—lawyers naturally rushed to exploit it to the full. They not only demanded injunctions on every hand; they freely resorted to an ingenious method by which they could apply for injunctions and challenge the constitutionality of laws while preventing the government from entering the court and defending the threatened enactment. This was done by raising the question through friendly private lawsuits, in which stockholders would sue their own companies to enjoin them from obeying the law. These cases obviously did not present any authentic conflict of interests. As Robert H. Jackson remarked, "Both sides wanted the same thing. There was no real issue between them." But they were cunningly designed to keep the federal government out of court when federal legislation was under challenge.

Nor was this all. Beyond the actual testing in the courts, the conservative leaders worked hard to discredit the new legislation in the mind of the public. In particular, they sponsored a technique of constitutional prejudgment, in which eminent counsel, on their own, would hand down private decisions against irksome statutes. Thus by the end of 1935 elaborate opinions were in circulation holding the TVA Act, the Holding Company Act and the Labor Relations Act unconstitutional—the first, circulated by the Edison Electric Institute; the second, by Wendell Willkie of Commonwealth and Southern; the third, by the American Liberty League—and all were signed by the leaders of the American bar. "Whether the purpose of such emanations is to influence the federal courts when such legislation shall be presented for consideration," said the *United States Law Review* editorially, "or whether it is to arouse public sentiment so that confidence in the courts will be impaired should the legislation be held constitutional, is not clear. But neither purpose has anything to commend it."

[The conduct of some of the federal district courts provoked congressional appraisal of the administration of the courts in two areas: (1) that of the power of the single federal judge; and (2) that of assuring that the government of the United States shall be afforded full opportunity to provide adequate litigatory preparations in defending the constitutionality of federal legislation. That opportunity for the latter was, on occasion, "thwarted by the use of subtle legal forms available to a private litigant,"[1] is demonstrated in *In re American States Public Service Company.*

[1] Felix Frankfurter and Adrian Fisher, "The Work of the Supreme Court—1935 and 1936 Terms," *Harvard Law Review*, LI (1938), 615.

124

In this case the lower courts considered the constitutionality of the Public Utility Holding Company Act of 1935 upon a trustee's petition for instructions under 77B. The Government did not receive notice of the proceedings until the petitions had been filed, and the issues joined and largely concluded by admissions of fact and law in the pleadings. Counsel for the Government appeared as amicus curiae *ten days after the filing of the petitions, but were denied a continuance for the purpose of investigation. The Government was allowed to cross-examine on the issue of jurisdiction but was not allowed to share in building the record of the substantive issues. The district court held the Act unconstitutional in its entirety; the circuit court of appeals held the Act unconstitutional as applied to the particular company. When* certiorari *was asked the Government submitted a statement in opposition, fundamentally because under the circumstances of the litigation the record was inadequate for a decision upon the constitutional problem. It was urged that the parties, through collaboration in the pleadings and in the presentation of testimony, had not made an accurate representation of the facts underlying the relation of the Act to the reorganization and the constitutionality of the Act as applied to the debtor. The Supreme Court denied* certiorari.[2]

Situations of this kind led to the passage of the Judiciary Act of 1937. Frankfurter and Fisher provided a classic account of the background and main events in its passage.]

2. The Judiciary Act of 1937 and the District Judges*

Inevitably law reflects the forces of economic and social dislocation implied in a great depression and its consequent readjustments. This is true not merely of substantive legal doctrines. A general tendency toward enlarged governmental activity and the centripetal influences within economic enterprise which make for increasing exercise of national authority, have their repercussions in judicial organization and administration. The broader questions of jurisdiction and procedure affecting the federal courts have always presented some of the most delicate problems in the working of our constitutional government. It would indeed be surprising if the recent stresses and strains in our national life had not reflected themselves in the workings of the federal judicial system. All the devices by which procedural changes come to pass have played their part. Rules of the Supreme Court for the conduct of its own business and that of the "inferior courts," resourceful employment of the

---

[2] 12 F. Supp. 667 (D. Md., 1935). Described by Frankfurter and Fisher, *ibid.*, note 67.

* Felix Frankfurter and Adrian Fisher, "The Work of the Supreme Court—1935 and 1936 Terms," *Harvard Law Review*, LI (1938), 598–619. [Footnotes and charts omitted.] Reproduced with permission of the authors and the publisher. Copyright (1938) by the Harvard Law Review Association.

Court's discretionary powers, fluctuations in the Court's attitude toward its jurisdiction, are all registered in the latest volumes of the United States Reports. In addition to these readjustments through judicial self-determination, Congress, during the last term of Court, deemed it necessary to intervene by redistributing power within the federal judicial system. By modifying, in an important way, the Judiciary Act of 1925, Congress has illustrated the historic truth that every judiciary enactment since the great statute of 1789 is but one of a series, a part of the continuous living process of making the federal courts appropriate instrumentalities for the changing needs of the Union.

Ordinary problems of judicial administration make little appeal to the imagination of legislators. The Supreme Court is entangled as much as it is in the political history of the United States because its work is so largely an expression of statecraft and interwoven with the political problems of our national life. Except on the rare occasions when the Court itself needs congressional relief to master its docket, judiciary legislation invariably is the political answer of Congress to what are believed to be judicial obstructions to needed activities of government. Barring the tariff and land grants, the establishment of the Interstate Commerce Commission, in 1887, was the first major intervention of the Federal Government in the area of economic enterprise. For the past half century our major domestic issues have been phases of a single central problem, namely, the interplay between enterprise and government. Taxation, utility regulation, control of the security market, banking and finance, industrial relations, agricultural controls, are issues that derive from the circumstances of modern, large-scale, industrialized society, and ultimately turn on conceptions of the relation of individuals one to another in the context of our society. For Congress they present a blend of law and policy; to the Supreme Court, under our Constitution, they come as legal problems. Clashes between courts and Congress affecting the ultimate fate of such legislation often have their origin in procedure. Who may raise legal questions about laws, what tribunals may dispose of them and when they will be finally adjudicated, are all contingencies of legislation. To effectuate its own policies—as well as those of the states when challenged in the federal courts—Congress has deemed it necessary, from time to time, to modify procedural practices of the federal courts, to exercise its constitutional power to define the authority of the inferior federal courts and to regulate the appellate jurisdiction of the Supreme Court.

Since the intermediate federal appellate tribunals were established in 1891, they have been utilized to relieve the Supreme Court of its obligatory jurisdiction, leaving with the circuit courts of appeals final adjudication in those types of cases for which *certiorari* was a sufficient safeguard of the national interest. First by the Act of 1916 and then by the more comprehensive measure of 1925, the flow of cases coming to the Court as of right was greatly dammed. What issues may, as a matter of course, be brought before the Supreme Court is partly a technical, professional matter, but also, by touching the feelings of the general community, becomes a more dominant concern of legislative policy. In placid periods, when the distribution of jurisdiction is pre-eminently a matter of the internal economy of the judicial system, Congress is naturally responsive to the authoritative wishes of the Court. And so, the adjustments of 1891, 1916, and 1925, to enable the Court to meet adequately the swelling tide of its business, were made by Congress at the Court's own insistence.

On the other hand, for different categories of litigation, Congress had to formulate its own notions of jurisdictional policy to give effect to the social and economic movements which got under way in the administration of Theodore Roosevelt. Orders of the Interstate Commerce Commission often have ramifying economic consequences. Such issues have special claims for prompt, final adjudication, and their complexity, as well as their prior scrutiny by the Commission, requires at *nisi prius* the wisdom and experience of more than a single judge. By the Act of February 11, 1903, in cases involving orders of the Interstate Commerce Commission, Congress initiated the device of an original court of three judges and direct review by the Supreme Court. In other spheres, the ignition of public excitement through judicial action deemed adverse to the public interest, has led to successive extensions of the Supreme Court's historic scope of review and to a recession from the general tendency to curtail its obligatory jurisdiction.

First, the traditional practice against reviewing rulings in favor of the accused, even where no double jeopardy was at stake, had consequences unknown to the common law when Congress affixed penal sanction to legislation involving far-reaching issues of policy. The Criminal Appeals Act of 1907 put an end to the power of a single judge to hold up the enforcement of a law for years by invalidating it improperly. Then, the growing range of economic control by the states brought them into conflict with the federal courts. The initial shift from a fundamentally *laissez-faire* emphasis in government to its modern regulatory activities largely affected public utilities. At first it expressed itself through legislative rate regulation. To federal judges the invalidation of such measures presented only a simple application of conventional doctrines to prevent irreparable damages. To the general public it was nullification of vital state policy by a single federal judge. Congress promptly responded to this feeling, and by the Act of 1910 applied the safeguards against too irresponsible judicial restraint of the Interstate Commerce Commission to the protection of state laws. Thereafter "no interlocutory injunction suspending or restraining the enforcement, operation or execution of any statute of a state" because of unconstitutionality could be issued except by a three-judge district court, and an appeal could be taken directly to the Supreme Court. That Congress should have used this device only when statutes were called into question, and not for orders of state commissions, is a striking instance of the narrowly empiric nature of the legislative process. For by 1910 it had become abundantly clear that effective utility regulation demanded expert administration, and the movement for the establishment of utility commissions was well under way. But for many judges these new administrative agencies only served to render the trend towards social legislation still more uncongenial. Courts seemed as unaware of the emergence of modern administrative law as an indispensable evolution of the Rule of Law, as the great common-law judges in the days of Coke were unresponsive to the proper role of emerging equity. And so, by the Act of March 4, 1913, protection against frustration of state regulation by a single federal judge and direct review by the Supreme Court was extended to administrative as well as legislative action.

Shortly after the amendment of 1913, the general movement of social legislation led to the first extension of the Supreme Court's appellate jurisdiction over state court decisions. Probably no single episode in American judicial history illustrates better the limited relevance of doctrines derived from specialized political preoccupation in legal arrangement when the emphasis of government shifts from politics to economics. The authority of the Supreme Court to review state decisions was, naturally enough, confined by the famous Section 25 of the first Judiciary Act to instances where the state courts denied a federal claim. The assumption that state courts would not find in the Federal Constitution a bar to state laws was valid enough at a time of historic jealousy against national authority. Moreover, the psychological environment in which state court judges move is very different from what it was a hundred years ago, now that economics and law have become more closely interrelated and the vague contours of the Fourteenth Amendment have greatly extended the orbit of judicial discretion. And so, when, in 1911, the New York Court of Appeals temporarily arrested the progress of the now commonplace workmen's compensation legislation, partly by invoking the Fourteenth Amendment, the inability to secure authoritative interpretation of that clause from the Supreme Court inevitably led to legislation. The Act of March 23, 1914, sponsored by Senator Elihu Root, extended the Supreme Court's review to a state court ruling even when it sustained a claim under the United States Constitution. This was accomplished by allowing the use of *certiorari* to the Supreme Court in such cases.

Although today dramatic ingredients may bulk large, the Judiciary Act of August 24, 1937, will surely take its place as part of the sequence of congressional adjustments of judicial administration which begot the Acts of 1903, 1910, 1913, 1914. That the fate of acts of Congress should depend, even temporarily, upon the view of a single judge; that the United States should have no standing to defend effectively a law of the utmost national importance simply because the canons of legal procedure make the controversy merely a private litigation; that the ultimate validity of a statute may be a long drawn out process depending in part upon the state of the Supreme Court's docket and its notions of exigency, have long been sources of anxiety to students of public law and have occasioned remedial proposals in Congress. To be sure, in a period when legislative energies run strong and the judiciary interposes powerful and persistent restraints, the pace of procedural reform is accelerated. At no time in the country's history did the judiciary play a more permeating part in the affairs of the country. At no time in the country's history was there a more voluminous outpouring of judicial rulings in restraint of acts of Congress than the body of decisions in which the lower courts, in varying degree, invalidated every measure deemed appropriate by Congress for grappling with the great depression. Friction between Congress and the judiciary was intensified by the atmosphere which enveloped some of the opinions of the lower court judges. There were utterances more appropriate to the hustings than to the bench, reminiscent of political harangues by early Federalist judges which involved the federal judiciary for the first time in the conflict of politics.

As in similar periods when the judiciary interposed obstacles to legislative policies having wide popular support, the traditional scope of judicial review in constitutional controversies came under scrutiny and numerous bills proposing drastic modifications were introduced in both houses of Congress. The past further repeated itself in that narrower measures for reform were urged to remove inadequacies in the existing federal procedure when applied to cases of large public moment. Speedy justice has been the aim of Anglo-American law reformers since Magna Carta, and evils entailed through avoidable delay in adjudication were deemed to be especially far-reaching when the operation of economic measures affecting large regions or even the whole nation depended upon judicial validation. The motive power for such reform is usually some concrete experience, close to the interests of a particular legislator. The prosecution of its program by the Tennessee Valley Authority had a strong regional hold on Senator Black of Alabama. The decision of Judge Grubb on November 28, 1934, put at hazard a scheme of public development which, after more than a decade of political struggle, received overwhelming congressional approval. Clothed as abstract issues of governmental power, the litigation affected vast investments and touched the lives of millions of people. Yet ultimate decision, argued Senator Black, had to take the tortuous path of reaching the Supreme Court through the circuit court of appeals.

By a bill introduced on March 6, 1935, Senator Black addressed himself to the single, narrow purpose of securing prompt. definitive disposition of decrees restraining the operation of federal laws. The crux of his proposal was to eliminate the circuit court of appeals in these cases and to route them from the district court directly to the Supreme Court. The bill was referred to the Senate Committee on the Judiciary and the Court invited to express its views. On behalf of the Court, the Chief Justice appeared with two of his colleagues and gave reasons against the enactment of the measure. The public interest with which Senator Black was concerned seemed to the Court sufficiently safeguarded through its power to jump a circuit court of appeals by the discretionary use of *certiorari*. To open the door to every case that came within the ambit of the Black bill, seemed to the Chief Justice to be an inroad on the philosophy of selective jurisdiction underlying the Act of 1925 without compensating advantage. Not to have its docket thrown out of balance was a driving consideration with the Court. Probably, also, it regarded the illumination which serious questions should derive from passing through a circuit court of appeals as valuable to the perspective and thoroughness of the Court's own deliberative process. The bill never emerged from Committee.

The fate of acts of Congress in the lower courts and some of the circumstances attending their invalidation were not calculated to allay congressional concern over procedural inadequacies. The existing scheme of procedure did not preclude delay in securing the final word from the Supreme Court. Thereby uncertainty hung over many of the most important activities of government. Moreover, the ability of the government adequately to represent the national interest within the framework of purely private litigation, while an old problem, emerged with new intensity. Chairman Sumners of the House Committee therefore renewed the proposal of the Black bill and widened its scope. His bill provided both for direct review and for participation by the United States in litigation in which, under settled practice, it would have no standing as a party. But attention was diverted from these attempts to adapt the ways of private litigation to their serious public implications by the dramatic emergence of the great political controversy to which the President's proposal regarding the Supreme Court gave rise. Only after this issue was no longer before Congress, did the Senate address itself to these seemingly technical aspects of litigation. Their important relation to the whole process of constitutional litigation then became manifest, and the Senate Committee on the Judiciary unanimously reported the Judiciary Act of 1937 in substantially its present form.

In sum, the new Act gave matured expression to the combined aims of the Black and Sumners bills. The decision in *In re American States Public Service Co.* vividly demonstrated that the power of the United States to share in the control of litigation, whereby the constitutionality of legislation of the profoundest national import would be effectively tested, ought not to be thwarted by the use of subtle legal forms available to a private litigant. Section I of the Act therefore put the exclusion of the United States from such litigation beyond the power of any judge. Again, the denial by the Supreme Court of a speedy test of the Public Utility Holding Company Act of 1935, sought both by the utility interests and by the Government in the *Electric Bond & Share* case, reinforced the momentum of the proposals for direct review. This is the essence of Section 2 of the Act. Finally, the inevitable irritation of Congress at the free-handed way in which single judges throughout the country enjoined the enforcement of some of the most vital measures ever enacted, made inevitable the requirement of Section 3 for a court of three judges to set aside the will of Congress. This feeling fused with considerations derived from the gravity of the issues presented by such litigation and from the desire for their thorough exploration before they reached the Supreme Court.

The new judiciary Act contains inevitable frailties of draftsmanship. Like all its predecessors, it will have to be supplemented by authoritative construction. But the operations of the new procedure, as has been true of all important judiciary acts, will depend mostly on the general environment in which it moves. Thus it becomes sheer speculation to estimate the extent to which clashes between Congress and the judiciary would have differed had the enactment of last August governed constitutional adjudications since March 4, 1933. The materials for prophecy of its future consequences for American constitutional law are no less exiguous. Some obvious factors in the administration of the Act will limit the freedom of the federal courts and that of the Government as litigant. The requirement of three judges entails an absorption of judicial resources which may have unexpected repercussions upon judicial efficiency, should there be a plethora of litigation. Again, the course of litigation is not automatic. It depends not a little on the strategy of litigants. To the extent that the new Act makes mandatory appeals to the Supreme Court from rulings adverse to the validity of legislation, it circumscribes the discretion of the Attorney General. But these are all factors contingent upon larger forces quite outside any judiciary act. They depend upon the future of legislation, its range and volume; they depend on the impregnating political and psychological atmosphere. The Judiciary Act of 1937 is part of a continuous history of interplay between the judiciary and the other branches of the government. Insofar as the Act leaves creative scope for the courts, its ultimate significance in that historic process will be determined by the Supreme

Court's attitude toward the inarticulate major premise which underlay the enactment of that statute.

D. THE ROLE OF THE INFERIOR FEDERAL JUDGES IN THE AMERICAN LEGAL PROCESS

[Conflicts between inferior federal judges and the Supreme Court are not limited to fundamental differences over public policy but sometimes embody sharp clashes between men who are proud of their ability as judges. In some instances, a latent clash of concepts over the proper mode of performing trial or appellate judicial tasks is at the root of these disagreements. In order to appraise the federal judicial system properly, it should be clearly understood that the phrase "inferior federal judges" is technically correct as a description of the position of district and appeals judges, but that the word "inferior" as used here connotes no qualitative meaning. It should further be noted that the supervisory power of the Supreme Court is often overrated. For while it is true that it ultimately may overrule an inferior federal court, a variety of factors makes this practically impossible in most situations. The next two excerpts, although drawn from newspapers rather than academic journals, provide accurate appraisals of the realities of intra-court relations and useful descriptions of the organization of the appeals courts and the judges who man them. The third item, chosen from a law journal, is an eloquent and forthright appraisal of the perceived differences in judicial roles of the trial judge, the intermediate appellate judge and the Supreme Court justice. In short, it provides an excellent discussion of how judges often view their craft.

The disappearance of Federal Appeals Judge W. Lynn Parkinson in the fall of 1960 inadvertly provided the occasion for a rare newspaper interview with the Chief Judge of the Court of Appeals of the 7th Circuit. His frank comments about the ability of the appeals judges to control the docket also indicated the extent to which his court acted as a court of final appeal in most cases.]

1. The Eleven Federal Courts of Appeals: Courts of Final Appeals in 95 Per Cent of the Issues*

Attorneys who practice before the U.S. Court of Appeals here find the dilatory continuance a useless weapon in their courtroom arsenal.

And backlogs are virtually unknown in the high court—despite an understaffed bench caused by the disappearance last fall of Judge W. Lynn Parkinson.

*"U.S. Appeals Court Here Sets Brisk Legal Pace," *Chicago Daily News*, March 31, 1960, p. 7.

"It really isn't fair, however, to try to compare our court with the federal, state and city trial courts," said Chief Judge John S. Hastings.

The third generation Hoosier lawyer explained then what enables the appeals court to function so efficiently with such a small staff.

Currently, only five full-time judges sit in the graystone mansion-like building overlooking the lake at 1200 Lake Shore dr.

Each judge has a law clerk and a secretary—thus, with clerical personnel and one bailiff, the court functions with a staff of about 20.

It operates on three scheduled terms, starting in September, January and April, with rotating three-judge panels sitting to hear oral arguments on two cases daily.

"But our court is never closed—although it is fair to say that in August and September we seldom sit except on emergency matters," the graying judge said.

The court heard a total of 349 cases in 1959, appeals from the seven federal court districts of this circuit in Illinois, Indiana and Wisconsin and from agencies such as the Federal Trade Commission, the U.S. Tax Court and the National Labor Relations Board.

In addition, the court receives a steady flow of petitions from inmates in both state and federal prisons who are seeking writs of habeas corpus, and hears appeals on motions for injunctions or other orders that were rejected by the district courts.

"The reason why continuances are seldom given here," said the chief judge, "is just that we are an appeals court, not a trial court.

"The appellee files comprehensive briefs before the case is given a hearing date.

"Before we sit in hearing on an appeal, we have already studied the briefs of both sides and researched the legal citations given so we will understand the case thoroughly.

"We always have much homework to do—studying of the briefs and then, after the hearing, preparation of our opinions."

"Perhaps you don't realize it," the former Washington (Ind.) lawyer continued, "but this is the court of last appeal for some 95 per cent of the cases in the federal courts.

"Last year, the U.S. Supreme court granted petitions for rehearing in only 16 cases out of a total of 83 cases that were taken to the high court from this circuit.

"Of these 16, only about half will be reversed—thus, about 5 per cent of our decisions are reversed."

But, he added, smiling, "Of course, this doesn't necessarily mean that we are right that much of the time.

"It might mean that, although the Supreme court might not have agreed with our decisions on more cases, they only found this handful which they felt were of sufficient importance to federal law to warrant their consideration."

[The Courts of Appeals in the eleven federal circuits possess distinctive characteristics reflecting the traditions of the bar, the quality of its members, and the political and economic forces dominant within the circuit boundaries. James E. Clayton, court reporter for the *Washington Post and Times Herald* provided the following appraisal of the federal Court of Appeals for the District of Columbia.]

2. The Court of Appeals for the District of Columbia*

Like most other units of government in the District, the United States Court of Appeals here has a unique spot in the structure of American public affairs.

It is equal in all respects to 10 other Federal Courts of Appeals. At the same time, it is, in many respects, a state supreme court equal to the highest courts in the 50 states.

It holds this dual role alone among American courts. And that role, plus the jurisdiction over decisions of Federal administrative agencies which it gains merely because it is located here, makes this Court of Appeals the Naton's second most important court in the eyes of most lawyers and judges.

For a body of such significance, this Court and its nine members are relatively unknown.

ONLY THREE FROM HERE

Its judges include men who were once law school professors and politicians, who are Northerners and Southerners, who follow liberal and conservative political leanings. Only three of them claimed the District as home before their appointments.

Their only common ground seems to be that they all once went to a law school.

This broad sweep of the bench makes it the only national court except for the Supreme Court. The spread of political views has also brought the Court some of its most severe criticism.

Most lawyers admit that this Court is probably the best balanced one in the Nation when all nine judges are sitting. Of the nine, four are generally considered political liberals (all Democrats), three conservatives (one Democrat and two Republicans) and two in the middle (one Democrat and one Republican).

'LUCK OF THE DRAW'

But the Court seldom sits as a 9-man bench. Instead, it transacts most of its business in 3-man panels. All Federal Courts of Appeals do this and the criticism of "justice by the luck of the draw" is aimed at all of them.

The criticism is spoken with particular bitterness by some lawyers and lower court judges here because of the difference in outlook of the nine judges.

The assignment of judges is literally made by "the draw," with the Court's Clerk, Joseph W. Stewart, pulling the lots. This assures that each judge has an equal amount of work but it does not assure that any particular panel will be divided between liberal and conservative judges.

* James E. Clayton in the *Washington Post and Times Herald*, August 3, 1959, p. A 13.

Thus, more than one lower court judge has been known to tell losers in a case before him, "I don't think you can win on appeal but go ahead, you never know what the draw will do for you."

FULL COURT CAN INTERVENE

Such comments overlook the fact that few decisions would be different if the entire court sat in each case.

When a panel writes its opinion, the other judges know of it before it is announced. If a majority of the court is in disagreement with the result, a full bench hearing can be called, and sometimes is before the decision is announced.

Because no one has come up with a better way of selecting the panels, the judges continue the drawing, aware of the criticism but unable to avoid it.

UNUSUAL AUTONOMY

These nine men, whether sitting in panels or as a full bench on exceptional cases, have the last say on a good many matters of great interest to the individual citizen. This is true even though all their decisions are subject to review by the Supreme Court.

Years ago, Supreme Court Justice Stanley F. Reed wrote: "Matters relating to law enforcement in the District are entrusted to the Courts of the District. Our policy is not to interfere with the local rules which they fashion, save in exceptional situations where egregious error has been committed."

Since the Supreme Court has applied a similar policy to cases dealing with ordinary civil law, the Court of Appeals has almost, but not quite, the autonomy of a state supreme court in run-of-the-mill civil and criminal matters.

Even at that, more cases from the local Court of Appeals are reviewed annually by the Supreme Court than from any other Federal Court of Appeals. This, in itself, shows the importance of matters which are decided here.

SHIFT FROM NEW YORK

In fiscal 1957, for example, the Supreme Court agreed to hear 30 cases from this Court of Appeals and 73 from the other nine appellate courts. It refused to hear 111 cases decided here.

In years past, the Second Circuit Court of Appeals, which operates out of New York City, was rated as the nation's No. 2 court. It had this status because it made crucial decisions on Wall Street business matters and because of the unusual caliber of its judges—Learned and Augustus Hand and Jerome M. Frank, among others.

Many of those crucial decisions shifted to administrative agencies here in the 1930s and to review by this Court of Appeals. More recently, the revered judges in the Second Circuit have left the bench.

134

ACCENT ON LIBERTIES

During the same period, the emphasis in law also shifted from business and property matters to civil liberties. Passport, security cases, contempt of Congress charges became more important. And all of these are handled almost exclusively through the Court of Appeals here.

In these new areas, where there was little precedent, the philosophy of the judges on the Court of Appeals here appeared clearly in their decisions. It was then that the political labels were attached and criticism directed at individual judges.

Judge Henry W. Edgerton was, for years, the leader of the liberal bloc. Judge David L. Bazelon, 20 years younger, is usually rated in that post now, but he and Edgerton vote together in almost every case.

They are usually joined by Judges Charles Fahy and George T. Washington to make up the Court's liberal wing.

These men have voted, generally, to expand the concept of criminal insanity here and to restrict Congressional investigation power and the State Department's control over passports. They frequently criticize police practice and procedures.

The other wing of the Court is led by Judge Wilbur K. Miller. He is joined regularly by Judge Walter M. Bastian and, more times than not, by Judge John A. Danaher. They have voted, generally, in favor of an older concept of insanity, to uphold congressional power and State's control of passports, and to accept police procedures.

In between are Chief Judge E. Barrett Prettyman and Judge Warren E. Burger. Their votes regularly decide the way that full bench decisions go and they often vote together. That means there are 5 to 4 votes when the liberals lose and 6 to 3 votes when they win. . . .

[Appeals Judge Calvert Magruder provides a tart and insightful appraisal of the position of the intermediate appeals judge in relation to the trial judge and the Supreme Court of the United States.]

3. The Trials and Tribulations of an Intermediate Appellate Court*

Of course the functions of an appellate judge differ from those of a trial judge. When I was appointed, one of my two elderly colleagues was Judge James M. Morton. He had been for years a very successful and able United States District Judge in the trial court of the federal system. He regarded his so-called "promotion" to the court of appeals as a sort of dignified retirement merited by his age and infirmities. The story is told that Judge Morton once made a statement, at some bar

---

* Judge Calvert Magruder, "The Trials and Tribulations of an Intermediate Appellate Court," *Cornell Law Quarterly*, XLIV (Fall, 1958), 1–11. [Footnotes omitted.] Reproduced with permission of the publisher. Copyright © 1958 by Cornell University.

association gathering, to the effect that "any solemn chump can get away with being an appellate judge, but it takes an honest-to-God he-man to be a good trial judge." My comment on that differentiation would be that it was not quite fair to the appellate judge. I would agree that it is easier for any "solemn chump" to "get away" with being an appellate judge than to "get away" with being a trial judge. But merely "getting away" with something, of course, is not the whole story. I would contend that one needs to be much more than a "solemn chump" to deserve the accolade of being a *good* appellate judge.

The circuit judge does share with the district judge the common factor that we are both judges, and therefore it becomes important to observe our relationships as judges with the lawyers. As you are aware, there are certain amenities which the lawyer customarily observes. Whatever may be his private opinion of the judge, the lawyer maintains what sometimes may seem to be an obsequious and exaggerated deference to "his Honor," who may be wrong in the particular instance, or who may be making an ass of himself—only the lawyer does not say so, openly and bluntly, in so many words.

But these amenities which lead the lawyer to refrain from showing the judge up are, or ought to be, a two-way street. It would be hitting below the belt for a judge, secure in the immunity with which he is cloaked by the courtesy of lawyers, to bawl him out when he knows the lawyer will feel a reluctance to answer back. The judge needs to be, on his part, respectful to the feelings of the lawyer and should refrain from the temptation, sometimes prompted by arrogance, to humiliate the lawyer before his client or before the public.

Of course, judges are recruited from the ranks of the lawyers, and wrapping a black robe around a lawyer does not invest him with any more wisdom or legal competence than he had before. The judge's aura of immunity resulting from the exercise by lawyers of these professional amenities certainly has some aspect of fraud and fakery, so that perhaps it may be wondered why such customs have been accepted tacitly as the proper professional practice.

The answer is, I suppose, that this is but a phase of institutional prestige that envelops all public officials, not only judges—a prestige that tends to condition the uninstructed general public more readily to accept as binding what the public official may do. When one has done his best to perform a public task, it is always comforting to be buttressed by a little prestige, meretricious or otherwise. A public official, even on occasions the President of the United States, may give utterance to some banality, some truism, which the ordinary man in the street would not have the nerve to say, because of its transparent emptiness. But coming from the public official, such a comment may be quoted with the utmost solemnity by the press, as implying that the trite remark constitutes the very embodiment of prescience and wisdom. This all contributes to building up the prestige of the office, and renders the acts of the official more readily acceptable to the general public.

This institutional prestige, therefore, serves a useful purpose, and is not a thing lightly to be cast into the discard by the protected official. Public officials, judges included, must not, then, be too frank in "letting down their hair" in public. The important caution is that the public official must not let himself be deceived, by this deference and prestige that surround him, into thinking that he is any better than he really is.

In an intermediate appellate court, such as mine, the maintenance of this institutional prestige of the courts imposes upon us a certain judicial etiquette in our dealing with judges lower in the federal system, whose acts we are called upon to review on appeal. We also have imposed upon us certain amenities in our dealings with the Supreme Court of the United States, which of course has the final say, and which may, and often does, say that we were wrong.

As to the trial judges, we must always bear in mind that they may be as good lawyers as we are, or better. They are under the disadvantage of often having to make rulings off the cuff, so to speak, in the press and urgency of a trial proceeding, and the main reason we on appeal may have a better chance of being right is that we have more time for reflection and study. Hence, we should approach our task of judicial review with a certain genuine humility. We should never unnecessarily try to make a monkey of the judge in the court below, or to trespass on his feelings or dignity and self-respect. Sometimes we may have contributed to an erroneous ruling below by an incautious statement made by us in an earlier opinion, in which case we should take care to point out that this is so, and that we may have been to blame for misleading the district court, which was only trying to follow us. Sometimes we may have occasion to reverse a judge of the district court on a ground not presented to it, or considered below. If so, we should be at pains to point that out. And if the district court has written a careful and full opinion, with which we agree, and which we feel unable to improve upon, we should affirm on the opinion of the court below.

In recent years we have been somewhat embarrassed by appeals, in criminal as well as in civil cases, where the main point raised by appellant was that biased and partial actions by the trial judge so outrageously interfered with the orderly development of the case by counsel as to deny to appellant the essence of a fair trial before an impartial tribunal. If we think that appellant's point is well taken, we have no escape but to say so, however much this determination is inevitably a slap in the face of the district judge. But we have assured the bar of our reluctance to accept as true such a serious charge without the court's being thoroughly acquainted with the whole atmosphere of the trial, which can only be achieved by a careful reading of the trial transcript from beginning to end.

Now as to our relations with our superior tribunal, the Supreme Court of the United States. Here too, we have to play the game according to certain well-accepted rules, and it makes no difference what our private opinion might be as to whether certain justices of the Supreme Court know more, or less, than we do about the law. We should always express a respectful deference to controlling decisions of the Supreme Court, and do our best to follow them. We should leave it to the Supreme Court to overrule its own cases.

I have always thought that the prevailing majority of our court did the right thing in *United States* v. *Girouard*, where we accepted a never-overruled precedent in the Supreme Court, though we got reversed for doing so. Of course the Supreme Court, in reversing our judgment, pursuant to the institutional obligation it owed to us, was careful to point out that we had merely followed an undistinguishable and never-overruled precedent by the Supreme Court, which that Court then proceeded to overrule. On the other hand, it appears to me that the three-judge court in the fourth circuit, in the second *Flag Salute* case, did an unseemly thing in counting noses, so as to speculate as to whether the Supreme Court, as reconstructed, would be likely to adhere to its ruling in the first *Flag Salute* case, decided only a few years earlier. It was no less unseemly, though in the result Judge Parker guessed right as to what the Supreme Court would ultimately do. Statistics will show that in these two cases the Court of Appeals for the First Circuit got itself reversed whereas the Fourth Circuit got affirmed. But that only goes to show that statistics do not necessarily tell the full story.

But what are we supposed to do when we have no controlling precedent in the Supreme Court on all fours with our case, as the saying goes, but where we find expressions in previous opinions which may serve to indicate the slant which the justices might have as to the particular problem?

Well, there are at least two ways in which we could deal with a situation like that, and we have tried both of them. Just why, in a particular case, we may have chosen to follow one rather than the other course, may indeed be difficult to determine.

(1) The first method is perhaps the more modest one. Since we are only a half-way house of judicial review, it might be said that we should focus on previous cases in the Supreme Court to see what consequences would flow from them as a matter of logic, and examine the dicta in that Court, all with the purpose of concluding, if possible, how the Supreme Court would probably deal with the problem. That course I chose in the famous, or notorious, case of *Sampson* v. *Channell,* where I concluded that, from the logic and reasoning of the Supreme Court in *Erie Railroad Co.* v. *Tompkins,* it would follow that in a diversity case the federal district court should apply, as part of the substantive law of the state wherein the district court sits, the local rules of conflict of laws as understood and applied in the state tribunals.

(2) The second method is to assume that the Supreme Court, in a matter on which it has not specifically ruled, is entitled to the benefit of whatever illumination the court of appeals may be able to throw upon the question of what ought to be the law, untrammeled by dicta or logic-chopping from previous opinions of the Supreme Court which might point to the opposite conclusion. That method we pursued in *McClennen* v. *Commissioner.* We thought the Court was shaky in some of the things it said in *Bull* v. *United States,* but in any event we thought the case could be distinguished. Treating the case with the utmost respect as a "peculiar case on its facts and in the way the case came up," we even professed to find, perhaps with tongue in cheek, that there were implications in *Bull* v. *United States* pointing to the conclusion we were inclined to reach in the case then before us.

It may be that a bit of psychiatric introspection would disclose why I chose to follow one method in *Sampson* v. *Channell* and a different method in *McClennen* v. *Commissioner.* I do not tax my brain too much with such speculations, because whatever conclusion one might come up with would be suspect as a mere rationalization. All too often we have to realize that the case might be written up either way, in a lawyer-like opinion. The judge may not recognize that this is so, or even be conscious of the inner springs which lead him to choose one result rather than the other. Perhaps here effective advocacy does its more subtle work in persuading the judge that he wants the case to come out one way rather than the other.

In the case of *Sampson* v. *Channell,* subsequent events proved that I had guessed right as to what the Supreme Court would do, both on the conflicts point and on the question whether the rule as to burden of proof was to be treated as a matter of substance or procedure for the particular purpose at hand. But of course that does not prove that I chose the right method in *Sampson* v. *Channell.* If the conclusion reached in that case is as wrong and unfortunate as I understand they now say it is in the class on federal jurisdiction at Harvard Law School, assuming I was competent to write a persuasive opinion the other way, who knows but that I might have succeeded in persuading even the Supreme Court to take that view, in a matter which, after all, they had never focused on before.

For what it is worth, and maybe it is worth nothing, I submit this ex post facto rationalization of why I did what I did in these two cases.

Perhaps I liked the result which I arrived at, following the method I chose in *Sampson* v. *Channell.* When I was law clerk to Justice Brandeis, he said, speaking for the Court in *Kryger* v. *Wilson*:

> *It is apparent from the above statement that there has been no lack of due process. . . . The most that the plaintiff in error can say is that the state court made a mistaken application of doctrines of the conflict of laws in deciding that the cancellation of a land contract is governed by law of the* situs *instead of the place of making and performance. But that, being purely a question of local common law, is a matter with which this court is not concerned.*

I have always thought that proposition was pretty good, for the Supreme Court of the United States has too much other essential work to do to become also the final arbiter in conflicts questions. Its necessarily episodic dealing with conflicts problems is not likely to contribute helpfully to the development of the subject. And if the Supreme Court was to become the final arbiter of conflicts problems only in diversity cases, then its influence on the state courts in non-diversity cases, in the direction of developing a uniform law, would likely be nil, as was proved by the broader experience under *Swift* v. *Tyson.* While the prescription that one must follow the substantive law of the state in diversity cases would seem to take lots of fun out of the federal judge's function in diversity cases, yet this is perhaps so only theoretically. For the federal judge, if he professes solemnly to be seeking out the rule that is applicable in the state tribunal, can usually reach the result he thinks ought to be reached, since more likely than not he will find the state law pronouncements on the particular point to be ambiguous or inconclusive.

On the other hand, when it came to *McClennen* v. *Commissioner,* I thought I knew something about the law of partnership, and I felt pretty confident as to what the tax consequences should be in that estate tax case. To reach the result I thought ought to be reached, it was necessary to deal somewhat roughly, though very respectfully, of course, with the Supreme Court case of *Bull v. United States,* which was the main reliance of the taxpayer. Certiorari was not applied for by the losing taxpayer in the *McClennen* case.

We cannot adopt the easy, slap-dash view that what the court of appeals does is really not important, because the Supreme Court has the last word. When Congress created the system of intermediate courts of appeals, in 1891, it was with the idea of taking a load off the Supreme Court of the United States, so that that Court might perform better its primary function of mediator in the federal system. The Supreme Court retains a discretionary power of ultimate review, upon certiorari, but as you well know the Supreme Court is just too busy to grant a writ of certiorari in all cases. Therefore, we have to do our job thoroughly and well, in order to fulfill what is expected of us. It is obvious that if we get too bad, the Supreme Court will have to load itself up with routine cases, to the detriment of its more important business.

I don't think we have become too bad, and the result is that in the vast majority of cases that are brought to us, what we say becomes the final word on appeal. If I may quote briefly from some statistics: in the five-year period from October 1951 to September 1956, inclusive, out of a total of 570 cases docketed in our court, the Supreme Court was applied to for a writ of certiorari in only 110, and the number of certiorari petitions which the Supreme Court granted was only 12. As a result of review by the Supreme Court of our work during this five-year period, seven of our judgments were affirmed, and five were reversed, which made an average reversal of only one case per year over the five-year period.

It is probably only a coincidence that three of the five opinions of ours which were reversed were written by me on behalf of the court. Now, I don't enjoy getting reversed any more than any other judge, and when that happens, my first impulse is to repair to the nearest tavern and "cuss out" the Supreme Court. Sometimes, after we have given long study to a case and written a careful opinion, we find ourselves reversed by the Supreme Court in an opinion that strikes us as superficial and hastily prepared. We eventually cool off, when we come to realize that the opinion may indeed be superficial and hastily drawn from the very necessities and pressures under which the Supreme Court has to do its work. Another thing that tends to cool us off is the realization that, were our positions reversed, and were we required to perform our work in the environment and under the pressures prevailing in the Supreme Court, we probably could not do so good a job as they do.

I do say without hesitation that where a court of appeals has written a full opinion which evidences a careful and painstaking study of the case, the Supreme Court of the United States owes it an institutional obligation not to reverse us except upon filing a reasoned opinion undertaking to show that our conclusion was mistaken. The only exceptions to this proposition that I can think of at the moment are two: (1) Where the Supreme Court can cite, and rely upon, a supervening decision of its own in another case, which obviously covers our case and which serves well enough to indicate why it thinks we went wrong; (2) where the court of appeals has lost the confidence of the Supreme Court, which wishes curtly to manifest that lack of confidence to the world.

In this connection one case that still burns me up is *Pino* v. *Nicolls*. The question there was the validity of an order for the deportation of an alien, on the statutory ground that the deportee at some time after his entry into the United States had been "convicted of two crimes involving moral turpitude, not arising out of a single scheme of criminal misconduct, regardless of whether confined therefore and regardless of whether the convictions were in a single trial." There was no issue as to one of the two offenses, namely, carnal abuse of a female child. The only question presented to us on appeal was whether, as the records stood in the Third District Court of Eastern Middlesex, Massachusetts, it could be said that the alien stood convicted of the crime of petit larceny. It was not suggested to us that the crime of petit larceny was not a crime involving moral turpitude, within the meaning of the federal statute. We held, in a lengthy opinion, which after all turned upon the niceties of local Massachusetts law, that the alien did stand convicted in the Third District Court of Eastern Middlesex of the crime of petit larceny.

The Supreme Court in its wisdom granted a writ of certiorari. Upon review, the Supreme Court unanimously reversed our judgment, in a five-line per curiam opinion that magisterially stated: "On the record here we are unable to say that the conviction has attained such finality as to support an order of deportation within the contemplation of 241 of the Immigration and Nationality Act. The judgment is reversed."

Now, why were we treated that way by the Supreme Court? There was no question of a controlling supervening decision of the Supreme Court. And I am sure as a court we had not forfeited the confidence of the Supreme Court; so we have not believed, even for a moment, that the Supreme Court was taking an occasion to manifest sharply its lack of confidence in us.

Of course, it is possible that the members of the Supreme Court, for one reason or another, wanted to save the alien from deportation, but that no extensive opinion supporting that conclusion could obtain acceptance by a majority of the justices. That possibility I can understand, for the justices of the Supreme Court, like the rest of us, are only human. Maybe the justices felt that they could not avoid doing what they did. Whether there were other available ways of handling the situation I don't know. Oftentimes the Supreme Court announces two or more opinions by minority groups on the Court, no one opinion commanding the support of a majority, though a majority do concur in the announced judgment. Perhaps something like that might have been done in this case. However that may be, it is certainly true that the Supreme Court owed the court of appeals the obligation of furnishing a reasoned statement for reversing us, and whatever might have been the explanation of why the justices did not fulfill that obligation, it is still true that the Supreme Court must be charged with an institutional failure in its summary treatment of the court of appeals in that case.

Realistically, we must recognize that there are certain types of cases in which, if we dare to "stick our necks out," we are pretty sure to get reversed.

One such case is where a fellow claims to be a seaman. Because seamen as a class are supposed to be defenseless and unable to look out for themselves, the expression has grown up that "seamen are wards of the admiralty." But I wouldn't suppose that a man is entitled to this special protective arm of the judiciary merely on his claim to be a seaman. At all events, in *Grimes* v. *Raymond Concrete Pile Co.,* a plaintiff had claimed to be entitled, as a seaman, to sue for damages under the Jones Act. If he were not a seaman he could not maintain such an action, and his exclusive remedy would have been a claim for workmen's compensation under the Longshoremen's and Harbor Workers' Compensation Act, as provided by Congress in the Defense Bases Act. We held, as a matter of law, that the man could not, on the proven facts, reasonably be found to be a seaman, and so we affirmed the judgment of the district court. The Supreme Court granted certiorari and reversed us on April 7, 1958, in a per curiam opinion informing us briefly:

> *We hold, in agreement with the Court of Appeals, that 42 U.S.C. 1654 saves the remedy under the Jones Act created for a member of a crew of any vessel. We hold further, however, in disagreement with the Court of Appeals, that the petitioner's evidence, presented an evidentiary basis for a jury's finding whether or not the petitioner was a member of a crew of any vessel.*

This time we picked up a few dissents.

If, upon retrial of the case, a jury holds that the plaintiff *was* a seaman, we shall have to accept that determination of fact under the Jones Act, unless, of course, the record contains different evidence, because the Supreme Court has told us that whether the man was, or was not, a seaman, constituted, on the evidence presented, a factual issue which had to be submitted to the jury. We always try faithfully to follow a decision of our superiors. But if another case comes up, where a party's claim to be a seaman seems to us to be as preposterous as in the *Grimes* case, as in our humble view the dissenting opinion by Mr. Justice Harlan in the latter case well demonstrated, I am afraid that we shall again "stick our necks out" and say, as a matter of law, that the man is not a seaman, thereby courting another probable reversal by the Supreme Court.

Another familiar situation where we are pretty likely to get reversed is where, in a case under the Federal Employers' Liability Act, we either affirm the trial court in giving judgment for the railroad, pursuant to a verdict directed for the defendant, or reverse a judgment for the plaintiff on the ground that the district court committed error in submitting the issues of negligence or causation to the jury. In *New York, New Haven & Hartford Railroad Co.* v. *Dox* we explained what we have to do in cases of this sort, as long as the Supreme Court continues to tell us that the plaintiff has the burden of establishing negligence and causation in suits under the Federal Employers' Liability Act. Pointing out, what cannot be denied, that a "plaintiff's right to a jury trial, as guaranteed by the Seventh Amendment to the Federal Constitution, is not an unqualified right to have the jury pass on issues of negligence and proximate cause in all cases . . . ," we said that in such cases an intermediate appellate court has an inescapable function to perform in deciding whether the plaintiff proved enough to get his case to the jury. "We have to perform that function honestly and conscientiously, let the chips fall where they may, in so far as possible further appellate review is concerned."

We are not obliged, as part of our institutional obligation to the Supreme Court, to express agreement with everything the Supreme Court may choose to do. It is true, the Supreme Court has the final word, so far as the disposition of the particular case is concerned. That is indeed an awesome power, though it is unavoidable, for there needs be some ultimate tribunal; and in one sense it is no doubt true, as Stone, J., dissenting, said of the Supreme Court in *United States* v. *Butler,* that "the only check upon our own exercise of power is our own sense of self-restraint."

[Judge Magruder's comments suggest that the mode of operation of a court and, to use Karl Llewellyn's compelling phrase, the "craft-tradition" developed within its confines may be factors of prime significance in the extension (or curtailment) of institutional power and influence. The next major portion of the book is devoted to this aspect of the judicial process.]

5 Traditions and Procedures of Judicial Institutions

A. PROCEDURES OF THE SUPREME COURT

1. The Supreme Court Begins its October Term*

The Supreme Court reconvened yesterday but stayed in session just long enough to make it official. Only business transacted at the 16-minute session was admission of 39 lawyers to practice before the Court.

Promptly at noon the nine justices appeared through the red draperies behind the bench. Court Crier George E. Hutchinson sounded the traditional cry Oyez, oyez, oyez and admonished all persons having business with the Court to "draw near and give their attention for the Court is now sitting."

This began what is called the "October term," which will continue through next June.

SCHEDULES CONSIDERED

After the brief public session the justices began a series of conferences to decide which cases to review of the nearly 400 filed during their three-month recess. Results of the conferences will be announced next Monday when the Court will also begin hearing oral argument on cases already scheduled.

The first case to be argued is a sequel to the old tidelands oil dispute. The question is where does state jurisdiction stop and Federal control begin in the Gulf of Mexico. The Federal Government says it controls beyond 3 miles out. Some of

---

*Richard L. Lyons in the *Washington Post and Times Herald,* October 9, 1959, p. A 2. Reproduced with permission of the publisher. Copyright © 1959 by the *Washington Post and Times Herald.*

the states say their boundaries go out more than 10 miles. At issue is millions of dollars in oil lease revenues.

A capacity crowd of tourists and lawyers was on hand for the opening session. Retired Justices Stanley F. Reed and Harold H. Burton were on hand, as they often are on decision Mondays throughout the term. A third retired Justice, Sherman Minton, is ill.

Attorney General William P. Rogers and Solicitor General J. Lee Rankin were also present, dressed in traditional morning coats which Justice Department attorneys still wear when appearing before the Supreme Court.

The ceremony of admitting of new lawyers to practice before the Court is one the Court goes through each Monday despite the fact it often takes 30 minutes or more out of their four-hour regular session. One day two years ago 682 were admitted in one day.

Each lawyer is presented by a sponsor and is welcomed by the Chief Justice. The lawyers take an oath to conduct themselves "uprightly," pay $25, are given a certificate and then are eligible to file appeals and argue cases in the Supreme Court.

Yesterday was Chief Justice Earl Warren's sixth anniversary on the Court. Justice Hugo L. Black, senior justice in terms of service, took his seat 22 years ago last Sunday.

[For many, the internal traditions and procedures of the courts seem to embody a useless emphasis upon the pomp and circumstance of time-worn but presently irrelevant customs. The foregoing account of the opening of the Supreme Court recreated some of the spirit of the occasion but did not provide much information about the manner in which the Court operates internally. However, there is much to support the view of Frankfurter and Landis that "the formalities and modes of doing business, which we characterize as procedure, though lacking in dramatic manifestations, may, like the subtle creeping in of the tide, be a powerful force in the dynamic process of government."[1]

Jefferson, for example, grounded his opposition to the Marshall Court not simply upon his well-publicized rejection of judicial review and federal supremacy but also upon his distaste for the mode of decision-making initiated by Chief Justice John Marshall.]

2. On the Supreme Court, Letter from Thomas Jefferson to Thomas Ritchie*

The judiciary of the United States is the subtle corps of sappers and miners constantly working underground to undermine the foundations of our confederated

---

[1] Felix Frankfurter and James M. Landis, *The Business of the Supreme Court* (New York: Macmillan, 1927), p. vi.

*Dated December 25, 1820, published in Paul Leicester Ford (ed.), *The Writings of Thomas Jefferson* (New York: G. P. Putnam's Sons, 1899). pp. 170–71.

fabric. They are construing our constitution from a coordination of a general and special government to a general and supreme one alone. This will lay all things at their feet, and they are too well versed in English law to forget the maxim, *"boni judicis est ampliare jurisdictionem"* . . . Having found, from experience, that impeachment is an impracticable thing, a mere scare-crow, they consider themselves secure for life; they sculk from responsibility to public opinion, the only remaining hold on them, under a practice first introduced into England by Lord Mansfield. An opinion is huddled up in conclave, perhaps by a majority of one, delivered as if unanimous, and with the silent acquiescence of lazy or timid associates, by a crafty judge [Marshall] who sophisticates the law to his mind, by the turn of his own reasoning. A judiciary law was once reported by the Attorney General [Edmond Randolph] to Congress, requiring each judge to deliver his opinion seriatim and openly, and then to give it in writing to the clerk to be entered in the record. A judiciary independent of a king or executive alone is a good thing; but independence of the will of the nation is a solecism, at least in a republican government.

B. THE SIGNIFICANCE OF RULES AND TRADITIONS FOR SUBSTANTIVE PUBLIC POLICY

[Occasionally, situations have arisen in American constitutional law in which the invocation of a universally respected technical rule may result, because of the circumstances out of which the litigation arises, in a gross denial of justice to one class of litigants. The early case of *Mima Queen and Child* v. *Hepburn*[1] concerned the claim to freedom of a slave based on the contention that one of her ancestors had possessed freedom. The claim was rejected by the majority of the members of the Supreme Court on the ground that hearsay evidence is not admissible in proving the freedom of a slave's ancestor. Justice Gabriel Duvall dissented in a manner which invoked frank recognition of the harsh social realities confronting slaves who sought to assert their cherished legal right to freedom. He pointed out that

> *the reason for admitting hearsay evidence upon a question of freedom is much stronger than in cases of pedigree or in controversies relative to the boundaries of land. It will be universally admitted that the right to freedom is more important than the right of property. And people of color from their helpless condition under the uncontrolled authority of a master, are entitled to all reasonable protection.*
>
> *A decision that hearsay evidence in such cases shall not be admitted, cuts up by the roots all claims of the kind, and puts a final end to them, unless the claim should arise from a fact of recent date, and such a case will seldom, perhaps never, occur.*

[1] 7 Cranch 290 (1813).

In the mid-twentieth century, several states still retain costly appeal requirements which, while far less dramatic than the situation which provoked Duvall's
dissent in 1813, have the practical effect of discouraging many from pressing
legitimate suits. The following excerpt describes the one situation in the most
populous state in the Union.]

1. Justice Lost—By What Appellate Papers Cost*

Is there a veteran of New York legal practice who has not at some time stood
in the office of the clerk of an appellate court and gazed in wonder over range on
range of mountainous records and briefs? If these mountains are made of paper
all exquisitely printed, as they are in most offices in this State, he will be gazing
upon one of our major barriers against justice. This is a barrier against justice
as applied in practice for the ordinary litigant who seeks it. These mountains of
printed papers constitute not only a denial of justice but also a great economic
waste. The forbidding role of these barriers has been recognized for a long time,
but in New York little has been done to blast a passage through them.

Applied justice is lost to anyone who is barred, in actual fact, from any of the
basic legal remedies. An appeal to another judge or judges for a second hearing
and possible correction has come, in our system, to be considered a basic remedy.
If the mechanisms of civil appeal cost so much as to be out of proportion to the
amount involved, the losing party is in actual fact barred from this basic remedy.
Hence, justice is thwarted. In small civil cases, justice fails not only for litigants
of modest means, but also for wealthy litigants who are barred by the cost of appeal
from pursuing what they deem to be just claims. If an appeal is uneconomic, justice
may be denied as truly to a rich as to a poor litigant.

The risk of injustice is even greater in a criminal case. The damage to a defendant's reputation and earning power, the dislocation and trauma for his family,
and the injuries to personality that are wrought by a wrongful conviction for
crime are likely to be worse than the harm flowing from an erroneous judgment
in a civil case. If a convicted defendant, in order to appeal, must pay out more
money than he has, he is again barred from a basic remedy, and justice fails once
more.

RECENT SURVEY OF REASONS FOR FAILURE TO APPEAL

In an effort to ascertain the extent to which appeals are deterred by costs, in
general, and printing costs, in particular, we sent a questionnaire in July 1958, to all
lawyers in Onondaga, Oswego, and Oneida Counties plus the City of Rochester

---

* Bertram F. Willcox, Delmar Karlen and Ruth Roemer, "Justice Lost—By What Appellate Papers
Cost," *New York University Law Review*, XXXIII (November, 1958), 934–36. [Footnotes omitted.]
Reproduced with permission of the authors and the publisher. Copyright © 1958 by *New York
University Law Review*.

(but not the rest of Monroe County). All these areas are in the Fourth Department of the Appellate Division. Approximately 20 per cent of the 1773 lawyers replied. Almost half of those who replied do handle appeals. These attorneys reported filing 344 appeals (328 civil and 16 criminal appeals) during the year July 1, 1957 to July 1, 1958. They estimated that, in addition to the 328 cases appealed, another 411 appeals would have been desirable but were not taken for various reasons. With respect to the civil cases, this sample of lawyers reported that printing costs barred appeals in nearly half of the civil cases to which appeals were deemed desirable but not taken. With respect to criminal cases, these lawyers reported that in one-quarter of the criminal cases where an appeal was deemed desirable but not taken, the appeal was deterred by printing costs alone; that in three-quarters of the criminal cases in which an appeal was deemed desirable but not taken, the appeal was deterred by all costs. In only 46 of the civil cases (13 per cent) and 6 of the criminal cases (12 per cent) in which appeals were deemed desirable were they deterred by reasons other than costs.

C. DELAY IN THE COURTS

[Closely related to the problem which arises out of the costs of litigation is the possibility that economically powerful litigants may, through protracted invocation of technical remedies, defeat financially weaker litigants because the latter simply lack the resources to continue cases that often appear to involve interminable legal maneuvering. In some situations (the variety of anti-integration maneuvers devised by some of the public officials in the South provide the most striking contemporary examples) protracted litigation is rather openly pursued for the sake of delay, particularly where the ultimate judicial result is a foregone conclusion. Among the members of the Supreme Court, Justice Brennan has contributed, during his brief tenure, some of the most cogent analyses of the dimensions of the problem of calculated delay. In *Louisiana Power and Light Company* v. *Thibodaux City* Justice Brennan dissented in part on the ground that the majority's decision encouraged protracted delay.]

1. Tactical Delay*

Not only has the Court departed from any precedential basis for its action, but the decision encourages inefficiency in administration of the federal courts and leads to unnecessary delay, waste and added expense for the parties. This is particularly the stark truth in the instant case. The City of Thibodaux brought this

*Mr. Justice William Brennan for the majority in *Louisiana Power and Light Company* v. *Thibodaux City*, 360 U.S. 25, 42–44 (1958). [Footnotes omitted.]

proceeding in a Louisiana court to expropriate lands of the Power and Light Company for public purposes. The Power and Light Company, a Florida corporation, removed the action to the District Court, as was its privilege under 28 U.S.C. 1441. The crucial issue in the case is whether Louisiana Act 111 of 1900 empowers the City to exercise the State's right of eminent domain. Because the District Court rebuffed the City's plea to decide its authority under Act 111, and this Court sustains the District Court, the City must go back to the state court, not in the action originally brought there by the City, but in a new action to be initiated under Louisiana's declaratory judgment law. The Power and Light Company, which escaped a state court decision by removing the City's action to the District Court, is now wholly content with the *sua sponte* action of the District Court. This is understandable since the longer decision is put off as to the City's power to expropriate its property, the longer the Power and Light Company will enjoy the possession of it. Resolution of the legal question of the City's authority, already delayed, according to the City's estimate in its brief, a minimum of two additional years before a decision may be obtained from the State Supreme Court in the declaratory judgment action. Even if the City obtains a favorable decision, the City must suffer still further delay while the case comes back to the District Court for a decision upon the amount of damages to be paid the Power and Light Company. Thus at best the District Court will finally dispose of this case only after prolonged delay and considerable additional expense for the parties. Moreover, it is possible that the State Supreme Court will, for one reason or another, conclude that it will not render the parties this advisory opinion. All of this delay should have been avoided, and would have been, had the District Court performed what I think was its plain duty, and decided the question of the City's power when that question was ripe for decision a few months after the case was removed to the District Court. I think it is more than coincidence that both in this case and in *Mashuda* the party supporting abstention is the one presently in possession of the property in question. I cannot escape the conclusion in these cases that delay in the reaching of a decision is more important to those parties than the tribunal which ultimately renders the decision. The Court today upholds a procedure which encourages such delay and prevents "that promptness of decision which in all judicial actions is one of the elements of justice." *Forsyth* v. *Hammond*. . . One must regret that this Court's departure from the long-settled criteria governing abstention should so richly fertilize the Power and Light Company's strategy of delay which now has succeeded, I dare say, past the fondest expectation of counsel who conceived it. It is especially unfortunate in that departure from these criteria fashions an opening wedge for District Courts to refer hard cases of state law to state courts in even the routine diversity negligence and contract actions.

I would affirm the judgment of the Court of Appeals.

[Die-hard political opponents of integration in the South have often capitalized upon the availability of technical rules permitting delay as illustrated by the following example.]

2. *Division on the Court about Delay:* Harrison v. NAACP*

MR. JUSTICE HARLAN DELIVERED THE OPINION
OF THE COURT

In this case a three-judge District Court was convened . . . to hear federal constitutional challenges against five Virginia Statutes. It declared three invalid under
the Fourteenth Amendment, and permanently enjoined the appellants from en-
forceing them against the appellees; the other two statutes it found vague and
ambiguous and accordingly retained jurisdiction pending a construction by the
state courts. . . . Only the former disposition was appealed. The appeal raises two
questions: First, whether in the circumstances of this case the District Court should
have abstained from a constitutional adjudication, retaining the cause while the
parties through appropriate proceedings, afforded the Virginia courts an opportunity to construe the three statutes in light of state and federal constitutional requirements. Second, if such an abstention was not called for, whether the District
Court's constitutional holdings were correct. Because of our views upon the first
question we do not reach the second.

National Association for the Advancement of Colored People (NAACP) and
NAACP Legal Defense and Educational Fund, Incorporated (Fund), appellees
herein, are organizations engaged in furthering the rights of colored citizens. Both
are membership corporations organized under the laws of New York, and have
registered under the laws of Virginia as foreign corporations doing business within
the State. NAACP's principal relevant activities in Virginia are appearing before
legislative bodies and commissions in support of, or opposition to, measures affecting the status of the Negro race within the State, and furnishing assistance to
Negroes concerned in litigation involving their constitutional rights. Fund performs
functions similar to those of NAACP in the field of litigation, but is precluded
by its charter from attempting to influence legislation. The revenues of NAACP
are derived from both membership dues and general contributions, those of Fund
entirely from contributions.

NAACP and Fund brought this action against the Attorney General of Virginia
and a number of other Commonwealth officials, appellants herein, for declaratory
and injunctive relief with respect to Chapters 31, 32, 33, 35 and 36 of the Acts of
the Virginia Assembly, passed in 1956. . . . The complaint alleging irreparable
injury on account of these enactments, sought a declaration that each infringed
rights assured under the Fourteenth Amendment and an injunction against its
enforcement. Jurisdiction was predicated upon the civil rights statutes, . . . diversity
of citizenship, . . . and the presence of a federal question . . .

The Attorney General and his co-defendants moved to dismiss the action on the
ground, among others, that the District Court should not "exercise its jurisdiction
to enjoin the enforcement of state statutes which have not been authoritatively
construed by the state courts." The District Court, recognizing "the necessity of

*360 U.S. 167 (1959). [Footnotes omitted.]

maintaining the delicate balance between state and federal courts under the concept of separate sovereigns," stated that "the constitutionality of state statutes requiring special competence in the interpretation of local law should not be determined by federal courts in advance of a reasonable opportunity afforded the parties to seek ajudication by the state court," but considered that relief should be granted where "the statute is free from ambiguity and there remains no reasonable interpretation which will render it constitutional. . . ." On this basis, the court, one judge dissenting, held Chapters 31, 32, and 35 unconstitutional, and permanently enjoined their enforcement against NAACP and Fund. Chapters 33 and 36, on the other hand, the court unanimously found vague and ambiguous. It accordingly retained jurisdiction as to those Chapters, without reaching their constitutionality, allowing the complaining parties a reasonable time within which to obtain a state interpretation.

The Commonwealth defendants, proceeding under 28 USC 1253 appealed to this Court and the lower court's disposition of Chapters 31, 32, and 35. We noted probable jurisdiction. . . . NAACP and Fund did not appeal the disposition of Chapters 33 and 36.

The three Virginia statutes before us are lengthy, detailed, and sweeping. Chapters 31 and 32 are registration statutes. Chapter 31 deals with the rendering of financial assistance in litigation. It proscribes the public solicitation of funds, and the expenditure of funds from whatever source derived, for the commencement or further prosecution of an "original proceeding," by any person, broadly defined to include corporations and other entities, which is neither a party nor possessed of a "pecuniary right or liability" in such proceeding, unless a detailed annual filing is made with the State Corporation Commission. If such person is a corporation, the filing must include among other things, (1) certified copies of its charter and by-laws; (2) "A certified list of the names and addresses of the officers, directors, stockholders, members, agents and employees or other persons acting for or in [its] behalf"; (3) a certified statement of the sources of its income, however derived, including the names and addresses of contributors or donors if required by the Commission; (4) a detailed certified statement of the corporation's expenditures for the preceding year, the objects thereof, and whatever other information relative thereto may be required by the Commission; and (5) a certified statement of the "counties and cities in which it proposes to or does finance or maintain litigation to which it is not a party." Correspondingly broad disclosures are required of individuals who fall within the statutory proscription.

Violation of this Chapter is punishable as a misdemeanor for individuals, and by a fine of not more than $10,000 for corporations, plus a mandatory denial or revocation of authority to do business within the State in the case of a foreign corporation. An individual "acting as an agent or employee" of a corporation or other entity with respect to activity violative of the Chapter is deemed guilty of a misdemeanor. And directors, officers, and "those persons responsible for the management or control of the affairs" of a corporation or other entity are made jointly and severally liable for whatever fines might be imposed on it.

Chapter 32 deals with activities relating to the passage of racial legislation, with advocacy of "racial integration or segregation," and also with the raising and expenditure of funds in connection with racial litigation. Declaring that the "continued harmonious relations between the races are . . . essential to the welfare, health, and safety of the people of Virginia," the Chapter finds it "vital to the public interest" that registration be made with the State Corporation Commission by "persons, firms, partnerships, corporations and associations whose activities are causing or may cause interracial tension and unrest." Specifically, under 2 of this Chapter, annual filings are required of

"[e]very person, firm, partnership, corporation or association, whether by or through its agents, servants, employees, officers or voluntary workers or associates, who or which engages as one of its principal functions or activities in the promoting or opposing in any manner the passage of legislation by the General Assembly in behalf of any race or color, or who or which has as one of its principal functions or activities the advocating of racial integration or segregation or whose activities cause or tend to cause racial conflicts or violence, or who or which is engaged or engages in raising or expending funds for the employment of counsel or payment of costs in connection with litigation in behalf of any race or color, in this State. . . ."

The extent of such filing is comparable to that required by Chapter 31. The information so furnished is a matter of public record, to "be open to the inspection of any citizen at any time during the regular business hours of" the State Corporation Commission.

Failure to register subjects individuals to punishment as for a misdemeanor, and corporations to a fine not exceeding $10,000. Like Chapter 31, Chapter 32 also makes "responsible" persons liable jointly and severally for corporate fines. Further, "[e]ach day's failure to register and file the information required . . . shall constitute a separate offense and be punished as such." The Chapter is not applicable to persons or organizations which carry on the proscribed activities through matter which may qualify as second-class mail in the United States mails, or by radio or television, nor to persons or organizations acting in connection with any political campaign.

Chapter 35 is a "barratry" statute. Barratry is defined as "the offence of stirring up litigation." A "barrator" is thus a person or organization which "stirs up litigation." Stirring up litigation means "instigating," which in turn "means bringing it about that all or part of the expenses of the litigation are paid by the barrator," or by those, other than the plaintiffs, acting in concert with him, "unless the instigation is "justified" when "the instigator is related by blood or marriage to the plaintiff whom he instigates, or . . . is entitled by law to share with the plaintiff in money or property that is the subject of the litigation or . . . has a direct interest ["personal right or a pecuniary right or liability"] in the subject matter of the litigation or occupies a position of trust in relation to the plaintiff; or . . . is acting on behalf of a duly constituted legal aid society approved by the Virginia State Bar which offers advice or assistance in all kinds of legal matters to all members of the public who come to it for advice or assistance and are unable because of poverty to pay legal fees."

Individuals guilty of barratry as defined in the Chapter are punishable as for a misdemeanor and "shall" have their licenses "to practice law or any other profession . . . revoked for such period as provided by law." Corporations are subject to a fine of not more than $10,000 and, if they are foreign, mandatory revocation of their authority to do business within the State. Moreover, a "person who aids and abets a barrator by giving money or rendering services to or for the use or benefit of the barrator for committing barratry shall be guilty of barratry and punished. . . ." A host of exceptions to which the Chapter is not applicable is provided; none of these has thus far been asserted to include, or to be capable of including, appellees.

The majority below held Chapters 31 and 32 unconstitutional on similar grounds, centering its treatment of both around 2 of Chapter 32, the material provisions of which have already been set forth. . . . In essence 2 was found to infringe rights assured under the Fourteenth Amendment, in that, taken in conjunction with the registration requirements of the statute, (1) the clause relating to the promoting or opposing of racial legislation invaded rights of free speech because it was not restricted to lobbying activities; (2) the clause directed at advocacy of racial "integration or segregation" had the same infirmity because it was not supported by a compelling state interest or some clear and present danger; (3) the clause referring to activities causing or tending to cause racial conflicts or violence was too vague and indefinite to satisfy constitutional requirements; and (4) the clause aimed at the raising and expending of funds in connection with racial litigation unduly burdened the right of access to the courts, and did not serve an interest which could support a disclosure as broad as the one demanded.

Chapter 35, the "barratry" statute, was held to offend due process, in that it was found to be aimed not at the legitimate regulation of the practice of law but at preventing NAACP and Fund from continuing "their legal operations." In addition, the court held the Chapter to violate equal protection by unjustifiably discriminating between the racial litigation activities of the appellees and the general litigation efforts of "approved" legal aid societies.

These constitutional holdings were made in the context of findings that Chapters 31, 32, and 35, as well as Chapters 33 and 36 not presently before us, were passed by the Virginia Legislature "to nullify as far as possible the effect of the decision of the Supreme Court in Brown v Board of Education, . . . as parts of the general plan of massive resistance to the integration of schools of the state under the Supreme Court's decrees.". . . In the view we take of this case we do not reach appellants' objections to these findings.

According every consideration to the opinion of the majority below, we are nevertheless of the view that the District Court should have abstained from deciding the merits of the issues tendered it, so as to afford the Virginia courts a reasonable opportunity to construe the three statutes in question. In other words, we think that the District Court in dealing with Chapters 31, 32, and 35 should have followed the same course that it did with respect to Chapters 33 and 36.

This now well-established procedure is aimed at the avoidance of unnecessary interference by the federal courts with proper and validly administered state concerns, a course so essential to the balanced working of our federal system. To minimize the possibility of such interference a "scrupulous regard for the rightful independence of state governments . . . should at all times actuate the federal courts," Matthews v. Rodgers, . . . as their "contribution . . . in furthering the harmonious relation between state and federal authority . . ." Railroad Com. v. Pullman Co. . . . In the service of this doctrine, which this Court has applied in many different contexts, no principle has found more consistent or clear expression than that the federal courts should not adjudicate the constitutionality of state enactments fairly open to interpretation until the state courts have been afforded a reasonable opportunity to pass upon them. . . . This principle does not, of course, involve the abdication of federal jurisdiction, but only the postponement of its exercise; it serves the policy of comity inherent in the doctrine of abstention; and it spares the federal courts of unnecessary constitutional adjudication. . . .

The present case, in our view, is one which calls for the application of this principle, since we are unable to agree that the terms of these three statutes have no reasonable room for a construction by the Virginia courts which might avoid in whole or in part the necessity for federal constitutional adjudication, or at least materially change the nature of the problem.

It certainly cannot be said that Chapter 35 does not require a construction by the state courts. As appellants asserted here and in the court below, the Chapter might well be read as requiring a "stirring up" of litigation in the conventional common-law sense, in addition to the "unjustified" payment of litigation expenses. Were it to be so read, the statute might then not even apply to these appellees since the lower court found the evidence "uncontradicted that the initial steps which have led to the institution and prosecution of racial suits in Virginia with the assistance of the Association and the fund have not been taken until the prospective plaintiffs, made application to one or the other of the corporations for help.". . . Further the "personal right" component of "direct interest" in the statutory definition of "justified" instigation . . . might lend itself to a construction which would embrace non-party Negro contributors to litigation expense, including NAACP because of the relationship of that organization to its members. . . .

The possibility of limiting interpretation, characteristic of constitutional adjudication, also cannot be ignored. . . . The "advocacy" clause of Chapter 32, for example, might be construed as reaching only that directed at the incitement of violence. . . . Similar construction might be employed with respect to the clause in that Chapter relating to the influencing of legislation "in any manner." . . . And in connection with these and the membership and contributor list requirements of Chapter 31 and 32, . . . we note that Chapter 32 contains a separability clause, and that the Supreme Court of Appeals of Virginia treats legislative acts as separable, where possible, even in the absence of such an express provision. . . .

We do not intimate the slightest view as to what effect any such determinations might have upon the validity of these statutes. All we hold is that these enactments should be exposed to state construction or limiting interpretation before the federal courts are asked to decide upon their constitutionality, so that federal judgment will be based on something that is a complete product of the State, the enactment as phrased by its legislature and as construed by its highest court. The Virginia declaratory judgment procedure, . . . which the appellees are now pursuing with reference to Chapters 33 and 36, also provides an expeditious avenue here. And of course we shall not assume that the Virginia courts will not do their full duty in judging these statutes in light of state and federal constitutional requirements.

Because of its findings, amply supported by the evidence, that the existence and threatened enforcement of these statutes worked great and immediate irreparable injury on appellees, the District Court's abstention with respect to Chapters 33 and 36 proceeded on the assumption "that the defendants will continue to cooperate, as they have in the past, in withholding action under the authority of the statutes until a final decision is reached . . ." . . . In this Court counsel for the appellants has given similar assurances with respect to the three statutes presently before us, assurances which we understand embrace also the intention of these appellants never to proceed against appellees under any of these enactments with respect to activities engaged in during the full pendency of this litigation. While there is no reason to suppose that such assurances will not be honored by these or other Virginia officials not parties to this litigation, the District Court of course possesses ample authority in this action, or in such supplemental proceedings as may be initiated, to protect the appellees while this case goes forward.

Accordingly, the judgment below will be vacated and the case remanded to the District Court, with instructions to afford the appellees a reasonable opportunity to bring appropriate proceedings in the Virginia courts, meanwhile retaining its own jurisdiction of the case, and for further proceedings consistent with this opinion.

It is so ordered.

SEPARATE OPINION

Mr. Justice Douglas, with whom The Chief Justice and Mr. Justice Brennan concur, dissenting.

The rule invoked by the Court to require the Federal District Court to keep hands off this litigation until the state court has construed these laws is a judge-made rule. It was fashioned in 1941 in the decision of Railroad Co. v. Pullman Co. . . . as a device to avoid needless decisions under the Federal Constitution where a resolution of state law questions might make those adjudications unnecessary. Since that time, the rule of the Pullman Case has been greatly expanded. It has indeed been extended so far as to make the presence in federal court litigation of a state law question a convenient excuse for requiring the federal court to hold its hand while a second litigation is undertaken in the state court. This is a delaying tactic that may involve years of time and that inevitably doubles the cost of litigation. When used widespread, it dilutes the statute of the Federal District Courts, making them secondary tribunals in the administration of justice under the Federal Constitution.

With all due deference, this case seems to me to be the most inappropriate one of all in which to withhold the hand of the Federal District Court. Congress has ordained in the Civil Rights Act that "All persons within the jurisdiction of the United States shall have the same right in every State . . . to sue, be parties, give evidence . . . as is enjoyed by white citizens." . . . It has subjected, any citizen of the United States or other persons . . . to the deprivation of any rights . . . secured by the Constitution and laws" . . . and has given the District Courts "original jurisdiction" of actions "to redress the deprivation, under color of any State law, . . . of any right . . . secured by the Constitution of the United States or any Act of Congress providing for equal rights of citizens." . . . The latter section was invoked here. From the time when Congress first implemented the Fourteenth Amendment by the comprehensive Civil Rights Act of 1871 the thought has prevailed that the federal courts are the unique tribunals which are to be utilized to preserve the civil rights of the people. Representative Dawes, in the debate on the 1871 bill, asked "what is the proper method of thus securing the free and undisturbed enjoyment of these rights?" Looking to the Act which eventually became law he answered. "The first remedy proposed by this bill is a resort to the courts of the United States. Is that a proper place in which to find redress for any such wrongs? If there be power to call into the courts of the United States an offender against these rights, privileges and immunities; and hold him to account there, . . . I submit . . . that there is no tribunal so fitted, where equal and exact justice would be more likely to be meted out in temper, in moderation, in severity, if need be but always according to the law and fact, as that great tribunal of the Constitution." . . .

It seems plain to me that it was the District Court's duty to provide this remedy, if the appellees, who invoked that court's jurisdiction under the Civil Rights Act, proved their charge that the appellants, under the color of the Virginia statutes, had deprived them of civil rights secured by the Federal Constitution. . . .

Judge Soper, speaking for the three-judge District Court, said that the five statutes against which the suits were directed "were enacted for the express purpose of impeding the integration of the races in the public schools" of Virginia. . . . He reviewed at length the legislative history of the five Virginia statutes . . . concluding that "they were passed to nullify as far as possible the effect of the decisions" of this Court in Brown v Board of Education. . . . They were indeed "parts of the general plan of massive resistance" which Virginia inaugurated against those decisions. . . .

Of course Virginia courts were not parties to the formulation of that legislative program. But they are interpreters of Virginia laws and bound to construe them, if possible, so that the legislative purpose is not frustrated. Where state laws make such an assault as these do on our decisions and a State has spoken defiantly against the constitutional rights of the citizens, reasons for showing deference to local institutions vanish. The conflict is plain and apparent; and the federal courts stand as the one authoritative body for enforcing the constitutional rights of the citizens.

This Court has had before it other state schemes intended to emasculate constitutional provisions or circumvent our constitutional decisions. In Guinn v. United States, . . . a "Grandfather Clause" in an Oklahoma suffrage statute, exempting citizens who are qualified to vote on January 1, 1866, and their lineal descendants, from the requirements of a literacy test was said to have "no discernible reason other than the purpose to disregard the prohibitions of the [Fifteenth] Amendment," and was struck down because in "direct and positive disregard" of that Amendment. . . . Oklahoma sought to avoid the effects of that decision (rendered in 1959) by requiring all qualified voters in 1916 to register within a named 12-day period, else the right to vote would be lost to them permanently. Persons who voted in the 1914 elections were, however, exempt from the requirement. The new statute was invalidated, this Court noting that the Fifteenth Amendment barred "sophisticated as well as simple-minded" contrivances by a state to thwart equality in the enjoyment of the right to vote." . . . The Boswell Amendment to the Alabama Constitution required prospective voters to understand and explain a section of the Alabama Constitution to the satisfaction of a registrar. A three-judge court found it to be a device in purpose and in practice to perpetuate racial distinctions in regulation of suffrage. We affirmed the judgment without requiring any submission of the amendment to the state courts to see how they might narrow it. . . . All these cases originated in federal courts and implicated state laws evasive of our decisions; and we decided them without rerouting them through the state courts.

A similar history is evidence by the "White Primary" cases. It starts with Nixon v. Herndon . . . where a Texas statute prohibiting Negroes from participating in Democratic Party primary elections was characterized as a "direct and obvious infringement" of the Fourteenth Amendment's Equal Protection Clause. As a result of that decision, the Texas Legislature enacted a new statute authorizing the State Executive Committee of a political party to prescribe the qualifications for voters in its primary elections. Pursuant thereto the Democratic Party Committee adopted a resolution limiting the voting privilege to white Democrats. Finding that the Committee was an arm of the State, and that it discharged its power in such a way as to "discriminate invidiously between white citizens and black" this Court overturned the restriction. [In] Nixon v. Condon . . . we held that approval by the state party convention of the discriminating prohibition did not save it. . . . These cases too originated in federal courts and were aimed at state laws at war with our decisions. Here again, we decided them without making the parties first repair to the state courts for a construction of the state statutes.

We need not—we should not—give deference to a state policy that seeks to undermine paramount federal law. We fail to perform the duty expressly enjoined by Congress on the federal judiciary in the Civil Rights Acts when we do so.

To return to the present case: the error, if any, of the District Court was not in passing on the constitutionality of three of the five Virginia statutes now before us but in remitting the parties to the Virginia courts for a construction of the other two.

[It would be an oversimplification to attribute all of the difficulties in the administration of federal justice to the ideological controversies engendered in decision-making. Although there is little public discussion of it, tension has developed between Congress and the federal judiciary in areas where the former has attempted to instigate operational change. A recent field study of the contemporary operations of the United States courts provides a most comprehensive and perceptive analysis of such problem areas. This study was written as a report for the Senate Appropriations Committee, yet much of it is pertinent to this analysis because it portrays with sensitivity the mode of operation of the federal district courts and highlights a number of areas where judicial authorities have thwarted Congressional desires.]

3. Administrative Causes of Delay*

I. INTRODUCTION

This report summarizes the results of a field study of the operations of the United States courts. The objectives of the study were to obtain firsthand information, by actual review, of the manner in which appropriated funds are being spent and of the conditions existing in the respective courts, including the efficiency with which the Federal courts are being operated, the facts with respect to congested calendars, and the manner in which the judiciary is keeping its own house in order, as well as information and views regarding possible improvements.

There were early indications in the study of a grave lack of administrative direction in the operation of the business of the United States courts, with resultant serious and, in some cases, shocking conditions of delay and neglect of cases on court dockets. For this reason, the study was confined primarily to the operations of the United States district courts and to the functioning of the administrative organization within the judiciary to supervise court business under presently existing laws.

It hardly needs to be stated that under our system of government, the judicial branch, in a very real sense, is as important as the executive and legislative branches. In fact, it is the keystone in our constitutional form of government. The fiscal year 1959 appropriation of $47,813,650 for salaries and expenses of the Federal judiciary was only about one-sixteenth of 1 percent of the total Federal budget, but the importance of the judiciary cannot be measured in terms of money. It is the effectiveness of our system of justice which is the measure of its worth. Inefficiency and poor administration in the operation of the courts not only result in a waste of appropriated funds, but, far more important, have a most adverse effect upon the rights and interests of the public. Litigants who are denied a timely day in court, whether it results from inefficiency and poor administration or from any other cause, not only have their rights compromised but may suffer irreparable financial loss. Although calendar congestion and delay appear to be chronic ailments of many courts, and such conditions are by no means unique to the Federal courts, growing concern has been voiced by the public, the press, bar associations, government officials, and even by judges themselves, as to such delays and congestion, and demands have been made that something be done about it.

The study was initiated September 15, 1958, by attending the Judicial Conference of the United States. In addition to examining budget hearings and the reports of the Administrative Office of the United States Courts for recent years, the operations of the Administrative Office were examined and 23 United States district courts and 6 circuit courts throughout the country were actually visited. The municipal court of the District of Columbia and the headquarters office of the New Jersey State courts system were also visited. Sixty-five district and circuit court judges were interviewed, as well as the clerks of the courts visited and numerous attorneys and others having an interest in the subject matter.

*Paul Cotter, "Field Study of the Operations of the United States Courts," *Report to Senate Appropriations Committee* (Washington, D.C., Committee Print, 1959), pp. 1–5, 16–29.

The United States districts visited were: The northern and southern districts of California; Connecticut; Delaware; the District of Columbia; the southern district of Florida; the northern district of Illinois; the eastern district of Louisiana; Maryland; Massachusetts; the eastern district of Michigan; Nevada; New Jersey; the eastern and southern districts of New York; the northern district of Ohio; Oregon; the eastern and western districts of Pennsylvania; the eastern district of South Carolina; the western district of Tennessee; and the northern and southern districts of Texas.

Excellent cooperation was received from the judges and from the personnel of the Administrative Office and the various courts visited. It was this cooperation and the advice and information which was so willingly given that made the survey possible. It should be quite apparent that the limitations of time prohibited more than an overall sampling of the conditions and operations of the courts, and that the study necessarily had to be restricted to the major problems involved.

II. SUMMARY OF OVERALL REACTIONS

A district-by-district field study of the operations of the United States courts breeds a deep respect for the principles of our system of justice and real admiration for the judges of our Federal courts. Nowhere else in the world can be found a judicial system in which the judges are responsible for decisions relating to such a wide range of subject matter both in equity and in law, some encompassing fantastically complicated issues. Generally speaking, nowhere else can one interview a group so consistently capable, responsible, and dedicated. The conclusion is inescapable that the task of the Federal judge, if properly carried out, is a most difficult one, requiring not only great ability, objectivity, patience, perseverance, and the proper background of experience, but a strong constitution and long hours of hard work. And, for the most part, the judges of the Federal judiciary meet these standards. This needs to be emphasized in order to place in proper context what must be said regarding the serious administrative deficiencies and other conditions found to exist in the system and which contribute so greatly to court congestion and delay. Were it not for the high degree of individual responsibility on the part of a large majority of the judges, it might appear that the condition of our courts would be in a bad state indeed. Even so, much remains to be desired in the administration of the system.

In some of the courts having the worst conditions of delay and calendar congestion, this was found to be due not to an unduly heavy caseload, but almost solely to poor administration. Striking variations in the degree of efficiency in handling court business were found to exist in the respective courts and there was a minimum of exchange of intelligence between the courts as to procedures employed in effectively disposing of the workload. Some courts are doing a superlative job while others are hopelessly enmeshed in outmoded, inadequate, and, at times, amateurish and most unbusinesslike practices and procedures. There is no system of indoctrination, and it appears to follow that the judges of numerous courts are limited by their personal experience and by the procedures already employed by their particular court in solving common problems of court administration which in other courts have been found easily susceptible of solution. There is a great tendency to continue practices and procedures long outmoded and to resist change. In some courts, inertia and complacency predominate.

In sharp contrast to the judges who are working exhaustively for improvement in the operation of the whole court system, a larger percentage of the judges appear to view their responsibilities as limited to their own court and even to the particular calendar or cases to which they have been assigned. Many judges feel that within the scope of their judicial autonomy no one can or should give them administrative direction with respect to the business with which they may be charged. They feel that such administrative control is an impingement upon their judicial autonomy and would impair the freedom and independence which should surround their conduct of the court's business. In some judges, this attitude amounts almost to a phobia against any type of administrative supervision, which they term "regimentation." They appear to overlook entirely the fact that the decisions which they do render are subject to review and reversal by a higher court and that any workable system would require some supervision over cases which might be neglected or on which no action is being taken. They also appear to overlook the fact that existing law requires the judicial council of each circuit to take cognizance of the condition of the district court dockets and to make necessary orders for the effective and expeditious administration of the business of the courts within its circuit.

Independence and autonomy are not only proper with respect to the judicial area, but have contributed immensely to the success of the system. However, when these elements are extended to matters purely administrative, coupled with life tenure and the fact that the commissions of all judges are, for practical purposes, identical, the function of court administration is rendered exceedingly difficult. There is a high degree of disagreement between the judges as to procedures and methods, the majority having fiercely opinionated convictions as to how the work should be done and feeling their own way to be the best. It may be a natural consequence that the judiciary's system of self-government, through the Judicial Conference of the United States, the circuit judicial councils and conferences, and the operational setup of the district courts, has been tortuously slow and inadequate in bringing about reforms and improvements to meet changing times and conditions. There is a very serious lack of administrative control and direction throughout the whole system. The smaller courts (in number of judges) appear not to be as adversely affected by this lack as are the larger metropolitan area courts, where the identity and activity of the individual judges tend to be merged in the overall operations of the court. It is especially in these larger courts that better administration must be installed if there is to be improvement in the system.

There is great divergence of views as to the relative merits of the two types of calendar systems employed—the individual and the central calendars. Roughly one-half of the larger multiple-judge courts employ one system and the rest the other. Both systems have definite advantages and weaknesses. The central system requires infinitely greater administrative control, which, in most of the courts visited, was found to be lacking. Either system lacks effectiveness if pretrial conferences and other procedures for expeditious disposal of the caseload are not employed and unless there is equalization of the workload and full utilization of the judgepower.

The facts suggest that there is a serious question as to whether the chief judges of the district courts have the proper tools or authority to effectively administer the business of the courts, and there is also a question as to whether the responsibility for the administration of such courts should be saddled on the chief judges, who occupy these positions solely on the basis of seniority and, generally, at an advanced age.[1]

The most startling and paradoxical condition found, however, was the general disregard of a 20-year-old law which charges the judicial council of each circuit with the supervision of district court dockets; requires the Administrative Office of the United States Courts to submit to these councils quarterly reports based on examination of the district court dockets; and requires the judicial council of each circuit to take such action thereon as is necessary, and to make all necessary orders for the effective and expeditious administration of the business of the courts within its circuit. The law also requires the district court judges to promptly carry into effect all such orders. The reasons given for the failure to carry this law into effect will be given later in the report, but the end result of the failure is that in numerous district courts cases lie on the dockets for long periods without attention, or, one judge of a particular court may be relatively current in his work while another judge in the same court may be several months behind. In a few courts, the conditions can only be described as shocking. This failure to adequately supervise amounts almost to a complete blind spot in the administration of the courts' business, for only about 10 percent of the cases filed in any Federal district court are ever actually tried, and it is the 90 percent of the caseload which will be settled, abandoned, dismissed, or never reach trial, which causes congested calendars and long delays in those cases which eventually will be tried.

By reason of this failure to supervise district court dockets, the judicial councils of the circuits, and, in turn, the Judicial Conference of the United States, do not have the facts upon which to act. Because the Administrative Office does not make field examinations of the conditions of the dockets of the respective district courts, the statistics compiled—although extensive and informative—do not tell the whole story and, to some extent, are confusing. Information is not marshaled and published as to the manner in which, and the stage at which, cases are terminated; nor is any meaningful information given as to how the judges spend their time. In other words, it is impossible from the statistics furnished to form an opinion as to how effectively a court is operating or whether, when a congested calendar condition prevails or there are long delays, it is the fault of the particular court or judges thereof, some temporary condition, or that there are insufficient judges in that district. Some of the judges are overworked while a minority of the judges appear to do too little. In some instances these conditions exist in the same court. There is also an uneven condition in the workload between respective courts. In several districts, temporary

[1] Since the presentation of Cotter's study, Congress has passed a statute providing for compulsory retirement of chief judges (as chief judges, however, not as court of appeals judges).

assistance from visiting judges could clear up the backlog and eliminate delay. Yet, statistics on the assignment of judges indicate an almost complete lack of organization of judicial manpower to deal effectively with the problems of calendar congestion and delay in courts needing such assistance.

* * *

Of the courts visited, there was a marked variance in the attitude which the judges had toward the cases pending on the dockets. Some judges and courts took charge of the cases as soon as they were filed, and, by periodic calendar calls, pretrial conferences, and various other methods, brought about a timely disposition of the cases by trial, settlement, or dismissal. Other courts took the position that it was up to the attorneys to decide when they wished a trial; that the court was available if and when; and that the running of time would take care of many of the problems presented. The majority of the courts visited appeared to take something of a middle course.

Without exception, however, the courts which maintained tight calendar control and which were in command of the cases from the time of filing until disposition, were the courts with the good records. On the other hand, courts which showed undue deference to the bar; where procedures for the orderly and timely processing of the cases to conclusion were absent; or where complacency prevailed, invariably had records of long delay in litigation and congested calendars. It also generally followed that in these courts with poor direction and control, the costs of the jury system and the whole operation were substantially higher.

A. TECHNIQUES OF DISTRICT COURT DOCKET MANAGEMENT

The methods employed to bring about the timely preparation and disposition of cases were not found to be unique to a particular court, region, or type of case. Although such methods may require minor adaptation to fit the conditions of a particular district and the composition of its caseload, the key to effective court administration, particularly in the handling of large caseloads, regardless of the calendar system employed, was found to be the positive management of cases on the docket from the time they are filed until they are disposed of. Generally, lawyers are prone to procrastinate and many cases would remain on the dockets indefinitely if procedures and rules were not put into effect to force, with reasonable firmness, cases to trial, settlement, or other disposition.

As completely distinguished from the standard Federal procedural rules of civil and criminal practice, each of the United States district courts has its own set of local rules governing the management of the business of that particular court. In the courts visited, these rules varied greatly from district to district. But, again, at the risk of over-simplification, there appeared to be a few rules and principles and procedures in the management of cases in district courts which, when taken together and properly put into effect, would not only result in the efficient disposition of the cases but are essential to this end. These are as follows:

(1) A system whereby cases, once filed, are reviewed periodically to assure that they are progressing normally toward trial or other disposition. Practically all of the

courts visited had local rules with this objective in mind, but these rules not only varied greatly from court to court, but there was even greater variance in the manner in which they were enforced.

After a case is filed, an appropriate time must elapse for the answer to be filed and issue joined. While this is governed by standard rules of procedure, the time period between filing and issue can vary considerably, depending upon the type of action, its degree of complexity, the number of preliminary motions, etc.

Once issue is joined, the case may automatically be placed on a trial calendar, a reserve calendar, or a pretrial calendar, depending upon the rules in effect in the particular court. On the other hand, many of the courts visited employed, with variations, a rule which required a certificate, signed by counsel for all parties in the case, stating that issue had been joined and the case was ready for trial, before the case could be advanced from the docket to a trial calendar.

Some courts review their pending cases almost continuously, or at frequent periods, whether or not they are on the docket or have progressed to a trial calendar. This is frequently done by a calendar call at which time the judge ascertains from the attorneys the nature and present status of the case. He may also issue instructions regarding the timing and preparation for trial and may explore the possibilities of settlement.

Most courts have a rule to the effect that if no action has been taken on a case within a given period, it will automatically be dismissed, unless good cause is shown as to why it should not be. Generally, these rules apply to both those cases which are on the docket and those which have progressed to a trial calendar. These rules vary in the different courts, allowing periods of inactivity ranging from 3 months to 2 years. Generally, this screening of the inactive cases is done by the clerk of court, but to show cause why the case should not be dismissed, counsel must come before a judge. There is a great variance in the efficiency of this screening process in the different courts and, even more important, in the attitude of the judges in dealing with these slow-moving cases. It is obvious that it is quite as important to nudge along a case which has been lying dormant, whether it is on the docket or on a trial calendar, if timely disposition is to be made of it. It is also apparent that if the local rule of the court permits a case to lie dormant on the docket for a period of 2 years without any action being taken, as, for example, in the southern district of New York and the eastern district of Pennsylvania, there can be an accumulation of cases which do not get timely disposition. It is equally apparent that where the rule calls for dismissal after 6 months or a year, if the rule is not enforced (a condition which was found in a number of courts), the same result will obtain. It also appeared that in a number of courts the screening of cases was so mechanical that the filing of one motion within the time period of the rule would meet the requirements and the case could remain pending almost indefinitely on the docket.

(2) A system whereby motions and other preliminary matters arising in connection with the cases on the court dockets can be heard and disposed of with dispatch, giving all parties fair consideration, and yet keeping such ancillary matters within reasonable bounds.

Apart from the trial of cases, there is a whole field of practice before the courts which can be most time consuming. It arises on motions for hearings on points of law, and in connection with such pretrial procedures as interrogatories, depositions, inspections, examinations, etc. An adroit counsel in a court which does not have good coordination, firmness, and control, can frequently prolong proceedings of an action for months, or even years, by the use of plausible motions, continuances, etc. It would appear that the practices employed in some courts lend themselves to such delays, while at the same time, too much of the time of the judges is taken up with these matters. While the principles of the modern rules of Federal procedure promote the free use of pretrial procedures to give the parties on both sides of an action all pertinent information in the interest of preventing surprise and making for a fairer trial, it was indicated that the courts and judges with the best records for efficiency have little difficulty in keeping these preliminary proceedings within reasonable bounds and a particular time limit, with apparent satisfaction to all parties. However, this cannot be said of numerous of the courts visited.

In some of the courts, all motions were submitted and decided on briefs, and rarely were oral arguments heard. In these district courts it was stated that motions took up very little time. In other districts, the judges received briefs on many of the motions but also heard oral arguments from counsel before ruling. In these latter courts it was contended, with considerable logic, that full justice could not be done without a more complete discussion and the give and take of oral arguments. In many of the courts, briefs are rarely required for such preliminary motions and only upon request of the judge.

In some central calendar courts, the judge, after sitting 2 weeks in the motions part is given 2 weeks to complete the writing of his opinions on matters which he has heard (e.g., southern district, New York). In other courts (e.g., eastern district, New York), they are given a month. In the District of Columbia, the judge who sits in the motions part upon completion of his assignment is rotated directly to another part and is presumed to write whatever opinions are necessary on the matters he has heard as he goes along. A number of the judges interviewed indicated that they rule on all but a very small percentage of the motions they hear from the bench immediately after arguments are heard, but that, in all complicated matters, this requires considerable advance preparation, frequently after hours, so they will be familiar with the cases and the issues involved prior to the hearing.

In some courts, the impression was received that insufficient time and attention were given to preliminary hearings and pretrial matters. In other courts, some of the judges reportedly held matters which they had already heard for an unduly long time before handing down a decision. In the majority of the courts visited, it appeared much could be done by way of improving techniques respecting the handling of motions and preliminary pretrial procedures in more expeditiously bringing the cases on the docket and calendars to an orderly state of preparation for trial.

(3) The employment of more uniform use of the pretrial conference and the techniques which have been developed in connection therewith, particularly the requiring of counsel to prepare their cases, exchange evidence, consult with each other, discuss settlement, and otherwise face the realities of their cases prior to

appearing at such conferences. The use of these techniques has demonstrated so clearly their value in the expeditious preparation, trial, and disposition of cases on court dockets that there is little excuse for their not being employed more universally throughout the Federal court system. If the judiciary, through its own machinery, does not require more general use of such procedure, consideration should be given to making its use mandatory by statute. Due to its importance, the pretrial conference will be treated separately later in this report.

(4) The employment of calendar systems and calendar practices which will not only bring about the trial and disposition of cases with efficiency, but which will do so in such a manner as to place the least possible burden and expense upon litigants and their counsel, as well as upon the jurors who are called to serve under our system of justice. This will also be discussed under a separate subsection below.

(5) The installation and use of a statistical system which will reflect not only the volume and types of business in the respective courts, the accomplishments and backlogs, and cases which may not be receiving proper attention, but also how the individual judges are spending their time. The value of adequate statistics as a tool of administration is so important that this subject will be treated separately later in the report under "The Administrative Office and Meaningful Statistics."

In addition to rules, procedures, or techniques for the operation of the district courts, there is need for a system which will provide supervision, when required, by the circuit judicial councils, assistance when problems arise in a particular court through the assignment of judges from other courts, and cohesion and integration of the whole system through the judicial councils and judicial conferences of the respective circuits and the judicial Conference of the United States. These processes were so lacking in the system that they will also be treated later in this report.

It should be stated, here, however, that the techniques of management of the business of the United States district courts vary so greatly in efficiency from court to court that general improvement will only come (1) by analysis of the administrative deficiencies of the courts where the problems occur, (2) by supplying those courts with the techniques of courts which have successfully solved such problems, and (3) by example, through the assignment of judges who have proved the effectiveness of such techniques for temporary duty in those courts needing improvement.

B. THE PRETRIAL CONFERENCE

The pretrial conference and the techniques employed in connection therewith were widely cited as the greatest single advance of modern times in the handling of the business of the courts. Rule 16 of the Federal Rules of Civil Procedure (Title 28, United States Code) provides:

> In any action the court may in its discretion direct the attorneys for the parties to appear before it for a conference to consider (1) the simplification of the issue, (2) the necessity or desirability of amendments to the pleadings, (3) the possibility of obtaining admissions of fact and of documents which will avoid unnecessary proof, (4) the limitation of the number of expert witnesses, (5)

the advisability of a preliminary reference of issues to a master for findings to be used as evidence when the trial is to be by jury, (6) such other matters as may aid in the disposition of the action.

It further provides:

The court shall make an order which recites the action taken at the conference . . . and such order when entered controls the subsequent course of the action, unless modified at the trial to prevent manifest injustice.

In other words, the pretrial conference is a method of sifting the issues and reducing the delays and expense of trials so that a suit will go to trial only on questions as to which there is an honest dispute of law and fact. It is contended that when efficienctly used, it not only contributes to the efficiency of the administration of justice, but saves time and expense and eliminates unnecessary attendance and long waits of witnesses, in addition to accelerating trial. While the primary object of the pretrial conference is not the settlement of cases, it has long been recognized that when properly conducted, settlement is an important byproduct and often the logical result of pretrial.

As is true of other methods and procedures, there is great divergence of views among the judges as to the value of pretrial—some use it in all civil cases, some do not use it at all. It will be noted that the use of the procedure is made optional, but, apparently, rule 16 requires that if a pretrial conference is held, "The court shall make an order which recites the action taken at the conference," etc.

Some of the judges interviewed felt that the employment of the pretrial conference not only enabled them to dispose of the caseload they do, but resulted in an improved quality of justice. Other judges felt it was mostly a waste of not only their time but the time of counsel, particularly in the simpler type of cases. They contended that they could call counsel to the bench just before trial and accomplish whatever was necessary by way of stipulations, simplification of the issues, etc., and thus avoid a separate conference. Numerous judges who use the pretrial conference extensively do not hesitate to advise counsel for both parties what they feel the case is worth based upon the facts presented at the conference, regardless of whether the case is to be tried by a jury or before the court itself. While they consider that bringing pressure for settlement is reprehensible, they do not resitate to call back the parties for a second and third conference, if there is a possibility of working out an equitable disposition. Other judges will not even discuss settlement with counsel.

In the eastern district of Louisiana, the court which has the largest civil case filings and terminations per judge in the whole system, the pretrial conference is used extensively and effectively and is given much credit for the results this court has obtained. Yet, in the western district of Tennessee, a court which has an excellent record of accomplishment and a short median time between filing and trial, the judge does not employ the pretrial technique or discuss settlement with counsel. Some judges and courts go through a meticulous procedure of covering all facets of the case and write up a somewhat extensive pretrial order. It appeared that some courts, by overformalizing the pretrial conference, have made it unpopular. Some courts have rejected the pretrial conference entirely after a short experience, or they hold only a "settlement conference", making no record of the proceeding. The courts which appeared to be doing the most efficient work, however, make a succinct record or order based on the conference, and in these courts, the conference and order on the average case were accomplished in approximately one-half hour's time.

A number of courts are now employing a type of order in connection with pretrial which requires counsel for the litigants, prior to pretrial to exhaust all discovery; to confer with each other for the purpose of marking all exhibits and documents for identification and to exchange same or permit inspections of the documents; to stipulate in writing the uncontested facts, the issues of fact and law in dispute; to exchange lists of witnesses and copies of medical reports; and to discuss the possibilities of settlement. By requiring these various steps by counsel preparatory to the conference, the court is taking a positive position in bringing about the preparation of the cases and the actual conference not only accomplishes its primary objectives, but the judge can rule on pending motions and otherwise order the completion of the preparation, thus obviating time-consuming separate motions before the court with resultant further delays. This placing of the responsibility on counsel for taking the necessary steps in the preparation of their cases, when properly enforced, makes them face the realities with respect to the merits of their cases and appeared to be one of the most effective devices for attacking the congested calendar. . . . This type of rule is not to be confused with the rule employed by some courts requiring counsel to certify that their cases are ready for trial and that discovery has been completed before the case is placed on the trial calendar. While the latter rule operates to prevent congested calendars and penalizes the litigant whose counsel does not make timely preparation, it is devoid of the elements of positive management for effective disposition of the caseload.

While it was generally contended that the holding of the pretrial conference should not occur too far in advance of the trial date (if the case goes to trial), it is quite obvious, as less than 10 percent of the cases filed go to trial, that by requiring counsel to fully prepare their cases soon after issue is joined and following this up with a pretrial conference, a far greater percentage of the cases will be settled or otherwise disposed of at a much earlier date, with less delay to the litigant and less congestion of the docket.

Success in the use of the pretrial conference reportedly depends upon the ability and personality of the judge and the amount of effort put into it. It was frequently stated that the great divergence of views among the judges as to the value of the pretrial conference was due to a difference in concept as to its objectives. Whatever the reasons, 20 years have elapsed since the rule went into effect and although its use is slowly increasing, it appears that educational methods and persuasion to bring about fuller utilization of pretrial have, to date, fallen far short of success. Were it not for the proven qualities of pretrial processes as an invaluable management technique in the handling of the congested calendar, it might appear that more patience should be given the methods of propaganda and persuasion in bringing about its more universal use. Certainly, where a judge or court is reaching cases on the docket in an expeditious fashion and is staying current with the workload, it would seem of little consequence whether the pretrial conference is used or not. The situation most usually encountered, however, in the districts visited, was congestion and delay in the handling of a workload of relatively moderate proportions and the failure to employ techniques which would correct the situation. Accordingly, it would seem that the only rational course to more effective management of court business is to make the pretrial process, in its most efficient form, mandatory, except in the case where a judge, by order, explicitly decrees otherwise. The result of the experiment presently being conducted in the badly congested eastern district of New York, if it meets expectations, should be further proof of the efficacy of such action.

C. CALENDAR SYSTEMS AND CALENDAR PRACTICES

The calendar, in practice, is recognized generally as one of the most important factors affecting the efficiency of district court operations. It not only permits counsel to follow the progress of their cases toward actual trial, it is the implementation of all the court rules toward this end.

In some of the courts visited this operation of the calendar, the setting of cases for trial, the handling of motions and other preliminary matters, amounted almost to a work of art. In other courts, its operation was little less than chaotic and by following inept and outmoded procedures and by lacking proper control, the resultant inefficiency contributed not only to a waste of the court's time and Government funds, but to a great waste of the time of the counsel practicing before the court, a needless waste of jurors, and generally unsatisfactory conditions.

There are two distinct types of calendar systems employed—the individual and the central or master calendar system. In the individual calendar system, cases are assigned proportionately and by lot to the individual judges of a court as the actions are filed and, thereafter, until their disposition, they become the responsibility of the judge to whom assigned. In the central calendar system, the cases are not assigned to individual judges as they are filed, but are moved up, generally in the order of the date of filing or calendaring, from the docket to a central or master calendar and assigned to the individual judges only shortly before trial. In the central calendar system, particularly in the larger multiple-judge courts, the court, by local rule, is divided into various parts, i.e., the assignment part, the motions part, the criminal part, civil jury, and nonjury, and the judges, generally under a system of rotation, take turns sitting in the various parts. All preliminary motions and other matters arising in a particular case prior to assignment of the case for trial are heard by the judge who is sitting in the motions part, the pretrial part, etc., although this judge will not necessarily be the one who tries the case. Also, several different judges may hear preliminary matters on the same case under the central calendar system. The exception to this is the protracted or highly complicated cases, which, pursuant to recommendation of the Judicial Conference of the United States, and in accordance with the rules of most district courts employing the central calendar system, are assigned to a particular judge at an early stage to permit a continuity of understanding of the many facets of such cases, thus avoiding needless duplication.

168

As can be seen, under the individual calendar system, each judge goes his own way with the caseload assigned to him, while the central calendar system requires coordination and teamwork to a high degree.

One-judge courts, of necessity, are individual calendar courts and many of the smaller multiple-judge courts, particularly in districts where court is held at a number of locations, more readily lend themselves to the individual calendar system. However, a number of the two- and three-judge courts visited employed the central calendar system with success. Of the larger courts visited, Massachusetts, New Jersey, eastern Michigan, northern Illinois, and southern California employ the individual calendar system. The eastern and southern districts of New York, the eastern and western districts of Pennsylvania, northern Ohio, Washington, D.C., and the northern district of California employ the central or master calendar system.

1. Individual Calendar versus Central Calendar System. There is a sharp divergence of opinion among the judges as to the merits and weaknesses of the two systems. One group feels that experience has proven the central calendar system to be the most effective, particularly in the large multiple-judge courts and in the handling of run-of-the-mill cases. On the other hand, proponents of the individual calendar system characterize the central calendar system as a device favoring the indolent judge. While no attempt will be made to resolve these differences, for a better understanding of the operations of the respective courts and their effectiveness in administering the court's business, the advantages and disadvantages with respect to each system will be set forth.

(A) THE INDIVIDUAL CALENDAR SYSTEM. As in a one-judge court, each judge of a multiple-judge court under the individual calendar system knows exactly what his workload is and can employ whatever methods and time he has at his disposal in handling it. It is contended by the proponents of this system that this places the responsibility on each judge for handling an equitable segment of the caseload of the court and gives a competitive incentive to each judge to do his share of the work and stay abreast of the other judges. It permits him to become familiar with all of the cases assigned to him and to work on the whole caseload, assessing the merits of the various cases, narrowing the issues, dismissing cases without merit at an early stage, holding pretrial conferences, etc., and it is contended that even though a case scheduled to be tried is suddenly settled, there is always work to be done in chambers. It is said that lawyers prefer to have the same judge throughout a case for motions and other matters preliminary to the trial, and by the same token, lawyers cannot go shopping around for a judge of their choice under this system. Generally, it is contended that this system makes for greater responsibility and better justice and that in the case of the judge who is not doing his share of the work, this fact soon becomes glaringly apparent.

Some of the disadvantages and weaknesses of the system cited are that it does not make as efficient use of courtrooms, jurors, and supporting personnel of the courts as does the central calendar system, and, in particular, that it does not make as effective use of the judge-power; that each judge of an individual calendar court has his own calendar, calendar calls, motions part, jury panel, etc., which condition is less efficient than under the central system; that each judge is on an island by himself and it is more difficult to employ uniform procedures within the court. Perhaps the most cogent and frequently heard complaint against the individual calendar system was that it too frequently resulted in a very uneven and inequitable condition for the litigants in the courts where employed, as a result of some judges being faster than others in disposing of their share of the cases, yet feeling no responsibility for helping the judge who was behind to catch up with his workload. It was not uncommon to find in the individual calendar courts one judge who was reaching for trial the cases assigned to him within less than a year from the date of filing, while other judges in the same court were as much as 3 or 4 years behind. Examples of the wide range in median times (from filing to disposition of civil cases in which a trial was held, terminated during fiscal year of 1958) between judges of the same court in some of the larger individual calendar courts visited are as follows: In the district of Massachusetts, the median times for the individual judges ranged from 11 months to 40 months; in eastern Michigan, from 9 months to 30.6 months; and in the northern district of Illinois, from 16.6 months to 38.4 months.

The result is that one set of litigants in these courts obtain trials within a relatively short time, while another group in the same court, purely because their cases happened to be assigned to a judge who is slower or less conscientious, or who may have been ill or had a larger number of trials of protracted cases, must wait several years. In only one district court visited (New Jersey) was any uniform practice in effect of making a crash program of the less complicated delinquent cases once a year to clear up the backlog of the judges who may have gotten behind.

In the majority of the individual calendar courts visited, the judges who were relatively current with the caseloads assigned them appeared to feel little or no responsibility for the cases assigned to other judges of the same court who were far behind.

Also, in a number of the individual calendar courts, it appeared to be the practice to load a newly appointed judge with the oldest and the most undesirable and difficult cases screened from the calendars of the other judges.

It should not be too difficult to install a system or practice in these individual calendar courts to correct the gross inequities referred to above, without impairing the desirable features of the system. If the courts where these conditions exist do not themselves undertake to correct them, certainly the judicial councils have the authority to order them to do so. It is difficult to understand why the judicial councils have not already taken action in this regard.

(B) THE CENTRAL CALENDAR SYSTEM. This system apparently is based upon the premise that two or more judges working from a common calendar can dispose of more cases more efficiently than they can by working from separate lists. It is common knowledge that the imminence of trial is the most forceful influence in inducing the settlement of cases. It is contended that where the judges of a court work as a team, with one of the judges handling the calendar and assigning the cases out to the others for trial, a steady stream of cases can be sent to the judges available for the trial of cases; that in the event of settlement as a case is reached for trial, another case can be sent out to the judge immediately without loss of time;

that the system is limited only to the number of judges, courtrooms, and lawyers available, and that it will follow that not only more cases will be tried but that more settlements will occur.

In practice, however, it was found that in only a minor percentage of the courts using the central calendar system was there even a close approach to the ideal. It appeared that this resulted from a lack of coordination and direction which rules alone could not supply. Also, as previously pointed out, there is much more to the operation of a court than the mere trial of cases, and the management of the cases prior to reaching trial and the manner of handling pretrial procedures, motions for continuance, etc., appeared quite as important in the measure of efficiency of a particular court as the conduct of trials.

It was contended that as the judges of the central calendar system have no individual responsibility for a proportionate segment of the caseload (or, for that matter, for any cases until they are assigned them), it is easier for the indolent or less conscientious judge to do less than his share, thus substantially lowering the production of the court as a whole, without being held individually responsible for the increased backlog, as would be the case under the individual calendar system. In a number of the central calendar courts visited, there were strong indications that such conditions existed. Some courts reportedly had changed from the central calendar system to the individual calendar system because one or more of the judges weren't carrying their share of the load and the other judges had tired of it.

It was also contended that under the rotation system employed in the central calendar courts, a judge who is not too effective, for example, in pretrial work, in the assignment part, or in some other key position of the court operation, can adversely affect the work of the whole court.

Another problem in the central calendar courts, which have numerous protracted and complicated cases, is that if these cases are assigned at an early stage to individual judges and become their sole responsibility, as is recommended, and if the respective judges of a court are assigned many cases of this type, they frequently will not be available to assist in the operation of the central calendar, to the serious detriment of its efficiency. Most of the chief judges attempt to assign individually as few of these cases as possible so that this will not happen, but some cases are so complicated that they just do not adapt to the central calendar system. There were examples cited in some central calendar courts where as many as 18 different judges had passed on motions or some other proceedings of a single case.

In the southern district of New York, where the problem of the complicated case exists to a high degree, a system was considered whereby the court would concentrate on its more complicated cases during one period and on the run-of-the-mill cases through the central calendar system at another time, but apparently this has never been carried into effect.

Of the larger central calendar courts visited, the District Court of the District of Columbia was one of the most impressive in its operation of the calendar and the effective progression of cases to trial or other disposition. It has employed a compulsory pretrial rule almost since the new rules of civil procedure went into effect. The pretrial conference is used not only for its primary objectives, but as a means of requiring counsel to prepare their cases, exchange evidence, and consult with each other prior to the conference. The conference itself tends to gather in the loose ends and bring about the completion of the remaining preliminary proceedings. This court employs a calendar call of all cases which are at issue, but a case gets only one call. The objectives of the call are to screen out cases which do not belong in that court, to determine the status of the cases, to encourage the filing of certificates of readiness for trial, and to effect settlements if there is a disposition in that direction. However, if a case has not been certified as ready prior to or at the time of the calendar call, the responsibility is placed upon counsel, by local rule, to complete preparation and certification of readiness within 6 months, otherwise the case will be dismissed, unless good cause is shown as to why it should not be. Further, in this court it is necessary for counsel to get permission of the court for a continuance, as contrasted with many courts which permit continuance by consent of counsel of both parties or with the permission of the clerk of court or the calendar commissioner. When the cases were reached for trial in court, it appeared that they were assigned to the judges in the trial parts in a constant flow without calendar breakdown or delays between the termination or settlement of one case and the beginning of the next one, and that this was accomplished with a minimum of waiting on the part of lawyers, litigants, and witnesses. There also appeared to be good coordination between the motions part, the pretrial part, the calendar call, and the assignment part, with the court working as a coordinated team. It would be well for some of the larger central calendar courts to adopt and put into effect certain of the techniques employed by this court.

The general reaction to the central calendar operation, particularly with respect to the larger courts, was that a better administrative system would have to be devised if it is ever to be fully effective. Administrative direction in the district courts will be taken up later in the report.

2. Lenient Attitude toward Continuances. A common problem in many district courts having calendar congestion is that the bulk of civil practice consists of negligence cases which are handled by a few lawyers or law firms. This appeared to apply equally to plaintiff as well as defense counsel and the same counsel handle the bulk of the same type of cases in the corresponding State courts. This creates a situation where relatively few counsel have a large percentage of the cases on the civil calendars and are continually seeking continuances on the basis of being engaged in other cases before other courts and judges, thus creating bottlenecks. Some of the courts, such as the districts of eastern Louisiana and Maryland, apparently have been successful in minimizing this problem by settling pretrial conferences and trials for specific dates well in advance and closely adhering to the schedule. A few courts have promulgated rules which tend to force lawyers or firms with an excessive number of cases on the docket to employ more trial counsel. The District Court for the District of Columbia has such a rule and a copy of it is attached as exhibit 2.

While continuances in all types of cases for good cause are, at times, necessary, this practice in some courts appeared to have been badly abused by counsel who use it as an instrument of delay.

172

As previously indicated, there is great discrepancy between the attitudes of different courts and individual judges in the whole management of the cases on the docket and calendars, and the granting of continuances has a most serious effect upon delay and congestion, as well as upon the efficiency of the operation of a court. All judges desire the respect of the bar which practices before the court. Some judges appear to be able to maintain this respect while at the same time being reasonably firm and requiring cases on their calendars to be promptly prepared and tried. It would appear that others, in an effort to maintain the good will of the counsel who frequently appear before them do so by being unnecessarily lenient toward requests for continuances and deferments at the expense of the litigants and the timely disposal of cases. In this regard, the eastern district of New York might be cited as a prime example of a court where the bar had almost gotten out of hand, but there are a number of other courts and judges that appeared to be entirely too lenient in the matter of granting continuances. Some courts grant continuances almost automatically. It would appear that within the self-governing system of the judiciary, orders and procedures could easily be put into effect to deter excesses in the matter of granting continuances to the substantial improvement of the operation of many courts.

3. Excessive Jurors and Excessive Costs. Perhaps one of the most concrete examples of how an abuse of administrative autonomy can result in a waste of appropriated dollars and a serious imposition upon persons called to serve on juries, is the practice engaged in by many judges of requiring an excessive number of jurors to their needs and calling them on days when there are no jury trials.

While jury costs vary from district to district, depending upon the conditions prevailing with respect to the distance jurors must travel, the type of cases tried, etc.; while it is always necessary to call more jurors than will ever be needed and challenged; while larger jury panels are needed in criminal cases than in civil; and while in a few outstanding criminal or other cases it is necessary to call large numbers of jurors, generally these conditions are known in advance and can easily be provided for within a reasonable margin. It is reported that for the past several years an average of six jurors per jury trial have been challenged.

However, particular courts habitually call far in excess of the number of jurors ever needed. In numerous courts, when inquiry was made of the clerks as to why more efficient use was not made of jurors, the usual reply was that the judges insisted upon larger panels being summoned than were ever used. It was also admitted in a number of instances that the judges keep jury panels waiting around regardless of whether or not a trial is imminent. Some judges reportedly feel that their time is sufficiently important that they should have jury panels waiting and available in the prospect of a jury trial, while others feel that the presence of a waiting jury panel has a psychological effect in obtaining settlements just prior to trial. Generally speaking, however, it appeared to follow that the courts which lack good administrative direction and calendar control also had a poor record in the utilization of jurors.

An effective method employed to improve the utilization of jurors is the jury pool, in which the jurors for a multiple-judge court are assembled in one group and when a jury has been selected, those not used return to the pool for another assignment. Reportedly, there are 20 courts in the system which use the jury pool, but, paradoxically, some of the courts which have the worst records of juror utilization in the whole system (e.g., southern district of New York) employ a "pool." However, it appeared that in the case of New York, the "pool" was used as little more than an original gathering place and that not only was each judge drawing an excessive number of jurors from which to select a jury, but that excessive numbers of jurors were being held in reserve.

(A) FISCAL 1958 JURY COSTS. In fiscal year 1958, petit juror costs for the 86 districts amounted to $3,127,982.33. According to computations of the Administrative Office of the United States Courts, 5,124 jury trials were conducted (3,203 civil and 1,921 criminal) at a cost per jury trial of $610.45. Jury trials averaged 2.3 days in length, thus making the average petit jury costs per trial day $270.55. Jurors received reimbursement for 300,002 juror days, but actually served on only 168,287 days. In addition, jurors who were challenged and did not serve were paid for 29,628 juror days, which left 102,087 juror days on which jurors were called and paid but were not used. As the average petit juror per diem cost is approximately $10, including travel and subsistence allowance, over $1 million, or about one-third of the amount appropriated for the petit juror system, was paid to jurors who were called but neither challenged nor used. When it is considered that the courts with the good records for juror utilization, as well as those with the poor records, go into the making up of these averages, it can readily be seen that the waste of appropriations and the needless inconvenience to prospective jurors called reach shocking proportions in the courts with the poorest records of juror utilization. For example, from information obtained for fiscal year 1958 regarding jury costs for particular districts, it appeared that in the southern district of New York, which had one of the worst records in the system for juror utilization, total costs for petit jurors reportedly amounted to $289,792.93, of which 58.8 percent, or $170,398.24, represented payments to prospective jurors called but not used, while but 41.2 percent, or $119,394.69, was the amount paid jurors who actually served or were challenged. It further appeared that the petit juror cost per day per jury trial for the southern district of New York was $308.61 and for the northern district of Illinois, $301.72, while in the district of Maryland it amounted to but $138.57.

(B) ADMINISTRATIVE OFFICE STUDIES ON THE COSTS OF THE JURY SYSTEM. For the past 6 years, the Administrative Office of the United States Courts has conducted an annual study of the costs of operating the jury system. This study reflects, by district, the average panel called the first day of trial; the number of trials; the number of days on which panels were called and not used; the number of jurors present, broken down by the number serving or challenged and the number in reserve; the percentage of jurors serving or challenged; and the percentage serving or challenged of the jurors called for the first day of trial. The study points out that during fiscal 1958 there were 1,083 panels, aggregating 38,070 jurors, summoned and not used and that, in addition to the inconvenience to these prospective jurors, the cost to the United States was in excess of $380,000. This highly significant report, . . . pointed out that the figure in the last column of the schedule reflecting utilization in the respective courts by the percentage of jurors serving or challenged of the number called for the first day of trial is the most reliable for comparative purposes. In pointing out the great disparity which exists among the district courts in the handling of jurors, the report stated that the percentage of jurors used on the first day of trial ranged from a high of 83.9 percent in the court with the best record to a low of 18 percent in the court with the poorest record.

It is indicated that this report, and the previous one, at the direction of the Judicial Conference, have been circulated to the circuit and district judges and the clerks of district courts for the purpose of calling attention to those courts where jury costs appear to be excessive, as well as to the districts where an efficient system of jury operations has held down the costs. It is astonishing to note, however, that with few exceptions, the courts with the poor records of jury utilization have continued to maintain such records, and there has been little improvement in the overall conditions since these studies were begun.

In the face of such seeming indifference not only to a serious waste of appropriated funds but to a great imposition upon prospective jurors who are called but not used, it is suggested that the Congress consider the substantial curtailment of the appropriations for the petit jury system in order to require the courts, where indicated, to install and practice an improved system of juror utilization.

[In the contemporary era public debate has been focused not only upon the external manifestations of judicial work but also upon its internal operations. The foregoing critique emphasized primarily trial court problems. Because appellate court work is by nature the product of a group of judges rather than a single individual, a good deal of the modern controversy over the work of the courts has generally been directed to the appellate rather than the trial court level. The following article by Laurance M. Hyde is a summary of a study of appellate decision-making by a committee of the Section of Judicial Administration of the American Bar Association.]

D. DECISION-MAKING PROCEDURES IN
APPELLATE COURTS

1. An Appraisal*

Methods of work of appellate courts have often been described and discussed in bar association reports and in articles in bar journals and law reviews. These methods are not and should not be considered secret or confidential, although, of course, anything concerning any submitted case is very much so. In 1927, Hon.

* Laurance M. Hyde, "Appellate Court Decisions," *American Bar Association Journal,* XXVIII (December, 1942), 808–12. Reproduced with permission of the author and the publisher. Copyright (1942) by the American Bar Association.

Charles Evans Hughes, after his first service on the United States Supreme Court and before he became Chief Justice, delivered a series of lectures at Columbia University, in which he fully and clearly described in detail the Court's method of work. These have since been published in a book entitled, *The Supreme Court of the United States.*

In 1924 the American Judicature Society circulated a questionnaire, "Concerning Methods of Work in Supreme Courts." It then said: "We desire to make it clear that there is no implied criticism of the courts in any of these questions. Our object is not to criticize, but to co-operate. The integrity, industry, and ability of the supreme courts are not in question. The only question is whether the experience and practice of certain courts may not be helpful to other courts. . . . We attempted to have the broadest possible basis for our report by preparing a questionnaire and sending it to every appellate judge in the United States. We also sent copies of our questionnaires to the presidents of all bar associations represented in the House of Delegates so that they would have information as to the study we were making."

THE MATTER OF ONE-MAN OPINIONS

The principal reason for having appellate courts is to review decisions made by one man (the trial judge; on his rulings in law cases, on his decision of the whole case in equity) so that a final decision may be made which is the joint product of all of the minds of all of its judges. The term "one-man opinion," is a somewhat overworked and misconstrued expression. There is certainly a distinction to be made between one-man opinions and one-man decisions. In one sense, almost every opinion is and properly should be a one-man opinion because it is usually written in the language and method of expression of the author. Surely such individuality and originality makes for progress in the law as in anything else. The style and unusual manner of statement of such judges as Holmes and Cardozo (and many others) have been of highest value, greatly enriching the literature of the law. Criticism of one-man opinions should not be carried so far as to hinder such individuality of expression. Our study indicates much collaboration and co-operation in all courts, especially on the close and difficult questions. Nevertheless, certain methods have been found by experience to work well to bring about consideration of the views of all participating judges without unreasonable expenditure of judicial time, and to be important safeguards to make decisions a joint product.

REASONS FOR DIFFERENCES IN METHODS OF APPELLATE COURTS

It is apparent that appellate courts have two important problems: first, to decide cases correctly; second, to get the work done. Everyone will agree that the first is the most important. However, even a correct decision may not do the parties any good unless it comes in time. Therefore, an appellate court with a heavy case load per member must necessarily place the emphasis on quantity of work, and use methods which will get its work done so that it will not get behind with its docket. An appellate court which is up with its docket and has a light annual load of new cases can place more emphasis on quality and exactness of statement. Undoubtedly, overloading of work must necessarily tend toward one-man decisions, because of lack of time for consultation without getting behind with the court's work. Unquestionably, also, better opinions will be produced if the ideas and work of the author can be tested and tempered by the criticism and consultation of his associates. Thus each appellate court is constantly compelled to consider whether more time can be given to perfection of its product or whether its volume of work requires more emphasis to be placed on prompt preparation of opinions.

Another important factor, in the determination of methods to be used, is whether the court must travel from place to place to hold its sessions, or whether it has only one fixed permanent place where it always sits. Even if all sessions are at one place, methods must be different if the judges do not live there, but come together there only once or twice each month. These different situations explain to some extent the different methods of the courts, especially in such matters as formal conferences with tentative written opinions by all members before assignments, collaboration between members in preparing opinions, and holding conferences for adoption of opinions. Obviously, judges who all live in the same town and work daily in offices in the same building have more opportunities for informal conference and co-operation than those who do their work widely separated from each other. These factors must be taken into account in considering differences in methods used. Methods which work well where the judges are constantly together might not work at all where they are widely separated.

Tenure of judges is another matter that has much influence on methods. Where tenure is secure, so that judges may be sure that appellate work will be a life career, they can have time to study and utilize the best appellate methods. However, where the turnover of personnel is frequent, as is unually true in states closely divided politically if judges are elected on party tickets, judges are not likely to stay on the bench long enough to study and perfect appellate methods. To do the best judicial work, or even to learn the best methods for doing it, requires years of work and experience. Many judges do good work from the beginning of their service, but, as in any other work, all will learn to do better work in the hard school of experience. There is a vast waste of judicial talent in many of our states by turning men out of judicial office about as soon as they have begun to learn how to best do the job. This situation is perhaps the greatest of all handicaps to adoption of the best appellate methods.

METHODS FOR MAKING ORAL ARGUMENT MORE EFFECTIVE

Modern science and invention, giving us the power-operated printing press, supplemented by the shorthand method of taking dictation, the typewriter and the dictaphone, have made it practicable and easy to present arguments and authorities in printed form, which may be read and studied in chambers in connection with the trial record. Surely the system developed in this country of printed briefs is a great advance in appellate methods. However, presentation of the case by printed briefs has some weaknesses. It tends to encourage (or at least permits) the appellant to raise too many contentions. Too often an attorney, in preparing a great many points, does not think anything through and fails to make a clear presentation of the really important matters. In print every issue has the appearance of equal importance. Arbitrary limitations on the length of briefs (by rules) are unsatisfactory. Therefore, oral argument can aid to make matters stand out in the true light of their importance. Questions by the court can perform a most important function here. Thus the oral argument has not outlived its usefulness, but when properly used can be most helpful.

The use of printed briefs does also make it possible for members of the court to know something about the facts, issues and principles of law involved before the oral argument. Certainly judges who have examined briefs and records before the case is heard can better follow the oral argument and cause it to be concentrated upon the issues concerning which the court feels the need for information. A mere oration about the case cannot aid the court very much in deciding it. Real information about the facts and the issues is very helpful. Only the judges can know the matters about which they are in doubt, and they do know this much better if they have made a study of the case prior to the argument. If, by prior study, they can think of and ask questions about matters which the attorneys might not present, then the attorneys are given an opportunity to state their views on propositions which the judges would otherwise decide solely from their own research after the argument has ended. However, we have found a definite conflict of views about the advisability of such prior investigation. It is stated that a prior study would cause the judges to have preconceived notions about the merits of the case before they heard the argument, so that they would not hear the case with completely open minds. Those who take this view say it is fairer to litigants, and their counsel, for judges to get their first information about facts and issues from counsel's oral statements. Surely, however, qualified judges do not finally decide close complicated cases under either method until they have considered and carefully studied every viewpoint of which they can think themselves or have brought to their attention by others.

METHODS USED IN PREPARATION OF OPINIONS

The most complete method, for insuring full investigation and consideration of every participating judge, undoubtedly is that described by Chief Justice Hughes as used in the United States Supreme Court. We have found that it is used in a number of state supreme and intermediate appellate courts. It is also used in a modified form (with three members sitting in each case) in most of the United States circuit courts of appeals. (The methods used in the Eighth and Tenth Circuits are thus described.)

The unit of work is one week during which the same three judges usually sit together. (1) At the end of each day, there is an informal discussion of the cases heard that day. This discussion has two purposes: First, to ascertain if the decision in any case is so clear that it needs no further consideration (which rarely occurs); and, second, to fix the oral argument in the minds of the judges. (2) Next each judge independently investigates each case—reading the record and briefs—and prepares a written memorandum thereon. (3) When all three judges have prepared such memoranda, a conference is held. At this conference, each case is taken up, memoranda of the judges therein are read and there is a full discussion as to how each case shall be decided and as to the grounds for each decision. (4) The cases are then, for the first time, assigned for opinions; so as to equalize the work in writing the opinions, assignments of particular cases are made to the judge who seems to have the best and clearest grasp of a particular case (as shown by his memorandum and discussion during conference) or by his experience in that class of litigation. When the cases are assigned for opinions, the judges exchange the above conference memoranda. Thus, when a judge starts to prepare an opinion he has available his own memoranda, his notes made at conference, and the memoranda of the two other judges which they worked out before and had at the conference. With these aids, he can form the opinion along the lines of thought of all of the three judges and of the discussion at the conference. When an opinion is prepared, it is sent to the two other judges for suggestions and criticisms. The purpose of this method is to secure the independent thought and investigation of each judge. Memoranda are usually quite complete and frequently are extended discussion of every point in the case necessary to be decided. Thus, when the three judges gather for conference, each is thoroughly informed and prepared on each case and, therefore, can discuss it intelligently and fully. The result is that every decision is the product of three minds which have investigated *separately,* and thereafter, have considered *together* every point presented by counsel.

PERSONNEL—METHODS FOR MOST EFFICIENT UTILIZATION

The matter of personnel is something with which courts have very little to do. They must do the work which comes to them with whatever force is available. In most states, this is fixed by constitutional provisions which are very difficult to change. In many states there are no provisions for methods of obtaining additional judges. Therefore, the court cannot substitute someone for a judge who is incapacitated temporarily or expand the court to take care of substantial increase of business. In most states, there is no administrative head to the judicial system, but each judge or each court is considered completely separate without responsibility except in its own jurisdiction. No person or court is made responsible for the efficient operation of the whole judicial system. This condition comes from court organization devised for pioneer conditions and is responsible for much of today's delay and public dissatisfaction concerning the administration of justice.

Several states have devised a means of increasing personnel by providing commissions of appeals, created by statute, which furnish additional judges for appellate courts. One method is to have the commissioners sit with the court at hearings and assign cases to them just as they are assigned to the judges. When commissioners' opinions are written they are submitted to a regular conference and those which receive the vote of a majority of the judges are adopted as the opinion of the court. They are published under the name of the author, like the judges' opinions, but each is followed by a per curiam order stating that it has been adopted as the opinion of the court and showing which of the judges concurred in it. The advantage of the commissioner system is that the same men work permanently with the court, and have no other duties to take part of their time, as would be true of trial judges used temporarily. This practically amounts to increasing the number of judges of the court.

Another handicap of many appellate courts is that there is provision made for hearing and deciding cases with less than the whole membership participating. If every member must hear every case and participate in deciding it, obviously the court must either dispose of fewer cases or decide them with less consideration by every member than they might otherwise get. A court which has discretion to control the number of cases it hears can keep within a limit which will allow full participation by all its members. A court which must take what comes is often compelled to cut down on the amount of participation to keep up with its docket. The best solution is to provide for divisions or for hearings of cases by three judges as is done in the United States circuit courts of appeals. Certainly it is better to obtain full consideration for a case by three judges who read briefs and records and have time for real conference discussion than to have more judges charged with the responsibility of deciding but without time for such full consideration. Provisions can be made for control of the docket by the court en banc so that cases of great public importance can be heard only en banc and cases assigned to divisions can be brought back to banc whenever deemed advisable by the whole court. Transfer to banc, upon application of the losing party, also may be required whenever the division judges are not unanimous. One trouble with many provisions for divisions is that they are too rigid, requiring the same judges to sit always in the same divisions. In many cases, they are elected or appointed to a certain division and cannot be changed. Another handicap to the most efficient utilization of personnel, as well as efficient operation in other respects, is the custom of many courts of rotating the office of Chief Justice in periods varying from six months to two years. No one man holds the office long enough to be responsible for efficiency. No one can have real responsible administrative authority under such circumstances. There can be no systematically sustained effort to discover defects or outmoded procedure and so improvements are not often made.

ESSENTIALS OF THE APPELLATE PROCESS

In our questionnaire we suggested a criterion for proper appellate methods which was stated in a 1941 resolution of the Board of Governors of the California Bar Association in describing and commending the methods of the United States Circuit Court of Appeals, 9th Circuit. This contemplates a court of seven members, but one in which only three judges ordinarily sit in each case. We requested comments, suggestions, or criticisms of these stated essentials, which we summarize as follows:

180

(1) *The court practically abolishes terms of court by making the last day of the term the beginning of the next.*

Most appellate courts have abolished the effect of terms by remaining in session (adjournment from day to day or by some method to prevent final adjournment) from the beginning of one term to the beginning of the next, except in some instances of complete adjournment during summer months. Continuous session of appellate courts so that they can always be open to transact business surely is required under modern conditions.

(2) *The court sits in fifty of the fifty-two weeks of the year—the seven judges arranging their vacations so that this is possible.*

Many courts, particularly those in warmer summer climates, do not favor holding hearings during the warmest summer months. This is a matter of local convenience.

(3) *Cases decided on the merits are upon written opinion, thus making certain for litigants the disciplined reasoning of its judges.*

Although the problem of an ever-increasing volume of published opinions is recognized, nevertheless, most courts still use this method and think it should be done, at least in all but the most simple cases. The method is suggested of a complete memorandum for the benefit of parties, but not released for publication in reports when no new law is pronounced.

(4) *To study the briefs of counsel before hearings.*

Certainly oral argument can be made more helpful and effective if it can be directed to the points upon which the judges desire information. Such prior study would also seem to have possibilities for determining the cases in which time for argument could profitably be extended. In this connection it is suggested that better briefs would be helpful, particularly if the prolix generalities of the assignment of error practice were abolished and a rule similar to that used in Pennsylvania adopted; requiring a brief statement of the questions involved to be printed on the first page of the brief.

(5) *To grant freely extended time to counsel for arguments; and*

(6) *To give a true conference between bench and counsel in the course of the presentation of the appeal.*

Both of these relate to the oral argument. Participation of the judges in the argument by questions to indicate the matters concerning which they are in doubt undoubtedly make the oral argument of more value in the decision of the case. This is also the chief advantage of oral argument over printed argument submitted in briefs and is a most effective means of preventing one-man decisions. The principal problem is to get all the argument which would be helpful in cases where it is needed, without hearing useless argument in cases where it merely wastes time. Limitations on oral argument are mainly due to volume of cases and lack of time.

(7) *Thereafter to have, before decision, a conference (and often conferences) in chambers of three fully prepared judges.*

A conference immediately after the oral argument is used by several courts and is bound to be helpful to fix the points and issues in the minds of the judges, to determine points of argument, and to suggest the matters as to which further study is most necessary. A conference at which anything more than a mere tentative decision is to be reached certainly requires discussion based on the independent investigation of each participating judge. This is even more effective if each judge prepares a written memorandum stating his views. Of course, there may often be some simple cases which do not require the full conference treatment and this might be determined at the preliminary conference.

(8) *To assign the case for opinion writing only after reaching a decision based upon such consideration.*

As heretofore stated, the method of the United States Supreme Court, most of the United States circuit courts of appeals and of several state courts, is to have a conference of all participating judges after they have carefully studied the briefs and records and to then agree upon the decision to be reached before assigning it to a member of the court for preparation of the opinion. The courts which use this method deem it to be essential. Many state courts consider the rotation method of assignment preferable as the best means to equalize work.

(9) *For the careful study by the other two judges of the final form of the opinion before it is handed down.*

Even though the judges may be in full accord upon the decision to be reached, nevertheless difficult, laborious, painstaking effort is still required to write a worthwhile opinion in any close or complicated case. It is essential that the other participating judges consider carefully and criticize freely the statements made and the language used. It will also occasionally happen that the attempt to write out reasons, for the result agreed upon, will disclose that such result is incorrect. Some cases just will not write the way they first seem. Therefore, this final essential is perhaps the most essential of all in our judicial system, where opinions have the function not only to decide cases between litigants, but also to furnish a guide for future action to all citizens.

It seems that lawyers want shorter opinions (except in their own cases) and judges want shorter briefs and records; lawyers want longer arguments and judges want to ask questions to shut off mere oratory and to find out the real issues; lawyers want cases decided in less time but want all judges to do more work on each case; and many of them also want every judge on courts of seven to nine members to participate in every case. The answers to our questionnaire certainly show that appellate judges are almost everywhere required to do a tremendous amount of work to keep up with their docket. They also show that appellate courts do their work well enough to balance these conflicting elements with reasonable satisfaction to the Bar.

[The perceptive appraisals of the modes of internal operation of trial and appellate courts by Paul Cotter and Justice Laurance Hyde both underscored the crucial importance of judicial personnel. The question of what is the proper method for selecting judges is, therefore, intimately related to the problem of improving the day to day operation of our court systems. The next portion of the text is devoted to materials on the selection of federal judges.]

6 *The Selection of Federal Judges*

A. THE APPOINTING PROCESS

[The selection process has frequently been the focus of attempted change in the twentieth century. The attempts have had as their objectives not only the alteration of the mode of choosing judges, but more importantly, the transformation of the ideology of the courts. Consequently, it is not surprising that the selection process has long been at the heart of the recurring controversies that have characterized many eras of American history.

The nomination of a member of the Supreme Court is solely the responsibility of the President. However, the President normally solicits the recommendations of persons in his cabinet and in public affairs. His authority is clearly established in Article II, Section 2, Clause 2, of the Constitution. In Section 2, Clause 3, his power to make recess appointments is established. It should be noted, however, that his power to nominate inferior federal judges is not clearly spelled out.]

1. *Article II of the Constitution*

(2). He shall have power, by and with the advice and consent of the Senate, to make treaties, provided two thirds of the Senators present concur; and he shall nominate, and by and with the advice and consent of the Senate, shall appoint ambassadors, other public ministers, and consuls, judges of the Supreme Court, and all other officers of the United States, whose appointments are not herein otherwise provided for, and which shall be established by law: but the Congress may by law vest the appointment of such inferior officers, as they think proper, in the President alone, in the courts of law, or in the heads of departments.

(3). The President shall have power to fill up all vacancies that may happen during the recess of the Senate, by granting commissions which shall expire at the end of their next session.

[The President has never operated alone with respect to federal judicial appointments. The Senate, from the 1790's to the present, has played a key role, although its influence with respect to Supreme Court selections is far less strong than that over choice of inferior federal judges. The material which follows is a discussion of a relatively recent, and unsuccessful, attempt to invoke "senatorial courtesy."]

2. "Senatorial Courtesy" and Judicial Nominations*

On July 8 the Senate confirmed the nomination of Joe B. Dooley, of Amarillo, Texas, a member of our Association since 1928, to be United States District Judge for the Northern District of Texas. The vote was 48 to 36, after a motion to send the nomination back to the Committee on the Judiciary had been rejected by a vote of 39 to 46. Of the minority party, only Senators Harry F. Byrd, of Virginia, and Kenneth McKellar, of Tennessee, voted against confirmation.

The Committee on the Judiciary had reported Judge Dooley's nomination favorably on May 14. The vote in the Committee was 8 to 4, with one vote favoring no recommendation. Our Association Committee on nominations for judicial office had advised the Senate Committee that it regarded the nominee as well qualified and of judicial temperament. Chairman Alexander Wiley of the Senate Committee told the Senate on July 1:

> *I listened to practically all of the testimony which was given and my personal conclusion was that the nominee met the tests which have been applied by the Committee in relation to qualifications, character, pro-American philosophy, etc. The State Bar of Texas has a rule that the Bar as such will make no recommendations, but the Committee received endorsements of the nominee from the officials of the Bar.*

The nomination and confirmation of Judge Dooley had been strongly supported by Senator Tom Connally, of Texas. His junior colleague from Texas, Senator O'Daniel, stated that the nominee was "personally obnoxious" to him. Although nominated in the Democratic primaries as Governor and later as Senator, and

---

*Comment, *American Bar Association Journal*, XXXIII (August, 1947), 805–6. [Footnotes omitted.] Reproduced with permission of the publisher. Copyright (1947) by the American Bar Association.

elected as a Democrat, Senator O'Daniel is said to have been ignored by the Administration as to "patronage" and as to recommendations for appointment to office. This raised squarely the historic issue as to whether individual members of the Senate shall, in respect of a nominee for judicial office, give validity to the objection of one Senator from a State that the nominee who has been favorably reported on is "personally obnoxious" to him. The Judiciary Committee submitted a notable memorandum to the Senate on this issue. Stating that there are precedents for recognizing and for ignoring such an objection, Chairman Wiley made the following statement for the Committee on July 1, to "outline the main issue and specify some of the implications of either type of action which we may take":

There are three steps, as we know, that must be taken:

(A)   There must be nomination by The President.

(B)   His nomination must be "by and with the advice and consent of the Senate."

(C)   There must be execution of the commission by The President.

The Senate has the absolute right to reject any nomination, and the action of the Senate is not subject to reversal anywhere or by anyone.

The words "by and with the advice and consent of the Senate" do not mean "with the advice and consent" of any particular group or individual, but rather by the entire Senate as a going concern. The Senate is not obliged to give any reasons to anyone for its acts, nor is any Senator required to explain why he voted for confirmation or rejection.

Our principal problem comes from the application of the rule of so-called "Senatorial courtesy" in this situation. It is a difficult rule to apply because, as I have mentioned before, the precedents on it are conflicting.

In his book The President—Office and Powers, *Professor Corwin, on page 69 states the following:*

"Much more extensive is the control which is exerted over the President's freedom of choice by a set of usages which go by the name of 'senatorial courtesy'. If the President in nominating to an office within a state fails to consult the preferences of the Senator or Senators of his own party from that state, he is very likely to see the appointment defeated upon an appeal to the Senate by the slighted member or members. Reciprocally, the Senate will ordinarily interpose no objection to the President's nominees for Cabinet or diplomatic posts. While any attempt to find a basis in the written Constitution for this interesting understanding would be disappointing, since it is the advice and consent of the Senate which the Constitution requires and not that of individual Senators, yet there is no usage of the Constitution affecting the powers of the President which is more venerable."

INDIVIDUAL INTERPRETATION OF SENATORIAL COURTESY

The force of the "personal obnoxiousness" objection is one that each individual Senator will have to determine for himself on the merits of the given case. Under the Constitution, the Senate is called up to "advise and consent"; but each individual Senator, in turn, has the responsibility for interpreting that language. There can be no absolutely inflexible rule with respect to adhering to or ignoring the "personal obnoxiousness" objection. Let us consider the implications of both actions:

(A) If the obnoxiousness objection were always accepted, *then we would be giving a powerful and arbitrary weapon to the individual Senator, who could utilize this weapon continually to embarrass the Executive without any reference to the qualifications of nominees.*

(B) On the other hand, if we were to always reject *the "obnoxiousness" objection, it would mean that the Executive would have a virtually undisputed appointing power unless there was some very obvious and damaging evidence to disqualify his nominees. There would be no bar to mediocrity via the "personal obnoxiousness" objection, and there would be no bar to purely political appointees nominated solely to serve some purely partisan purpose.*

FACTORS IN EVALUATING OBNOXIOUSNESS

What, then, are the major factors that we must bear in mind in evaluating our actions along this line? I submit those factors are:

(A) The United States Constitution *itself, giving the "advice and consent" power to the Senate.*

(B) The broken practice *of respecting "personal obnoxiousness" and "Senatorial courtesy."*

(C) The obligation *which a* Senator *may feel to the objecting Senator to respect the latter's judgment.*

(D) Justice *for the nominee himself. We must bear in mind, of course, that when a nominee is rejected by the Senate for whatever reason, forever after he lives under, in a certain sense, a cloud of official disapproval.*

(E) Our obligations to the American public, which means our obligation to secure the appointment of fit public servants.

(F) The factor of whether or not a given nominee is to serve within the particular State of the objecting Senator.

(G) Whether or not this is the first instance in which the objecting Senator has raised the "personal obnoxiousness" issue or whether it is part of a long series of such objections.

(H) Whether or not circumstances permit open discussion of the reasons on which the objecting Senator bases his objection. We can well understand that if a nominee had insulted a given Senator's wife in some manner, the Senator might not want to bring that to the open attention of the Senate. Whether or not other Senators would be willing to accept the blanket statement of "personal obnoxiousness" from a particular Senator without his specifying the reasons for it would depend on one of the preceding points which I stated; namely, the obligation which other Senators feel to the objecting Senator.

We are presented with this situation in Texas where the nominee is apparently above reproach, where he is caught between two fires, so to speak. Here we have two Senators who have not been able to agree, and one Senator who has been totally neglected for six years in relation to patronage by the Administration. We have a judicial vacancy in Texas. The people need that vacancy filled. What, then, should the Senate do in fairness to all parties concerned and on the basis of the factors that I have mentioned?

[The preceding comment not only illustrates a modern application of the custom of "senatorial courtesy" but also underscores the modern attempts by the American Bar Association to establish its advisory role in the selection process. In the 1940's the House of Delegates of the American Bar Association adopted, as part of its by-laws, the following provision [Article X, Section 7 (K)] for a Standing Committee on the Federal Judiciary:

This committee shall have power, on behalf of the Association, to promote the nomination and confirmation of competent persons for appointment as judges of the courts of the United States and to oppose the nomination and confirmation of persons deemed by it to be not sufficiently qualified. It shall have power also to report to the House of Delegates or the Board of Governors on any questions relating to the behavior of Judges of such courts and any matters relating to the sufficiency of the number of Federal Judiciary.

The objectives and methods of this committee of the American Bar Association were described in 1957 by one of its members.]

3. The Work of the American Bar Association Federal Judiciary Committee*

In 1945, for the first time, a special Committee on Federal Judiciary broke ground for the Association in attempting to influence the selection of federal judges. At that time, when a vacancy existed, there was no way in which the organized Bar could present its recommendation for the vacancy to anyone in authority. The Special Committee undertook to canvass the district where a vacancy existed and then suggest various names to the Attorney General for appointment, but before the Committee had an opportunity to complete its canvass and make its recommendation, those in authority had usually agreed on an appointee and made the nomination. As a practical matter, therefore, the only time at which the Bar could be heard was after the nomination had been made. Any member of the Bar could then appear before the

*Edward J. Fox, Jr., "The Selection of Federal Judges: The Work of the Federal Judiciary Committee," *American Bar Association Journal*, XLIII (August, 1957), 685–88, 761. [Footnotes omitted.] Reproduced with permission of the author and publisher. Copyright © 1957 by the American Bar Association.

Senate Committee on the Judiciary when it was considering the confirmation of the nominee and either urge or attempt to defeat confirmation.

The Special Committee did notable work in establishing a cordial relationship with the Senate Committee and in presenting its recommendations. Its work was so well done and so effective that it held out much promise for the future.

In 1949 the Committee was made a Standing Committee. It continued to function over the same pattern set by the Special Committee and despite the almost overwhelming odds it, too, met with gratifying success.

During the last six months of the Truman Administration, the Committee through its Chairman, Howard F. Burns, of Cleveland, made a notable advance in its relations with the Department of Justice. This was done through the high-minded and non-partisan approach of Deputy Attorney General Ross Malone and with the full co-operation of Attorney General McGranery.

Mr. Burns and Deputy Attorney General Malone made an arrangement whereby all persons who were under sufficiently serious consideration for the office of judge to have an FBI report made on them would also have their names submitted to the Standing Committee on Federal Judiciary for a report on their professional qualifications. A similar arrangement was reached under the Eisenhower Administration with Attorney General Brownell and Deputy Attorney General Rogers. However there was a slight modification in the functioning of the Committee at that point. It decided to forgo the suggestion of names for vacancies and give its undivided effort to the investigation of the names submitted to it by the Attorney General. This change in procedure was suggested by the Attorney General. It was not forced on the Committee in any way. The change was agreed to by the full Committee and after a trial period it decided to continue this policy in the belief that it was the best way to accomplish its result. This decision puts the Committee in a totally objective position. Except on rare occasions, the Committee has always had ample time to complete its investigation and make its report to the Attorney General before the Attorney General made a recommendation to the President.

When a judicial vacancy occurs, literally scores of names are submitted to the Attorney General by persons seeking the appointment. Names are sent to him by ambitious individuals, hopeful friends, influential friends and on many occasions—and quite properly and logically—by bar associations. After he has culled out what he considers to be the best names, the Attorney General submits the top name or names for investigation to the FBI and to the Committee on Federal Judiciary.

PARTISAN POLITICS . . . A CONTINUING PROBLEM

It is no secret that high on the list of advisers of the Attorney General are the members of the Senate from the party of the President. Obviously the Senate contains members who are not of that party. If neither Senator is a member of the party in power, the state chairman, after consultation with any members of the House from his state may submit names. Occasionally the Attorney General may recommend a name that is submitted from what may be called an "outside source" but it is administratively difficult to ignore it because it has become traditional—in fact it is spoken of as a senatorial prerogative—for a Senator to pick the nominee for the federal Bench. If a person nominated by the President is not one of those originally recommended by the Senator from the state in which the vacancy exists, he may find himself in an extremely unenviable position.

When a nomination is sent to the Senate it is referred to the Committee on the Judiciary for its recommendation and the Clerk of the Committee notifies the Senators from the state of the nominee that the nomination has been made. This is done by a blue slip or form asking the Senators for their opinion and any information they may have regarding the nominee. Under a rule of the Committee, if no answer is received within one week, approval is assumed. If the slip is not returned, the Clerk of the Committee, despite its rule, inquires of the Senator whether the slip has been received. If a Senator has the slip but says that he is investigating the qualifications of the nominee, the hearing is usually continued to enable the Senator to complete his investigation.

In the absence of strong, clear and disqualifying evidence the nominee is generally recommended for confirmation if the Senator approves. If the slip is not returned, it becomes the task of the nominee and his supporters and his uncles and his cousins and his aunts to get the slip returned to the Committee, for if there is no blue slip in the file the chances are that there will be no judge.

Two Republican Senators from Pennsylvania failed to return their slips pending the "investigation" of a nominee. This investigation delayed the confirmation of a man nominated by President Eisenhower for well over one year.

An even more devastating way to block a nomination is to have a Senator say that the nominee is "personally obnoxious" to him. If such a statement is made by a Senator from the state of the nominee, senatorial courtesy prescribes that the other ninety-five Senators refuse confirmation. This procedure was followed by a Democratic Senator from Illinois and also by a Democratic Senator from Iowa thus blocking the confirmation of two judges nominated by President Truman.

Senators have supported their position by arguing that they know the capabilities and characters of judges and lawyers in their own state better than the President who, however excellent his intentions, necessarily cannot know the Bench and Bar of forty-eight states. This is the premise on which the Senators have built the custom of recommending names for judicial vacancies.

The Constitution, however, lays on the President the duty of choosing the nominee for judge. In spite of this mandate, the original choice seems to me to lie almost wholly in the hands of the Senators or, if no Senator can be consulted, in the hands of the chairman of the state committee.

The real vice of the situation is that the office of judge is considered political patronage and as such is still a part of the spoils system.

How far this present method of selecting judges has departed from the intention of the original framers of the Constitution appears in No. LXVI of *The Federalist*. Hamilton is discussing the competence of the Senate to act as a court of impeachment. It had been suggested that it would not be proper for the Senate to sit as judges to impeach a person whose appointment it had previously approved. Hamilton pointed out, however, that:

It will be the office of the President to nominate, *and with the advice and consent of the Senate to* appoint. *There will of course be no exertion of choice, on the part of the Senate. They may defeat one choice of the executive, and oblige him to make another; but they cannot themselves choose . . . they can only ratify or reject the choice he may have made. They might even entertain a preference to some other person, at the very moment they were assenting to the one proposed: because there might be no positive ground of opposition to him; and they could not be sure, if they withheld their assent, that the subsequent nomination would fall upon their own favorite, or upon any other person in their estimation more meritorious than the one rejected. Thus it could hardly happen, that the majority of the Senate would feel any other complacency toward the object of an appointment, than such as the appearances of merit might inspire, and proofs of the want of it destroy* [emphasis by Hamilton].*

It must never be assumed that Senators do not have as high standards for the federal Bench as the members of the American Bar Association. Perhaps they are conditioned differently by what they see and what many others do not see. For instance, over the last fifty years, appointments to the federal Bench have been made from the party of the President in well over 90 per cent of the cases. No magic results from the use of a fifty-year span. Judges have come from the party of the President at least as far back as the time of John Adams and his "midnight judges". Nevertheless, it is a little hard to see why, in principle, during a certain four-year period, only Democrats are appointed to the Bench and during another four-year period only Republicans are appointed. Political tags do not belong on judges.

Perhaps it is natural to suggest for a judicial vacancy either a good friend or someone who has rendered valuable service to the party. While I personally deplore such an attitude, if the appointee has the necessary professional qualifications and he is the free choice of the President, little real harm is done. However, service to the party or friendship with a Senator is not of itself enough to qualify a man for appointment to the federal Bench. Fortunately, most of the Senators recognize this. Some of them do not. This occasional lapse furnishes one of the reasons why the services of this Committee are so important to the Bench and to the Bar and to the public.

THE COMMITTEE'S WORK . . . METHOD OF SCREENING

The Committee is composed of eleven members, one from each Circuit. When a name is submitted to the Chairman of the Committee by the Attorney General, the name is promptly transmitted to the person in the appropriate Circuit whose duty it is to investigate the qualifications of the person under consideration. When the information is collected the member sends a detailed report and recommendation to the Committee with the request that the members send their votes to the Chairman promptly. At times members of the Committee from outside the Circuit have sources of information which they consider reliable and they supplement the investigation being made.

It is a uniform rule of the Committee that all officers and directors of the Association who might be expected to know the persons under consideration as well as members of the House of Delegates from the district or circuit in which the vacancy exists are asked for their opinion. The members themselves have their own additional sources of information in their own district as well as in their circuit and inquiry is made from these sources. Investigation is not limited to members of the Bar. On several occasions during the last two years of my term, members of the Committee traveled hundreds of miles for personal interviews with persons under consideration and those favoring or opposing their nomination.

All communications with members of the Committee are in the strictest confidence. Names of the informants are not even given to the other members of the Committee unless permission is first obtained.

It sometimes happens that while the committee and the FBI are investigating, rumors of an impending appointment leak out. Here the Committee meets a serious obstacle. Members of the Bar have been known to say "this man isn't qualified but he is going to be appointed. I have to live with him and represent clients before him and I won't say anything against him." At times the Committee has received a glowing endorsement of the man under investigation with a note at the bottom "cc Mr. Candidate". Purported assistance of this sort is of no help to the Committee.

Members of the Bar can make one of their greatest contributions toward the attainment of a strong Bench by wholehearted co-operation with the Committee. If the person under investigation lacks the necessary qualifications, he must be side-tracked either at the Attorney General's office or before the Senate Committee. It is easier to do it before the Attorney General, but in either event it must be done by information furnished by those who practice with the candidate and know him best. Fearless judges seldom come from a timid Bar and if the Bar is unwilling to speak, an unqualified person may be appointed.

Attorney General Brownell stated publicly that judges would be chosen from among those members of the Bar who were "the best qualified men available" for appointment and so when the votes are in, the Committee reports to the Attorney General that in its opinion the person under investigation either is or is not among those best qualified for the office.

The Committee is obliged to recognize however that no positive test or formula can be applied to a person to determine in advance whether he will be a good judge. It expresses its opinion to the Attorney General and in turn it must recognize the right of the Attorney General to differ with its opinion.

If the investigation is not conducted properly or if the case is not stated persuasively and objectively and supported by credible evidence, the fault lies with the Committee and the members of the Bar. If, on those few occasions when the Attorney General and the Committee disagree and the nomination is made, the Committee, i.e., the Bar, still has an opportunity to be heard before the Committee on the Judiciary of the Senate.

Here the Committee again files a report on each nomination. It may say that in its opinion the nominee is qualified. This report is based on a standard different from its report to the Attorney General. A man may be qualified to be judge even if he does not come from that small group considered "the best qualified men available." Honesty, however, requires the Committee to report him qualified.

The Committee may also report that it will neither recommend nor oppose confirmation. This can mean that members of the Bar have not expressed their opinion of the nominee with sufficient unanimity to enable the Committee to form a recommendation.

The Committee may recommend that a nominee not be confirmed. If such a recommendation is made, the Committee cannot safely rest its case on a unfavorable written report to the Senate Committee which is based necessarily on hearsay evidence. No lawyer would be willing to submit an important case on such a record, and what more important case can there be?

JUDICIAL CANDIDATES . . . SPECIFIC SUGGESTIONS

If the Committee reports that a man should not be confirmed, it needs courageous support from the Bar to defeat the nomination. Members of the Bar must be willing to appear before the Senate Committee in the presence of the nominee and his Senator and state frankly and fully why the man is not qualified for appointment. With help of this sort from the Bar, nominations have successfully been opposed by the Committee.

The Deputy Attorney General and the Chairman of the Committee form the contact between the Attorney General and the Committee and this should be a close relationship. To my knowledge it can be a very pleasant one. At times a request is made for a preliminary report on whether a full-scale investigation should be made on some lawyer. Specific suggestions relating to particular phases of the lawyer's life or practice are suggested for investigation and it often happens that if this preliminary investigation turns out badly, nothing further is heard of it.

Statements of Attorneys General and of Deputy Attorneys General to members of the Committee warrant the belief that the opinion of the Committee is valued highly in the Department of Justice and that its services are extremely helpful.

When Senator Patrick J. McCarran was Chairman of the Committee on the Judiciary, the Standing Committee had occasion to appear before it. At the conclusion of the hearing Senator McCarran made a rather lengthy and very gracious statement about the Standing Committee saying ". . . you have on a number of occasions effectively brought about results here" and "have brought results most useful to us." Other chairmen have made similar comments.

Possibly President Eisenhower had the work of the Committee in mind when he said at Philadelphia in 1955:

"To the officers and members of the American Bar Association I express my grateful acknowledgement of the assistance they have rendered as a public service in aiding me and my trusted advisers in the review of professional qualifications of individuals under consideration for federal judicial positions. You have helped secure judges who I believe will serve in the tradition of John Marshall."

When Chief Justice Vinson died the services of the Committee were offered to the Attorney General but the Committee was told that the appointment of a

Justice to the Supreme Court was a personal appointment of the President and that if the help of the Committee was needed, it would be consulted.

When the next vacancy occurred, the Committee was not consulted but the Chairman of the Committee was invited by the Deputy Attorney General to testify before the Senate Committee in favor of the confirmation of Judge Harlan.

Deputy Attorney General Rogers, speaking in Baltimore before the Regional Meeting of the Association in October, 1956, said that when Mr. Justice Brennan's name was discussed with the President, he asked what the American Bar Association Committee thought about him. When he was told that the Committee had not been asked for its opinion, he directed that the nomination be held up until the Committee could report . . .

[In addition to the often competing roles of advocates of "senatorial courtesy" and proponents of increased influence of the organized bar, aggressive candidates for high judicial posts usually seek to marshal assistance from political allies and influencial private organizational leaders. That some active candidates for appointment to the Supreme Court cultivated a public attitude of disinterest was perhaps best illustrated by Joseph Rucker Lamar. His wife reported that shortly before he was nominated by William Howard Taft, Lamar remarked to a friend, apparently without humor, "I had a singular dream the other night. I dreamed that the President had appointed me to the Supreme Court of the United States."[1]

The supernatural quality of that comment was somewhat distilled by the following exchange between Archie Butt and President Taft:

"Well Archie, I am feeling better, for I have got the Supreme Court off my mind. I am going to name Lamar for one of the vacancies."

Butt answered. "Is it possible?"

"Yes," answered Taft. "Do you think he will accept?"

Then Butt laughed, for he "knew it was the fondest hope of both Mr. Lamar and his wife."[2]]

4. Does the Office Seek the Man?: Henry Billings Brown*

Mrs. Brown, as one of the heirs of her father, inherited what was then a large fortune, and she, with the other heirs, became partners in a lumber business. Mr. Pitts was but fifty-eight. The Browns appear to have become independent of

---

[1] Clarinda Pendleton Lamar, *The Life of Joseph Rucker Lamar, 1857–1916* (New York: G. P. Putnam's Sons, 1926), p. 168.

[2] Henry F. Pringle, *The Life and Times of William Howard Taft* (New York: Farrar & Rinehart, 1939), I, 398.

* Charles A. Kent, *Memoir of Henry Billings Brown* (New York: Duffield & Co., 1915), pp. 61, 73, 76–79, 88.

his [Brown's] law business, and to this must be attributed his subsequent pursuit of office. . . .

At the time Mr. Brown became District Judge, he had, in conjunction with Mr. Pond, a large and growing practice. He was a successful lawyer, but I do not think that either he or his best friends thought him more deserving of judicial honours than some others. His great distinction was that he had a great ambition to be a judge, and was able to accept the position with the small salary then paid. . . .

Justice Brown's life should be an encouragement to young lawyers. It shows how a man without perhaps extraordinary abilities may attain and honour the highest judicial position by industry, by good character, pleasant manners and some aid from fortune. . . .

Justice Brown's appointment to the Supreme Bench was not obtained without considerable effort on his part. One quite formidable opponent was Alfred Russell, the former United States District Attorney, when Brown was his assistant, who had the warm support of one of the then United States senators from Michigan, Mr. McMillan, and of many lawyers in Detroit and in the East. I have heard that one considerable ground for Justice Brown's appointment was his reputation as an admiralty judge and the lack in the Supreme Court of men specially familiar with this branch of the law. In seeking a position on the Supreme Bench, as in other matters, Justice Brown did not hesitate to use all honourable means to attain the object of his ambition.

5. Seeking the Office: Horace Lurton*

[This letter written by Horace Lurton on November 25, 1909, to one Dickinson certainly belies the tradition that the office should seek the man.]

I enclose certain editorials that have appeared in various papers that have reached me.

My New York friends advise me very positively that both Senators Depew and Root will support my confirmation. I have a letter from Senator Overman, of North Carolina, saying that both North Carolina Senators will stand strongly by me. I have like information from the Alabama Senators and both Kentucky Senators. Judge Severans says that Senator Burrows told him that there would not be any difficulty in the way of a confirmation. A friend in Cincinnati writes me that Senator Foraker will go himself to Washington and personally see a number of Senators in the interest of confirmation. Governor Harmon writes me that he will also be on the scene and will take an active hand in bringing about the confirmation. Luke Wright came from Memphis and spent the evening with me. This was

*Quoted in Daniel S. McHargue, *Appointments to the Supreme Court, 1789–1932* (Los Angeles: Doctoral Dissertation, University of California, 1949), pp. 364–66. [Footnotes omitted.] Reproduced with permission of the author.

altogether voluntary upon his part and I was very glad to so know his attitude. He said he would write to a number of Senators and that he would go on to Washington when the Senate convened and render such assistance as he found himself able to do. Governor Patterson had written a strong letter to every one of the Democratic Senators. Governor Porter, much to my surprise, has manifested a large interest in the matter. Governor McMillin has exerted his influence and will go to Washington, if necessary. The newspapers report Senators Clarke and Borah as having promised the President to support the nomination. Judd has opened up a correspondence with Senator Sutherland, of Utah. General Torrance, the most influential lawyer of Minnesota, the Ex-Commander in Chief of the Grand Army of the Republic has actively interested himself with the Minnesota Senators. I have a number of letters from influential men of Missouri who tell me that they have no uneasiness whatever about their Senators. Judge Severens, in connection with several of my friends in Michigan, is looking after Senator Smith of that State. A very close friend of Senator Stephenson of Wisconsin, tells me that he will stand absolutely responsible for his favorable consideration of the matter. I have another friend who has also the necessity of very careful management, in consequence of the supposed friction between LaFollette and the President and LaFollette and his colleague, and will endeavor to manage wisely. My friends at Cincinnati, Cleveland, Memphis, Atlanta and Dallas, are all hard at work. A dozen men at Nashville are doing what they think they can do.

According to all that I know there will be no serious objection to the confirmation if the President shall see fit to send my name to the Senate.

The New England Senators are an unknown quantity. There are a good many New York lawyers of prominence who I have no doubt would assist in this matter, but I feel a hesitancy in personally writing them about it. Mr. Kingsley, President of the New York Life Insurance Company, has volunteered to put every influence of the New York Life Insurance Company to work and I have particularly suggested the New England Senators as his field.

Our old friend, John Wesley Gaines, states that he is going to Washington to look after the Radicals. Col. Shook has more influence with him than anyone else and is going to caution him to keep on his own side of the road, for he might do me much more harm than good, though I am quite aware that with some of the Senators he might have considerable influence, especially if any attack is made upon me on account of any supposed leaning toward corporations. He has armed and equipped himself with my opinions and if he can be prevented from promiscuous endeavors may prove useful with some of the extreme men of the Senate.

[Finally, it should not be forgotten that Congress may determine the number and size of the inferior federal courts and the size of the Supreme Court of the United States. In the 1961 Senate debate on a bill to create 73 new federal judgeships, Republican Senator Everett Dirksen of Illinois exclaimed plaintively, "These are choice political plums." Later, in urging delay upon the majority party, he remarked that "We are picking plums off this juicy plum tree so fast that we almost forced one judge on a committeeman who did not want him." One of the sharpest demonstrations of Congressional power over the number and size of federal courts occurred after the bitter attempt by lame duck Federalists to deny the Presidency to Thomas Jefferson despite his electoral defeat of President John Adams in 1800.]

6. The Federalist Judiciary Act of 1801*

[Beveridge concluded a dramatic account of the Federalist attempt to deny the Presidency to Jefferson in this vein:]

So it came about that the party of Washington, as a dominant and governing force in the development of the American Nation, went down forever in a welter of passion, tawdry politics, and disgraceful intrigue. All was lost, including honor.

But no! All was not lost. The Judiciary remained. The newly elected House and President were Republican and in two years the Senate also would be "Jacobin"; but no Republican was as yet a member of the National Judiciary. Let that branch of the Government be extended; let new judgeships be created, and let new judges be made while Federalists could be appointed and confirmed, so that, by means, at least, of the National Courts, States' Rights might be opposed and retarded, and Nationalism defended and advanced—thus ran the thoughts and the plans of the Federalist leaders.

Adams, in the speech to Congress in December of the previous year, had urged the enactment of a law to this end as "indispensably necessary." In the President's address to the expiring Federalist Congress on December 3, 1800, which Marshall wrote, the extension of the National Judiciary, as we have seen, was again insistently urged. Upon that measure, at least, Adams and all Federalists agreed. "Permit me," wrote General Gunn to Hamilton, "to offer for your consideration, the policy of the federal party extending the influence of our judiciary; if neglected by the federalists the ground will be occupied by the enemy, the very next session of Congress, and, sir, we shall see—and many other scoundrels placed on the seat of justice."

Indeed extension of the National Judiciary was now the most cherished purpose of Federalism. A year earlier, after Adam's first recommendation of it, Wolcott narrates that "the steady men" in the Senate and House were bent upon it, because "there is no other way to combat the state opposition [to National action] but by an efficient and extended organization of judges."

Two weeks after Congress convened, Roger Griswold of Connecticut reported the eventful bill to carry out this Federalist plan. It was carefully and ably drawn and greatly widened the practical effectiveness of the National Courts. The Supreme Court was reduced, after the next vacancy, to five members—to prevent, said the

*Albert J. Beveridge, *Life of John Marshall* (Boston: Houghton Mifflin, 1916), pp. 547–52. [Footnotes omitted.] Reproduced with permission of the publisher. Copyright (1916) by Houghton Mifflin Co.

Republicans, the appointment of one of their party to the Nation's highest tribunal. Many new judgeships were created. The Justices of the Supreme Court, who had sat as circuit judges, were relieved of this itinerant labor and three circuit judges for each circuit were to assume these duties. At first, even the watchful and suspicious Jefferson thought that "the judiciary system will not be pushed, as the appointments, if made, by the present administration, could not fall on those who create them."

But Jefferson underestimated the determination of the Federalists. Because they felt that the bill would "greatly extend the judiciary power and of course widen the basis of government," they were resolved, writes Rutledge, to "profit of our short lived majority, and do much good as we can before the end of this session" by passing the Judiciary Bill.

In a single week Jefferson changed from confidence to alarm. After all, he reflected, Adams could fill the new judgeships, and these were life appointments. "I dread this above all the measures meditated, because appointments in the nature of freehold render it difficult to undo what is done," was Jefferson's second thought.

The Republicans fought the measure, though not with the vigor or animosity justified by the political importance they afterwards attached to it. Among the many new districts created was an additional one in Virginia. The representatives from that State dissented; but, in the terms of that period, even their opposition was not strenuous. They said that, in Virginia, litigation was declining instead of increasing. "At the last term the docket was so completely cleared in . . . ten days . . . that the court . . . had actually decided on several [suits] returnable to the ensuing term."

That, replied the Federalists, was because the courts were too far away from the citizens. As for the National revenues, they could be collected only through National tribunals; for this purpose, two Federal Courts in Virginia, as provided by the bill, were essential. But, of course, sneered the Federalists, "Virginia would be well satisfied with one court in preference to two or with no court whatever in preference to one."

But there was a defect in the bill, intimated the Virginia Republicans, that affected tenants and landowners of the Northern Neck. A clause of section thirteen gave the newly established National Court jurisdiction of all causes arising under the Constitution where original or exclusive jurisdiction was not conferred upon the Supreme Court or Admiralty Courts. The National Court of the New Virginia District was to be held at Fredericksburg. Thus all suits for quitrents or other claims against those holding their lands under the Fairfax title could be brought in this near-by National Court, instead of in State Courts. This criticism was so attenuated and so plainly based on the assumption that the State Courts would not observe the law in such actions, that it was not pressed with ardor even by the impetuous and vindictive Giles.

But Nicholas went so far as to move that the jurisdiction of National Courts should be limited to causes exceeding five hundred dollars. This would cut out the great mass of claims which the present holders of the Fairfax title might lawfully have against tenants or owners. The Marshalls were the Fairfax assignees,

197

as we have seen. No Republican, however, mentioned them in debate; but some one procured the insertion in the record of an insinuation which nobody made on the floor. In brackets, the "Annals" after the brief note of Nicholas's objection, states: [It is understood that the present assignees of the claims of Lord Fairfax, are General Marshall, General Lee, and a third individual and that they maintain their claims under the British Treaty.]"

For three weeks the debate in the House dragged along. Republican opposition, though united, was languid. At last, without much Republican resistance, the bill passed the House on January 20, 1801, and reached the Senate the next day. Two weeks later the Senate Republicans moved a substitute providing for fewer circuits, fewer judges, and a larger Supreme Court, the members of which were to act as circuit judges as formerly. It was defeated by a vote of 17 to 13. The next day the bill was passed by a vote of 16 to 11.

[One of the first actions of the incoming Jeffersonian Republicans was passage of an act repealing the Federalist Judiciary Act of 1801. After repealing the Federalist Act, the Jeffersonians were confronted with the possibility that their repealing act would be held unconstitutional on the ground that it removed, in effect, federal circuit judges from office despite the fact that they were guaranteed life tenure on good behavior under the Constitution. They immediately passed an additional statute abolishing the June term of the Supreme Court and providing that the Court convene once each year beginning on the second Monday of February. The immediate effect of the enactment was to forestall a meeting of the Supreme Court for fourteen months. Despite the delay, the Jeffersonian repealing act was challanged in the federal courts and reached the Supreme Court in 1803.]

7. A Challenge of the Constitutionality of the Repealing Act of 1802*

The court of the fifth circuit ought not to have taken cognizance of the motion; because the court of the fourth circuit did exist, and not because it did not exist, as alleged in the plea.

If the acts of 8th March and 29th April, 1802, are constitutional, then it is admitted there is no error in the judgment; because, in that case, the courts ceased to exist, the judges were constitutionally removed, and the transfer from the one court to the other was legal. But if those acts are unconstitutional, then the court of the fourth circuit still exists, the judges were not removed, and the transfer of jurisdiction did not take place. The legislature did not intend to transfer causes

* Federalist Attorney Charles Lee's oral argument in *Stuart* v. *Laird,* 1 Cranch 299, 303–304 (1803).

from one existing court to another. If then the courts still exist, the causes, not being intended to be removed from existing courts, were not removed.

But we contend that those acts were unconstitutional so far as they apply to this cause.

1st. The first act (March 8, 1802) is unconstitutional in as much as it goes to deprive the courts of all their power and jurisdiction, and to displace judges who have been guilty of no misbehavior in their offices.

By the constitution the judges both of the supreme and the inferior courts are to hold their office during good behavior. So much has been recently said, and written and published upon this subject, that it is irksome to repeat arguments which are so familiar to everyone.

There is no difference between the tenure of office of a judge of the supreme court and that of a judge of an inferior court. The reason of that tenure, to wit, the independence of the judge, is the same in both cases; indeed the reason applies more strongly to the case of the inferior judges, because to them are exclusively assigned cases of life and death.

It is admitted that congress have the power to modify, increase or diminish the power of the courts and the judges. But that is a power totally different from the power to destroy the courts and to deprive them of all power and jurisdiction. The one is permitted by the constitution, the other is restrained by the regard which the constitution pays to the independence of the judges. They may modify the courts, but they cannot destroy them, if thereby they deprive a judge of his office. This provision of the constitution was intended to place the judges not only beyond the reach of executive power, of which the people are always jealous, but also to shield them from the attack of that party spirit which always predominates in popular assemblies. That this was the principle intended to be guarded by the constitution is evident from the contemporaneous exposition of that instrument, published under the title of *The Federalist,* and written, as we all know, by men high in the esteem of their country. . . .

Mr. Lee also cited and read the speeches of Mr. Madison in the convention of Virginia, . . . of Mr. Nicholas, . . . and of Mr. Marshall . . .

The words *during good behavior* can not mean *during the will of congress.* The people have a right to the services of those judges who have been constitutionally appointed, and who have been unconstitutionally removed from office. It is the right of the people that their judges should be independent; that they should not stand in dread of any man, who, as Mr. Henry said in the Virginia convention, has the congress at his heels.

[The Supreme Court's response to Lee's argument was presented by Justice Paterson. (Chief Justice Marshall took no part in the decision because he had presided over the Circuit Court from which the case arose.) Paterson rejected Lee's request for reversal in a manner fully cognizant of Congress' paramount authority.]

8. The Supreme Court Avoids a Clash with Congress: Courts Abolished*

Congress have constitutional authority to establish from time to time such inferior tribunals as they may think proper; and to transfer a cause from one such tribunal to another. In this last particular, there are no words in the constitution to prohibit or restrain the exercise of legislative power.

The present is a case of this kind. It is nothing more than the removal of the suit brought by Stuart against Laird from the court of the fourth circuit to the court of the fifth circuit, which is authorized to proceed upon and carry it into full effect. This is apparent from the ninth section of the act entitled, "an act to amend the judicial system of the United States," passed the 29th of April, 1802. The forthcoming bond is an appendage to the cause, or rather a component part of the proceedings.

2d. Another reason for reversal is, that the judges of the Supreme Court have no right to sit as circuit judges, not being appointed as such, or in other words, that they ought to have distinct commission for that purpose. To this objection, which is of recent date, it is sufficient to observe, that practice and acquiescence under it for a period of several years, commencing with the organization of the judicial system, affords an irresistable answer, and has indeed fixed the construction. It is a contemporary interpretation of the most forcible nature. This practical exposition is too strong and obstinate to be shaken or controlled. Of course, the question is at rest, and ought not now to be disturbed.

[In modern times, Congress ordinarily cooperates closely with the federal justices and judges while attending with shrewd calculation to partisan needs. The passage of the congressional statute creating 73 new federal judgeships provides a striking illustration of the interplay of factors governing legislative-judicial relations in the mid-twentieth century. First, the administrative arm of the federal judiciary, the Judicial Conference, is consulted with respect to the needs of the federal judicial system. Second, the Department of Justice usually supports the recommendation of the Judicial Conference in such matters.]

9. The Judges' Bill of 1961: On the Need for New Judgeships*

MR. KENNEDY. I appreciate this opportunity to appear before the committee today in support of the Judicial Conference recommendations embodied in H.R. 2226,

*Stuart v. Laird, 1 Cranch 299, 309 (1803).

*Testimony of Attorney General Robert Kennedy, *Hearings before Subcommittee 5 of the House Judiciary Committee on Bills to Provide for the Appointment of Additional Circuit and District Judges,* March 1 and 2, 87th Cong., (Washington, D.C.: United States Government Printing Office, 1961).

a bill sponsored by Chairman Celler, which provides for the creation of additional circuit and district judgeships in the U.S. courts.

H.R. 2226 embodies—with certain additions—the recommendations of the Judicial Conference of the United States which were approved at its most recent session, September 21–23, 1960. The recommendations of the Judicial Conference have the full support of President Kennedy, and the Department of Justice.

There are at present 68 circuit judgeships. The Judicial Conference recommends 9 additional circuit judgeships which, if approved, would bring the number of circuit judgeships to 77.

There are now 245 district judgeships. The Conference recommends 50 district judgeships which, if approved, would bring the total number to 295. In addition the Judicial Conference would change three temporary district judgeships to permanent judgeships.

The last bill creating additional judgeships was enacted by the 83d Congress, February 10, 1954.—30 judgeships were approved. The committee reports published at the time stated that the legislation was intended to take care of the minimum requirements for alleviating the most urgent needs of the Federal judiciary . . . and it was recognized that in many instances the need for additional manpower will shortly become so acute as to require additional legislation to provide judges. . . .

The congressional awareness of this manpower problem was a key factor in the passage of the 1958 jurisdiction bill. While this law resulted in a decrease of 14 percent in the number of civil cases filed in 1959, there is evidence that the respite was temporary and inadequate to affect any reversal in the trend of increasing judicial business. In 1960 there was an increase of about 4 percent in number of cases filed. Moreover, there seems to be little hope that this increasing trend will be reversed without the creation of more judgeships.

The Department of Justice has a particular interest in doing everything it can to insure that the business of the Federal courts is disposed of promptly, because 35 percent of the cases filed in these courts involve the United States as a party litigant.

In the courts of appeals, the Government is a litigant in over half of the cases which are disposed of after hearing or submission. In fact, in eight cases disposed of by the appellate courts, the Government is represented in one criminal case, one administrative agency review, and two civil actions.

Thus, it is obvious that the efficiency of the Department of Justice (1) in protecting the interest of the United States in civil cases, (2) in prosecuting criminal actions, and (3) in insuring the most economic use of the personnel and resources provided by the Congress, depends to a very real extent upon the ability of the courts to receive, handle, and dispose of the judicial business.

Unfortunately, at the present time, the district courts and courts of appeals are not sufficiently manned to keep pace with the rapid increase in litigation.

The civil business of the courts has skyrocketed in the last 20 years. Since 1941, the number of cases filed annually in the 86 district courts which have Federal jurisdiction, exclusively, has increased more than 60 percent. The backlog of cases has risen almost 130 percent. But in contrast, during this entire 20-year period there has been but a 25-percent increase in the number of judgeships in these districts. Where there were 150 civil cases pending per judgeship in March 1941, there are now 260 civil cases per judgeship.

If we just compare the demands upon the courts this year with those of a year even as recent as 1950—the contrast is striking:

In 1950, private civil cases—which by far are most burdensome—accounted for 22,600 of the total cases filed in the 86 districts; by 1960, this number has risen to 30,048, an increase of 33 percent. This increase would have been still larger except for the effect which the Jurisdiction Act of 1958 had on private case filings. In fiscal 1958, the last full year before the act became effective, 37,725 private cases were filed in the 86 districts.

On June 30, 1950, there were 27,771 private civil cases pending; by June 30, 1960, the backlog of private civil cases had climbed to 40,932, an increase of nearly 50 percent.

But, between the years 1950 and 1960, the number of all district judgeships only increased from 221 to 245, an increase of only 11 percent, for an increase of only 24 judges for the entire Nation. During 1941, the average number of cases terminated by each district judge was 196. By 1960, the average number of cases disposed of had risen to 252.

If we look at the courts of appeals, we find that in 1950 they received 2,830 cases; by 1960, they received 3,899 cases, an increase of over 37 percent. The cases pending in the courts of appeals on June 30, 1950, were 1,675; by June 30, 1960, the cases pending totaled 2,220, or an increase of 32 percent.

But, during this 10-year period, only 3 circuit judgeships were created for the entire Nation, making a total of 68, or an increase of less than 8 percent.

That, very briefly, is the account for a decade—the 1950's.

But, I believe that for your purposes, the committee will be more particularly interested in what has happened in the last 6 months—July through December.

DISTRICT COURTS

The district courts had 61,251 civil cases pending on July 1, 1960. During the next 6 months 28,425 civil cases were filed, but only 25,928 terminated. Thus, filings outstripped terminations and as a result, the total number of civil cases awaiting action on January 1 was 63,748, or an increase of 2,497 over July 1.

On the criminal side, 7,691 were pending on July 1. During the period, 13,703 cases were filed and 13,283 were terminated by final disposition, leaving a total of 8,144 cases pending on December 31, an increase of 453.

As a result, on January 1 of this year, the U.S. district courts faced a combined civil criminal backlog of 71,922 cases, for an increase of 3,285 cases in the 6-month period.

At this point, I want to mention the attention that is usually given in judicial statistics of the civil cases; and this is so because of the volume of such cases and, also, the time it takes to dispose of them.

However, I believe we have a definite obligation to give greater attention to the serious delays in criminal matters. The pending criminal case load is over 45 cases. In the eastern district of North Carolina, 242 cases are pending, and in the southern district of Florida, 657 criminal are pending.

COURTS OF APPEALS

The courts of appeals, I must report, are confronted with the largest backlog in a decade. Filings during the period from July 1 through December 31, 1960, increased 12½ percent to 2,182 cases, compared to 1,939 cases filed during the same months a year ago. At the same time, the number of cases disposed of increased from 1,599 to 1,759. Even so, 400 fewer cases were disposed of than were filed, and the pending caseload rose during the 6-month period from 2,220 cases on July 1, 1960, to 2,643 on December 31, 1960. This represents an increase in the pending caseload of 423 cases, or almost 20 percent.

Thus, the increase in judicial business in continuing, and it is the result of the trends which mark a growing nation.

POPULATION INCREASE

Since 1950, the population of our country has increased from 150 million to nearly 180 million, an increase of 20 percent, or 30 million people.

Our gross national product has grown from $285 billion in 1950 to an estimated $498 billion, an increase of 80 percent.

Motor vehicle registrations have spiraled from 49 million to 71 million, an increase of 45 percent.

Yet, even these statistics of a nation bursting at the seams are not entirely revealing—they do not disclose the full stress which has been put upon the courts. And I might add here, Mr. Chairman, that in 40 years the population of the United States will have doubled so that this problem and difficulty is going to increase and not decrease.

An increase in our national wealth, of course, carries with it a proportionate increase in commercial transactions. However, the litigation growing out of such transactions creates problems disproportionately greater. As our economy increases, commercial transactions not only increase in number, but in complexity. Thus, the burdens upon the courts do not grow at an even rate—they multiply.

New legislation enacted by Congress also produces increases in the workload of the courts. Legislation enacted by the 86th Congress has already led to additional litigation in the Federal Courts. Examples of such legislation are the Labor-Management Reporting and Disclosure Procedure Act of 1959, enacted in September 1959 . . . , which established new controls affecting labor unions and their relationships with union members; and the disclosure of welfare and pension plans.

The Judicial Conference of the United States and the Department of Justice, is convinced that a minimum of 50 district judgeships, and 9 circuit judgeships, are required to enable the Federal Courts to keep up with the current annual inflow of civil and criminal business.

These recommendations for the creation of new judgeships span the length and breadth of this country, because the problem of congestion and delay is not confined to a few localities—it is a national problem. The recommendations, therefore, are not concentrated in any one district, in any one State, or in any one circuit.

Six new judgeships have been recommended for the southern district of New York—the greatest for any one district; but the southern district is unique in terms of volume and character of the matters that come before it. Not only does this court handle a greater volume of business than any other Federal district court, but, situated as it is at the hub of the Nation's largest economic, shipping and financial center, this court had pending on January 1, 1961, 11,667 civil cases out of the national pending caseload of 63,748 cases. Even so, bare statistical data does not give the full measure of the judicial workload because there is an unusually large percentage of highly complicated matters, including Government antitrust cases, patent suits, admiralty proceedings, and private antitrust suits, pending in this particular court.

Mr. Chairman and members of the Committee, this is the evidence as we have found it. The Department of Justice favors the creation of new judgeships as recommended by the Judicial Conference.

MR. McCULLOCH. In the busy days since the inauguration, have you or your assistants had time to make an independent investigation other than the investigation and recommendation of the Judicial Conference?

MR. KENNEDY. We have not made an independent investigation, Congressman. We have reviewed this whole matter with representatives of the Judicial Conference and we are accepting their recommendations.

MR. McCULLOCH. Each of their recommendations?

MR. KENNEDY. That is correct, and I understand that they are now in the process of perhaps adding several more, which we, of course, also support.

[Interested private groups are invited to present supporting or contrary arguments at such committee hearings. The following testimony before the House Judiciary Committee not only indicates the active participation of lawyers' organizations in the governmental process, but also underscores the particularly heavy demands made upon federal judges in a complex metropolitan region.]

10. Report on the Need for Additional Judges for the Southern District of New York*

The bar associations submitting this report are deeply concerned over a threatened breakdown in the administration of justice in the U. S. District Court for the

*Statement submitted by the Association of the Bar of the City of New York, New York County Lawyers' Association, Bronx County Bar Association, Empire State Chapter of the Maritime Law Association of the United States, and the New York Patent Law Association, *Hearings before Subcommittee 5 of the House Judiciary Committee on Bills to Provide for the Appointment of Additional Circuit and District Judges,* March 1 and 2, 1961, 87th Cong. (Washington, D.C.: United States Government Printing Office, 1961), pp. 246–53. [Footnoes omitted.]

Southern District of New York because of an insufficient number of judges in that court to handle its ever-growing business. Our members, whose practice constitutes the primary work of the Court, firmly believe that unless Congress promptly enacts legislation creating six additional judgeships for the southern district of New York, as recommended by the Judicial Conference of the United States, such a breakdown may occur.

While the need for additional judges is a problem which is not confined to the southern district of New York alone, the southern district is unique in terms of the volume and character of the matters that come before it, and should be treated as such. Not only does this court handle a greater volume of business than any other Federal district court, but situated as it is at the hub of the Nation's largest economic, shipping and financial center, this court is constantly being called upon to decide matters of vital and unusual importance to the country at large— matters involving more complex and difficult factual and legal problems than those found on the dockets of most other Federal district courts. Such matters, whether disposed of before or after trial, inevitably require more time than the relatively simpler cases that characterize most other Federal dockets.

As of July 1, 1959, out of the Nation's total Federal civil caseload of 56,430 cases this district alone had pending before it 10,937 civil cases. But, as indicated above, bare statistical data concerning the number of cases pending does not give the full measure of judicial output because in this caseload there is an unusually large percentage of highly complicated matters which will take far more time to dispose of than the ordinary cases. This load includes—

33 Government antitrust cases, or over one-third such cases pending in the country.

237 patent suits, constituting almost one-fifth of all such cases in the United States.

2,376 admiralty proceedings (exclusive of Jones Act personal injury cases) representing over two-fifths of all admiralty matters on file in the Federal courts.

117 private antitrust suits, or about 20 percent of all such litigation in the Federal courts, and approximately 25 Robinson-Patman Act cases.

Likewise high is the percentage of other cases that involve complex fields of industry, services, and enterprises, ranging from bottled baby foods and bananas to copyright music, color photography, and prizefight promotion. These suits are of the type referred to colloquially by bench and bar as "the big case." Estimates of trial time required range from several weeks to almost a year per case and the amounts of damages claimed run in many cases to over a million dollars each.

The implications of this unique type of caseload may be gathered by reference to some examples. In the admiralty field, for instance, the much publicized limitation of liability proceedings affecting the SS *Andrea Doria* and the M/V *Stockholm* are recorded statistically as only two cases. However, they actually represent a vast number of separate suits, 1 for each claim, and in these 2 cases there were approximately 3,500 claims filed, many of which involved settlement of infants' and deceased persons' claims.

The recent Bethlehem-Youngstown Steel Merger case, a Government antitrust suit tried in the southern district before Judge Edward Weinfeld in 1958, is another typical example. There a motion for summary judgment . . . required the court to consider affidavits, exhibits, and briefs exceeding 400 pages. Despite complete cooperation on all sides to shorten the trial through pretrial conferences and stipulations (One of which was 600 pages long) the trial record ran to 12,000 pages and required the judge to spend a very substantial part of 6 months in chambers before handing down an 88-page decision . . . plus 199 pages of findings of fact and conclusions of law.

The statistics in the Government suit against the investment bankers, *United States* v. *Henry S. Morgan et al.* . . . . tried before Judge Medina, reveal the true character of the "big case." That case involved—

6,848 pages of pretrial depositions, interrogatories, and orders.

10,640 pretrial exhibits, consisting of 43,252 pages.

196 pretrial and interim motions, briefs and memorandums, plus 2,967 pages marked for identification.

417 pages devoted to the court's opinion.

Yet the *Morgan* case would be counted as but one case in statistical records.

In his "Field Study of the Operations of the U.S. Courts," report to Senate Appropriations Committee, April 1959, Mr. Paul J. Cotter stated that "the problem of complicated case exists to a high degree" in this district, and that it has the largest number of "long and complicated cases" in the country. Such litigation demands much more of a judge's time and intellect than the hours spent on the trial itself. Before trial the parties usually present difficult factual and legal questions by way of a series of motions accompanied by voluminous papers and briefs which must be studied for a considerable length of time in chambers before they can intelligently be decided. During trial many more hours must be spent analyzing minutes and exhibits and preparing jury charges; and in nonjury cases (which are customary in the complicated patent and admiralty proceedings, and in many antitrust suits) the judge must after the trial study the exhibits, transcript, and briefs before drafting and filing his findings, conclusions, and opinion.

In addition to the many protracted cases on its civil docket, the southern district of New York has also been the venue for an unusually large number of so-called big criminal cases, such as the recently concluded Appalachin trial and the *Genovese Narcotics* case which was tried in April 1959. It should be noted that the southern district handles approximately 1,100 criminal prosecutions annually, which cannot be deferred, since the Constitution guarantees the accused a prompt disposition; and that this consumes the full time of four judges, making them unavailable for civil cases.

To handle this enormous and complex caseload, which in sheer numbers constitutes 20 percent of the civil cases pending in all the Federal district courts, Congress has allocated to the southern district of New York only 18 judges, or 7 percent of the total number of Federal district judges in the country. According to the Director of the Administrative Office of the U.S. Courts, Warren Olney III, "No district is as undermanned as the southern district of New York."

The 10,937 pending cases in the southern district breaks down to an average of 608 cases pending per judge. There are 12 Federal districts, including the southern district of New York, which have 5 or more judges. All of these districts are located in metropolitan areas and handle approximately 45 percent of all new civil cases filed in the 86 districts having purely Federal jurisdiction. The average caseload pending before each judge in these 12 districts was 321 cases as of June 30, 1959. In other words, each of the judges in the southern district of New York has on the average almost twice the number of cases pending before him as the judges of these other metropolitan districts. The situation as of June 30, 1958, was much the same: At that time in the same 12 metropolitan districts, the average number of cases pending per judge was 336, while in the southern district of New York the average case load per judge was 578. And the average case load of the judges in all 86 districts having exclusive Federal jurisdiction was 249 and 270 in those years.

Of course, if this unduly large number of cases pending per judge in the southern district of New York could be attributed to inefficiency or a lack of industriousness on the part of its judges, the creation of additional judgeships obviously would not be the solution to the problem. But the record establishes conclusively that this is not the case. In the fiscal year ending June 30, 1959, the judges in the southern district of New York on the average disposed of 334 cases per judge, as compared to an average of 253 cases per judge in the 12 metropolitan districts described above. A comparison for the fiscal year ending June 30, 1958, likewise reveals that the southern district disposed of a substantially greater number of cases per judge than the average of the other metropolitan districts. The average number of cases disposed of per judge for all 86 districts having exclusive Federal jurisdiction was even lower: In 1959 the figure was 236 cases disposed of per judge, and in 1958 the average number of cases disposed of per judge was 231.

Yet, despite the fact that through a prodigious effort the judges in the southern district of New York disposed of a much higher than average number of cases in both 1958 and 1959, their caseload continues to swell: In the fiscal year ending June 30, 1958, 6,732 new cases were filed in the southern district and 4,896 cases were disposed of. Last year 6,549 new cases were filed and a total of 6,011 cases disposed of. Thus, from July 1, 1957, to June 30, 1959, the backlog of pending cases has increased by 2,374 cases in this district even though its judges are working harder than ever. Any further efforts to increase the output per judge pose the risk that judges will be forced unconsciously to sacrifice the quality of justice expected of them in an effort to keep up with the increasing workload. There is a limit to the burden that can be handled efficiently, even by the most conscientious judge. If he exceeds that limit his very attempt to keep up with the excessive burden is self-defeating since mental exhaustion will undoubtedly have an adverse effect upon all of his work, not just the excess.

The steady increase in this district's backlog does not completely reflect the seriousness of the situation. With an inadequate number of judges to handle the entire caseload before it, there is a natural tendency on the part of the court to dispose of the shorter cases first and defer the more complicated and protracted ones, since trial of these cases would consume months of the time of the judges involved and result in a sharp increase in the number of cases forming the backlog. This tendency to handle the shorter cases first, however, increases the hard core of the protracted and complicated cases, especially when one realizes that from 2 to 3 percent of the current filings, or approximately 150 new cases each year, are of the complicated and protracted type. Recently Chief Judge Ryan has assigned 4 or 5 complicated and protracted cases apiece for all purposes to each of the 18 judges and we may therefore expect that when trial of some of these cases is commenced in 1960 the delay in handling of regular run of the mill cases will be increased.

Nor have efforts on the part of Congress to stem the engulfing tide of new cases being brought in the Federal courts met with success in the southern district of New York. When Congress passed the Jurisdictional Act of July 25, 1958, which raised the minimum jurisdictional amount from $3,000 to $10,000 in diversity cases, it was anticipated that this would result in a sharp decrease in the number of such cases being brought in the Federal courts, because, of the 67,115 cases filed during the fiscal year ending June 30, 1958, throughout the United States, 25,709 were diversity cases. From the standpoint of the country as a whole, the statute had its desired effect since there was an overall decline of 32.6 percent in the number of such cases filed in the fiscal year 1959. Unfortunately, this decline occurred in districts other than the southern district of New York. In this district, while the number of private civil cases filed in the fiscal year 1959 declined slightly from the previous year (5,388 filed in 1959 as compared to 5,764 filed in 1958), the total number of civil cases commenced in the southern district for 1959 remained substantially the same as it was in 1958; viz, 6,549 as compared with 6,727. Furthermore, an examination of the docket in the southern district for the first 4 months of the current fiscal year (1959–60) reveals that 2,357 new civil cases have been filed, or an average of approximately 600 suits per month, which would mean that we may expect the total for the current year to exceed 7,100 new civil actions.

Thus, while the number of civil actions being commenced in most other districts is on the decline, the number in the southern district of New York is still increasing despite the new act. It should also be noted that the great majority of cases pending in the southern district consist principally of private civil suits by or against the Government, a fact of considerable significance in assessing the court's workload, since it is generally accepted that "private civil cases . . . take much more time of the judges than Government cases."

Other new Federal legislation enacted by Congress at its last session may also lead to additional litigation in the southern district of New York. One example of this legislation is the Labor Management Report and Disclosure Act of 1959 (the so-called Landrum-Griffin bill) enacted in September 1959 . . . which establishes new controls affecting labor unions and their relationships with union members. Both labor and management representatives have predicted that this act will lead to a flood of litigation by individual union members and employees seeking to enforce rights accorded them under the law. The southern district of New York, which is the situs of the headquarters of many important unions, will undoubted be invoked in such cases. We may further anticipate that future sessions of Congress will pass additional legislation in other fields that will likewise add to this important court's burden.

What has been the result thus far of this tremendous caseload in the southern district? The median interval between issue and trial in the district during the fiscal year ending June 30, 1959, was 19.1 months as distinguished from a average median interval of 10.3 months in the 86 districts having exclusive Federal jurisdiction. And the time between the filing of a complaint and trial was 26.7 months in the southern district as compared with 15.3 months in these same 86 districts during that same period.

The delay of over 26 months between filing and trial in the southern district causes hardships to litigants and brings the court into disrepute in the eyes of the public. In patent infringement cases, for example, this inordinate delay has serious consequences for it has encouraged willful and wanton infringement of important patents toward the end of their term. Infringers, secure in the knowledge that if suit is brought in the southern district of New York no determination of the issues involved is probable until after the expiration date of the patent, have deliberately embarked on infringement activities toward the end of the term of many patents, thus foreshortening the effective term of such patents by several years.

In areas of industry engaged in highly competitive research, patented inventions frequently become obsolete in a matter of years; and in these areas the value of a patent is seriously reduced if speedy relief against infringers is not available, and, absent value in the patent, the incentive for invention and development of new products disappears.

But the problem in the southern district of New York is far more serious than one of delay alone. If the present rate of filing continues without abatement, or increases as the first 4 months of 1959–60 indicate will be the case, and the court is given no relief in the form of judges, we face a deterioration in the very quality of justice that this distinguished court will be able to dispense in the future. Because it is inevitable that when the caseload on the individual judges becomes too heavy, not only does court congestion occur but the quality of the justice which is dispensed must ultimately be adversely affected.

We believe that this problem cannot be met by measures short of the enactment of legislation creating six additional judgeships. The court has welcomed any reasonable alternative suggestions including the use of visiting judges from other districts and the adoption of various procedural reforms calculated to increase the court's work product. But past experience has shown that the services of visiting judges, although welcomed with open arms, have limited utility since their help is of a temporary and transitory nature and they cannot therefore be assigned to deal with the court's No. 1 problem, which is the extraordinary number of complicated and protracted cases pending on its calendar. These judges invariably return after a few weeks to their respective home districts which are often hundreds or thousands of miles from New York. To ask them to continue to handle a matter after they have returned to their home districts would not only be unfair to them and to the lawyers and litigants involved but would also be impractical.

With respect to procedural reforms, efforts are continually being made toward improving the court's efficiency. These include studies presently underway of measures designed to eliminate waste of time on the part of the court and counsel in the hearing and disposition of motions and of possible revisions in the court's pretrial procedures. Even with such improvements, however, the court could never expect to increase its already prodigious work product to a point where it could keep abreast of the annual intake of new cases, much less to dispose of the huge backlog of pending litigation before it.

After reviewing the manner in which the present 18 judges are assigned, we are convinced that a minimum of 6 additional judgeships is required to enable the court to keep up with the current annual inflow of civil and criminal business. Any plan for assignment of the 24 judges would still necessitate continuation of the services of retired senior and visiting judges who would be utilized on shorter trials in order to enable a portion of the regularly assigned judges to handle the many complicated and protracted cases instituted in this district. Adequate space and facilities are available to accommodate the six additional judges recommended.

On behalf of our members we urge Congress as strongly as we can to enact promptly legislation creating six additional judgeships for the southern district of New York before the problem has grown to such gargantuan proportions that the damage will be irreparable.

B. THE POLITICS OF NON-PARTISANSHIP

1. Partisan Considerations in Judicial Selection: The Views of Senator Alexander Wiley*

The present political character of the membership of the federal bench is . . . grossly lopsided on the side of democratic leftists. I shall strive to restore a balance so as to assure for the bench an adequate supply of able jurists (including a fair proportion of Republicans), all of whom will be of unimpeachable judicial standing and dedicated to our Constitutional system of checks and balances. . . .

In the past, the opinions of the American Bar Association and other recognized legal groups have not been accorded the weight and respect which are their first due. Instead, as I have indicated, political considerations have too often dominated the appointment of federal judges. So long as I am chairman of the [Senate] judiciary committee, full weight will be given to the recommendation of recognized and respected legal groups, in contrast to those of political officials.

2. The American Bar Association and the Partisanship of Judges*

MR. McCULLOCH. Mr. Chairman, I would like to ask a question. I hope that the statement that you did not have time to deliver will touch upon the selection of judges for the positions that we are about to create.

*"Nomination of Judges: Association's Views to be Given Weight," *American Bar Association Journal*, XXXIII (August, 1947), 110–11. [Footnotes omitted.] Reproduced with permission of the publisher. Copyright (1947) by the American Bar Association.

*Testimony of Mr. Bernard Segal (with an assist from Republican Congressman McCulloch), *Hearings before Subcommittee 5 of the House Judiciary Committee on Bills to Provide for the Appointment of Additional Circuit and District Judges,* March 1 and 2, 1961, 87th Cong. (Washington, D.C.: United States Government Printing Office, 1961), p. 433.

In that connection as I recall you are the chairman of the Standing Committee on the Federal Judiciary of the American Bar Association and I have the August of 1960 report and here is one paragraph of that report,

> This association has long urged that the best judicial appointments will not result until they are made without regard to the political affiliation of the nominees and without limitation to the political party of the President.

Do you still remain of that opinion?

Mr. Segal. I wrote that Mr. McCulloch. I feel it very strongly. I think eventually we must get to nonpartisanship if we hope to retain the respect of the American people for the judiciary. I do not think you can hope to have the respect we all seek for our courts when people again and again say as they do to me, "Well, you know, Bernie, that when a Republican President is in office, only Republicans can get appointed to the Federal Bench, and when a Democratic President is in, only Democrats can get appointed."

I believe even if you get equally competent judges under these circumstances, the judiciary suffers by virtue of that attitude on the part of the people. I think there is an intermediate position to nonpartisanship, because I don't believe we will achieve nonpartisanship yet. Therefore, I should hope for bipartisanship of appointments at this time, as an intermediate step between the present unfortunate partisanship and the goal of nonpartisanship.

Mr. McCulloch. You made this recommendation to the platform committee of both the parties prior to the nominations in the summer of 1960?

Mr. Segal. I did. I should say in all justice to the Democratic National Committee that there was a dislocation due to a fog that delayed a plane which resulted in Mr. Cecil Burney of Corpus Christi, Texas, getting to Mr. Perlman and Mr. Bowles at so late a time that the ABA recommendation could not receive the consideration it otherwise could have received.

The Republican plank was one which I participated in preparing, just as I was in readiness to do for a Democratic plank.

Mr. McCulloch. We think you did yeoman service for our party.

3. The Attorney General Replies*

Mr. McCulloch. Do you have any opinion concerning the advisability of the Federal judiciary being reasonably in balance with respect to the politics of the judges prior to their appointments?

Mr. Kennedy. I think that the best qualified individuals should be selected as judges, Congressman.

Mr. McCulloch. I think that is a very good answer. I would like, Mr. Chairman, to have for the record the best information available concerning the percentage of

*Hearings before Subcommittee 5 of the House Judiciary Committee on Bills to Provide for the Appointment of Additional Circuit and District Judges, March 1 and 2, 1961, 87th Cong. (Washington, D.C.: United States Government Printing Office, 1961), pp. 402–3.

appointments of Federal judges both in the appellate and in the trial courts down through the years. This information is furnished by the Library of Congress.

During William Howard Taft's term as President there were 62 judicial appointments. Out of this total there were 47 judges appointed, who at the time of their appointment were Republicans. I made the distinction "who at the time of their appointment" because I am hopeful that in all matters of litigation after appointment judges are not partisan. There were 10 who were Democrats and 5 with political affiliations unknown.

President Wilson made 72 appointments, 71 were Democrats when appointed and 1 was a Republican.

President Harding appointed a total of 51 judges. Forty-nine of them were Republicans when appointed and two were Democrats.

President Coolidge appointed a total of 84 judges. Seventy-seven were Republicans when appointed, four were Democrats, and the politics of three were unknown.

President Hoover appointed a total of 69 judges. Fifty-seven were Republicans when appointed and twelve were Democrats.

President Franklin D. Roosevelt made 225 appointments. Two hundred and seventeen were Democrats when appointed and eight were Republicans.

President Truman made a total of 141 appointments. One hundred and eighteen were Democrats when appointed and thirteen were Republicans. And I might say that at the close of the Truman administration there was the greatest imbalance in the Federal judiciary with respect to the politics of the judges at the time of appointment. At that time approximately 84 percent of the Federal judges were Democrats.

President Eisenhower made a total of 186 appointments. One hundred and seventy-five were Republicans when appointed and eleven Democrats. President Eisenhower, of course, needs no defense from me; but I suppose if I were called upon to defend him, I would say that in view of his very definitely stated opinion that the appointments during his term was a studied attempt to bring into a reasonable balance the politics of the individuals who are appointed as Federal judges.

THE CHAIRMAN. I might say in that connection that from the figures that have been read to us, there has been made quite manifest the partisanship of the appointments of judges by Republican Presidents as well as Democratic Presidents. It is nothing new in the judicial system. But as I stated before I am quite sure that our present President will appoint efficient, erudite, objective, and honest judges. I don't think we need to have any fear on that score. It is true that this committee approved the bill in the last Congress and the leadership was reluctant to embrace it. Very frankly I believe they contemplated a change in the Executive and the leadership gambled as it were—and won—that a new administration will make the appointments. That is nothing new in our political history. I am quite sure that the gentleman from Ohio will undoubtedly have certain recommendations to make and I am sure that he will be heard attentively here as well as in the White House on those suggestions.

[Before the measure passed the House and Senate by voice votes, Representative Emanuel Celler (Dem., N.Y.), chairman of the House Judiciary Committee, said the judgeships should not be handed out as prizes to deserving Democrats, but he added:

"Being a realist, candor impels me to say that being a Democrat will not hurt one's chances for appointment."

C. OTHER ASPECTS OF THE APPOINTMENT PROCESS

After Congress has acted in its periodic determinations of the size of the federal courts, a key factor governing the characteristics of judicial selection is the strategy of the chief executive. The quality of the judicial appointees is, of course, a paramount consideration, but a successful nominating record can be compiled by a President only if he combines keen awareness of the qualitative needs with a precise sense of political timing and propriety. More often than not, the President's choices must literally run a gauntlet of hostile critics among members of the Senate Judiciary Committee. In recent years particular concern has been expressed over the special problem raised by recess appointments.]

1. Recess Appointments to the Supreme Court— Constitutional but Unwise?*

SENATOR McCARTHY. You, of course, I assume, will agree with me—and a number of the members of the committee—that communism is not merely a political way of life, it is a conspiracy designed to overthrow the United States Government.

MR. BRENNAN. Will you forgive me an embarrassment, Senator. You appreciate that I am a sitting Justice of the Court. There are presently pending before the Court some cases in which I believe will have to be decided the question what is communism, at least in the frame of reference in which those particular cases have come before the Court.

I know, too, that you appreciate that having taken an oath of office it is my obligation not to discuss any of those pending matters. With that qualification, whether under the label communism or any other label, any conspiracy to overthrow the Government of the United States is a conspiracy that I not only would do anything appropriate to aid suppressing, but a conspiracy which, of course, like every American, I abhor.

SENATOR McCARTHY. Mr. Brennan, I don't want to press you unnecessarily, but the question was simple. You have not been confirmed yet as a member of the Supreme Court. There will come before the Court a number of questions involving the all-important issue of whether or not communism is merely

*Note, *Stanford Law Review*, X (December, 1957), 124–47. [Footnotes omitted.] Reproduced with permission of the publisher. Copyright © 1957 by the *Stanford Law Review*.

a political party or whether it represents a conspiracy to overthrow this Government.

I believe that the Senators are entitled to know how you feel about that and you won't be prejudicing then any cases by answering that question.[1]

Senator McCarthy's interrogation of Justice William Brennan, who was at the time a recess appointee to the Supreme Court, dramatizes the inherent conflict between the practice of making recess appointments to constitutional courts and the independence of the judiciary. This conflict arises from the fact that it is universally accepted that article III provides for life tenure for constitutional judges, while clause 3 of article II, section 2 has been exercised to fill up vacancies on constitutional courts with judges holding only temporary commissions. However, such recess appointments have been questioned only in the last four years, in connection with the appointments of Chief Justice Warren and Justice Brennan. Apparently those who wrote the Constitution saw no conflict between clause 3 of article II, section 2 and article III.

THE RECESS APPOINTMENT POWER

During the Federal Convention of 1789, advocates of a strong executive sought to give the exclusive power to appoint major federal officers, including Supreme Court Justices, to the President. Those who favored a weak executive argued that the Senate, the House of Representatives, or both should have the power. The issue was resolved by providing that the President shall "nominate, and by and with the Advice and Consent of the Senate, shall appoint . . . Judges of the Supreme Court. . . ."

In addition to the quoted provision, an ancillary clause was approved, apparently without debate. That was clause 3 of article II, section 2 and it reads: "The President shall have Power to fill up all Vacancies that may happen during the Recess of the Senate, by granting Commissions which shall expire at the End of their next Session."

Apparently its purpose was to assure the President the capacity for filling vacancies at any time to keep the Government running smoothly.

THE PROBLEMS RAISED

When the President uses the general power granted to him by clause 3 to make recess appointments to the Supreme Court and to other constitutional courts, two basic problems are raised: (1) Should a recess appointment of an article III judge be upheld as constitutional? (2) If so, how can such an appointment be made most consistent with the requirements of article III? A consideration of these problems requires, first, a discussion and analysis of recent arguments made against such

[1] From *Hearing before the Senate Committee on the Judiciary on Nomination of William Joseph Brennan, Jr.,* 85th Cong., 1st sess., (Washington, D.C.: United States Government Printing Office, 1957), pp. 17–18.

TABLE OF RECESS APPOINTMENTS *To The Supreme Court*

Recess Appointees	Date Appointed	Date Nomination Received by Senate	Date Confirmed	Sat on the Court Before Confirmed
Thomas Johnson	Aug. 5, 1791	Nov. 1, 1791	Nov. 7, 1791	No
John Rutledge	July 1, 1795	Dec. 10, 1795	Dec. 15, 1795 (rejected)	Yes
Bushrod Washington	Sept. 29, 1798	Dec. 19, 1798	Dec. 20, 1798	No
Henry Brockholst Livingston	Nov. 10, 1806	Dec. 15, 1806	Dec. 17, 1806	No
Smith Thompson	Sept. 1, 1823	Dec. 8, 1823	Dec. 9, 1823	No
John McKinley	April 22, 1837	Sept. 19, 1837	Sept. 25, 1837	No
Levi Woodbury	Sept. 20, 1845	Dec. 23, 1845	Jan. 3, 1846	Uncertain
Benjamin Curtis	Sept. 22, 1851	Dec. 12, 1851	Dec. 20, 1851	Yes
David Davis	Oct. 17, 1862	Dec. 3, 1862	Dec. 8, 1862	Uncertain
Earl Warren	Oct. 2, 1953	Jan. 11, 1954	March 1, 1954	Yes
William Brennan, Jr.	Oct. 16, 1956	Jan. 14, 1957	March 19, 1957	Yes

appointments by constitutional scholars, and of the validity of those arguments in light of historical practice and of the practical importance of recess appointments, and second, a tracing of the development of the advice and consent power of the Senate and an evaluation of the importance of that development to a solution of both questions posed.

CONSTITUTIONALITY: SCHOLARSHIP AND HISTORY

THE ARGUMENT OF CONSTITUTIONAL SCHOLARS

Although the conflict between clause 3 and article III has not been drawn in question in the courts or in the legal periodicals, constitutional scholars have indicated concern over the apparent inconsistency of the recess appointment power with article III, and one has suggested that recess appointments violate the Constitution.

The argument against the constitutionality of recess appointments is based upon two contentions. The first stems from the "during good Behaviour" clause of article III. It is said that this clause provides life tenure for a judge sitting on a constitutional court. Thus, since a recess appointee, who holds his commission only until the end of the next session of the Senate, does not have the life tenure required by article III, use of the recess appointment power to fill vacancies on constitutional courts seems improper.

The second contention is that the actions of the recess appointee during the recess may be influenced by the fact or possibility of a Presidential decision to nominate the appointee for permanent appointment subject to confirmation by the Senate. It is observed that the framers agreed that judges must be "as independent as the lot of humanity will admit," and the pressure resulting from the possibility of nomination with appointment dependent on the result of senatorial investigation, does not permit that independence. It is concluded, therefore, that any recess appointment to a constitutional court violates the "spirit of the Constitution, and possibly also its letter."

This argument is not without merit. The records of the Constitutional Convention and the authoritative writings of those who participated in the drafting of the Constitution clearly indicate that the independence of the judiciary was considered essential to successful government. Hamilton said that tenure during good behavior— thus inferentially an independent judiciary—"is the best expedient which can be devised in any government, to secure a steady, upright, and impartial administration of the laws." It was thought that the requisite independence could be vouchsafed only by providing life tenure to those who served as judges on the federal bench.

The "during good Behaviour" clause admits to no other meaningful reading than that once a constitutional judge is appointed he shall sit for life, unless he is impeached or retires. It might be argued that the clause means only that good behavior is required of a jurist sitting on a federal court whether pursuant to a temporary or a permanent commission. However, this argument is untenable. The "good Behaviour" clause has been the constitutional basis for the practice of granting lifetime commissions to constitutional judges for over 150 years. This practice has merely put into effect the well-established intention of the framers that "good Behaviour" would mean life tenure. It would appear, therefore, that life tenure is one of the essential attributes of article III judges.

If life tenure is required by article III, is seems that the recess appointment power is inconsistent with that requirement insofar as it allows a judge to sit on an article III court while holding only a temporary commission. The language of the two parts of the Constitution cannot be reconciled unless clause 3 is interpreted to constitute an exception to article III in the case of recess appointments, or unless clause 3 is interpreted not to include the power to make recess appointments to constitutional courts.

It is arguable that to determine the essential attributes of a federal judge, only article III should be consulted. Article III is the particular part of the Constitution dealing with the federal courts and federal judges, and it is there that the judiciary is created and given its powers and complexion. On the other hand, article II deals with and creates the *executive* department of the government. Clause 3, of article II, section 2, deals only with the President's power to fill up vacancies and consequently is concerned only by inference with the judiciary of the United States. This argument lends weight to the conclusion that clause 3 does not include the power to make recess appointments to constitutional courts.

HISTORICAL PRACTICE TO 1862

Between 1791 and 1862, there were nine recess appointments to the Supreme Court. There is no evidence that the constitutionality of ony of those nine appointments was questioned, although they were made during a critical period of constitutional interpretation.

Two particularly outstanding incidents during this period were those involving Chief Justice John Rutledge and Justice Benjamin Curtis. Rutledge was given a recess appointment on July 1, 1795, and took his seat shortly thereafter. On December 15, 1795, Rutledge was rejected by the Senate. While he was on the Court, Rutledge participated in two decisions and delivered the opinion of the Court in the first. There is, however, no evidence that anyone contested the propriety of his sitting on the Court temporarily and not for life as article III is taken to require.

On September 22, 1851, Justice Curtis received his recess appointment to the Court. He immediately assumed his duties as a Justice by going on circuit, and soon thereafter he was faced with determining whether a jury could find the Federal Fugitive Slave Act unconstitutional as argued by defendant's counsel. Curtis found that the jury had no such power. It is to Curtis' credit that he could withstand denunciations by the radical antislavery interests in the North and consider such a controversial statute at a time when he had yet to be confirmed by the Senate. Furthermore, Curtis took his seat on the Court on December 1, 1851, and participated in the business of the Court although he was not confirmed until December 20. Although the influence which may have been brought to bear on Curtis while he was on circuit or on the Court could have tended to deprive him of the independence required by article III, there is again no evidence of anyone objecting to the practice of recess appointments.

But perhaps the most significant historical fact is that by the end of 1823, there had been five recess appointments to the Supreme Court. During this period, when those who wrote the Constitution were alive, not one dissenting voice was raised against the practice. It would seem that the framers must have looked upon recess appointments as an exceptional expedient to fill vacancies on the Court and not as a violation of article III.

It appears reasonable to consider those five appointments, and the four additional ones made before the end of 1862, as examples of the growth of a constitutional practice. Justice Frankfurter has said:

> *The Constitution is a framework of government. Therefore the way the framework has consistently operated fairly establishes that it has operated according to its true nature. Deeply embedded traditional ways of conducting government cannot supplant the Constitution or legislation, but they give meaning to the words of a text or supply them.*

It is logical to conclude that by 1862 historical practice had established that use of clause 3 to make recess appointments to constitutional courts was not inconsistent with article III.

Since 1862, there have been but two recess appointments to the Supreme Court, those of Chief Justice Warren and Justice Brennan. It remains to be considered whether in the elapsed ninety-one years conditions have arisen to make the exercise of that power unwise. Such consideration requires analysis of the development of the advice and consent power of the Senate and the impact of that development on the asserted constitutionality of recess appointments.

THE ADVICE AND CONSENT OF THE SENATE

THE ROLE OF PARTISAN POLITICS, 1789–1894

The advocates of a strong executive felt that inclusion of a Presidential appointive power in article II represented a significant victory. They viewed the power to nominate as equivalent to the power to appoint, and the Senate, it was thought, had a mere veto power.

Early in the nation's history, however, the Senate began an expansion of its confirmation power. The Senators of the President's party initiated the device of senatorial courtesy to perpetuate or obtain patronage. The opposition party often used the necessity of confirmation as a political weapon to embarrass the President. It was soon apparent that strictly partisan politics would play a large role in any confirmation by the Senate.

The first incident to dramatize the importance of partisan politics to the confirmation of justices was the rejection of Chief Justice Rutledge because of a speech he made in opposition to the Jay Treaty, which was considered by many Federalists to be the "touchstone of true Federalism." That incident is considered to have established the precedent for Senate inquiry into the political views and ideas of nominees. Moreover, it was a precedent for the rejection of nominees whose views contrasted with those of the majority of the Senate.

During the nineteenth century, the Senate continued to use the confirmation power to inquire into the political beliefs of Supreme Court nominees. Professional qualifications were largely ignored. The attitude of the Senate was perhaps justified, however, for the President often made his selection solely on the theory of placing on the Court a justice who would perpetuate the President's policies through interpretation of the Constitution while on the bench. From 1844 to 1861, the Senate-President conflict led to the strictly partisan rejection of three nominees to the Court, and the failure of six others to obtain confirmation. Five of those instances occurred in the last year of a president's term when he was apparently attempting to perpetuate his administration's policies through the Court.

From 1862 to 1894, six additional nominees failed to receive confirmation by the Senate. One was nominated by Johnson, three by Grant, and two by Cleveland. The period of emphasis on partisan politics reached a climax in 1894, when Senator Hill through the device of senatorial courtesy succeeded in blocking the confirmation of two of President Cleveland's nominees, W. B. Hornblower and W. H. Peckham, simply because of a bitter personal fued between Hill and the President. That marked the first and last time a Senator successfully used the device of senatorial courtesy to block a nomination to the Court. But partisan politics had taken its toll: from the years 1789 to 1894 eighty-four nominees were considered for the Court and twenty failed to receive confirmation.

A CHANGE IN EMPHASIS, 1894–1957

Toward the end of the nineteenth century the Senate began using the confirmation power to inquire into the economic and social as well as political philosophies of a nominee. The reasons for the practice of scrutinizing the ideas of a nominee rather than his political background can be found in the industrial, economic and sociological developments of the period. In the last quarter of the nineteenth century, interstate and foreign commerce developed rapidly, and this expansion was paralleled by the growth of industrial empires. Along with the development of interstate commerce and the general industrial and economic surge came the birth of strong class interests, in labor and in agriculture to name but two. And as an incident to bigness came government regulation. These changes generated conflicts that in any other nation would have been dealt with either by the executive or legislative branches of the government or by both, but which in the United States must eventually come before the judiciary. Thus, the Supreme Court became more than a place of last resort for questions of private law: it became a battleground where the social and economic edicts of the Congress were to be tested. It was inevitable, therefore, that the Senate, in an attempt to insure a sympathetic judiciary, came to use the advice and consent power to pass on the social and economic philosophies of the nominees. John P. Frank has said:

> *The new issues that came before the Court caused new factors to weigh in the selection of its membership. After 1877, in greater degree than ever before,*

219

politicians and the public examined a prospective Justice's economic as well as his political views. The chief objections to appointees considered earlier in this discussion were levelled at their political sins or personal characteristics. After 1877 the farmers objected to Matthews as a railroad lawyer; labor fought Lurton because it considered him biased. "Friends of property" quailed at Holmes' appointment and revolted at the choice of Brandeis.

Indeed the Brandeis hearings vividly dramatize the change in the role of the confirmation power. The opposition to Brandeis came primarily from a group of New England railroad and shoe manufacturing interests which had felt the power of Brandeis' social and economic philosophy as expressed in his role as a "people's lawyer." The hearings before the Senate Committee on the Judiciary were made public, contrary to custom, for the express purpose of minimizing the charges that would be brought against Brandeis. Nevertheless, the hearings lasted from February 9 to March 15, 1916, a period of about five weeks.

The issue before the committee was whether a conservative group would be able to block the appointment of a liberal nominee. But President Wilson, in order to save his nominee, personally intervened and made the confirmation a party issue. The vote in the committee and the Senate split along party lines and Brandeis was finally confirmed. The Brandeis hearings were an indication that in the future a nominee of strong social or economic convictions would face a trying experience before the Senate.

Nine years later, in 1925, Justice Stone became the first nominee to appear in person before the Judiciary Committee and was asked to explain his political and social philosophies. Much of the opposition to Stone's appointment was generated by strictly partisan politics coupled with charges that Stone had harrassed Senator Wheeler with a dilatory prosecution and that he had been guilty of unethical conduct in the case of *Ownbey* v. *Morgan*. However, a third charge against Stone was that he was a representative of Morgan interests. Senator Norris announced that he would vote against Stone because Supreme Court decisions flow fundamentally from the viewpoint of justices, and Stone's views, he thought, were biased because of his Morgan associations. Striking evidence of the fact that Norris' opposition was not based on party politics was his apology and admission of error at the confirmation of Stone as Chief Justice in 1941.

And in 1930, J. J. Parker, because of his allegedly unpopular social views, became the only nominee to have been rejected since 1894. The testimony of organized Negro and labor groups convinced the Committee on the Judiciary and eventually the Senate that Parker would not be able properly to fulfill the function of a Supreme Court Justice because of his bias against Negroes and unions. It is interesting to note that the opposition to Justice Brandeis was based on alleged radicalism, whereas the opposition to Parker was based on his alleged reactionism.

Investigation of nominees has continued to be directed toward the social and economic as well as political views of the individual. In 1939, Justice Frankfurter appeared in person before the Committee on the Judiciary to undergo examination by Senator McCarran and finally to answer the question put by Senator Neely as to whether or not he was a Communist. Justice Harlan, in 1955, was questioned extensively and was asked to justify his membership in an organization dedicated to a federal union of the North Atlantic countries. Most recently Justice Brennan was called upon to define Communism and to indicate how he would react toward cases which would come before him involving that political philosophy.

And as an incident to increasing emphasis on social and economic views there has emerged the practice of bringing the nominee before the Committee on the Judiciary in person, a practice which now appears to be firmly established. Also, full opportunity to testify is now given to witnesses both for and against a nominee, with apparently little restriction as to their number or character.

CONSTITUTIONALITY OF RECESS APPOINTMENTS TODAY

It would be inaccurate to say that increasingly close Senate scrutiny into the economic and social philosophies of conventional nominees to constitutional courts is a violation of the independence of the Judiciary. Desire for confirmation may induce the nominee to compromise or appear innocuous while before the Committee on the Judiciary, but once he is confirmed and appointed, life tenure places him beyond the influence of Congress or the Executive. This is especially true of Justices of the Supreme Court, where the importance of the Court and the protection of article III seem to combine to give all Justices a sense of genuine independence. . . .

However, the case of the recess appointee expecting an advice and consent nomination is different. As he sits on the Court he has full knowledge that he has yet to face the process of confirmation as it has developed. Paul Freund, at the time of the recess appointment of Chief Justice Warren, feared the effect, in terms of judicial independence, of a Justice sitting on the Court "with one eye over his shoulder on Congress."

There is evidence to support the conclusion that the Supreme Court shares the fear of Professor Freund. On December 9, 1952, *Brown* v. *Board of Education,* the school desegregation case, was argued before the Court. The Court delayed its decision because of the character of the issue and perhaps because of the failing health of Chief Justice Vinson. On June 8, 1953, the Court ordered the *Brown* case restored to the docket and reargument was assigned for October 12, 1953. Chief Justice Vinson died on September 8, 1953, and Earl Warren was given a recess appointment on October 2. The *Brown* case was finally reargued on December 8, 1953.

When the Senate reconvened in January, 1954, the *Brown* case was still undecided. Thus, whatever the southern Senators may have thought Warren's views on desegragation would be, they could not make an issue of them at the confirmation hearings.

On March 1, 1954, Warren was confirmed as Chief Justice. The *Brown* decision was handed down six weeks later by the Court. Chief Justice Warren wrote the unanimous opinion which struck down the "separate but equal" doctrine as unconstitutional.

On October 16, 1956, Justice Brennan received his recess appointment to the

Court. On October 17, 1956, *Jencks* v. *United States* was argued, and on November 14, and 15, 1956, *United States* v. *E. I. du Pont de Nemours & Co.* was argued. Justice Brennan was confirmed by the Senate on March 25, 1957. The decisions in the *du Pont* and *Jencks* cases were both handed down on June 3, 1957, Justice Brennan writing the opinion in each case.

It would not seem presumptuous to suggest that the motivation for the delay in the *Brown, du Pont* and *Jencks* cases might have been a desire to immunize Chief Justice Warren and Justice Brennan from possible strong attacks by Southern Senators, large corporate interests, and law enforcement agencies, both federal and local. No doubt the delay in handing down the decisions in such controversial cases could be attributed to the difficulties involved in opinion writing and the fact that nine men of differing sociological and economic inclinations had the task of deciding highly controversial issues. Yet, the other possibility exists and so long as there is a chance that the Court will be motivated by concern over the repercussions of their opinions in the Senate, the independence of the judiciary is impaired. There is little doubt that the recess appointee himself does not have the requisite independence of article III, and that he must consider the possible effects of his action on the Senate and on the defeated litigants or disgrunted parties who may appear before the Judiciary Committee.

A good argument can be made that regardless of the status of recess appointments in 1862, factors exists today, which, had they been present at the turn of the eighteenth century, would have caused the framers to object to recess appointments as being an impairment of the independence of the Judiciary. Those factors include: (1) The change in the business of the Supreme Court; (2) the change in emphasis of the Senate's advice and consent power; (3) subjection of nominees to examination in person by the Committee on the Judiciary or other Senators, at hearings where the testimony of any interested party is admitted; (4) participation of Justices Warren and Brennan in several decisions prior to confirmation.

The change in the business of the Supreme Court allows any influence exerted on a nominee to have a much more far-reaching and damaging effect. Certainly there were many great policy decisions during the early nineteenth century; yet it is generally true that decisions by the Court had little importance for anyone but the actual parties. In contrast, the large majority of decisions today are based on public law and affect several persons or interests. It is also possible that since most of the decisions during the early nineteenth century had to be based on well established principles of common law, the chances for influence were to some degree limited. The requirements of pure legal analysis and stare decisis may have served as a safeguard against outside influence.

The changed use of the advice and consent power of the Senate contributes to the possibility of influence on a nominee. During most of the nineteenth century, whether a nominee was to be confirmed by the Senate depended largely upon the nominee's political affiliations, his popularity, and the strength of the President. There was little he could do after the time he was issued a temporary commission that would materially alter the Senate's disposition toward him. A recess appointee today, however, might be able, if he so desired, successfully to compromise his economic and social beliefs long enough to be confirmed by the Senate. This is possible because the individual policy of a nominee is likely to be unknown at the time he receives his recess appointment.

Interrogation of a nominee and uncontrolled testimony of witnesses, in addition to increasing the possibility of senatorial influence on a nominee's actions, tend to put him in the national spotlight and subject him to prejudiced attacks which reflect on the dignity of the judiciary. The publicity incident to public hearings and interrogation reflects on the whole Court to a much greater extent when the one being interrogated is sitting as a member of that Court.

Finally, the participation by a Justice in several decisions while he has "one eye over his shoulder on Congress" could deprive the litigants of a fair hearing. Of the nine recess appointees prior to Chief Justice Warren, only two, Rutledge and Curtis, sat on the Court before confirmation, and neither participated in the Court's business nearly so extensively as Chief Justice Warren and Justice Brennan. Only preconfirmation participation in a case gives the questions of influence and independence significant practical importance. The participation of Rutledge and Curtis was so minor that it is probable those questions were never so vividly presented as they are today.

These four factors, along with possible influence on the Court and the ever-present pressure on the nominee, combine to form a setting quite different from that which confronted those who wrote the Constitution. It appears fair to conclude that although the President has power to make recess appointments, the exercise of that power today is unwise.

The Constitution, however, should not be interpreted not to give the President the power to make recess appointments to constitutional courts. The lapse of ninety-one years between the recess appointment of Justice Davis and that of Chief Justice Warren and the factors which have come into play during that time should not be taken to have changed the meaning of clause 3 intended by the framers and established by early historical practice.

This conclusion is further compelled by a very practical necessity. Article III provides that judges "both of the supreme and inferior Courts shall hold their Offices during good Behaviour." If the President were foreclosed from filling up vacancies on constitutional courts, all vacancies on federal district courts and courts of appeals as well as the Supreme Court would remain unfilled until the next session of Congress. The impact of prolonged vacancies on an already overworked federal judiciary would be more damaging to the capacity for effective action of the President and of the federal government than any alleged violation of article III by recess appointments. And the unfairness to a litigant having the decision of his case prolonged because of the lack of federal judges outweighs the possibility that a recess appointee will decide the case unfairly because of outside influences.

The problem that emerges, therefore, is not how to theorize away the existence of the recess appointment power, but rather whether the exercise of that power can be made consistent with article III.

PROPOSED SOLUTIONS

In fact, there appears to be no practical way to make recess appointments to constitutional courts completely consistent with the requirements of article III. However, some suggestions that do attempt at absolute consistency should be reviewed here.

A solution suggested by Professor Hart and concurred in by Professors Brown and Sutherland of the Harvard Law School is to call a special session of the Senate for each recess vacancy. This solution is practically and politically unfeasible for two reasons. First, a Senator's time is limited, and since he is subject to popular election, he must spend sufficient time at "home" to keep his political fences mended. The impracticality of recalling the Senate in an election year is apparent. An example is that President Eisenhower would have been required to call a special session of the Senate when he appointed Justice Brennan on October 16, 1956, three weeks before the Presidential election. It is doubtful that any President would call a special session of the Senate under comparable circumstances.

A special session would also tend unduly to emphasize the confirmation power of the Senate. If a special session were to be called for every recess appointment, it would be an invitation to make the nominee himself a political issue.

Another suggestion is to require that the individual given the recess appointment not be nominated to fill the vacancy permanently. However, it might be difficult to obtain qualified men to undertake for only a brief term the great responsibility attendant to a seat on the Supreme Court because of the limited reward. But the strongest objection to this solution is that no individual serving on the Court for only three or four months could possibly succeed in doing the job required of him, and the machinery of the Court would be disrupted because of the lack of continuity where a recess appointee heard the argument of a case and then was not present for the complete process of opinion writing and decision. The same objection would, of course, apply to any plan which temporarily elevated a circuit judge to the Supreme Court and disqualified him from filling the vacancy permanently, or which returned a retired Justice to the Court during the recess.

Although all positive solutions to the problem of consistency appear impractical, there remains one practical solution which would assure a minimum of conflict with article III. The Constitution does not *require* that the President make recess appointments. It reads "The President shall have Power . . .," not "he shall exercise the Power in all events." Therefore the President should view the recess appointment power as being strictly discretionary and to be exercised only in cases of clearest emergency. Theoretically such an emergency would be found to exist only in the case of death or incapacitation of several Justices or judges or in a situation in which the work load of the Court or the lower federal courts becomes unmanageable. If an emergency of either type were to arise, a responsible Senate should not be antagonized against the appointment and might be expected to proceed to a quick confirmation with a minimum of publicity after the recess. In addition, of course, this solution would leave the President free to fill up vacancies on the inferior constitutional courts, where an emergency of the second type is more likely to exist.

It can be argued that this solution is nothing more than a rationalization of what already exists, or that the President may purport to find an emergency in any case of vacancy because of the work load of the constitutional courts. This argument can be met only by saying that it is the responsibility of the Executive not to abuse discretionary power. A developed practice of avoiding the making of recess appointments except in clearest cases of emergency would act as a strong reminder to the Executive that the interest in having an independent judiciary outweighs the interest in making an advantageous political appointment.

Furthermore, it may safely be predicted that the Senate will continue to be strongly interested in the political and social philosophies of a Supreme Court nominee so long as the subject matter of Congressional legislation and that of judicial decisions overlap. It is equally safe to predict that the last "explosive issue" has not been decided by the Supreme Court. These two factors alone should compel the President to exercise the recess appointment power only in unusual circumstances.

[Private individuals and groups have often attempted to persuade the President and members of the Senate to appoint or deny appointment to potential judges and justices on the basis of their ideological attitudes. And in some extremely controversial situations they have resorted to legal action designed to deny a place on the bench to individuals whom they violently opposed. The appointment of Senator Hugo Lafayette Black to the Supreme Court aroused fierce opposition which continued even after his confirmation. The two petitions that follow were presented to the Supreme Court in the October term of 1937. Both were denied by the Court.]

2. An Attempt to Deny a Supreme Court Seat by Legal Means*

PETITION FOR AN ORDER TO SHOW CAUSE

"Comes now the above named Albert Levitt, Petitioner, and presents this petition that the Supreme Court order Hugo L. Black to show affirmative cause why he should be permitted to serve as an Associate Justice of the Supreme Court of the United States, under the appointment which he now holds, and in support thereof respectfully shows:

"1. That the said Albert Levitt is a Member of the Bar of the Supreme Court of the United States, is an humble officer of said Court, and as such is under a duty, and has the right, to present to this Honorable Court any information or knowledge which he may have, that any person has engaged in, or is about to engage in, any unlawful activity which will interfere with or prevent the proper and lawful administration of justice in the Supreme Court of the United States.

"2. That the said Albert Levitt is a practicing attorney at law with the right to plead causes before the Supreme Court of the United States and, as such, has the right to ask that only those persons who have been lawfully appointed as Chief

*Ex Parte Albert Levitt, reproduced in George Washington Law Review, VI (1937–1938), 88–89. [Footnotes omitted.] Reproduced with permission of the publisher. Copyright (1937) by the George Washington Law Review.

Justice of the United States or as Associate Justices of the United States Supreme Court should be permitted to sit as judges in causes and controversies which come before the Supreme Court of the United States for trial and judgment."

The provisions of Article 1, section 6, clause 2 of the Constitution of the United States, of section 215 of the Judicial Code (28 U. S. C. 321), of the New Retirement Act of March 1, 1937, and of section 260 of the Judicial Code (28 U. S. C. 375) were then set forth.

* * *

"7. That, the said Act of March 1, 1937, did increase the emoluments of the Justices of the Supreme Court of the United States, including the emoluments of every Associate Justice of the Supreme Court of the United States.

"8. That on March 1, 1937, Hugo L. Black was a Senator within the meaning of the Constitution, Article 1, Section 6, Clause 2, and so was ineligible to be appointed to any civil office under the authority of the United States the emoluments of which had been increased by the above mentioned Act of March 1, 1937, as the term for which Hugo L. Black had been elected Senator did not expire until January 1, 1939.

9. That, on the 2nd day of June, 1937, Willis Van Devanter then an Associate Justice of the Supreme Court of the United States did retire from regular active service on the bench of the Supreme Court of the United States in accordance with the provisions of the Act of March 1, 1937, above set out.

"10. That, the retirement of Associate Justice Willis Van Devanter did not annul or vacate his commission as an Associate Justice of the Supreme Court of the United States.

"11. That, the above mentioned Willis Van Devanter still is an Associate Justice of the Supreme Court of the United States within the meaning of Section 215 of the Judicial Code of the United States . . .

"12. That, the Supreme Court of the United States lawfully still consists of only one Chief Justice and eight Associate Justices, including Associate Justice Willis Van Devanter.

"13. That, there is not now, and there has not been since the retirement of the said Willis Van Devanter, any vacancy upon the bench of the Supreme Court of the United States.

"14. That, on or about the 16th day of August, 1937, the President of the United States did purport to appoint the said Hugo L. Black, . . . to be an Associate Justice of the Supreme Court of the United States, and . . . the Senate of the United States Congress did purport to confirm the above purported appointment . . .

"15. That the above mentioned purported appointment and purported confirmation of Hugo L. Black to be an Associate Justice of the Supreme Court of the United States were and are unlawful, null and void, because the said Hugo L. Black was ineligible to be appointed as an Associate Justice of the Supreme Court of the United States by reason of the prohibition found in the Constitution of the United States, Article I, Section 6, Clause 2, and, further, because there was no vacancy then existing upon the bench of the Supreme Court of the United States which the

President of the United States could lawfully fill with the advice and consent of the United States Senate; and, further, because the Senate of the United States had no authority to confirm the purported appointment of Hugo L. Black to be an Associate Justice of the Supreme Court of the United States for the reason that the said Hugo L. Black was ineligible to be so appointed and confirmed.

* * *

"17. That the said Hugo L. Black cannot lawfully serve as an Associate Justice of the Supreme Court of the United States.

"18. That the said Hugo L. Black cannot lawfully be installed as an Associate Justice of the Supreme Court of the United States.

"19. That the installation of Hugo L. Black as an Associate Justice of the Supreme Court of the United States and his purporting to serve as an Associate Justice of the Supreme Court of the United States will interfere with and prevent the due, proper and lawful administration of justice in the Supreme Court of the United States.

"Therefore, and by reason of all the foregoing facts, your petitioner respectfully prays that this Honorable Court issue an order that the said Hugo L. Black affirmatively show cause why he should be permitted to serve as an Associate Justice of the Supreme Court of the United States under the purported appointment which he now holds; and your petitioner further prays for such other relief and assistance as may be provided by the Constitution and the laws of the United States, under the facts herein stated.

Respectfully submitted,
Albert Levitt,
Pro. se."

3. Another Attempt to Oust Justice Black

"PETITION FOR REHEARING OF ORDER DENYING PETITION FOR WRITS OF CERTIORARI*

"Come now petitioners in the foregoing numbered and stated causes, by their attorneys of record undersigned, and jointly and severally pray leave of this Honorable Court to file the following petition for rehearing of the order or orders entered by this Honorable Court on October 18, 1937, wherein the petition for writs of certiorari in these causes was denied. This petition for rehearing urges and assigns to the court, in support thereof, the following grounds and reasons:

* * *

"Because the petition for writs of certiorari in these cases was considered by this Honorable Court and order handed down denying said petition on October 18, 1937. That Honorable Hugo L. Black participated as an Associate Justice of this Court

*Frank J. Ryan et al. reproduced in George Washington Law Review, VI (1937–1938), 89–91. [Footnotes omitted.] Reproduced with permission of the publisher.

in the consideration of said petition and in the determination thereof, and sat with this Court at the time said order was handed down on said date. That the determination of the petition and the order denying same is invalid, ineffectual, null and void in that the court was illegally and unconstitutionally constituted for the reason that said Honorable Hugo L. Black was not and is not eligible under the Constitution of the United States to be an Associate Justice of this Court, or to sit in judgment and to participate as such Justice in the determination of the petition for writs of certiorari in these cases, in the manner and under the circumstances under which his appointment and confirmation as such Associate Justice was made. That the facts under which said Honorable Hugo L. Black presumed to sit as Associate Justice and under which petitioners respectfully aver he is ineligible to perform the duties thereof are as follows:

"(a) Said Honorable Hugo L. Black (who will be hereinafter respectfully referred to as Justice Black, but without waiving the challenge to his eligibility herein made) was appointed by the President of the United States to be an Associate Justice of this Court on August 12, 1937. . . .

"(b) That said Justice Black was confirmed by the Senate of the United States on August 17, 1937. . . .

"(c) That pursuant thereto said Justice Black presumed to take the oath of Office prescribed for an Associate Justice of this Court by the Constitution of the United States and did thereafter sit with the other members of this Court in judgment upon the petitions pending in these causes and in the determination thereof.

"(d) That the appointment of said Justice Black aforesaid was made by the President to fill the supposed vacancy in the office of Associate Justice created upon this Court due to the retirement on May 18, 1937, of Associate Justice Willis Van Devanter and the acceptance of such retirement on said date by the President. . . .

"(e) That said retirement of Associate Justice Van Devanter was pursuant the provisions of the Act of March 1, 1937, c 21, 50 Stat. 24, same being Title 28, Section 375a U.S. Code (hereinafter referred to as the Retirement Act), which Act is as follows, to wit:

[The provisions of said Act and of Section 260 of the Judicial Code were then set forth.]

* * *

"(g) That said Associate Justice Van Devanter has at all times since May 18, 1937, remained in the status of an Associate Justice of this Court who has retired under the provisions of said Retirement Act and is at this time occupying such status.

"(h) That no other or further vacancy existed as Associate Justice of the Supreme Court of the United States on March 1, 1937, or since said date either by resignation, death, impeachment, incapacity, or otherwise, other than the supposed vacancy created by the retirement of Associate Justice Willis Van Devanter as aforesaid.

[The provisions of Section 215 of the Judicial Code and of Article 1, Section 6, Clause 2, of the Constitution were then set forth.]

* * *

"(k) That at the time said Retirement Act of March 1, 1937 was introduced, considered and passed by the Congress of the United States and at the time of Justice Van Devanter's retirement as aforesaid and at the time of his own appointment and confirmation as Associate Justice of this Court as aforesaid, and at all times intervening therebetween, said Justice Black was a duly elected, qualified, acting and serving United States Senator from the State of Alabama within the meaning of Article I, Section 6, clause 2 of the Federal Constitution, and that in fact Justice Black as such Senator voted for the bill. . . .

"(1) That in law and in fact there does not now exist, nor has there existed since the retirement of Associate Justice Van Devanter, any vacancy in the office of Associate Justice of this Court.

"(m) That upon his retirement as aforesaid the said associate Justice Van Devanter did not cease to be an Associate Justice of this Court nor has he relinquished his title or commission as such Justice, either by death, resignation, impeachment, or otherwise, but on the contrary said Justice Van Devanter has at all times since said date remained as such Associate Justice and has retained his title and commission as such, though retired from active service under the provisions of the Retirement Act."

* * *

"(o) That because of the provisions of said Article I, Section 6, Clause 2 of the Constitution aforesaid, the said Justice Black was ineligible to be appointed or confirmed as Associate Justice aforesaid, or to take the oath of office thereof, or to perform any of the duties of an Associate Justice for the reason that the emoluments of said office as Associate Justice were increased by said Retirement Act.

"(p) That if it be considered that said Retirement Act created a new office of Associate Justice of this Court, to become effective upon the retirement of a Justice under the provisions thereof, such as the retirement of Justice Van Devanter aforesaid, then Justice Black was and is likewise ineligible to be appointed or confirmed as Associate Justice aforesaid, or to take the oath of office thereof, or to perform any of the duties of an Associate Justice, for the reason that he was a Senator at the time such office was created.

"(q) That such participation by Justice Black in the hearing and determination of the petition in these causes rendered void the decision and order thereon and warrants the same to be opened up and set aside by the duly qualified and eligible Chief Justice and Associate Justices of this Court, sitting as the Supreme Court of the United States, in the absence of Justice Black. . . .

"Wherefore petitioners herein respectfully aver that they have been directly injured in these causes and their legal and constitutional rights have been adversely and wrongfully affected by such participation of Justice Black, and because thereof these petitioners have such standing in this Court and such legal and constitutional rights in causes duly pending herein as to be enabled to properly raise the question of Justice Black's eligibility as aforesaid and to duly challenge the validity of the order denying the petition herein and to procure a reconsideration, rehearing and redetermination of said petition by the duly constituted Supreme Court of the United States.

* * *

"Wherefore petitioners by counsel respectfully pray leave of this Honorable Court to file this petition for rehearings and pray the Court to reconsider its order denying the petition for writs of certiorari and, upon reconsideration in the absence of Mr. Justice Black, to grant said petition and assign the causes for argument and determination on the merits.

> W. K. Zewadski,
> Wm. C. Pierce,
> of Tampa, Florida
> Attorneys for Petitioners."

[In most situations, the attention focused upon the judicial selection process by private organizations results from public policy conflicts which have developed in Congress or before the Courts. For example, Charles B. Shuman, President of the American Farm Bureau Federation, made the following recommendations to President Dwight D. Eisenhower:]

4. Private Interests and Appointments*

February 16, 1959

The Honorable Dwight D. Eisenhower,
President of the United States,
The White House,
Washington, D.C.

Dear President Eisenhower:

In my letter of January 29 I advised that a more detailed answer to your letter of January 13 would follow. We are happy to know that you have given attention to the resolutions adopted last December by the elected voting delegates of our member State Farm Bureaus to the 40th annual meeting of the American Farm Bureau Federation.

The question that you raised was concerned with the following underscored portion of our policy resolution on the Supreme Court of the United States:

> *We are seriously concerned over the present tendency of the Supreme Court to legislate, the acquiesence of the Executive Branch in such decisions, and the tendency of Congress to yield certain of the legislative powers to the Supreme Court. These attitudes destroy the system of checks and balances which is a fundamental concept of the Constitution. (Underscoring added.)*

The interpretation which you have given to the underscored phrase is not what our delegates had in mind in adopting this resolution, although it is easy to understand

*Reproduced with permission of Charles B. Shuman, President, American Farm Bureau Federation.

how you could have made this interpretation. We certainly would be the first to agree with you that it is not the function of the President to criticise or pass judgment publicly on individual cases decided by the Supreme Court.

You have asked for our comments as to what we believe the President can properly do, under the constitutional division of powers, if he is not in agreement with certain decisions of the Supreme Court.

Our concern is that in several instances the Executive Branch has not only accepted a legal concept developed by the Supreme Court which strikes down State authority, but in addition has opposed any legislative action to restore such state authority. This may be illustrated by the legislative history of H.R. 3 during the last session of Congress. This bill would have provided as follows:

> *No Act of Congress shall be construed as indicating an intent on the part of Congress to occupy the field in which such Act operates, to the exclusion of all State laws on the same subject matter, unless such Act contains an express provision to that effect, or unless there is a direct and positive conflict between such Act and a State law so that the two cannot be reconciled or consistently stand together.*

This organization actively supported H.R. 3. It was also supported by the American Bar Association, the Annual Governors' Conference, the Organization of (State) Chief Justices, the National Association of (State) Attorneys General, and many other national associations. In view of the closeness of the Senate vote, the opposition of the Justice Department to the bill was decisive.

Congress recently considered legislation to reassert the principle of state control of water resources to reverse recent federal court decisions abandoning previous cases upholding state control. The Justice Department also opposed this legislation. This is another example of what the voting delegates had in mind last December in referring to the "acquiescence of the Executive Branch."

The Supreme Court in abandoning the rule of *"stare decisis"* no longer abides by, or adheres to, decided cases. This is contrary to what the framers of the Constitution had intended. If the decision in any case based upon legal precedents is unacceptable, the necessary changes may be made by Congressional Act or Constitutional Amendment. Attorneys for the Executive Branch should avoid urging the Courts to decide cases contrary to legal precedent.

Attorneys of the Executive Branch also might be urged to exercise more self-restraint in encouraging the Supreme Court to render decisions which tend to be more legislative rather than judicial. As a general rule, we recommend seeking congressional action, rather than encouraging the Court to "stretch" the legislative intent. The necessary safeguards to deal with this problem must be continually reviewed and strengthened by those persons charged with administrative responsibilities in the Executive Branch.

We believe that it would be quite appropriate for the President and the rest of the Executive Branch to join with Congress in prescribing proper limitations upon the appellate jurisdiction of the Supreme Court. As you know, the Constitution expressly gives the Congress the responsibility of defining the appellate jurisdiction of the Supreme Court. Since this would involve an act of Congress, you as President would be called upon to approve it. The Constitution will not be preserved, in our opinion, if the Supreme Court continues to usurp functions of the Congress and such usurpation is not challenged, within their constitutional powers, by both the Legislative and Executive Branches, Thomas Jefferson expressed his concern as follows: ". . . there is no danger I apprehend so much as the consolidation of our government by the noiseless and therefore unalarming, instrumentality of the Supreme Court."

In considering the resolution on the Supreme Court, the delegates were no doubt influenced by the Report of the Committee on Federal-State Relationships adopted by the Conference of State Chief Justices on August 23, 1958 by a 36-8 vote. We have appended hereto excerpts from this report which declared that the Supreme Court ". . . too often has tended to adopt the role of policy maker without proper judicial restraint." The delegates have also been influenced by many statements made by you (such as your address at the Conference of State Governors on June 24, 1957), urging the States and local governments to resist centralization of power in the Federal Government and to reassert their powers and responsibilities.

One of the most important responsibilities of the President, in my opinion, rests in his power to fill vacancies on the Supreme Court. The delegates to our 38th annual meeting adopted a resolution recommending "that appointees to the U.S. Supreme Court be selected from those qualified through previous judicial experience in a State Supreme Court or a United States Court."

We believe that the Supreme Court could play an important role in reversing the trend toward the ever growing centralized powers of the Federal Government, particularly if future appointees are men of strong convictions and qualifications— men who believe in and will hold firmly to the Constitution and its division, delegation and restraint of government power and authority.

We sincerely appreciate this opportunity to express our views of this subject.

Very truly yours,

Charles B. Shuman, President
American Farm Bureau
Federation

[Of all the external forces influencing the legal process in America, the organized bar is by far the most important. The subsequent portion of the text is devoted in its entirety to assessment of the role of the bar.]

7 The Crucial Role of the Bar

A. THE LAWYER IN THE APPELLATE PROCESS

[The lawyer owes an obligation to his client but has a simultaneous commitment to the public as an officer of the courts. His duties to the courts embrace, according to the Canons of Professional Ethics of the American Bar Association, the maintenance of "a respectful attitude" and, of equal importance, the presentation to the courts of all relevant decisions including those adverse to the cause of his client. The assumption underlying this obligation is essentially similar to that imposed upon the public prosecutor. As indicated in the canons, "the primary duty of a lawyer engaged in public prosecution is not to convict, but to see that justice is done. The suppression of facts or the secreting of witnesses capable of establishing the innocence of the accused is highly reprehensible."

The following article by Frederick Bernays Wiener serves a twofold purpose. It etches concisely the crucial role of the American lawyer in the important appellate process and places in contemporary perspective the comparable role of the British lawyer.]

1. The Conduct of an American Appeal*

In the United States there is a unified legal profession and a dual system of courts. England, on the other hand, has a divided legal profession but a unified

*Frederick Bernays Wiener, "The Conduct of an American Appeal," *American Bar Association Journal*, XLVI (August, 1960), 829–34. Reproduced with permission of the author and the publisher. Copyright © 1960 by the American Bar Association.

system of courts. Those two fundamental differences necessarily condition appeals in this country quite as much as they affect other aspects of American law practice. But, as will be seen, perhaps the most basic difference between an appeal in the United States and one in England is that in America the contending appellate advocates are always required to file written—generally printed—arguments with the appellate court, while their oral arguments are sharply curtailed by rigid time limits.

Our own dual complement of courts—a federal judicial system and a separate judicial system in each of now fifty states—makes generalizations in respect of appeals somewhat difficult. Nonetheless, a general survey that sets forth respectively the progress of a federal appeal and of an appeal in most states can be ventured with some confidence, though delineation of local details and differences must necessarily be omitted.

THE BASIC APPELLATE STRUCTURE

In the federal system, the United States District Court is the court of general and original jurisdiction. There is at least one such court in every state, and there are up to four in others. Except for a relatively limited number of cases, in which by reason of their public importance an appeal can be taken directly to the United States Supreme Court, appeal from a final judgment of the United States District Court lies to the United States Court of Appeals in one of eleven Circuits as of right. Certain classes of interlocutory judgments may also be appealed, some as of right, some by permission.

The Courts of Appeals also review the orders of numerous administrative and regulatory bodies such as the Tax Court, the National Labor Relations Board, and most other federal regulatory commissions.

Most judgments of United States Courts of Appeals are reviewable by the Supreme Court only on its granting of a writ of certiorari—in short, by permission and not as of right. This includes criminal cases, either at the instance of the appellant, or, when a judgment of conviction has been reversed, on petition for a writ of certiorari filed by the United States.

Judgments of the United States Court of Claims (rendered in suits against the United States based on the Constitution, or on a federal statute, or on a contract) and of the United States Court of Customs and Patent Appeals are similarly reviewable by the Supreme Court only by certiorari. Convictions by court martial are reviewed by a civilian Court of Military Appeals, whose judgments are not subject to further review by other courts of the United States. Judgments in military cases are reviewable only collaterally, by way of habeas corpus or by a suit for back pay.

Within each state, there is a state court of general jurisdiction. In some states that tribunal will be designated as the Superior Court, in others it is termed the Court of Common Pleas, in still others the Circuit Court, while in New York the court of general and original jurisdiction is called the Supreme Court. Every state also has a court of last resort, generally known as the Supreme Court, but sometimes styled, as in New York, Kentucky and Maryland, the Court of Appeals. In many states, because of the volume of appeals, there is an intermediate appellate court as well. Indeed, more and more states are revising their judicial systems to include such a tribunal, to ease the work load of their courts of last resort.

Final judgments of state courts may be reviewed by the Supreme Court of the United States if there is a federal question in the case, *i.e.,* one arising under the Constitution or laws of the United States, and if that federal question has been timely and properly raised below. State cases not involving federal questions cannot be reviewed by the Supreme Court of the United States. Thus—without going into details, because the fringes of the problem are very complex—an action on a contract or a dispute over title to real estate litigated in a state court can go no farther than the highest court of the state unless some federal question is involved. But if the contract involves the interpretation of a federal statute, such as a price control act, or if the land title involves the effect of a treaty, then the requisite federal question is present, and the United States Supreme Court may review. Final judgments of the highest court of a state in criminal cases are thus reviewable by the Supreme Court of the United States whenever there is presented a substantial constitutional question, of which the most usual instance in such cases is a showing that the proceedings would deprive the defendant of life or liberty without due process of law.

CONTACTS WITH COUNSEL

There are no barristers or solicitors in the United States, nor do we have any rank corresponding to Queen's Counsel. A lawyer is admitted to practice originally by the highest court in his own state, and that normally entitles him to practice in all the courts of that state. He may then go on to seek admission to the Bars of the various federal courts, many of which require that the applicant shall have been a member of a state bar for a given number of years. Three years after admission to practice before the highest court of his own state, a lawyer is eligible to be admitted to the Bar of the Supreme Court of the United States.

Any lawyer may, of course, talk freely to his client, to his witnesses and to the lawyers on his own and the other side. (Trial counsel who does not personally interview all his own witnesses in advance of trial is considered derelict in his duty.) On appeal, such contacts are necessarily more limited, because what the witnesses have said is in the record; but the same freedom is there.

How, then, is counsel retained for an appeal? Usually, the lawyer—or the firm, because law partnerships are normal and not in any sense at all exceptional—who handled the trial goes on to deal with the appeal. If for any reason it is desired to associate or retain different counsel on appeal, such new counsel can be approached either by trial counsel or by the client himself. And such approaches may be and are often extremely informal. If I may refer to my personal experience as appellate counsel, it is the fact that my most important (and most lucrative) appeals came to me over the telephone.

It is of course desirable to reduce the terms of the retainer of appellate counsel to writing. Retainers on a partially contingent basis—*i.e.,* payment of an additional fee in the event of success on appeal—are quite common. I suspect that appellate retainers on a wholly contingent basis are not unusual. However unwise they may be for a lawyer, they are not at all unethical. The larger firms are less inclined to accept contingent retainers, but that disinclination does not rest on ethical grounds. They eschew such arrangements only because they disapprove (or do not find it necessary to assume) the financial risks inherent in betting on the outcome of an appeal.

It should be added that an American lawyer is under no obligation whatever to take an appeal tendered to him; he is free to turn it down on any ground—the inadequacy of the fee, the fact that he wants to go on vacation or is too busy, or simply because he does not want to represent the prospective client. Most of the larger law firms do not handle the usual criminal appeals (except when appointed by an appellate court to represent an indigent) and this does not expose them to censure or disapproval. Any lawyer is free to turn down any case or class of case.

TAKING THE APPEAL

In the federal system, an appeal to a Court of Appeals is taken by filing a notice of appeal in the District Court, within the time specified, and by filing the record of the case with the Court of Appeals.

Appeals to the United States Supreme Court—the word "appeal" is a technical one in that connection—are similarly taken, but the appellant must thereafter file a jurisdictional statement with the Supreme Court, which may dismiss or affirm the appeal without a hearing if a showing of substantiality warranting oral argument is not made.

Review by certiorari is sought by filing the record in the Supreme Court, together with a petition for certiorari, the latter being a printed argument which aims to show that the questions presented have sufficient public importance to justify consideration of the case.

The appellee in a case on appeal, and the respondent in a case on certiorari, may then file his printed argument in opposition to review. The Court considers both, and enters an order either affirming the judgment on appeal, dismissing the appeal, denying certiorari—or else noting probable jurisdiction of the appeal or granting certiorari, either of which latter orders involves setting the cause down for argument.

Appeal practice in state courts varies; some proceed by notice of appeal, others still use the old bills of exceptions and writs of error. Many states provide for discretionary appeals, *i.e.,* by permission of either the lower or the higher court concerned, or, in some instances, by a single judge of the latter.

THE RECORD

In virtually all American trials, all testimony is taken down verbatim by a stenographer—some are shorthand reporters, some use a stenotype machine, some a sound-mask. The trial judge never functions as a shorthand writer—and probably 80 per cent of American lawyers would not know what is meant by the English term "judge's notes."

At any rate, when the appeal is perfected, all of the pleadings and all of the transcript of testimony are taken to the appellate court, either in the form of a certified copy, or—now more frequently—by transmitting the original papers to the clerk of the appellate court.

In many state courts, and in many federal criminal cases, the appeal is heard on the single set of original unprinted papers. In other states, and in some federal circuits, virtually the entire record must be printed before the appeal is heard. In still other states, and in an increasing number of federal circuits, the pertinent portions of the record are printed in an appendix by the appellant (or by both parties jointly, if agreement is possible). Where no agreement on a joint appendix is reached, the appellee is free to print an additional appendix containing any omitted extracts which he deems important.

In the Supreme Court of the United States, decision to grant or refuse review is made on the record as transmitted from the court below, which may or may not be printed. But no case is argued on the merits until after the record as settled by both parties has been printed under the clerk's supervision.

COMPOSITION OF THE APPELLATE COURT

The composition of the Supreme Court of the United States is constant, and so is that of many state appellate courts.

The composition of United States Courts of Appeals fluctuates. Generally three judges sit, but since nine of the eleven circuits have more than three judges, the composition of the panel varies. Moreover, District Judges, retired Circuit Judges, and judges from other circuits are eligible to, and frequently do, sit. Resolution of intracircuit conflicts is effected by hearings in banc, which in some circuits means a bench of nine judges.

Many state appellate courts sit in divisions or panels, with provision for replacement of temporarily disqualified members.

WRITTEN ARGUMENTS

A distinctive feature of American appellate practice is the written—generally printed—argument or, as it is called here, the brief—which is wholly unlike the document, also called a brief, that an English barrister receives from a solicitor. The nearest British analogy is the printed "case" in the House of Lords.

The brief should be—but, alas; only too frequently is not—a complete, self-contained written argument on behalf of the respective parties to the appeal. It sets forth the facts out of which the case arises, the pertinent statutes, regulations and constitutional provisions involved, and then makes a carefully arranged legal argument on the issues involved.

Since the rules of most federal circuits—and of some state courts—limit the length of briefs as well as the length of reply briefs, it will be apparent that an appellate brief is not a document that can be lightly thrown together.

A good brief requires—and will reflect—a combination of learning, logic and literary qualities.

ORAL ARGUMENT

The other distinctive feature of American appellate practice is the limited oral argument—thirty, forty-five, or sixty minutes on a side. More time can be obtained only on a compelling showing of necessity, based on the complexity of the case.

This means that the appellate advocate on his feet must be prepared to strike at once at the jugular. He cannot indulge in peripheral musings, he cannot read long quotations from earlier decisions, and he must frankly relegate to the written arguments in his brief all discussion of matters too complicated to be usefully conveyed orally to the judges of the appellate court.

It was Dr. Johnson who remarked that "When a man knows he is to be hanged in the morning, it concentrates his mind wonderfully." Well, when an advocate knows that he has only half, or three-quarters, or a single hour, he had better concentrate his argument wonderfully—because unless he does, he will never be able to get through all that he needs to tell the court.

In the Supreme Court of the United States, a case on the summary calendar gets thirty minutes on a side, and one on the regular calendar sixty minutes per side. Yet the Justices say, with remarkable unanimity, that they derive great help from these abbreviated arguments, and the Court's current rules and practice join in discouraging submission without oral argument.

More and more state courts of last resort require that all cases be orally argued.

Only rarely will any American appellate court listen to more than two counsel on a side; in many situations and cases only one will be heard; and the Supreme Court of the United States has expressed in its rules its preference for argument by a single advocate on a side. This has the advantage that always attends avoidance of a dispersion of effort, and of course dispenses with the elaborate apparatus of juniors and Q. C.'s so familiar to the English Bar. Indeed, there is no requirement that the lawyer who argues the case be accompanied by others, regardless of his own seniority or standing at the Bar.

Most American appellate judges wear plain black robes. American lawyers have never worn wig or gown, at least since wigs went out of fashion *circa* 1800, and counsel arguing an appeal in any court normally wears a business suit. Formal dress —morning coat, or, more precisely, a cutaway—is no longer required anywhere. Government lawyers and "leaders of the Bar" wear formal dress in the Supreme Court of the United States. Years ago, the Massachusetts Bar invariably appeared before the Supreme Judicial Court of that commonwealth in cutaways, on occasion worn with a soft shirt and a colored tie; I understand that, "apart from a few", the old custom has disappeared since World War II. Twelve years ago I ventured to appear in formal dress in the United States Court of Appeals for the First Circuit, in Boston, and was told privately by the then Chief Judge that they were similarly favored by only a single resident advocate.

DECISIONS

American courts distinguish between "opinions"—the views expressed by the judges either for the court or for themselves if dissenting—and the "judgment", which is the formal document affirming, modifying or reversing the ruling below. A learned English law teacher considers the American terminology more precise; no matter, precise or otherwise, we use is as just indicated.

Our appellate opinions are always written, and never delivered in open court after argument; only very, very rarely will there be an oral affirmance *per curiam* without opinion, and then only in appeals that are utterly and clearly without merit.

It is not the practice in American courts for each judge to file a separate opinion; rather one member of the tribunal writes the "Opinion of the Court". But there is no limitation on dissents, and concurring opinions are becoming more frequent.

In almost all courts, state and federal, the opinions when agreed upon are filed with the clerk, who then sends copies to counsel. Only in the Supreme Court of the United States is oral announcement made of the substance of the written opinions. Frequently the oral delivery does not exactly parallel what has been written; this may not enhance the *elegantia juris,* but certainly it assists the lawyers in the courtroom in understanding—and in attempting to predict—the judicial trend.

American appeals are apt to be time-consuming, what with printing the record, printing the briefs, and then waiting for the decision. But "Reflection is a slow process. Wisdom, like wine, requires maturing". These words, from a non-concurring opinion, emphasize the dangers inherent in decision by deadline—and indeed, that very case, in which a different result was reached a year later on rehearing, stands as a warning against hasty decision.

COSTS AND COUNSEL FEES

In the United States, the costs paid by the losing party do not include attorneys' fees (except, by statute, in very limited classes of cases). In some state courts, the costs include the printing of the briefs; that item is not included in most federal bills of costs. But costs everywhere cover the price of printing the record or the appendix, and this is an item which can be quite frightening. *E.g.,* in a regulatory case in the Supreme Court of the United States, a bill of $12,500 for printing the record is about par for the course. *E.g.,* in a criminal appeal in which the record was drastically compressed because only pretrial issues were presented, the cost of printing the record was $2,750. The cost of printing makes American appeals an expensive luxury, particularly since the party winning against the United States or any agency thereof is not entitled to costs.

Counsel fees are another story. There is no set fee for an appeal and no real minimum, except in some communities, where the local bar association may have adopted a schedule. It is safe to say that few lawyers will undertake an appeal for a fee of less than $500, except of course as a favor for a friend or as a matter of "principle." (The foregoing sentence was passed with approval by two appellate lawyers to whom I showed a draft of the present paper; one has practiced alone in New York for many years, the other was a member of a large Washington firm. But a third lawyer, the senior partner in a large Chicago firm, wrote, "I do not think that in Chicago a fee on appeal, even for the appellee, should ever be less than

$1,250. Actually, $3,500 for the appellant in almost any kind of a case is more in keeping with the time a careful job demands. It is terribly hard to generalize, but surely your $500 minimum is a rural figure.")

Much will depend on whether the lawyer on appeal is new to the case or whether the appeal is a further step in a litigation with which he is already intimately familiar. Other variables are the size of the record, the importance of the case to the client, and, inescapably, the client's state of solvency. The ability or reputation of the lawyer or the law firm is of course a significant factor. It is impossible to generalize, and, since we have no Taxing Masters, data as to fees are hard to come by. Probably it is safe to venture that fees in matters in the Supreme Court of the United States will run from the low four to the high five figures—a not inconsiderable spread. It is believed that the highest fee paid for a single appeal in recent years, in the Steel Seizure case, was either $100,000 or $125,000. This, of course, was for professional services in connection with a single argument. Higher contingent fees are probably not uncommon, depending of course on the nature and extent of the contingency so far as the client is concerned.

POOR PERSONS' CAUSES

In law as in medicine, the rich can afford the services, the middle-income group cannot, and the poor get theirs gratis.

The last few years have seen a rapid expansion in poor persons' cases—the *in forma pauperis* matters. If an individual can show that he has no means, he can proceed without payment of costs and on typewritten papers; he can similarly appeal at public expense; and, in criminal cases, the public pays for such printing or reproduction of the record as may be necessary, and the appellant will be provided with court-appointed counsel, who must appear as advocates and not simply as friends of the court. Such appointments must be accepted, and frequently involve leaders of the Bar whose services the indigent defendant could never hope to retain with his own resources. The problem here, of sifting out the cases that are meritorious, or at least arguably substantial, from those that are wholly frivolous, has not yet been solved, if indeed it is capable of solution.

BY WAY OF CONCLUSION

No American court considers itself powerless, like the House of Lords, to overrule its earlier decisions, and, particularly in the Supreme Court of the United States, many, many of the earlier landmarks have been overruled. State courts of last resort, which deal primarily with questions of private law, questions that do not normally involve constitutional issues and hence are susceptible of correction by a legislature, are more inclined to hew to the line of *stare decisis*. Nonetheless, the power to blaze new trails (and to overrule prior decisions in the process) is there, and is exercised on occasion.

Consequently, the American appellate lawyer not only is more free to argue principle in preference to precedent, but he is far less apt to be awed by what a particular judge has said on the precise point in the past. Nowhere in American opinions will be found the judicial deference to the exact phraseology of prior judicial utterance that is commonplace in the English reports. The result is that an American appellate lawyer has far wider scope for influencing the path of the law.

The two quotations which follow are from addresses by Mr. Justice Holmes, made while on circuit in Massachusetts over seventy years ago, in response to resolutions of the Bar on the passing of its members:

> *The external and immediate result of an advocate's work is but to win or lose a case. But remotely what the lawyer does is to establish, develop, or illuminate rules which are to govern the conduct of men for centuries; to set in motion principles and influences which shape the thought and action of generations which know not by whose command they move. The man of action has the present, but the thinker controls the future; his is the most subtle, the most far-reaching power.*

> * * *

> *And the record which remains of them is but the names of counsel attached to a few cases.*
>
> *Is that the only record? I think not. Their true monument is the body of our jurisprudence,—that vast cenotaph shaped on the genius of our race, and by powers greater than the greatest individual, yet to which the least may make their contribution and inscribe it with their names. The glory of lawyers, like that of men of science, is more corporate than individual. Our labor is an endless organic process. The organism whose being is recorded and protected by the law is the undying body of society. When I hear that one of the builders has ceased his toil, I do not ask what statute he has placed upon some conspicuous pedestal, but I think of the mighty whole, and say to myself, He has done his part to help the mysterious growth of the world along its inevitable lines towards its unknown end.*

Thoughts such as those are for the future. Speaking more immediately, and on a more mundane plane, what I like about arguing an appeal is its stimulation, its excitement, its opportunity to persuade an audience—and the constant, indeed eternal hope, that it will win the case.

Those aspects, I feel certain, apply equally to the argument of any appeal in Britain. Thus there is, inescapably, an essential bond of professional understanding between English-speaking appellate lawyers on both shores of the Atlantic.

B. THE BAR AND CONSTITUTIONAL DEVELOPMENT

[Precisely because the lawyer plays such an influential role in the judicial (and particularly, the appellate) process, the characteristics of the American legal

241

profession are of prime significance. In actions before the Supreme Court of the United States, the briefs submitted and oral arguments presented often concern more than the narrow interests of contending litigants. As Chief Justice Vinson once observed, the issues taken by the Supreme Court under its broad discretionary authority involve "tremendously important principles, upon which are based the plans, hopes, and aspirations of a great many people throughout the country."[1] The able advocate has, on occasion, an unparalleled opportunity to influence the course of constitutional history. The mediocre, conversely, may wreck the hopes of the just as well as the unjust. Ironically, truly great advocacy does not always win the day in the immediate case. But frequently the able exposition of challenging social as well as legal concepts provides the groundwork for later successes. A distinctive example is provided by the oral presentation of the cause of the small butchers of New Orleans by attorney John Archibald Campbell in the *Slaughterhouse Cases*.]

2. A Losing but Influential Brief*

A. FACTUAL BACKGROUND—FROM THE MAJORITY OPINION OF JUSTICE SAMUEL FREEMAN MILLER

The records show that the plaintiffs in error relied upon, and asserted throughout the entire course of the litigation in the State courts, that the grant of privileges in the charter of defendant, which they were contesting, was a violation of the most important provisions of the thirteenth and fourteenth articles of amendment of the Constitution of the United States. The jurisdiction and the duty of this court to review the judgment of the State court on those questions is clear and is imperative.

The statute thus assailed as unconstitutional was passed March 8th, 1869, and is entitled "An act to protect the health of the city of New Orleans, to locate the stock-landings and slaughter-houses, and to incorporate the Crescent City Live-Stock Landing and Slaughter-House Company."

The first section forbids the landing or slaughtering of animals whose flesh is intended for food, within the city of New Orleans and other parishes and boundaries named and defined, or the keeping or establishing any slaughter-houses or *abbattoirs* within those limits except by the corporation thereby created, which is also limited to certain places afterwards mentioned. Suitable penalties are enacted for violation of this prohibition.

The second section designates the corporators, gives the name to the corporation, and confers on it the usual corporate powers.

The third and fourth sections authorize the company to establish and erect within certain territorial limits, therein defined, one or more stock-yards, stock-

---

[1] Quoted in Robert L. Stern and Eugene Gressman, *Supreme Court Practice* (2nd ed.; Washington, D.C.: Bureau of National Affairs, Inc., 1954), p. 108.

* *Brief of Archibald Campbell in The Slaughterhouse Cases*, 16 Wallace 36, 48–50, 58–60, (1873). [Footnotes omitted.]

landings, and slaughter-houses, and imposes upon it the duty of erecting, on or before the first day of June, 1869, one grand slaughter-house of sufficient capacity for slaughtering five hundred animals per day.

It declares that the company, after it shall have prepared all the necessary buildings, yards, and other conveniences for that purpose, shall have the sole and exclusive privilege of conducting and carrying on the live-stock landing and slaughter-house business within the limits and privilege granted by the act, and that all such animals shall be landed at the stock-landings and slaughtered at the slaughter-houses of the company, and nowhere else. Penalties are enacted for infractions of this provision, and prices fixed for the maximum charges of the company for each steamboat and for each animal landed.

Section five orders the closing up of all other stock-landings and slaughter-houses after the first day of June, in the parishes of Orleans, Jefferson, and St. Bernard, and makes it the duty of the company to permit any person to slaughter animals in their slaughter-houses under a heavy penalty for each refusal. Another section fixes a limit to the charges to be made by the company for each animal so slaughtered in their building, and another provides for an inspection of all animals intended to be so slaughtered, by an officer appointed by the governor of the State for that purpose.

These are the principal features of the statute, and are all that have any bearing upon the questions to be decided by us.

B. CAMPBELL ARGUES FOR THE BUTCHERS OF NEW ORLEANS

[The learned counsel read Sir Edward Coke's report of the judgment in this case (on monopolies), which was given fully in the brief at length, seeking to apply it to the cases before the court.]

It was from a country which had been thus oppressed by monopolies that our ancestors came. And a profound conviction of the truth of the sentiment already quoted from M. Thiers—that every man has a right to his own faculties, physical and intellectual, and that this is a right, one of which no one can complain, and no one deprive him—was at the bottom of the settlement of the country by them. Accordingly, free competition in business, free enterprise, the absence of all exactions by petty tyranny, of all spoliation of private right by public authority—the supression of sinecures, monopolies, titles of nobility, and exemption from legal duties— were exactly what the colonists sought for and obtained by their settlement here, their long contest with physical evils that attended the colonial condition, their struggle for independence, and their efforts, exertions, and sacrifices since.

Now, the act of the Louisiana legislature was in the face of all these principles; it made it unlawful for men to use their own land for their own purposes; made it unlawful to any except the seventeen of this company to exercise a lawful and necessary business for which others were as competent as they, for which at least one thousand persons in the three parishes named had qualified themselves, had framed their arrangements in life, had invested their property, and had founded all their hopes of success on earth. The act was a pure MONOPOLY; as such against common right, and void at the common law in England. And it was equally void by our own law. The case of *The Norwich Gaslight Company* v. *The Norwich City Gaslight Company,* a case in Connecticut, and more pointedly still, *The City of Chicago* v. *Rumpff,* a case in Illinois, and *The Mayor of the City of Hudson* v. *Thorne,* a case in New York, were in entire harmony with Coke's great case, and declared that monopolies are against common right.

How, indeed, do authors and inventors maintain a monopoly in even the works of their own brain in that which in a large sense may be called their own? Only through a provision of the Constitution preserving such works to them. Many State constitutions have denounced monopolies by name, and it is certain that every species of exclusive privilege is an offence to the people, and that popular aversion to them does but increase the more largely that they are granted.

II. *But if this monopoly were not thus void at common law, it would be so under both the thirteenth and the fourteenth amendments.*

[THE THIRTEENTH AMMENDMENT]. The thirteenth amendment prohibits "slavery and involuntary *servitude.*" The expressions are ancient ones, and were familiar even before the time when they appeared in the great Ordinance of 1787, for the government of our vast Northwestern Territory; a territory from which great States were to arise. In that ordinance they are associated with enactments affording comprehensive protection for life, liberty, and property; for the spread of religion, morality, and knowledge; for maintaining the inviolability of contracts, the freedom of navigation upon the public rivers, and the unrestrained conveyance of property by contract and devise, and for equality of children in the inheritance of patrimonial estates. The ordinance became a law after Great Britain, in form the most popular government in Europe, had been expelled from that territory because of "injuries and usurpations having in direct object the establishment of an absolute tyranny over the States." Feudalism at that time prevailed in nearly all the kingdoms of Europe, and serfdom and servitude and feudal service depressed their people to the level of slaves. The prohibition of "slavery and involuntary servitude" in every form and degree, except as a sentence upon a conviction for crime, comprises much more than the abolition or prohibition of African slavery. Slavery in the annals of the world had been the ultimate solution of controversies between the creditor and debtor; the conqueror and his captive; the father and his child; the state and an offender against its laws. The laws might enslave a man to the soil. The whole of Europe in 1787 was crowded with persons who held as vassals to their landlord, and serfs on his dominions. The American constitution for that great territory was framed to abolish slavery and involuntary servitude in all forms, and in all degrees in which they have existed among men, except as a punishment for crime duly proved and adjudged.

Now, the act of which we complain has made of three parishes of Louisiana "enthralled ground." "The seventeen" have *astricted* not only the inhabitants of those parishes, but all other portions of the earth who may have cattle or animals for sale or for food, to land them at the wharves of that company (if brought to that territory), to keep them in their pens, yards, or stables, and to prepare them for market in their abattoir or slaughter-house. Lest some competitor may present more tempting or convenient arrangements, the act directs that all of these shall be closed on a particular day, and prohibits any one from having, keeping, or establishing any other; and a peremptory command is given that all animals shall be sheltered, preserved, and protected by this corporation, and by none other, under heavy penalties.

Is not this "a servitude?" Might is not be so considered in a strict sense? It is like the "thirlage" of the old Scotch law and the *banalities* of seignioral France; which were servitudes undoubtedly. But, if not strictly a servitude, it is certainly a servitude in a more popular sense, and, being an enforced one, it is involuntary servitude. Men are surely subjected to a servitude when, throughout three parishes, embracing 1200 square miles, every man and every woman in them is compelled to refrain from the use of their own land and exercise of their own industry. . . .

[THE FOURTEENTH AMENDMENT]. . . . the fourteenth amendment does define citizenship and the relations of citizens to the State and Federal government. It ordains that "all persons born or naturalized in the United States and subject to the jurisdiction thereof are citizens of the United States and of the State where they reside." Citizenship in a State is made by residence and without reference to the consent of the State. Yet, by the same amendment, when it exists, no State can abridge its privileges or immunities. The doctrine of the "States-Rights party," led in modern times by Mr. Calhoun, was that there was no citizenship in the whole United States, except *sub modo* and by the permission of the States. According to their theory the United States had no integral existence except as an incomplete combination among several integers. The fourteenth amendment struck at, and forever destroyed, all such doctrines. It seems to have been made under an apprehension of a destructive faculty in the State governments. It consolidated the several "integers" into a consistent whole. Were there Brahmans in Massachusetts, "the chief of all creatures, and with the universe held in charge for them," and Soudras in Pennsylvania, "who simply had life through the benefolence of the other," this amendment places them on the same footing. By it the national principle has received an indefinite enlargement. The tie between the United States and every citizen in every part of its own jurisdiction has been made intimate and familiar. To the same extent the confederate features of the government have been obliterated. The States in their closest connection with the members of the State, have been placed under the oversight and restraining and enforcing hand of Congress. The purpose is manifest, to establish through the whole jurisdiction of the United States ONE PEOPLE, and that every member of the empire shall understand and appreciate the fact that his privileges and immunities cannot be abridged by State authority; that State laws must be so framed as to secure life, liberty, property from arbitrary violation and secure protection of law to all. Thus, as the great personal rights of each and every person were established and guarded, a reasonable confidence that there would be good government might seem to be justified. The amendment embodies all that the statemanship of the country has conceived for accommodating the Constitution and the institutions of the country to the vast additions of territory, increase of the population, multiplication of States and Territorial governments, the annual influx of aliens, and the mighty changes produced by revolutionary events, and by social, industrial, commercial development. It is an act of Union, an act to determine the reciprocal relations of the millions of population within the bounds of the United States—the numerous State governments and the entire United States administered by a common government—that they might mutually sustain, support, and co-operate for the promotion of peace, security, and the assurance of property and liberty.

Under it the fact of citizenship does not depend upon parentage, family, nor upon the historical division of the land into separate States, some of whom had a glorious history, of which its members were justly proud. Citizenship is assigned to nativity in any portion of the United States, and every person so born is a citizen. The naturalized person acquires citizenship of the same kind without any action of the State at all. So either may by this title of citizenship make his residence at any place in the United States, and under whatever form of State administration, he must be treated as a citizen of that State. His "privileges and immunities" must not be impaired, and all the privileges of the English Magna Charta in favor of freemen are collected upon him and overshadow him as derived from this amendment. The States must not weaken nor destroy them. The comprehensiveness of this amendment, the natural and necessary breadth of the language, the history of some of the clauses; their connection with discussions, contests, and domestic commotions that form landmarks in the annals of constitutional government; the circumstances under which it became part of the Constitution, demonstrate that the weighty import of what it ordains is not to be misunderstood.

From whatever cause originating, or with whatever special and present or pressing purpose passed, the fourteenth amendment is not confined to the population that had been servile, or to that which had any of the disabilities or disqualifications arising from race or from contract. The vast number of laborers in mines, manufactories, commerce, as well as the laborers on the plantations, are defended against the unequal legislation of the States. Nor is the amendment confined in its application to laboring men. The mandate is universal in its application to persons of every class and every condition. There are forty millions of population who may refer to it to determine their rank in the United States, and in any particular State. There are thirty-seven governments among the States to which it directs command, and the States that may be hereafter admitted, and the persons hereafter to be born or naturalized will find here declarations of the same weighty import to them all. To the State governments it says: "Let there be no law made or enforced to diminish one of the privileges and immunities of the people of the United States;" nor law to deprive them of their life, liberty, property, or protection without trial. To the people the declaration is: "Take and hold this your certificate of status and of capacity, the Magna Charta of your rights and liberties." To the Congress is says: "Take care to enforce this article by suitable laws."

The only question then is this: "When a State passes a law depriving a thousand people, who have acquired valuable property, and who, through its instrumentality, are engaged in an honest and necessary business, which they understand, of their right to use such their own property, and to labor in such their honest and necessary business, and gives a monopoly, embracing the whole subject, including the right

246

to labor in such business, to seventeen other persons—whether the State has abridged any of the privileges or immunities of these thousand persons?"

Now, what are "privileges and immunities" in the sense of the Constitution? They are undoubtedly the personal and civil rights which usage, tradition, the habits of society, written law, and the common sentiments of people have recognized as forming the basis of the institutions of the country. The first clause in the fourteenth amendment does not deal with any interstate relations, nor relations that depend in any manner upon State laws, nor is any standard among the States referred to for the ascertainment of these privileges and immunities. It assumes that there were privileges and immunities that belong to an American citizen, and the State is commanded neither to make nor to enforce any law that will abridge them.

[Campbell's argument failed to carry the Court, but the four dissenting justices adopted the essence of Campbell's contentions. Within a few years his broad assertion of economic freedom from governmental control became the dominant theme in American constitutional interpretation. Indeed this was influential, with some important qualifications, until 1937.

C. THE BENCH AND THE BAR

Because of the crucial role, for good or ill, that the lawyer plays in relation to the courts, strong suggestions have occasionally been made to place lawyers directly in public service. Christian Doerfler's suggestion (reproduced below) reflected the idealism of the Progressive Era. Although his broad recommendation was not adopted, the modern public defender system partially fulfills the role which Doerfler envisioned for the twentieth century attorney.]

1. The Duty of the Lawyer as an Officer of the Court*

The profession of law is one of the most highly respected of all the learned professions. To successfully practice that profession requires, not only the highest of intellectual accomplishments, but the highest standard of morality and fair dealing. The profession does not, *in the eyes of the public,* occupy that high and dignified stand that it is entitled to, and I believe that this is due, not solely to a prejudice on the part of the public entertained towards the profession, but also to the law itself and to the members of the profession. While I have constantly had in mind the ideal which I set before me at the beginning of my administration, I am constrained to plead that I have done comparatively little to advance this high standard. Let us

*Christian Doerfler, "The Duty of the Lawyer as an Officer of the Court," *Green Bag,* XXIV (1912), 74–78.

for a moment consider the cause or the reasons why the profession does not occupy morally in the eyes of the public the stand which it ought to. In the first place, attorneys generally are too closely identified with the success and failure of litigation. It has been my observation and also that of a great many members of the profession, that an attorney in a case is more interested in the outcome or results of litigation than is the client. *He has not only at stake to a great extent his fee involved, but his reputation as an attorney.* The result of this is that every possible point is strained by counsel to the utmost limit for the purpose of securing and acquiring the desired end. *The object of the attorney is to attain success.* While attending a lecture at the law school at the University while I was a student there, one of the most noted lecturers of that institution made the statement that *"A good lawyer wins lawsuits."* Now, while that is, of course, a very desirable object to attain, it is oftentimes accomplished at the sacrifice of the highest purpose for which the profession exists. It must always be remembered that the profession of law is instituted among men for the purpose of *aiding the administration of justice.* A proper administration of justice does not mean that a lawyer should succeed in winning a lawsuit. *It means that he should properly bring to the attention of the court everything by way of fact and law that is available and legitimate for the purpose of properly presenting his client's case.* I have oftentimes thought and I will still believe that the profession of law as it is now practised, and has been practised from time immemorial, is to a great extent at fault for the failure in securing justice. *As long as private individuals are at liberty to use an officer who is a quasi-public officer as a representative, and pay him out of their private means, so long will the ends of justice to a great extent be diverted from that source.* As stated before, an attorney at law is a *quasi*-public officer. His duty as far as his client is concerned is simply to legitimately present his side of the case. His duty as far as the public is concerned and as far as he is an officer of the court is to aid and assist *in the administration of justice.* How to obviate this difficulty is one to which I have given a great deal of thought and attention. I will simply make a suggestion and that is this: *That the duty that counsel owes to the court and to the public be increased, and that the duty which he owes to his client be decreased proportionately, so that private interests shall not have the power to induce an officer of the court to trespass upon the rights of the public.* In that respect I make this suggestion that is might be worthy of this Association and of the profession in general to consider the proposition to make the members of the profession officers of the public almost exclusively, and that remuneration be derived from the public in the same manner as judges are now paid. Then again, as part of the expenses of the litigation, the client engaging the services of an attorney could then be required to pay into the public treasury a certain sum of money for the services of counsel. Counsel would then be directly responsible to the public, and his only object in the practice of his profession would then be to aid in the proper administration of justice. . . .

[What controls, if any, are imposed upon the bar to insure its responsibility to the public? As was indicated above, suggestions such as Doerfler's did not gain wide acceptance. But for many decades increasing attention had been placed upon the interrelationship of attorneys and the courts before which they practice. Blewett Lee's early study etched the salient legal aspects of that evolving relationship.]

2. The Courts and Admission to the Bar*

[The portions reproduced follow a detailed historical analysis.]

It is reasonable to conclude, from an examination of the historical records, that for more than six hundred years it has been the practice of the courts to admit attorneys upon their own examination, and that at the time the Colonies separated from the mother country the power of examination and admission of attorneys was vested in the courts.

The fundamental question after all is, however, the nature of the attorney's office, and the relation in which he stands to the court. Perhaps the most interesting cases on this point are those in the Federal courts.

The state and congressional statutes of the reconstruction period immediately following the Civil War, which imposed test oaths upon attorneys as a prerequisite of practicing in the courts, that the applicant, for example, had never voluntarily borne arms against the United States, compelled a very serious examination of the relation of the attorney to the court. Such statutes were sustained in the earlier cases of *Cohen* v. *Wright* and *Ex parte* Yale, but were ultimately and decisively overthrown by the Federal courts. One of the most interesting of the early cases was *In re* Shorter, where an application was made for leave to practice in the Federal courts without taking the test oath prescribed by the act of Congress of January 24, 1865. In that case Busteed, District Judge, makes the following comment on the thirty-fifth section of the Judiciary Act of September 24, 1789, to which we have just referred:—

This act, it will be remembered, was passed shortly after the adoption of the national Constitution, and when the principles upon which it was founded were familiar to the minds of every statesman and politician. It was intended by the legislature to carry into effect that provision of the organic law which provides that 'the judicial power of the United States shall be vested in one supreme court, and in such inferior courts as Congress may from time to time establish.' The thirty-fifth section of this act is a clear concession to the courts of exclusive jurisdiction over the subject of the admission of attorneys and counsellors to practise, and may, I think, be taken as an acknowledgment by Congress that this is a matter within the 'judicial power of the United States.' It is certain that

*Blewett Lee, "The Courts and Admission to the Bar," *Harvard Law Review*, XIII (December, 1899), 245–55. [Footnotes omitted.] Reproduced with permission of the publisher. Copyright (1899) by the Harvard Law Review Association.

the courts have uniformly acted upon this understanding, and until the passage of the law of January 24, 1865,—nearly eighty years,—Congress has not attempted to exercise any control over the subject.

The court then quotes Chief Justice Taney, in *Ex parte* Secombe, that, "It has been well settled by the rules and practice of common-law courts that it rests exclusively with the court to determine who is qualified to become one of its officers as an attorney and counsellor, and for what cause he ought to be removed," and makes the following comment: "If Congress may, *ex mero motu,* exact that a man who has aided in the Rebellion shall thereafter be absolutely disqualified from practising law in the national courts, notwithstanding that he has been previously admitted under their rules, why may not Congress exact that a man shall be allowed to practise in those courts without any other qualification than having fought under the banners of the Republic? If the former may be decreed as a penalty, why not the latter as a reward? Where shall the power of the courts over the conduct and qualifications of attorneys end, and where the power of Congress begin? How shall the conflict of jurisdiction that might arise be settled? It must not be forgotten that Congress does not originate either the national courts themselves or the office, privilege, or franchise of an attorney and counsellor in those courts. If it did, I am not prepared to say that it could not annex such conditions to the enjoyment of the privilege as it might consider wise and just." On this and other grounds the court held the requirements of the test oath unconstitutional.

In the celebrated case of *Ex parte* Garland, the Supreme Court of the United States held the same act of Congress unconstitutional upon other grounds. We quote from the opinion of the court a passage relied upon by the Supreme Court of Illinois, as follows:—

They [attorneys] are officers of the court, admitted as such by its order, upon evidence of their possessing sufficient legal learning and fair private character. It has always been the general practice in this country to obtain this evidence by an examination of the parties. In this court the fact of the admission of such officers in the highest court of the States to which they respectively belong, for three years preceding their application, is regarded as sufficient evidence of the possession of the requisite legal learning, and the statement of counsel moving their admission sufficient evidence that their private and professional character is fair. The order of admission is the judgment of the court that the parties possess the requisite qualifications as attorneys and counsellors, and are entitled to appear as such and conduct causes therein. From its entry the parties become officers of the court, and are responsible to it for professional misconduct. They hold their office during good behavior, and can only be deprived of it for misconduct ascertained and declared by the judgment of the court after opportunity to be heard has been afforded. (Ex parte Heyfron, 7 How. (Miss) 127; Fletcher v. Daingerfield, 20 Cal. 430.) Their admission or their exclusion is not the exercise of a mere ministerial power. It is the exercise of judicial power, and has been so held in numerous cases. It was so held by the Court of Appeals of New York in the matter of the application of Cooper for admission. (Matter of Cooper, 22 N.Y. 81) Attorneys and counsellors, said that court, are not only officers of the court, but officers whose duties relate almost exclusively to proceedings of a judicial nature. And hence their appointment may, with propriety, be intrusted to the courts, and the latter in performing this duty may very justly be considered as engaged in the exercise of their appropriate judicial functions.

Illustrations of the attorney's peculiar relationship to the court are to be found in the power of the court to compel him to serve poor persons gratuitously, and his privilege from arrest on civil process while attending courts. His admission is an act of quasi public character to which any person may object. The discretion of the court in refusing admission cannot be controlled by mandamus. In the case of *Ex parte* Secombe, the Supreme Court refused to grant a mandamus to the judges of the Supreme Court of Minnesota Territory, to compel them to reinstate Secombe as an attorney of that court. Chief Justice Taney, speaking for the court, said, "We are not aware of any case where a mandamus has issued to an inferior tribunal, commanding it to annul its decision, where the decision was in its nature a judicial act within the scope of its jurisdiction and discretion." If, as the decisions generally agree, in admitting an attorney the court acts judicially, this would seem to be an end of the controversy, for manifestly the Legislature cannot, without usurping judicial power, bind the court in advance to decide the case a certain way.

An interesting case upon the general question is Petition of Splane. In this case Splane relied upon the act of May 7, 1885, providing that any attorney or counsellor at law who should "have been duly admitted to practise in any Court of Common Pleas and in the Supreme Court of this Commonwealth shall be admitted to practise in any other court of this Commonwealth upon motion simply, by exhibiting to the court (1) a certificate of admission to the Supreme Court, and (2) filing a certificate of the presiding judge of the county or district from which he came, setting forth that he is of reputable professional standing and unobjectionable character."

The court was of the opinion that the petitioner had not presented a certificate from the presiding judge of the proper county or district, and that the act contemplated the county or district in which the attorney had last practised. The act provided, in terms, that the court *shall* admit attorneys in the cases there recited; but the court do not base their opinion upon non-compliance with the terms of the act alone. After pointing out that in the admission of an attorney the court acts not ministerially, but judicially, they say:—

If there is anything in the Constitution that is clear beyond controversy, it is that the Legislature does not possess judicial powers. They are lodged exclusively in the judiciary as a co-ordinate department of the government. The executive and legislative departments can no more encroach upon the judicial department than the latter can encroach upon them. Each department, in our beautiful system of government, has its own appropriate sphere, and, so long as it confines itself to its own orbit, the machinery of government moves without friction. . . .

We are clearly of opinion that the act of 1887, though probably not so intended, is an encroachment upon the judiciary department of the government.

The constitutional question is suggested, but not decided, in Goodell's case, where a woman applied for admission to the bar, and a very strong intimation is given that the court would not submit to a statue requiring them to admit persons whom they considered improper. In the same volume of reports they refused to obey a statute requiring them to admit non-residents as attorneys.

The judicial nature of the act of admission is brought out still more clearly by its converse, the act of disbarment, which is a part of the same power. It is manifest that the power of the court to disbar is taken away when its power over admission is destroyed. Of course it is possible for the Legislature to make disbarment a punishment for an offence, and the courts will enforce it accordingly; but this does not militate against the doctrine that the courts have an inherent power to disbar. This power follows from the fiduciary nature of the attorney's relation to the court, and Chief Justice Doe is probably justified in concluding, in his admirable discussion of the history and nature of the attorney's office, the power existed at common law. The earliest general statute upon the subject of disbarment, summarized in Chief Justice Cartwright's opinion, treats disbarment as part of the same subject as admission.

The power to disbar has been said by the Supreme Court of the United States to be possessed by all courts which have authority to admit attorneys to practise. It exists independent of any rule or statute. The powers of admission and disbarment are necessarily inseparable, and equally inherent in courts of justice. . . .

[Lee's article reflects the ascendant antagonism toward the legislatures of his period. Yet it also underscores the still prevailing assumption that judges may, through the manner in which they apply their power to admit to the bar, raise the standards of the profession. By mid-twentieth century, the role of the courts in the bar admission process is often formal and ceremonial as the following excerpt indicates. Admission to the bar as well as disbarment has become, in practice, the prerogative of the private profession. The cases of *Lathrop* v. *Donohue* and *Cohen* v. *Hurley,* reproduced subsequently, underscore the power of the organized bar as a private government endowed with powers of considerable public importance.

In view of the fact that the organized bar plays an increasingly influential role in judicial selection at both the state and federal levels of government, the question has been raised whether control of bar admissions by the courts is merely a formality. The interaction of bar organization and sitting judge involves, of course, a two-way relationship. The rationale for broad assertion of bar influence was given recently with respect to judicial selection, but has also been asserted in connection with other areas of judicial administration. This view of the bar's proper function is followed by a contrary view. Finally, an example of bar participation (in an advisory capacity) in Supreme Court determination of its internal rules is included.

First, the opinion of the American Bar Association:

> *The efforts of the organized Bar to secure good judges is one of the greatest services of the profession to the public. Because lawyers are the only group of citizens that are in daily contact with the courts, they are the only group that are really able to judge the qualifications necessary for good judicial material.*[1]]

3. A Contrary View of the Role of the Bar*

Though constituting the primary function of government, there is probably no single thing that our governments do with less efficiency and economy than the administration of the law. Both our system of courts and their methods of procedure are almost universally recognized as unsatisfactory. In their practical operations our courts are expensive both to the government and to litigants. They perform their work with great dilatoriness, and miscarriages of justice are frequent. So long has this unsatisfactory condition of affairs existed that an attitude of mind has obtained that these evils are inherent in the nature of the task to be performed; that anything like the same promptness and efficiency in the conduct of business of the courts such as is demanded of the administrative branch, is impossible. . . .

In large part responsibility for existing unsatisfactory conditions is due to the fact that consideration of the judicial branch has been confined almost wholly to the legal profession, the members of which are not primarily interested in matters of administrative organization and technique, or fitted by their training and studies to handle such matters in a competent manner.

4. The Bar in an Advisory Role, Revised Rules of the Supreme Court†

A general idea of the Bar's appraisal of the needs and possibilities for changes in the form and content of the Rules was obtained from the following gentlemen:

Warner W. Gardner, Esq., of the District of Columbia Bar

Henry M. Hart, Esq., of Cambridge, Massachusetts. Professor of Law at Harvard University

Charles A. Horsky, Esq., of the District of Columbia Bar

James Wm. Moore, Esq., of New Haven, Connecticut, Professor of Law at Yale University

[1] From *American Bar Association Journal*, XLIII (August, 1957), 685. Reproduced with permission of the publisher. Copyright © 1957 by the American Bar Association.

*William Franklin Willoughby, *The Principles of Judicial Administration* (Washington: The Brookings Institution, 1929), pp. xii–xiii. [Footnotes omitted.] Reproduced with permission of the publisher. Copyright (1929) by the Brookings Institution.

†Order Adopting Revised Rules of the Supreme Court of the United States, 348 U.S. 945–947 (1954).

Robert L. Stern, Esq., of Washington, D. C., at the time Acting Solicitor General

Herbert Wechsler, Esq., of New York City, Professor of Law at Columbia University

Frederick Bernays Wiener, Esq., of the District of Columbia Bar

Harold B. Willey, Esq., Clerk of the Supreme Court of the United States

The Court expresses its high appreciation for the services of all the gentlemen named. Their expert knowledge and painstaking collaboration have aided the Court in the formulation of Rules designed to promote the simplification of procedure in this Court.

Special mention must be made of the services of Mr. Wiener who, for more than a year as Reporter to the Committee of the Court on the Revision of the Rules devoted himself to the preparation of drafts for the Committee.

We acknowledge, also, our indebtedness to our Clerk, Mr. Willey, for the experience and skill he contributed to the work of draftsmanship.

The Court directs that this order be spread upon the Journal of the Court.

MR. JUSTICE BLACK.

The revised rules contain some changes made necessary by legislation, with which I am of course in accord. There are also a few other changes which I think represent desirable improvements. But I believe it would be far better to make these changes simply by amending the old rules rather than by adopting a whole new set. The old rules and our interpretations of them are familiar to the bar, and, according to my observation, work about as well as could be expected of any rules. The principal function of procedural rules should be to serve as useful guides to help, not hinder, persons who have a legal right to bring their problems before the courts. But new rules without settled meanings breed mistakes and controversies that frequently make the way of litigants unnecessarily perilous. Volumes of new Rules Decisions in recent years attest to this. Judicial statistics would show, I fear, an unfortunately large number of meritorious cases lost due to inadvertent failure of lawyers to conform to procedural prescriptions having little if any relevancy to substantial justice. So much for my general objection to frequent, sweeping rules revisions.

I particularly object to the present revision because a number of the changes put unnecessarily burdensome conditions and restrictions on rights of review and appeal Congress has provided. Our rules should make appellate review easier, not harder.

Finally, I have never favored the almost insuperable obstacles our rules put in the way of briefs sought to be filed by persons other than the actual litigants. Most of the cases before this Court involve matters that effect far more people than the immediate record parties. I think the public interest and judicial administration would be better served by relaxing rather than tightening the rule against *amicus curiae* briefs.

[A good deal of the controversy over the proper role of the bar arises out of sharply conflicting notions of the social and political roles of lawyers. Lawyers are usually proud of their reputation for conservatism, but this very reputation may, on occasion, lead to popular distrust. The following excerpt by an anonymous book reviewer in 1838 contains conflicting historic views on the role of lawyers. The book reviewed was Alexis de Tocqueville's *Democracy in America.*]

D. LAWYERS IN AMERICAN SOCIETY

1. *Two Views from the 1830's: Alexis de Tocqueville and a Critic**

In the chapters immediately following those on the omnipotence of majorities, M. de Tocqueville enlarges upon certain circumstances which, as he supposes, temper and mitigate their power. The principal of these is the influence of the *legal profession.* His theory upon this subject, as upon the one just alluded to, is somewhat eccentric, and is not, in our opinion, much more tenable. According to M. de Tocqueville, the *influence of the legal profession* is, in our institutions, the real and only principle of *aristocracy.*

"If I were requested," says our author, "to point out the seat of the aristocratic principle in the United States, I should answer, without hesitation, that it is not to be found among the wealthy, who are not combined together by any common bond of interest. The seat of the American aristocracy is with the judges on the bench and the lawyers at the bar.

"The more I reflect upon what I have witnessed in the United States, the more fully am I satisfied that the lawyers are the most powerful class in the community, and the only real counterpoise to the influence of the democracy. In the United States we perceive at once how well the spirit that pervades the bar is fitted by its virtues, and even its defects, to neutralize the vices inherent in a popular government.

"When the people are under the influence of some temporary excitement or accidental delusion, the lawyers make them feel an almost invisible rein which checks their fury and keeps them within bounds. To the democratic instinct of the mass they oppose their aristocratic tendencies; to its love of innovation their superstitious respect for antiquity; to its vast designs their narrow views; to its contempt for all rule, their taste for forms, and to its fiery ardor their habits of slow and cautious action.

"The courts of justice are the instruments through which the legal profession exercises its influence upon the democracy in the most apparent way, but it also operates by several other channels. As the lawyers are the only class of educated men who are not distrusted by the people, they are naturally called upon to fill most of the places in the Legislative and Executive departments of the Government. They consequently have a great share in making and administering the laws. They are often obliged to give way to the torrent of public opinion, but it is easy to see what they would do if they were at liberty.

"The lawyers form, in the United States, a power, which is very little feared, and

* Anonymous [Critique of Alexis de Tocqueville's *Democracy in America*], *The United States Magazine and Democratic Review* (July, 1838), pp. 341–49.

is even not much noticed; which carries no flag of its own; which yields flexibly to every passing exigency, and follows, without resistance, the movement of the body politic; but which, nevertheless, surrounds and embraces that body in all its members, —penetrates into all the classes that compose it,—works upon it secretly, and finally gives it any shape which suits its own pleasure."

This theory is rather more plausible than the one just alluded to, of the *omnipotence of majorities,* and agrees a good deal better, with a merely superficial view of the mode in which the public affairs are conducted in this country. It is no doubt true that the legal profession furnishes a large proportion of the persons employed in the administration of the Government in all its departments, Executive, Legislative, and Judicial. It is also true that a very large proportion of the lawyers so employed habitually act with the political party which represents for the time, under whatever name, the *aristocratic* principle, and supply that party with its acknowledged and ostensible leaders. From these apparent facts it is not very unnatural for a hasty observer to conclude with M. de Tocqueville that the legal profession forms, in fact, the real and substantial basis of the aristocracy, so far any thing of the kind can be said to exist in this country. The opinion of M. de Tocqueville is accordingly not uncommon among ourselves, and has contributed largely, in connection with other causes, to generate the unpopularity of the lawyers as a class. For it is far from being true, as he supposes, that they are less distrusted by the people than other educated men. It is notorious, on the contrary, that as a class, and with the rare exceptions of those who openly espouse the democratic cause, they are decidedly unpopular. A democratic lawyer is, of course, more popular than any other person would be under the same circumstances, precisely for the reason that he resists the tendencies of his own profession in support of what are regarded as the rights and interests of the people.

But though a superficial view of the facts alluded to above might lead to the conclusion that the legal profession forms, in fact, the basis of the aristocracy, or rather of the *aristocratic tendencies,* which are developed, to a greater or less extent, in this country,—a more thorough examination of the subject shows very plainly that this is not the real state of the case. The members of the legal profession in this country are not the aristocracy but the agents, organs, or, to use a more appropriate term, the *attorneys,* of the aristocracy. The aristocracy is constituted by the owners of *accumulated wealth,* and chiefly by the moneyed men of the great commercial cities. These are generally persons educated in the habits of practical life, and not very capable of pleading their own cause before the public. The lawyers undertake to do this for them; they occupy the foreground; they fill the legislative halls and the various departments of the Government; they talk and write upon all occasions, in season and out of season; in short, they take the responsibility, and bear the unpopularity, of keeping up a perpetual warfare upon the democratic tendencies that are constantly in action, and in the end generally carry all before them. The conspicuous position which the lawyers hold in the fore front of the battle, gives them an imposing and formidable aspect. In reality, however, they are merely present in a representative character, and would declaim as loudly and as long for democracy as they now do against it, if they could be as well paid for their trouble.

In saying this we would not be understood to mean any personal disparagement to the individuals composing the legal profession, for many of whom we entertain a high respect. It is no disparagement to any class of men to say that they carry into other pursuits the spirit and genius of their habitual calling. It is only saying that they are subject to the common law of human nature. An individual of strong or eccentric character may escape from the bias imparted by his professional pursuits; perhaps may take, by reaction, a directly opposite one. This occurs as often in the legal profession as in any other. But the members of every profession, considered as such, must, in general, exhibit, on all occasions, their peculiar professional character. The soldier will be frank and fearless in the ball-room as well as on the field of battle; the mere politician shrewd and cunning,—as Cardinal de Retz was said to be,—upon a question of turnips and cabbages,—*politique aux choux et aux raves;* and the attorney will argue cases at the dinner table or in Congress as naturally as he does at the bar.

We remarked above that the real aristocracy of this country is constituted by the owners of accumulated wealth, and particularly the moneyed men of the great commercial cities. This is also the case in all other countries. The basis of the feudal aristocracy of Europe was the possession of the land, which was formerly the only important element of wealth. The progress of trade and the accumulation of capital have introduced in Europe a new aristocracy of money, which has gradually shorn the former of some of its beams, and opened the way for the entrance of the democratic principle into the Government at the expense of both. The possession of accumulated wealth is the only thing which can give an individual substantial political power; that is, the power of *commanding the services of others.* Superiority in intellectual and physical qualities, natural or acquired,—strength, talent, learning, skill, dexterity in the arts,—are only so many means of *rendering service* to others with greater facility or effect. But to render services is a very different thing from commanding them. The exercise of these valuable qualities may produce wealth, and bring with it political power; but their possessors, as such, are the *servants,* and not the *masters* or rulers, of those who employ them. This is the position of the lawyers as a class in relation to the moneyed men. The only lucrative part of a lawyer's business is that which is connected with the management of property, and especially property accumulated in large masses, and employed in an active way. The lawyers, as a class, depend for success in life upon being employed by the owners of property, and particularly of accumulated property. They are, therefore, virtually, with all their superiority of education, and, as a body, of intellectual power, the mere agents, factors, or, in one word, servants of the moneyed men. Their political career, if they go at all into politics,—which the most prudent carefully avoid,—is entirely subordinate to the professional, which furnishes their means of subsistence; and they fall, accordingly, without effort, into any political course which the interest of their employers may happen to dictate.

* * *

We find, accordingly, that the principal seat of the opposition to the democratic tendencies of our institutions has always been among the moneyed men of the cities. It does not always happen that they are able to control the numerical majority of the voters around them. Cities are the points where the two extremes of society come into contact, and the larger numbers of the working class often more than counter-balance, at the polls, the wealthy few, although these have so many means of influencing the working voters within their immediate neighbourhood, that a contrary result is, by no means, uncommon, and is, perhaps, on the whole, a more natural one. It occasionally happens, however, that Boston, New York, Philadelphia, or Baltimore, will present the appearance of a democratic city, but even in such cases they are still the headquarters of the aristocratic principle, and the points from which it diffuses its influence through the country. The city newspaper press is almost wholly under the command of the moneyed men; the proprietors depend for support upon the patronage of this class, and are, of course, compelled, like the lawyers, to wear their political livery. A few independent editors sustain themselves, with difficulty, in a different course; but a large majority of the leading journals in all the great cities are, as is well known, in the interest of the Opposition. The city press is, in short, the great battery by the aid of which the moneyed men carry on the war which they are constantly waging against the democratic tendencies of our institutions, the party which favors these tendencies, and the administrations which they bring into power. Through this channel the moneyed men proclaim their good pleasure to their submissive partisans, exhale their griefs at the progress of democratic principles, and pour forth torrents of abuse upon all who make themselves conspicuous on the popular side. It is the city press which gives the moneyed men their political importance, such as it is; disguises their weakness, in part from the people, and entirely from themselves; and deludes them constantly with new hopes of approaching triumph, which are as regularly followed by fresh defeats at every election, or returning flow of the popular flood.

The young members of the bar are the principal agents of the moneyed men in managing the press; the seniors, who are willing to run the dangerous career of political life, go forward and plead the same cause in the legislative bodies of the States and the Union. All, however, as we remarked before, sustain a representative character. They argue the case because they are well paid for it, and cheerfully exchange for this kind of 'solid pudding' the 'empty praise' which attends upon the vigorous and successful champions of the rights of the people.

It is not, therefore, the legal profession, as M. de Tocqueville supposes, but the moneyed men of the cities, that form the basis of the American aristocracy, or rather of the opposition to the democratic tendency of our institutions, for that is the only shape in which aristocracy can possibly exhibit itself in this country. In keeping up this perpetual warfare upon the spirit of the institutions under which they live, the moneyed men and their agents, the lawyers, are probably not actuated by any worse motive than the influence of their personal position.

E. THE SPECIALIZED BAR

[In modern times it is frequently argued that the very complexity of the bar militates against simple acceptance of the positions of either de Tocqueville or his critic. For example, Justice Harlan, who has emerged as a militant defender of the organized bar, wrote in 1961 that the modern lawyer has a threefold responsibility—as businessman, as advocate for his client, and as aide to the courts. Yet Karl Llewellyn felt that the modern trend toward specialization made difficult the fulfillment of the last function and the engendering of a sense of social responsibility commensurate with the lawyer's influence in society.]

1. The Results of Specialization*

The most significant fact about the modern metropolitan bar [is that] most of its best brains, most of its inevitable leaders, have moved mass-wise out of court work, out of a general practice akin to that of the family doctor, into highly paid specialization in the service of large corporations. They are the ablest of legal technicians. I doubt if the world has ever known abler. But their main work is in essence the doing of business. They negotiate, in their own office or another's, or they do business for their clients with tax officials or a supervisory commission, or they devise a plan to get a given business policy accomplished with a minimum of legal risk.

Now, any man's interests, any man's outlook, are shaped in greatest part by what he *does*. His perspective is in terms of what he knows. His sympathies and ethical judgments are determined essentially by the things and the people he works on and for and with. Individual exceptions there are; rarely indeed do they work deflection of the mass movement. Hence the practice of corporation law not only works for business men toward business ends, but develops within itself a business point of view —toward the work to be done, toward the value of the work to the community, indeed, toward the way in which to do the work.

CORPORATION LAW PRACTICE

Corporation law practice becomes itself a business. Services are to be provided, in quantity, with speed. Peak-load demands must be met. That means a large staff, a highly organized office, a high overhead, more intense specialization. To carry such overhead, fees must be earned; they must be earned steadily. A good will must be built up, attracting enough clients to distribute somewhat the particular peak demands. Names with pulling power, though they be dead men's names, head stationery still.

And—a key phenomenon—the "law factory" emerges; the mass of the work is done by the ablest young men from the best law schools, while the product goes out under the name and over the name of three senior partners. The young man learns, makes contacts, gets opportunity, hopes for a partnership, and sweats twelve hours a day. From 2 a.m. on, he is free to sleep or drink. The old man, if he has survived the killing apprenticeship, cashes in on his own experience, recorded (the forms in the

* Karl N. Llewellyn, "The Bar Specializes—With What Results?" *Annals of the American Academy of Political and Social Science*, CLXVII (May, 1933), 177–80. [Footnotes omitted.] Reproduced with permission of the author and the publisher. Copyright (1933) by the American Academy of Political and Social Science.

files!) or trade-secret in his head, on his own good will, and on the young man's labor. He plans. He guides. He worries. He may still slave. He often makes final decisions. He always is responsible. But above all, he is, and he is valued as, a business-*getter*. The measure of him is the business he can summon from the vasty corporation deep. He is to attract more orders for services than he or twenty like him can supply. He is to make the necessary office space for clerks and juniors run into acreage. He cashes in, then, as an enterpriser, putting his own label on the work of others.

This is understood on all hands, is expected, is accepted. No customer complains. It is, however, business. Indeed, if the corporation lawyer is to be more than a technician-dog whistled up to fetch and carry, he must become a business man of high acumen and make his business policy judgments, with his executive and negotiating power, a thing his clients need.

I am not decrying this; I am describing it. No conspiracy produced the situation; it grew. It grew, in response to conditions, out of the responses not of "a bar," but of thousands of individual lawyers, over half a century, to stimuli those lawyers did not plan. "The Bar" is in this country an almost meaningless conglomeration. What we have is lawyers, by their tens of thousands—individual lawyers without unity of tradition, character, background, or objective; as single persons, many of them powerful; as a guild, inert beyond easy understanding. So that the metropolitan specialization on corporate work is a growth, a cumulation of individual responses to environmental sweeps. It is a scheme of things—not a scheme of men.

VALUE OF SPECIALIZATION

And that specialization has had value. It still has value. Without some such mobilization of the best brains to the task, it is hard to see how an ancient law, rooting in landed property, received and developed in a pioneer agricultural regime, could have withstood the strain of adjustment first to a commercial, then to an industrial, finally to an investment-credit economy.

* * *

IMBALANCE THROUGH SPECIALIZATION

Two results we have already seen: that the legal work of Those-who-have is done with singular skill; and that the new tools (e.g., holding-company structure) of integrated business have been created, with astounding ingenuity, out of pre-industrial legal materials. But these are not all. The draining off of best brains into a single channel has meant that the fitting of law to new conditions has been concentrated on *only one phase* of new conditions: to wit, the furtherance of the business and financing side, *from the angle of the enterpriser and the financier*. It has been focused on organizing their control of others, and on blocking off control of them by others.

The cure of evils in the labor bargain has had to be sought by lay agitation and by legislation on lay urging. And it is corporation lawyers that are then met contending against minimum wage, or the invalidity of yellow-dog clauses, or prohibition of payment in company script, as being infringements of liberty of contact. The cure of evils in the investment market is left for other hands, while corporation counsel hedge borrower, underwriter, and trustee about with more legal defenses than a layman can conceive.

The readjustment of the law, then, is made lopsided by the best brains. Their work, their interest, and their outlook drive them into lack of social perspective. They rival both the technical proficiency and the insight into the country's legal needs of the Great Brass Brain that calculates the tides. Where we need vision, there is vacuum.

As lopsided as their outlook is the field of labor of the best lawyers. Court work has been rare among them; especially rare has been work in the *trial* courts. They have practiced in court, if at all, before appellate judges. But courts are made and shaped more by the character of the bar before them than by any other single factor. Courts, over the long haul, tend in their standards and in their performance to fit the character *of the bar with whom they deal*. We hear relatively little complaint of the appellate courts; and that little is for a one-sidedness in social outlook which mirrors that of the appellate bar. The trial courts, deprived of the best lawyers, are our crying shame. Here, too, is a result of specialization.

THE POOR MAN'S CASE

What now of the civil litigation of the needy? The high-powered law factory runs up an overhead the poor man's case can rarely carry. The poor man's case is a single case—means no repeats on orders. The poor man's case is therefore shelved or fed out to some youngster who has given up hope for partnership and gone in on his own. Or, scared off by mahogany and fear of thousand-dollar fees, the poor man takes his case to other doors than that of Kingpin and Bluesock.

To whom does the poor man take his case? If there is money in the case, though little in the pocket, it can be carried forward on contingent fee. And then we hear of unethical business-getting practices. The steady retainer income that pays rent goes upward by capillary attraction (how thoroughly, we learned the year the income tax payments were made public); there is left a struggle of hard-pressed lesser lawyers for existence—"the ambulance-chasing evil." Men with built-up secure good will lead the attack. But permanent disbarment seems to call for guild courage which the guild can rarely muster. Still, the poor man's case gets taken. Something, if it is won, will be left in it for him whose case it was.

But if there is little money in the case, its owner has his troubles. Even a modest fee eats up the stake. Again specialization calls forth counter-specialization. We have the legal aid societies to help the poor. And they help well. But they are overtaxed with work. They dare not make their presence too well known, for fear of being swamped. We have the small claims court, simplifying, speeding, process and procedure, and doing huge good where we have it. We have the occasional charity case (and where does it run to the Scriptural tithe of time?) in the large office—a relic of the fine tradition of our early bar. But no man with eyes can believe these *fill* the need. The poor man's rights in small things (most men's rights in small things!) on the civil side remain, for most, on paper. How many suits are brought in *forma pauperis?* How many laymen know the form exists?

[Llewellyn's analysis was written in 1933. In the intervening decades, the trend toward specialization has probably contributed some degree of counter-vailing "brain power" in legal relations. The powerful corporate law firms, described below by a friendly *Fortune* magazine writer, do undoubtedly exercise far-reaching influence. But other types of lawyers have developed special talents which often serve to operate against complete dominance by corporate lawyers. Labor lawyers provide an obvious example. Specialists in litigation concerning the Negro provide another. Government lawyers in particular have emerged as having highly significant influence in litigatory matters during the past three decades. The first of the diverse elements that comprise the bar to be described is the most influential segment, the corporate bar.]

2. The Wall Street Lawyers*

For members of the big law firms of downtown New York, a corps of practitioners generally known as Wall Street lawyers, these are agreeably busy times. In one thirty-day period last autumn, for example, Wall Street lawyers analyzed and approved an antitrust consent decree for Combustion Engineering, Inc.; represented American Express in the organization of an international car-rental system jointly owned with the Hertz Corp.; and helped set the stage for an $11-million swap involving two of New York's largest hotels, the Ambassador and the Sheraton-Astor. During this period they were called on to handle the legal aspects of one big projected merger—Climax Molybdenum and American Metal—and to defend in court an even bigger one—Bethlehem Steel and Youngstown Sheet & Tube—the legality of which had been challenged by the Justice Department. Working with bankers and company counsel, Wall Street lawyers also completed the laborious preparation of prospectuses and SEC registration statements for more than a dozen major corporate security issues, including a $288-million offering of common stock by Standard Oil (New Jersey).

As it has been over the years, the Wall Street legal corps was simultaneously active in non-business affairs, too. In Washington, to give just one instance, a Wall Street lawyer, Edwin L. Weisel, was serving as counsel to a Senate subcommittee, one of whose principal witnesses was a former Wall Street lawyer, CIA Director Allen W. Dulles, who testified on Soviet progress in missile technology. The law

*Spencer Klaw, "The Wall Street Lawyers," *Fortune* (February, 1958), pp. 140–44, 192, 197–98, 202. Reprinted from the February, 1958, issue of *Fortune* magazine by special permission; © 1958 Time Inc.

firms of downtown New York have traditionally supplied the federal government with investigators, administrators, and policy makers. Wall Street lawyers, of whom John Foster Dulles and the late Henry L. Stimson are two outstanding examples, have been picked for major jobs by every President from McKinley to Eisenhower, and hundreds more have served two or three-year tours in Washington at slightly lower levels of government. Members of Wall Street law firms also sit on the boards of big foundations, among them the Carnegie Corporation and the Rockefeller Institute for Medical Research, and of universities, charities, civic organizations, and cultural institutions.

But it is in the world of business, which provides them with their principal livelihood, that Wall Street lawyers have their most pervasive influence. Indeed, many have moved from the position of corporate legal adviser to that of corporate executive. Today, Prudential Insurance, U.S. Steel, International Nickel, J. P. Morgan, Phelps Dodge, Chrysler, and Chase Manhattan are among the companies headed by former Wall Street lawyers. Even as a corporate adviser, the Wall Street lawyer often exerts considerable influence in the conduct of business enterprises (although these days, to be sure, he is no longer called on, as one New York attorney likes to put it, to teach the robber barons how to rob). The complexities of doing business within the framework of federal regulation and taxation have in fact created an unprecedented demand for his services, and the Wall Street lawyer, who will be examined here primarily in terms of how he earns his living, has never before had so many affairs of great moment to handle.

WATCHING THE SUN RISE OVER WALL STREET

What makes a lawyer a Wall Street lawyer? He doesn't have to have a Wall Street address, of course, but for purposes of this article he has to be a member of one of the big institutional law firms that are the distinguishing feature of the downtown Manhattan legal community. In all, there are about 1,700 such lawyers— partners or salaried associates of the twenty large firms that offer legal services of comparable scope and quality. The contemporary Wall Street lawyer characteristically practices as a member of a legal team consisting of fifteen to thirty partners, many of them specialists, and perhaps twenty-five to eighty or more associates. The individual practitioner and the small partnership have been giving way to the big institutional law firm in cities other than New York, but most lawyers all over the U.S. still regard the big law office of the New York financial district as being, as lawyers like to say, *sui generis*.

The big Wall Street firm generally handles bigger transactions, draws bigger clients, charges bigger fees (not infrequently $100 an hour or more for a senior partner's time), and takes in more money (up to $6 million a year) than law firms in other cities. Its legal craftsmanship is of the highest quality, and it is able and willing to assign whole squads of legal foot soldiers to a single antitrust case or bond issue. In some of the oldest firms, hard work and long hours are such an honorable tradition that young associates boast of watching the sun come up over Wall Street. Indeed, the prosperity of the partners in a big Wall Street firm depends in part on what Karl

Marx would have classified as the systematic expropriation of surplus labor value. By hiring talented young lawyers, working them to a fare-thee-well, and in effect reselling their services to clients at a healthy markup, the partners—who often work just as hard as their associates—are able to earn an average of $80,000 or so each year, and in some cases as much as $200,000 or more.

This does not mean that the one hundred or more law-school graduates who come to Wall Street each year are being cruelly exploited. On the contrary, the Wall Street firm offers bright young lawyers a post-graduate education of great value, at a salary starting at $6,500 and rising to around $18,000 after eight or ten years. For perhaps one out of every six or seven who qualify for starting jobs, the payoff is membership in the firm. For others, the reward is a partnership in a smaller New York firm or in a large firm in some other city. For still others, it is a job with a corporation—very often with one of the firm's clients, an arrangement that has the effect, of course, of strengthening the bonds between client and law firm.

There are some observers who feel that the big Wall Street firms have had their day. Their influence, the argument runs, has diminished with the decentralization of economic power that has deprived the Wall Street financial community of some of its old imperial splendor. Certainly Wall Street law firms have been facing stiff competition in recent years, both for business and for manpower. Law firms in other cities have begun to offer services to clients, and training to young lawyers, comparable to those once available only on Wall Street. For manpower the big New York firms are also getting competition from their own clients: many companies in the past twenty years have established or greatly expanded legal departments of their own, and in staffing them they have been able to offer benefits—notably tax-sheltered pension funds and in some cases stock options—not available to the employees or members of a partnership.

Nevertheless, the lights are burning late at night in the big law firms on Wall and Broad streets, a sure sign of prosperity. New firms have grown up to compete for business with the big old firms, while most of the big old firms have been getting even bigger. Simpson, Thacher & Bartlett, for instance, has doubled in size since 1936, and so has Cahill, Gordon, Reindel & Ohl. Indeed, the big Wall Street law firms have probably never had it so good.

HOT POTATOES AND MASSIVE SITUATIONS

The large institutional law firm is a fairly recent phenomenon. Its early history has been summarized in one mouth-filling sentence by Robert T. Swaine in his history of the firm of Cravath, Swaine & Moore. "The expansion of personnel and the tendency toward specialization, which began in the larger offices of New York and other cities in the early 1920's," Swaine notes, "accelerated during the boom, and, with little hesitation at the 1929 market collapse, continued as depression-induced bankruptcies and New Deal agencies engulfed business and created such demands on the profession that competent legal assistance was at a premium." Bankruptcies are no longer a major item of business. But the prosperity of the big Wall Street law firms, as Swaine suggests, has in effect been underwritten by New Deal and post-New Deal legislation, and for twenty years their main stock in trade has been advice on how to do business in a heavily taxed and closely regulated economy.

Corporations do not, of course, have to go to Wall Street for such advice. But in three important fields—antitrust work, corporate financing, and corporate reorganization (e.g., mergers)—and, to a lesser extent, in the field of tax law, the big New York firms are the recognized experts. "Take a merger problem," a Wall Street lawyer explained recently. "A company is planning a merger, and it wants to know if it will violate Section 7 of the Clayton Antitrust Act. This is a very hot potato, and the company's house lawyer, who may be an absolutely first-rate man, usually is still anxious to have someone else take the responsibility. Well, it makes sense to come to us. We're specialists. We've had a number of these Section 7 cases in the firm since the act was amended in 1950, and we've been doing antitrust work for years. We know what the law is, and we have a feeling for what it's likely to become. Another thing, we know all the people down at Justice who are involved. I'm not talking about influence—we don't deal in that—but it's our business to know what those people are thinking, and we've got a book on every one of them."

The big Wall Street firm has what amounts, indeed, to a national practice. Most of its corporate clients, naturally enough, are drawn from the New York area, where sixty-five of the two hundred largest industrial corporations have their headquarters. But they come from faraway points too. In a recent survey of forty-eight large companies located outside New York, twenty-six reported that they used Wall Street firms either regularly or on special occasions, usually in connection with financing, major litigation, mergers, or serious tax or antitrust problems. "Whenever a large, massive situation comes up," a senior partner of one big Wall Street firm observes complacently, "they come to New York. We have the shock troops to throw in— that's one of the services we sell."

One sort of massive situation that has come up with increasing frequency in the past ten years is the big antitrust case. To prepare and conduct a sound defense may require three to four years' work by as many as fifteen lawyers. In one recent case, in which R.C.A. and General Electric were sued by Zenith for alleged patent monopoly, two New York law firms each rented an entire floor at the Palmer House in Chicago, where the suit was being tried, to accommodate lawyers, files, clerks, and stenographers. Litigation is not always profitable. "It's so damn expensive," one lawyer explains, "that often you just can't charge the client anything above your actual costs. But it's a service we have to provide, and at worst it can be looked on as a sort of loss leader." (The boom in antitrust litigation has, however, tended to improve the standing of the litigating partners of the big firms. At one time, mere barristers were rather overshadowed by office-lawyer partners, like the late Nelson Cromwell of Sullivan & Cromwell, and Paul D. Cravath of Cravath, Swaine & Moore, who seldom, if ever, went near a courtroom. Today, the reputation of some large firms—notably Cahill, Gordon, Reindel & Ohl, whose senior partner, John T. Cahill, was once a highly successful U.S. prosecutor—stems largely from their litigating skills.)

Another massive situation in which Wall Street firms specialize is the issuing of new securities. ("Anyone can read the SEC regulations," a Wall Street lawyer says.

"Nine-tenths of the real work is reading between the lines, and that's what we're experienced at.") Registering a big stock or bond issue with the SEC is a complicated business, on which a team of lawyers, consisting of at least one partner and perhaps three associates, may work day and night for many weeks. Of course, this is not everybody's dish. "There's only a limited amount of creative splendor," says one New York lawyer, "that you can put into an SEC registration statement." But however unrewarding from a literary point of view, the composition of prospectuses and registration statements is a very profitable affair, and stock and bond issues are looked on with affection in the big Wall Street offices, where they are often referred to as lettuce, green vegetables, or the green-goods business.

The big Wall Street firms have traditionally chosen their associates (and future partners) mainly from the law schools of Harvard, Yale, and Columbia, and, to a lesser extent, from Michigan, Virginia, and Pennsylvania. Before World War II, the most promising seniors flocked to Wall Street each year at Christmas time and made the rounds of the big offices looking for jobs. "I didn't particularly want to work in New York," says a successful midwestern lawyer who graduated close to the top of his Harvard Law School class in 1937, "but I did want to practice law, and the Wall Street firms were the only ones who would take you on and pay you a decent salary even if you had no clients and no connections."

In the last few years this situation has changed. Hundreds of law students still make the annual Christmas trek to Wall Street, but many of them have already been tentatively sized up, or even offered jobs, by partners who have visited their law schools on recruiting trips. In 1956–57, 194 law firms and corporations sent recruiters to Harvard; at Yale, during one thirty-day period at the height of last fall's rushing season, recruiters included representatives of five corporations, seventeen big Wall Street firms, ten other New York firms, and twenty-four law firms located elsewhere in the country.

Since 1949 the big New York firms have raised their top starting salaries from $3,600 to $6,500 (they were about $2,100 prewar) and many large firms outside New York have been fairly closely matching these figures.

In the face of this competition, the big Wall Street firms are now hiring graduates of law schools at Minnesota, Chicago, Iowa, and other universities that used to be considered outside the pale. But the bulk of their associates still come from the traditional Ivy League recruiting grounds, where Wall Street continues to get a good share of the able and talented graduates. A recent Harvard Law School compilation, for instance, shows that of the five top men in the classes of 1950 through 1956, thirty-five in all, sixteen went to work for large New York firms. "The secret of Wall Street's power," says Dean Eugene V. Rostow of the Yale Law School, a former associate of Cravath, Swaine & Moore, "is its concentration of skill and experience. There is still a powerful pull toward Wall Street."

Who are the desirable recruits in Wall Street's eyes? One important criterion is academic standing, and a personable senior who has served on his school's law review—i.e., who is in the top 5 or 10 per cent of his class—can usually take his pick of the big Wall Street firms. (In contrast to pre-World War II days, this now applies even to Jewish students, though some Wall Street firms that in recent years have been hiring Jews have not yet made any of them partners. Many firms also take on women as associates, but partnerships are still for men only.)

But Wall Street firms also hire men with mediocre marks. In a sampling of recent Yale Law School graduates hired by big Wall Street firms, one-fourth—nine out of thirty-five—were in the bottom two-thirds of their class, and three of these were in the bottom quarter. Actually, it takes a fair amount of brains just to get through a first-rate law school, and a Wall Street firm will often choose an attractive and socially mature student with a B-minus average in preference to a brilliant scholar with awkward manners and bearing. "Brilliant intellectual powers are not essential," the late Paul D. Cravath, generally considered the principal architect of the big institutional law firm, once told a group of Harvard law students in discussing the qualifications for becoming a lawyer of affairs. He added: "Too much imagination, too much wit, too great cleverness, too facile fluency, if not leavened by a sound sense of proportion, are quite as likely to impede success as to promote it. The best clients are apt to be afraid of those qualities. They want as their counsel a man who is primarily honest, safe, sound, and steady."

A few big firms—an outstanding example is Davis, Polk, Wardwell, Sunderland, & Kiendl, sometimes known as the Tiffany of law firms—reputedly have a predilection for young men who are listed in the *Social Register*. These firms are called "white-shoe outfits," a term derived from the buckskin shoes that used to be part of the accepted uniform at certain eastern prep schools and colleges.

The law-school graduate who signs up with a big Wall Street firm can count on working hours that would be regarded as pretty outrageous by management trainees at, say, General Electric or du Pont. At some Wall Street firms, indeed, night and weekend work was considered, as recently as the 1940's, to be not only normal but salutary. It is a tradition at Cravath, Swaine & Moore, for instance, that when Hoyt A. Moore (now, at eighty-seven, the firm's oldest active partner) was urged by his colleagues to take on extra help because the staff was under such pressure, Moore replied, "That's silly. No one is under pressure. There wasn't a light on when I left at two o'clock this morning."

Cravath himself often used to tell an associate to meet him at his house on East Thirty-eighth Street at eleven-thirty or so in the evening, when Cravath would have returned from the opera or the theatre. "Many nights," Robert Swaine writes in his history of the Cravath firm, "young lawyers from the office sat there awaiting his return, spent an hour or two past midnight going over papers or discussing a question of law with him, and then returned to the office with instructions to be back at eight o'clock in the morning with a new draft or the answer."

Since World War II the rigors of an associate's life have been greatly tempered— he now gets a full month's vacation, for example—and when a partner of one Wall Street firm remarked some time ago to a group of Harvard students that he kept a blanket in his bottom desk drawer so that he could catch cat-naps when working through the night, most of his audience recognized that he was joking.

Nevertheless, in most big offices, unless an associate drops anchor in the relatively quiet waters of the estates-and-trusts department, he is likely to average one or two late evenings a week at the office, and a good deal of weekend work. At least one firm, Sullivan & Cromwell, keeps a suite in a Manhattan hotel to accommodate partners and associates who miss the last train home. And while few if any firms these days regard long hours in themselves as a desirable feature of a young man's legal training, it is usually made clear early in the game that slackers are not likely to be rewarded with partnerships.

"Sooner or later," the managing partner of one firm explains with chilling affability, "the young men come into my office and ask, 'Can I take Monday off next week?' I say, 'I don't know; *can* you?' They usually look surprised, and I say, 'If it won't interfere with your work, take Monday, Tuesday, Wednesday, Thursday, and Friday off. But if you have work to be done, you'd better be here all night if necessary.' They never ask the question again."

Cravath, Swaine & Moore is known as the hardest-working of the big firms. The firm's offices are at 15 Broad Street, in the same building as several other big law firms, among them Davis Polk, and there is a standard joke about how to tell the Cravath lawyers from the Davis Polk lawyers. Going down in the elevator, the joke runs, the Cravath lawyers talk about what they were doing at the office so late the night before, while the Davis Polk lawyers talk about what they're going to have for lunch.

A shrewd Wall Street observer points out, however, that any such differences may reflect nothing more than superficial contrasts in institutional styles. "The Davis Polk lawyer," this observer comments, "may have worked just as late the night before as the Cravath fellow. He just doesn't boast about it. Davis Polk people pride themselves on being gentlemen, and a gentleman doesn't brag about being a greasy grind."

The prize for which the young associate theoretically strives is, of course, a partnership. But only one out of every half-dozen or so who begin their apprenticeship in a big Wall Street firm is ever rewarded, figuratively speaking, with the key to the partners' lavatory.

Some associates are not really interested in becoming partners. They come to Wall Street for a two or three-year legal internship, and then move on to law firms in other cities. Other associates become fascinated by the business problems of a client, decide they would really like to make business decisions themselves, and leave to go to work for the client in an executive job. (At last count, former associates of just one Wall Street firm, Sullivan & Cromwell, included the presidents of eight large companies, among them International Nickel, American Radiator & Standard Sanitary, and Marine Midland; and vice presidents of a dozen more, including National Dairy Products, Crown Zellerbach, and Eastman Kodak.)

Some associates would like to become partners, but eventually conclude that the chances are slim. (Few Wall Street firms have an absolutely rigid up-or-out policy, but most of them discourage men from staying on indefinitely as associates.) Men with six or seven years of experience in a big Wall Street office are in great demand, however, to staff or even head corporate legal departments, and they usually have no trouble landing a good job—in most cases, as noted earlier, with a client.

For those who achieve a partnership in a big Wall Street firm the financial rewards, compared with the earnings of the average U.S. lawyer, are quite dazzling.

A very large Wall Street firm with, say, eighty or more partners and associates, may gross from $4 million to $6 million a year. Roughly half of this amount, however, is siphoned off in overhead expenses, which in the case of one large firm were divided as follows during its last fiscal year:

Employees' salaries:

Legal	$1,030,000
Non-legal	825,000
Total salaries	**$1,855,000**
Pensions, social security, etc.	195,000
Rent, depreciation, maintenance, etc.	270,000
Stationery, library, and telephone	95,000
Other expenses	95,000
Total expenses	**$2,510,000**

Assuming that such a firm grosses $5 million, nets $2,500,000 and has thirty partners, the average take per partner would come to about $83,000. By comparison, a U.S. Commerce Department survey in 1954 placed the average earnings of U.S. lawyers at $10,220, and of lawyers practicing in large firms (nine or more partners) at $36,100.

Average figures, of course, are rather meaningless. Earnings vary from firm to firm, from year to year, and from partner to partner. Generally, though, a new partner in one of the very large Wall Street firms is given a percentage of the firm's profits calculated to yield from $25,000 to $30,000 a year. In many firms working capital is provided by the senior partners, who from time to time leave some of their earnings in the kitty, and new men are not required to contribute. In a few offices, however, a new partner is expected to put some money into the working-capital fund, usually a sum proportionate to his share in the firm's proceeds.

The distribution of earnings within a partnership is a very delicate matter. In many large firms it is handled by a committee of senior partners whose recommendations are usually accepted without question by their younger colleagues. Practices vary widely from firm to firm, but, generally speaking, a partner in a big firm can count on earning at least $60,000 a year by the time he is in his early fifties, and if he consistently attracts important new clients, a good deal more. In some Wall Street firms, indeed, there may be several senior partners whose shares in the firm's earnings range from $100,000 to $200,000 a year. But taxes being what they are, many senior partners prefer to spread the money around among the younger men. And in one large firm all partners, after their first seven or eight years in the firm, are put on an equal footing, each drawing around $80,000 a year.

The partners' share of the work in a big Wall Street firm is big, too. Partners often put in long hours on weekends when—as they point out with a certain masochistic relish—their businessmen clients are out playing golf.

Wall Street's Twenty Biggest Law Firms

Below, ranked in order by total number of lawyers (partners plus salaried associates), are the twenty largest law offices of downtown New York. There are also a number of smaller Wall Street firms—e.g., Hughes, Hubbard, Blair & Reed (thirty-nine lawyers) and Debevoise, Plimpton & McLean (thirty-five lawyers)—that are organized and that operate like the bigger firms. Figures are as of last December [1957].

	Partners	Associates	Total
Shearman & Sterling & Wright	35	90	125
Cravath, Swaine & Moore	28	88	116
White & Case	34	75	109
Dewey, Ballantine, Bushby, Palmer & Wood	23	82	105
Simpson Thacher & Bartlett	23	74	97
Davis Polk Wardwell Sunderland & Kiendl	30	67	97
Milbank, Tweed, Hope & Hadley	28	66	94
Cahill, Gordon, Reindel & Ohl	28	56	84
Sullivan & Cromwell	32	52	84
Chadbourne, Parke, Whiteside & Wolff	21	49	70
Breed, Abbott & Morgan	22	44	66
Winthrop, Stimson, Putnam & Roberts	17	46	63
Cadwalader, Wickersham & Taft	17	44	61
Willkie Owen Farr Gallagher & Walton	20	40	60
Donovan Leisure Newton & Irvine	21	37	58
Lord, Day & Lord	16	40	56
Dwight, Royall, Harris, Koegel & Caskey	21	34	55
Mudge, Stern, Baldwin & Todd	20	35	55
Kelley, Drye, Newhall & Maginnes	22	28	50
Cleary, Gottlieb, Friendly & Hamilton	15	31	46

Some Wall Street lawyers take a fierce pride in how hard they work. "I would rather work twelve hours a day as a lawyer and go to bed tired after a day full of interest," Paul Cravath once proclaimed, "than to work six dull hours as a stockbroker and have six hours left for bridge and society." But most partners seem to regard their heavy work load as a necessary price they pay for success in a very competitive field. "Wills-and-estates work is pretty leisurely," a tired-looking young partner observed recently. 'But corporate practice is different. The lawyer can't just work from nine to five the way the client does. The client wants his problems solved quickly. He calls you Friday, and he wants an answer by Monday. And in this league there's a terrific professional drive to do work as accurately and expertly as possible."

Like other lawyers, those who practice on Wall Street are concerned with attracting and holding clients. Many Wall Street firms have members who specialize in what one senior partner calls "trapping," i.e., cultivating prospective clients through social contacts. But law firms cannot ethically operate new-business departments, and apart from buying theatre tickets on occasion for an out-of-town client, Wall Street lawyers do little business entertaining.

Actually, trapping seldom snares major clients. Most big companies are quite hardheaded when casting about for a Wall Street law firm, and their choice is likely to be made on the basis of the reputation of a particular senior partner. The best business-getters on Wall Street, in fact, are men who reputations as trial lawyers, politicians, government officials, business advisers, or public citizens are such that they attract important clients to the firm without having to lift a finger to woo them. The late John W. Davis, one-time Ambassador to the Court of St. James and Democratic candidate for the presidency in 1924, was an outstanding example of what one Wall Street lawyer calls "the public partner."

Because of the institutional character of the big Wall Street firms, not every partner has to be a good business producer for a firm to prosper. The new generations of corporate managers are often content to pass along their legal business to the new partners of the same law firms that served the company before. The First National City Bank, for instance, has been a client of Shearman & Sterling & Wright since 1897, while Davis Polk Wardwell Sunderland & Kiendl has represented J. P. Morgan & Co. for upwards of seventy years.

Many Wall Street lawyers sit on the boards of client companies. This is frowned on by some critics, who argue that a lawyer can't give a company really objective legal advice if he is also a director, but the client often expects it, the law firm likes this further hold on the client's legal business, and so the practice is quite widespread. John Cahill, for example, is on the boards of W. R. Grace & Co. and of R.C.A. (R.C.A. alone gives Cahill's firm around $425,000 of business each year.) Sullivan & Cromwell partners are on the boards of some dozen major companies.

Even old clients can be lost, however, and remembering not to take them for granted is often the Wall Street lawyer's hardest job. "The greatest mistake," says Arthur Dean, senior partner of Sullivan & Cromwell, "is to think you're entitled to be consulted. Some lawyers get to be fortyish, fiftyish, living in the suburbs, playing golf on weekends—then suddenly the client is faced with some new and very tough problem, and he takes his business somewhere else. In many cases where a law firm loses a client, you'll find the lawyers had too comfortable an existence."

The fees charged by the big Wall Street firms, like most lawyers' fees, usually bear at least some relation to the time expended on the client's behalf, and partners and associates are required to keep close track of their time. A value is assigned to each lawyer's time, and these time charges may range from $5 to $35 an hour for an associate and from $50 to $100 or more for a partner. When a bill is being prepared, the hourly time charges of each lawyer who worked on the job in question are first added up. Then the total arrived at may be halved—or doubled—depending on factors such as the difficulty and novelty of the legal problems dealt with, and, in litigation, whether the client won or lost. "When we win a big case," a Wall Street lawyer points out, "we expect to share in our own success."

The size of the matter handled is also taken into account. In the green-goods business, for instance, legal charges are usually related to the size as well as to the complexity of a security issue. Thus total legal fees, paid by both issuer and underwriters, might range from $20,000 to $35,000 in the case of a small ($5 million to $10 million) stock or bond issue, up to several hundred thousand dollars in the case of a big and complicated financing. (Trans-Canada Pipe Lines, for example, recently paid legal fees of approximately $237,500 in connection with a $112,500,000 issue of subordinated debentures and common stock; this sum excludes the amount, not a matter of public record, paid to counsel for the underwriters.)

Generally, Wall Street firms refuse to haggle with clients about bills; if a client complains about a fee, it is suggested that he pay whatever he thinks the job is worth. Bills are almost never itemized, and even within the office the time charges assigned to each partner and associate are sometimes treated as highly confidential—at least in so far as the associates are concerned. "But you usually find out sooner or later," one associate recalls. "I remember the day I hit on the formula. At the time, the firm was paying me about $3.75 an hour, and they were charging the client $21 for my services. I didn't know whether to feel flattered or sore."

Despite the fees they get, Wall Street lawyers, like most other Americans, feel that they don't make enough money—or, at any rate, that they aren't able to keep enough of what they do make. Lawyers are legally prohibited from practicing as corporations, of course, and so, unlike the executives of a corporation, members of a partnership get no stock options and no tax-sheltered pension funds. In the circumstances, a job offer from a corporation can look very attractive even to an $80,000-a-year partner in a Wall Street firm.

This is particularly true if the position offered is an executive one. Offers of jobs as company counsel, even in quite large corporations, are not usually so appealing. As a rule, they neither pay so well nor offer such exciting prospects for further advancement as, say, an administrative vice-presidency. To be sure, there has been a marked improvement over the past twenty years in the professional and social standing of coporate counsel. But Wall Street lawyers, like many others in private practice, are proud of the fact that they are not dependent on any single client, and tend therefore to be a little patronizing about what used to be called the "kept" lawyer who works for one company.

(Company lawyers, incidentally, don't take this lying down. One of their most effective spokesmen, Leon E. Hickman, vice president and general counsel of Alcoa, has observed tartly: "The files of Alcoa are replete with brilliantly reasoned opinions of general practitioners that have little or no value because of the incompleteness or the distorted emphasis of their factual assumptions.")

Their patronizing attitude toward company lawyers does not prevent private practitioners from envying some company lawyers the money they make. A notable example, one that brings a glazed expression into the eyes of some Wall Street lawyers, is that of William T. Gossett, a former member of the Wall Street firm of Hughes, Hubbard, Blair & Reed, who resigned in 1947 to become general counsel of the Ford Motor Co. (He is also a vice president and director.) In 1956, the latest year for which figures have been made public, Gossett's salary amounted to $125,000. In addition, he had "supplemental compensation" due him amounting to $145,000, and the company reported that under its stock-option plan, Gossett had bought 37,500 shares of Ford stock at $21 a share. Ford stock as of the beginning of the year was selling at about $37.

The lure of corporate benefits has not resulted in any exodus from the big Wall Street firms or, as noted earlier, in any discernible falling off in the quality of their young apprentices and future partners. For all their complaints about high taxes, Wall Street lawyers seem quite content with their lot.

Most of them profess to find their satisfaction in the practice of law, and not in making business decisions for clients or in acting as their conscience-keepers— two roles that have sometimes been attributed to them. Many Wall Street lawyers naturally have a highly developed business sense, and in complicated transactions it is often impossible to sort out the legal from the business aspects. But even those Wall Street lawyers who are widely respected for their shrewd judgment in business affairs tend to minimize the lawyer's role as a maker of business policy. "If a lawyer wants to make business decisions," says one such partner, "let him resign from the practice of law and go into business."

Wall Street lawyers also deny performing any great prodigies in the public-relations or conscience-keeping line. In many cases, of course, a lawyer may be better read, better informed about social trends, and generally less parochial in his outlook than his client, and therefore in a position to advise him not only about the legal implications of his acts, but about other possible repercussions as well—e.g., unwelcome attentions from a congressional investigating committee. But a Wall Street lawyer, dealing largely with sophisticated executives of big banks, investment houses, and industrial corporations, may not often find himself in this position.

"In getting out a big securities issue," says a specialist in this field, "ethical problems hardly ever come up. It strikes me that the managers of big business are leaning over backward these days to do the right thing. It's the little fellows who are always trying to gouge each other's eyes out."

Wall Street law firms are often asked for advice in situations not covered by existing law (a possible conflict of interest, say, between a corporation and one of its officers), and in such cases the client will be advised to do what is "right"—that is, to conform to what the lawyer believes the law ought to be. But in general, Wall Street lawyers spend very little time urging clients to behave themselves.

For the typical Wall Street lawyer there appears to be excitement enough in dealing in large (and gratifyingly complex) economic affairs, and in occupying a position from which the upper echelons of public service are readily accessible and which is at the same time close to the very center of U.S. business life. "When I came downtown in 1923," a highly successful Wall Street practitioner recalled recently, "everyone was talking about the golden Nineties. Now they're talking about the golden Twenties. Glamour is an elusive thing, and I don't know if they'll ever be talking about the golden Fifties. But for my money, this is still one hell of a business."

[Although comprising a far smaller contingent in the legal profession, the lawyers who have served primarily as the attorneys for organized labor have often been very influential in public policy formulation since 1937.]

273

3. The Lawyers of Labor*

U.S. Secretaries of Labor in the past have included union leaders, politicians, a welfare worker, and even a businessman. Arthur Goldberg is the first labor lawyer to hold the job. The term "labor lawyer" has a special meaning. Goldberg was far more than a lawyer who happened to have labor unions as his clients. But although he sat in the highest councils of the United Steelworkers and the A.F.L.-C.I.O., he was clearly not a labor leader in the same sense as George Meany or David McDonald.

Labor lawyers form a category all their own. Their province includes the strategy and diplomacy of the bargaining table, and the rapidly expanding, highly complex, and not yet clarified body of law that deals with organized labor and the conditions of work in American industry. Labor law is one of the newest of the specialized disciplines of the bar, and its versatile and influential practitioners are well worth examining now that the most successful of them has taken his place in the President's Cabinet.

The proliferation of labor lawyers is a fairly recent phenomenon. "Before 1935 if there were ten lawyers known as union lawyers, I'd be surprised," says Gerhard van Arkel, a former general counsel of the National Labor Relations Board, who now practices labor law in Washington. "The A. F. of L. had one lawyer part time; most of the international unions had no counsel at all." Today the American Bar Association lists a total of 2,000 specialists in labor law. Some of these represent corporations or function as independent arbitrators. About 500 are attorneys serving unions, either as salaried "house counsel" or as lawyers in private practice who are retained on a fee basis. The Teamster's international body alone has spent more than $1,500,000 in legal fees in the past three years, and at present all Teamster organizations together retain about 250 attorneys (mostly on a part-time basis), the majority of whom are specialists in labor law.

In pre-New Deal days, law in the labor field was hard to distinguish from the main body of criminal and common law. Union attorneys spent their time getting pickets out of jail, opposing injunctions, and defending unions against damage suits. Many of the early labor lawyers emerged from poverty and were passionate warriors in the class struggle. Morris Hillquit, general counsel of the International Ladies' Garment Workers, died of the tuberculosis he contacted as a boy in the sweatshops of New York. He was a founder of the Socialist party and at one time its national chairman. Hillquit's Socialist colleague, Louis Waldman, an immigrant from the Ukraine, was fired from his $2-a-week job in a chandelier factory after refusing to sign a false affidavit clearing his employer of blame in an accident. Later he was fired as a cutter of ladies' garments and blacklisted by employers for his union activities. He struggled through years of night school before he gained his law degree.

The best-known courtroom voice for labor in those days belonged to Clarence Darrow, who resigned a lucrative job as a railroad lawyer in 1894 to defend Eugene

* "The Lawyers of Labor," *Fortune* (March, 1961), pp. 213–14, 216, 218. Reprinted from the March, 1961, issue of *Fortune* magazine by special permission; © 1961 Time Inc.

V. Debs against charges of conspiracy arising from the Pullman strike. Darrow's peroration in another case was typical of the emotional content of early labor law: ". . . so long as inhumanity and injustice exist, so long as employers grow rich and powerful through greed and robbery, so long as they build palaces on the underpaid labor of men and women, so long as children are robbed of life and sunshine and joy, you will find other conspirators, thank God, to take the place of these as fast as the prison doors close on them."

That kind of flaming advocacy began to go out of fashion with the passage of the Wagner Act, which gave unions legal rights Darrow and Hillquit had not dreamed of. The act and the decisions growing out of it became a separate and formidable branch of law, creating a demand for people to specialize in it. Many of the bright young lawyers who swarmed to Washington went to work for the National Labor Relations Board. With this experience under their belts, they then moved on to work on the legal staffs of unions, or into private labor practice.

A leading lawyer of the new era was the late Joseph Padway, a Wisconsin Progressive who became general counsel for the A. F. of L. in 1938. His Milwaukee firm produced David Previant, who is special counsel to the Teamsters; Padway's Washington associates included Henry Kaiser, now lawyer to the Musicians union, and J. Albert Woll, now general counsel to the merged A.F.L.-C.I.O.

Gradually the practice of labor law took on new respectability. Attorneys for unions became more like corporation lawyers, even down to the law schools they came from. David Feller, who with his two partners will succeed Goldberg as general counsel for the Steelworkers, is a product of Harvard College and Harvard Law School; he was law clerk to the late Chief Justice Vinson. His partners are graduates respectively of Yale and Harvard.

At the heart of labor law today are the 150,000 collective-bargaining agreements that set wages, hours, working conditions, job security, and grievance procedures for some 18 million American workers. Regulating the collective-bargaining process are a variety of state labor laws and the all-important federal acts: Wagner, Taft-Hartley, and Landrum-Griffin (the last of which has been called a "full-employment act for lawyers"). Adding further to the labor lawyer's job has been the growth in the unions' size and wealth and the burgeoning of huge welfare and pension funds. "Labor law is the most variable, unpredictable, and challenging mechanism in the whole field of law," says Herman Cooper, an attorney whose numerous clients include the National Maritime Union and Actors' Equity. "You have a chance to be a creative participant today in what the law will be tomorrow. More cases in labor law go to the Supreme Court than from any other area, and the labor cases have more guts to them."

Nowadays almost every union local retains legal counsel, usually from a law firm that has a clientele of several unions. The lawyer for the local helps the officers to chart their way through legal shoals as they establish their bargaining positions and conduct strikes. He also argues grievance and unfair-labor-practice cases and, in some instances, takes part in actual bargaining with the employer.

The parent union, the international, generally retains its own counsel also. He advises the locals' lawyers and assists them in handling difficult negotiations, a strike, or an arbitration. The internationals often retain Washington law firms, which are especially well equipped to give advice on federal law, to lobby in Congress, and to argue cases before the Supreme Court. Washington lawyer Louis Sherman, for example, was able to lobby changes in the Taft-Hartley Act desired by his clients, the building-trades unions, and recently won a unanimous decision of the Supreme Court reversing a ruling of the NLRB.

Management, too, has increasingly required the services of specialists in labor law, and a growing number of corporation lawyers have specialized in the field. In the past there was often deep antagonism between management lawyers and union lawyers. Today it is normal to find respect and even friendship between them. Both sides agree on the value of this relationship. As one management lawyer puts it with splendidly mixed metaphor, "They lubricate collective bargaining by acting as a conduit through which feelers are extended and arrangements are made."

One reason for the increased harmony is that some of the ideological fervor has cooled. Recently a labor lawyer said of a colleague, a former Communist, "Now all he thinks about is how to make more money." The young men who go from the law schools to union practice today think of themselves less as shock troops in class warfare and more as legal technicians.

But some union lawyers, especially the veterans, do help in shaping the general policy of client unions. Traditionally, labor leaders are jealous of any effort by hired advisers to share their authority, but where the leadership is uncertain of its course a capable and trusted lawyer may find his counsel sought on any subject. Insiders believe that Herman Cooper was the brains of the Actors' Equity strike last year. Benjamin Robinson is considered the real power in the Lithographers union, of which he is chief counsel, and lawyer Henry Mayer concedes that over the years his activities in the telephone workers' and teachers' unions have sometimes gone far beyond legal matters. In general, lawyers have had the most prestige and authority in the younger industrial unions of the C.I.O. The "old-line" craft unions of the A.F.L., whose leaders admit to no need for advice on organization or bargaining, believe in keeping lawyers in their place. On the other hand, the A.F.L. unions give their lawyers more work of a purely legal nature than do the C.I.O. unions. And the A.F.L. pays its legal help better.

On the whole, however, no lawyer expects to get rich quick out of union practice. "The unions are horrible employers," says one lifelong labor attorney, and another remarks wistfully that his unions seems to regard his work not as a job but as a social contribution.

Attorney Benjamin Wyle of New York recalls that thirteen years ago, when he was a lawyer on the staff of the Textile Workers Union, he spent five days opposing an insurance-company lawyer on a case. Wyle received his normal salary for the week, $75. The company lawyer received $5,000 for his time. Wyle's experience may be extreme, but even today, when union chiefs are paid like corporation executives, union legal fees normally run between 25 and 50 per cent of what a corporation pays for equivalent service.

A salaried union house counsel is doing well if he gets $20,000 a year. Private practice on a fee basis is more remunerative, but to earn good money the union lawyer ordinarily has to handle more clients than his management counterpart. "Union lawyers frequently assume such a large volume of work that they cannot adequately prepare their cases," says David Benetar, a New York labor-law specialist for a number of corporations. "Thus the company lawyer is likely to go to court or to the bargaining table better prepared than his opposite number."

To fill out their incomes some lawyers take on what is called "derivative business"—i.e., general law practice that comes to them through their labor connections. Wyle, who is now in private practice, recently defended a union member charged with murder. Herman Cooper and other union lawyers contribute legal columns to the newspapers of client unions, thereby reminding the rank and file where they can obtain legal services when the need arises.

The most lucrative form of derivative business is the handling of personal-injury claims for workers. Under state workmen's conpensation acts, the fees for these cases are relatively low, but the volume is very high, and some law offices, set up to handle them on an assembly-line basis, have waiting rooms that could be mistaken for clinics. Injury suits for maritime workers are handled under a federal law known as the Jones Act. The lawyer gets a "contingency fee" ranging from 25 to 50 per cent of the settlement. Cooper, long established in the maritime field, handles an unusually large volume of Jones Act cases, and frankly envious colleagues estimate his volume of fees from this alone at $300,000 to $400,000 a year, although Cooper calls this "unfriendly exaggeration."

It is not only union parsimony that puts a strain on the lawyers who work for organized labor. A number of them have had their loyalty to their clients put to the test by the disclosure of corruption, strong-arm methods, and dictatorial rule in some unions. The McClellan Committee hearings tended at first to cast suspicion on the lawyers themselves, but the hearings showed that racketeers ordinarily do not retain labor-relations specialists; they hire racket lawyers. In the view of Jerome Adlerman, who was assistant to Robert Kennedy during the McClellan hearings and now has succeeded Kennedy as counsel, "By and large union lawyers as a group have high standards, as high as any other group within the bar."

But when the leadership of a union he is representing is accused of corruption, the union lawyer is faced with difficult and sometimes painful choices. His personal inclination to withdraw from an unsavory situation may conflict with a belief that he has a professional responsibility to stay on. David Previant, long-time counsel to Hoffa's Teamsters, who is often asked about this point, states the position this way: "A lawyer would indeed be lacking in courage as well as fidelity to his oath if he should withdraw at a time when he is most needed." Previant, who is widely respected by his professional colleagues, generally leaves the personal defense of accused Teamster officials to criminal lawyers, notably the well-known courtroom pleader Edward Bennett Williams.

When union officers accused of corruption are challenged by insurgents from the rank and file, the lawyer is placed in an especially difficult position. Is he working for the leadership or for the union as a whole? Realistically speaking, he is retained not by the union as an abstract entity but by the officers in power. Thus he can hardly help being used to fight the insurgents and the reform they are calling for. But in the public mind this identifies him with the corruption itself. If in a showdown the insurgents win, he will probably be tossed out along with the deposed leaders.

But such ethical predicaments and job risks do not seem to dim the enthusiasm of the majority of labor lawyers for their work. "I couldn't go back to wills and real estate," says one C.I.O. lawyer. "This is my life."

[The development of special bar groups in contemporary America is not simply predicated upon greater demands for technical specialization but, in some instances, upon the needs of minority groups. This is especially true for those minority groups whose needs for legal services are left unfulfilled by majority antagonism or indifference. The growth of the Negro bar may be traced in large part to this sort of situation. Clement Vose has provided an excellent treatment of the Negro bar.]

4. The Negro Bar*

It is evident that an interest group which works primarily through the courts is highly dependent on lawyers. And it is essential when the issues are national in character but local in origin that able lawyers be on the job regularly in widely scattered places. Also, the delicacies of coordination demand that these lawyers be similarly motivated, compatible, and in basic agreement on objectives and procedures. These criteria have marked the Negro interest's activity in litigation. The great success of Thurgood Marshall as full-time special counsel of the NAACP, rests in part on the competence and camaraderie of Negro attorneys across the country who, for years, knew each other in law school, in business, and in fraternal and professional associations. To say this is not to discount the vital contributions made by white attorneys and professors, but merely to stress the leading roles played by Negro lawyers who felt themselves responsible for improving the legal status of all Negroes. Many have made substantial contributions of time to support the NAACP. The associational patterns of Negro lawyers were perhaps more casual and informal than can be shown here. Yet some attention to the unity of the Negro bar is necessary if the methods of the National Association for the Advancement of Colored People are to be understood.

The single most important training place for Negro attorneys has been the law school of Howard University, in the District of Columbia. Organized in 1868 with almost complete financial support by the national government, the Howard Law School in recent years has had an annual student enrollment of 100 and a faculty of twelve. In the summer of 1956, the school occupied a new well-equipped building on the campus. Faculty interest in civil-rights problems has been shared by students and

---

* Clement E. Vose, *Caucasians Only: The Supreme Court, the NAACP, and the Restrictive Covenant Cases* (Berkeley and Los Angeles: University of California Press, 1959), pp. 45–47. [Footnotes omitted.] Reproduced by permission of the author and the publisher. Copyright © 1959 by the University of California Press.

alumni. The school's publicity emphasizes that Howard has "the oldest and most fully developed civil rights course in any American law school." This course, begun early in the 1940's by Charles Houston and James Nabrit, has always centered on current problems in race-relations law. Professors and students have worked on litigation in process and their findings and recommendations have been relied upon in the presentation of briefs and arguments by the NAACP. Graduates of Howard Law School practice in many sections of the country. Asked to list those who have distinguished themselves in civil-rights activities, Dean George M. Johnson named twenty-two graduates and then added twenty-eight who have handled significant civil-rights cases in connection with their general practice. Nevertheless, the part played by Howard Law School in the training of attorneys interested in civil-rights cases should be seen in perspective. A number of distinguished Negro lawyers have graduated from other institutions, for example, Charles Houston and William Hastie from Harvard. Besides, many white lawyers, as students, faculty members, and practicing attorneys have been interested in and supporters of efforts to improve the general legal status of Negroes.

A study of Negro lawyers made in 1951 showed that there were 2,000 Negroes engaged in active legal practice. One-third of these were concentrated in three cities with 350 Negro lawyers in Chicago, and 200 each in Washington and New York. In 1951, the count stood at 11 in Alabama, 19 in Florida and 71 in Virginia but the number of Negro lawyers in Southern states has been increasing rapidly in recent years. The closeness of these attorneys in cities across the country to the problems of racial conflict and their part in channeling this conflict into the courts is significant. They are on the scene; it is part of their everyday life.

Not only are Negro attorneys participating in the affairs of their own community, but they also have professional contact with each other across the country. Excluded from the American Bar Association a small group of Negro attorneys in 1925 formed their own organization, the National Bar Association. The purposes of the association include

> . . . *working for a more equitable representation of all racial groups in the judiciary of our Cities, States and Nation, promoting legislation that will improve the economic condition of all the citizens of the United States, aiding all citizens, regardless of race or creed, in their effort to secure a free and untrammeled use of the franchise guaranteed by the Constitution of the United States . . . protecting the civil and political rights of the citizens and residents of the several States of the United States, and working for the integration of the American Bar.*

In the annual summer meetings of the association mainly problems of civil rights are discussed, especially for the legal profession itself. For a time the association published the *National Bar Journal*. Many of its most active members are graduates of the Howard Law School and have also served on the National Legal Committee of the NAACP. The interlocking nature of these organizations has been an important factor in the consciousness of Negro lawyers with respect to the legal barriers to equal treatment.

[In the 1960's, attorneys in the service of the federal government often play crucial roles in the treatment of major public policy questions. For example, the implementation of desegregation, the new civil rights act, and meaningful enforcement of anti-trust policies depend in many respects upon aggressive and competent action by government lawyers. Deputy Attorney General Byron White, now an Associate Justice of the Supreme Court, in testimony before the House Judiciary Committee in 1961, provided a succinct statement on the activities of attorneys in the Justice Department. White's remarks were made in behalf of a bill to raise substantially the salaries of Justice Department attorneys.]

5. The Government Lawyer: The Work of the Justice Department*

The Department represents the United States in all cases in the Federal courts in which the United States or any department or agency thereof is a party. Out of 72,691 cases pending in the Federal courts on June 30, 1960, the United States was a party in 25,718 of these cases, or approximately 35 percent. The United States, moreover, was a party in approximately half the cases pending before the Supreme Court. Although many lawyers are employed throughout the Federal Government, whenever the United States sues or is sued in court, the Department of Justice provides the lawyer to handle the suit. Many disputes, of course, are settled in the departments or agencies. However, it is the big case, the hard case, or the case involving important policy that comes to the Department of Justice.

Not only are major policy and legal questions involved in many of these cases for which the Department has responsibility, but also the amounts of money involved are rather staggering. The Tax Division of the Department of Justice, for example, is defending refund suits brought by taxpayers involving $489,220,708, and suing to collect $111,640,161 in various cases against taxpayers. The Civil Division is defending suits in which $807,292,332 is claimed against the Government. That same Division is pressing claims on behalf of the United States against others in suits in which $180,936,383 is at stake. The Lands Division has responsibility for defending claims before the Indian Claims Commission in excess of a billion dollars and is engaged in condemnation proceedings in which more than $50 million is involved.

The Department of Justice is also the chief law enforcement agency of the United States and is responsible for investigating and prosecuting violations of all the Federal criminal laws. The Federal Bureau of Investigation investigates and the Criminal Division of the Department of Justice tries or supervises the trial of the resulting cases where the ordinary criminal laws are involved. The Internal Security Division handles violations of the laws affecting the national security. The Antitrust Division originates, tries and disposes of the very important violations of the antitrust laws. These cases have a major effect upon the economic structure of our country, and are of tremendous importance to the proper functioning of our free enterprise system.

*Deputy Attorney General Byron R. White, Department of Justice, *Hearing before Subcommittee 5 of the House Judiciary Committee on Salaries of Attorneys in the Deparment of Justice*, June 16, 1961, 87th Cong., (Washington, D.C.: United States Government Printing Office, 1961), pp. 3, 4.

The Civil Rights Division is concerned with the civil rights laws and with guaranteeing to all our citizens that their rights under these laws and the Constitution are not abridged. There is little doubt that the success or failure of the Department of Justice in enforcing the laws of the United States has a major impact upon our society.

The Department of Justice, through its Office of Legal Counsel, is also the legal adviser to the President and the other departments and agencies of the Federal Government. This Office furnishes formal and informal opinions dealing with the most complex and sensitive legal problems.

The Department of Justice, through the office of the Deputy Attorney General, also analyzes and comments upon legislation when it is requested to do so by Congress, and we like to believe that the exercise of this responsibility is of significant assistance to the Congress. All the divisions, moreover, from time to time provide assistance to the Members of Congress in answering mail from constituents concerning subjects which are related to the work of the particular division.

[The fate of the bill to increase the salaries of government attorneys underscores congressional recognition of the important public policy roles played by government lawyers. The conservative coalition, composed of southern Democrats and northern Republicans, defeated H.R. 6242 by a margin of 223 to 172. Opposition to government lawyers because of their roles in implementing positive federal governmental action has been fundamental to the conservative coalition since the New Deal. In 1951, Representative Charles A. Halleck summed up his objections in an address to the American Bar Association entitled, "The Role of the Lawyer in Government: A Warning to the American Bar."[1] Representative Halleck's contentions were underscored by the following editorial in the *American Bar Association Journal*.]

6. The Role of the Lawyer in Government: The View of the American Bar Association*

Representative Charles Halleck, in his very readable address to the Section of Legal Education and Admissions to the Bar which is published in this issue of the Journal, stresses an aspect of the lawyer's activity, influence and duty, in American life today to which some but not nearly enough attention has been given.

As the Federal Government has expanded in many directions, reaching further and further into the fortunes, lives, and liberties of the citizen, the problem of operating big government without excessive impairment of individual freedom, and of maintaining the authority of the Congress against the encroachment of the bureaucracy, has become acute. The tendency of big government always is toward

[1] *American Bar Association Journal*, XXXVII (December, 1951), 889–92. Halleck did vote for H.R. 6242, however.

*Editorial, "A Dangerous Tendency," *American Bar Association Journal*, XXXVII (December, 1951), 915. Reproduced with permission of the publisher. Copyright (1951) by the American Bar Association.

totalitarian rule from the man at the top, and away from government by the people through laws enacted by their representatives and enforced by their courts.

Mr. Halleck cites some familiar instances in which the will of the Congress, plainly expressed in the statute, has been thwarted by technical misinterpretation on the part of bureaucrats. This has been made possible through the unavoidable delegation to administrative agencies of authority to implement the generality of far-reaching statutes by rules and regulations which have the force of law.

As Mr. Halleck points out, the devices by which such agencies pervert legislation to take an oblique, or even a right-about, direction spring from the brains of subservient lawyers within the agencies, many of them holding obscure and minor positions, but exercising great powers through their guidance of superiors. These lawyers, in some cases, seem to lack a proper appreciation of the fundamental concept and significance of the separation and independence of the legislative, executive, and judicial branches of the American republic as expressed in the Constitution. Their ingenuity is aimed at accomplishing a result, desired by those above, without regard to the impact of that result, proximately or remotely, on the American way of life as patterned by the Constitution.

In private practice an honorable lawyer will refuse to steer his client in ways to circumvent the law. To steer him so may not always constitute a crime, but it is always a blunder. Too many lawyers in government positions, though by no means all of them, seem to suppose that a government agency is justified in stretching, straining and distorting the law if it can do so without running counter to the courts.

This is a dangerous tendency, as Mr. Halleck indicates: dangerous to our defense against external aggression, but doubly dangerous to our internal security and freedom. To backfire against that tendency, we must look for aid to the law schools. They can help by training students in the fundamental principles of the Constitution and the common law; by maintaining strict and ever improving standards of legal education; by insisting on the American ideals of duty and government and the lawyer's duty to safeguard them whether his client be an individual, a corporation, or a government.

[Suspicion of the "government lawyer" arises not only because of ideological differences among subdivisions of the bar but also because it is sometimes assumed that the federal government maintains a monolithic unity in litigation. The following selection suggests that unity may be the rule, but conflicting legal positions between agencies are not unknown.]

7. Suspicion of the "Government Lawyer" and "Inconsistency" in Government Litigation*

In the past several years there has been both judicial and extrajudicial comment on what has seemed to be a surprising phenomenon—that the United States Govern-

*Robert L. Stern, " 'Inconsistency' in Government Litigation," *Harvard Law Review,* LXIV (March, 1951), 759–69. [Footnotes omitted.] Reproduced with permission of the author and the publisher. Copyright (1951) by the Harvard Law Review Association.

ment has occasionally taken conflicting positions in cases in the Supreme Court, either by appearing on both sides of a question or in opposition to what appears to be the Government's own interest. The object of this paper is to show why such rare situations arise and how they are handled.

Most Government litigation is under the supervisory control of the Attorney General and the Solicitor General in the Department of Justice. In the Supreme Court, the litigation is in the direct charge of the Solicitor General. In the lower courts, most Government cases are handled by Department of Justice lawyers (including the United States Attorneys), although some are handled by attorneys for independent agencies. A great many lawyers who represent the Government in the lower courts work in specialized fields, and none of them can possibly be aware of all the problems which confront the other Government attorneys or how such problems are handled. There is no central source of knowledge of Government litigation in the various fields, except that of the Solicitor General's Office as to the relatively few cases which reach the Supreme Court. Three types of cases give rise to possible charges of inconsistency. In the first, there is no conflict of governmental interests, but the Government takes a different position in the Supreme Court from that taken below. The second class of cases involves suits to set aside orders of the Interstate Commerce Commission and a few other agencies. In the third class, there are conflicting governmental interests or conflicting views of different agencies, but the litigation is subject to the control of the Department of Justice, and the Department determines the position which the Government should take.

DIFFERENT GOVERNMENT POSITION TAKEN IN SUPREME COURT

Cases reaching the Supreme Court level are usually handled by a new set of attorneys in the appellate sections of the various Divisions of the Department of Justice and the Solicitor General's Office. Such attorneys often have greater time and facilities for studying a problem, as well as a broader perspective, than the attorneys who handled the cases in the lower courts, and sometimes they reach different conclusions. If the Department has lost the case, this different conclusion may mean merely that no appeal or petition for certiorari will be filed, but if the opposing party is taking the case to the Supreme Court, the Department must state its position. In such cases the Solicitor General may confess error when he believes the position taken below to have been incorrect.

AGENCY AUTHORIZED BY STATUTE TO APPEAR SEPARATELY

Several of the cases in which conflicting governmental positions have been presented to the Supreme Court have involved the Interstate Commerce Commission. By special statutory provision, suits to set aside orders of that Commission are brought against the United States, represented by Department of Justice attorneys from the Antitrust Division, but the Commission is given authority to intervene as a separate party, with complete autonomy with respect both to the presentation of its case and the right to appeal. The result is that if the Commission and the Department of Justice cannot agree as to what position should be taken, or whether a case should be appealed, no single authority has power to determine what should be done, and each agency can insist that its own views be presented to the courts. This does not mean that the Commission and the Department ignore each other and do not attempt to cooperate. In the vast majority of cases their attorneys work together. Although the Department of Justice regards itself as primarily the representative of the Commission, and, of course, gives great weight to the views which the Commission desires to have presented, differences of opinion occasionally arise which cannot be reconciled.

The cases in which the Department and the Commission take conflicting positions fall into three categories. In the first, no other governmental interest comes into the picture. The conflicting position arises because the Department of Justice attorneys, appearing on behalf of the United States, are so convinced that the Commission's position is wrong that they are unwilling to accommodate their views to those of the Commission. This was the situation in the recent *Henderson* and *Railway Labor Executives Asscciation* cases. In the former case, the Commission had held lawful the segregation of Negroes in railroad dining cars. In the latter case, the Commission had limited the protection to be given employees displaced by a consolidation of terminal facilities to the period of four years following the effective date of the Commission's order authorizing the consolidation. The Commission was following what it thought was required by the literal language of the statute, even though it was aware that construction of the new terminal would take five years, and that most of the employees to be displaced would not therefore lose their jobs until five years after the effective date of the order. In each of these cases, Department of Justice attorneys, from the Antitrust Division, joined with the Commission in the district court in successfully defending the Commission's decision. The cases first came to the attention of the Solicitor General's Office and the Assistant Attorney General in charge of the Antitrust Division when the losing party appealed to the Supreme Court. A fresh examination of the law by the attorneys charged with responsibility for the appeals in both the Antitrust Division and the Solicitor General's Office convinced them that the Commission's position was unsound as a matter of law; in the first case, because contrary both to the Constitution and the provisions of the Interstate Commerce Act forbidding discrimination, and in the second case, because the literal construction of the statute adopted by the Commission seemed to lead to an absurd result. The outcome was that in each case the Department abandoned the position which it had taken in the district court, and urged in the Supreme Court that the Commission's order be set aside. In each case, the Supreme Court so held.

In the second class of cases in which the Department has appeared separately from the Commission, another governmental agency was involved and its views were in conflict with those of the Commission. Thus, the Department of Agriculture, pursuant to express statutory authority to appear as a party, has opposed, before the Commission and in the courts, decisions regarded as favoring the railroads as against barge lines which could haul agricultural commodities more cheaply. The Office of Price Administration had similar litigation with the Commission. The Department of Labor has differed with the Commission's interpretation of a provision in the Interstate Commerce Act which was incorporated by reference in an exemption from the Fair Labor Standards Act.

In such cases, the Department of Justice must decide which position—if either—it should support. Since the Department is charged with responsibility for representing one agency as much as the other, its problem is not, as in cases of the first class, merely whether it can conscientiously support the Commission; it must determine, as impartially as it can, which position it believes to be correct. If the Department agrees entirely with the Commission, the views of the opposing agency (which can appear only through or with the consent of the Department) may not be presented at all. If it disagrees with the Commission, as in one of the barge line cases above, it will appear separately on behalf of the agency opposing the Commission; the Commission, by reason of its statutory autonomy, will still have an opportunity to present its own views. Or the Department may take an intermediate position of its own, as in the Fair Labor Standards Act case mentioned above where the Commission appeared separately and the Wage and Hour Administrator was also authorized to appear on his own behalf. The Department, without expressing its own views, may also, by authorizing the appearance of the agency opposing the Commission, decide to let the two agencies fight the matter out themselves as in the other barge line case.

The third class of cases is really a branch of the second, except that the conflicting governmental interest is one which must be represented by the Department of Justice itself or not at all. The Department has opposed the Commission when it thought the Commission was acting contrary to the policy of the antitrust laws which the Department itself is charged with enforcing. And the Department has represented the War Department in seeking to recover from the railroads reparations for allegedly excessive freight rates, both before the Commission and in a suit in the courts seeking to set aside the Commission's ruling in favor of the railroads. Since the Department is also charged with representing the interests of the United States in the enforcement of the Interstate Commerce Act, it should not, in such cases, act merely as an advocate for the interest opposing the Commission, but should support whichever governmental interest it believes entitled to prevail under the law.

The statutory provisions applicable to the Interstate Commerce Commission have been adopted by Congress for several other agencies. Thus, the Federal Communications Commission, the United States Maritime Commission (now the Federal Maritime Board), and the Department of Agriculture, in certain types of cases, have the same statutory autonomy as the Interstate Commerce Commission. Although in theory the same difficulties could arise as with the Interstate Commerce Commission, in practice this has occurred in only one current case, involving the Maritime Commission. Not many cases, either absolutely or in comparison to those under the Interstate Commerce Act, have arisen under these statutes, and these cases have not otherwise resulted in any disagreement or conflict in governmental interests.

CONFLICTING INTERESTS WHERE CONTROL OVER LITIGATION IS IN DEPARTMENT OF JUSTICE

In this class of cases, there are conflicting governmental interests, or conflicting views of different agencies, but the litigation is subject to the control of the Department of Justice, and it determines the position which the Government should take. In the exercise of its discretion, however, the Department may believe it sound policy to permit an agency taking a different position to make its views known to the courts.

The recent cost-plus contract cases presented, in clear-cut form, this problem of conflicting governmental interests. Under the World War II cost-plus contracts, the Government was bound to indemnify contractors for all expenses, including the cost of labor. After the war, many employees brought suits against contractors for additional sums claimed to be due under the Fair Labor Standards Act. If they won, the Government would have to repay the contractor. The Department of Justice had both a duty to defend the Government against monetary claims and a duty to enforce the Fair Labor Standards Act, the latter being delegated to the Labor Department in so far as civil cases in the lower courts were concerned. In each suit against a cost-plus contractor under the Fair Labor Standards Act, the Government had to reconcile its financial and law-enforcement interests before its position could be determined This reconciliation was usually accomplished by consultation with the agencies concerned, and with the Department of Justice. Since the Department possessed the ultimate power to decide what position should be taken in the courts, how a matter was presented to the courts depended upon the Department's reaction to the merits of the particular controversy.

In the so-called "overtime on overtime" litigation, the Department took the position from the beginning that the employees were not entitled to more than time and one-half the daytime rate for hours over forty per week even though the same time and one-half was paid for all or part of the first forty hours when worked at night or on weekends or holidays. The Wage and Hour Administration interpreted the statute differently. Defense of the cases in the lower courts, as well as in the Supreme Court, was undertaken by the Department of Justice, and since that agency's position was contrary to that of the Labor Department, the latter's attorneys did not appear. In the Supreme Court, though not in the lower courts, the Department of Justice advised the Court that the Administrator of the Wage and Hour Division believed the decision below to be correct, but did not otherwise set forth the arguments in behalf of the Administrator's position, which were, of course, marshalled by counsel for the employees. The Supreme Court, in a five-to-three decision, ultimately decided in favor of the employees and the Wage and Hour Administrator, and against the position taken by the Department of Justice, but the decision was later overturned by Congress.

The "coverage" cost-plus cases took an entirely different course. The principal questions in issue were whether employees of private contractors operating munitions plants for the Government and producing goods for war purposes to be transported by the Government across state lines were employees of the contractors or of the Government, and whether they were engaged in the production of goods for interstate commerce. During the war all Government agencies concerned—the Department of Justice, the Wage and Hour Administration and the War Department—agreed that contractors should pay such employees in accordance with the Fair Labor Standards Act. Nevertheless, after the war, a great many workers made claims for additional compensation, contending, for various reasons, that they had not been paid all to which they were entitled under the Act. If the employees at such plants were not covered at all, these claims could be defeated without going into their individual merits. The Department of the Army, faced with claims which it thought —with some justification prior to the Portal-to-Portal Act—might run into hundreds of millions of dollars, wished to have the so-called coverage defenses raised. It asserted that it had previously treated the employees as subject to the Fair Labor Standards Act only for reasons of labor policy, and not because of a conviction that they were covered as a matter of law, and therefore, it was not being inconsistent. The Department of Justice, agreeing with the Department of Labor that these defenses lacked merit, at first refused to permit them to be made in cases handled by Government attorneys and advised private counsel that the Department believed the defenses unsound. But after several lower courts held the defenses valid when raised by private counsel, the Department, though unconvinced, felt obliged to allow the defenses to be maintained, through counsel retained by the contractors with the approval and at the expense of the Army. The Government's financial interest was thus protected until the matter could finally be settled by the Supreme Court. In view of its own interpretation of the law, however, the Department instructed Government attorneys not to appear on behalf of the defendants in such cases. As in other non-Government civil cases, the attorneys for the Wage and Hour Administrator were free to appear as amici curiae in the lower courts. When the cases reached the Supreme Court, the Solicitor General filed briefs as amicus curiae in opposition to the defenses raised by the contractors. The briefs stated, however, that the Department of the Army was of a different view for the reasons set forth in briefs submitted by the attorneys for the contractors. In *Powell* v. *United States Cartridge Co.,* the Supreme Court upheld the Department's position that the defenses were without merit, with Justices Frankfurter and Jackson dissenting.

These cost-plus cases show that when competing governmental interests appear, the Department of Justice, as impartially as it can, must decide for itself which position it thinks to be correct, taking both interests into account. In most cases, only the position sponsored by the Department is presented to the courts. Occasionally, when other agencies are involved, the Department is requested or believes it advisable also to present to the Supreme Court the views of an agency with which it disagrees. In such situations, the Department may merely call attention to the agency's opposing position, as it did in the cost-plus cases, with knowledge that the arguments will be developed in the brief of the adverse party. The Department sometimes has authorized the agency to appear separately on its own behalf in opposition to the Department. It has authorized a representative of Congress to appear in support of the validity of an act which the Department believed to be unconstitutional. It has submitted a brief setting forth its views and those of the Government agency which it was representing, but included therein a full statement of the opposing position submitted to it by another governmental department. It has filed a brief setting forth its own views which differed in part from those of two disagreeing governmental agencies, but has also permitted the agencies to state their own position. It has also authorized two agencies to state their opposing positions without making any presentation of its own views. In one recent case, the Solicitor General authorized the Federal Trade Comission to file its own brief and to argue on its own behalf in the Supreme Court. The

Department did not submit any statement of its own position, but its officials had previously indicated before congressional committees that they disagreed with the holding of the Commission in the case.

The question may be asked whether efficient and orderly management of the Government's law business would not eliminate the presentation of conflicting positions to the courts. This would only be possible where Government litigation was subject to centralized control, as it is not in the Interstate Commerce Commission cases. But even where the ultimate authority over litigation policy rests in the Attorney General and the Solicitor General, the most orderly course may not always be the most wise. Many of the administrative agencies are important policy-making bodies. Not even the President has authority to tell them how to decide particular cases. They are not subject to the supervisory authority of the Department of Justice. Whatever control it has over them is derived entirely from its right to decide what position should be taken in the courts, particularly in the Supreme Court. This authority might lead the Department of Justice, when there is a conflict in views among governmental agencies or when it thinks that a particular agency's position is indefensible, to refuse to support an agency. In such situations, the Department may feel obligated to advise the Court as to the position which, in its opinion, is correct, but may also feel loath to preclude presentation of the opposing view. If that position has been publicly stated, it will inevitably be brought to the Court's attention by one party or another, and the Court may well desire to have the position of the agency concerned stated officially. It may be equally desirable that the Court should be informed as to previously unexpressed views of an interested agency, even though the Department of Justice may not agree with those views. This does not mean that in all circumstances the Department believes itself obliged to present the views of other agencies with which it disagrees, but there are some occasions in which such a course seems advisable.

These problems, however, only result in the presentation of conflicting positions to the courts in a few cases. In the large portion of Government litigation handled exclusively by the Department of Justice, in which no other agency is concerned, whatever differences there may be among Government attorneys are resolved within the Department—although, as has been noted, the Department may, on rare occasions, change its position when the case reaches the Supreme Court. Where other agencies are concerned, there is a strong effort to accommodate views which may at first appear to differ. The Department recognizes that, subject to the overriding obligation of its attorneys to support the Constitution and laws of the United States, its function is to represent the agencies; it will take an opposing view only when it believes an agency's position to be completely without merit. The agencies, in turn, are reluctant to ask the Solicitor General for authority to present their views in the Supreme Court in opposition to his, doubtless partly because they feel that the Court will not look very favorably on arguments which the Government's chief law-enforcement officer is unwilling to espouse.

These factors are significant even where the Department of Justice lacks statutory authority over the agencies. As a consequence, differences actually reach the courts only in a very small number of cases. In such cases, determination by the judiciary is often more satisfactory than an effort by the Department of Justice to force its own views on the disagreeing agency by refusing to present the agency's position to the courts. The Attorney General has no authority to give binding legal advice to the independent agencies. Only the judiciary has authority to give the conclusive answer to the question in dispute.

[Low salaries and limited opportunities for advancement often plague the federal government's efforts to attract—and hold—talented young graduates of the top law schools. In recent years the Justice Department has had remarkable success in attracting such individuals, but, as Byron R. White indicates below, has not fared so well in its efforts to keep them.]

8. The Need for Higher Salaries*

The beginning salaries for lawyers in the Department are good and the Department has little trouble in recruiting amply qualified graduates from our law schools. The honors program provides the Department with a very bright, energetic group of young but relatively inexperienced lawyers. However, the great bulk of these new hands leave the Department in 2 or 3 years. For example, in the category of men with less than 5 years' experience with the Department, 73 resigned in fiscal 1959, 74 in 1960, and 48 during the first 11 months of this fiscal year. If the Department is successfully to handle litigation for the Government it must retain more of these young lawyers for a greater length of time, and an ample number of them for their entire career. As our older lawyers appointed in the late thirties and early forties retire, and these are fine lawyers, we must replace them to a large extent with well-trained attorneys from within the Department.

[Salary and advancement are not the only factors, however; strong ideological commitment or enthusiasm for an exciting new governmental approach to domestic and foreign problems often attract, and keep, the more adventurous among the top law school graduates.]

9. How to Attract the "Bright Young Men"†

. . . "The essential postulate of Mr. Justice Brandeis," said Felix Frankfurter, "is effective and generous opportunity for the unflagging operation of reason." As a

*Deputy Attorney General Byron R. White, Department of Justice, *Hearing before Subcommittee 5 of the House Judiciary Committee on Salaries of Attorneys in the Department of Justice,* June 16, 1961, 87th Cong. (Washington, D.C.: United States Government Printing Office, 1961), p. 7.
†The selection from Arthur Schlesinger, Jr., *The Politics of Upheaval,* Vol. III of *The Age of Roosevelt* (Boston: Houghton Mifflin, 1960), pp. 222–30, is reprinted by permission of and arrangement with the author and Houghton Mifflin Company, the authorized publishers. [Footnotes omitted.]

person, he shone with an intellectual and moral luminosity. He had the mien of a figure from the Old Testament, with his strong and beautiful face, his great, dark, kindly eyes, his pensive and brooding expressions. After meeting him, Harold Ickes wrote, "I felt as if I were sitting at the feet of one of the fine old prophets." Franklin Roosevelt used to refer to him as Isaiah.

VII

There gathered round him a group of the able young men of the country. Each year Felix Frankfurter would send along to Brandeis (as he also did to Holmes) a top Harvard Law School graduate to serve, sight unseen, as clerk. "We are the fortunate ones," Dean Acheson later said, "but what he has meant to us is not very different from what he has meant to hundreds of young men and women who have grown up under his influence."

Brandeis inspired them with a sense of social responsibility. When his law clerks suggested a joint visit on his eightieth birthday, he told them that, even more, he would welcome a message from each telling what public service he had lately performed. He inspired his young men with the idea of making their life in their own community; when they asked him what they should do, he always told them to go back to their "hinterland." A young Oregon newspaperman asked whether he should accept a job in New York. "Dear Richard Neuberger," the Justice replied: "Stay in Oregon. Cordially, Louis D. Brandeis." (Another, subjected to the same counsel, replied gloomily, "But Mr. Justice—Fargo, North Dakota!" And another: "But I have no hinterland. I'm from New York City." The Justice replied bleakly, "That is your misfortune." In time Oregon sent Neuberger east anyway.) Above all, Brandeis inspired everyone he could with his faith that the wellspring of moral vitality was individual identity, and that identity could be made safe only through the decentralization of power.

A wide variety of people came to him. The weekly teas were attended by government lawyers and economists, by writers and reformers, by congressmen and senators (for example: Harry S. Truman of Missouri), each waiting for a few moments' chat with the Justice, as Mrs. Brandeis sternly kept the guests in circulation. But the main channel of Brandeis's influence on the New Deal was through his intimate friend from the Harvard Law School, Felix Frankfurter, and Frankfurter's Washington representatives, Thomas G. Corcoran and Benjamin V. Cohen.

Frankfurter, like Brandeis, was in the tradition of Jefferson and Wilson. Competitive enterprise had to be at the basis of the American system, "not because of the opportunity it affords a few to make fabulous or unearned fortunes, but because of the encouragement and freedom of action it gives to men to shape their own lives and to plan their own destinies." In view of the "limitation of men," said Frankfurter, the general interest would be best served, "not by the minute orders of an all-directing state, governed by non-existent supermen but through the multitudinous activities, experiments and strivings of all those whom Lincoln called the common people." The greatest threat to the competitive system was the trend toward concentration. "If that trend is not reversed there is a danger of a private socialism in this country

290

as alien to traditional Americanism as state socialism. . . . In a truly democratic community the average citizen must have a stake worth preserving in the economic system."

In one vital area Frankfurter extended with brilliance the implications of Brandeis's views. Where the idea of the disinterested expert had been implicit in the "Brandeis brief" and in Brandeis's whole approach to social policy, Frankfurter now used the idea as the basis for a philosophy of government service. He was deeply impressed by the intricate problems thrown up by industrial civilization; "merely to analyze these issues requires a vast body of technical knowledge." Obviously such complex matters could not be left to Jacksonian theories of versatile improvisation. Frankfurter used to quote with contempt William Jennings Bryan's apothegm, "Any man with real goodness of heart can write a good currency law." Democracy, he said, depended on knowledge and wisdom beyond all other forms of government. It was the "reign of reason on the most extensive scale"; the grandeur of its aims was only matched by the difficulties of their achievement.

If democracy were to meet the challenge of modern society, it had to have traditions of public service powerful enough to enlist the best brains of the country. Frankfurter was a confirmed Anglophile; and for him the British Civil Service supplied the answer. "Without a permanent professional public service, highly trained, imaginative and courageously disinterested, the democratic aims of our society cannot be solved." For years he had carried on the fight for such a public service, with little success. "The whole tide of opinion," he wrote sadly in 1930, "is against public administration as a career for talent." "The whole mental and moral climate of our times—the impalpable but terrific pressure of current standards of achievement . . . [are] overwhelmingly on the side of private gain."

The New Deal brought a stunning change. Partly because government now provided the greater challenge, partly because jobs were not available elsewhere, the young men flocked to Washington. Frankfurter rejoiced: "The political law of gravitation has operated as it usually operates when new problems call for new endeavor." It was not accident, he asserted, that the founders of the republic had mostly been youngish men. Disinterested enthusiasm, freedom from imprisoning dogmatism, capacity for fresh insight, unflagging industry, ardor for difficulties, resilience, co-operativeness, release "from complicated ramifications of private life"— these were qualities which the times demanded and which, in the main, youthful years could best supply. The one-man employment office was now working overtime. And Frankfurter, with his flair and sparkle and sense of excitement, attracted the brightest of the young men.

Brandeis, with his classical severity of temperament, won respect by purity of character, whereas Frankfurter, with his Viennese exuberance, won affection by charm and high spirits. He loved food, drink, gossip, and parties; his technique of influence was not systematic cross-examination, but mischievous provocation and challenge; he was sparkling, contentious and diffuse. His intellectual gaiety had captivated Roosevelt, whom Frankfurter had known when he was a junior at Carter, Ledyard, and Milburn and had worked with on labor matters during the First World War, as it captivated Henry Stimson, Holmes, and Brandeis, and as it captivated the generations of students he was now guiding into public service. In 1933 Roosevelt had proposed that Frankfurter enter the government as Solicitor General, but Frankfurter replied that he could be of more use to the administration as a professorial free-lance than as a full-time public servant. In the winter of 1933–34 he was out of the country as Eastman Professor at Oxford. By the fall of 1934 he was back at Harvard, commuting regularly on the Federal to Washington.

VIII

With his concern for public administration and his admiration for the more systematic practices of Downing Street, Frankfurter was particularly troubled over the helter-skelter responsibility imposed on an American President. The problem of subduing any Roosevelt to any system seemed, as ever, insuperable. But Frankfurter argued to the President that he could diminish his burdens somewhat if he would take on an able young man as a trouble-shooter and general aide. Moreover, Frankfurter continued, he thought he knew the man.

Frankfurter's candidate was Thomas G. Corcoran, a member of the legal staff of the Reconstruction Finance Corporation. Corcoran's legal brilliance, adorned by Irish ebullience and wit, had first attracted Frankfurter's attention ten years before at the Harvard Law School. In 1926 Frankfurter sent him on to Washington as clerk to Justice Holmes. Holmes is supposed to have described him as "quite noisy, quite satisfactory, and quite noisy." From Frankfurter, Corcoran gained a sense of the responsibilities of government and the high dignity of public service ("Make me civil service commissioner ten years from now," he used to say in the early thirties, "and I'll be content.") From Holmes, Corcoran took away an appreciation of style in public life and a conviction of the indispensability of variety and experiment in a free state, as well, perhaps, as more than a trace of Holmes's corrosive skepticism. Five years of Wall Street practice perfected Corcoran's education. Cotton and Franklin was a first-class firm, aware of all the devices of high finance without being under the compulsion to regard them as high statesmanship. But the yearning for public service still touched Corcoran more deeply than anything else. When Eugene Meyer, staffing RFC in 1932, applied for suggestions to George Franklin, who had been his general counsel in the War Finance Corporation, Franklin nominated Corcoran, and Corcoran leaped at the opportunity.

After Roosevelt came in, Frankfurter commended Corcoran to Moley, and Moley soon found him indispensable in dealing with the securities and stock exchange legislation. It was then that Corcoran fell in with Benjamin V. Cohen, the gentle and sagacious lawyer whom Frankfurter had summoned in 1933, along with James M. Landis, to rescue the securities bill. Cohen subsequently went to work for Harold Ickes, first in the Public Works Administration and later in the National Power Policy Committee. Corcoran and Cohen made an ideal combination. Corcoran's brashness supplemented Cohen's shyness, as his perpetual high spirits offset Cohen's occasional moodiness. In the same way Cohen's wisdom balanced Corcoran's impetuosity, and Cohen's rectitude, Corcoran's opportunism. Cohen was the man of ideas and reflection; Corcoran, though he had plenty of ideas, was preeminently the salesman and promoter. The idea of the Corcoran-Cohen team—this alliterative partnership of an Irishman and a Jew—caught the popular fancy. They reminded *Fortune* of "those minor state counselors in Shakespearian comedies who serve the Duke, make astute comments, and are always perturbed at developments."

On questions of policy, Cohen and Corcoran were both in the Brandeis tradition. Experiments in central planning of the NRA-AAA type left them cold. What they cared about was the revitalization of competitive enterprise through an attack on the chicanery of finance; and they took pride at outwitting the Wall Street lawyers in their own field. The New Deal, said Cohen in 1934, "recognizes that far-reaching reforms are necessary to preserve that individualism which was achieved in a simpler and less complicated society through laissez faire." He added that "reform of the existing order to effect a revival of true individualism, was intellectually more difficult than the attempt to govern by central plan. "It involves a penetrating understanding of the complicated character and functioning of modern economic life, a delicate sense of balance, and alert sensitivity to constant change." The New Deal was "deliberately flexible and unlogical in its approach to conditions rather than theories" because it recognized "that necessity of dealing with multitudinous concrete instances which is the essence of government."

Cohen, from the beginning a disciple of Keynes as well as of Brandeis, argued that government spending was the only way of making up for the timidity of private capital. Corcoran agreed. In 1934, trying to persuade Amos Pinchot to become a director of RFC, Corcoran suggested that the right way to restore buying power and bring about recovery was to pour money into circulation in the greatest possible quantities and at the highest possible speed. The ideal thing, he said with characteristic high spirits, would be for fleets of airplanes to fly over the country, discharging money as they went, so that anyone needing cash could pick it up from the ground.

IX

Cohen and Corcoran gathered around them a brilliant group of younger lawyers, whom Corcoran placed in key agencies. "What is a government?" Corcoran once asked. "It's not just the top man or the top ten men. A government is the top one one hundred or two hundred men. What really makes the difference is what happens down the line before—and after—the big decisions are taken." The old Frankfurter employment agency was now enlarged to epic proportions under Corcoran's tireless direction. "The spectacle of a good man jobless or a good job manless," as Joseph Alsop and Robert Kintner put it, "drives him to a frenzy." Whenever an agency needed a lawyer, Corcoran was ready with a candidate, someone he had known at Harvard or in Wall Street, or someone Frankfurter or Brandeis told him about, or anyone who had a reputation for legal ability and aggressive liberalism.

While nominally domiciled in the RFC, Corcoran by 1934 was operating all over Washington. Soon introduced into the White House circles, he made an instant impression. He knew the law and the Constitution, was a master of legal technicality and artifice, had a unique ability to direct the operations of a team, was single-minded in his determination to get things done, and never slept. More than this, he had an extravagant personal charm which served as a cloak for his boundless talents as a manipulator and an *intrigant*.

With older men he seemed almost to overdo deference. One senator objected that the ingratiating Corcoran had said "sir" to him twice in the same sentence. But toward his contemporaries he mixed a light-hearted cynicism with an idealist's respect for hard work in a compound that most of them found beguiling; and he won the devotion of his juniors with his combination of solicitude, discipline, and inspiration. His personal warmth was as irresistible as his intellectual resourcefulness was unlimited. This compact chunk of a man, an accordion strap swung over his stocky shoulders, his rich voice singing songs at once gay and melancholy ("Tim Toolan" in a Pawtucket brogue or "Vive la Garibaldi" in San Francisco Italian, or "The Yellow Rose of Texas"), soon became a fixture at New Deal parties. The party over, Corcoran (who never smoked and rarely drank) might well go on to read to Justice Holmes, now in his nineties, or spend the rest of the night, sustained by dextrose and hot coffee, working on a brief or preparing for a hearing in the morning.

With the tacit consent of Jesse Jones and the active cooperation of RFC's general counsel, Stanley Reed, Corcoran turned RFC into a base for operations which extended through the government. A fluid and emergency-minded organization, RFC was a reservoir of expert talent for any contingency. It provided not only lawyers, but comptrollers, treasurers, bank examiners, personnel experts, public-relations experts, secretaries—not to speak of telephone operators who could get anyone anywhere in the world in five minutes. If furnished Corcoran the facilities he needed—the office space, the all-night secretaries, the long-distance wires, the mimeograph machines. It supplied a means of bringing down new men, looking them over, and putting them on a payroll until something opened up for them. It became in effect the springboard from which the old departments (especially Justice, Interior, and the Federal Reserve) could be reorganized and the new agencies required by the new legislation launched and staffed. "In a practical sense," Corcoran later put it, with slight but pardonable exaggeration, "the new organizations were all 'spin-offs' from an RFC prototype."

Stanley Reed became the particular protector of the Harvard Law School crowd. RFC and, after Reed became Solicitor General in 1935, Justice served as the intelligence switchboard and the operational base for the web of Frankfurter-Corcoran relationships through the new agencies. Whenever a crucial law had to be drafted or crucial brief written, Corcoran conjured up a task force from his young men around the government, who then completed the job in a spurt of intense concentration and furious energy. Little could have been harder than to raise the standards of legal performance in a government hectically expanding in size and purpose. Corcoran's invention of the *ad hoc* task force provided in its time an effective solution.

For its success, this solution required a flexible conception of the way government should operate. This Roosevelt, of course, had; and men like Ickes, Hopkins, Jones, and Reed, instead of insisting on the sacredness of channels and flow charts, were prepared to tolerate, even encourage, the Corcoran-style operation so long as it produced results. For its success it also required flexible conception of the way lawyers should operate. "We lawyers," one of the most resourceful of the New Deal lawyers, Oscar Cox, once said, "are frequently—and many times justly—accused of having negative minds. Too often we are disposed to search out the reasons why something necessary can *not* be done rather than to seek out the means whereby it *can* be done." This was precisely what Corcoran sought to change. He saw the government lawyer as the man whose job it was to find constitutional ways to do what had to be done. As Roosevelt himself used to challenge his successive chiefs of the Department of Justice: "If you are a good Attorney General, tell me how I can do it."

The New Deal lawyer was thus a freewheeler and an activist. He was also, most probably, a young man. The New Deal's readiness to bet on youth created problems; it also nurtured ability and assured loyalty. Charles E. Wyzanski, Jr., a twenty-six-year-old graduate of the Harvard Law School, was told, on his first day in Washington as a prospective solicitor for the Department of Labor, that his immediate job was to draw up a public-works bill. Frances Perkins brought him up to meet the President after they had all taken part in a White House conference on public works, and Wyzanski thought he should explain that he had voted for Hoover. "I don't care," Roosevelt replied. "What I want you to do is to have on my desk tomorrow morning a draft of a bill carrying out this idea that you've heard discussed." Wyzanski, appalled, called Tom Corcoran, who gave him a quick briefing on the things to watch out for. By the next morning a bill was on the President's desk. "This was such an initiation," Wyzanski later said, "as no man would ever forget. I never could be so scared again. . . . This in one moment was plunging into the furnace. If you lived and got out of it, there could be no other fire which you would have to particularly fear in Washington."

Those who lived and got out of it were bound together by a sense of common experience on the firing line. The result was a group of lawyers dispersed through Washington agencies and departments, but united by a strong loyalty to Corcoran and Cohen, to each other, and to the New Deal. Some even lived with Tom and Ben in a convivial house in Georgetown—"the little red house on R Street" which, to the devotees of Dr. Wirt, was the headquarters of revolution. Tom's pretty secretary Peggy Dowd, whom, when he had time, he eventually married, was the Missy LeHand of the second echelon, stroking the brows and sustaining the spirits of a volatile collection of talents. The existence of the Harvard Law School network gave Corcoran a unique instrument both for finding out what was going on and for getting things done. He used the instrument to the hilt.

X

Corcoran and Cohen, like Brandeis and Frankfurter, were working mainly behind the scenes. Moreover, all four men, as lawyers were more inclined to respond to specific cases than to develop a general rationale. Accordingly, the most rounded presentation of the Brandeis position in 1935 came from a nonlawyer outside government, David Cushman Coyle.

A civil engineer by profession, Coyle had turned some years before to the semipopular writing of economics. His engineering background gave him special qualifications with which to discuss national planning. Thus no one understood better the fallacies packed in the expression "social engineering," a phrase Coyle exposed with relish as based on false analogies. Engineering operations required conditions which free society could not fulfill: definite physical objectives, accepted technical procedures, and the capacity to impose absolute discipline within the area of activity.

F. THE SOCIAL AND POLITICAL ROLE OF
THE ORGANIZED BAR

[The public debate over the social role of the organized bar in America has in recent years become a key issue in constitutional adjudication. The movement for an integrated bar has, in particular, stimulated sweeping appraisal by the Supreme Court of the United States. The occasion was *Lathrop* v. *Donohue,* decided in 1961. The majority, concurring, and dissenting opinions embody, often in cutting fashion, sharply different views of the social and political role of the organized bar. To provide these contrasting views, the opinions are reproduced in full.]

1. The "Integrated Bar" and Fundamental Freedoms*

Mr. Justice Brennan announced the judgment of the Court and an opinion in which The Chief Justice, Mr. Justice Clark and Mr. Justice Stewart join.

The Wisconsin Supreme Court integrated the Wisconsin Bar by an order which created "The State Bar of Wisconsin" on January 1, 1957, under Rules and Bylaws promulgated by the court. . . . The order originally was effective for a two-year period, but in 1958 was continued indefinitely. . . . Alleging that the "rules and by-laws required the plaintiff to enroll in the State Bar of Wisconsin and to pay dues to the treasurer of the State Bar of Wisconsin on the penalty of being deprived of his livelihood as a practicing lawyer, if he should fail to do so," the appellant, a Wisconsin lawyer, brought this action in the Circuit Court of Dane County for the refund of $15 annual dues for 1959 paid by him under protest to appellee, the Treasurer of the State Bar. He attached to his complaint a copy of the letter with which he had enclosed his check for the dues. He stated in the letter that he paid under protest because "I do not like to be coerced to support an organization which is authorized and directed to engage in political and propaganda activities. . . . A major portion of the activities of the State Bar as prescribed by the Supreme Court of Wisconsin are of a political and propaganda nature." His complaint alleges more specifically that the State Bar promotes "law reform" and "makes and opposes proposals for changes in . . . laws and constitutional provisions and argues to legislative bodies and their committees and to the lawyers and to the people with respect to the adoption of changes in . . . codes, laws and constitutional provisions." He alleges further that in the course of this activity "the State Bar of Wisconsin has used

Lathrop v. *Donohue,* 367 U.S. 820 (1961).

its employees, property and funds in active, unsolicited opposition to the adoption of legislation by the Legislature of the State of Wisconsin, which was favored by the plaintiff, all contrary to plaintiff's convictions and beliefs." His complaint concludes: "The plaintiff bases this action on his claim that the defendant has unjustly received, held, and disposed of funds of the plaintiff in the amount of $15.00, which to the knowledge of the defendant were paid to the defendant by the plaintiff unwillingly and under coercion, and that such coercion was and is entailed in the rules and by-laws of the State Bar of Wisconsin continued in effect by the aforesaid order of the Supreme Court of the State of Wisconsin . . . ; and the said order insofar as it coerces the plaintiff to support the State Bar of Wisconsin, is unconstitutional and in violation of the Fourteenth Amendment of the Constitution of the United States. . . ."

The appellee demurred to the complaint on the ground, among others, that it failed to state a cause of action. The demurrer was sustained and the complaint was dismissed. The Supreme Court of Wisconsin, on appeal, stated that the Circuit Court was without jurisdiction to determine the questions raised by the complaint. However, treating the case as if originally and properly brought in the Supreme Court, the court considered appellant's constitutional claims, not only on the allegations of the complaint, but also upon the facts, of which it took judicial notice, as to its own actions leading up to the challenged order, and as to all activities, including legislative activities, of the State Bar since its creation. The judgment of the Circuit Court dismissing the complaint was affirmed . . . The Supreme Court held that the requirement that appellant be an enrolled dues-paying member of the State Bar did not abridge his rights of freedom of association, and also that his rights to free speech were not violated because the State Bar used his money to support legislation with which he disagreed.

An appeal was brought here by appellant under 28 U.S.C. 1257 (2), which authorizes our review of a final judgment rendered by the highest court of a State "By appeal, where is drawn in question the validity of a [state] statute. . . ." We postponed to the hearing on the merits the question whether the order continuing the State Bar indefinitely under the Rules and Bylaws is a "statute" for the purposes of appeal under 1257 (2). . . .

We think that the order is "a statute" for the purposes of 1257 (2). Under that section, the legislative character of challenged state action, rather than the nature of the agency of the State performing the act, is decisive of the question of jurisdiction. It is not necessary that the state legislature itself should have taken the action drawn in question. In construing the similar jurisdictional provision in the Judiciary Act of 1867, . . . we said: "Any enactment, from whatever source originating, to which a State gives the force of law is a statute of the State, within the meaning of the clause cited relating to the jurisdiction of this court." . . . We likewise said of the provision of the Act of 1925, . . . which is the present 1257 (2): ". . . the jurisdictional provision uses the words 'a statute of any State' in their larger sense and is not intended to make a distinction between acts of a state legislature and other exertions of the State's law-making power, but rather to include every act legislative in character to which the State gives its sanction." . . . Thus this Court has upheld jurisdiction on appeal of challenges to municipal ordinances . . . certain types of orders of state regulatory commissions . . . and some orders of other state agencies. . . . It is true that in these cases the state agency the action of which was called in question was exercising authority delegated to it by the legislature. However, this fact was not determinative, but was merely relevant to the character of the State's action. The absence of such a delegation does not preclude consideration of the exercise of authority as a statute.

We are satisfied that this appeal is from an act legislative in nature and within 1257 (2). Integration of the Bar was effected through an interplay of action by the legislature and the court directed to fashioning a policy for the organization of the legal profession. The Wisconsin Legislature initiated the movement for integration of the Bar in 1943 when it passed the statute, chapter 315 of the Wisconsin Laws for that year, now Wis. Rev. Stat. 256.31, providing:

> *"(1) There shall be an association to be known as the 'State Bar of Wisconsin' composed of persons licensed to practice law in this state, and membership in such association shall be a condition precedent to the right to practice law in Wisconsin.*
>
> *"(2) The supreme court by appropriate orders shall provide for the organization and government of the association and shall define the rights, obligations and conditions of membership therein, to the end that such association shall promote the public interest by maintaining high standards of conduct in the legal profession and by aiding in the efficient administration of justice."*

The State Supreme Court held that this statute was not binding upon it because "[t]he power to integrate the bar is an incident to the exercise of the judicial power." . . . The court twice refused to order integration . . . before taking the actions called in question on this appeal . . . Nevertheless, the court in rejecting the first petition, . . . recognized that its exercise of the power to order integration of the Bar would not be adjudicatory, but an action in accord with and in implementation of the legislative declaration of public policy. The court said:

> *"It is obvious that whether the general welfare requires that the bar be treated as a corporate body is a matter for the consideration of the legislature. . . . While the legislature has no constitutional power to compel the court to act or, if it acts, to act in a particular way in the discharge of the judicial function, it may nevertheless with propriety, and in the exercise of its power and the discharge of its duty, declare itself upon questions relating to the general welfare which includes the integration of the bar. The court, as has been exemplified during the entire history of the state, will respect such declarations and, as already indicated, adopt them so far as they do not embarrass the court or impair its constitutional functions."*

Integration of the Bar in Wisconsin bore no resemblance to adjudication. The State Supreme Court's action disposed of no litigation between parties. Rather the court sought to regulate the profession by applying its orders to all present members of the

Bar and to all persons coming within the described class in the future. . . . As such, the action had the characteristics of legislation. We conclude that the appeal is cognizable under 1257 (2). We therefore proceed to the consideration of the merits.

The core of appellant's argument is that he cannot constitutionally be compelled to join and give support to an organization which has among its functions the expression of opinion on legislative matters and which utilizes its property, funds and employees for the purposes of influencing legislation and public opinion toward legislation. But his compulsory enrollment imposes only the duty to pay dues. The Supreme Court of Wisconsin so interpreted its order and its interpretation is of course binding on us. The court said: "The rules and by-laws of the State Bar, as approved by this court, do not compel the plaintiff to associate with anyone. He is free to attend or not attend its meetings or vote in its elections as he chooses. The only compulsion to which he has been subjected by the integration of the bar is the payment of the annual dues of $15 per year." . . . We therefore are confronted, as we were in *Railway Employees Department* v. *Hanson* . . . only with a question of compelled financial support of group activities, not with involuntary membership in any other aspect. . . .

A review of the activities of the State Bar authorized under the Rules and Bylaws is necessary to decision. The purposes of the organization are stated as follows in Rule 1, 2: "to aid the courts in carrying on and improving the administration of justice; to foster and maintain on the part of those engaged in the practice of law high ideals of integrity, learning, competence and public service and high standards of conduct; to safeguard the proper professional interests of the members of the bar; to encourage the formation and activities of local bar associations; to provide a forum for the discussion of subjects pertaining to the practice of law, the science of jurisprudence and law reform, and the relations of the bar to the public, and to publish information relating thereto; to the end that the public responsibilities of the legal profession may be more effectively discharged." To achieve these purposes standing committees and sections are established. The Rules also assign the organization a major role in the State's procedures for the discipline of members of the bar for unethical conduct. A Committee on Grievances is provided for each of the nine districts into which the State is divided. Each committee receives and investigates complaints of alleged misconduct of lawyers within its district. Each committee also investigates and processes petitions for reinstatement of lawyers and petitions for late enrollment in the State Bar of lawyers who fail to enroll within a designated period after becoming eligible to enroll.

The State Legislature and the State Supreme Court have informed us of the public interest sought to be served by the integration of the Bar. The statute states its desirability "to the end that such association shall promote the public interest by maintaining high standards of conduct in the legal profession and by aiding in the efficient administration of justice." This theme is echoed in the several Supreme Court opinions. The first opinion after the passage of the statute noted the "widespread general recognition of the fact that the conduct of the bar is a matter of general public interest and concern." . . . But the court's examination at that time of existing procedures governing admission and discipline of lawyers and the prevention of the unauthorized practice of the law persuaded the court that the public interest was being adequately served without integration. The same conclusion was reached when the matter was reviewed again in 1946. At that time in addition to reviewing the desirability of integration in the context of the problems of admission and discipline, the court considered its utility in other fields. The matter of post-law school or post-admission education of lawyers was one of these. The court believed, however, that while an educational program was a proper objective, the one proposed was "nebulous in outline and probably expensive in execution." . . . The court also observed, "There are doubtless many other useful activities for which dues might properly be used, but what they are does not occur to us and no particular one seems to press for action." . . .

The court concluded in 1956, however, that integration might serve the public interest and should be given a two-year trial. It decided to "require the bar to act as a unit to promote high standards of practice and the economical and speedy enforcement of legal rights," . . . because it had come to the conclusion that efforts to accomplish these ends in the public interest through voluntary association had not been effective. "[T]oo many lawyers have refrained or refused to join, . . . membership in the voluntary association has become static, and . . . a substantial minority of the lawyers in the state are not associated with the State Bar Association." . . . When the order was extended indefinitely in 1958 the action was expressly grounded on the finding that, "Members of the legal profession by their admission to the bar become an important part of [the] process [of administering justice]. . . . An independent, active, and intelligent bar is necessary to the efficient administration of justice by the courts." . . .

The appellant attacks the power of the State to achieve these goals through integration on the ground that because of its legislative activities, the State Bar partakes of the character of a political party. But on their face the purposes and the designated activities of the State Bar hardly justify this characterization. The inclusion among its purposes that it be a forum for a "discussion of . . . law reform" and active in safeguarding the "proper professional interests of, the members of the bar," in unspecified ways, does not support it. Only two of the 12 committees, Administration of Justice, and Legislation, are expressly directed to concern themselves in a substantial way with legislation. Authority granted the other committees directs them to deal largely with matters which appear to be wholly outside the political process and to concern the internal affairs of the profession.

We do not understand the appellant to contend that the State Bar is a sham organization deliberately designed to further a program of political action. Nor would such a contention find support in this record. Legislative activity is carried on under a statement of policy which followed the recommendations of a former president of the voluntary Wisconsin Bar Association, Alfred LaFrance. He recommended that the legislative activity of the State Bar should have two distinct aspects: (1) "the field of legislative reporting or the dissemination of information concerning legislative proposals. . . . This is a service-information function that is both useful to the general membership and to the local bar associations" and (2) "promotional or positive legislative activity." As to the latter he advised that "the rule of substantial unanimity should be observed. Unless the lawyers of Wisconsin are substantially for or against a proposal, the State Bar should neither support nor oppose the proposal." . . . "We must remember that we are an integrated Bar, that the views of the minority must be given along with the views of the majority where unanimity does not appear. The State Bar represents all of the lawyers of this state and in that capacity we must safeguard the interests of all." . . . The rules of policy and procedure for legislative activity follows these recommendations.

Under its charter of legislative action, the State Bar has participated in political activities in these principal categories:

(1) its executive director is registered as a lobbyist in accordance with state law. For the legislative session 1959–1960, the State Bar listed a $1,400 lobbying expense; this was a percentage of the salary of the executive director, based on an estimate of the time he spent in seeking to influence legislation, amounting to 5% of his salary for the two years. The registration statement signed by the then president of the State Bar added the explanatory note: "His activities as a lobbyist on behalf of the State Bar are incidental to his general work and occupy only a small portion of his time."

(2) The State Bar, through its Board of Governors or Executive Committee, has taken a formal position with respect to a number of questions of legislative policy. These have included such subjects as an increase in the salaries of State Supreme Court justices; making attorneys notaries public; amending the Federal Career Compensation Act to apply to attorneys employed with the Armed Forces the same provisions for special pay and promotion available to members of other professions; improving pay scales of attorneys in state service; court reorganization; extending personal jurisdiction over nonresidents; allowing the recording of unwitnessed conveyances; use of deceased partners' names in firm names; revision of the law governing federal tax liens; law clerks for State Supreme Court justices; curtesy and dower; securities transfers by fiduciaries; jurisdiction of county courts over the administration of *inter vivos* trusts; special appropriations for research for the State Legislative Council.

(3) The standing committees, particularly the Committees on Legislation and Administration of Justice, and the sections have devoted considerable time to the study of legislation, the formulation of recommendations, and the support of various proposals. For example, the president reported in 1960 that the Committee on Legislation "has been extremely busy, and through its efforts in cooperation with other interested agencies has been instrumental in securing the passage of the Court Reorganization bill, the bill of the Judicial Council expanding personal jurisdiction, and at this recently resumed session a bill providing clerks for our Supreme Court, and other bills of importance to the administration of justice." . . . A new subcommittee, on federal legislation, was set up by this committee following a study which found need for such a group "to deal with federal legislation affecting the practice of law, or lawyers as a class, or the jurisdiction, procedure and practice of the Federal courts and other Federal tribunals, or creation of new Federal courts or judgeships affecting this state, and comparable subjects . . ." . . . Furthermore, legislative recommendations and activities have not been con-

fined to those standing committees with the express function in the bylaws of considering legislative proposals. . . . Many of the positions on legislation taken on behalf of the State Bar by the Board of Governors or the Executive Committee have also followed studies and recommendations by the sections. . . .

(4) A number of special committees have been constituted, either *ad hoc* to consider particular legislative proposals, or to perform continuing functions which may involve the consideration of legislation. Thus special committees have considered such subjects as extension of personal jurisdiction over non-residents, law clerks for State Supreme Court justices, and revision of the federal tax lien laws. The Special Committee on World Peace through Law, which has encouraged the formation of similar committees on the local level, has sponsored debates on subjects such as the repeal of the Connally reservation, believing that "the general knowledge of laymen as well as of lawyers concerning the possibility of world peace through law is limited and requires a constant program of education and discussion." . . .

(5) The Wisconsin Bar Bulletin, sent to each member, prints articles suggesting changes in state and federal law. And other publications of the State Bar deal with the progress of legislation.

But it seems plain that legislative activity is not the major activity of the State Bar. The activities without apparent political coloration are many. The Supreme Court provided in an appendix to the opinion below, "an analysis of [State Bar] . . . activities and the public purpose served thereby." . . . The court found that "The most extensive activities of the State Bar are those directed toward postgraduate education of lawyers," and that "Postgraduate education of lawyers is in the public interest because it promotes the competency of lawyers to handle the legal matters entrusted to them by those of the general public who employ them." . . . It found that the State Bar's participation in the handling of grievances improved the efficiency and effectiveness of this work. It found that the public interest was furthered by the Committee on Unauthorized Practice of Law which was carrying on "a constant program since numerous trades and occupations keep expanding their services and frequently start offering services which constitute [*sic*] the practice of the law." . . . The court also concluded that the Legal Aid Committee had "done effective and noteworthy work to encourage the local bar associations of the state to set up legal-aid systems in their local communities. . . . Such committee has also outlined recommended procedures for establishing and carrying through such systems of providing legal aid." . . . In the field of public relations the court found that the "chief activity" of the State Bar was the "preparation, publication and distribution to the general public of pamphlets dealing with various transactions and happenings with which laymen are frequently confronted, which embody legal problems." . . . Moreover, a number of studies have been made of programs, not involving political action, to further the economic well-being of the profession.

This examination of the purposes and functions of the State Bar shows its multi-faceted character, in fact as well as in conception. In our view the case presents a claim of impingement upon freedom of association no different from that which we decided in *Railway Employees Dept.* v. *Hanson* . . . We there held that 2, . . .

Eleventh of the Railway Labor Act . . . did not on its face abridge protected rights of association in authorizing union-shop agreements between interstate railroads and unions of their employees conditioning the employees' continued employment on payment of union dues, initiation fees and assessments. There too the record indicated that the organizations engaged in some activities similar to the legislative activities of which the appellant complains. . . . In rejecting Hanson's claim of abridgment of his rights of freedom of association, we said, "On the present record, there is no more an infringement or impairment of First Amendment rights than there would be in the case of a lawyer who by state law is required to be a member of an integrated bar." . . . Both in purport and in practice the bulk of State Bar activities serve the function, or at least so Wisconsin might reasonably believe, of elevating the educational and ethical standards of the Bar to the end of improving the quality of the legal service available to the people of the State, without any reference to the political process. It cannot be denied that this is a legitimate end of state policy. We think that the Supreme Court of Wisconsin, in order to further the State's legitimate interests in raising the quality of professional services, may constitutionally require that the costs of improving the profession in this fashion should be shared by the subjects and beneficiaries of the regulatory program, the lawyers, even though the organization created to attain the objective also engages in some legislative activity. Given the character of the integrated bar shown on this record, in the light of the limitation of the membership requirement to the compulsory payment of reasonable annual dues, we are unable to find any impingement upon protected rights of association.

However, appellant would have us go further and decide whether his constitutional rights of free speech are infringed if his dues money is used to support the political activities of the State Bar. The State Supreme Court treated the case as raising the question whether First Amendment rights were violated "because part of his dues money is used to support causes to which he is opposed." . . . The Court in rejecting appellant's argument reasoned that "[t]he right to practice law is not a right but is a privilege subject to regulation. . . . The only limitation upon the state's power to regulate the privilege of the practice of law is that the regulations adopted do not impose an unconstitutional burden or deny due process." . . . The Court found no such burden because ". . . the public welfare will be promoted by securing and publicizing the composite judgment of the members of the bar of the state on measures directly affecting the administration of justice and the practice of law. The general public and the legislature are entitled to know how the profession as a whole stands on such types of proposed legislation. . . . The only challenged interference with his liberty is the exaction of annual dues to the State Bar, in the nature of the imposition of an annual license fee, not unreasonable or unduly burdensome in amount, part of which is used to advocate causes to which he is opposed. However, this court, in which is vested the power of the state to regulate the practice of law, has determined that it promotes the public interest to have public expression of the views of a majority of the lawyers of the state, with respect to legislation affecting the administration of justice and the practice of law, the same to be voiced through their own democratically chosen representatives comprising the board of governors of the State Bar. The public interest so promoted far outweighs the slight inconvenience to the plaintiff resulting from his required payment of annual dues." . . .

We are persuaded that on this record we have no sound basis for deciding appellant's constitutional claim insofar as it rests on the assertion that his rights of free speech are violated by the use of his money for causes which he opposes. Even if the demurrer is taken as admitting all the factual allegations of the complaint, even if these allegations are construed most expansively, and even if, like the Wisconsin Supreme Court, we take judicial notice of the political activities of the State Bar, still we think that the issue of impingement upon rights of free speech through the use of exacted dues is no more concretely presented for adjudication than it was in *Hanson*. Compare *International Association of Machinists* v. *Street,* decided today . . . Nowhere are we clearly apprised as to the views of the appellant on any particular legislative issues on which the State Bar has taken a position, or as to the way in which and the degree to which funds compulsorily exacted from its members are used to support the organization's political activities. There is an allegation in the complaints that the State Bar had "used its employees, property and funds in active unsolicited opposition to the adoption of legislation by the Legislature of the State of Wisconsin which was favored by the plaintiff, all contrary to the plaintiff's convictions and beliefs," but there is no indication of the nature of this legislation, nor of appellant's views on particular proposals, nor of whether any of his dues were used to support the State Bar's positions. There is an allegation that the State Bar's revenues amount to about $90,000 a year, of which $80,000 is derived from dues, but there is no indication in the record as to how political expenditures are financed and how much has been expended for political causes to which appellant objects. The facts of which the Supreme Court took judicial notice do not enlighten us on these gaps in the record. The minutes of the Board of Governors and Executive Committee of the State Bar show that the organization has taken one position or another on a wide variety of issues, but those minutes give no indication of appellant's views as to any of such issues or of what portions of the expenditure of funds to propagate the State Bar's views may be properly apportioned to his dues payments. Nor do the other publications of the State Bar. The Supreme Court assumed, as apparently the trial court did in passing on the demurrer, that the appellant was personally opposed to some of the legislation supported by the State Bar. But its opinion still gave no description of any specific measures he opposed, or the extent to which the State Bar actually utilized dues funds for specific purposes to which he had objected. Appellant's phrasing of the question presented on appeal in this Court is not responsive to any of these inquires as to facts which may be relevant to the determination of constitutional questions surrounding the political expenditures. It merely asks whether a requirement of financial support of an association which "among other things uses its property, funds and employees for the purpose of influencing a broad range of legislation and public opinion" can be constitutionally imposed on him. This statement of the question, just as does his complaint, appears more a claim of the right to be free from compelled financial support of the organization because of its political activities, than a challenge by appellant to the use of his dues money for particular political causes of which he disapproves. Moreover, although the court below purported to decide as against all Fourteenth Amendment claims that the appellant could be compelled to pay his annual dues, even though "part of [it] . . . is used to advocate causes to which he is opposed," on oral argument here appellant disclaimed any necessity to show that he had opposed the position of the State Bar on any particular issue and asserted that is was sufficient that he opposed the use of his money for any political purposes at all. In view of the state of the record and this disclaimer, we think that we would not be justified in passing on the constitutional question considered below. "[T]he questions involving the power of . . . [the State] come here not so shaped by the record and by the proceedings below as to bring those powers before this Court as leanly and as sharply as judicial judgment upon an exercise of . . . [state] power requires." . . .

We, therefore, intimate no view as to the correctness of the conclusion of the Wisconsin Supreme Court that the appellant may constitutionally be compelled to contribute his financial support to political activities which he opposes. That issue is reserved, just as it was in *Hanson*. . . Upon this understanding we four vote to affirm. Since three of our colleagues are of the view that the claim which we do not decide is properly here and has no merit, and on that ground affirm, the judgment of the Wisconsin Supreme Court is

Affirmed.

———

Mr. Justice Harlan, with whom Mr. Justice Frankfurter joins, concurring in the judgment.

I think it most unfortunate that the right of the Wisconsin Integrated Bar to use, in whole or in part, the dues of dissident members to carry on legislative and other programs of law reform—doubtless among the most useful and significant branches of its authorized activities—should be left in such disquieting Constitutional uncertainty. The effect of that uncertainty is compounded by the circumstance that it will doubtless also reach into the Integrated Bars of twenty-five other States.

I must say, with all respect, that the reasons stated in the plurality opinion for avoiding decision of this Constitutional issue can hardly be regarded as anything but trivial. For, given the unquestioned fact that the Wisconsin Bar uses or threatens to use, over appellant's protest, some part of its receipts to further or oppose legislation on matters of law reform and the administration of justice, I am at a loss to understand how it can be thought that this record affords "no sound basis" for adjudicating the issue simply because we are not "clearly apprised as to the views of the appellant on any particular legislative issues on which the State Bar has taken a position, or as to the way in which and the degree to which funds compulsorily exacted from its members are used to support the organization's political activities." . . . I agree with my Brother Black that the Constitutional issue is inescapably before us.

Unless one is ready to fall prey to what are at best but alluring abstractions on rights of free speech and association, I think he will be hard put to it to find any solid basis for the Constitutional qualms which, though unexpressed, so obviously underlie the plurality opinion, or for the views of my two dissenting Brothers, one of whom finds unconstitutional the entire Integrated Bar concept . . . and the other of whom holds the operations of such a Bar unconstitutional to the extent that they involve taking "the money of protesting lawyers" and using "it to support causes they are against."

For me, there is a short and simple answer to all of this. The *Hanson* case . . . decided by a unanimous Court, surely lays at rest all doubt that a State may Constitutionally condition the right to practice law upon membership in an integrated bar association, a condition fully as justified by state needs as the union shop is by federal needs. Indeed the conclusion reached in *Hanson* with respect to compulsory union membership seems to me *a fortiori* true here, in light of the supervisory powers which the state, through its courts, has traditionally exercised over admission to the practice of law . . . and over the conduct of lawyers after admission. . . The Integrated Bar was in fact treated as such an *a fortiori* case in the *Hanson* opinion itself. . . . So much, indeed, is recognized by the plurality opinion which rejects the contention that Wisconsin could not Constitutionally require appellant, a lawyer, to become and remain a dues-paying member of the State Bar.

That being so, I do not understand why it should become unconstitutional for the State Bar to use appellant's dues to fulfill some of the very purposes for which it was established. I am wholly unable to follow the force of reasoning which, on the one hand, denies that compulsory dues-paying membership in an Integrated Bar infringes "freedom of association" and, on the other, in effect affirms that such membership, to the extent it entails the use of a dissident member's dues for legitimate Bar purposes, infringes "freedom of speech." This is a refinement between two aspects of what, in circumstances like these, is essentially but a single facet of the "liberty" assured by the Fourteenth Amendment . . . that is too subtle for me to grasp.

Nevertheless, since a majority of the Court here, as in the *Street* case . . . has deemed the "free speech" issue to be distinct from that of "free association," I shall also treat the case on that basis. From a Constitutional standpoint, I think that there can be no doubt about Wisconsin's right to use appellant's dues in furtherance of any of the purposes now drawn in question. Orderly analysis requires that there be considered, *first*, the respects in which it may be thought that the use of a member's dues for causes he is against impinges on his right of free speech, and *second*, the nature of the state interest offered to justify such use of the dues exacted from him. I shall also add some further observations as to the overall Constitutionality of the Integrated Bar concept.

I

To avoid the pitfall of disarming, and usually obscuring, generalization which too often characterizes discussions in this Constitutional field, I see no alternative (even at the risk of being thought to labor the obvious) but to deal in turn with each of the various specific impingements on "free speech" which have been suggested or intimated to flow from the State Bar's use of an objecting member's dues for the purposes involved in this case. As I understand things, it is said that the operation of the Integrated Bar tends (1) to reduce a dissident member's "economic capacity" to espouse causes in which he believes; (2) to further governmental "establishment" of political views; (3) to threaten development of a "guild system" of closed, self-regulating professions and businesses; (4) to "drown out" the voice of dissent by requiring all members of the Bar to lend financial support to the views of the majority; and (5) to interfere with freedom of belief by causing "compelled affirmation" of majority-held views. With deference, I am bound to say that, in my view, all of these arguments border on the chimerical.

1. REDUCTION IN THE "ECONOMIC CAPACITY" TO ESPOUSE VIEWS

This argument which, if indeed suggested at all, is intimated only obliquely, is that the mere exaction of dues money works a Constitutionally cognizable inhibition of speech by reducing the resources otherwise available to a dissident member for the espousal of causes in which he believes. The untenability of such a proposition becomes immediately apparent when it is recognized that this rationale would make every governmental exaction the material of a "free speech" issue. Even the federal income tax would be suspect. And certainly this source of inhibition is as great if the Integrated Bar wastes its dues on dinners as if it spends them on recommendations to the legislature. Yet I suppose that no one would be willing to contend that every waste of money exacted by some form of compulsion is an abridgment of free speech.

2. "ESTABLISHMENT" OF POLITICAL VIEWS

The suggestion that a State-created Intergrated Bar amounts to a governmental "establishment" of political belief, is hardly worthy of more serious consideration. Even those who would treat the Fourteenth Amendment as embracing the identical protections afforded by the First would have to recognize the clear distinction in the wording of the First Amendment between the protections of speech and religion, only the latter providing a protection against "establishment." And as to the Fourteenth, viewed independently of the First, one can surely agree that a State could not "create a fund to be used in helping certain political parties or groups favored" by it "to elect their candidates or promote their controversial causes" . . . any more than could Congress do so, without agreeing that this is in any way analogous to what Wisconsin has done in creating its Integrated Bar, or to what Congress has provided in the Railway Labor Act, considered in the *Street* case . . .

In establishing the Integrated Bar Wisconsin has, I assume all would agree, shown no interest at all in favoring particular candidates for judicial or legal office or particular types of legislation. Even if Wisconsin had such an interest, the Integrated Bar does not provide a fixed, predictable conduit for governmental encouragement of particular views, for the Bar makes its own decisions on legislative recommendations and appears to take no action at all with regard to candidates. By the same token the weight lent to one side of a controversial issue by the prestige of government is wholly lacking here.

In short, it seems to me fanciful in the extreme to find in the limited functions of the Wisconsin State Bar those risks of governmental self-prepetuation that might justify the recognition of a Constitutional protection against the "establishment" of political beliefs. A contrary conclusion would, it seems to me, as well embrace within its rationale the operations of the Judicial Conference of the United States, and the legislative recommendations of independent agencies such as the Interstate Commerce Commission and the Bureau of the Budget.

3. DEVELOPMENT OF A "GUILD SYSTEM"

It is said that the Integrated Bar concept tends towards the development of some sort of a "guild system." But there are no requirements of action or inaction connected with the Wisconsin Integrated Bar, as contrasted with any unintegrated bar, except for the requirement of payment of $15 annual dues. I would agree that the requirement of payment of dues could not be made the basis of limiting the profession of law to the comparatively wealthy. . . . Nor, doubtless, could admission to the profession be restricted to relatives of those already admitted. But there is no such "guild" threat presented in this situation.

True, the Wisconsin Bar makes recommendations to the State Supreme Court for regulatory canons of legal ethics, and it may be supposed that the Bar is not forbidden to address the State Legislature for measures regulating in some respects the conduct of lawyers. But neither activity is the kind of direct self-regulation that was stricken down in *Schechter Corp.* v. *United States* . . . The Wisconsin Supreme Court has retained *all* of the traditional powers of a court to supervise the activities of practicing lawyers. It has delegated *none* of these to the Integrated Bar. As put by the State Supreme Court:

> *The integrated Bar has no power to discipline or to disbar any member. That power has been reserved to and not delegated by this court. The procedure under sec. 256.28, Stats., for filing complaints for discipline or disbarment in this court is unaffected by these rules. Rule 11 and Rule 7 provide an orderly and easy method by which proposals to amend or abrogate the Rules of the State Bar may be brought before this court for hearing on petition. Rule 9 provides the rules of professional conduct set forth from time to time in the canons of the professional ethics of the American Bar Association, as supplemented or modified by pronouncement of this court, shall be the standard governing the practice of law in this state. Prior to the adoption of the rules this court has not expressly adopted such canons of professional ethics in toto.*
>
> *"The by-laws of the State Bar provide for the internal workings of the organization and by Rule 11, sec. 2, may be amended or abrogated by resolution adopted by a vote of ⅔ of the members of the Board of Governors or by the members of the association themselves through the referendum procedure. As a further protection to the minority a petition for review of any change in the By-laws made by the Board of Governors will be entertained by the court if signed by 25 or more active members.*
>
> *Independently of the provisions in the Rules for invoking our supervisory jurisdiction, this court has inherent power to take remedial action, on a sufficient showing that the activities or policies of the State Bar are not in harmony*

*with the objectives for which integration was ordered or are otherwise contrary
to the public interest. . . .*

Moreover, it is by no means clear to me in what part of the Federal Constitution
we are to find the prohibition of *state-authorized* self-regulation of and by an economic group that the *Schechter* case found in Article I as respects the Federal Government. Is state-authorized self-regulation of lawyers to be the occasion for judicial
enforcemnt of Art. IV, 4, which provides that "The United States shall guarantee
to every State in this Union a Republican Form of Government . . .

4. "DROWNING OUT" THE VOICE OF DISSENT

This objection can be stated in either of two ways. First: The requirement of
dues payments to be spent to further views to which the payor is opposed tends to
increase the volume of the arguments he opposes and thereby to drown out his
own voice in opposition, in violation of his Constitutional right to be heard. Second:
The United States Constitution creates a scheme of federal and state governments each
of which is to be elected on a one-man-one-political-voice basis. Of course several
persons may voluntarily cumulate their political voices, but no governmental force
can require a single individual to contribute money to support views to be adopted
by a democratically organized group even if the individual is also free to say what he
pleases separately.

It seems to me these arguments have little force. In the first place, their supposi-
tion is that the voice of a dissenter is less effective if he speaks it first in an attempt
to influence the action of a democratically organized group and then, if necessary,
in dissent to the recommendations of that group. This is not at all convincing. The
dissenter is not being made to contribute funds to the furtherance of views he opposes
but is rather being made to contribute funds to a group expenditure about which
he will have something to say. To the extent that his voice of dissent can convince
his lawyer associates, it will later be heard by the State Legislature with a magnified voice. In short, I think it begs the question to approach the Constitutional issue
with the assumption that the majority of the Bar has a permanently formulated
position which the dissenting dues payor is being required to support, thus increasing the difficulty of effective opposition to it.

Moreover, I do not think it can be said with any assurance that being required
to contribute to the dispersion of views one opposes has a substantial limiting effect
on one's right to speak and be heard. Certainly these rights would be limited if
state action substantially reduced one's ability to reach his audience. But are these
rights substantially affected by increasing the opposition's ability to reach the same
audience? I can conceive of instances involving limited facilities, such as television
time, which may go to the highest bidder, wherein increasing the resources of the
opposition may tend to reduce a dissident's access to his audience. But before the
Constitution comes into play, there should surely be some showing of a relationship between required financial support of the opposition and reduced ability to
communicate, a showing I think hardly possible in the case of the legislative recommendations of the Wisconsin Bar. And, aside from the considerations of freedom

from compelled affirmations of belief to the discussed later, I can find little basis for a right not to have one's opposition heard.

Beyond all this, the argument under discussion is contradicted in the everyday operation of our society. Of course it is disagreeable to see a group, to which one has been required to contribute, decide to spend its money for purposes the contributor opposes. But the Constitution does not protect against the mere play of personal emotions. We recognized in *Hanson* that an employee can be required to contribute to the propagation of personally repugnant views on working conditions or retirement benefits that are expressed on union picket signs or in union handbills. A federal taxpayer obtains no refund if he is offended by what is put out by United States Information Office. Such examples could be multiplied.

For me, this "drowning out" argument falls apart upon analysis.

5. "COMPELLED AFFIRMATION" OF BELIEF

It is argued that the requirement of Bar dues payments which may be spent for legislative recommendations which the payor opposes amounts to be compelled affirmation of belief of the sort this Court struck down in *West Virginia Board of Education* v. *Barnette* . . . While I agree that the rationale of *Barnette* is relevant, I do not think that it is in any sense controlling in the present case.

Mr. Justice Jackson, writing for the Court in *Barnette*, did not view the issue as turning merely "on one's possession of particular religious views or the sincerity with which they are held." . . . The holding of *Barnette* was that no matter how strong or weak such beliefs might be, the Legislature of West Virginia was not free to require as concrete and intimate an expression of belief in any cause as that involved in a compulsory pledge of allegiance. It is in the light that one must assess the contention that, "Compelling a man by law to pay his money to elect candidates or advocate laws or doctrines he is against differs only in degree, if at all, from compelling him by law to speak for a candidate, a party, or a cause he is against" . . . One could as well say that the same mere difference in degree distinguishes the *Barnette* flag salute situation from a taxpayer's objections to the views a government agency presents, at public expense, to Congress. What seems to me obvious is the large difference in degree between, on the one hand, being compelled to raise one's hand and recite a belief as one's own, and, on the other, being compelled to contribute dues to a bar association fund which is to be used in part to promote the expression of views in the name of the organization (not in the name of the dues payor), which views when adopted may turn out to be contrary to the views of the dues payor. I think this is a situation where the difference in degree is so great as to amount to a difference in substance.

In *Barnette* there was a governmental purpose of requiring expression of a view in order to encourage adoption of that view, much the same as when a school teacher requires a student to write a message of self-correction on the blackboard one hundred times. In the present case there is no indication of a governmental purpose to further the expression of any particular view. More than that, the State Bar's purpose of furthering expression of views, is unconnected with any desire to induce belief or conviction by the device of forcing a person to identify himself with the expression of such views. True, purpose may not be controlling when the identification is intimate between the person who wishes to remain silent and the beliefs foisted upon him. But no such situation exists here where the connection between the payment of an individual's dues and the views to which he objects is factually so remote. Surely the Wisconsin Supreme Court is right when it says that petitioner can be expected to realize that "everyone understands or should understand" that the views expressed are those "of the State Bar as an entity separate and distinct from each individual." . . .

Indeed, I think the extreme difficulty the Court encounters in the *Street* case . . . in finding a mechanism for reimbursing dissident union members for their share of "political" expenditures, is wholly occasioned by, and is indicative of, the many steps of changed possession, ownership, and control of dues receipts and the multiple stages of decision making which separate the dues payor from the political expenditure of some part of his dues. I think these many steps and stages reflect as well upon whether there is an identification of dues payor and expenditure so intimate as to amount to a "compelled affirmation." Surely if the Court in *Street* can only with great difficulty—if at all—identify the contributions of particular union members with the union's political expenditures, we should pause before assuming that particular Bar members can sensibly hear their own voices when the State Bar speaks as an organization.

Mr. Justice Cardozo, writing for himself, Mr. Justice Brandeis, and Mr. Justice Stone in *Hamilton* v. *Regents* . . . thought that the remoteness of the connection between a conscientious objection to war and the study of military science was in itself sufficient to make untenable a claim that requiring this study in state universities amounted to a state establishment of religion. These Justices thought the case even clearer when all that was involved was a contribution of money:

> *Manifestly a different doctrine would carry us to lengths that have never yet been dreamed of. The conscientious objector, if his liberties were to be thus extended, might refuse to contribute taxes in furtherance of a war . . . or in furtherance of any other end condemned by his conscience as irreligious or immoral. The right of private judgment has never yet been so exalted above the powers and the compulsion of the agencies of government.*

Nor do I now believe that a state taxpayer could object on Fourteenth Amendment grounds to the use of his money for school textbooks or instruction which he finds intellectually repulsive, nor for the mere purchase of a flag for the school. In the present case appellant is simply required to pay dues into the general funds of the State Bar. I do not think a subsequent decision by the representatives of the majority of the bar members to devote some part of the organization's funds to the furtherance of a legislative proposal so identifies the individual payor of dues with the belief expressed that we are in the *Barnette* realm of "asserted power to force an American citizen publicly to profess any statement of belief or to engage in any ceremony of assent to one. . . ."

It seems to me evident that the actual core of appellant's complaint as to "compelled affirmation" is not the identification with causes to which he objects that might arise from some conceivable tracing of the use of his dues in their support, but is his forced association with the Integrated Bar. That, however, is a bridge which, beyond all doubt and any protestations now made to the contrary, we crossed in the *Hanson* case. I can see no way to uncross it without overruling *Hanson*. Certainly it cannot be done by declaring as a rule of law that lawyers feel more strongly about the identification of their names with proposals for law reform than union members feel about the identification of their names with collective bargaining demands declared on the radio, in picket signs, and on handbills.

II

While I think that what has been said might well dispose of this case without more, in that Wisconsin lawyers retain "full freedom to think their own thoughts, speak their own minds, support their own causes and wholeheartedly fight whatever they are against." . . . I shall pass on to consider the state interest involved in the establishment of the Integrated Bar, the other ingredient of adjudication which arises whenever incidental impingement upon such freedoms may fairly be said to draw in question governmental action. . . .

In this instance it can hardly be doubted that it was Constitutionally permissible for Wisconsin to regard the functions of an Integrated Bar as sufficiently important to justify whatever incursions on these individual freedoms may be thought to arise from the operations of the organization. The Wisconsin Supreme Court has described the fields of the State Bar's legislative activities and has asserted its readiness to restrict legislative recommendations to those fields:

> *This court takes judicial notice of the activities of the State Bar in the legislative field since its creation by this court in 1956. In every instance the legislative measures advocated or opposed have dealt with the administration of justice, court reform, and legal practice. Neither the above-quoted by-laws nor the stated purposes set forth in section 2 of Rule 1 for which the bar was integrated would permit the State Bar to be engaged in legislative activities unrelated to these three subjects. . . . However, as we pointed out in our opinion in the 1958* In re Integration of the Bar Case, *this court will exercise its inherent power to take remedial action should the State Bar engage in an activity not authorized by the rules and by-laws and not in keeping with the stated objectives for which it was created. If the lawyers of the state wish by group action to engage in legislative activities not so authorized they will have to do so within the framework of some voluntary association, and not the State Bar. . . .*

Further, the same court has declared its belief that the lawyers of the State possess an expertise useful to the public interest within these fields:

> *We are of the opinion that the public welfare will be promoted by securing and publicizing the composite judgment of the members of the bar of the state on measures directly affecting the administration of justice and the practice of*

law. The general public and the legislature are entitled to know how the profession as a whole stands on such type of proposed legislation. This is a function an integrated bar, which is as democratically governed and administered as the State Bar, can perform much more effectively than can a voluntary bar association. . . .

I do not think that the State Court's view in this respect can be considered in any way unreasonable.

"The composite judgment of the members of the bar of the state on measures directly affecting the administration of justice and the practice of law" may well be as helpful and informative to a state legislature as the work of individual legal scholars and of such organizations as the American Law Institute, for example, is to state and federal courts. State and federal courts are, of course, indifferent to the personal beliefs and predilections of any of such groups. The function such groups serve is a rationalizing one and their power flows from and is limited to their ability to convince by arguments from generally agreed upon premises. They are exercising the techniques and knowledge which lawyers are trained to possess in the task of solving problems with which the legal profession is most familiar. The numberless judicial citations to their work is proof enough of their usefulness in the judicial decision-making process.

Legislatures too have found that they can benefit from a legal "expert's effort to improve the law in technical and non-controversial areas." . . . In the words of the Executive Secretary of the New York Law Revision Commission, there are areas in which "lawyers as lawyers have more to offer, to solve a given question, than other skilled persons or groups." . . . The Acts recommended by the Commissioners on Uniform State Laws have been adopted on over 1,300 occasions by the legislatures of the fifty States, Puerto Rico, and the District of Columbia. . . . There is no way of counting the number of occasions on which state legislatures have utilized the assistance of legal advisory groups. Some indication may be obtained by noting that thirty-one jurisdictions have permanent legislative service agencies which recommend "substantive" legislative programs and forty-two jurisdictions utilize such permanent agencies in recommending statutory revision.

In this light I can only regard as entirely gratuitous a contention that there is anything less than a most substantial state interest in Wisconsin having the views of the members of its Bar "on measures directly affecting the administration of justice and the practice of law." Nor can I take seriously a suggestion that the lawyers of Wisconsin are merely being polled on matters of their own personal belief or predilection, any more than Congress had in mind such a poll when it made it the duty of federal circuit judges summoned to attend the Judicial Conference of the United States "to advise . . . as to any matters in respect of which the administration of justice in the courts of the United States may be improved. . . ."

III

Beyond this conjunction of a highly significant state need and the chimerical nature of the claims of abridgment of individual freedom, there is still a further approach to the entire problem that combines both of these aspects and reinforces my belief in the Constitutionality of the Integrated Bar.

I had supposed it beyond doubt that a state legislature could set up a staff or commission to recommend changes in the more or less technical areas of the law into which no well-advised laymen would venture without the assistance of counsel. A state legislature could certainly appoint a commission to make recommendations to it on the desirability of passing or modifying any of the countless uniform laws dealing with all kinds of legal subjects, running all the way from the Uniform Commercial Code to the Uniform Simultaneous Death Law. It seems no less clear to me that a reasonable license tax can be imposed on the profession of being a lawyer, doctor, dentist, etc. . . . . In these circumstances, wherein lies the unconstitutionality of what Wisconsin has done? Does the Constitution forbid the payment of some part of the Constitutional license fee directly to the equally Constitutional state law revision commission? Or is it that such a commission cannot be chosen by a majority vote of all the members of the state bar? Or could it be that the Federal Constitution requires a separation of state powers according to which a state legislature can tax and set up commissions but a state judiciary cannot do these things?

I end as I began. It is exceedingly regrettable that such specious contentions as appellant makes in this case should have resulted in putting the Integrated Bar under this cloud of partial unconstitutionality.

MR. JUSTICE WHITTAKER, CONCURRING IN RESULT

Believing that the State's requirement that a lawyer pay to its designee an annual fee of $15 as a condition of its grant, or of continuing its grant, to him of the *special privilege* (which is what it is) of practicing law in the State—which is really all that is involved here—does not violate any provision of the United States Constitution, I join in the result of the Court's opinion.

MR. JUSTICE BLACK, DISSENTING

I do not believe that either the bench, the bar or the litigants will know what has been decided in this case—certainly I do not. Two members of the Court, saying that "the Constitutional issue is inescapably before us," vote to affirm the holding of the Wisconsin Supreme Court that a State can, without violating the Federal Constitution, compel lawyers over their protest to pay dues to be used in part for the support of legislation and causes they detest. Another member, apparently agreeing that the constitutional question is properly here, votes to affirm the holding of the Wisconsin Supreme Court because he believes that a State may constitutionally require a lawyer to pay a fee to its "designee" as a condition to granting him the "special privilege" of practicing law, even though that "designee," over the lawyer's protest, uses part of the fee to support causes the lawyer detests. Two other members of the Court vote to reverse the judgment of the Wisconsin court on the ground that the constitutional question is properly here and the powers conferred on the Wisconsin State Bar by the laws of that State violate the First and Fourteenth Amendments. Finally, four members of the Court vote to affirm on the ground that the constitutional question is actually not here for decision at all. Thus the only proposition in this case for which there is a majority is that the constitutional question is properly here, and the five members of the Court who make up that majority express their views on this constitutional question. Yet a minority of four refuses to pass on the question and it is therefore left completely up in the air—the Court decides nothing. If ever there were two cases that should be set over for reargument in order for the Court to decide—or at least to make an orderly attempt to decide—the basic constitutional question involved in both of them, it is this case and the companion case of *International Association of Machinists* v. *Street*. In this state of affairs, I find it necessary to set out my views on the questions which I think are properly presented and argued by the parties.

In my judgment, this Court cannot properly avoid decision of the single, sharply defined constitutional issue which this case presents. The appellant filed a complaint in a Wisconsin Circuit Court, charging that he is being compelled by the State of Wisconsin, as a prerequisite to maintaining his status as a lawyer in good standing, to be a member of an association known as the State Bar of Wisconsin and to pay dues to that association; that he has paid these dues only under protest; that the State Bar of Wisconsin is using his money along with the moneys it has collected from other Wisconsin lawyers to engage in activities of a political and propagandistic nature in favor of objectives to which he is opposed and against objectives which he favors; and that, as a consequence of this compelled financial support of political views to which he is personally antagonistic, he is being deprived of rights guaranteed to him by the First and Fourteenth Amendments of the Federal Constitution. Upon demurrer to this complaint, the Circuit Court held that it must be dismissed without leave to amend because, in the opinion of that court, "it would be impossible to frame a complaint so as to state facts sufficient to constitute a cause of action against either the State Bar of Wisconsin or the defendant Donohue."

On appeal, the Supreme Court of Wisconsin, relying upon its powers of judicial notice, found as a fact that the State Bar does expend some of the moneys it collects as dues to further and oppose legislation and that court also accepted, at its full face value, the allegation of the complaint that many of these expenditures furthered views directly contrary to those held by the appellant. The Wisconsin Supreme Court nevertheless affirmed the judgment of the trial court on the ground that the public interest in having "public expression of the views of a majority of the lawyers of the state, with respect to legislation affecting the administration of justice and the practice of law . . . far outweighs the slight inconvenience to," and hence any abridgment of the constitutional rights of those who disagree with the views advocated by the State Bar.

The plurality decision to affirm the judgment of the Wisconsin courts on the ground that the issue in the case is not "shaped . . . as leanly and as sharply as judicial judgment upon an exercise of . . . [state] power requires" is, in my judgment, wrong on at least two grounds. First of all, it completely denies the appellant an opportunity to amend his complaint so as to "shape" the issue in a manner that would be acceptable to this Court. Appellant's complaint was dismissed by the Wis-

consin courts, without giving him a chance to amend it and before he had an opportunity to bring out the facts in the case, solely because those courts believed that it
would be impossible for him to allege any facts sufficient to entitle him to relief. The
plurality now suggests, by implication, that the Wisconsin courts were wrong on this
point and that appellant could possibly make out a case under his complaint. Why
then is the case not remanded to the Wisconsin courts in order that the appellant will
have at least one opportunity to meet this Court's fastidious pleading demands? The
opinions of the Wisconsin courts in this case indicate that the laws of that State—as
do the laws in most civilized jurisdictions—permit amendments and clarifications of
complaints where defects exist in the original complaint which can be cured. And
even if Wisconsin law were to the contrary, it is settled by the decisions of this Court
that a federal right cannot be defeated merely on the ground that the original complaint contained a curable defect. On this point, the judgment of the Court affirming
the dismissal of appellant's suit, insofar as that judgment rests upon the plurality
opinion, seems to me to be totally without justification, either in reason, in precedent
or in justice.

My second ground of disagreement with the plurality opinion is that I think we
should consider and decide now the constitutional issue raised in this case. No one
has suggested that this is a contrived or hypothetical lawsuit. Indeed, we have it on
no less authority than that of the Supreme Court of Wisconsin that the Wisconsin
State Bar does in fact use money extracted from this appellant under color of law to
engage in activities intended to influence legislation. The appellant has alleged, in a
complaint sworn to under oath, that many of these activities are in opposition to the
adoption of legislation which he favors. In such a situation, it seems to me to be
nothing more than the emptiest formality to suggest that the case cannot be decided
because the appellant failed to allege, as precisely as four members of this Court
think he should, what it is that the Bar does with which he disagrees. And it
certainly seems unjust for the appellant to be thrown out of court completely without
being given a chance to amend his complaint and for a judgment against him to be
affirmed without consideration of the merits of his cause even though that judgment
may later be held to constitute a complete bar to assertion of his First Amendment
rights. Even if the complaint in this case had been drawn in rigid conformity to the
meticulous requirements of the plurality, we would be presented with nothing but
the very same question now before us: Can a State, consistently with the First and
Fourteenth Amendments, force a person to support financially the activities of an
organization in support of views to which he is opposed? Thus, the best, if not the
only, reason I can think of for not resolving that question now is that a decision on
the constitutional question in this case would make it impossible for the Court to rely
upon the doctrine of avoidance with respect to that same constitutional question to
justify its strained interpretation of the Railway Labor Act in the *Street* case.

On the merits, the question posed in this case is, in my judgment, identical to
that posed to but avoided by the Court in the *Street* case. Thus, the same reasons that
led me to conclude that it violates the First Amendment for a union to use dues
compelled under a union-shop agreement to advocate views contrary to those advocated
by the workers paying the dues under protest lead me to the conclusion that an

integrated bar cannot take the money of protesting lawyers and use it to support causes they are against. What I have said in the *Street* case would be enough for me to dispose of the issues in this case were it not for the contention which has been urged by the appellee throughout this case that there are distinguishing features that would justify the affirmance of this case even if the statute in the *Street* case were struck down as unconstitutional.

The appellee's contention in this respect rests upon two different arguments. The first of these is that the use of compelled dues by an integrated bar to further legislative ends contrary to the wishes of some of its members can be upheld under the so-called "balancing test," which permits abridgment of First Amendment rights so long as that abridgment furthers some legitimate purpose of the State. Under this theory, the appellee contends, abridgments of speech "incidental" to an integrated bar must be upheld because the integrated bar performs many valuable services for the public. As pointed out above, the Wisconsin Supreme Court embraced this theory in express terms. And the concurring opinion of Mr. Justice Harlan, though not purporting to distinguish the *Street* case, also adopts the case-by-case "balancing" approach under which such a distinction as, indeed, any desired distinction is possible.

The "balancing" argument here is identical to that which has recently produced a long line of liberty-stifling decisions in the name of "self-preservation." The interest of the State in having "public expression of the views of a majority of the lawyers" by compelling dissenters to pay money against their will to advocate views they detest is magnified to the point where it assumes overpowering proportions and appears to become almost as necessary a part of the fabric of our society as the need for "self-preservation." On the other side of the "scales," the interest of lawyers in being free from such state compulsion is first fragmentized into abstract, imaginary parts, then minimized part by part almost to the point of extinction, and finally characterized as being of a purely "chimerical nature." As is too often the case, when the cherished freedoms of the First Amendment emerge from this process, they are too weightless to have any substantial effect upon the constitutional scales and must therefore be sacrificed in order not to disturb what are conceived to be the more important interests of society.

I cannot agree that a contention arising from the abridgment of First Amendment freedoms which results from compelled support of detested views can properly be characterized as a "chimercial nature" or, in the words of the Wisconsin Supreme Court, as involving nothing more than a "slight inconvenience." Quite the contrary, I can think of few plainer, more direct abridgments of the freedoms of the First Amendment than to compel persons to support candidates, parties, ideologies or causes that they are against. And, as stated many times before, I do not subscribe to the theory that abridgments of First Amendment freedoms can ever be permitted on a "balancing" basis. I reiterate my belief that the unequivocal language of the First Amendment was intended to mean and does mean that the Framers of the Bill of Rights did all of the "balancing" that was to be done in this area. It is my firm belief that, in the long run, the continued existence of liberty in this country depends upon the abandonment of the constitutional doctrine that permits this Court to reweigh the values weighed by the Framers and thus to weaken the protection of the Bill of

Rights. This case reaffirms that belief for it shows that the balancing test cannot be and will not be contained to apply only to those "hard" cases which at least some members of this Court have regarded as involving the question of the power of this country to preserve itself. For I assume that no one would argue that the power at stake here is necessary to that end.

Moreover, if I felt that I had the power to reweigh the "competing" values involved, I would have no difficulty reaching the conclusion that the loss inflicted upon our free way of life by invasion of First Amendment freedoms brought about by the powers conferred upon the Wisconsin integrated bar far outweighs any state interest served by the exercise of those powers by that association. At stake here is the interest of the individual lawyers of Wisconsin in having full freedom to think their own thoughts, speak their own minds, support their own causes and wholeheartedly fight whatever they are against, as well as the interest of the people of Wisconsin and, to a lesser extent, the people of the entire country in maintaining the political independence of Wisconsin lawyers. How is it possible that such formidable interests so vital to our free way of life can be said to be outweighed by any interest—much less the wholly imaginary interest urged here by the State which would have us believe that it will never know what its lawyers think about certain political questions if it cannot compel them to pay their money to support views they abhor? Certainly, I feel entirely confident in saying that the Framers of the First Amendment would never have struck the balance against freedom on the basis of such a demonstrably specious expediency.

In saying all this, I do not mean to suggest that the Wisconsin State Bar does not provide many useful and entirely lawful services. Quite the contrary, the record indicates that this integrated bar association, like other bar associations both integrated and voluntary, does provide such services. But I think it clear that these aspects of the Wisconsin State Bar are quite beside the point so far as this case is concerned. For a State can certainly insure that the members of its bar will provide any useful and proper services it desires without creating an association with power to compel members of the bar to pay money to support views to which they are opposed or to fight views they favor. Thus, the power of a bar association to advocate legislation at the expense of those who oppose such legislation is wholly separable from any legitimate function of an involuntary bar association and, therefore, even for those who subscribe to the balancing test, there is nothing to balance against this invasion of constitutionally protected rights.

The second ground upon which the appellee would have us distinguish compelled support of hated views as practiced by an integrated bar from compelled support of such views as practiced by the unions involved in the *Street* case is that lawyers are somehow different from other people. This argument, though phrased in various ways, amounts to nothing more than the contention that the practice of law is a high office in our society which is conferred by the State as a privilege and that the State can, in return for this privilege, impose obligations upon lawyers that it could not impose upon those not given "so high a privilege." Were it not for this Court's recent decision in *Cohen* v. *Hurley,* I would regard this contention as utterly frivolous. But it is true that the Court did hold in the *Cohen* case that lawyers could be treated differently from other people, at least insofar as a constitutional privilege against self-incrimination is concerned. As I pointed out in my dissenting opinion in that case, it is a short step from that position to the position now urged in the concurring opinion of Mr. Justice Whittaker—that lawyers must also give up their constitutional rights under the First Amendment in return for the "privilege" that the State has conferred upon them.

I do not believe that the practice of law is a "privilege" which empowers Government to deny lawyers their constitutional rights. The mere fact that a lawyer has important responsibilities in society does not require or even permit the State to deprive him of those protections of freedom set out in the Bill of Rights for the precise purpose of insuring the independence of the individual against the Government and those acting for the Government. What I said in the *Cohen* case is, in my judgment, equally applicable here:

> . . . [*One*] *of the great purposes underlying the grant of those freedoms was to give independence to those who must discharge important public responsibilities. The legal profession, with responsibilities as great as those placed upon any group in our society, must have that independence. If it is denied them, they are likely to become nothing more than parrots of the views of whatever group wields governmental power at the moment. Wherever that has happened in the world, the lawyer, as properly so called and respected, has ceased to perform the highest duty of his calling and has lost the affection and even the respect of the people.*

As I see it, the single, sharply defined constitutional issue presented in this case does not raise a difficult problem. This appellant is not denying the power of the State of Wisconsin to provide that its bar shall engage in non-political and non-controversial activities or even the power of the State to provide that all lawyers shall pay a fee to support such activities. What he does argue, and properly I think, is that the State cannot compel him to pay his money to further the views of a majority or any other controlling percentage of the Wisconsin State Bar when that controlling group is trying to pass laws or advance political causes that he is against. If the "privilege" of being a lawyer renders that argument unsound, it is certainly one of the more burdensome privileges Government can confer upon one of its citizens. And lawyers might be well advised to reconsider the wisdom of encouraging the use of a slogan which, though high-sounding and noble in its outward appearance, apparently imposes heavy burdens upon their First Amendment freedoms.

I would reverse this case and direct the Supreme Court of Wisconsin to refund the dues exacted under protest from the appellant in order to permit the Wisconsin State Bar to advocate measures he is against and to oppose measures he favors. I think it plain that lawyers have at least as much protection from such compulsion under the Constitution as the Court is holding railroad workers have under the Railway Labor Act.

[The dissenting opinion of Mr. Justice Douglas is omitted.]

[Perhaps the greatest question must remain unanswered until clarified by future developments: What ideological role will evolve out of the formalization of professional organizational control over lawyers by their state bar associations? Despite Justice Harlan's disclaimers, persistent arguments have been raised alleging the growth of a medieval guild-like system. Conversely, equally persistent contradictory arguments have been presented by bar leaders. At best, little empirical evidence has been presented by the protagonists of either position. Another salient, unanswered question about the role of the bar also remains. Given the tendencies which have influenced the organized bar during the past few decades, what impact have these developments had upon the behavior of higher American appellate judges?]

8 The Supreme Court and Social Change

A. INTRODUCTION

[When one turns from the characteristics of the bar to the behavior of judges, a new factor must be taken into account—the impact, if any, of the institutional traditions of higher appellate courts. This portion of *Constitutional Law in the Political Process* is not designed to provide a complete and detailed description of judicial policy-making in the subject matter areas discussed below; rather it is to illustrate the wide variety of policy alternatives available to the Supreme Court in major problem areas. It is also designed to underscore the salient responses of the Court to issues which are crucial in the contemporary setting of urban, industrial America.

Although it is often reiterated that the Supreme Court's decisions are subject to possible annulment by constitutional amendment, it should be recognized that in fact the Court may, through interpretation, emasculate provisions of a constitutional amendment.]

1. The Supreme Court Annuls a Constitutional Amendment, *The* Slaughterhouse Cases*

[JUSTICE MILLER FOR THE MAJORITY]

This statute is denounced not only as creating a monopoly and conferring odious and exclusive privileges upon a small number of persons at the expense of the great body of the community of New Orleans, but it is asserted that it deprives a large

*Majority and Dissent in the *Slaughterhouse Cases,* 16 Wallace 60–82, 93–97, 109–111 (1873).

and meritorious class of citizens—the whole of the butchers of the city—of the right to exercise their trade, the business to which they have been trained and on which they depend for the support of themselves and their families; and that the unrestricted exercise of the business of butchering is necessary to the daily subsistence of the population of the city.

But a critical examination of the act hardly justifies these assertions.

It is true that it grants, for a period of twenty-five years, exclusive privileges. And whether those privileges are at the expense of the community in the sense of a curtailment of any of their fundamental rights, or even in the sense of doing them an injury, is a question open to considerations to be hereafter stated. But it is not true that it deprives the butchers of the right to exercise their trade, or imposes upon them any restriction incompatible with its successful pursuit, or furnishing the people of the city with the necessary daily supply of animal food.

The act divides itself into two main grants of privilege,—the one in reference to stock-landings and stock-yards, and the other to slaughter-houses. That the landing of livestock in large droves, from steamboats on the bank of the river, and from railroad trains, should, for the safety and comfort of the people and the care of the animals, be limited to proper places, and those not numerous, it needs no argument to prove. Nor can it be injurious to the general community that while the duty of making ample preparation for this is imposed upon a few men, or a corporation, they should, to enable them to do it successfully, have the exclusive right of providing such landing-places, and receiving a fair compensation for the service.

It is, however, the slaughter-house privilege, which is mainly relied on to justify the charges of gross injustice to the public, and invasion of private right.

It is not, and cannot be successfully controverted, that it is both the right and the duty of the legislative body—the supreme power of the State or municipality—to prescribe and determine the localities where the business of slaughtering for a great city may be conducted. To do this effectively it is indispensable that all persons who slaughter animals for food shall do it in those places *and nowhere else.*

The statute under consideration defines these localities and forbids slaughtering in any other. It does not, as has been asserted, prevent the butcher from doing his own slaughtering. On the contrary, the Slaughter-House Company is required, under a heavy penalty, to permit any person who wishes to do so, to slaughter in their houses; and they are bound to make ample provision for the convenience of all the slaughtering for the entire city. The butcher then is still permitted to slaughter, to prepare, and to sell his own meats; but he is required to slaughter at a specified place and to pay a reasonable compensation for the use of the accommodations furnished him at that place.

The wisdom of the monopoly granted by the legislature may be open to question, but it is difficult to see a justification for the assertion that the butchers are deprived of the right to labor in their occupation, or the people of their daily service in preparing food . . .

* * *

It cannot be denied that the statute under consideration is aptly framed to remove from the more densely populated part of the city, the noxious slaughter-houses, and

large and offensive collections of animals necessarily incident to the slaughtering business of a large city, and to locate them where the convenience, health, and comfort
of the people require they shall be located. And it must be conceded that the means
adopted by the act for this purpose are appropriate, are stringent, and effectual. But it
is said that in creating a corporation for this purpose, and conferring upon it exclusive
privileges—privileges which it is said constitute a monopoly—the legislature has
exceeded its power. If this statute had imposed on the city of New Orleans precisely
the same duties, accompanied by the same privileges, which it has on the corporation
which it created, it is believed that no question would have been raised as to its
constitutionality. In that case the effect on the butchers in pursuit of their occupation
and on the public would have been the same as it is now. Why cannot the legislature
confer the same powers on another corporation, created for a lawful and useful public
object, that it can on the municipal corporation already existing? That wherever a
legislature has the right to accomplish a certain result, and that result is best attained
by means of a corporation, it has the right to create such a corporation, and to
endow it with the powers necessary to effect the desired and lawful purpose seems
hardly to admit of debate. . . .

* * *

It may, therefore, be considered as established, that the authority of the legislature
of Louisiana to pass the present statute is ample, unless some restraint in the exercise
of that power be found in the constitution of that State or in the amendments to the
Constitution of the United States, adopted since the date of the decisions we have
already cited.

If any such restraint is supposed to exist in the constitution of the State, the
Supreme Court of Louisiana having necessarily passed on that question, it would
not be open to review in this court.

The plaintiffs in error accepting this issue, allege that the statute is a violation of
the Constitution of the United States in these several particulars:

That it creates an involuntary servitude forbidden by the thirteenth article of
amendment;

That it abridges the privileges and immunities of citizens of the United States;

That it denies to the plaintiffs the equal protection of the laws; and,

That it deprives them of their property without due process of law; contrary to
the provisions of the first section of the fourteenth article of amendment.

This court is thus called upon for the first time to give construction to these
articles.

We do not conceal from ourselves the great responsibility which this duty devolves
upon us. No questions so far-reaching and pervading in their consequences, so
profoundly interesting to the people of this country, and so important in their bearing
upon the relations of the United States, and of the several States to each other and
to the citizens of the States and of the United States, have been before this court
during the official life of any of its present members. We have given every opportunity for a full hearing at the bar; we have discussed it freely and compared views
among ourselves; we have taken ample time for careful deliberation, and we now

propose to announce the judgments which we have formed in the construction of those articles, so far as we have found them necessary to the decision of the cases before us, and beyond that we have neither the inclination nor the right to go.

Twelve articles of amendment were added to the Federal Constitution soon after the original organization of the government under it in 1789. Of these all but the last were adopted so soon afterwards as to justify the statement that they were practically contemporaneous with the adoption of the original; and the twelfth, adopted in eighteen hundred and three, was so nearly so as to have become, like all the others, historical and of another age. But within the last eight years three other articles of amendment of vast importance have been added by the voice of the people to that now venerable instrument.

The most cursory glance at these articles discloses a unity of purpose, when taken in connection with the history of the times, which cannot fail to have an important bearing on any question of doubt concerning their true meaning. Nor can such doubts, when any reasonably exist, be safely and rationally solved without a reference to that history; for in it is found the occasion and the necessity for recurring again to the great source of power in this country, the people of the States, for additional guarantees of human rights; additional powers to the Federal government; additional restraints upon those of the States. Fortunately that history is fresh within the memory of us all, and its leading features, as they bear upon the matter before us, free from doubt.

The institution of African slavery, as it existed in about half the States of the Union, and the contests pervading the public mind for many years, between those who desired its curtailment and ultimate extinction and those who desired additional safeguards for its security and perpetuation, culminated in the effort, on the part of most of the States in which slavery existed, to separate from the Federal government, and to resist its authority. This constituted the war of the rebellion, and whatever auxiliary causes may have contributed to bring about this war, undoubtedly the overshadowing and efficient cause was African slavery.

In that struggle slavery, as a legalized social relation, perished. It perished as a necessity of the bitterness and force of the conflict. When the armies of freedom found themselves upon the soil of slavery they could do nothing less than free the poor victims whose enforced servitude was the foundation of the quarrel. And when hard pressed in the contest these men (for they proved themselves men in that terrible crisis) offered their services and were accepted by thousands to aid in suppressing the unlawful rebellion, slavery was at an end wherever the Federal government succeeded in that purpose. The proclamation of President Lincoln expressed an accomplished fact as to a large portion of the insurrectionary districts, when he declared slavery abolished in them all. But the war being over, those who had succeeded in re-establishing the authority of the Federal government were not content to permit this great act of emancipation to rest on the actual results of the contest or the proclamation of the Executive, both of which might have been questioned in after times, and they determined to place this main and most valuable result in the Constitution of the restored Union as one of its fundamental articles. Hence the thirteenth article of amendment of that instrument. Its two short sections seem hardly to admit of construction, so vigorous is their expression and so appropriate to the purpose we have indicated.

"1. Neither slavery nor involuntary servitude, except as a punishment for crime, whereof the party shall have been duly convicted, shall exist within the United States or any place subject to their jurisdiction.

"2. Congress shall have power to enforce this article by appropriate legislation."

To withdraw the mind from the contemplation of this grand, yet simple declaration of the personal freedom of all the human race within the jurisdiction of this government—a declaration designed to establish the freedom of four millions of slaves—and with a microscopic search endeavor to find in it a reference to servitudes, which may have been attached to property in certain localities, requires an effort, to say the least of it.

That a personal servitude was meant is proved by the use of the word "involuntary," which can only apply to human beings. The exception of servitude as a punishment for crime gives an idea of the class of servitude that is meant. The word servitude is of larger meaning than slavery, as the latter is popularly understood in this country, and the obvious purpose was to forbid all shades and conditions of African slavery. It was very well understood that in the form of apprenticeship for long terms, as it had been practiced in the West Indies Islands, on the abolition of slavery by the English government, or by reducing the slaves to the condition of serfs attached to the plantation, the purpose of the article might have been evaded, if only the word slavery had been used. The case of the apprentice slave, held under a law of Maryland, liberated by Chief Justice Chase, on a writ of habeas corpus under this article, illustrates this course of observation. And it is all that we deem necessary to say on the application of that article to the statute of Louisiana, now under consideration.

The process of restoring to their proper relations with the Federal government and with the other States those which had sided with the rebellion, undertaken under the proclamation of President Johnson in 1865, and before the assembling of Congress, developed the fact that, notwithstanding the formal recognition by those States of the abolition of slavery, the condition of the slave race would, without further protection of the Federal government, be almost as bad as it was before. Among the first acts of legislation adopted by several of the States in the legislative bodies which claimed to be in their normal relations with the Federal government, were laws which imposed upon the colored race onerous disabilities and burdens, and curtailed their rights in the pursuit of life, liberty, and property to such an extent that their freedom was of little value, while they had lost the protection which they had received from their former owners from motives both of interest and humanity.

They were in some States forbidden to appear in the towns in any other character than menial servants. They were required to reside on and cultivate the soil without the right to purchase or own it. They were excluded from many occupations of gain, and were not permitted to give testimony in the courts in any case where a white man was a party. It was said that their lives were at the mercy of bad men, either because the laws for their protection were insufficient or were not enforced.

These circumstances, whatever of falsehood or misconception may have been mingled with their presentation, forced upon the statesmen who had conducted the Federal government in safety through the crisis of the rebellion, and who supposed that by the thirteenth article of amendment they had secured the result of their labors, the conviction that something more was necessary in the way of constitutional protection to the unfortunate race who had suffered so much. They accordingly passed through Congress the proposition for the fourteenth amendment, and they declined to treat as restored to their full participation in the government of the Union the States which had been in insurrection, until they ratified that article by a formal vote of their legislative bodies.

Before we proceed to examine more critically the provisions of this amendment, on which the plaintiffs in error rely, let us complete and dismiss the history of the recent amendments, as that history relates to the general purpose which pervades them all. A few years' experience satisfied the thoughtful men who had been the authors of the other two amendments that, notwithstanding the restraints of those articles on the States, and the laws passed under the additional powers granted to Congress, these were inadequate for the protection of life, liberty, and property, without which freedom to the slave was no boon. They were in all those States denied the right of suffrage. The laws were administered by the white man alone. It was urged that a race of men distinctively marked as was the negro, living in the midst of another and dominant race, could never be fully secured in their person and their property without the right of suffrage.

Hence the fifteenth amendment, which declares that "the right of a citizen of the United States to vote shall not be denied or abridged by any State on account of race, color, or previous condition of servitude." The negro having, by the fourteenth amendment, been declared to be a citizen of the United States, is thus made a voter in every State of the Union.

We repeat, then, in the light of this recapitulation of events, almost too recent to be called history, but which are familiar to us all; and on the most casual examination of the language of these amendments, no one can fail to be impressed with the one pervading purpose found in them all, lying at the foundation of each, and without which none of them would have been even suggested; we mean the freedom of the slave race, the security and firm establishment of that freedom, and the protection of the newly-made freeman and citizen from the oppressions of those who had formerly exercised unlimited dominion over him. It is true that only the fifteenth amendment, in terms, mentions the negro by speaking of his color and his slavery. But it is just as true that each of the other articles was addressed to the grievances of that race, and designed to remedy them as the fifteenth.

We do not say that no one else but the negro can share in this protection. Both the language and spirit of these articles are to have their fair and just weight in any question of construction. Undoubtedly while negro slavery alone was in the mind of the Congress which proposed the thirteenth article, it forbids any other kind of slavery, now or hereafter. If Mexican peonage or the Chinese coolie labor system shall develop slavery of the Mexican or Chinese race within our territory, this amendment may safely be trusted to make it void. And so if other rights are assailed by the States which properly and necessarily fall within the protection of these articles, that protection will apply, though the party interested may not be of African descent. But what we do say, and what we wish to be understood is, that in any fair and just construction of any section or phrase of these amendments, it is necessary to look to the purpose which we have said was the pervading spirit of them all, the evil which they were designed to remedy, and the process of continued addition to the Constitution, until that purpose was supposed to be accomplished, as far as constitutional law can accomplish it.

The first section of the fourteenth article, to which our attention is more specially invited, opens with a definition of citizenship—not only citizenship of the United States, but citizenship of the States. No such definition was previously found in the Constitution, nor had any attempt been made to define it by act of Congress. It had been the occasion of much discussion in the courts, by the executive departments, and in the public journals. It had been said by eminent judges that no man was a citizen of the United States, except as he was a citizen of one of the States composing the Union. Those, therefore, who had been born and resided always in the District of Columbia or in the Territories, though within the United States, were not citizens. Whether this proposition was sound or not had never been judicially decided. But it had been held by this court, in the celebrated Dred Scott case, only a few years before the outbreak of the civil war, that a man of African descent, whether a slave or not, was not and could not be a citizen of a State or of the United States. This decision, while it met the condemnation of some of the ablest statesmen and constitutional lawyers of the country, had never been overruled; and if it was to be accepted as a constitutional limitation of the right of citizenship, then all the negro race who had recently been made freemen, were still, not only not citizens, but were incapable of becoming so by anything short of an amendment to the Constitution.

To remove this difficulty primarily, and to establish a clear and comprehensive definition of citizenship which should declare what should constitute citizenship of the United States, and also citizenship of a State, the first clause of the first section was framed.

"All persons born or naturalized in the United States, and subject to the jurisdiction thereof, are citizens of the United States and of the State wherein they reside."

The first observation we have to make on this clause is, that it puts at rest both the questions which we stated to have been the subject of differences of opinion. It declares that persons may be citizens of the United States without regard to their citizenship of a particular State, and it overturns the Dred Scott decision by making *all persons* born within the United States and subject to its jurisdiction citizens of the United States. That its main purpose was to establish the citizenship of the negro can admit of no doubt. The phrase, "subject to its jurisdiction" was intended to exclude from its operation children of ministers, consuls, and citizens or subjects of foreign States born within the United States.

The next observation is more important in view of the arguments of counsel in the present case. It is, that the distinction between citizenship of the United States and citizenship of a State is clearly recognized and established. Not only may a man be a citizen of the United States without being a citizen of a State, but an important element is necessary to convert the former into the latter. He must reside within the State to make him a citizen of it, but it is only necessary that he should be born or naturalized in the United States to be a citizen of the Union.

It is quite clear, then, that there is a citizenship of the United States, and a citizenship of a State, which are distinct from each other, and which depend upon different characteristics or circumstances in the individual.

We think this distinction and its explicit recognition in this amendment of great weight in this argument, because the next paragraph of this same section, which is the one mainly relied on by the plaintiffs in error, speaks only of privileges and immunities of citizens of the United States, and does not speak of those of citizens of the several States. The argument, however, in favor of the plaintiffs rests wholly on the assumption that the citizenship is the same, and the privileges and immunities guaranteed by the clause are the same.

The language is, "No State shall make or enforce any law which shall abridge the privileges or immunities of citizens of *the United States*." It is a little remarkable, if this clause was intended as a protection to the citizen of a State against the legislative power of his own State, that the word citizen of the State should be left out when it is so carefully used, and used in contradistinction to citizens of the United States, in the very sentence which precedes it. It is too clear for argument that the change in phraseology was adopted understandingly and with a purpose.

Of the privileges and immunities of the citizen of the United States, and of the privileges and immunities of the citizen of the State, and what they respectively are, we will presently consider; but we wish to state here that it is only the former which are placed by this clause under the protection of the Federal Constitution, and that the latter, whatever they may be, are not intended to have any additional protection by this paragraph of the amendment.

If, then, there is a difference between the privileges and immunities belonging to a citizen of the United States as such, and those belonging to the citizens of the State as such, the latter must rest for their security and protection where they have heretofore rested; for they are not embraced by this paragraph of the amendment.

The first occurrence of the words "privileges and immunities" in our constitutional history, is to be found in the fourth of the articles of the old Confederation.

It declares "that the better to secure and perpetuate mutual friendship and intercourse among the people of the different States in this Union, the free inhabitants of each of these States, paupers, vagabonds, and fugitives from justice excepted, shall be entitled to all the privileges and immunities of free citizens in the several States; and the people of each State shall have free ingress and regress to and from any other State, and shall enjoy therein all the privileges of trade and commerce, subject to the same duties, impositions, and restrictions as the inhabitants thereof respectively."

In the Constitution of the United States, which superseded the Articles of Confederation, the corresponding provision is found in section two of the fourth article, in the following words: "The citizens of each State shall be entitled to all the privileges and immunities of citizens of the several States."

There can be but little question that the purpose of both these provisions is the same, and that the privileges and immunities intended are the same in each. In the article of the Confederation we have some of these specifically mentioned, and enough perhaps to give some general idea of the class of civil rights meant by the phrase.

Fortunately we are not without judicial construction of this clause of the Constitution. The first and the leading case on the subject is that of *Corfield* v. *Coryell,* decided by Mr. Justice Washington in the Circuit Court for the District of Pennsylvania in 1823.

"The inquiry," he says, "is, what are the privileges and immunities of citizens of the several States? We feel no hesitation in confining these expressions to those privileges and immunities which are *fundamental*; which belong of right to the citizens of all free governments, and which have at all times been enjoyed by citizens of the several States which compose this Union, from the time of their becoming free, independent, and sovereign. What these fundamental principles are, it would be more tedious than difficult to enumerate. They may all, however, be comprehended under the following general heads: protection by the government, with the right to acquire and possess property of every kind, and to pursue and obtain happiness and safety, subject, nevertheless, to such restraints as the government may prescribe for the general good of the whole."

This definition of the privileges and immunities of citizens of the States is adopted in the main by this court in the recent case of *Ward* v. *The State of Maryland,* while it declines to undertake an authoritative definition beyond what was necessary to that decision. The description, when taken to include others not named, but which are of the same general character, embraces nearly every civil right for the establishment and protection of which organized government is instituted. They are, in the language of Judge Washington, those rights which are fundamental. Throughout his opinion, they are spoken of as rights belonging to the individual as a citizen of a State. They are so spoken of in the constitutional provision which he was construing. And they have always been glad to be the class of rights which the State governments were created to establish and secure.

In the case of *Paul* v. *Virginia,* the court, in expounding the clause of the Constitution, says that "the privileges and immunities secured to citizens of each State in the several States, by the provision in question, are those privileges and immunities which are common to the citizens in the latter States under their constitution and laws by virtue of their being citizens."

The constitutional provision there alluded to did not create those rights, which it called privileges and immunities of citizens of the States. It threw around them in that clause no security for the citizen of the State in which they were claimed or exercised. Nor did it profess to control the power of the State governments over the rights of its own citizens.

Its sole purpose was to declare to the several States, that whatever those rights, as you grant or establish them to your own citizens, or as you limit or qualify, or impose restrictions on their exercise, the same, neither more or less, shall be the measure of the rights of citizens of other States within your jurisdiction.

It would be the vainest show of learning to attempt to prove by citations of authority, that up to the adoption of the recent amendments, no claim or pretence was set up that those rights depended on the Federal government for their existence or protection, beyond the very few express limitations which the Federal Constitution imposed upon the States—such, for instance, as the prohibition against ex post facto laws, bills of attainder, and laws impairing the obligation of contracts. But with the exception of these and a few other restrictions, the entire domain of the privileges and immunities of citizens of the States, as above defined, lay within the constitutional and legislative power of the States, and without that of the Federal government. Was it the purpose of the fourteenth amendment, by the simple declaration that no State should make or enforce any law which shall abridge the privileges and immunities of *citizens of the United States*, to transfer the security and protection of all the civil rights which we have mentioned, from the States to the Federal government? And where it is declared that Congress shall have the power to enforce that article, was it intended to bring within the power of Congress the entire domain of civil rights heretofore belonging exclusively to the States?

All this and more must follow, if the proposition of the plaintiffs in error be sound. For not only are these rights subject to the control of Congress whenever in its discretion any of them are supposed to be abridged by State legislation, but that body may also pass laws in advance, limiting and restricting the exercise of legislative power by the States, in their most ordinary and usual functions, as in its judgment it may think proper on all such subjects. And still further, such a construction followed by the reversal of the judgments of the Supreme Court of Louisiana in these cases, would constitute this court a prepetual censor upon all legislation of the States, on the civil rights of their own citizens, with authority to nullify such as it did not approve as consistent with those rights, as they existed at the time of the adoption of this amendment. The argument we admit is not always the most conclusive which is drawn from the consequences urged against the adoption of a particular construction of an instrument. But when, as in the case before us, these consequences are so serious, so far-reaching and pervading, so great a departure from the structure and spirit of our institutions; when the effect is to fetter and degrade the State governments by subjecting them to the control of Congress, in the exercise of powers heretofore universally conceded to them of the most ordinary and fundamental character; when in fact it radically changes the whole theory of the relations of the State and Federal governments to each other and of both these governments to the people; the argument has a force that is irresistible, in the absence of language which expresses such a purpose too clearly to admit of doubt.

We are convinced that no such results were intended by the Congress which proposed these amendments, nor by the legislatures of the States which ratified them.

Having shown that the privileges and immunities relied on in the argument are those which belong to citizens of the States as such, and that they are left to the State governments for security and protection, and not by this article placed under the special care of the Federal government, we may hold ourselves excused from defining the privileges and immunities of citizens of the United States which no State can abridge, until some case involving those privileges may make it necessary to do so.

But lest it should be said that no such privileges and immunities are to be found if those we have been considering are excluded, we venture to suggest some which owe their existence to the Federal government, its National character, its Constitution, or its laws.

One of these is well described in the case of *Crandall* v. *Nevada*. It is said to be the right of the citizen of this great country, protected by implied guarantees of its Constitution, "to come to the seat of government to assert any claim he may have upon that government, to transact any business he may have with it, to seek its protection, to share its offices, to engage in administering its functions. He has the right of free access to its seaports, through which all operations of foreign commerce are conducted, to the sub-treasuries, land offices, and courts of justice in the several States." And quoting from the language of Chief Justice Taney in another case, it is said "that *for all the great purposes for which the Federal government* was established, we are one people, with one common country, *we are all citizens of the United States;*" and it is, as such citizens, that their rights are supported in this court in *Crandall* v. *Nevada*.

Another privilege of a citizen of the United States is to demand the care and protection of the Federal government over his life, liberty, and property when on the high seas or within the jurisdiction of a foreign government. Of this there can be no doubt, nor that the right depends upon his character as a citizen of the United States. The right to peaceably assemble and petition for redress of grievances, the privilege of the writ of *habeas corpus*, are rights of the citizen guaranteed by the Federal Constitution. The right to use the navigable waters of the United States, however they may penetrate the territory of the several States, all rights secured to our citizens by treaties with foreign nations, are dependent upon citizenship of the United States, and not citizenship of a State. One of these privileges is conferred by the very article under consideration. It is that a citizen of the United States can, of his own volition, become a citizen of any State of the Union by a *bona fide* residence therein, with the same rights as other citizens of that State. To these may be added the rights secured by the thirteenth and fifteenth articles of amendment, and by the other clause of the fourteenth, next to be considered.

But it is useless to pursue this branch of the inquiry, since we are of opinion that the rights claimed by these plaintiffs in error, if they have any existence, are not privileges and immunities of citizens of the United States within the meaning of the clause of the fourteenth amendment under consideration.

"All persons born or naturalized in the United States, and subject to the jurisdiction thereof, are citizens of the United States and of the State wherein they reside. No State shall make or enforce any law which shall abridge the privileges or immunities of citizens of the United States; nor shall any State deprive any person of life, liberty, or property without due process of law, nor deny to any person within its jurisdiction the equal protection of the laws."

The argument has not been much pressed in these cases that the defendant's charter deprives the plaintiffs of their property without due process of law, or that it denies to them the equal protection of the law. The first of these paragraphs has been in the Constitution since the adoption of the fifth amendment, as a restraint upon the Federal power. It is also to be found in some form of expression in the constitutions of nearly all the States, as a restraint upon the power of the States.

This law, then, has practically been the same as it now is during the existence of the government, except so far as the present amendment may place the restraining power over the States in this matter in the hands of the Federal government.

We are not without judicial interpretation, therefore, both State and National, of the meaning of this clause. And it is sufficient to say that under no construction of that provision that we have ever seen, or any that we deem admissible, can the restraint imposed by the State of Louisiana upon the exercise of their trade by the butchers of New Orleans be held to be a deprivation of property within the meaning of that provision.

"Nor [shall any State] deny to any person within its jurisdiction the equal protection of the laws."

In the light of the history of these amendments, and the pervading purpose of them, which we have already discussed, it is not difficult to give a meaning to this clause. The existence of laws in the States where the newly emancipated negroes resided, which discriminated with gross injustice and hardship against them as a class, was the evil to be remedied by this clause, and by it such laws are forbidden.

If, however, the States did not conform their laws to its requirements, then by the fifth section of the article of amendment Congress was authorized to enforce it by suitable legislation. We doubt very much whether any action of a State not directed by way of discrimination against the negroes as a class, or on account of their race, will ever be held to come within the purview of this provision. It is so clearly a provision for that race and that emergency, that a strong case would be necessary for its application to any other. But as it is a State that is to be dealt with, and not alone the validity of its laws, we may safely leave that matter until Congress shall have exercised its power, or some case of State oppression, by denial of equal justice in its courts, shall have claimed a decision at our hands. We find no such case in the one before us, and do not deem it necessary to go over the argument again, as it may have relation to this particular clause of the amendment.

In the early history of the organization of the government, its statesmen seem to have divided on the line which should separate the powers of the National government from those of the State governments, and though this line has never been very well defined in public opinion, such a division has continued from that day to this.

The adoption of the first eleven amendments to the Constitution so soon after the original instrument was accepted, shows a prevailing sense of danger at that time from the Federal power. And it cannot be denied that such a jealousy continued to exist with many patriotic men until the breaking out of the late civil war. It was then discovered that the true danger to the perpetuity of the Union was in the capacity of the State organizations to combine and concentrate all the powers of the State, and of contiguous States, for a determined resistance to the General Government.

Unquestionably this has given great force to the argument, and added largely to the number of those who believe in the necessity of a strong National government.

But, however pervading this sentiment, and however it may have contributed to the adoption of the amendments we have been considering, we do not see in those amendments any purpose to destroy the main features of the general system. Under the pressure of all the excited feeling growing out of the war, our statesmen have still believed that the existence of the States with powers for domestic and local government, including the regulation of civil rights—the rights of person and of property—was essential to the perfect working of our complex form of government, though they have thought proper to impose additional limitations on the States, and to confer additional power on that of the Nation.

But whatever fluctuations may be seen in the history of public opinion on this subject during the period of our national existence, we think it will be found that this court, so far as its functions required, has always held with a steady and an even hand the balance between State and Federal power, and we trust that such may continue to be the history of its relation to that subject so long as it shall have duties to perform which demand of it a construction of the Constitution, or of any of its parts. . . .

[JUSTICE FIELD IN DISSENT]

. . . if the exclusive privileges conferred upon the Louisiana corporation can be sustained, it is not perceived why exclusive privileges for the construction and keeping of ovens, machines, grindstones, wine-presses, and for all the numerous trades and pursuits for the prosecution of which buildings are required, may not be equally bestowed upon other corporations or private individuals, and for periods of indefinite duration.

It is not necessary, however, as I have said, to rest my objections to the act in question upon the terms and meaning of the thirteenth amendment. The provisions of the fourteenth amendment, which is properly a supplement to the thirteenth, cover, in my judgment, the case before us, and inhibit any legislation which confers special and exclusive privileges like these under consideration. The amendment was adopted to obviate objections which had been raised and pressed with great force to the validity of the Civil Rights Act, and to place the common rights of American citizens under the protection of the National government. It first declares that "all persons born or naturalized in the United States, and subject to the jurisdiction thereof, are citizens of the United States and of the State wherein they reside." It then declares that "no State shall make or enforce any law which shall abridge the privileges or immunities of citizens of the United States, nor shall any State deprive any person of life, liberty, or property, without due process of law, nor deny to any person within its jurisdiction the equal protection of the laws."

The first clause of this amendment determines who are citizens of the United States, and how their citizenship is created. Before its enactment there was much diversity of opinion among jurists and statesmen whether there was any such citizenship independent of that of the State, and, if any existed, as to the manner in which it originated. With a great number the opinion prevailed that there was no citizenship independent of the citizenship of the State. Such was the opinion of Mr. Calhoun and the class represented by him. In his celebrated speech in the Senate upon the Force Bill, in 1833, referring to the reliance expressed by a senator upon the fact that we are citizens of the United States, he said: "If by citizen of the United States he means a citizen at large, one whose citizenship extends to the entire geographical limits of the country without having a local citizenship in some State or Territory, a sort of citizen of the world, all I have to say is that such a citizen would be a perfect nondescript; that not a single individual of this description can be found in the entire mass of our population. Notwithstanding all the pomp and display of eloquence on the occasion, every citizen is a citizen of some State or Territory, and as such, under an express provision of the Constitution, is entitled to all privileges and immunities of citizens in the several States; and it is in this and no other sense that we are citizens of the United States."

* * *

The amendment does not attempt to confer any new privileges or immunities upon citizens, or to enumerate or define those already existing. It assumes that there are such privileges and immunities which belong of right to citizens as such, and ordains that they shall not be abridged by State legislation. If this inhibition has no reference to privileges and immunities of this character, but only refers, as held by the majority of the court in their opinion, to such privileges and immunities as were before its adoption specially designated in the Constitution or necessarily implied as belonging to citizens of the United States, it was a vain and idle enactment, which accomplished nothing, and most unnecessarily excited Congress and the people on its passage. With privileges and immunities thus designated or implied no State could ever have interfered by its laws, and no new constitutional provision was required to inhibit such interference. The supremacy of the Constitution and the laws of the United States always controlled any State legislation of that character. But if the amendment refers to the natural and inalienable rights which belong to all citizens, the inhibition has a profound significance and consequence.

What, then, are the privileges and immunities which are secured against abridgment by State legislation?

In the first section of the Civil Rights Act Congress has given its interpretation to these terms, or at least has stated some of the rights which, in its judgement, these terms include; it has there declared that they include the right "to make and enforce contracts, to sue, be parties and give evidence, to inherit, purchase, lease, sell, hold, and convey real and personal property, and to full and equal benefit of all laws and proceedings for the security of person and property." That act, it is true, was passed before the fourteenth amendment, but the amendment was adopted, as I have already said, to obviate objections to the act, or speaking more accurately, I should say, to obviate objections to legislation of a similar character, extending the protection of the National government over the common rights of all citizens of the United States. Accordingly, after its ratification, Congress re-enacted the act under the belief that whatever doubts may have previously existed of its validity, they were removed by the amendment.

The terms, privileges and immunities, are not new in the amendment; they were in the Constitution before the amendment was adopted. They are found in the second section of the fourth article, which declares that "the citizens of each State shall be entitled to all privileges and immunities of citizens in the several States," and they have been the subject of frequent consideration in judicial decisions. In *Corfield* v. *Coryell,* Mr. Justice Washington said he had "no hesitation in confining these expressions to those privileges and immunities which were, in their nature, fundamental; which belong of right to citizens of all free governments, and which have at all times been enjoyed by the citizens of the several States which compose the Union, from the time of their becoming free, independent, and sovereign;" and, in considering what those fundamental privileges were, he said that perhaps it would be more tedious than difficult to enumerate them, but that they might be "all comprehended under the following general heads: protection by the government; the enjoyment of life and liberty, with the right to acquire and possess property of every kind, and to pursue and obtain happiness and safety, subject, nevertheless, to such restraints as the government may justly prescribe for the general good of the whole." This appears to me to be a sound construction of the clause in question. The privileges and immunities designated are those *which of right belong to the citizens of all free governments.* Clearly among these must be placed the right to pursue a lawful employment in a lawful manner, without other restraint than such as equally affects all persons. . . .

* * *

In all these cases there is a recognition of the equality of right among citizens in the pursuit of the ordinary avocations of life, and a declaration that all grants of exclusive privileges, in contravention of this equality, are against common right, and void.

This equality of right, with exemption from all disparaging and partial enactments, in the lawful pursuits of life, throughout the whole country, is the distinguishing privilege of citizens of the United States. To them, everywhere, all pursuits, all professions, all avocations are open without other restrictions than such as are imposed equally upon all others of the same age, sex, and condition. The State may prescribe such regulations for every pursuit and calling of life as will promote the public health, secure the good order and advance the general prosperity of society, but when once prescribed, the pursuit or calling must be free to be followed by every citizen who is within the conditions designated, and will conform to the regulations. This is the fundamental idea upon which our institutions rest, and unless adhered to in the legislation of the country our government will be a republic only in name. The fourteenth amendment, in my judgment, makes it essential to the validity of the legislation of every State that this equality of right should be respected. How widely this equality has been departed from, how entirely rejected and trampled upon by the act of Louisiana, I have already shown. And it is to me a matter of profound regret that its validity is recognized by a majority of this court, for by it the right of free labor, one of the most sacred and imprescriptible rights of man, is violated. As stated by the Supreme Court of Connecticut, in the case cited, grants of exclusive privileges, such as is made by the act in question, are opposed to the whole theory of free government, and it requires no aid from any bill of rights to render them void. This only is a free government, in the American sense of the term, under which the inalienable right of every citizen to pursue his happiness is unrestrained, except by just, equal, and impartial laws.

[The majority opinion on the privileges and immunities clause of the Fourteenth Amendment technically still stands, but the social and political world it originally sought to maintain was swept away in the succeeding era of the "Robber Barons." Key factors in the transition were judicial doctrinal developments, chiefly under the due process clause of the Fourteenth Amendment, which tended to curtail state governmental regulation of business enterprise in the public interest. Narrow construction of the commerce clause accomplished much the same result with respect to the federal government. The majority in the *Slaughterhouse Cases* therefore had only limited success in restraining the social forces dominant in the post-Civil War period.

In other situations, the reluctance of the courts to meet new conditions often may prove decisive because no other political institution is fully capable of accomplishing change or because private power effectively inhibits the normal processes of legislative and executive action. The long-lived yet largely unsuccessful efforts to establish a legal "right to privacy" provide an excellent illustration. The triumph of commercial advertising as a pervasive institutional influence may, as Potter has indicated, be a concomitant of abundance. But Warren and Brandeis, over seven decades ago, hopefully suggested a qualitatively more satisfactory alternative.

Over seventy years ago, Samuel Warren and Louis Brandeis perceptively argued that sweeping and fundamental changes in American society, largely resulting from the industrial revolution, necessitated a drastic re-evaluation of conventional legal doctrines relating to the intellectual freedoms. The occasion was an article in the fourth volume of the *Harvard Law Review*. Today this essay is justly considered a classic assertion of the view that law may be and should be altered from time to time to insure the basic conditions of freedom when changing circumstances render the traditional safeguards obsolete.]

2. Basic Freedoms in a Rapidly Changing Society: The Right to Privacy*

That the individual shall have full protection in person and in property is a principle as old as the common law; but it has been found necessary from time to time to define anew the exact nature and extent of such protection. Political, social, and economic changes entail the recognition of new rights, and the common law, in its eternal youth, grows to meet the demands of society. Thus, in very early times, the law gave a remedy only for physical interference with life and property, for trespasses *vi et armis*. Then the "right to life" served only to protect the subject from battery in its various forms; liberty meant freedom from actual restraint; and the right to property secured to the individual his lands and his cattle. Later, there

*Samuel D. Warren and Louis D. Brandeis, "The Right to Privacy," *Harvard Law Review*, IV (December, 1890), 193–96, 219–20. [Footnotes omitted.] Reproduced with permission of the publisher. Copyright (1890) by the Harvard Law Review Association.

came a recognition of man's spiritual nature, of his feelings and his intellect. Gradually the scope of these legal rights broadened; and now the right to life has come to mean the right to enjoy life,—the right to be let alone; the right to liberty secures and exercise of extensive civil privileges; and the term "property" has grown to comprise every form of possession—intangible, as well as tangible.

Thus, with the recognition of the legal value of sensations, the protection against actual bodily injury was extended to prohibit mere attempts to do such injury; that is, the putting another in fear of such injury. From the action of battery grew that of assault. Much later there came a qualified protection of the individual against offensive noises and odors, against dust and smoke, and excessive vibration. The law of nuisance was developed. So regard for human emotions soon extended the scope of personal immunity beyond the body of the individual. His reputation, the standing among his fellow-men, was considered, and the law of slander and libel arose. Man's family relations became a part of the legal conception of his life, and the alienation of a wife's affections was held remediable. Occasionally the law halted,—as in its refusal to recognize the intrusion by seduction upon the honor of the family. But even here the demands of society were met. A mean fiction, the action *per quod servitium amisit,* was resorted to, and by allowing damages for injury to the parents' feelings, an adequate remedy was ordinarily afforded. Similar to the expansion of the right to life was the growth of the legal conception of property. From corporeal property arose the incorporeal rights issuing out of it; and then there opened the wide realm of intangible property, in the products and processes of the mind, as works of literature and art, goodwill, trade secrets, and trademarks.

This development of the law was inevitable. The intense intellectual and emotional life, and the heightening of sensations which came with the advance of civilization, made it clear to men that only a part of the pain, pleasure, and profit of life lay in physical things. Thoughts, emotions, and sensations demanded legal recognition, and the beautiful capacity for growth which characterizes the common law enabled the judges to afford the requisite protection, without the interposition of the legislature.

Recent inventions and business methods call attention to the next step which must be taken for the protection of the person, and for securing to the individual what Judge Cooley calls the right "to be let alone." Instantaneous photographs and newspaper enterprises have invaded the sacred precincts of private and domestic life; and numerous mechanical devices threaten to make good the prediction that "what is whispered in the closet shall be proclaimed from the house-tops." For years there has been a feeling that the law must afford some remedy for the unauthorized circulation of portraits of private persons; and the evil of the invasion of privacy by the newspapers, long keenly felt, has been but recently discussed by an able writer. The alleged facts of a somewhat notorious case brought before an inferior tribunal in New York a few months ago, directly involved the consideration of the right of circulating portraits; and the question whether our law will recognize and protect the right to privacy in this and in other respects must soon come before our courts for consideration.

Of the desirability—indeed of the necessity—of some such protection, there can, it is believed, be no doubt. The press is overstepping in every direction the obvious bounds of propriety and of decency. Gossip is no longer the resource of the idle and of the vicious, but has become a trade, which is pursued with industry as well as effrontery. To satisfy a prurient taste the details of sexual relations are spread broadcast in the columns of the daily papers. To occupy the indolent, column upon column is filled with idle gossip, which can only be produced by intrusion upon the domestic circle. The intensity and complexity of life, attendant upon advancing civilization, have rendered necessary some retreat from the world, and man, under the refining influence of culture, has become more sensitive to publicity, so that solitude and privacy have become more essential to the individual; but modern enterprise and invention have, through invasions upon his privacy, subjected him to mental pain and distress, far greater than could be inflicted by mere bodily injury. Nor is the harm wrought by such invasions confined to the suffering of those who may be made the subjects of journalistic or other enterprise. In this, as in other branches of commerce, the supply creates the demand. Each crop of unseemly gossip, thus harvested, becomes the seed of more, and, in direct proportion to its circulation, results in a lowering of social standards and of morality. Even gossip apparently harmless, when widely and persistently circulated, is potent for evil. In both belittles and perverts. It belittles by inverting the relative importance of things, thus dwarfing the thoughts and aspirations of a people. When personal gossip attains the dignity of print, and crowds the space available for matters of real interest to the community, what wonder that the ignorant and thoughtless mistake its relative importance. Easy of comprehension, appealing to that weak side of human nature which is never wholly cast down by the misfortunes and frailties of our neighbors, no one can be surprised that it usurps the place of interest in brains capable of other things. Triviality destroys at once robustness of thought and delicacy of feeling. No enthusiasm can flourish, no generous impulse can survive under its blighting influence. . . .

[Warren and Brandeis hoped that the new direction in law would be developed by the tribunals of the states, a theme discussed in their concluding remarks.]

* * *

The remedies for an invasion of the right of privacy are also suggested by those administered in the law of defamation, and in the law of literary and artistic property, namely:—

1. An action of tort for damages in all cases. Even in the absence of special damages, substantial compensation could be allowed for injury to feelings as in the action of slander and libel.

2. An injunction, in perhaps a very limited class of cases.

It would doubtless be desirable that the privacy of the individual should receive the added protection of the criminal law, but for this legislation would be required. Perhaps it would be deemed proper to bring the criminal liability for such publication within narrower limits; but that the community has an interest in preventing such invasions of privacy, sufficiently strong to justify the introduction of such a remedy, cannot be doubted. Still, the protection of society must come mainly through a recognition of the rights of the individual. Each man is responsible for his own acts and omissions only. If he condones what he reprobates, with a weapon at hand equal to his defence, he is responsible for the results. If he resists, public opinion will rally to his support. Has he then such a weapon? It is believed that the common law provides him with one, forged in the slow fire of the centuries, and to-day fitly tempered to his hand. The common law has always recognized a man's house as his castle, impregnable, often, even to its own officers engaged in the execution of its commands. Shall the courts thus close the front entrance to constituted authority, and open wide the back door to idle or prurient curiosity?

[In point of fact, the state courts have been slow to move in the direction suggested by Warren and Brandeis, while the federal courts have only belatedly begun to explore the problem. As the authors of "The Right to Privacy" cogently pointed out, the problem has two aspects—the impact upon the individual of intrusions upon privacy and the broad social consequences of a regime of public exposure to unfettered triviality. These problems have not been solved in the seven decades that have passed since the writing of this insightful essay. In 1951 the question whether there is a right to privacy came before the federal judiciary. The opinion of three distinguished judges of the federal Court of Appeals for the District of Columbia is presented below.]

3. The Captive Audience Case: Is There a Right to Privacy?*

Before EDGERTON, BAZELON, and FAHY, Circuit Judges.
EDGERTON, Circuit Judge.
Appellee Capital Transit Company (Transit) operates streetcars and buses in the District of Columbia. In 1948 Transit made a contract with appellee Washington Transit Radio, Inc., (Radio) by which Radio was to install and maintain loudspeakers in Transit vehicles and provide broadcasts at least 8 hours daily except Sunday. In October, 1949, loudspeakers were in operation in 212 vehicles and it was planned to increase the number to 1,500.

Though Transit and Radio call the broadcasts "music as you ride", they include not only music but also "commercials, announcements, and time signals". The contract permits six minutes of "commercial announcements" per hour. These vary from 15 to 35 seconds in length and are usually scheduled about once in five minutes, though the interval varies.

Appellee Public Utilities Commission received protests against Transit's use of radio. It ordered an investigation and held a hearing "to determine whether or not the installation and use of radio receivers on the street cars and busses of Capital

*Pollak v. Public Utilities Commission of the District of Columbia, 191 Federal Reporter (2nd Series) 450, 453–459 (1959). [Footnotes and most citations omitted.]

Transit Company is consistent with public convenience, comfort and safety. . . ." Appellants, who ride Transit vehicles, and other persons and organizations were allowed to intervene and took part in the hearing. The Commission found that transit radio does not reduce safety, "tends to improve the conditions under which the public rides," and "is not inconsistent with public convenience, comfort, and safety." The Commission's final order "dismissed" its investigation.

Appellants and others appealed to the District Court from the Commission's order. Appellants' petition of appeal states that appellants are "obliged to use the street cars and busses of Capital Transit Company in connection with the practice of their profession and on other occasions and are thereby subjected against their will to the broadcasts in issue. These broadcasts make it difficult for petitioners to read and converse. . . ." Each of the appellees, i.e. the Commission, Transit, and Radio, moved to dismiss the petitions of appeal as not stating claims on which relief could be granted and as not within the court's jurisdiction. The court dismissed the petitions on the ground that "no legal right of the petitioners . . . has been invaded . . ." This appeal followed.

Appellants' chief contention is that Transit radio deprives them of liberty without due process of law in violation of the Fifth Amendment of the Constitution.

[1, 2] The jurisdiction of the Public Utilities Commission, the District Court, and this court are clear. All public utilities are required by Act of Congress to "furnish service and facilities reasonably safe and adequate and in all respects just and reasonable" and the term "service" is used "in its broadest and most inclusive sense." . . . The Commission is authorized to fix and enforce standards of service. . . .

[3–5] Since the Commission's order was its final decision that Transit may use loudspeakers in its streetcars and buses, the order was appealable. "Any . . . person . . . affected by any final order or decision of the Commission, other than an order fixing or determining the value of the property of a public utility in a proceeding solely for that purpose, may" appeal to the District Court and from that court to this. . . . "Administrative determinations which are not commands may for all practical purposes determine rights as effectively as the judgment of a court, and may be reexamined by courts under particular statutes providing for the review of 'orders' " . . . Since the appellants use the service of Transit and intervened before the Commission they are "affected by" the Commission's order and may appeal.

[6, 7] Transit passengers commonly have to hear the broadcasts whether they want to or not. The Commission made no finding on this point but the fact is well known. It was proved by many witnesses. It is in legal effect admitted by appellees' motions to dismiss the petition of appeal, since the petition states that appellants "are subjected against their will to the broadcasts in issue. These broadcasts make it difficult for petitioners to read and converse . . ." The brief of appellee Radio admits the fact in these terms: "it is impossible to give effect to this alleged right [not to listen] without frustrating the desire of other passengers to listen . . ." Appellee Transit says in its brief: "The record shows that *every precaution is taken* in the installation of the equipment and its maintenance *to minimize the sound level at the operators' position* and to distribute sound evenly throughout the public spaces in the vehicle . . ." WWDC-FM, the transmitting station, advertised in 1949 that

Transit Radio was "delivering a guaranteed audience." The passengers are known in the industry as a "captive audience". Formerly they were free to read, talk, meditate, or relax. The broadcasts have replaced freedom of attention with forced listening.

The dismissed petition of appeal states that appellants are "obliged to use the street cars and busses" of Transit. Most people have to use mass transportation. In the District of Columbia this means they have to use Transit and hear the broadcasts. Even as between the District and the adjoining Pentagon region in Virginia the Supreme Court has said: " . . . most government employees, in going to and returning from their work, were compelled to begin or complete their trips by utilizing buses or streetcars of Capital Transit." . . .

[8] Though statutes and the law of torts forbid invasions of liberty by private individuals, the constitutional guarantees of liberty are directed against government action. But acts of individuals are beyond the reach of these guarantees only when they are "unsupported by state authority in the shape of laws, customs, or judicial or executive proceedings." . . . For example, since Smith v. Allwright . . . was decided a state cannot "by permitting a party to take over a part of its election machinery . . . avoid the provisions of the Constitution forbidding racial discrimination in elections . . ." . . . A private corporation that owns the streets of a town may no more abridge the freedoms of press and religion than a municipality regularly organized. . . . The Supreme Court has recently said: "When authority derives in part from Government's thumb on the scales, the exercise of that power by private persons becomes closely akin, in some respects, to its exercise by Government itself." . . .

[9] The forced listening imposed on Transit passengers results from government action. By authorizing Transit and forbidding others to operate local streetcars and buses, Congress made it necessary to ride the vehicles in which Transit makes it necessary to hear the broadcasts. Streetcars and buses cannot operate in city streets without a franchise. Congress has given Transit not only a franchise but a virtual monopoly of the entire local business of mass transportation of passengers in the District of Columbia.

[10, 11] Furthermore the forced listening has been sanctioned by the governmental action of the Commission. If the Commission had found it contrary to public comfort or convenience, or unreasonable, it would have stopped. Because the Commission decided otherwise it continues. To suggest that a "negative" order cannot be the final step in a misuse of government power is to assert a distinction the Supreme Court has repudiated. " . . . An order of the Commission dismissing a complaint on the merits and maintaining the *status quo* is an exercise of administrative function, no more and no less, than an order directing some change in status." . . . Even failure to enter any order may be a denial of constitutional rights. . . . By dismissing its investigation the Commission declined to prevent valid action of Congress from having an unintended and unnecessary result.

[12] No occasion had arisen until now to give effect to freedom from forced listening as a constitutional right. Short of imprisonment, the only way to compel a man's attention for many minutes is to bombard him with sound that he cannot ignore in a place where he must be. The law of nuisance protects him at home. At home or at work, the constitutional question has not arisen because the government has taken

no part in forcing people to listen. Until radio was developed and someone realized that the passengers of a transportation monopoly are a captive audience. there was no profitable way of forcing people to listen while they travel between home and work or on necessary errands. Exploitation of this audience through assault on the unavertible sense of hearing is a new phenomenon. It raises "issues that were not implied in the means of communication known or contemplated by Franklin and Jefferson and Madison." But the Bill of Rights, as appellants say in their brief, can keep up with anything an advertising man or an electronics engineer can think of. In United States v. Classic, Mr. Justice Stone said for the Supreme Court: "in determining whether a provision of the Constitution applies to a new subject matter, it is of little significance that it is one with which the framers were not familiar. For in setting up an enduring framework of government they undertook to carry out for the indefinite future and in all the vicissitudes of the changing affairs of men, those fundamental purposes which the instrument itself discloses." . . .

[13, 14] If Transit obliged its passengers to read what it liked or get off the car, invasion of their freedom would be obvious. Transit obliges them to hear what it likes or get off the car. Freedom of attention, which forced listening destroys, is a part of liberty essential to individuals and to society. The Supreme Court has said that the constitutional guarantee of liberty "embraces not only the right of a person to be free from physical restraint, but the right to be free in the enjoyment of all his faculties. . . ." One who is subjected to forced listening is not free in the enjoyment of all his faculties.

[15] Both the decision and the opinions in Kovacs v. Cooper . . . give great weight to the public interest in freedom from forced listening. The Supreme Court upheld a municipal ordinance prohibiting loud and raucous sound trucks in public streets. Mr. Justice Reed's opinion, for three Justices, said . . . "The unwilling listener is not like the passer-by who may be offered a pamphlet in the street but cannot be made to take it. In his home or on the street he is practically helpless to escape this interference with his privacy by loud speakers except through the protection of the municipality." Kovacs had broadcast, along with music, comment on a labor dispute. He contended that the ordinance abridged his freedom of speech. The Supreme Court's decision upholding the ordinance means that the public interest in freedom from forced listening is so important as to outweigh even the public interest in making more effective, by amplifying, a communication protected by the First Amendment. It would seem to follow that the public interest in freedom from forced listening outweighs the private interest in making more effective, by amplifying, a communication not protected by the First Amendment. The Amendment does not protect commercial advertising.

Validation of the forced listening involved here would result in this curious paradox. Although a municipality may forbid speech protected by the First Amendment from being broadcast in a street, where no one need hear it more than a few minutes, speech not protected by the First Amendment may be broadcast in a streetcar where passengers must hear it for a substantial time.

[16, 17] Of course freedom from forced listening, like other freedoms, is not absolute. No doubt the government may compel attention, as it may forbid speech,

in exceptional circumstances. But a deprivation of liberty to which the government is a party is unconstitutional when it is "arbitrary or without reasonable relation to some purpose within the competency of the state to effect." . . . Forcing Transit passengers to hear these broadcasts has no reasonable relation to any such purpose. Some discomforts may perhaps be inevitable incidents of mass transportation, but forced listening is neither incidental nor inevitable. It deprives the appellants and other passengers who object to the broadcasts of their liberty for the private use of Transit, Radio, and passengers who like the broadcasts. This loss of freedom of attention is the more serious because many people have little time to read, consider, or discuss what they like, or to relax. The record makes it plain that the loss is a serious injury to many passengers. They suffer not only the discomfort of hearing what they dislike but a sense of outrage at being compelled to hear whatever Transit and Radio choose.

[18, 19] Willing hearers are entertained by the broadcasts. But the profit of Transit and Radio and the entertainment of one group of passengers cannot justify depriving another group of passengers of their liberty. The interest of some in hearing what they like is not a right to make others hear the same thing. Even if an impartial survey had shown that most passengers liked the broadcasts or were willing to tolerate them on the supposed chance of a money benefit, that would not be important, since the will of a majority cannot abrogate the constitutional rights of a minority. More-over there is no evidence that any large group of passengers actually wish to go on being entertained by broadcasts forced upon other passengers at the cost of their comfort and freedom.

[20] It has been argued that when freedom of attention is abridged, and that when Transit sells the forced attention of its passengers to Radio for advertising purposes it deprives them of property as well as liberty. Also, it may well be doubted whether Transit can perform its statutory duty of providing comfortable service for all by giving more than comfortable service to some and less than comfortable service to others. But we need not consider these issues. In our opinion Transit's broadcasts deprive objecting passengers of liberty without due process of law. Service that violates constitutional rights is not reasonable service. It follows that the Commission erred as a matter of law in finding that Transit's broadcasts are not inconsistent with public convenience, in failing to find that they are unreasonable, and in failing to stop them.

This decision applies to "commercials" and to "announcements." We are not now called upon to decide whether occasional broadcasts of music alone would in-fringe constitutional rights. . . .

The judgment of the District Court is therefore reversed with instructions to vacate the Commission's order and remand the case to the Commission for further proceedings in conformity with this opinion.

Reversed.

[Judge Edgerton's decision gave promise of the beginnings of a federally-safeguarded right to privacy. But this proved to be short-lived. In its October,

1951, term, the Supreme Court of the United States reversed the decision of the Court of Appeals on the grounds set forth in the opinion that follows.]

4. The Supreme Court Reverses: The Captive Audience Remains in Custody*

MR. JUSTICE BURTON DELIVERED THE OPINION OF THE COURT

[Since the description of the circumstances of case is essentially the same as the background provided by Judge Edgerton in the Court of Appeals decision, Justice Burton's background presentation is omitted.]

4. *No violation of the First Amendment.*—Pollak and Martin contend that the radio programs interfere with their freedom of conversation and that of other passengers by making it necessary for them to compete against the programs in order to be heard. The Commission, however, did not find, and the testimony does not compel a finding, that the programs interfered substantially with the conversation of passengers or with rights of communication constitutionally protected in public places. It is suggested also that the First Amendment guarantees a freedom to listen only to such points of view as the listener wishes to hear. There is no substantial claim that the programs have been used for objectionable propaganda. There is no issue of that kind before us. The inclusion in the programs of a few announcements explanatory and commendatory of Capital Transit's own service does not sustain such an objection.

5. *No violation of the Fifth Amendment.*—The court below has emphasized the claim that the radio programs are an invasion of constitutional rights of privacy of the passengers. This claim is that no matter how much Capital Transit may wish to use radio in its vehicles as part of its services to its passengers and as a source of income, no matter how much the great majority of its passengers may desire radio in those vehicles, and however positively the Commission, on substantial evidence, may conclude that such use of radio does not interfere with the convenience, comfort and safety of the service but tends to improve it, yet if one passenger objects to the program as an invasion of his constitutional right of privacy, the use of radio on the vehicles must be discontinued. This position wrongly assumes that the Fifth Amendment secures to each passenger on a public vehicle regulated by the Federal Government a right of privacy substantially equal to the privacy to which he is entitled in his own home. However complete his right of privacy may be at home, it is substantially limited by the rights of others when its possessor travels on a public thoroughfare or rides in a public conveyance. Streetcars and busses are subject to the immediate control of their owner and operator and, by virtue of their dedication to public service, they are for the common use of all of their passengers. The Federal Government in its regulation of them is not only entitled, but is required, to take into consideration the interests of all concerned.

Public Utilities Commission v. *Pollak,* 343 U.S. 451, 453, 463–466. [Footnotes omitted.]

In a public vehicle there are mutual limitations upon the conduct of everyone, including the vehicle owner. These conflicting demands limit policies on such matters as operating schedules and the location of car or bus stops, as well as policies relating to the desirability or nature of radio programs in the vehicles. Legislation prohibiting the making of artifically amplified raucous sounds in public places has been upheld. . . . Conversely, where a regulatory body has jurisdiction, it will be sustained in its protection of activities in public places when those activities do not interfere with the general public convenience, comfort and safety. The supervision of such practices by the Public Utilities Commission in the manner prescribed in the District of Columbia meets the requirements both of substantive and procedural due process when it is not arbitrarily and capriciously exercised.

The contention of Pollak and Martin would permit an objector, with a status no different from that of other passengers, to override not only the preference of the majority of the passengers but also the considered judgment of the federally authorized Public Utilities Commission, after notice, investigation and public hearings, and upon a record reasonably justifying its conclusion that the policy of the owner and operator did not interfere with public convenience, comfort and safety but tended, in general, to improve the utility service.

We do not agree with that contention. The proctection afforded to the liberty of the individual by the Fifth Amendment against the action of the Federal Government does not go that far. The liberty of each individual in a public vehicle or public place is subject to reasonable limitations in relation to the rights of others.

This Court expresses no opinion as to the desirability of radio programs in public vehicles. In this case that is a matter for decision between Capital Transit, the public and the Public Utilities Commission. The situation is not unlike that which arises when a utility makes a change in its running schedules or in the locations of its stops in the interests of the majority of the passengers but against the vigorous protests of the few who are inconvenienced by the change.

The court below expressly refrained from passing on the constitutionality of the receipt and amplification in public vehicles of occasional broadcasts of music alone. Pollak and Martin, in No. 295, contend that broadcasts even so limited are unconstitutional. However, in view of our holding that the programs before us, containing music, commercial advertising and other announcements are constitutionally permissible, it is clear that programs limited to a like type of music alone would not be less so.

The judgment of the Court of Appeals, accordingly, is reversed and the case is remanded to the District Court.

Reversed.

[Justice Frankfurter took no part in the consideration or decision, stating that his feelings were "so strongly engaged as a victim of the practice in controversy that I had better not participate in judicial judgment upon it."

Justice Black and Douglas wrote separate dissenting opinions. That of Justice Douglas comprised a striking assertion of the need for acceptance of a constitutional right of privacy.]

SEPARATE OPINION OF MR. JUSTICE BLACK

I concur in the Court's holding that this record shows no violation of the Due Process Clause of the Fifth Amendment. I also agree that Capital Transit's musical programs have not violated the First Amendment. I am of the opinion, however, that subjecting Capital Transit's passengers to the broadcasting of news, public speeches, views, or propaganda of any kind and by any means would violate the First Amendment. To the extent, if any, that the Court holds the contrary, I dissent.

MR. JUSTICE DOUGLAS, DISSENTING

This is a case of first impression. There are no precedents to construe; no principles previously expounded to apply. We write on a clean slate.

The case comes down to the meaning of "liberty" as used in the Fifth Amendment. Liberty in the constitutional sense must mean more than freedom from unlawful governmental restraint; it must include privacy as well, if it is to be a repository of freedom. The right to be let alone is indeed the beginning of all freedom. Part of our claim to privacy is in the prohibition of the Fourth Amendment against unreasonable searches and seizures. It gives the guarantee that a man's home is his castle beyond invasion either by inquisitive or by officious people. A man loses that privacy of course when he goes upon the streets or enters public places. But even in his activities outside the home he has immunities from controls bearing on privacy. He may not be compelled against his will to attend a religious service; he may not be forced to make an affirmation or observe a ritual that violates his scruples; he may not be made to accept one religious, political, or philosophical creed as against another. Freedom of religion and freedom of speech guaranteed by the First Amendment give more than the privilege to worship, to write, to speak as one chooses; they give freedom not to do nor to act as the government chooses. The First Amendment in its respect for the conscience of the individual honors the sanctity of thought and belief. To think as one chooses, to believe what one wishes are important aspects of the constitutional right to be let alone.

If we remembered this lesson taught by the First Amendment, I do not believe we would construe "liberty" within the meaning of the Fifth Amendment as narrowly as the Court does. The present case involves a form of coercion to make people listen. The listeners are of course in a public place; they are on streetcars traveling to and from home. In one sense it can be said that those who ride streetcars do so voluntarily. Yet in a practical sense they are forced to ride, since this mode of transportation is today essential for many thousands. Compulsion which comes from circumstances can be as real as compulsion which comes from a command.

The streetcar audience is a captive audience. It is there as a matter of necessity, not of choice. One who is in a public vehicle may not of course complain of the noise of the crowd and the babble of tongues. One who enters any public place sacrifices some of his privacy. My protest is against the invasion of his privacy over and beyond the risks of travel.

The government may use the radio (or television) on public vehicles for many purposes. Today it may use it for a cultural end. Tomorrow it may use it for political purposes. So far as the right of privacy is concerned the purpose makes no difference. The music selected by one bureaucrat may be as offensive to some as it is soothing to others. The news commentator chosen to report on the events of the day may give overtones to the news that please the bureau head but which rile the streetcar captive audience. The political philosophy which one radio speaker exudes may be thought by the official who makes up the streetcar programs to be best for the welfare of the people. But the man who listens to it on his way to work in the morning and on his way home at night may think it marks the destruction of the Republic.

One who tunes in on an offensive program at home can turn it off or tune in another station, as he wishes. One who hears disquieting or unpleasant programs in public places, such as restaurants, can get up and leave. But the man on the streetcar has no choice but to sit and listen, or perhaps to sit and to try *not* to listen.

When we force people to listen to another's ideas, we give the propagandist a powerful weapon. Today it is a business enterprise working out a radio program under the auspices of government. Tomorrow it may be a dominant political or religious group. Today the purpose is benign; there is no invidious cast to the programs. But the vice is inherent in the system. Once privacy is invaded, privacy is gone. Once a man is forced to submit to one type of radio program, he can be forced to submit to another. It may be but a short step from a cultural program to a political program.

If liberty is to flourish, government should never be allowed to force people to listen to any radio program. The right of privacy should include the right to pick and choose from competing entertainments, competing propaganda, competing political philosophies. If people are let alone in those choices, the right of privacy will pay dividends in character and integrity. The strength of our system is in the dignity, the resourcefulness, and the independence of our people. Our confidence is in their ability as individuals to make the wisest choice. That system cannot flourish if regimentation takes hold. The right of privacy, today violated, is a powerful deterrent to any one who would control men's minds.

B. THE POLITICAL CONSEQUENCES OF JUDICIAL SELF-RESTRAINT: URBAN VERSUS RURAL POLITICAL ASCENDANCY

1. Legislative Apportionment in the Federal Courts*

. . . The districts from which members of the forty-eight state legislatures are elected are, on the average, substantially less representative of population today than they were a generation ago. In congressional districts, too, disparities in population are increasing.

The consequences of this gap between population and representation are more

*Anthony Lewis, "Legislative Apportionment and the Federal Courts," *Harvard Law Review*, LXXI (1957–1958), 1057–66. [Footnotes omitted.] Reproduced with permission of the author and publisher. Copyright © 1958 by the Harvard Law Review Association.

significant than is generally recognized for our national life. In the last two decades the United States has become an urban country. Two out of three Americans live now in what the Census Bureau defines as an urban area. It is evident that one of our major national failures since World War II has been the failure to meet the problems of rapid urbanization. The decay of the center city, disorderly suburban growth, and crises in education, housing, and transportation have become familiar facts in every metropolitan area. A fundamental reason that these problems have not been adequately met is urban political weakness, stemming in large part from the underrepresentation of urban areas in the state and national legislatures.

. . . The evidence is overwhelming that neither Congress nor the state legislatures can be relied on to ensure equitable representation, indeed that there are virtually insurmountable, built-in obstacles to legislative action. . . .

I. MALAPPORTIONMENT: CAUSES, EXTENT, EFFECTS

There are two chief varieties of malapportionment, using that term generally to describe representation which does not equitably reflect population.

First, districts may be made up of unequal populations. For example, in a 1951 revision of congressional districts by the Republican-controlled California legislature, five of the districts in Los Angeles County were given substantially less than the average population; all elected Republicans. Four districts were given much more than the average population; all elected Democrats. The five Republicans represented 1,243,000 persons, the four Democrats 1,787,000. A Democratic district had, on the average, 180 per cent of a Republican district's population. Second, districts may be of approximately equal population but gerrymandered—their physical shape manipulated for political reasons. For example, party A wins a bare majority in each of a city's three districts. Now party B, in control of reappointment, creates three new districts, odd in shape though equal in population. One district winds about to include most of the A supporters in the city. Party A wins easily in that district but now loses the other two seats. The first type of malapportionment, population inequalities in the districting process, will be the major concern of this paper.

Malapportionment stems from two distinct causes: affirmative provisions of state constitutions of statutes, and the failure of legislatures to act on apportionment.

Some state constitutions provide for representation in one house of the legislature based not on population at all but on geographic area. For example, seats may be apportioned by counties or by towns. But failure of the legislatures to act is by far the more significant source of unequal representation. The constitutions of 40 states require reapportionment of one or both houses of the legislature every 10 years or more frequently, and 3 other state constitutions authorize decennial redistricting. Yet 23 of the 48 states have not reapportioned for 10, 20, 50 years or more. For example, Alabama's legislature is constitutionally obligated to reapportion every 10 years but last did so in 1901. Under 40 state constitutions population is the basis of apportionment, with some qualifications, in at least one house of the legislature. But the frequent redistricting required to make these standards a reality has not been forthcoming.

Inaction affects congressional districts as much as those of the state legislatures.

Only 17 states have made general changes in their congressional districts since World War II. Of those, 8 were forced to redistrict because they lost seats in the 1950 census, and 7 were encouraged to redistrict because they gained seats in that census. Only 2 states revised their congressional districts without the special incentive to action of a change in size of delegation.

The extent of malapportionment in the state legislatures was charted in a recent study. For example: In Florida, in part because of constitutional provisions and in part because of legislative inaction, about 17 per cent of the population elects a majority of each house. In Oklahoma, entirely as a result of legislative inaction, a majority of the upper house is elected by 29 per cent of the population and a majority of the lower house by 33 per cent.

As for congressional districts, a conservative standard of equality would require that a state's most populous district be no more than 50 per cent greater than the least populous. At present the congressional districts in 30 states fail to meet even this moderate requirement. Legislation pending in Congress to require equitably distributed House districts lays down a standard which would invalidate the districts in all 30 of those states.

The direct effect of maldistricting is to tighten the grip of the historically dominant party—Republicans in the North, Democrats in the South. In Michigan, for example, Democratic candidates for the state senate in 1954 had an aggregate plurality of 52,000 votes over the Republican candidates, but the Republicans won 23 seats to the Democrats' 11. In Florida the Republicans polled 26 per cent of the gubernatorial vote in 1956 against a popular Democratic incumbent but won only 1 of 38 senate and 6 of 95 house seats. Thus malapportionment is a factor in making one-party states the rule rather than the exception as far as the legislatures are concerned—with all the resultant evils of unresponsive political leadership and loss of public confidence in government.

The effect of unequal districts on party strength in the House of Representatives is difficult to measure, but a table of votes cast and seats won in 1956 suggests that the Democrats are hurt. Outside the South they had 47 per cent of the votes but won only 39 per cent of the seats, in part because of maldistricting.

Malapportionment has an almost universal rural bias. One estimate is that in 1947 residents of urban areas made up 59 per cent of the United States population but elected only about 25 per cent of the state legislators in the country. Some conservative urban organizations and individuals, seeing in rural control a conservative influence, have opposed fairer representation for their own cities. The Los Angeles Chamber of Commerce fought a reapportionment which would have given more than one state senator to the 4,125,000 citizens of Los Angeles County. (One rural senatorial district in northern California has a population of 13,568.)

With respect to congressional districts the bias is rural also. The most populous and hence most underrepresented districts are usually in urban and suburban areas. One reason for the tendency of urban political interests to focus on the President is their underrepresentation in the House. The Senate, too, has become more urban-minded than the House, probably because senators need the votes of what is an urban majority in most states.

The potential evil effects of congressional maldistricting, as well as its political appeal to state legislatures, would be vastly increased by a proposed constitutional amendment to permit the choosing of some presidential electors by congressional districts instead of at large.

There is an important secondary effect of the rural-dominated state legislatures on federal-state-city relations. When the legislatures ignore urban needs, the cities turn to Washington. President Eisenhower's Commission on Intergovernmental Relations explored the problem in detail. It concluded that there had been a decline in the power and influence of state governments and that this must be attributed in part to the failure "to maintain an equitable system of representation." Assiduous efforts by the Eisenhower administration to reduce grants in aid to the states for programs such as public housing have been urgently opposed by city governments on the ground that federal funds, if withdrawn, would not be replaced by the rural-minded legislatures.

[The problems attendant upon urban underrepresentation have increased rather than diminished since 1958 when Anthony Lewis wrote the analysis quoted above. The failure of the state legislatures and the national Congress to provide for fair representation through periodic reapportionment and balanced redistricting has impelled many "under-represented urban-dwellers to turn to the state and federal courts for assistance. For many years, the courts were reluctant to enter what Justice Felix Frankfurter referred to in 1946 as this 'political thicket.' "]

2. *Judicial Reluctance to Enter this "Political Thicket"**

. . . Petitioners are three qualified voters in Illinois districts which have much larger populations than other Illinois congressional districts. They brought this suit against the Governor, the Secretary of State, and the Auditor of the state of Illinois, as members ex officio of the Illinois Primary Certifying Board, to restrain them, in effect, from taking proceedings for an election in November, 1946, under the provisions of Illinois law governing congressional districts. . . . Formally, the appellees asked for a decree, with its incidental relief, . . . declaring these provisions to be invalid because they violated various provisions of the United States Constitution and 3 of the Reapportionment Act of August 8, 1911, . . . in that by reason of subsequent changes in population the congressional districts for the election of Representatives in the Congress created by the Illinois Laws of 1901, . . . lacked compactness of territory and approximate equality of population. The District Court . . . dismissed the bill. . . .

We are of opinion that the petitioners ask of this Court what is beyond its competence to grant. This is one of those demands on judicial power which cannot be met by verbal fencing about "jurisdiction." It must be resolved by considerations

*Mr. Justice Frankfurter in *Colegrove* v. *Green,* 328 U.S. 549 (1946). [Footnotes omitted.]

on the basis of which this Court, from time to time, has refused to intervene in controversies. It has refused to do so because due regard for the effective working of our government revealed this issue to be of a peculiarly political nature and therefore not meet for judicial determination.

This is not an action to recover for damage because of the discriminatory exclusion of a plaintiff from rights enjoyed by other citizens. The basis for the suit is not a private wrong, but a wrong suffered by Illinois as a polity. . . . In effect this is an appeal to the federal courts to reconstruct the electoral process of Illinois in order that it may be adequately represented in the councils of the nation. Because the Illinois legislature has failed to revise its Congressional Representative districts in order to reflect great changes, during more than a generation, in the distribution of its population, we are asked to do this, as it were, for Illinois.

Of course no court can affirmatively remap the Illinois districts so as to bring them more in conformity with the standards of fairness for a representative system. At best we could only declare the existing electoral system invalid. The result would be to leave Illinois undistricted and to bring into operation, if the Illinois legislature chose not to act, the choice of members for the House of Representatives on a statewide ticket. The last stage may be worse than the first. The upshot of judicial action may defeat the vital political principle which led Congress, more than a hundred years ago, to require districting. This requirement, in the language of Chancellor Kent, "was recommended by the wisdom and justice of giving, as far as possible, to the local subdivisions of the people of each state, a due influence in the choice of representatives, so as not to leave the aggregate minority of the people in a state, though approaching perhaps to a majority, to be wholly overpowered by the combined action of the numerical majority, without any voice whatever in the national councils." . . . Assuming acquiescence on the part of the authorities of Illinois in the selection of its Representatives by a mode that defies the direction of Congress for selection by districts, the House of Representatives may not acquiesce. In the exercise of its power to judge the qualifications of its own members, the House may reject a delegation of Representatives-at-Large. . . . Nothing is clearer than that this controversy concerns matters that bring courts into immediate and active relations with party contests. From the determination of such issues this Court has traditionally held aloof. It is hostile to a democratic system to involve the judiciary in the politics of the people. And it is not less pernicious if such judicial intervention in an essentially political contest be dressed up in the abstract phrases of the law.

The petitioners urge with great zeal that the conditions of which they complain are grave evils and offend public morality. The Constitution of the United States gives ample power to provide against these evils. But due regard for the Constitution as a viable system precludes judicial correction. Authority for dealing with such problems resides elsewhere. Article I, section 4 of the Constitution provides that "The Times, Places and Manner of Holding Elections for . . . Representatives, shall be prescribed in each State by the Legislature thereof; but the Congress may at any time by Law make or alter such Regulations, . . ." The short of it is that the Constitution has conferred upon Congress exclusive authority to secure fair representation by the states in the popular House and left to that House determination whether states have fulfilled their responsibility. If Congress failed in exercising its powers, whereby standards of fairness are offended, the remedy ultimately lies with the people. Whether Congress faithfully discharges its duty or not, the subject has been committed to the exclusive control of Congress. An aspect of government from which the judiciary, in view of what is involved, has been excluded by the clear intention of the Constitution cannot be entered by the federal courts because Congress may have been in default in exacting from states obedience to its mandate. . . .

To sustain this action would cut very deep into the very being of Congress. Courts ought not to enter this political thicket. The remedy for unfairness in districting is to secure state legislatures that will apportion properly, or to invoke the ample powers of Congress. The Constitution has many commands that are not enforceable by courts because they clearly fall outside the conditions and purposes that circumscribe judicial action. Thus, "on Demand of the Executive Authority," Art. IV, sec. 2, of a state it is the duty of a sister state to deliver up a fugitive from justice. But the fullfillment of this duty cannot be judicially enforced. . . . The duty to see to it that the laws are faithfully executed cannot be brought under legal compulsion. . . . Violation of the great guaranty of a republican form of government in states cannot be challenged in the courts. . . . The Constitution has left the performance of many duties in our governmental scheme to depend on the fidelity of the executive and legislative action and, ultimately, on the vigilance of the people in exercising their political rights.

Dismissal of the complaint is affirmed.

[Mr. Justice Jackson took no part in the consideration or decision of this case. Mr. Justice Rutledge concurred in a separate opinion. Mr. Justice Black dissented in an opinion concurred in by Justices Douglas and Murphy.]

3. For Judicial Activism*

It is difficult for me to see why the 1901 State Apportionment Act does not deny appellants equal protection of the laws. The failure of the Legislature to reapportion the congressional election districts for forty years, despite census figures indicating great changes in the distribution of the population, has resulted in election districts the populations of which range from 112,000 to 900,000. One of the appellants lives in a district of more than 900,000 people. His vote is consequently much less effective than that of each of the citizens living in the district of 122,000. And such a gross inequality in the voting power of citizens irrefutably demonstrates a complete lack of effort to make an equitable apportionment. The 1901 State Apportionment Act if applied to the next election would thus result in a wholly indefensible discrimination against appellants and all other voters in heavily populated districts. The equal protection clause of the Fourteenth Amendment forbids such discrimination. It does not permit the States to pick out certain qualified citizens or groups

*Mr. Justice Black in *Colegrove* v. *Green*, 328 U.S. 549, 569–574 (1946). [Footnotes omitted.]

of citizens and deny them the right to vote at all. . . . No one would deny that the equal protection clause would also prohibit a law that would expressly give certain citizens a half-vote and others a full vote. The probable effect of the 1901 State Apportionment Act in the coming election will be that certain citizens, and among the appellants, will in some instances have votes only one-ninth as effective in choosing representatives to Congress as the votes of other citizens. Such discriminatory legislation seems to me exactly the kind that the equal protection clause was intended to prohibit.

The 1901 State Apportionment Act in reducing the effectiveness of appellants' votes abridges their privilege as citizens to vote for Congressmen and violates Article I of the Constitution. Article I provides that Congressmen "shall be . . . chosen . . . by the People of the several States . . ." It thus gives those qualified a right to vote and a right to have their vote counted. . . . This Court in order to prevent "an interference with the effective choice of the voters" has held that this right extends to primaries. . . . While the Constitution contains no express provision requiring that congressional election districts established by the States must contain approximately equal populations, the constitutionally guaranteed right to vote and the right to have one's vote counted clearly imply the policy that state election systems, no matter what their form, should be designed to give approximately equal weight to each vote cast. To some extent this implication of Article I is expressly stated by 2 of the Fourteenth Amendment which provides that "Representatives shall be apportioned among the several States according to their respective numbers . . ." The purpose of this requirement is obvious: It is to make the votes of the citizens of the several States equally effective in the selection of members of Congress. It was intended to make illegal a nation-wide "rotten borough" system as between the States. The policy behind it is broader than that. It prohibits as well congressional "rotten boroughs" within the States, such as the ones here involved. The policy is that which is laid down by all the constitutional provisions regulating the election of members of the House of Representatives, including Article I which guarantees the right to vote and to have that vote effectively counted: All groups, classes, and individuals shall to the extent that it is practically feasible be given equal representation in the House of Representatives, which, in conjunction with the Senate, writes the laws affecting the life, liberty, and property of all the people.

It is true that the States are authorized by 2 of Article I of the Constitution to legislate on the subject of congressional elections to the extent that Congress has not done so. Thus the power granted to the State Legislature on this subject is primarily derived from the Federal and not from the State Constitution. But this federally-granted power with respect to elections of Congressmen is not to formulate policy but rather to implement the policy laid down in the Constitution, that, so far as feasible, votes be given equally effective weight. Thus, a state legislature cannot deny eligible voters the right to vote for Congressmen and the right to have their vote counted. It can no more destroy the effectiveness of their vote in part and no more accomplish this in the name of "apportionment" than under any other name. For legislation which must inevitably bring about glaringly unequal representation in the Congress in favor of special classes and groups should be invalidated, "whether accomplished ingeniously or ingenuously." . . .

Had Illinois passed an Act requiring that all of its twenty-six Congressmen be elected by the citizens of one county, it would clearly have amounted to a denial to the citizens of the other counties of their constitutionally guaranteed right to vote. And I cannot imagine that an Act that would have apportioned twenty-five Congressman to the State's smallest county and one Congressman to all the others, would have been sustained by any court. Such an Act would clearly have violated the constitutional policy of equal representation. The 1901 Apportionment Act here involved violates that policy in the same way. The policy with respect to federal elections laid down by the Constitution, while it does not mean that the courts can or should prescribe the precise methods to be followed by state legislatures and the invalidation of all Acts that do not embody those precise methods, does mean that state legislatures must make real efforts to bring about approximately equal representation of citizens in Congress. Here the Legislature of Illinois has not done so. Whether that was due to negligence or was a wilful effort to deprive some citizens of an effective vote, the admitted result is that the constitutional policy of equality of representation has been defeated. Under these circumstances it is the Court's duty to invalidate the state law.

It is contended, however, that a court of equity does not have the power, or even if it has the power, that it should not exercise it in this case. To do so, it is argued, would mean that the Court is entering the area of "political questions." I cannot agree with that argument. There have been cases, such as *Coleman* v. *Miller, supra, . . .* where this Court declined to decide a question because it was political. In the *Miller* case, however, the question involved was ratification of a constitutional amendment, a matter over which the Court believed Congress has been given final authority. To have decided that question would have amounted to a trespass upon the constitutional power of Congress. Here we have before us a state law which abridges the constitutional rights of citizens to cast votes in such way as to obtain the kind of congressional representation the Constitution guarantees to them.

It is true that voting is a part of elections and that elections are "political." But as this Court said in *Nixon* v. *Herndon, supra,* it is a mere "play upon words" to refer to a controversy such as this as "political" in the sense that courts have nothing to do with protecting and vindicating the right of a voter to cast an effective ballot. The *Classic* case, among myriads of others, refutes the contention that courts are impotent in connection with evasions of all "political" rights. . . . *Wood* v. *Broom* . . . does not preclude the granting of equitable relief in this case. There this Court simply held that the State Apportionment Act did not violate the Congressional Reapportionment Act of 1929, . . . since that Act did not require election districts of equal population. The Court expressly reserved the question of "the right of the complainant to relief in equity." *Giles* v. *Harris* . . . also did not hold that a court of equity could not, or should not, exercise its power in a case like this. As we said with reference to that decision in *Lane* v. *Wilson* . . . it stands for the principle that courts will not attempt to "supervise" elections. Furthermore, the author of the *Giles* v. *Harris* opinion also wrote the opinion in *Nixon* v. *Herndon,* in which a voter's right to cast a ballot was held to give rise to a justiciable controversy.

In this case, no supervision over elections is asked for. What is asked is that this

Court do exactly what it did in *Smiley* v. *Holm, supra.* It is asked to declare a state apportionment bill invalid and to enjoin state officials from enforcing it. The only difference between this case and the *Smiley* case is that there the case originated in the state courts while here the proceeding originated in the Federal District Court. The only type of case in which this Court has held that a federal district court should in its discretion stay its hand any more than a state court is where the question is one which state courts or administrative agencies have special competence to decide. This is not that type of question. What is involved here is the right to vote guaranteed by the Federal Constitution. It has always been the rule that where a federally protected right has been invaded the federal courts will provide the remedy to rectify the wrong done. Federal courts have not hesitated to exercise their equity power in cases involving deprivation of property and liberty. . . . There is no reason why they should do so where the case involves the right to choose representatives that make laws affecting liberty and property.

Nor is there any more difficulty in enforcing a decree in this case than there was in the *Smiley* case. It is true that declaration of invalidity of the State Act and the enjoining of state officials would result in prohibiting the State from electing Congressmen under the system of the old congressional districts. But it would leave the State free to elect them from the State at large, which, as we held in the *Smiley* case, is a manner authorized by the Constitution. It is said that this would be inconvenient for the State to conduct the election in this manner. But is has an element of virtue that the more convenient method does not have—namely, it does not discriminate against some groups to favor others, it gives all the people an equally effective voice in electing their representatives as is essential under a free government, and it is constitutional.

Mr. Justice Douglas and Mr. Justice Murphy join in this dissent.

4. The Courts Should Intervene: A Lay Dissent*

II. STATE EXPERIENCE: JUDICIAL INTERVENTION CAN WORK

The political thicket of malapportionment has not, as a rule, scared off the courts of the states. They have granted relief in a large number of lawsuits brought by private citizens against state officials to challenge apportionments. Districts have been held in violation of state constitutional requirements that they be of approximately equal population, be compact in shape, be made up of contiguous territory, or follow town boundaries. Occasionally, plaintiffs in the state courts have relied on asserted federal rights.

A series of cases in Massachusetts in 1916 illustrate state-court practice. The Suffolk County Apportionment Commissioners, authorized by law to assign the county's

*Anthony Lewis, "Legislative Apportionment and the Federal Courts," *Harvard Law Review,* LXXI (1957–1958), 1066–98. [Footnotes omitted.] Reproduced with permission of the author and the publisher. Copyright © 1958 by the Harvard Law Review Association.

54 legislative seats to districts, had created districts varying in population from 1,957 to 6,182 persons per representative. A suit against the commissioners in the Supreme Judicial Court asserted a violation of a provision of the state constitution requiring apportionment of "the representation assigned to each county equally, as nearly as may be, according to the relative number of legal voters in the several districts of each county." Plaintiffs sought mandamus to require a new apportionment. The Suffolk Commissioners were ordered by the court to redistrict, and did.

The next apportionment showed districts varying in population from 2,427 to 5,596 persons per representative. A second suit was brought, and mandamus issued to the commissioners again. The court found a third apportionment, with districts ranging in population from 2,427 to 4,282, valid.

There is virtually no discussion of judiciability in the state cases. The courts have not often articulated the political-question theory, nor cited *Colegrove,* as a ground for declining jurisdiction. But the state courts have put on a strangely mixed performance in their handling of remedial problems. A common practice when invalidating a challenged districting statute has been to bring back to life some previous apportionment, and then to hold the revived districts immune from legal attack. A series of Kentucky cases illustrates this odd practice. In *Ragland* v. *Anderson* the court invalidated a 1906 statute. The opinion's powerful language, citing the battle of Yorktown, has often been quoted. The holding required return to an 1893 apportionment, which was then attacked in *Adams* v. *Bosworth.* The court denied relief, saying that the plaintiffs should have challenged the 1893 act immediately after its passage and would not be allowed to "sleep on their rights." The 1893 districts were then used until the passage of a 1918 act which went unchallenged in the courts. In 1930 the legislature again redistricted, but the statute was held void in *Stiglitz* v. *Schardien.* The court's language, adverting to justice, civilization, and tyranny, was even more colorful than in *Ragland.* Its remedy was to return to the 1918 districts.

The Illinois congressional districts at issue in *Colegrove* v. *Green* were themselves a product of such a remedial practice. The Supreme Court of Illinois had invalidated a 1931 reapportionment establishing districts with a maximum population variation of 158,738 to 541,785. It ordered a return to the previous statute, that of 1901, under which the districts varied in population from 138,000 to 839,000. There was no new apportionment before *Colegrove* was decided in 1946.

The performance of the state courts has been especially weak in fashioning remedies for the wrongful refusal of legislatures to reapportion. The courts have generally declined to grant relief in suits involving long-standing districts. They advance the ground of laches expressed in the Kentucky cases, combined occasionally with the view that time cannot make an apportionment invalid. And they have rejected, on the ground of the separation of powers, a large number of direct efforts to compel legislative action. Plaintiffs have sought mandamus against the legislature itself, or an injunction against the secretary of state to bar use of the challenged districts. They have asked the courts to restrain payment of legislators' salaries until they redistrict, and to issue a writ of quo warranto requiring members of a malapportioned legislature to show by what right they hold office. Other plaintiffs have asked the courts in effect to do the redistricting themselves by requiring state officials to issue election mandates giving populous areas additional seats or refusing to give less populous areas the seats given them by the apportionment. One criminal defendant sought to reverse his conviction on the ground that the law he had violated had been passed by a malapportioned legislature and hence was invalid. Another man resorted to what might be called self-help. The reasons for the state courts' difficulties with these remedies are apparent. To compel a legislature by mandamus to draft a new apportionment or to use other methods of direct compulsion on individual legislators are not usual exercises of judicial power, though many state courts have successfully done this. Nor is return to an earlier apportionment a satisfactory solution.

But there is a simple, appropriate, and effective remedy: requiring an election at large until valid districts are drawn. This was the relief granted in *Brown* v. *Saunders*. A statute revising Virginia's congressional districts was invalidated as in violation of a state constitutional requirement that the districts contain "as nearly as practicable, an equal number of inhabitants." The state's representatives were chosen at large, and valid new districts were drawn before the next Congress.

III. A FEDERAL RIGHT TO EQUALITY OF REPRESENTATION EXISTS

A. CONGRESSIONAL DISTRICTS

An individual right to equal representation in the House of Representatives can be drawn from article I of the Constitution. The existence of such a right is strongly supported by the legislative history of the article—the proceedings of the Constitutional Convention and the ratification debates.

Section 2 of article I reads, in pertinent part:

> *The House of Representatives shall be composed of Members chosen every second Year by the People of the several States.*

A reading of the contemporaneous material demonstrates that the word "People" was not used accidentally; the House was intended to represent the people rather than the states.

In the heart of the convention debate between large and small states on the form of representation in Congress, William Samuel Johnson of Connecticut thus put the compromise that was adopted: "[I]n *one* branch the *people,* ought to be represented; in the *other,* the *States.*" William Pierce of Georgia, noted Madison,

> *was for an election by the people as to the 1st branch & by the States as to the 2d branch; by which means the Citizens of the States wd. be represented both* individually & collectively.

The same belief in a personal, individual right to representation in the House was reflected in the connection between taxation and representation often made by speakers in the convention. (The two are themselves connected in article I.) The thesis that the people would be represented in the House was also expounded in the state ratifying conventions and in *The Federalist.*

A second proposition demonstrated by the historical material is that the framers specifically anticipated the possibility of malapportionment of congressional districts and provided federal power to prevent it in the clause of article I giving Congress ultimate authority to regulate the time, place, and manner of congressional elections. In the convention, Madison supported the clause as a weapon against maldistricting. Without it, he said,

> *the inequality of the representation in the Legislatures of particular States would produce a like inequality in their representation in the Natl. Legislature, as it was presumable that the Counties having the power in the former case would secure it to themselves in the latter.*

Similar defenses of the clause were made in the ratifying conventions. In South Carolina, Charles Cotesworth Pinckney said it was

> *absolutely necessary that Congress should have this superintending power, lest, by the intrigues of a ruling faction in a state, the members of the House of Representatives should not really represent the people of the state.*

In the Massachusetts convention, Francis Dana pointed to examples of maldistricting in Rhode Island and Great Britain, and Rufus King noted similar examples in Connecticut and South Carolina. In Virginia, Madison, in defense of the clause, equated malapportionment with deprivation of suffrage.

All this indicates that the framers, in considering the possibility of maldistricting, envisaged a congressional corrective power. Congress first exercised the power in order to require election of representatives by districts in 1842. In 1872 Congress added the requirement that districts be of approximately equal population, and this provision continued through the act of 1911. It was never enforced by Congress, and the Supreme Court held in *Wood* v. *Broom*—the first case in the federal courts involving congressional districts—that the provision had been impliedly repealed when Congress enacted a permanent apportionment statute in 1929.

The fact that the Constitution casts the right to equal representation in the House in terms of affirmative congressional power should not preclude judicial enforcement of the right in the absence of legislation. Such judicial action is commonplace in other areas. There is, notably, the commerce clause, which is phrased in the most general language and entirely in terms of congressional power. Among the framers and contemporary commentators, "the conception that the mere grant of the commerce power to Congress dislodged state power finds no expression." There was no hint that the federal courts were empowered, in the absence of congressional legislation, to invalidate state laws impinging on national commerce. Yet since Marshall's first essay in *Gibbons* v. *Ogden,* use of the commerce clause for judicial invalidation of state action has become "central to our whole constitutional scheme." There is, in fact, more substantial support in the constitutional history for the presumption that, in the silence of Congress, the Constitution gives a right to equality of representation in the House than there is for the analogous presumption as to freedom of interstate commerce.

The leading modern cases exploring the scope of the right to vote for members of Congress given by article I are *United States* v. *Classic* and *United States* v. *Saylor*. Both were criminal prosecutions of state election officials under Civil Rights Acts dating back to 1870—the former for miscounting votes, the latter for stuffing ballot boxes. The statutes invoked do not mention voting but merely make it a crime to violate a person's constitutional rights, defined in the broadest terms. To uphold the indictments, the Supreme Court had to find, in the acts charged, violations of some specific right given by the Constitution. It found that right in article I—a guarantee of the integrity of the ballot. The Court held in *Classic*:

> *Obviously included within the right to choose, secured by the Constitution, is the right of qualified voters within a state to cast their ballots and have them counted at Congressional elections.*

Saylor went further to hold that article I protects the voter's ballot against the diluting effect of stuffed ballot boxes.

In a suit challenging inequitably apportioned congressional districts, the substantive federal right could be analogized from *Classic* and *Saylor*: if the declaratory language of article I guarantees the ballot against the random hazards of miscounting and stuffing, it should protect also against the continued diluting effect of maldistricting. It may be said that there is a difference in that in the *Classic* and *Saylor* situations the voters were qualified under state law and that the acts assailed were violations of state law as well as the Constitution, while in the maldistricting case the attack is against a deliberate act of the state. But the historical material shows that supervision over congressional redistricting was intended to fall within the area of federal power, not within the states' exclusive authority over voting "qualifications." Moreover, the fact that an action violates state law does not of itself affect its validity under the Federal Constitution. Of course there is an important difference of standards in the two situations. One miscounted ballot plainly constitutes a wrong, while a difference in district populations would have to be substantial before it could be regarded as invalid. But the substantive right would be based on the same premise of article I— the worth of the individual vote.

As for the technical right of action, a suit for equitable relief from an unconstitutional act can be based directly on the Constitution. But in any event a Civil Rights Act parallel to the criminal statute involved in *Classic* authorizes civil actions, including "suits in equity," against state officials who deprive persons of constitutional rights.

In addition to article I, a federal right to equality of representation in the House may be based on the various provisions in section I of the fourteenth amendment. The first of these, the half-forgotten privileges-and-immunities clause, has been held to protect only rights of national citizenship, not state-given rights. It would appear, by a specific negative on state action, to reinforce rights implicit in other portions of the Constitution. In an attack on unequal congressional districts the clause would simply support the argument based on article I.

The equal-protection and due-process clauses offer a supplementary argument. Here the assertion is that for a state to discriminate geographically among its voters is, as in the case of racial discrimination, to deny the equal protection of the laws; or that it is to deprive the citizen of political liberty or of the intangible property of his vote without due process. In any case, as to congressional districts, there should be no practical difference in legal consequences whether reliance is placed on article I or on the fourteenth amendment.

B. STATE LEGISLATIVE DISTRICTS

There is no constitutional assumption that representation in the state legislatures should be based on units of equal population. Indeed the states would seem constitutionally free to choose any reasonable form of representation they wish; by population, by area, or by occupations as in guild socialism.

A system of state legislative representation could, however, be so unreasonable as to offend the equal-protection and due-process clauses. Were a state, for example, to provide that each resident of an urban area have one-quarter of a vote in legislative elections while a rural citizen may cast a full vote, a court might easily find such blatant discrimination in violation of the fourteenth amendment.

Suppose the state constitution requires legislative districts of equal population, but failure to reapportion has so unbalanced the districts that the urban resident's vote is in fact worth only one-quarter as much as the rural resident's. The violation of the state constitution would not itself amount to a violation of the fourteenth amendment. But in an argument on the merits the apportionment would stand exposed as based on something other than a rational principle. It might lack the rational basis needed to pass muster under the fourteenth amendment.

IV. THE SUPREME COURT'S REASONS FOR DENYING RELIEF ARE NOT PERSUASIVE

The Supreme Court has articulated on three occasions—principally in *Colegrove* v. *Green,* more briefly in two subsequent cases—its grounds for rejecting constitutional challenges to malapportionment. . . .

[Summary of *Colegrove* omitted.]

* * *

MacDougall v. *Green* challenged an Illinois law which required a new party seeking a place on the statewide ballot to have petitions with at least 200 signatures from each of at least fifty different counties and at least 25,000 signatures in all. The Progressive Party of 1948 had 75,000 signatures in the state but did not have the requisite geographical distribution. Plaintiffs, would-be Progressive candidates and voters, sought an injunction against enforcement of the geographic requirement—in effect seeking an order to put the party on the ballot. The principal basis of attack on the statute was the fourteenth amendment. The case was argued on Oct. 18, 1948, fifteen days before the election, and decided three days later. The Court, with all nine members now sitting, denied relief in a per curiam opinion. Mr. Justice Rutledge concurred specially in view of the lateness of the date and the probable disruptive effects of an injunction on the election. Mr. Justice Douglas dissented in an opinion joined by Justices Black and Murphy.

In *South* v. *Peters*, plaintiff voters attacked the Georgia county-unit system, used for counting primary-election votes in statewide contests. Under the system the candidate leading the popular vote in each county receives its "unit vote"—two units in each of the state's 121 smallest counties, four units in 30 counties, six in the 8 largest counties. The system is weighted against the large counties, whose share of the unit vote is much less than their proportion of the population. Violations of the fourteenth amendment and of the provision of the seventeenth amendment that senators be "elected by the people" were alleged. Plaintiffs sought to enjoin use of the county-unit system, forcing an ordinary tabulation by popular vote. The Supreme Court affirmed dismissal of the suit in a per curiam opinion with these words of explanation:

> *Federal courts consistently refuse to exercise their equity powers in cases posing political issues arising from a state's geographical distribution of electoral strength among its political subdivisions.*

Mr. Justice Douglas, joined by Mr. Justice Black, dissented.

The view that prevailed in *Colegrove* v. *Green* rests on something more than the formal doctrine of "political questions." Indeed, the political-question doctrine alone would be an unconvincing basis of decision since malapportionment so plainly resembles state discrimination of the kind often remedied by the federal courts more than it does the contests of physical power which have been deemed political. The course chosen in *Colegrove* seems a deliberate withholding of judicial power because of problems foreseen in its exercise. Those problems relate to the justiciability of the issue, to the efficacy of judicial remedies for malapportionment, and to legislative responsibility.

A. JUSTICABILITY

One passage in the *Colegrove* opinion—"The basis for the suit is not a private wrong but a wrong suffered by Illinois as a polity"—may indicate a concern about the plaintiffs' standing, *i.e.*, whether they have some special interest of their own to vindicate.

The Supreme Court has decided on the merits so many suits brought by plaintiffs who have had standing only as voters that the question might really be regarded as settled. A case decided by a unanimous Court in 1932, *Smiley* v. *Holm*, posed the problem squarely. Minnesota's governor had vetoed a bill creating new congressional districts after the state delegation had been reduced by the 1930 census. The legislature, asserting that under the Constitution districts should be laid out by legislatures without gubernatorial participation, declared the new districts in effect despite the veto. Plaintiff, a "citizen, elector, and taxpayer," sued in the state court to restrain the secretary of state from using the new districts and to force an election at large instead. The Minnesota courts denied relief. The Supreme Court reversed, the injunction issued, and the election was held at large. The same result was reached by the Court in two companion cases. Certainly these plaintiffs had no more personal an interest in the legality of their states' congressional districts than did the plaintiffs in *Colegrove*.

The prevailing opinion in Colegrove compared two successful actions at law to vindicate Negroes' voting rights with a similar suit in equity which did not succeed. This language follows: "In effect this is an appeal to the federal courts to reconstruct the electoral process of Illinois. . . ." But the great negro-voting cases which were actions for damages in fact called on the Supreme Court to "reconstruct the electoral process" of the southern states. And any suggestion that equity is an inappropriate instrument for vindication of political rights runs squarely against the success of equity in numerous Supreme Court cases arising in the state courts and the latest of the negro-voting cases in the federal courts, *Terry* v. *Adams*. This was a class action by negro plaintiffs who were barred from a special pre-primary conducted in one Texas county by the "Jaybird Democratic Association." They sought and won a declaratory judgment and such further injunctive relief as necessary to prohibit the Jaybird primary or require their participation in it. Neither the opinion announcing the judgment of the Court and the concurring opinions nor the dissenting opinion questioned either the plaintiffs' standing or their right to invoke the power of an equity court. Finally, it must be noted that the Civil Rights Act specifically authorizes suits in equity for vindication of constitutional rights; there is no apparent reason to exclude political rights.

But the real problem of justiciability in an apportionment case is not a technical one of standing or equity. It lies in the question: What is or is not equality of representation? A slight difference in population among districts would not render them invalid. But how is a court to determine when the disparity passes the allowable limits? The view has been expressed that such a judgment is not the normal judicial task and should not be undertaken unless the legislature lays down fixed mathematical standards. Proposed legislation introduced by Representative Emanuel Celler would provide such standards. It would require that each state's congressional districts be compact in form and vary in population by no more than twenty per cent from the average, derived by dividing the state's total population by the number of its representatives.

Of course the judicial function would be simplified in many cases if Congress laid down explicit criteria. But in the area of commerce, for example, Congress has refused to do so despite virtual urging by the Supreme Court, and the Court has continued to weigh such imponderables as the burden of state taxation on interstate commerce. It is fair to say that it is a central duty of the Supreme Court—indeed, of all courts—to decide cases in which precise standards are not, perhaps, cannot be fixed.

The state courts have done exactly this kind of job in apportionment cases. No state constitution or statute lays down mathematical standards for equality of representation. Nor have the state courts, in many cases in which they have found apportionments invalid, used abstract mathematical criteria themselves. Instead they have spoken in general terms:

> *It is not insisted that the equality of representation is to be made mathematically exact. This is manifestly impossible. All that the Constitution requires is*

that equality in the representation of a State which an ordinary knowledge of its population and a sense of common justice would suggest.

Another view considers whether the inequality is "necessary" or, as said by Chief Judge Rugg in one of the Massachusetts cases, "might have been avoided." This may entail looking to the ready availability of alternative districting plans. It is reminiscent of Professor Paul A. Freund's thesis that courts should consider in civil-liberties cases whether government could reach its end by other, less damaging means, as the Supreme Court has weighed alternatives in commerce cases. And state courts have tacitly looked to the motive of those responsible for malapportionment:

An apportionment which gives, and is intended to give, to one political party or another a decided and unfair advantage . . . where such disparity can be avoided, must for that reason be condemned.

The standards used by the state courts in apportionment cases are remarkably similar to the flexible test developed by the Supreme Court to measure state action against the equal-protection clause, the test of rational basis. The touchstone, as Mr. Justice Frankfurter has put it, is that classifications made by the state must be "rooted in reason." The classifications must have a genuine relationship to a non-discriminatory legislative purpose. And the Supreme Court has frequently looked past the declared intent of state action to find the real motive. Thus it has examined the claimed purpose of protecting the public health and safety and found instead an intention to exclude Chinese laundrymen from employment. The view that the equal-protection clause is in essence "a demand for purity of motive" has been persuasively argued.

The approach used in cases involving the equal-protection clause would be the appropriate test for the federal courts to employ in apportionment suits. A challenged apportionment would have the benefit of a presumption of constitutionality. But once the plaintiff had made a prima facie showing of inequality beyond a reasonable legislative discretion, as a practical matter the burden would be on the state to show a rational, nondiscriminatory basis for the apportionment.

Consider a small state with two representatives and somewhat more urban than rural population. A division of the state into one urban and one rural district, the latter substantially less populous, could readily be defended as assuring adequate representation to each element of the citizenry. But suppose that in a large state such as Illinois it appeared that some urban districts averaged four times the population of other urban districts. It is difficult to suggest a rational basis for the disparity. The burden should be on Illinois to demonstrate a nondiscriminatory purpose for the classification.

B. REMEDIES

A second basis for the result in *Colegrove* was the thesis that courts cannot provide an effective remedy for malapportionment. For one thing, the prevailing opinion observed, "no court can affirmatively re-map the Illinois districts. . . ." But this is true in many areas of Supreme Court adjudication. The Court does not, for example, give affirmative orders when it reverses the action of a federal administrative agency because of some basic legal error in its proceedings. It simply lays bare the error and forces further action by the agency. Nor does the Court redraft a city license system for street-corner orators when it finds the system in violation of the Constitution. Judicial invalidation of a statute returns the problem to the legislature.

The remedy of requiring an election at large until the legislature creates valid districts was criticized on two grounds in *Colegrove*: elections at large may be politically undesirable, and a court decree requiring such election may be unenforceable because of resistance by the state or refusal of the House to seat representatives so chosen. But the remedy of the election at large is simply a spur to legislative action, not an end in itself. It would be so burdensome for all the representatives in a large state or the entire membership of the legislature to carry on statewide campaigns that redistricting almost inevitably would result from a decree requiring an election at large. Actual experience in the use of the remedy confirms this fact.

Four times large states have been required by court orders to elect their entire congressional delegations at large. This followed from the Supreme Court decisions in *Smiley* v. *Holm* and *Carroll* v. *Becker,* the Virginia court's decision in *Brown* v. *Saunders,* and the decision of a federal district court in *Hume* v. *Mahan.* In all four instances the states proceeded to elect their representatives at large, and the House seated each delegation without recorded objection. And in the three cases in which the decrees were final the legislatures redistricted before the next election.

The history of Illinois after the *Colegrove* decision is suggestive. Just a year later the state's congressional districts were revised by the legislature for the first time in over forty years. Governor Green, who pushed the reapportionment bill through the legislature, recently attributed its passage in part to the fear that the Supreme Court might otherwise take jurisdiction in some future case and require an election at large. Senator Douglas has similarly explained the 1947 Illinois congressional reapportionment.

A recent Hawaiian case, *Dyer* v. *Kazuhisa Abe,* gives significant evidence of the effectiveness of the threat that an election at large will be required. A suit brought in a federal district court attacked the districts of the territorial legislature, unchanged since 1901, as in violation of the fourteenth amendment and of a provision of the Hawaii Organic Act requiring regular reapportionment. An injunction was sought to require an election at large.

In the reported opinion the court denied a motion to dismiss. After trial the judge announced orally his decision to grant the requested relief. Congress then rendered the case moot. In an amendment to the Organic Act it laid out new Hawaiian legislative districts, shifted authority to redistrict from the legislature to the governor, and authorized the territorial supreme court to compel the governor's action by mandamus. The meagre legislative history contains no reference to *Dyer* v. *Kazuhisa Abe,* but it seems reasonable to see more than coincidence in the fact that the first reapportionment in fifty years followed so closely upon the initial success of the litigation. In these examples of the use or threatened use of the election at large there is no hint of the unenforceability of a decree or of resistance by either the state legislatures or Congress. And the legislatures have in fact moved independently toward affirmative approval of a judicial role in apportionment.

Ten states, Hawaii, and Alaska have adopted constitutional provisions to take the responsibility for apportionment away from the political branch. A constitutional amendment to the same effect has been approved by the legislature of Washington and will be submitted to the voters in 1958. In seven of these thirteen plans, a special board, or the secretary of state, is designated to reapportion if the legislature does not do so on schedule. In the remaining six the apportionment job has been taken from the legislature entirely and given to a board, the secretary of state, or the governor.

In eight of these states and territories the courts are specifically authorized by the plans—or have actually exercised the power—to compel reapportionment by mandamus or other writ, to compel adherence to standards of equality and/or to revise the districts themselves. In two other of these states the courts have indicated that they would review apportionments in appropriate cases. In the remaining three states there has been no test of a court role. And the threat of elections at large is used in two of the state plans as a device to force reapportionment. The Illinois house and the Missouri senate must be elected at large if new apportionments are not made by fixed dates.

C. LEGISLATIVE RESPONSIBILITY

The philosophy underlying the opinion in *Colegrove* v. *Green* is summed up in one sentence of the opinion:

> *It is hostile to a democratic system to involve the judiciary in the politics of the people.*

The argument is that in a democracy excessive reliance on the courts weakens the responsibility of the legislature and of the voters. And so those injured by unfair districts are remitted to the state legislatures and to Congress for relief. If this is not a cynical resolution of the problem—and it surely is not so intended—its premise must be that there is a reasonable chance of action in the legislative branches. But the historical evidence indicates that there is no basis whatsoever for this premise.

Legislative fairness in districting is inhibited by factors built into our political structure. Once a group has the dominant position—as the rural legislators generally have —its overriding interest is to maintain that position. The motives of most individual legislators are just as selfish. Any substantial change in districts means that the members must face new constituents and deal with uncertainties—in short, undergo risks that few politicians would voluntarily put upon themselves. Voting for a fair apportionment bill would in many cases mean voting oneself out of office. That is too much to ask of most politicians. The result is that the state legislatures do not reapportion fairly or, more commonly, do not reapportion at all. Some recent examples of the performance of state legislatures on apportionment problems indicate how futile it is to remit the disenfranchised for relief to the body which has failed to enfranchise them.

The Maryland constitution provides that there shall be submitted to the voters every twenty years a proposal for a constitutional convention, to be called by the General Assembly if the voters approve. The voters overwhelmingly endorsed a convention at their most recent opportunity, in 1950, but the malapportioned Assembly refused to call one for fear it might revise the constitution's apportionment provisions.

If the Florida legislature fails to reapportion in regular session, the constitution requires the legislators to sit in special session until they act. A special session was called in June 1955, and sat, with several recesses, until the new legislature was elected in 1956. The special session made minor, automatic changes in the allotment of house seats but was unable to agree upon a formula for the reapportionment of the senate acceptable to the governor. The legislature then moved to amend the constitution to drop the required continuous special session for apportionment.

In Washington the legislature had not been reapportioned since an initiative measure of 1930. In 1956 an initiative measure got on the ballot. Neither party organization supported it, but it passed. Thereupon the newly elected legislature—elected from the old districts—passed an act "amending" the initiative statute beyond recognition by creating less equitable districts. A suit was brought in the state supreme court seeking mandamus to require use of the initiative measure. The court, dividing five to four, denied the writ. At least one other state court has prevented legislative sabotage of a popularly initiated reapportionment. The last general redistricting of the Colorado legislature was accomplished by initiative in 1932. The legislature passed its own, less equitable statute in 1933, but the courts threw it out.

A recent analysis of malapportionment in the state legislatures demonstrates what can be expected if the problem is left to the legislatures themselves. It shows that the upper houses in 38 states were less representative of population in 1955 than in 1937, and the lower houses less representative in 35 of the 46 states for which data were available.

The state legislatures have also had full control over congressional districts, and the results are similar. A table appended to Mr. Justice Frankfurter's opinion in *Colegrove* listed the most and least populous districts in each state in 1946. A comparison with the same figures for 1957 shows that the disparity has increased in 27 states. 10 states cannot be rated because of elections at large. In only 11 states have the congressional districts become more equitable. And all but 2 of those states were encouraged to redistrict because they lost or gained seats in the 1950 census. As to any hope for reform through the state legislatures, a state court was surely correct when it said many years ago:

> *It would be idle and useless to recommit such an apportionment to the voluntary action of the body that made it.*

That Congress can effectively enforce equitable districting—the alternative suggestion in *Colegrove*—is flatly negatived by history and by political horse sense. Twice in the House, in 1901 and 1910, seating of a member has been challenged on the ground that his district did not meet standards of equality. Both challenges were rejected. Committee reports advanced four reasons for not excluding elected members from their seats as a device to enforce district equality: (1) Such action would leave the voters in the affected districts without any representation for two years. (2) It would put enforcement of the equality requirement in the hands of the transitory House majority and might lead to politicking on a larger scale with the apportionment problem. (3) Members would be prey to constant uncertainty, not knowing when their seats might become pawns in some party struggle in the House. (4) To enforce equality "spasmodically" by occasional challenges to seating would be unfair and ineffective; it should be done "universally," as to all districts.

These objections to enforcement by the House seem unanswerable. Other suggestions for congressional enforcement seem equally to lack merit. It has been suggested, for example, that Congress direct the withholding of federal-aid funds from states with inequitable districts, or that Congress draw all the districts itself or set up a national board to do so. The political absurdity of these proposals needs no comment.

It is difficult to see how a policy of equal congressional representation can be enforced as it should be enforced—before elections, nationally, nonpolitically—without the use of the judiciary. Representative Celler's proposed apportionment legislation recognizes the necessity for a judicial role. It would provide for enforcement of its standard of equality in these terms:

> *Any establishment of congressional districts in any State shall be subject to review, at the suit of any citizen of such State, by the district court of the United States for the district in which such citizens* [sic] *resides. . . .*

Surely the Supreme Court would carry out the function of enforcing equality in congressional districts if Congress so ordered. But a realist must recognize that legislation like the Celler bill has little chance of passage. Members of Congress are no more likely to vote themselves out of office than are state legislators. The real alternatives would seem to be intervention by the federal courts or continued inaction.

V. THE COURT SHOULD ACT

Unequal districts have been part of the American political scene, as Mr. Justice Frankfurter observed in *Colegrove,* for generations. Why, then, should the federal courts undertake at this time to deal with the problem? The preliminary observation may be made that no legitimate interests or expectations have become settled as a result of past judicial inaction. But there are affirmative reasons for intervention now by the federal courts.

First, the provisions of a Constitution drawn with "purposeful vagueness" have always been interpreted and enforced by the Supreme Court in accordance with the changing needs of government and society. Interests which at one time received no judicial protection have been given that protection when their importance emerged. It was almost sixty years, for example, before the Supreme Court found any protection for free speech in the fourteenth amendment.

The effects of malapportionment are much graver today than they were a century ago. In a day when the federal government subsisted primarily on tariff revenues, unequal representation could be regarded as an insignificant evil; government itself had a less significant impact on society. But when the federal and state governments spend a third of the national income, when they are relied upon to regulate every aspect of a complex industrial civilization, the consequences of unequal representation are correspondingly more severe. The rapid growth of our population and change in its character make even more urgent the need for regular, equitable adjustment of representation.

Second, in weighing the appropriateness of judicial intervention, courts consider not only the gravity of the evil assailed but the unlikelihood of its correction by other means. This is the teaching of the Supreme Court's tentative efforts to outline a modern philosophy of judicial review. These efforts at articulation began with the suggestion by Mr. Justice Stone, in his footnote to *Carolene Products,* that courts should be "more exacting" in their view of restrictions on political liberties. Just before he went on the Court, Robert H. Jackson commented:

> [*W*]*hen the channels of opinion and of peaceful persuasion are corrupted or clogged, these political correctives can no longer be relied on, and the democratic system is threatened at its most vital point. In that event the Court, by intervening, restores the processes of democratic government; it does not disrupt them. . . .*
>
> [*A*] *court which is governed by a sense of self-restraint does not thereby become paralyzed. It simply conserves its strength to strike more telling blows in the cause of a working democracy.*

Particular formulations have been the subject of dispute, but there would seem to be general agreement in the Supreme Court today that what Mr. Justice Frankfurter has called "the indispensable conditions of a free society" deserve special judicial protection. Perhaps the most useful conception suggested so far is that the courts should be free to step in when the political process provides no inner check, as in the case of legislation affecting interests which have no voice in the legislature.

The Supreme Court has applied these principles especially in the area of free speech. If speech by a dissident minority is of sufficient importance to the political health of society to deserve special judicial protection, surely there is greater warrant for intervention by the courts when "the streams of legislation . . . become poisoned at the source." Of what use is the right of a minority—or a majority, as is often the case in malapportioned districts—to apply persuasion if the very machinery of government prevents political change?

Malapportionment is a disease incurable by legislative physic. No one would suggest that the federal courts can provide a quick, complete remedy. What they have to offer is chiefly their educational and moral influence. Judge Wyzanski has said that the Supreme Court

> *has perhaps been primarily an educational force rather than an absolute restraint. And no estimate of the role of the Court can overlook the contribution which judicial opinions have made to political thinking.*

Judging by the available evidence, it appears that the political branches would respond to moral leadership from the judiciary on the apportionment issue. The benefits that the courts can bring to the process will follow from their merely taking jurisdiction and requiring argument on the merits. Perhaps a spirit of commonsense self-limitation would weigh against the federal courts' granting relief in many cases. But for the first time those responsible for unequal representation would have to seek a justification better than the mere possession of power.

The federal courts cannot remake politics. But they can be a conscience, expressing ideas which take root in public and political opinion. Professor Freund has put it:

> The question is not whether the courts can do everything but whether they can do something. Moreover, the cleavage between growth from within and alteration imposed from without is not absolute. Education and the practice of self-improvement may be fostered by judicious judicial intervention.

Americans have traditionally looked to the courts for moral values, as they have tended to think politically in terms of moral judgments. Whatever their merits, these are our traditions. Only by putting them to use, with the help of the federal courts, can we begin to solve the problem of unequal representation.

C. THE TREND TOWARD JUDICIAL ACTION ON REAPPORTIONMENT

1. A Judicial Warning in New Jersey*

Failure of many state legislatures (including Iowa's) to provide for fair representation through periodic reapportionment has impelled many under-represented urban-dwellers to turn to the state and federal courts for assistance.

For many years, the courts were reluctant to enter what Justice Felix Frankfurter referred to in 1946 as this "political thicket."

But a startling change in attitude has developed during the last few years. The change was harbingered by a federal district court action in 1958 (*Magraw* vs. *Donovan*) which stimulated the Minnesota state legislature to enact a reapportionment bill.

The supreme court of New Jersey last June similarly indicated what it would consider appropriate action if the state legislature failed to act in its 1961 session. The occasion was the decision in *Asbury Park Press, Inc.* vs. *J. Russell Wooley, County Clerk of the County of Monmouth.*

The basis for this prospective judicial intervention should be of interest to urban dwellers throughout the nation, for the reasoning of the New Jersey jurists was not limited to the scope of the New Jersey constitution but suggested that either deliberate malapportionment or legislative inaction resulting in unequal representation constituted violation of the "equal protection of the laws" clause of the 14th Amendment.

Because of the distinguished character of the New Jersey supreme court (Arthur

*John R. Schmidhauser, "Comment," *Cedar Rapids Gazette,* January 1, 1961, p. 4.

Vanderbilt served as its chief justice until his death and William Brennan served as an associate justice until his elevation to the U.S. Supreme Court in 1956), its views could well be influencial beyond its jurisdiction. Writing for a unanimous court, Justice Francis stated that:

> . . . *No man can boast of a higher privilege than the right granted to the citizens of our state and nation of equal suffrage and thereby to equal representation in making of the laws of the land. Under our Constitution that right is absolute. It is one of which he cannot be deprived, either deliberately or by inaction on the part of the legislature. Inaction which causes an apportionment act to have unequal and arbitrary effects throughout the state is just as much a denial of equality as if a positive statute had been passed to accomplish the result. In our view, such deprivation not only offends against the state constitution but may very well deny equal protection of the laws in violation of the 14th Amendment . . . . As the court of appeals of Kentucky declared in Stiglite vs. Schardion . . .*
>
> *Equality of representation in the legislative bodies of the state is a right preservative of all other rights. The source of the laws that govern the daily lives of the people, the control of the public purse from which the money of the taxpayers is distributed, and the power to make and measure the levy of taxes, are so essential, all inclusive, and vital that the consent of the governed ought to be obtained through representatives chosen at equal, free, and fair elections. If the principle of equality is denied, the spirit, purpose, and the very terms of the Constitution are emasculated. The failure to give a county or a district equal representation is not merely a matter of partisan strategy. It rises above any question of party, and reaches the very vitals of democracy itself.*
>
> *. . . The judicial branch of the government has imposed upon it the obligation of interpreting the Constitution and of safeguarding the basic rights granted thereby to the people. In this sphere of activity the courts recognize that they have no power to overturn a law adopted by the legislature within its constitutional limitations, even though the law may be unwise, impolitic or unjust. The remedy in such cases lies with the people.*
>
> *But when legislative action exceeds the boundaries of the authority delegated by the Constitution, and transgresses a sacred right guaranteed to a citizen, final decision as to the invalidity of such action must rest exclusively with the courts. It cannot be forgotten that ours is a government of laws and not men, and that the judicial department has imposed upon it the solemn duty to interpret the laws in the last resort. However delicate that duty may be, we are not at liberty to surrender or to ignore, or to waive it.*

2. Intervention by the Justice Department*

The United States Government threw its weight yesterday on the side of those who want the Federal Courts to intervene when state legislatures refuse year after year to reapportion their membership.

Washington Post, March 15, 1961, p. A 1.

In a brief filed with the Supreme Court, Solicitor General Archibald Cox asked the Justices to reverse the decision of a Federal Court in Tennessee. That Court restated the long-standing proposition that Federal Courts will not intervene in reapportionment disputes.

The reapportionment problem in many states is critical, Cox said. It is part of the reason, he charged, that state legislatures "Have in very large part failed to adapt themselves to modern problems and majority needs, and this failure has resulted in public cynicism, disillusionment, and loss of confidence."

Cox argued that the Supreme Court has never said that Federal Courts are powerless to intervene in reapportionment disputes. He said that a 1946 decision (*Colegrove* v. *Green*), often cited as meaning that Federal Courts must stay out of these fights, means only that they should stay out of most of them.

Where malapportionment is particularly bad, Cox said, the Courts must intervene to protect the constitutional right to vote.

Many states, including Maryland, have serious problems of reapportionment. A court case aimed at forcing reapportionment in Maryland was recently dismissed.

Cox asked the Supreme Court to overrule the Colegrove case if it disagreed with his interpretation of it. If the Court refused to do that, he added, it should refuse to extend that case, which concerned congressional apportionment, to state legislatures.

The Tennessee case will be argued here later this spring. It seeks a court order forcing an election at large if there is no reapportionment. The Constitution of Tennessee says the Legislature must reapportion its seats every 10 years. The last reapportionment act was passed in 1901.

3. The Court Acts: Baker v. Carr*

MR. JUSTICE BRENNAN DELIVERED THE OPINION OF THE COURT

This civil action was brought . . . to redress the alleged deprivation of federal constitutional rights. The complaint, alleging that by means of a 1901 statute of Tennessee apportioning the members of the General Assembly among the state's 95 counties, "these plaintiffs and others similarly situated, are denied the equal protection of the laws accorded them by the Fourteenth Amendment to the Constitution of the United States by virtue of the debasement of their votes," was dismissed by a three-judge court convened . . . in the Middle District of Tennessee. The court held that it lacked jurisdiction of the subject matter and also that no claim was stated upon which relief could be granted . . . We noted probable jurisdiction of the appeal. . . . We hold that the dismissal was error, and remand the cause to the District Court for trial and further proceedings consistent with this opinion.

The General Assembly of Tennessee consists of the Senate with 33 members and the House of Representatives with 99 members.

* * *

Baker v. *Carr*, 369 U.S. 186 (1962). [Citations omitted.]

. . . Tennessee's standard for allocating legislative representation among her counties is the total number of qualified voters resident in the respective counties, subject only to minor qualifications. Decennial reapportionment in compliance with the constitutional scheme was effected by the General Assembly each decade from 1871 to 1901. . . . In 1901 the General Assembly abandoned separate enumeration in favor of reliance upon the Federal Census and passed the Apportionment Act here in controversy. In the more than 60 years since that action, all proposals in both Houses of the General Assembly for reapportionment have failed to pass.

Between 1901 and 1961, Tennessee has experienced substantial growth and redistribution of her population. In 1901 the population was 2,020,616, of whom 487,380 were eligible to vote. The 1960 Federal Census reports the State's population at 3,567,089, of whom 2,092,891 are eligible to vote. The relative standings of the counties in terms of qualified voters have changed significantly. It is primarily the continued application of the 1901 Apportionment Act to this shifted and enlarged voting population which gives rise to the present controversy.

Indeed, the complaint alleges that the 1901 statute, even as of the time of its passage, "made no apportionment of Representatives and Senators in accordance with the constitutional formula . . . , but instead arbitrarily and capriciously apportioned representatives in the Senate and House without reference . . . to any logical or reasonable formula whatever." It is further alleged that "because of the population changes since 1900, and the failure of the legislature to reapportion itself since 1901," the 1901 statute became "unconstitutional and obsolete." Appellants also argue that, because of the composition of the legislature effected by the 1901 apportionment act, redress in the form of a state constitutional amendment to change the entire mechanism for reapportioning, or any other change short of that, is difficult or impossible. The complaint concludes that "these plaintiffs and others similarly situated, are denied the equal protection of the laws accorded them by the Fourteenth Amendment to the Constitution of the United States by virtue of the debasement of their votes." They seek a declaration that the 1901 statute is unconstitutional and an injunction restraining the appellees from acting to conduct any further elections under it. They also pray that unless and until the General Assembly enacts a valid reapportionment, the District Court should either decree a reapportionment by mathematical application of the Tennessee constitutional formulae to the most recent Federal Census figures, or direct the appellees to conduct legislative elections, primary and general, at large. They also pray for such other and further relief as may be appropriate.

I. THE DISTRICT COURT'S OPINION AND ORDER OF DISMISSAL

Because we deal with this case on appeal from an order of dismissal granted on appellees' motions, precise identification of the issues presently confronting us demands clear exposition of the grounds upon which the District Court rested in dismissing the case. The dismissal order recited that the court sustained the appellees' grounds "(1) that the Court lacks jurisdiction of the subject matter, and (2) that the complaint fails to state a claim upon which relief can be granted. . . ."

In the setting of a case such as this, the recited grounds embrace two possible reasons for dismissal:

First: That the facts and injury alleged, the legal bases invoked as creating the rights and duties relied upon, and the relief sought, fail to come within that language of Article III of the Constitution and of the jurisdictional statutes which define those matters concerning which United States District Courts are empowered to act;

Second: That, although the matter is cognizable and facts are alleged which establish infringement of appellants' rights as a result of state legislative action departing from a federal constitutional standard, the court will not proceed because the matter is considered unsuited to judicial inquiry or adjustment.

We treat the first ground of dismissal as "lack of jurisdiction of the subject matter." The second we consider to result in a failure to state a justiciable cause of action.

The District Court's dismissal order recited that it was issued in conformity with the court's *per curiam* opinion. The opinion reveals that the court rested its dismissal upon lack of subject-matter jurisdiction and lack of a justiciable cause of action without attempting to distinguish between these grounds. . . .

The court proceeded to explain its action as turning on the case's presenting a "question of the distribution of political strength for legislative purposes." For,

> *from a review of [numerous Supreme Court] . . . decisions there can be no doubt that the federal rule, as enunciated and applied by the Supreme Court, is that the federal courts, whether from a lack of jurisdiction or from the inappropriateness of the subject matter for judicial consideration, will not intervene in cases of this type to compel legislative reapportionment. . . .*

The court went on to express doubts as to the feasibility of the various possible remedies sought by the plaintiffs. . . . Then it made clear that its dismissal reflected a view not of doubt that violation of the constitutional rights was alleged, but of a court's impotence to correct that violation:

> *With the plaintiffs' argument that the Legislature of Tennessee is guilty of a clear violation of the state constitution and of the rights of the plaintiffs the Court entirely agrees. It also agrees that the evil is a serious one which should be corrected without further delay. But even so the remedy in this situation clearly does not lie with the courts. It has long been recognized and is accepted doctrine that there are indeed some rights guaranteed by the Constitution for the viloation of which the courts cannot give redress. . . .*

In light of the District Court's treatment of the case, we hold today only (a) that the court possessed jurisdiction of the subject matter; (b) that a justiciable cause of action is stated upon which appellants would be entitled to appropriate relief; and (c) because appellees raise the issue before this Court, that the appellants have standing to challenge the Tennessee apportionment statutes. Beyond noting that we have no cause at this stage to doubt the District Court will be able to fashion relief if violations of constitutional rights are found, it is improper now to consider what remedy would be most appropriate if appellants prevail at the trial.

II. JURISDICTION OF THE SUBJECT MATTER

The District Court was uncertain whether our cases withholding Federal judicial relief rested upon a lack of federal jurisdiction or upon the inappropriateness of the subject matter for judicial consideration—what we have designated "nonjusticiability." The distinction between the two grounds is significant. In the instance of non-justiciability, consideration of the cause is not wholly and immediately foreclosed; rather, the court's inquiry necessarily proceeds to the point of deciding whether the duty asserted can be judicially identified and its breach judicially determined, and whether protection for the right asserted can be judicially molded. In the instance of lack of jurisdiction the cause either does not "arise under" the Federal Constitution, laws or treaties (or fall within one of the other enumerated categories of Art. III, § 2), or is not a "case or controversy" within the meaning of that section; or the cause is not one described by any jurisdictional statute. Our conclusion . . . that this cause presents no nonjusticiable "political question" settles the only possible doubt that it is a case or controversy. Under the present heading of "Jurisdiction of the Subject Matter" we hold only that the matter set forth in the complaint does arise under the Constitution and is within 28 U.S.C. 1343.

Article III, § 2 of the Federal Constitution provides that "the judicial power shall extend to all Cases, in Law and Equity, arising under this Constitution, the Laws of the United States, and Treaties made, or which shall be made, under their Authority; . . ." It is clear that the cause of action is one which "arises under" the Federal Constitution. The complaint alleges that the 1901 statute effects an apportionment that deprives the appellants of the equal protection of the laws in violation of the Fourteenth Amendment. Dismissal of the complaint upon the ground of lack of jurisdiction of the subject matter would, therefore, be justified only if that claim were "so attenuated and unsubstantial as to be absolutely devoid of merit," *Newburyport Water Co.* v. *Newburyport* . . . or "frivolous," *Bell* v. *Hood* . . . That the claim is unsubstantial must be "very plain." *Hart* v. *Keith Vaudeville Exchange* . . . Since the District Court obviously and correctly did not deem the asserted federal constitutional claim unsubstantial and frivolous, it should not have dismissed the complaint for want of jurisdiction of the subject matter. And of course no further consideration of the merits of the claim is relevant to a determination of the court's jurisdiction of the subject matter. . . .

* * *

An unbroken line of our precedents sustains the federal courts' jurisdiction of the subject matter of federal constitutional claims of this nature. The first cases involved the redistricting of States for the purpose of electing Representatives to the Federal Congress. When the Ohio Supreme Court sustained Ohio legislation against an attack for repugnancy to Art. 1, § 4, of the Federal Constitution, we affirmed on the merits and expressly refused to dismiss for want of jurisdiction "in view . . . of the subject-matter of the controversy and the Federal characteristics which inhere in it. . . ." *Ohio ex rel. Davis* v. *Hildebrant* . . . When the Minnesota Supreme Court affirmed the dismissal of a suit to enjoin the Secretary of State of Minnesota from acting under Minnesota redistricting legislation, we reviewed the constitutional merits of the legislation and reversed the State Supreme Court. *Smiley* v. *Holm* . . . And see companion cases from the New York Court of Appeals and the Missouri Supreme Court, *Koenig* v. *Flynn* . . . ; *Carroll* v. *Becker,* . . .

The appellees refer to *Colegrove* v. *Green* . . . as authority that the District Court lacked jurisdiction of the subject matter. Appellees misconceive the holding of that case. The holding was precisely contrary to their reading of it. Seven members of the court participated in the decision. Unlike many other cases in this field which have assumed without discussion that there was jurisdiction, all three opinions filed in *Colegrove* discussed the question. Two of the opinions expressing the views of four of the Justices, a majority, flatly held that there was jurisdiction of the subject matter. MR. JUSTICE BLACK joined by MR. JUSTICE DOUGLAS and Mr. Justice Murphy stated: "It is my judgment that the District Court had jurisdiction . . . ," . . . Mr. Justice Rutledge, writing separately, expressed agreement with this conclusion. . . . Indeed, it is even questionable that the opinion of MR. JUSTICE FRANK-FURTER, joined by Justices Reed and Burton, doubted jurisdiction of the subject matter. Such doubt would have been inconsistent with the professed willingness to turn the decision on either the majority or concurring views in *Wood* v. *Broom* . . .

Several subsequent cases similar to *Colegrove* have been decided by the Court in summary *per curiam* statements. None was dismissed for want of jurisdiction of the subject matter. *Cook* v. *Fortson* . . . ; *Turman* v. *Duckworth* . . . ; *Colegrove* v. *Barrett* . . . ; *Tedesco* v. *Board of Supervisors* . . . ; *Remmey* v. *Smith* . . . ; *Cox* v. *Peters* . . . ; *Anderson* v. *Jordan* . . . ; *Kidd* v. *McCanless* . . . ; *Radford* v. *Gary* . . . ; *Hartsfield* v. *Sloan* . . . ; *Matthews* v. *Handley* . . .

Two cases decided with opinions after *Colegrove* likewise plainly imply that the subject matter of this suit is within District Court jurisdiction. In *MacDougall* v. *Green,* . . . the District Court dismissed for want of jurisdiction . . . a suit to enjoin enforcement of the requirement that nominees for state-wide elections be supported by a petition signed by a minimum number of persons from at least 50 of the State's 102 counties. This Court's disagreement with that action is clear since the Court affirmed the judgment after a review of the merits and concluded that the particular claim there was without merit. In *South* v. *Peters* . . . we affirmed the dismissal of an attack on the Georgia "county unit" system but founded our action on a ground that plainly would not have been reached if the lower court lacked jurisdiction of the subject matter . . . The express words of our holding were that "federal courts consistently refuse to exercise their equity powers in cases posing political issues arising from a state's geographical distribution of electoral strength among its political subdivisions. . . ."

We hold that the District Court has jurisdiction of the subject matter of the federal constitutional claim asserted in the complaint.

III. STANDING

A federal court cannot "pronounce any statute, either of a State or of the United States, void, because irreconcilable with the Constitution, except as it is called upon to adjudge the legal rights of litigants in actual controversies," *Liverpool Steamship Co.* v. *Commissioners of Emigration, . . .* Have the appellants alleged such a personal stake in the outcome of the controversy as to assure that concrete adverseness which sharpens the presentation of issues upon which the court so largely depends for illumination of difficult constitutional questions? This is the gist of the question of standing. It is, of course, a question of federal law.

The complaint was filed by residents of Davidson, Hamilton, Knox, Montgomery, and Shelby Counties. Each is a person allegedly qualified to vote for members of the General Assembly representing his county. These appellants sued "on their own behalf and on behalf of all qualified voters of their respective counties, and further, on behalf of all voters of the State of Tennessee who are similarly situated. . . ." The appellees are the Tennessee Secretary of State, Attorney General, Coordinator of Elections, and members of the State Board of Elections; the members of the State Board are sued in their own right and also as representatives of the County Election Commissioners whom they appoint.

We hold that the appellants do have standing to maintain this suit. Our decisions plainly support this conclusion. Many of the cases have assumed rather than articulated the premise in deciding the merits of similar claims. And *Colegrove* v. *Green, supra,* squarely held that voters who allege facts showing disadvantage to themselves as individuals have standing to sue. A number of cases decided after *Colegrove* recognized the standing of the voters there involved to bring those actions.

These appellants seek relief in order to protect or vindicate an interest of their own, and of those similarly situated. Their constitutional claim is, in substance, that the 1901 statute constitutes arbitrary and capricious state action, offensive to the Fourteenth Amendment in its irrational disregard of the standard of apportionment prescribed by the State's Constitution or of any standard, effecting a gross disproportion of representation to voting population. The injury which appellants assert is that this classification disfavors the voters in the counties in which they reside, placing them in a position of constitutionally unjustifiable inequality *vis-à-vis* voters in irrationally favored counties. A citizen's right to a vote free of arbitrary impairment by state action has been judicially recognized as a right secured by the Constitution, when such impairment resulted from dilution by a false tally, cf. *United States* v. *Classic . . .* ; or by a refusal to count votes from arbitrarily selected precincts, cf. *United States* v. *Mosley . . .* ; or by a stuffing of the ballot box, cf. *Ex parte Siebold . . .* ; *United States* v. *Saylor . . .*

* * *

IV. JUSTICIABILITY

In holding that the subject matter of the suit was not justiciable, the District Court relied on *Colegrove* v. *Green, supra,* and subsequent *per curiam* cases. The court stated: "From a review of these decisions there can be no doubt that the federal rule . . . is that the federal courts . . . will not intervene in cases of this type to compel legislative reapportionment." . . . We understand the District Court to have read the cited cases as compelling the conclusion that since the appellants sought to have a legislative apportionment held unconstitutional, their suit presented a "political question" and was therefore nonjusticiable. We hold that this challenge to an apportionment presents no nonjusticiable "political question." The cited cases do not hold the contrary.

Of course the mere fact that the suit seeks protection of a political right does not mean it presents a political question. Such an objection "is little more than a play upon words." *Nixon* v. *Herndon* . . . Rather, it is argued that apportionment cases, whatever the actual wording of the complaint, can involve no federal constitutional right except one resting on the guaranty of a republican form of government, and that complaints based on that clause have been held to present political questions which are nonjusticiable.

* * *

It is apparent that several formulations which vary slightly according to the settings in which the questions arise may describe a political question, although each has one or more elements which identifies it as essentially a function of the separation of powers. Prominent on the surface of any case held to involve a political question is found a textually demonstrable constitutional commitment of the issue to a coordinate political department; or a lack of judicially discoverable and manageable standards for resolving it; or the impossibility of deciding without an initial policy determination of a kind clearly for nonjudicial discretion; or the impossibility of a court's undertaking independent resolution without expressing lack of the respect due coordinate branches of government; or an unusual need for unquestioning adherence to a political decision already made; or the potentiality of embarrassment from multifarious pronouncements by various departments on one question.

Unless one of these formulations is inextricable from the case at bar, there should be no dismissal for non-justiciability on the ground of a political question's presence. The doctrine of which we treat is one of "political questions," not one of "political cases." The courts cannot reject as "no law suit" a bona fide controversy as to whether some action denominated "political" exceeds constitutional authority.

* * *

We come, finally to the ultimate inquiry whether our precedents as to what constitutes a nonjusticiable "political question" bring the case before us under the umbrella of that doctrine. A natural beginning is to note whether any of the common characteristics which we have been able to identify and label descriptively are present. We find none. The question here is the consistency of state action with the Federal Constitution. We have no question decided, or to be decided, by a political branch of government coequal with this Court. Nor do we risk embarrassment of our government abroad, or grave disturbance at home if we take issue with Tennessee as to the constitutionality of her action here challenged. Nor need the appellants, in order to succeed in this action, ask the Court to enter upon policy determinations for which judicially manageable standards are lacking. Judicial standards under the

Equal Protection Clause are well developed and familiar, and it has been open to courts since the enactment of the Fourteenth Amendment to determine, if on the particular facts they must, that a discrimination reflects *no* policy, but simply arbitrary and capricious action.

This case does, in one sense, involve the allocation of political power within a State, and the appellants might conceivably have added a claim under the Guaranty Clause. Of course, as we have seen, any reliance on that clause would be futile. But because any reliance on the Guaranty Clause could not have succeeded it does not follow that appellants may not be heard on the equal protection claim which in fact they tender. True, it must be clear that the Fourteenth Amendment claim is not so enmeshed with those political question elements which render Guaranty Clause claims nonjusticiable as actually to present a political question itself. But we have found that not to be the case here.

* * *

We conclude then that the nonjusticiability of claims resting on the Guaranty Clause which arises from their embodiment of questions that were thought "political," can have no bearing upon the justiciability of the equal protection claim presented in this case. Finally, we emphasize that it is the involvement in Guaranty Clause claims of the elements thought to define "political questions," and no other feature, which could render them nonjusticiable. Specifically, we have said that such claims are not held nonjusticiable because they touch matters of state governmental organization. Brief examination of a few cases demonstrates this.

When challenges to state action respecting matters of "the administration of the affairs of the State and the officers through whom they are concluded" have rested on claims of constitutional deprivation which are amenable to judicial correction, this Court has acted upon its view of the merits of the claim. For example, in *Boyd* v. *Nebraska ex rel. Thayer,* . . . we reversed the Nebraska Supreme Court's decision that Nebraska's Governor was not a citizen of the United States or of the State and therefore could not continue in office. In *Kennard* v. *Louisiana ex rel. Morgan* . . . and *Foster* v. *Kansas ex rel. Johnston,* . . . we considered whether persons had been removed from public office by procedures consistent with the Fourteenth Amendment's due process guaranty, and held on the merits that they had. And only last Term, in *Gomillion* v. *Lightfoot,* . . . we applied the Fifteenth Amendment to strike down a redrafting of municipal boundaries which effected a discriminatory impairment of voting rights, in the face of what a majority of the Court of Appeals thought to be a sweeping commitment to state legislatures of the power to draw and redraw such boundaries.

Gomillion was brought by a Negro who had been a resident of the City of Tuskegee, Alabama, until the municipal boundaries were so recast by the State Legislature as to exclude practically all Negroes. The plaintiff claimed deprivation of the right to vote in municipal elections. The District Court's dismissal for want of jurisdiction and failure to state a claim upon which relief could be granted was affirmed by the Court of Appeals. This court unanimously reversed. This court's answer to the argument that States enjoyed unrestricted control over municipal boundaries was:

Legislative control of municipalities, no less than other state power, lies within the scope of relevant limitations imposed by the United States Constitution ... The opposite conclusion, urged upon us by respondents, would sanction the achievement by a State of any impairment of voting rights whatever so long as it was cloaked in the garb of the realignment of political subdivisions. "It is inconceivable that guaranties embedded in the Constitution of the United States, may thus be manipulated out of existence."

* * *

Since, as has been established, the equal protection claim tendered in this case does not require decision of any political question, and since the presence of a matter affecting state government does not render the case non-justiciable, it seems appropriate to examine again the reasoning by which the District Court reached its conclusion that the case was nonjusticiable.

We have already noted that the District Court's holding that the subject matter of this complaint was nonjusticiable relied upon *Colegrove* v. *Green, supra,* and later cases. Some of those concerned the choice of members of a state legislature, as in this case; others, like *Colegrove* itself and earlier precedents, *Smiley* v. *Holm, . . . Koenig* v. *Flynn, . . .* and *Carroll* v. *Becker . . .* concerned the choice of Representatives in the Federal Congress. . . . The Court followed these precedents in *Colegrove* although over the dissent of three of the seven Justices who participated in that decision. On the issue of justiciability, all four Justices comprising a majority relied upon *Smiley* v. *Holm,* but in two opinions, one for three Justices . . . and a separate one by Mr. Justice Rutledge . . .

* * *

Indeed, the refusal to award relief in *Colegrove* resulted only from the controlling view of a want of equity. Nor is anything contrary to be found in those *per curiams* that came after *Colegrove.* This Court dismissed the appeals in *Cook* v. *Fortson* and *Turman* v. *Duckworth . . .* as moot. *MacDougall* v. *Green . . .* held only that in that case equity would not act to void the State's requirement that there be at least a minimum of support for nominees for state-wide office, over at least a minimal area of the State. Problems of timing were critical in *Remmey* v. *Smith . . . ,* dismissing for want of a substantial federal question a three-judge court's dismissal of the suit as prematurely brought . . . ; and in *Hartsfield* v. *Sloan . . . ,* denying mandamus sought to compel the convening of a three-judge court—movants urged the Court to advance consideration of their case, "inasmuch as the mere lapse of time before this case can be reached in the normal course of . . . business may defeat the cause, and inasmuch as the time problem is due to the inherent nature of the case. . . ." *South* v. *Peters . . . ,* like *Colegrove* appears to be a refusal to exercise equity's powers . . .

Tedesco v. *Board of Supervisors . . .* indicates solely that no substantial federal question was raised by a state court's refusal to upset the districting of city council seats, especially as it was urged that there was a rational justification for the challenged districting. . . . Similarly, in *Anderson* v. *Jordan . . . ,* it was certain only that the state court had refused to issue a discretionary writ, original mandamus in the

Supreme Court. That had been denied without opinion, and of course it was urged here that an adequate state ground barred this Court's review. And in *Kidd* v. *Mc-Canless* . . . , the Supreme Court of Tennessee held that it could not invalidate the very statute at issue in the base at bar, but its holding rested on its state law of remedies, *i.e.*, the state view of *de facto* officers, and not on any view that the norm for legislative apportionment in Tennessee is not numbers of qualified voters resident in the several counties. Of course this court was there precluded by the adequate state ground, and in dismissing the appeal, . . . we cited *Anderson, supra,* as well as *Colegrove.* Nor does the Tennessee court's decision in that case bear upon this, for just as in *Smith* v. *Holm* . . . and *Magraw* v. *Donovan,* . . . a state court's inability to grant relief does not bar a federal court's assuming jurisdiction to inquire into alleged deprivation of federal constitutional rights. Problems of relief also controlled in *Radford* v. *Gary,* . . . affirming the District Court's refusal to mandamus the Governor to call a session of the legislature, to mandamus the legislature then to apportion, and if they did not comply, to mandamus the State Supreme Court to do so. . . . Lastly, *Colegrove* v. *Barrett,* . . . in which Mr. Justice Rutledge concurred in this Court's refusal to note the appeal from a dismissal for want of equity, is sufficiently explained by his statement in *Cook* v. *Fortson, supra*: "The discretionary exercise or nonexercise of equitable or declaratory judgment jurisdiction . . . in one case is not precedent in another case where the facts differ.". . .

We conclude that the complaint's allegations of a denial of equal protection present a justiciable constitutional cause of action upon which appellants are entitled to a trial and a decision. The right asserted is within the reach of judicial protection under the Fourteenth Amendment.

The judgment of the District Court is reversed and the cause is remanded for further proceedings consistent with this opinion.

Reversed and remanded.

Mr. Justice Whittaker did not participate in the decision of this case.

[The separate concurring opinions of Justices Tom Clark, Potter Stewart, and William O. Douglas are omitted as is the dissenting opinion of Justice Felix Frankfurter (which is joined in by Justice John Marshall Harlan).]

D. JUDICIAL ACTION CONFRONTS THE LOCAL POLITICAL ORDER

[Generations of students in constitutional law have read with satisfaction the broad doctrine of *Tumey* v. *Ohio*—due process is violated when a judge has a personal pecuniary interest in the outcome of a proceeding over which he presides. Yet the practice which the decision presumably prohibits is still utilized in one form or another in many jurisdictions. The resistance of the local political order to the doctrine is predicated in part upon tradition, in part upon the rewards of a lucrative system of fees, and finally upon widespread public indifference.]

1. *Doctrine Prohibiting Judicial Pecuniary Interest:*
Tumey *v*. Ohio*

MR. JUSTICE TAFT DELIVERED THE OPINION OF THE COURT

The question in this case is whether certain statutes of Ohio, in providing for the trial by the mayor of a village of one accused of violating the Prohibition Act of the State, deprive the accused of due process of law and violate the Fourteenth Amendment to the Federal Constitution, because of the pecuniary and other interest which those statutes give the mayor in the result of the trial.

The fees which the Mayor and Marshal received in this case came to them by virtue of the general statutes of the state applying to all state cases, liquor and otherwise. The Mayor was entitled to hold the legal fees taxed in his favor. . . . Moreover, the North College Hill village council sought to remove all doubt on this point by providing . . . that he should receive or retain the amount of his costs in each case, in addition to his regular salary, as compensation for hearing such cases. But no fees or costs in such cases are paid him except by the defendant if convicted. There is, therefore, no way by which the Mayor may be paid for his service as judge, if he does not convict those who are brought before him; nor is there any fund from which marshals, inspectors and detectives can be paid for their services in arresting and bringing to trial and furnishing the evidence to convict in such cases, except it be from the initial $500 which the village may vote from its treasury to set the court going, or from a fund created by the fines thereafter collected from convicted defendants.

By an Act of 1913 . . . the Mayor's court in villages in Hamilton County and in half a dozen other counties with large cities, was deprived of jurisdiction to hear and punish misdemeanors committed in the county beyond the limits of the corporation. The Prohibition Act, known as the Crabbe Act, adopted in 1920 . . . changed this, and gave to the Mayor of every village in the State jurisdiction within the county in which it was situated to try violations of that Act.

Counsel for the State in their brief explain the vesting by state legislatures of this country of jurisdiction in village courts as follows: "The purpose of extending the jurisdiction in the first instance was to break up places of outlawry that were located on the municipal boundary just outside of the city. The Legislature also faced the situation that in some of the cities the law enforcement agencies were failing to perform their duty, and, therefore, in order that those forces that believe in enforcement and upholding of law might have some courts through which process could be had, it gave to mayors county-wide jurisdiction." It was further pointed out in argument that the system by which the fines to be collected were to be divided between the State and the village was for the proper purpose of stimulating the activities of the village officers to such due enforcement.

The Village of North College Hill in Hamilton County, Ohio, is shown by the federal census to have a population of 1104. That of Hamilton County, including the City of Cincinnati, is more than half a million. The evidence discloses that Mayor

*273 U.S. 510–535 (1926). [Footnotes and citations omitted.]

Pugh came to office after ordinance No. 125 was adopted, and that there was a division of public sentiment in the village as to whether the ordinance should continue in effect. A petition opposing it and signed by a majority of the voters was presented to Mayor Pugh. To this the Mayor answered with the declaration that, if the village was in need of finances, he was in favor of and would carry on "the Liquor Court," as it was popularly called, but that if the court was not needed for village financial reasons, he would not do so. It appears that substantial sums were expended out of the village treasury, from the fund made up of the fines thus collected, for village improvements and repairs. The Mayor was the owner of a house in the village.

Between May 11, 1923 and December 31, 1923, the total amount of fines for violation of the prohibition law, collected by this village court, was upwards of $20,000, from which the State received $8,992.50, North College Hill received $4,471.25 for its general uses, $2,697.25 was placed to the credit of the village safety fund, and the balance was put in the secret service fund. Out of this, the person acting as prosecutor in the liquor court received in that period $1,796.50; the deputy marshals, inspectors and other employes, including the detectives, received $2,697.75 and $438.50 was paid for costs in transporting prisoners, serving writs and other services in connection with the trial of these cases. Mayor Pugh received $696.35 from these liquor cases during that period, as his fees and costs, in addition to his regular salary.

That officers acting in a judicial or quasi-judicial capacity are disqualified by their interest in the controversy to be decided is, of course, the general rule. . . . Nice questions, however, often arise as to what the degree or nature of the interest must be. One is in respect of the effect of the membership of a judge in a class of taxpayers or others to be affected by a principle of law, statutory or constitutional, to be applied in a case between other parties and in which the judge has no other interest. Then the circumstance that there is no judge not equally disqualified to act in such a case has been held to affect the question. . . . We are not embarrassed by such considerations here, for there were available in this case other judicial officers who had no disqualification either by reason of the character of their compensation or their relation to the village government.

All questions of judicial qualification may not involve constitutional validity. Thus matters of kinship, personal bias, state policy, remoteness of interest, would seem generally to be matters merely of legislative discretion. . . . But it certainly violates the Fourteenth Amendment, and deprives a defendant in a criminal case of due process of law, to subject his liberty or property to the judgment of a court the judge of which has a direct, personal, substantial, pecuniary interest in reaching a conclusion against him in his case.

The Mayor of the Village of North College Hill, Ohio, had a direct, personal, pecuniary interest in convicting the defendant who came before him for trial, in the twelve dollars of costs imposed in his behalf, which he would not have received if the defendant had been acquitted. This was not exceptional, but was the result of the normal operation of the law and the ordinance. Counsel for the State do not deny this, but assert the validity of the practice as an exception to the general rule. . . . They rely upon the cases of *Ownbey* v. *Morgan* . . . *Murray's Lessee* v. *Hoboken Land and Improvement Company* . . . These cases show that, in determining what due process of law is, under the Fifth or Fourteenth Amendment, the Court must look to those settled usages and modes of proceeding existing in the common and statute law of England before the emigration of our ancestors, which were shown not to have been acted on by them after the settlement of this country. Counsel contend that in Ohio and in other States, in the economy which it is found necessary to maintain in the administration of justice in the inferior courts by justices of the peace and by judicial officers of like jurisdiction, the only compensation which the State and county and township can afford is the fees and costs earned by them, and that such compensation is so small that it is not to be regarded as likely to influence improperly a judicial officer in the discharge of his duty, or as prejudicing the defendant in securing justice, even though the magistrate will receive nothing if the defendant is not convicted.

We have been referred to no cases at common law in England prior to the separation of colonies from the mother country showing a practice that inferior judicial officers were dependent upon the conviction of the defendant for receiving their compensation. Indeed, in analogous cases it is very clear that the slightest pecuniary interest of any officer, judicial or quasi-judicial in the resolving of the subject matter which he was to decide, rendered the decision voidable. . . .

As early as the 12th Richard II, A.D. 1388, it was provided that there should be a commission of the justices of the peace, with six justices in the county once a quarter, which might sit for three days, and that the justices should receive four shillings a day "as wages," to be paid by the sheriffs out of a fund made up of fines and amercements, and that that fund should be added to out of the fines and amercements from the courts of the Lords of the Franchises, which were hundred courts allowed by the King by grant to individuals.

It was required that the justices of the peace should be knights, esquires or gentlemen of the land—qualifications that were not modified until 1906. The wages paid were used "to defray their common diet," and soon became obsolete. . . . The wages paid were not dependent on conviction of the defendant. They were paid at a time when the distinction between torts and criminal cases was not clear . . . and they came from a fund which was created by fines and amercements collected from both sides in the controversy. There was always a plaintiff, whether in the action for a tort or the prosecution for an offense. In the latter he was called the prosecutor. If he failed to prove his case, whether civil or criminal, he was subject to amercement *pro falso clamore,* while if he succeeded, the defendant was *in misericordia.* . . . Thus in the outcome someone would be amerced in every case, and the amercements generally went to the Crown, and the fund was considerable. The Statute of Richard II remained on the statute book until 1855, when it was repealed by the 18th and 19th Victoria. Meantime the hundred courts by franchise had largely disappeared. The wages referred to were not part of the costs. The costs at common law were the amounts paid either by the plaintiff or prosecutor or by the defendant for the witnesses or services of the court officers. . . . For hundreds of years the justices of the peace of England seem not to have received compensation for court work. Instead of that, they were required, upon entering upon the office, to pay certain fees. . . . Local judges in towns are paid salaries.

There was at the common law the greatest sensitiveness over the existence of any pecuniary interest, however small or infinitesimal, in the justices of the peace. In Hawkins, 2 Pleas of the Crown, we find the following:

"The general rule of law certainly is that justices of the peace ought not to execute their office in their own case . . . ; and even in cases where such proceeding seems indispensably necessary, as in being publicly assaulted or personally abused, or their authority otherwise contemned while in the execution of their duty, yet if another justice be present, his assistance should be required to punish the offender (Stra. 240).

"And by the common law, if an order of removal were made by two justices, and one of them was an inhabitant of the parish from which the pauper was removed, such order was illegal and bad, on the ground that the justice who was an inhabitant was interested, as being liable to the poor's rate. . . ."

And this strict principle, unless there is relief by the statute, is seen in modern cases. . . .

There was, then, no usage at common law by which justices of the peace or inferior judicial officers were paid fees on condition that they convicted the defendants, and such a practice certainly can not find support as due process of law in English precedent. It may be that the principle, as stated in Blackstone, Book 3rd, page 400, that the King shall neither pay nor receive costs, because it is the King's prerogative not to pay them to a subject and is beneath his dignity to receive them, was misunderstood and led, as suggested by Mr. Lewis in his edition of Blackstone, . . . to the practice in some States, in minor cases, of allowing inferior judges no compensation except by fees collected of the convicted defendant; but whether it did or not, the principle relied on did not support the practice. That practice has prevailed, and still prevails, in Arkansas, Kentucky, Nebraska, North Carolina, Georgia, Ohio and Texas, and it seems at one time to have obtained in Indiana, Oregon, Illinois and Alabama.

In two of these States only has the question been considered by their courts, and it has been held that provision for payment to the judge of fees, only in case of conviction, does not disqualify him. Those are *Bennett* v. *State* . . . *Wellmaker* v. *Terrell* . . . There is no discussion in either of the question of due process of law. The existence of a statute authorizing the practice seems to have been the controlling consideration. Two other cases are cited. In *Ex parte Guerrero* . . . the judge was paid a regular salary, fixed by law. The fund out of which this was paid was increased by fees and fines collected in his court, but there is no evidence that payment of his salary was dependent on the amount of his collections or convictions. In *Herbert* v. *Baltimore County* . . . the action was by a justice of the peace against a county for services in criminal cases. A new law limited him to $10 a month. The statement of the case does not distinctly show that in convictions he would have had a larger compensation from his costs collected out of the defendant, but this may be assumed from the argument. His contention was that the new law was invalid because it did not give the defendants before him due process. The court held against him, chiefly on the ground that he must be satisfied with the compensation the law afforded him. Responding to his argument that the new law was invalid because justices would be induced to convict when in justice they should acquit, the court said:

"We can not recognize the force of this suggestion, founded as it is upon the assumption that the justices will violate their oaths and the duties of their office and not upon anything that the law authorizes to be done."

So far as the case goes, it is an authority for the contention of the State, but the issue thus raised was not considered at length and was not one which in such an action the court would be patient to hear pressed by the justice whose constitutional rights were not affected. . . .

In the case of *Probasco* v. *Raine, Auditor* . . . the question arose whether the fee of 4 per cent, payable to county auditors for placing omitted property on the duplicate list for taxation, which required investigation and quasi-judicial consideration, was invalid. The court held that it was not, and that the objection urged there could not be based on the argument that a man could not be a judge in his own case; that the auditor had no case to be adjudged, but that on the contrary he was the taxing officer before whom other parties were cited to appear and show cause why they should not bear their equal burden of taxation. The court said that the action of the auditor was not final so as to cut off further inquiry, but that the whole case might be gone into anew by proper proceedings in court. An exactly opposite conclusion was reached by the United States Circuit Court for the Northern District of Ohio in *Meyers* v. *Shields*. . . .

In other States than those above mentioned, the minor courts are paid for their services by the State or county regardless of acquittal or conviction, except that in Virginia the minor courts receive one-half of the usual fees where there is acquittal. Four States have put into their constitutions a provision that the State must pay the costs in such cases, in case of acqualal. They are California, Florida, Louisiana and South Carolina.

The strict common law rule was adopted in this country as one to be enforced where nothing but the common law controlled, and citizens and taxpayers have been held incompetent to sit in suits against the municipal corporation of which they have been residents. . . . With other courts, however, and with the legislatures, the strict rule seemed to be inconvenient, impracticable and unnecessary, and the view was taken that such remote or minute interest in the litigation might be declared by the Legislature not to be a reason for disqualification of a judge or juror.

A case, much cited, in which this conclusion was reached and in which the old English corporation cases were considered, was that of *City Council* v. *Pepper*. . . The recorder of the City of Charleston sentenced a non-resident of the city for violation of a city ordinance requiring him to take out a license for what he did or to pay a fine not exceeding $20. The contention was that the defendant was a non-corporator and non-resident and not subject to the jurisdiction of the city court; that the recorder was a corporator and interested in the penalty and therefore was not competent to try the cause. The Court said . . . in respect to *Hesketh* v. *Braddock* . . .

"It will be remarked that that case depends altogether upon the common law, and if the city court depended upon the same for its jurisdiction, the objection might be fatal. But the establishment and jurisdiction of the city court commences with the Act of 1801. By that Act it is clothed with the power of trying all offences against the by-laws of the city, and for that purpose is given concurrent jurisdiction with the court of Sessions. This grant of power is from all the people of the State, through their Legislature, and surely they have the power to dispense with the common law objection, that the corporators were interested, and ought not to be intrusted with the enforcement of their laws against others. The authority given to the city court to try all offenders against the city ordinances, impliedly declares, that notwithstanding the common law objection, it was right and proper to give it the power to enforce the city laws against all offenders. That there was great reason in this can not be doubted, when it is remembered that the interest of the corporators is so minute as not to be even thought of, by sheriff, juror or judge. It is very much like the interest which similar officers would feel in enforcing a State law, the sanction of which was a penalty. The sum thus to be recovered goes in exoneration of some part of the burden of government to which every citizen is subjected; but such an interest has no effect upon the mind. It is too slight to excite prejudice against a defendant. The same thing is the case here. For the judge, sheriff and jurors, are members of a corporation of many thousand members. What interest, of value, have they in a fine of twenty dollars? It would put a most eminent calculator to great trouble to ascertain the very minute grain of interest which each of these gentlemen might have. To remove so shadowy and slight an objection, the Legislature thought proper to clothe the city court, consisting of its judge, clerk, sheriff and jurors, with authority to try the defendant, and he can not now object to it." . . .

Mr. Justice Cooley, in his work on Constitutional Limitations, . . . points out that the real ground of the ruling in these cases is that "interest is so remote, trifling and insignificant that it may fairly be supposed to be incapable of affecting the judgment of or of influencing the conduct of an individual. And where penalties are imposed, to be recovered only in a municipal court, the judge or jurors in which would be interested as corporators in the recovery, the law providing for such recovery must be regarded as precluding the objection of interest." But the learned judge then proceeds:

"But except in cases resting upon such reasons, we do not see how the legislature can have any power to abolish a maxim which is among the fundamentals of judicial authority."

Referring then to a remark in the case of the *Matter of Leefe* . . . that the people of the State when framing their constitution might possibly establish so great an anomaly, if they saw fit, the learned author says:

"Even this must be deemed doubtful since the adoption of the fourteenth article of the amendments to the Federal Constitution, which denies to the state the right to deprive one of life, liberty or property, without due process of law."

From this review we conclude, that a system by which an inferior judge is paid for his service only when he convicts the defendant has not become so embedded by custom in the general practice either at common law or in this country that it can be regarded as due process of law, unless the costs usually imposed are so small that they may be properly ignored as within the maxim *de minimis non curat lex*.

The Mayor received for his fees and costs in the present case $12, and from such costs under the Prohibition Act for seven months he made about $100 a month, in addition to his salary. We can not regard the prospect of receipt or loss of such an emolument in each case as a minute, remote, trifling or insignificant interest. It is certainly not fair to each defendant, brought before the Mayor for the careful and judicial consideration of his guilt or innocence, that the prospect of such a loss by the Mayor should weigh against his acquittal.

These are not cases in which the penalties and the costs are negligible. The field of jurisdiction is not that of a small community engaged in enforcing its own local regulations. The court is a state agency, imposing substantial punishment, and the cases to be considered are gathered from the whole county by the energy of the village marshals, and detectives regularly employed by the village for the purpose. It is not to be treated as a mere village tribunal for village peccadilloes. There are doubtless mayors who would not allow such a consideration as $12 costs in each case to affect their judgment in it; but the requirement of due process of law in judicial procedure is not satisfied by the argument that men of the highest honor and the greatest self-sacrifice could carry it on without danger of injustice. Every procedure which would offer a possible temptation to the average man as a judge to forget the burden of proof required to convict the defendant, or which might lead him not to hold the balance nice, clear and true between the State and the accused, denies the latter due process of law.

But the pecuniary interest of the Mayor in the result of his judgment is not the only reason for holding that due process of law is denied to the defendant here. The statutes were drawn to stimulate small municipalities in the country part of counties in which there are large cities to organize and maintain courts to try persons accused of violations of the Prohibition Act everywhere in the country. The inducement is offered of dividing between the State and the village the large fines provided by the law for its violations. The trial is to be had before a mayor without a jury, without opportunity for retrial and with a review confined to questions of law presented by a bill of exceptions, with no opportunity by the reviewing court to set aside the judgment on the weighing of evidence, unless it should appear to be so manifestly against the evidence as to indicate mistake, bias or willful disregard of duty by the trial court. The statute specifically authorizes the village to employ detectives, deputy marshals and other assistants to detect crime of this kind all over the county, and to bring offenders before the Mayor's court, and it offers to the village council and its officers a means of substantially adding to the income of the village to relieve it from further taxation. The mayor is the chief executive of the village. He supervises all the other executive officers. He is charged with the business of looking after the finances of the village. It appears from the evidence in this case, and would be plain if the evidence did not show it, that the law is calculated to awaken the interest of all those in the village charged with the responsibility of raising the public money and expending it, in the pecuniarily successful conduct of such a court. The mayor represents the village and can not escape his representative capacity. On the other hand, he is given the judicial duty, first, of determining whether the defendant is guilty at all, and second, having found his guilt, to measure his punishment between $100 as a minimum and $1,000 as a maximum for first offenses, and $300 as a minimum and $2,000 as a maximum for second offenses. With his interest, as mayor, in the financial condition of the village, and his responsibility therefor, might not a defendant with reason say that he feared he could not get a fair trial or a fair sentence from one who would have so strong a motive to help his village by conviction and a heavy fine? The old English cases, cited above, of the days of Coke and Holt and Mansfield, are not nearly so strong. A situation in which an official perforce occupies two practically and seriously inconsistent positions, one partisan and the other judicial, necessarily involves a lack of due process of law in the trial of defendants charged with crimes before him. . . . It is, of course, so common to vest the mayor of villages with inferior judicial functions that the mere union of the executive power and the judicial power in him can not be said to violate due process of law. The minor penalties usually attaching to the ordinances of a village council, or to the misdemeanors in which the mayor may pronounce final judgment without a jury, do not involve any such addition to the revenue of the village as to justify the fear that the mayor would be influenced in his judicial judgment by that fact. The difference between such a case and the plan and operation of the statutes before us is so plain as not to call for further elaboration.

Counsel for the State argue that it has been decided by this Court that the legislature of a State may provide such system of courts as it chooses; that there is nothing in the Fourteenth Amendment that requires a jury trial for any offender; that it may give such territorial jurisdiction to its courts as it sees fit; and therefore that there is nothing sinister or constitutionally invalid in giving to a village mayor the jurisdiction of a justice of the peace to try misdemeanors committed anywhere in the county, even though the mayor presides over a village of 1,100 people and exercises jurisdiction over offenses committed in a county of 500,000. This is true and is established by the decisions of this Court in *Missouri* v. *Lewis* . . . It is also correctly pointed out that it is completely within the power of the legislature to dispose of the fines collected in criminal cases as it will, and it may therefore divide the fines as it does here, one-half to the State and one-half to the village by whose mayor they are imposed and collected. It is further said with truth that the legislature of a State may, and often ought to, stimulate prosecutions for crime by offering to those who shall initiate and carry on such prosecutions rewards for thus acting in the interest of the State and the people. The legislature may offer rewards or a percentage of the recovery to informers. . . . It may authorize the employment of detectives. But these principles do not at all affect the question whether the State by the operation of the statutes we have considered has not vested the judicial power in one who by reason of his interest, both as an individual and as chief executive of the village, is disqualified to exercise it in the trial of the defendant.

It is finally argued that the evidence shows clearly that the defendant was guilty and that he was only fined $100, which was the minimum amount, and therefore that he can not complain of a lack of due process, either in his conviction or in the amount of the judgment. The plea was not guilty and he was convicted. No matter what the evidence was against him, he had the right to have an impartial judge. He seasonably raised the objection and was entitled to halt the trial because of the disqualification of the judge, which existed both because of his direct pecuniary interest in the outcome, and because of his official motive to convict and to graduate the fine to help the financial needs of the village. There were thus presented at the outset both features of the disqualification.

The judgment of the Supreme Court of Ohio must be reversed and the cause remanded for further proceedings not inconsistent with this opinion.

Judgment reversed.

[Renewed interest in justice of the peace courts was created when the Kentucky Court of Appeals in its 1956 opinion in *Roberts* v. *Noel* reached the conclusion that the United States Supreme Court in its 1927 decision in *Tumey* v. *Ohio* intended, and did outlaw all judicial systems in which the trial judge is compensated solely by fees paid by convicted persons. This decision has direct application to Kentucky justices of the peace who are compensated in this manner. The Court will not issue a mandate to enforce its ruling until the expiration of the terms of incumbent justices; however, it has ordered that, before such officials may proceed to try cases, they must inform defendants of their right to demand trial before an impartial court. On a national level, too, the decision has signal importance in that it is the first decision of a state court of last resort, at least so far as the author is aware, voiding entirely the criminal jurisdiction of justice courts. It seems proper, therefore, to re-examine the Supreme Court's decision in the *Tumey* case, together with subsequent interpretations of the decision by the Kentucky Court of Appeals and other state supreme courts.]

2. Pecuniary Interest of Justices of the Peace in Kentucky*

THE TUMEY DECISION

Those who question the constitutionality of misdemeanor cases conducted in justice courts presided over by justices having a pecuniary interest in their result generally rely upon the United States Supreme Court's decision in *Tumey* v. *Ohio*. What this case holds is not exactly clear; the Supreme Court itself has never given adequate explanation of it; and a reading of various state supreme court opinions interpreting it reveals considerable disagreement concerning its actual meaning.

In the case itself, one Tumey was tried and convicted, on a charge of possessing intoxicating liquor, in a mayor's court in North College Hill, Ohio, after his protest that he could not receive a fair trial because of the mayor's financial interest in his conviction. He was tried before the mayor without a jury, without opportunity for retrial, and with review of his case confined to questions of law. In the event of acquittal, the mayor received no compensation. In this particular case, his fees and costs amounted to $12. The village of North College Hill, of which the mayor was chief executive officer, was also in need of revenues, and half of the fines imposed by the mayor's court went to the village treasury. The operation of the mayor's "liquor

*Kenneth Vanlandingham, "Pecuniary Interest of Justices of the Peace in Kentucky: The Aftermath of *Tumey* v. *Ohio*," *Kentucky Law Journal*, XLV (Summer, 1957), 607–25. [Footnotes omitted.] Reproduced with permission of the author and the publisher. Copyright © 1957 by the *Kentucky Law Journal*.

court," which had county-wide jurisdiction, was evidently intended to provide increased village revenue. For the purpose of enforcing the prohibition law—and also increasing village revenue—the city council was empowered to use any part of the fines going to the city treasury to hire attorneys, detectives, or secret service officers.

In its opinion, the Supreme Court noted that, under the common law, the slightest pecuniary interest of any officer, judicial or quasi-judicial, in resolving the subject matter which he was to decide rendered the decision voidable. Finally, it stated, "From this review, we conclude that a system by which an inferior judge is paid for his services only when he convicts the defendant has not become so embedded by custom in the general practice either at common law or in this country that it can be regarded as due process of law, unless the costs usually imposed are so small that they may be properly ignored as within the maxim *de minimis non curat lex."* The Court also stated, "Every procedure which would offer a possible temptation to the average man as judge to forget the burden of proof required to convict the defendant, or which might lead him not to hold the balance, nice, clear and true between the State and the accused, denies the latter due process of law."

While the Supreme Court recognized Ohio's authority to create courts and to establish their jurisdiction, it held that such recognition did not at all affect the question of whether the state had by law vested judicial power in one, who by reason of his interest both as an individual and as chief administrative officer of the village, was disqualified to exercise it. Tumey, the Court said, still had the right to an impartial judge. He had seasonably raised an objection and was entitled to stop the trial because of the disqualification of the judge and because of his official motive to convict.

INTERPRETATION OF THE TUMEY CASE BY COURTS OUTSIDE KENTUCKY

Since the *Tumey* decision, attempts have been made in several states to invalidate convictions in justice courts where it appeared that justices were financially interested in returning convictions. The majority of such efforts have proved unsuccessful, however, because most state supreme courts hold that circumstances present in such cases are unlike those of the *Tumey* case. Some courts hold that the right to demand a jury trial and the right of appeal with a trial *de novo* removes a case from the *Tumey* class. According to such courts, if a fair trial is obtainable anywhere within a state judicial system due process of law can not be said to be denied. In some of these cases there also existed the procedural point that exhaustion of all state remedies is prerequisite to appeal to federal courts.

Other courts hold that, even though a justice be disqualified because of financial interest, in the absence of some constitutional or statutory requirement that courts be presided over by disinterested judges, a judgment rendered by him is not void, but voidable only, and has the effect of legality until declared illegal in a proper proceeding. Such judgment cannot be attacked collaterally nor challenged on a writ of habeas corpus. Still other courts, starting from the position that constitutional rights may be waived provided their waiver is not contrary to public policy, hold that, in the absence of some constitutional or statutory provision, failure of a defendant to make seasonable objection to trial before a disqualified judge, when he has or is presumed to have full knowledge of the disqualification, constitutes a waiver of his right to trial by a disinterested judge and estops him from raising the disqualification question on appeal. It should be pointed out that, in its opinion in the *Tumey* case, the United States Supreme Court twice noted that Tumey had raised the disqualification question prior to his trial. But a categorical answer cannot be given to its influence on the decision reached by the Court. Nevertheless, several state supreme courts interpreting and applying the Tumey decision lay considerable stress upon it.

Although in most instances, state supreme courts have upheld the constitutionality of their own justice of the peace systems by distinguishing them from that prevailing in Ohio at the time of the *Tumey* decision, in some instances federal and state courts have used the decision in the *Tumey* case to void or outlaw convictions in justice courts. In 1927, one federal district court in the case of *Ex parte Baer* released on a writ of habeas corpus a defendant who had been convicted and given a fine and jail sentence in a Kentucky county judge's court for liquor-law violations. Here, the court held that the defendant had been denied due process of law due to the judge's financial interest in the result of the trial. He had previously appealed to a state court for the writ, but it had been denied. He did not, prior to his trial, raise objection to the judge's disqualification, nor did he, before seeking the federal writ, exhaust his state remedies by appealing to the state's highest court. The court stated, however, that he could not be expected to know the justice's disqualification and, consequently, held that he had not waived it. Shortly after the *Baer* case, another federal district court in the case of *Ex parte Meeks* refused to issue a writ of habeas corpus to release from state jurisdiction a defendant convicted under circumstances similar to those in the *Baer* case, on the ground that, even if the principles announced in the *Tumey* case were applicable, the defendant had not objected to the judge's disqualification at the time of trial, nor did he appeal to the circuit court where a trial *de novo* before a disinterested judge was available. These two decisions are at direct variance with each other, with the latter decision being the most commonly accepted interpretation of the *Tumey* case.

A significant state decision interpreting *Tumey* v. *Ohio* is *Williams* v. *Brannen*, decided by the West Virginia Supreme Court of Appeals. Here, the court awarded a writ of prohibition to a defendant to prevent his trial before a justice who, according to his allegations, would have a pecuniary interest in convicting him. The justice drew his compensation from costs paid by defendants when convicted and from a fund accumulated by fines assessed in his court. He was compensated by the latter method in cases where he rendered a verdict of acquittal and in cases where costs for any proper reason could not be collected from those adjudged guilty. The implication of such a compensation system was that the justice was required to convict in an appreciable number of cases in order to create a fund to secure payment of fees in cases in which he collected no costs. The Court refused to make fine distinctions between the facts in this case and those in the *Tumey* case, holding them inconsequential in view of the Supreme Court's pronouncement in the *Tumey* case that, "Every procedure which would offer a possible temptation to the average man as a judge to forget the burden of proof required to convict the defendant, or which might lead him not to hold the balance nice, clear and true between the state and the accused denies the latter due process of law." It held that due process of law required that a justice's compensation must not depend upon a fund created by his own convictions and, consequently, declared unconstitutional the West Virginia statutory system of compensating justices. It rejected arguments that right to demand trial by jury and right of appeal with trial *de novo* made conditions in this case different from those in the *Tumey* case. Trial by jury, it said, meant trial before a jury under the direction of a disinterested judge, and right of appeal did not meet the situation because a defendant would ordinarily incur less costs by paying a moderate fine than by paying appeal costs. Further, the Court held that an accused was entitled to a fair and impartial trial in the first instance.

The decision of the West Virginia Court in the *Williams* case declaring unconstitutional the West Virginia statutory system of compensating justices was further explained—and, it seems, its impact lessened—in the court's later holding in *State* v. *Simmons.* The pertinent question in the *Williams* case, it said, concerned the qualification of the justice, not the jurisdiction of his court which, according to it, remained unimpaired. Accordingly, it held that, when a defendant did not raise in the trial court the question concerning the justice's disqualification, it was deemed waived and could not be raised for the first time on appeal. A judgment rendered under such circumstances, it said, was voidable only, not void. Thus it appears that, if the holding in the *Williams* case is considered in the light of the holding in the *Simmons* case, the former case is not at all unique but merely states in somewhat different language what other courts have said, namely, that a justice is disqualified to act when his method of compensation gives him a direct interest in influencing the result of a trial. But disqualified justices actually conduct cases, and the important unresolved question concerns the legality of this practice.

Another case meriting consideration in connection with the *Tumey* decision is *Ex parte Kelly,* decided by the Texas Court of Criminal Appeals. Here, the court reversed a conviction rendered in a justice court on the grounds that it violated both the United States and Texas Constitutions. Under Texas law, justices were compensated only in those cases in which they found defendants guilty. Right of appeal, moreover, was limited to cases wherein the fine imposed exceeded $100. Although the *Tumey* decision had considerable bearing in the *Kelly* case, perhaps the most significant factor influencing the Court's decision was the fact that the *Texas Constitution* (Art. V, sec. 11) forbids a judge to sit in any case wherein he has an interest. For this reason, the Court held the justice disqualified, and noted that, as a general rule, acts of a judge subject to a constitutional disqualification are void. In a subsequent decision, the Texas Court stated that, in the *Kelly* case, it did not outlaw the jurisdiction of justice courts; it merely held that its legislature, by providing that fees should be payable to justices only in cases wherein they convicted defendants, had disqualified justices who attempted to assess and collect such fees. It stated specifically that ". . . if the duly qualified justice should see fit to exercise his prerogative to try such cases without compensation, it would seem plain that there would be thus no disqualification . . ."

In summary, most courts interpret the *Tumey* principles primarily to disqualify judges from conducting cases wherein they have a pecuniary interest; but the jurisdiction of courts presided over by such judges is left unaffected; and, except in instances where constitutional or statutory provisions require disinterested judges, they recognize that such judges, when waiver to their disqualification exists, may render legal judgments. Further, some courts hold that due process of law is not denied in cases conducted by judges having an interest in the outcome provided appeals may be taken from judgments rendered in them.

KENTUCKY JUSTICE COURTS

Before considering the various interpretations of the *Tumey* decision made by the Kentucky Court of Appeals, it is necessary to discuss the Kentucky justice and the functioning of his court. The Kentucky justice has existed as a constitutional officer since the beginning of the Commonwealth. The present *Constitution* authorizes the voters of each county to elect on a district basis from three to eight of these officials. In addition to being a judicial officer, the justice in all save 13 counties, serves as a member of the fiscal court, and chief governing body of the county. He receives a *per diem* for serving on the fiscal court and fees for his judicial duties.

Kentucky has 678 justices of the peace, but the vast majority are inactive as judicial officers. They function primarily in urban counties where the county judge's time is too occupied with county administrative problems to permit him to hear cases, in a considerable number of county-seat towns, and by custom in certain rural counties, situated particularly in the mountain area of the state. During the 1954–55 fiscal year, 40,651 convictions in misdemeanor cases were returned by 161 justices situated throughout the state. Some justices were much more active than others. Justice courts functioning in 18 of Kentucky's 120 counties returned 23,101 convictions or 57 per cent of the total number. Disregarding county boundaries, it was found that 63 justices situated in 34 counties returned 26,026 convictions or 64 per cent of the total. On the other hand, 47 justices each returned ten or less convictions, with 12 of this number returning only one conviction each.

No legal training is required for holding the office of justice; anyone meeting the usual age and residence requirements may fill it; and in actual practice, justices usually possess but little formal education. Their courts are frequently criticized for their failure to maintain the dignity and decorum so essential to the judicial process.

Kentucky justice courts are courts of record and possess jurisdiction coextensive with the county. They are empowered by statute to conduct preliminary examinations in all felony cases except murder cases and to hear minor civil and criminal cases, their civil jurisdiction extending to all cases in which the value in controversy does not exceed $200 and their criminal jurisdiction extending to cases in which the punishment is limited to a fine of $500 or imprisonment for one year, or both. (Civil cases are conducted primarily by justices in a few urban counties and will not be discussed in this article). Justice courts, along with county and quarterly courts, the latter courts conducted by county judges, have exclusive jurisdiction to hear misdemeanor cases wherein the punishment imposed does not exceed a fine of $20. When

393

a jail sentence or a fine of $20 or above is imposed, appeal may be taken to the circuit court. In actual practice, however, justice courts possess final jurisdiction in most cases they conduct. This seems evidenced by the fact that during the fiscal year 1954–1955, only seven of the 63 justices returning 100 or more convictions each imposed fines averaging more than $20. Most persons appearing before justice courts are without counsel, and most cases are conducted without juries. But defendants may demand jury trials in all cases in which the punishment imposed by statute is a jail sentence or a fine above $16.

THE TUMEY DECISION AND THE KENTUCKY COURT OF APPEALS

PRIOR TO THE ROBERTS DECISION

In the same year that the United States Supreme Court decided the *Tumey* case, the constitutionality of the Kentucky justice of the peace system was challenged before the Kentucky Court of Appeals when the latter court had presented to it in the case of *Wagers* v. *Sizemore* the question of whether a trial before a Kentucky justice, who was financially interested in the result of the trial, denied a defendant due process of law. In the case, the defendant had been tried and convicted on a charge of obstructing a public highway after his protest that, due to the justice's financial interest in convicting him, he could not receive a fair and impartial trial. The justice's total fees in this instance were $6. Since the fine imposed was only $10, the court's judgment was non-appealable. The defendant was tried before a jury, but the justice argued the case to the jury and directed it to impose a fine. The Court of Appeals, after noting these facts, reversed the conviction, holding itself bound by the decision in the *Tumey* case. It noted that, prior to trial, the defendant had raised objection to the justice's qualification and held that since he had done so, the same objection could be made before the Court of Appeals.

In order to remedy the situation created by the *Tumey* and *Wagers* cases, the Kentucky General Assembly enacted legislation placing the compensation of the county judge, who, like justices, had until this time been compensated in misdemeanor cases by fees, on a salary basis. Legislation was also passed placing the compensation of justices in Jefferson County, containing the City of Louisville, on a salary basis. In a suit brought under the Declaratory Judgment Act of 1922 to test the constitutionality of legislation altering the method of compensating the county judge, the Court of Appeals also had presented to it in the case of *Adams* v. *Slavin,* the question of whether justices of the peace, in the absence of seasonable objection to their disqualification, had the right to preside at misdemeanor trials. In its opinion, the Court reviewed its decision in the *Wagers* case, stating that even if the cost statute involved in that case was invalid, the justice had an undoubted right to conduct the trial because he was not then a disqualified judge, being entitled to no costs or a part of the fine in the event of conviction. (This same conclusion, it should be recalled, was reached by the Texas Court of Criminal Appeals). In such an instance, it said, the judgment would not be void. The court next noted that the Supreme Court in the *Tumey* case expressly recognized the right of a state legislature to vest jurisdiction in state courts. Finally, it concluded that, "the sole ground on which both the *Tumey* and *Wagers* cases rest is that a defendant has the right to object to being tried by a judge who is financially interested in his being convicted, and that to try him after such objection is to deprive him of the protection of the due process clause of the Fourteenth Amendment." It then raised the question of whether a defendant was also deprived if he did not object to trial. It answered that constitutional rights, at least in misdemeanor cases, may be waived and stated, "We are of the opinion that where a defendant on a final trial for a misdemeanor fails to seasonably object to being tried by a justice of the peace, the latter may try him, and in the event of conviction tax the costs against him, as has been the custom for so many years in this Commonwealth."

The latter statement, until 1956 when the Court of Appeals, in the *Roberts* case, held justice courts, save those in Jefferson County, to be without jurisdiction to conduct misdemeanor cases, summed up Kentucky law with respect to misdemeanor trials in justice courts. Justices of the peace were really standing disqualified judges; and, as stated by the Kentucky Court of Appeals, they could not collect any fee whatever from a defendant in a misdemeanor case except through "agreement, acquiescence and grace." If an accused protested trial before a justice, the latter was required to transfer his case to an impartial court having jurisdiction to hear it. In the event a justice refused to transfer a case after due protest had been made, the proper remedy was an application to the Court of Appeals for a writ of prohibition to prevent trial. Unfortunately, the vast majority of individuals brought before justice courts had no legal counsel and were themselves too little aware of their legal rights to be able to assert them; and, consequently, such rights were in practice generally rendered meaningless.

THE ROBERTS DECISION

By its decision in the *Roberts* case, the Court of Appeals appears to have brought to an end the justice of the peace system as it has functioned in the past. This case originated out of an arrest for a public drunkenness charge. After the arrest, the defendant posted bond for appearance at his trial, but at the time when it was scheduled, he did not appear, being represented, however, by an attorney who objected to the jurisdiction of the court on the ground of the pecuniary interest which the justice had in the result of the trial. (Ordinarily, it seems that objection should have been made, not to the jurisdiction of the court, but to the judge's disqualification.) The justice overruled the objection for the reason that it was not supported by affidavit of the defendant, and stated that he would waive his costs and fees. He then entered an order forfeiting the appearance bond, empanelled a jury, and tried the defendant *in absentia*. The jury found the defendant guilty and fixed his fine at $20. The defendant thereupon appealed to the circuit court for an injunction to restrain enforcement of the judgment; and the injunction being granted, the justice appealed to the Court of Appeals.

The Court, it seems, could very well have decided the case upon grounds other than those on which it actually did. It could have merely sustained the injunction granted by the circuit court; or, on the other hand, it could have held that, inasmuch as the justice in the trial court had waived his costs and fees, no pecuniary interest existed and he therefore was within his legal rights in trying the case. And, indeed, if costs and fees may legally be waived, the latter argument seems logical. Not to be overlooked, moreover, is the fact that the judgment, being a fine of $20, was appealable to the circuit court where a trial *de novo* was available. The Court, however, rejected this argument, stating that an accused is entitled to a fair trial in the first instance. Instead, therefore, of deciding the case by following any of the alternatives noted, the Court stated, "We feel that the time has come to reconsider our interpretation and application of the decision in the Tumey case, as set forth in *Adams* v. *Slavin* . . ." It said that, in the *Adams* case, it had construed the *Tumey* opinion, not as declaring the system unconstitutional or as depriving absolutely of jurisdiction a judge who has a pecuniary interest in the outcome of a case he conducts, but only as recognizing the constitutional right of a defendant to object to trial before a disqualified judge. It added, however, that upon a re-examination of the opinion in the *Tumey* case, it was led to conclude that the Supreme Court "intended to, and did, declare the entire system unconstitutional." It stated that "no justification exists for perpetrating a system that is designed and calculated to deprive persons of due process of law." It could see no merit, moreover, in its previous holding in the case of *Adams* v. *Slavin* that an accused may waive his constitutional right to a trial conducted by an impartial judge. Here, it declared, "To say, as we did in the *Slavin* case, that the right to trial by a judge free from prejudice may be waived is unrealistic for as pointed out in *Ex parte Baer,* 20 Fed. 2d 912, the ordinary person is not aware of his right to object to the jurisdiction; he assumes that the court before which he has been is a lawfully constituted one." (From the language of this statement, it seems that the Court confuses waiver of jurisdiction with waiver of a judge's disqualification. The former can not be waived, but the latter, at least in some instances, can be. It should be added, moreover, that there is authority for the view that justice courts, such as Kentucky's, are lawfully constituted.

The Court recognized that argument might be made for the position that the only unconstitutional feature of the justice of the peace system was the cost statute, and that the jurisdiction of justice courts to try cases without compensation remained. It stated, however, that although this view had been accepted as sound by former Kentucky Courts, the Court as it was now constituted, believing that the legislature did not intend justices to serve without compensation, disagreed. It admitted that the legislature had authority to require justices to try misdemeanor cases without compensation; however, it held that the present cost statute and the statute conferring jurisdiction upon justice courts must be read together, stating that a system under which justices served without compensation could occasion such evils as fee-splitting and would not lead to a fair administration of justice. There is further support for the Court's position if the view is taken that county officers, including justices of the peace, can not legally waive legislative prescribed fees for performing official duties. This view is based on the fact that, all revenues, including fees, accruing to a particular office in excess of those actually required to operate it, belong to the county. The Court ended its opinion by expressly overruling its former ruling in the *Adams* case and by holding that, until some other method of compensation is provided, justices of the peace, save those in Jefferson county, are without jurisdiction to conduct criminal cases. A mandate making this ruling effective, however, will not be issued during the terms of incumbent justices, and such officials may continue to try cases provided they inform defendants of their right to demand trial before an impartial court.

THE TUMEY AND ROBERTS DECISIONS RECONSIDERED

In its decision in the *Roberts* case, the Kentucky Court of Appeals perhaps has accorded the *Tumey* decision greater significance than it has heretofore received from any state supreme court. One may agree with the end accomplished by the Kentucky Court in the *Roberts* case—most justice courts are bad and ought to be abolished or radically altered—without concurring entirely with some of the reasoning advanced in its opinion. The *Roberts* decision rests, of course, on the Kentucky Court's interpretation of the United States Supreme Court's opinion in the *Tumey* case. Although the exact meaning of that opinion may not be clear, it holds at least (1) that the Fourteenth Amendment applies to misdemeanor trials conducted in state courts and (2) that a judge is disqualified to try a case wherein he has a direct pecuniary interest. State supreme courts disagree, however, concerning the extent of the Supreme Court's holding in the case, the Kentucky Court of Appeals holding that it outlaws entirely a judicial system wherein judges are compensated solely by fees collected from individuals they convict; however, most other state courts urge that it stops short of this, holding that, the jurisdiction of a court may remain even though its judge is disqualified. The latter view is probably the correct one, since what the *Tumey* case seems to condemn is a certain type of judicial procedure. It recognizes the right of a state to create courts and to establish their jurisdiction, but holds that exercise of such jurisdiction under certain circumstances constitutes a bar to a valid conviction since it denies due process of law. In other words, jurisdiction must be distinguished from exercise of jurisdiction.

Of vital concern in connection with the *Tumey* decision is the matter of whether a defendant must raise the question of judicial disqualification in the trial court. The United States Supreme Court both at the beginning and end of its opinion in the *Tumey* case noted that the defendant in that case had done so. Although it is impossible to determine what significance the Supreme Court intended to place upon failure to object to disqualification, several state courts accord it great weight, holding that, unless seasonable objection is made in the trial court, disqualification is deemed waived. But even if these courts are interpreting the Supreme Court's opinion correctly, another question still arises. Assume for sake of argument that the objection to disqualification must be made; the average defendant in a justice court can scarcely be expected to make it. Indeed, prior to the *Tumey* case, making the objection did not occur even to lawyers. In Kentucky, proceedings in a justice court ordinarily consist in a defendant appearing without counsel before a disqualified justice, who has, as a practical matter, final jurisdiction in his case. It seems difficult to expect due process of law to obtain under such circumstances. Herein, however, may lie the key whereby a criterion may be found to distinguish between a valid and an invalid trial. No claim of denial of due process of law ought to be allowed, it seems, concerning any proceeding in a justice court where a defendant is represented by counsel, for in such situation constitutional rights can be effectively asserted. Moreover, the same principle ought to hold where a defendant who has no counsel is informed of his constitutional rights by the trial judge and while competent to act refuses counsel. In this connection it seems appropriate to note that the recent Court of Appeals order requiring incumbent justices to inform defendants of their right to demand trial before an impartial court may have the effect of making such trials as are actually conducted conform to due process of law. This is based on the assumption that justices will strictly observe the court order and that defendants will voluntarily and intelligently consent to trial.

Although the rule that constitutional rights are considered waived unless claimed at the earliest opportunity—usually in the trial court—is sound, it seems a questionable one when applied to misdemeanor cases in which a defendant is unrepresented by counsel or is not informed of his constitutional rights by the court. Such rights should not be presumed waived through acquiescence due to ignorance. The Kentucky Court of Appeals appears therefore to have decided correctly in the *Roberts* case when it held that a person unaware of his right to an impartial judge can not waive that right. According to the United States Supreme Court, "A waiver is ordinarily an intentional relinquishment or abandonment of a known right or privilege." Accordingly, unless a defendant in a justice court is represented by counsel, or unless he is informed of his right to object and is himself competent to act, waiver of that right does not obtain, inasmuch as unknown rights can not be relinquished. Further, the Supreme Court has held that there is ". . . every reasonable presumption against waiver of fundamental constitutional rights." Such rights may be waived, but their waiver must be competent, voluntary, and intentional. In instances where a defendant has no counsel, it seems that the duty of determining whether a competent waiver has taken place falls upon the court; and, where the court fails to so determine, it seems that serious doubt arises concerning its jurisdiction to proceed.

RIGHT TO COUNCIL IN MISDEMEANOR CASES

A trial may be said to conform to the requirements of due process of law when an accused is afforded full opportunity to assert effectively his constitutional rights. Opportunity for assertion of such rights must be considered present when an accused is represented by counsel, or if, when not represented by counsel, he is informed of them by the court and is himself competent to act. The average defendant in a justice court, having no counsel and being himself generally unaware of his constitutional rights, is certainly in no position to assert them. It is therefore proper to inquire concerning a defendant's right to counsel in state misdemeanor cases.

In the past, the assumption seems to have been—and still prevails in many states— that a defendant in a non-capital criminal case, which, of course, includes a misdemeanor case, is not as a matter of right, entitled to be furnished counsel. Except in very serious cases—sometimes only in capital cases—state constitutional provision to the effect that a defendant has a right to be heard by himself and counsel have not been understood to impose upon the trial court the duty of furnishing counsel to an accused, or even of advising him of his need therefore; rather, such provisions have been taken to mean that a defendant has a right, if he chooses, to procure assistance of counsel. Prior to 1938, the Sixth Amendment was understood to have practically the same meaning in its application to cases in federal courts; but, as a consequence of the Supreme Court's decision in *Johnson* v. *Zerbst*, decided that year, the Amendment has been understood to impose a positive duty upon federal courts to furnish defendants in such courts with counsel. But the Supreme Court has never held that the due process clause of the Fourteenth Amendment imposes the same duty on state courts, holding instead that lack of counsel in state non-capital cases denies federal constitutional protection only when its absence results in a denial of the essentials of justice. In other words, if absence of a lawyer results in a defendant's not having a fair and adequate defense, or if it results in his actually being taken advantage of, or prejudiced, due process of law does seem denied.

In Kentucky, as in most states, the assumption seems to be that justice courts—and all lower courts as well—are not required to furnish counsel to an accused. Formerly, the Kentucky Court of Appeals took the position that counsel for an accused was absolutely necessary only in capital cases; but recently it has reversed itself and now holds that counsel is required in all felony cases. The Court's changed position was probably influenced by United States Supreme Court decisions concerning an accused's right to counsel in both state and federal courts. In its opinion requiring counsel for defendants in felony cases, the Kentucky [Court] quoted with approval the following statement of the Supreme Court:

> *There are some individuals who, by reason of age, ignorance, or mental capacity, are incapable of representing themselves adequately in a prosecution of a relatively simple nature. Their incapacity is purely personal and can be determined only by an examination and observation of the individual. Where such incapacity is present, the refusal to appoint counsel is a denial of due process of law under the Fourteenth Amendment.*

The Kentucky Court further held that common justice demands that every person accused of a felony be given a fair and impartial trial.

Although the stakes involved in misdemeanor cases are certainly less than those involved in felony cases, it seems that the requirements of due process of law demand that the same principles of justice be observed in them. Although as a matter of actual fact they do, constitutional standards of fairness ought not to depend on what court an accused is in. In the past all too little regard has been had for observance of procedures essential to due process in state misdemeanor cases simply because such cases concern petty matters and because but little formal protest has been made to the manner in which such cases have been conducted. Although trial of an accused without counsel in a misdemeanor case is not, in itself, unconstitutional, it may, when taken with other factors, result in a denial of due process of law. Due process of law requires that an accused in a misdemeanor case be given at least a fair trial. One of the elements of such a trial is right to counsel. Importance of counsel would seem to loom great in a trial conducted by a disqualified judge. Absence of counsel under such circumstances would seem to deny due process of law, because it would result in an accused being taken advantage of, for, surely the first duty of counsel, if present, would be to object to the disqualification and to demand trial before an impartial judge. One reason given by the Supreme Court for its refusal to read its interpretation of the Sixth Amendment into the due process clause of the Fourteenth Amendment is the fact that, should it do so, argument would be made that counsel should be assigned defendants in justice and all other minor courts. The Court takes the position that it is unreasonable to assume that a fair trial can not be had in a state court unless a defendant has counsel. But when it does so, it evidently presumes a trial conducted before an unprejudiced judge.

Finally, it seems that the United States Supreme Court in the *Tumey* case holds that any judge having a pecuniary interest in a case is disqualified from conducting it. It seems, however, that, although the disqualification does not, in itself, affect the jurisdiction vested in his court by the legislature, such jurisdiction if exercised when there has been no waiver to the disqualification, can be lost. This would seem to result when a court proceeds to conduct a case wherein an accused has not intelligently waived his right to counsel. If jurisdiction is assumed lost under such circumstances, right of appeal, as urged by some courts, is not the proper solution to the problem presented by convictions rendered by disqualified justices.

The decision of the Kentucky Court of Appeals in the *Roberts* case seems correct to the extent that it holds that right to trial before an unprejudiced judge may not be waived. It seems correct also in holding that the Kentucky legislature intends justices of the peace to collect fees in all misdemeanor cases they conduct. But there is considerable doubt concerning its holding that all Kentucky justices, save those in Jefferson County, are without jurisdiction to conduct misdemeanor cases. Such judicial officers, it seems, have jurisdiction to conduct cases when actual waiver to their disqualification exists.

E. THE SUPREME COURT AS INNOVATOR: THE DESEGREGATION SEQUENCE

[Because contemporary reactions to the school integration issue have been largely identified with a particular region, it is sometimes overlooked that initially racial segregation was (and still is) a nationwide problem. This is underscored by the fact that the "separate but equal" doctrine originated not in the South but in New England.]

1. Adoption of the "Separate but Equal" Doctrine*

I

In mid-nineteenth-century Massachusetts, color prejudice sought its last legal refuge in Boston's system of public schools. Yet no institution was safe from the pitiless criticism of conscience, for the age of the Universal Reformers pulsated with

*Leonard W. Levy, *The Law of the Commonwealth and Chief Justice Shaw* (Cambridge, Mass.: Harvard University Press, 1957), pp. 109–17. Reproduced with permission of the author and the publisher. Copyright © 1957 by the President and Fellows of Harvard College.

the spirit of social justice. Only the vision of a perfect society delimited the imagina-tion. Quite proper then that in William Lloyd Garrison's state the reformers should devote some measure of their energies toward improving the status of the free American Negro. The law prohibiting intermarriage had been rescinded in 1843, and railroads had been forced to abandon Jim Crow cars. Separate schools for Negroes had been abolished, where they had existed, in Salem, Lowell, New Bed-ford, Nantucket, and in the smaller towns. In the Supreme Judicial Court in 1849, Charles Sumner, arguing the cause of Sarah Roberts before Chief Justice Shaw, eloquently coupled the "civilization of the age" to an appeal for the abolition of segregated education in Boston.

For half a century schools for the exclusive use of Negro children had been main-tained in Boston. Both parties to the Roberts case agreed that the first school was originally established, in 1798, at the request of Negro citizens "whose children could not attend the public schools on account of the prejudice then existing against them." Boston had refused to incur the expense of the colored school, but it was made possible by the benefactions of white philanthropists. In 1806 the basement of the newly erected African Baptist Church in Belknap Street was secured as a permanent site. When Abiel Smith, "the merchant prince," died in 1815 and left an endowment of $4,000 for the school, it took his name. Not until 1812 had Boston assisted the school; the town's grant of $200 was continued yearly till 1815, when the Board of Select-men assumed control. Five years later, after the primary school for children of four to seven had become a part of the public-school system, Boston legally fixed the pat-tern of segregation by establishing a separate primary school for Negroes.

For more than twenty years thereafter, the Smith Grammar School and its primary-school appendages continued undisturbed. Meanwhile, the Boston Negro had been growing in political maturity. Once the battle against the Jim Crow car was won, Negro militants, urged on by the Massachusetts Anti-Slavery Society, turned their faces against the Jim Crow school, once a blessing, now a discriminatory abomina-tion. In 1846 they petitioned the primary school committee for the abolition of exclu-sive schools. Despite the protests of its two abolitionist members, Edmond Jackson and Henry I. Bowditch, the committee decided against the petition. Candidly naming racial differences as the reason for their action, the majority declared that segregated education for Negroes was "not only legal and just, but is best adapted to promote the education of that class of our population." That very year, the white master of Smith School officially reported that the institution was shamefully neglected, desper-ately in need of repairs.

For over four years the issue was the occasion of discord among public officials and among the Negroes themselves, who were bitterly divided. In the press, and at public meetings, it was long debated, and no less than two majority and two minority school committee reports were published. Without action by the legislature, which alone could end the controversy, all the circumstances were at hand for a court case.

II

Benjamin Roberts was one of the Negro leaders in the fight against segregation. Four times he tried to enter his five-year-old daughter Sarah in one of the white primary schools of the district in which he resided, and as many times she was rejected by authority of the school committee solely on the grounds of color. On the direct route from her home to the primary school for Negroes, Sarah passed no less than five other primary schools. Roberts was informed that his child might be admitted at any time to the colored school, but he refused to have her attend there. Determined to test the constitutionality of the school committee's power to enforce segregation, Roberts brought suit in Sarah's name under a statute which provided that any child illegally excluded from the public schools might recover damages against the city.

To argue Sarah's cause, Roberts retained Charles Sumner, a man of erudition, eloquence, and exalted moral fervor; he was to become New England's greatest senator and slavery's most implacable foe. The City of Boston was represented by its solicitor, Peleg W. Chandler, Massachusetts' foremost expert on municipal law and founder of one of the earliest legal journals, the *Law Reporter*.

Sumner's argument before Shaw turned on a "single proposition—*the equality of man before the law*." Quoting the paragraphs of the Massachusetts Constitution which courts of a later day were to construe as meaning the same as the "equal protection" clause of the Fourteenth Amendment, Sumner observed that every form of inequality and discrimination in civil and political institutions was thereby condemned. He alleged the unconstitutionality of the segregated school on the grounds of its "caste" nature, and proved that the school committee had been motivated by racial prejudice. The power of the committee, delegated by the state legislature, was merely to superintend the public schools and to determine "the number and qualifications of the scholars." A power to segregate could not be implied, argued Sumner, for the committee "cannot brand a whole race with the stigma of inferiority and degradation." To imply the existence of that power "would place the Committee above the Constitution. It would enable them, in the exercise of a brief and local authority, to draw a fatal circle, within which the Constitution cannot enter; nay, where the very Bill of Rights shall become a dead letter." Only factors of age, sex, and moral and intellectual fitness might be considered by the committee as qualifications, not complexion. Just as the law required the regulation and by-laws of municipal corporations to be reasonable, Sumner asserted, so must the acts of the school committee be reasonable. But an *a priori* assumption by the committee that an entire race possess certain qualities which make necessary a separate classification of that race, was an unreasonable exercise of the committee's discretion, and therefore an illegal one.

Anticipating the "separate but equal" doctrine, Sumner argued that the segregated school could not be an "equivalent" because of the inconveniences and the stigma of caste which it imposed, and because a public school, by definition, was for the equal benefit of all. The right of the Negro children was to "precise equality."

Before closing, Sumner discussed certain matters "not strictly belonging to the juridical aspect of the case," yet necessary for understanding it. His remarks, which have been validated by modern sociological scholarship, were in part as follows:

> *The white themselves are injured by the separation . . . With the law as their monitor . . . they are taught practically to deny that grand revelation of*

Christianity—the Brotherhood of Mankind. Their hearts, while yet tender with childhood, are necessarily hardened by this conduct, and their subsequent lives, perhaps, bear enduring testimony to this legalized uncharitableness. Nursed in the sentiment of Caste, receiving it with the earliest food of knowledge, they are unable to eradicate it from their natures . . . The school is the little world in which the child is trained for the larger world of life. It must, therefore, cherish and develop the virtues and the sympathies which are employed in the larger world . . . beginning there those relations of equality which our Constitution and laws promise to all . . . Prejudice is the child of ignorance. It is sure to prevail where people do not know each other. Society and intercourse are means established by Providence for human improvement. They remove antipathies, promote mutual adaptation and conciliation, and establish relations of reciprocal regard.

III

Chief Justice Shaw, delivering the unanimous opinion of the Court, upheld to the fullest extent the power of the school committee to enforce segregation. The case required for its disposition no fine analysis of difficult legal points, and Shaw confined himself, as did the counsel before him, primarily to general principles—and to predilections as well. That his opinion has had an enduring influence may be attributed in part to the sweep and force with which the principles were announced, and to the articulation given those predilections.

Pointing out that the plaintiff had access to a school for Negro children as well fitted and conducted in all respects as other primary schools, the Court rejected the contention that she had been unlawfully excluded from public-school instruction. The issue, rather, was one of power, "because, if they [the committee] have the legal authority," said Shaw, "the expediency of exercising it in any particular way is exclusively with them." The latter half of this unqualified proposition, which invested the school committee with discretionary powers to classify pupils by race, religion, economic status, or national origin, was stated as a fixed legal fact in support of which the Court risked no reasons. Similarly, other conclusions which were adopted regarding the points at issue were characterized by a singular absence of considered judgment.

For example, Shaw proceeded directly from *carte blanche* approval of the committee's discretionary powers, to an assumption—in itself, sufficient to decide the case —that all individuals did not possess the same legal rights. And whom else could he have had in mind but Negroes? His own words are given in full:

The great principle, advanced by the learned and eloquent advocate of the plaintiff, is, that by the constitution and laws of Massachusetts, all persons without distinction of age or sex, birth or color, origin or condition, are equal before the law. This, as a broad general principle, such as ought to appear in a declaration of rights, is perfectly sound; it is not only expressed in terms, but pervades and animates the whole spirit of our constitution of free government. But, when this great principle comes to be applied to the actual and various conditions of persons in society, it will not warrant the assertion, that men and women are legally clothed with the same civil and political powers, and that children and adults are legally to have the same functions and be subject to the same treatment; but only that the rights of all, as they are settled and regulated by law, are equally entitled to the paternal consideration and protection of the law, for their maintenance and security. What these rights are, to which individuals, in the infinite variety of circumstances by which they are surrounded in society, are entitled, must depend on laws adapted to their respective relations and conditions.

Stripped of its rhetoric, this paragraph set forth two contradictory propositions, perhaps more succinctly expressed by that favored class, the pigs of George Orwell's *Animal Farm:*

ALL ANIMALS ARE EQUAL
BUT SOME ANIMALS ARE MORE EQUAL THAN OTHERS

Having virtually decided the case by asserting unreasoned grounds for decision, the Chief Justice defined the question before the Court—an inversion of the order of logic. He stated the question in such a way as to make possible by his answer the "separate but equal" doctrine:

Conceding, therefore, in the fullest manner, that colored persons, the descendants of Africans, are entitled by law, in this commonwealth, to equal rights, constitutional and political, civil and social, the question then arises, whether the regulations in question, which provides separate schools for colored children, is a violation of any of these rights. [sic]

Thereupon, Shaw established in detail the undisputed facts that legal rights depend upon provisions of law; that the state constitution declared broad principles intended to direct the activities of the legislature; that the legislature, in turn, had defined only the general outlines and objects of an educational system; and that the school committee had been vested with a plenary power to make all reasonable rules for the classification of pupils. Shaw was impressed with the fact that the committee, after long deliberation, believed that the good of both races was best promoted by the separate education of their children. The Court, he said, perceived no ground to doubt that the committee formed its belief "on just grounds of reason and experience, and in the results of a discriminating and honest judgment."

In introducing into the jurisprudence of Massachusetts the power of a governmental body to arrange the legal rights of citizens on the basis of race, the Chief Justice was bound to show for the Court not only that the discrimination, in the face of an equality of rights clause, was not forbidden; he should have shown that such discrimination was reasonable. Instead, he contented himself with the thought that the prejudice which existed "is not created by law, and probably cannot be changed by law." He added, moreover, that it would likely be fostered "by compelling colored and white children to associate together in the same schools." This was the Court's answer to Sumner's contention that the maintenance of separate schools tended to perpetuate and deepen prejudice. It did not occur to Shaw to appraise the experience of other towns in Massachusetts, where children without regard to race attended the same schools with the most successful results. Thus the doctrine of "separate but equal" as a constitutional justification of racial segregation in public schools first entered American jurisprudence.

By 1855 the unceasing efforts of the abolitionists and Negroes proved to be of greater weight in Massachusetts than the opinion of its distinguished Chief Justice. A new statute was enacted which rooted out the last legal refuge of racial discrimination in Massachusetts.

IV

In constitutional history, however, Shaw's opinion had a continuing vitality. It was initially cited with approval by the high court of the Territory of Nevada in 1872. Two years later the California Supreme Court endorsed the doctrine by quoting most of Shaw's opinion, and concluded: "We concur in these views and they are decisive . . ." The courts of New York, Arkansas, Missouri, Louisiana, West Virginia, Kansas, Oklahoma, South Carolina, and Oregon have also relied upon the Roberts case as a precedent for upholding segregated education. It has been mentioned by lower federal courts twice in recent years, as well as on earlier occasions.

In the United States Supreme Court, the Roberts case was first discussed by Justice Clifford in *Hall* v. *DeCuir* as an authority for the rule that "equality does not mean identity." In *Plessy* v. *Ferguson,* decided in 1896, the Court turned to Shaw's opinion as a leading precedent for the validity of state legislation which required segregation of the white and colored races "in places where they are liable to be brought into contact . . ." When it is considered that the Plessy case itself became the leading authority on the constitutionality of the "separate but equal" doctrine, the influence of the Roberts case appears immeasurable. In 1927, in *Gong Lum* v. *Rice,* it was mentioned by a unanimous bench to support the proposition that segregation in education "has been many times decided" to be constitutional. Chief Justice Taft, the spokesman in the Gong Lum case, also added that the Massachusetts court had upheld "the separation of colored and white schools under a state constitutional injunction of equal protection, the same as the Fourteenth Amendment . . ."

Thus, Shaw's doctrine in the Roberts case became the law of the land and remained so more than a century after he originated it. Its uncritical acceptance by the highest courts of so many jurisdictions, in a nation whose Constitution is color-blind, long warranted its reexamination and repudiation. This historic step was finally taken by the Supreme Court of the United States on May 17, 1954. Chief Justice Warren, for a unanimous bench, stated:

> *Does segregation of children in public schools solely on the basis of race, even though the physical facilities and other 'tangible' factors may be equal, deprive the children of the minority group of equal educational opportunities? We believe that it does. . . . We conclude that in the field of public education the doctrine of 'separate but equal' has no place. Separate educational facilities are inherently unequal.*

[Leonard Levy's chapter suggests that influential doctrines do not always originate in the United States Supreme Court. The final repudiation of the "separate but equal" doctrine occurred in a group of cases which produced one of the sharpest group conflicts in the contemporary era. The intensity of group concern was in part demonstrated by the phalanx-like array of counsel on both sides, in *Brown* v. *Board of Education,* reproduced below.]

2. Repudiation of the "Separate but Equal" Doctrine: Brown *v.* Board of Education*

. . . *Robert L. Carter* argued the cause for appellants in No. 1 on the original argument and on the reargument. *Thurgood Marshall* argued the cause for appellants in No. 2 on the original argument and *Spottswood W. Robinson, III,* for appellants in No. 4 on the original argument, and both argued the causes for appellants in Nos. 2 and 4 on the reargument. *Louis L. Redding* and *Jack Greenberg* argued the cause for respondents in No. 10 on the original argument and *Jack Greenberg* and *Thurgood Marshall* on the reargument.

On the briefs were *Robert L. Carter, Thurgood Marshall, Spottswood W. Robinson, III, Louis L. Redding, Jack Greenberg, George E. C. Hayes, William R. Ming, Jr., Constance Baker Motley, James M. Nabrit, Jr., Charles S. Scott, Frank D. Reeves, Harold R. Boulware* and *Oliver W. Hill* for appellants in Nos. 1, 2 and 4 and respondents in No. 10; *George M. Johnson* for appellants in Nos. 1, 2 and 4; and *Loren Miller* for appellants in Nos. 2 and 4. *Arthur D. Shores* and *A. T. Walden* were on the Statement as to Jurisdiction and a brief opposing a Motion to Dismiss or Affirm in No. 2.

Paul E. Wilson, Assistant Attorney General of Kansas, argued the cause for appellees in No. 1 on the original argument and on the reargument. With him on the briefs was *Harold R. Fatzer,* Attorney General.

John W. Davis argued the cause for appellees in No. 2 on the original argument and for appellees in Nos. 2 and 4 on the reargument. With him on the briefs in No. 2 were *T. C. Callison,* Attorney General of South Carolina, *Robert McC. Figg, Jr., S. E. Rogers, William R. Meagher* and *Taggart Whipple.*

J. Lindsay Almond, Jr., Attorney General of Virginia, and *T. Justin Moore* argued the cause for appellees in No. 4 on the original argument and for appellees in Nos. 2 and 4 on the reargument. On the briefs in No. 4 were *J. Lindsay Almond, Jr.,* Attorney General, and *Henry T. Wickham,* Special Assistant Attorney General, for the State of Virginia, and *T. Justin Moore, Archibald G. Robertson, John W. Riely* and *T. Justin Moore, Jr.* for the Prince Edward County School Authorities, appellees.

H. Albert Young, Attorney General of Delaware, argued the cause for petitioners in No. 10 on the original argument and on the reargument. With him on the briefs was *Louis J. Finger,* Special Deputy Attorney General.

*347 U.S. 483–496 (1954). [Footnotes omitted.]

By special leave of Court, *Assistant Attorney General Rankin* argued the cause for the United States on the reargument, as *amicus curiae,* urging reversal in Nos. 1, 2 and 4 and affirmance in No. 10. With him on the brief were *Attorney General Brownell, Philip Elman, Leon Ulman, William J. Lamont* and *M. Magdelena Schoch. James P. McGranery,* then Attorney General, and *Philip Elman* filed a brief for the United States on the original argument, as *amicus curiae,* urging reversal in Nos. 1, 2 and 4 and affirmance in No. 10.

Briefs of *amici curiae* supporting appellants in No. 1 were filed by *Shad Polier, Will Maslow* and *Joseph B. Robinson* for the American Jewish Congress; by *Edwin J. Lukas, Arnold Forster, Arthur Garfield Hays, Frank E. Karelsen, Leonard Haas, Saburo Kido* and *Theodore Leskes* for the American Civil Liberties Union et al.; and by *John Ligtenberg* and *Selma M. Borchardt* for the American Federation of Teachers. Briefs of *amici curiae* supporting appellants in No. 1 and respondents in No. 10 were filed by *Arthur J. Goldberg* and *Thomas E. Harris* for the Congress of Industrial Organizations and by *Phineas Indritz* for the American Veterans Committee, Inc.

MR. CHIEF JUSTICE WARREN DELIVERED THE OPINION OF THE COURT

These cases come to us from the States of Kansas, South Carolina, Virginia and Delaware. They are premised on different facts and different local conditions, but a common legal question justifies their consideration together in this consolidated opinion.

In each of these cases, minors of the Negro race, through their legal representatives, seek the aid of the courts in obtaining admission to the public schools of their community on a nonsegregated basis. In each instance, they had been denied admission to schools attended by white children under laws requiring or permitting segregation according to race. This segregation was alleged to deprive the plaintiffs of the equal protection of the laws under the Fourteenth Amendment. In each of the cases other than the Delaware case, a three-judge federal district court denied relief to the plaintiffs on the so-called "separate but equal" doctrine announced by this Court in *Plessy* v. *Ferguson* . . . Under that doctrine, equality of treatment is accorded when the races are provided substantially equal facilities, even though these facilities be separate. In the Delaware case, the Supreme Court of Delaware adhered to that doctrine, but ordered that the plaintiffs be admitted to the white schools because of their superiority to the Negro schools.

The plaintiffs contend that segregated public schools are not "equal" and cannot be made "equal," and that hence they are deprived of the equal protection of the laws. Because of the obvious importance of the question presented, the Court took jurisdiction. Argument was heard in the 1952 Term, and reargument was heard this Term on certain questions propounded by the Court.

Reargument was largely devoted to the circumstances surrounding the adoption of the Fourteenth Amendment in 1868. It covered exhaustively consideration of the Amendment in Congress, ratification by the states, then existing practices in racial segregation, and the views of proponents and opponents of the Amendment. This discussion and our own investigation convince us that, although these sources cast some light, it is not enough to resolve the problem with which we are faced. At best, they are inconclusive. The most avid proponents of the post-War Amendments undoubtedly intended them to remove all legal distinctions among "all persons born or naturalized in the United States." Their opponents, just as certainly, were antagonistic to both the letter and the spirit of the Amendments and wished them to have the most limited effect. What others in Congress and the state legislatures had in mind cannot be determined with any degree of certainty.

An additional reason for the inconclusive nature of the Amendment's history, with respect to segregated schools, is the status of public education at that time. In the South, the movement toward free common schools, supported by general taxation, had not yet taken hold. Education of white children was largely in the hands of private groups. Education of Negroes was almost nonexistent, and practically all of the race were illiterate. In fact, any education of Negroes was forbidden by law in some states. Today, in contrast, many Negroes have achieved outstanding success in the arts and sciences as well as in the business and professional world. It is true that public school education at the time of the Amendment had advanced further in the North, but the effect of the Amendment on Northern States was generally ignored in the congressional debates. Even in the North, the conditions of public education did not approximate those existing today. The curriculum was usually rudimentary; ungraded schools were common in rural areas; the school term was but three months a year in many states; and compulsory school attendance was virtually unknown. As a consequence, it is not surprising that there should be so little in the history of the Fourteenth Amendment relating to its intended effect on public education.

In the first cases in this Court construing the Fourteenth Amendment, decided shortly after its adoption, the Court interpreted it as proscribing all state-imposed discriminations against the Negro race. The doctrine of "separate but equal" did not make its appearance in this court until 1896 in the case of *Plessy* v. *Ferguson, supra,* involving not education but transportation. American courts have since labored with the doctrine for over half a century. In this Court, there have been six cases involving the "separate but equal" doctrine in the field of public education. In *Cumming* v. *County Board of Education* . . . and *Gong Lum* v. *Rice* . . . the validity of the doctrine itself was not challenged. In more recent cases, all on the graduate school level, inequality was found in that specific benefits enjoyed by white students were denied to Negro students of the same educational qualifications. *Missouri ex rel. Gaines* v. *Canada* . . . ; *Sipuel* v. *Oklahoma* . . . ; *Sweatt* v. *Painter* . . . ; *McLaurin* v. *Oklahoma State Regents* . . . In none of these cases was it necessary to reexamine the doctrine to grant relief to the Negro plaintiff. And in *Sweatt* v. *Painter, supra,* the Court expressly reserved decision on the question whether *Plessy* v. *Ferguson* should be held inapplicable to public education.

In the instant cases, that question is directly presented. Here, unlike *Sweatt* v. *Painter,* there are findings below that the Negro and white schools involved have been equalized, or are being equalized, with respect to buildings, curricula, qualifications and salaries of teachers, and other "tangible" factors. Our recision, therefore, cannot turn on merely a comparison of these tangible factors in the Negro and white schools involved in each of the cases. We must look instead to the effect of segregation itself on public education.

In approaching this problem, we cannot turn the clock back to 1868 when the Amendment was adopted, or even to 1896 when *Plessy* v. *Ferguson* was written. We must consider public education in the light of its full development and its present place in American life throughout the Nation. Only in this way can it be determined if segregation in public schools deprives these plaintiffs of the equal protection of the laws.

Today, education is perhaps the most important function of state and local governments. Compulsory school attendance laws and the great expenditures for education both demonstrate our recognition of the importance of education to our democratic society. It is required in the performance of our most basic public responsibilities, even service in the armed forces. It is the very foundation of good citizenship. Today it is a principal instrument in awakening the child to cultural values, in preparing him for later professional training, and in helping him to adjust normally to his environment. In these days, it is doubtful that any child may reasonably be expected to succeed in life if he is denied the opportunity of an education. Such an opportunity, where the state has undertaken to provide it, is a right which must be made available to all on equal terms.

We come then to the question presented: Does segregation of children in public schools solely on the basis of race, even though the physical facilities and other "tangible" factors may be equal, deprive the children of the minority group of equal educational opportunities? We believe that it does.

In *Sweatt* v. *Painter, supra,* in finding that a segregated law school for Negroes could not provide them equal educational opportunities, this Court relied in large part on "those qualities which are incapable of objective measurement but which make for greatness in a law school." In *McLaurin* v. *Oklahoma State Regents, supra,* the Court, in requiring that a Negro admitted to a white graduate school be treated like all other students, again resorted to intangible considerations: ". . . his ability to study, to engage in discussions and exchange views with other students, and, in general, to learn his profession." Such considerations apply with added force to children in grade and high schools. To separate them from others of similar age and qualifications solely because of their race generates a feeling of inferiority as to their status in the community that may affect their hearts and minds in a way unlikely ever to be undone. The effect of this separation on their educational opportunities was well stated by a finding in the Kansas case by a court which nevertheless felt compelled to rule against the Negro plaintiffs:

> *Segregation of white and colored children in public schools has a detrimental effect upon the colored children. The impact is greater when it has the sanction of the law; for the policy of separating the races is usually interpreted as denoting the inferiority of the negro group. A sense of inferiority affects the motivation of a child to learn. Segregation with the sanction of law, therefore, has a tendency to [retard] the educational and mental development of negro children and to deprive them of some of the benefits they would receive in a racial[ly] integrated school system. . . .*

Whatever may have been the extent of psychological knowledge at the time of *Plessy* v. *Ferguson,* this finding is amply supported by modern authority. Any language in *Plessy* v. *Ferguson* contrary to this finding is rejected.

We conclude that in the field of public education the doctrine of "separate but equal" has no place. Separate educational facilities are inherently unequal. Therefore, we hold that the plaintiffs and others similarly situated for whom the actions have been brought are, by reason of the segregation complained of, deprived of the equal protection of the laws guaranteed by the Fourteenth Amendment. This disposition makes unnecessary any discussion whether such segregation also violates the Due Process Clause of the Fourteenth Amendment.

Because these are class actions, because of the wide applicability of this decision, and because of the great variety of local conditions, the formulation of decrees in these cases presents problems of considerable complexity. On reargument, the consideration of appropriate relief was necessarily subordinated to the primary question—the constitutionality of segregation in public education. We have now announced that such segregation is a denial of the equal protection of the laws. In order that we may have the full assistance of the parties in formulating decrees, the cases will be restored to the docket, and the parties are requested to present further argument on Questions 4 and 5 previously propounded by the Court for the reargument this Term. The Attorney General of the United States is again invited to participate. The Attorneys General of the states requiring or permitting segregation in public education will also be permitted to appear as *amici curiae* upon request to do so by September 15, 1954, and submission of briefs by October 1, 1954.

It is so ordered.

[As was indicated in the concluding paragraph, the Court refrained from implementing the decision pending further argument by the contending parties. Arthur J. Goldberg, now Associate Justice of the Supreme Court, Thomas E. Harris, and David E. Feller, counsel for the Congress of Industrial Organizations, presented an historic *amicus curiae* brief urging immediate integration rather than some form of gradual policy. In light of the limited success of the policy adopted by the Supreme Court, the viewpoint of Goldberg, Harris, and Feller is of considerable contemporary interest. Their brief provides a classic example of the kind of effort made by interest groups to shape public policy through judicial interpretation.]

3. Interest Groups and Policy Innovation: The CIO and Desegregation*

This Brief *amicus curiae* is submitted by the Congress of Industrial Organizations with the consent of the parties.

* Arthur J. Goldberg, Thomas E. Harris, and David E. Feller, *Brief for the Congress of Industrial Organizations as Amicus Curiae in Gebhart v. Belton,* submitted in the October term, 1953, in the Supreme Court of the United States.

The CIO is dedicated to the protection of our democratic system of government, and, hence of the civil rights of all Americans. Therefore, it supports the elimination of racial segregation and discrimination from every phase of American life.

The CIO's interest in the specific issues before the Court in this case is two-fold.

First, racial segregation in the public schools directly affects the millions of CIO members whose children attend these schools. The CIO is convinced that school segregation is harmful to the Negro children who are thus treated as inferior, to the white children in whom attitudes of racial hostility and discrimination are thus engendered and encouraged at an early age, and to the community as a whole. School segregation is a weakening and divisive force in American life. At the CIO's International Convention in November of this year, the delegates unanimously declared their opposition to school segregation, and their support for the position taken by the plaintiffs in these cases.

Secondly, the outcome of these cases will have indirect effects of great importance to the CIO. The CIO is endeavoring to practice non-segregation and non-discrimination in the everyday conduct of its union business. This effort has repeatedly been obstructed by statutes, ordinances, and regulations which require segregation in public meeting halls, public dining places, toilet facilities, etc. These laws seek to require CIO unions to maintain "equal but separate" facilities even in their own buildings, despite our membership's repudiation of segregation in any form. Since the constitutionality of these laws rests on basically the same line of reasoning which is put forward to justify school segregation, the decision of this Court in these school cases will, in all probability, have far-reaching implications as to the validity of these other segregation laws.

More broadly, school segregation, and the general pattern of government enforced segregation of which it is a part, fosters an atmosphere of inter-racial hostility which makes it more difficult for the CIO to carry out its own non-segregation policy. Further, this atmosphere of inter-racial hostility is used by anti-labor employers in opposing CIO organizing drives: invariably these employers stress the CIO's opposition to segregation and discrimination.

THE QUESTION DISCUSSED

In prior briefs *amicus curiae,* last year in *Brown* v. *Board of Education of Topeka,* and earlier in other school segregation cases, the CIO argued that segregation in public schools on the basis of race violates the Fourteenth Amendment *per se.* That is still our view, and we wholeheartedly subscribe to the arguments in support of it advanced by counsel for the appellants in Nos. 1, 2, and 4, and for the respondents in No. 10. Instead of repeating those arguments, however, we have concluded that it would be most helpful to the Court for us to confine our discussion to one particular issue on which the CIO has a certain amount of special experience and expert knowledge.

That issue, set out in paragraph 4 of the Court's Order of June 8, 1953, is what the Court should do if it concludes that segregation in the public schools violates the Fourteenth Amendment, i.e., whether the Court should order segregation terminated "forthwith" or permit "gradual adjustment."

This issue is very similar to the problem which the CIO and its affiliated unions have repeatedly faced as to how best to put into effect the non-segregation and non-discrimination policies of the national organizations in localities where segregation and discrimination have theretofore prevailed. It is our experience in the handling of this problem that we wish to lay before the Court.

ARGUMENT

Non-Segregation Could Be Effectuated With Less Disturbance By a "Forthwith" Decree Than By "Gradual Adjustment"

This memorandum seeks to summarize for the Court the experience and conclusions of unions and employers as to the best way to effectuate non-discrimination or non-segregation policies, and specifically as to how "forthwith" enforcement compares with "gradual adjustment." The bulk of this experience, both union and employer, relates to the institution or enforcement of a policy of non-discrimination and non-segregation in employment. The unions have, however, also had some experience with respect to desegregation in other fields, such as use of meeting halls and other union facilities.

As will be seen, all of this experience, union and employer, reinforces this central point: if a union or an employer wants to put into effect a policy of non-discrimination or non-segregation, it should do it "forthwith," firmly and decisively, and should avoid "gradual adjustment" or any other formula of indefinite postponement. If the policy of non-discrimination or non-segregation is put into effect concurrently with its announcement, and if it is enforced with firmness and decisiveness, there is every likelihood that the policy will be generally accepted and that any substanial degree of inter-racial friction will be avoided. The bulk of the people in any community or plant or office are influenced in their attitudes on racial discrimination by the current practice in the community or plant or office. If the practice is changed, and if the change be made unequivocally, they accept the new practice and their attitudes come to reflect it. Thus traditional Southern attitudes on racial segregation largely mirror, according to our experience, simply the prevailing practices, rather than deeply or strongly held individual convictions. Once the practice is changed, beliefs as to what the practice should be will change too.

Conversely, "gradual adjustment" to a new policy of non-segregation or non-discrimination is apt to work less well. Long drawn out discussion of a contemplated ultimate end of segregation or discrimination may serve only to exacerbate racial tensions. Division along racial lines may harden and people may be led to take more extreme and adamant stands than they would have if the issue had been disposed of promptly, once and for all. For example, in a plant where Negro workers have customarily been excluded from certain types of jobs it may prove extremely difficult to persuade the white workers, through a program of education and discussion, that the time has come to end this discrimination. Such a program may serve only to accentuate inter-racial tension by keeping the issue alive and in suspension. On the other hand, if the union and employer firmly announce that henceforth there will be no job discrimination, the new policy will, in our experience, be accepted by the workers with little friction, and the issue will be disposed of once and for all.

We do not mean that education and discussion do not serve a purpose in this field; they do. But they should accompany the effective implementation of a policy of non-discrimination and non-segregation. Absent such effective implementation, endless discussion and the indefinite postponements of "gradual adjustment" may serve only to freeze or accentuate attitudes. If no fixed terminal date for segregation is set, its proponents will regard the issue as really still open, and the controversy is likely only to become more intense with the passage of time.

Our experience suggests, we think, one further point: The CIO and its unions have put non-segregation and non-discrimination policies into effect in all parts of the country. No major strife has resulted within these organizations—and they are voluntary organizations, whose officers are elected by the membership and whose very existence depends upon the continued good will of the membership. If the non-segregation policies of these voluntary organizations, when promptly and firmly implemented, can win such acceptance, then, *a fortiori,* a definitive decree of the highest Court of the land will receive general acceptance.

I. UNION EXPERIENCE

We have stated the conclusions which the CIO has reached as the best procedure to follow in putting into effect a policy of non-discrimination or non-segregation. These conclusions rest on a very considerable body of experience. The CIO and its affiliated unions have some hundreds of thousands of members in Southern communities where racial segregation and discrimination, except for the changes the CIO has effected, permeate all aspects of life. It and its affiliates have other hundreds of thousands of members in border communities, or others, where some degree of segregation and discrimination is prevalent.

Yet the CIO has from its beginning stood out against these community prejudices. The CIO Constitution dedicates our organizations "to bring about the effective organization of the workingmen and women of America regardless of race, creed, color or nationality" and "to protect and extend our democratic constitutions and civil rights and liberties, and thus to perpetuate the cherished traditions of our democracy." Similar provisions are found in the constitutions of the international unions affiliated with the CIO. Accordingly the CIO and its affiliated unions have, from their inceptions, opposed discrimination in any form based on race or color.

The meetings of the CIO and its affiliates are never segregated, although, in many areas where we operate ours are the only unsegregated meetings held in the community. Negro members belong to the same local unions and have the same rights as white members. Local union officers are elected without regard to color. Scores of Negroes now hold local offices, or participate in collective bargaining as members of union negotiating committees. There are local unions that have Negro presidents.

The CIO conducts educational institutes at various places in the south for southern workers—white and Negro; male and female. These educational classes are entirely non-segregated. So also are the political meetings held from time to time by the CIO's Political Action Committee.

As discussed in more detail later, there is now no segregation in the use of CIO facilities, such as meeting halls, rest rooms, drinking fountains, etc. Where the CIO and its unions have their way, there is likewise no segregation in the use of plant eating places, locker rooms, rest rooms, etc. Sometimes, however, state laws or local ordinances require segregation in the use of these facilities, and employers usually comply with laws, unlike the CIO which disregards them as unconstitutional.

Many of the collective bargaining agreements which the CIO and its affiliates have negotiated specifically forbid discrimination on account of race in hiring, promotion, or any term or condition of employment; and whether or not the contracts contain such specific provisions we see to it that they are administered in a non-discriminatory manner.

We do not assert that this insistence by the CIO and its unions on no segregation and no discrimination on account of race has not sometimes been the subject of friction within the unions. Nor do we say that it has not sometimes made the CIO's organizing task more difficult in some communities. There has been some friction: Our unions have had to expel a few members and have even suspended the charter of an occasional local union for refusal to abide by these principles. Likewise, anti-union employers have repeatedly cited our anti-discrimination policies in opposing organizing campaigns of CIO unions, and their opposition has sometimes been successful.

We do assert, however, that there has been no *major* strife or difficulty or division within CIO unions or locals on this issue. We are confident, moreover, that the unequivocal stand taken by the CIO and its affiliated unions in opposition to segregation or discrimination, and their refusal to temporize on this issue, has resulted in more rapid acceptance of this policy by locals in the South, and in less friction with regard to it, than would have been the case had we followed a program of gradual adjustment to local *mores*.

We will set forth, with a minimum of comment, some of the experiences of the CIO and its unions on this subject.

At the outset we wish to call to the Court's attention the experience of the United Automobile, Aircraft and Agricultural Implement Workers of America, CIO, on this subject. The following quotation is from an article by Brendan Sexton, Educational Director of the UAW, entitled "The Intervention of the Union in the Plant," appearing in *The Journal of Social Issues.* . . . [Emphasis has] been added.

> *Where the problem of "up-grading" has created conflict, the union has been divided regarding the attitude it should take towards the recalcitrant group of workers. One group has advocated a "soft" educational approach, another a "hard" course of action. Those who favor education have argued that the abrupt introduction of Negroes into cohesive work groups can only produce aggravations, incite suspicions and provoke wildcat strikes and/or slowdowns. Those who argue for "action" insist that an informal work group should not be allowed to constitute itself, on the basis of its own sentiments or prejudices, the arbiter of a man's right to a job. The job is the man's right and the work group must bend to that broader democratic rule; the individual seeking that job should not*

have to bend to the wishes of the work-group. But more than demonstration of principle is involved, the action partisans would argue. Tactically, the approach is also correct, for the union and the company are also claimants to a man's loyalty, and by invoking the authority of the union and management, the work group can psychologically accept these wider claims. In some instances, this dispute has been complicated by two groups of extremists; on the one hand, the Communists and their supporters have espoused action largely for disruptive purposes; on the other hand, advocates of "do-nothingism" argue for education as a blind to postpone change. Apart from these extraneous motivations, the issue remains as a real moral and tactical dilemma.

The writer knows of no objective tests of either approach. In practice, the union has found that the greatest progress has been achieved where the action method has been used, followed by educational techniques. In those instances, the educational materials have served as a convenient and psychologically necessary rationalization to make acceptable the fact that his behavior has been changed by external sanction—the authority of the union.

There are many drawbacks to the use of "group discussion" as a technique of effecting change in a work plant. Actually we doubt that minority individuals would win many jobs or promotion if unions had put the question to a vote in the work group. Lazy prejudices are hard to change when the group is allowed to feel that being accepted by it is a privilege. The question arises, too, what is the locus of democratic opinion? Who should be permitted to vote on such a question? Should it be the workers in the specific department where the job is open, the general job classification to which the workers are assigned, the local union of which they are members?

In the UAW, as in many other unions, the basic issue is decided at international union conventions. And resolutions establishing a non-discrimination policy received all but unanimous support. Since this was accepted as basic union policy, all sub-units of the union are expected to carry out this policy. . . .

. . . Sometimes great resistance derelops when such a policy is imposed. In such instances both the action and education techniques must be applied judiciously. In an area in which prejudices are strong, however, prolonged discussion may only serve to generate and reinforce resistance to the application of the union policy.

In the passage of his article just quoted, Mr. Sexton sums up the conclusions which have been reached by the UAW-CIO, one of the country's largest unions, on how a union can best go about implementing a non-discrimination policy. Elsewhere in this article Mr. Sexton summarizes some of the experiences which led his union to this conclusion. Typical of these experiences is the following, described on page 9 of Mr. Sexton's article:

Members of Local 988 of the UAW-CIO, at the plant of the International Harvester Corporation in Memphis, Tennessee, struck against the upgrading of a Negro into a semi-skilled job in which the Negroes had hitherto not been employed. A good deal of education on the desirability of eliminating discrimination had been carried on in this local. In all likelihood this program was as effective as any union education program in any similar local. Moreover, this local union had seemed to be more advanced in its attitudes than many other 'Southern' locals in the UAW. It had elected Negroes as local union officers and bargaining committeemen and had, on at least two occasions, sent Negroes as delegates to international union conventions. Nevertheless, when a Negro was promoted to a welding job, the workers at the plant struck to enforce an informal ban against the admission of Negroes into this classification.

The union neither debated nor discussed the question with the workers affected. It sent to the local union an order adopted by the international executive board, signed by Walter Reuther, which "instructed" all workers to return to their jobs. The order called upon the authority of the constitution which had been adopted at the international union's convention. As a result of the order, the strike was called off. The Negro worker was upgraded and there has been no recurrence of trouble at this plant.

The experiences of the United Steelworkers of America, CIO, another of the country's largest unions, have been similar. The greatest aggregation of heavy industry in the South is found in and around Birmingham, Alabama. The mines and mills of the area—coal, iron, and steel—are all unionized, with tens of thousands of steelworkers and iron miners belonging to the United Steelworkers of America.

Despite a prevalent community pattern of segregation and discrimination, the Steelworker's locals have been unsegregated from their inception. White and Negro members belong to the same local unions, attend meetings together, and elect their local union officers without regard to the color of their skins. In the administration of collective bargaining agreements, the local union officers and the staff representatives of the International—some of whom, like some of the local union officers, are Negroes—are scrupulous to see that there is no discrimination in hiring, advancement, or any term or condition of employment on account of race.

In past years there was undeniably some friction in the Birmingham area over these union policies of no discrimination and no segregation. The union, nevertheless, adhered to these policies firmly and unequivocally, while at the same time undertaking to persuade its members of their soundness and justice. As part of the latter effort, the late Philip Murray, then President of the CIO and of the United Steelworkers of America, on one occasion addressed a mass meeting of thousands of persons in the Birmingham ball park.

The international union's firm adherence to its policies, coupled contemporaneously with discussion and explanation, has won general acceptance for those policies among the membership in the Birmingham area. They are no longer a source of friction or difficulty. Relations between white and Negro workers in the local unions and in the plants are now generally excellent. Indeed a few months ago the largest steel mill in the area was shut down when thousands of white workers joined a small number of Negro workers in protesting certain work conditions of the latter.

The experience of the Steelworkers' Union with regard to race segregation has not, incidentally, been confined to the South. In 1947 the Gary, Indiana, schools started admitting Negroes to elementary and high school classes theretofore reserved for whites, and hundreds of the white students, many of them children of steelworkers, declared a "holiday" from classes. The Steelworkers' Union went into action in support of the school authorities. The District Director, Joseph Germano, explained to a meeting at the union hall the policies of the union against discrimination or segregation, and the meeting voted to suspend from the union members whose children remained away from school. The children went back to school. . . .

The following quotation related to one of our smaller unions, the United Packinghouse Workers, CIO. It is from John Hope II, "The Self-Survey of the Packinghouse Union," in *The Journal of Social Issues* . . . :

> *An effort of a dissident white minority to stymie the desegregation of plant facilities, as required by the master contract of 1952, in a Southern branch plant of a major chain packer was defeated when the local officers who had courageously abided by their contractual obligations were re-elected over a lily-white slate of candidates who had sought to retire them from office purely on the race issue. In another Southern plant a brief protest of white women against newly hired Negro women using the same locker room was followed by their acceptance, and later by the insistence of white women that procrastination in the desegregation of the men's locker room be ended. Both are now integrated and no unfavorable consequences are apparent.*

These illustrations could be multiplied indefinitely.

We shall, however, cite but one further instance from the CIO's experience; an instance which relates not to segregation or discrimination on the job, but to segregation in union meeting halls, eating places, toilets, etc.

We have already mentioned that various state and local ordinances purport to require separate and segregated facilities. The existence of these laws, and uncertainty as whether they should be complied with, occasioned a certain amount of friction and confusion in CIO State and local councils for some years.

However, in April 1950, the General Counsel of the CIO advised its state and local councils that all such laws and ordinances were, in his opinion, unconstitutional, and that, in line with general CIO policy, "Therefore, no segregation in the use of facilities in buildings or office space under the control of CIO Industrial Union Councils should be permitted, and there should be no signs indicating such segregation."

This policy, once clearly laid down, received complete acceptance. There is now no segregation in the use of any CIO council facility—and there has been not the slightest friction or difficulty about it.

AFL and independent unions seem to have reached the same conclusions that we have: That a union policy against discrimination or segregation can be implemented without substantial strife or difficulty, if such a policy is unequivocally enunciated and unhesitatingly enforced.

For example, the *Indianapolis News,* for June 24 and 25, 1953, carries a story about a wildcat strike among a minority of Indianapolis railway operators against the proposed hiring of Negro drivers. It reports that the secretary-treasurer of the local union, a local of the Amalgamated Association of Street, Electric Railway & Motor Coach Employees of America, AFL, declared that "Our International Union prohibits any kind of discrimination," and ordered the strikers to return to work, on pain of suspension from the union. The newspaper account further relates that the strikers returned to work, and gave assurances that there would be no repetition of the walkout.

The United Mine Workers (Independent) has followed the same policy, and with the same results. Here is a quotation from Herbert R. Northrup, "Organized Labor and the Negro," . . . emphasis added:

> *It must be re-emphasized at this point that the UMW has an enviable record of practicing, as well as preaching, racial equality in its organization ever since it began to function. It is true that there have been instances of discrimination against Negroes in particular locals, both in the North and in the South.* But the officials of the national union have never, to the writer's knowledge, condoned such action, and have not hesitated to chastise individual locals for failing to live up to the letter of the non-discrimination policy. *Moreover, the UMW has always conducted both its organizing campaigns and its day-to-day union affairs without prejudice to any race.*

We close this enumeration of union experiences and viewpoints on how best to effectuate an anti-discrimination, anti-segregation, policy with a quotation from Hugo Ernst, President, Hotel and Restaurant Employees & Bartenders International Union, AFL, which appears in that Union's publication, *The Catering Industry Employee,* for July 1952:

> *I wish to speak out in the strongest possible terms concerning the question of our local unions and the admission of non-Caucasian members.*
>
> *This article is prompted by a newspaper clipping which was sent me the other day by a West Coast friend. It was from the front page of a daily paper, and it set forth the sorry details of a lawsuit filed against one of our local unions by an employer and three bartenders who work for him.*
>
> *The suit was filed because, although the employer was willing and ready to sign a union contract, and his workers were willing and ready to join the union, the union would not sign the contract and would not accept these bartenders as members. The bartenders are all three Negroes.*
>
> *By far the most damaging part of this story lies, not in the unfavorable publicity of that front-page story, but in the fact that there are still, in 1952, members of our International Union who will thus attack the principles of fair play on which every strong union must be built. "Our International Constitution is explicit on this matter of discrimination. Section 11, Article XI states:*
>
> *"No Local may reject a person prior to applying for membership; nor may any Local reject any applicant by reason of race, religion or color."*
>
> *Nothing could be plainer than that.*

Nobody can be denied membership in our union because he is a Negro, or because he is an Oriental, or an Indian or because he is a Catholic or a Jew or a Protestant or a Moslem or a Buddhist.

If he is employed at the trade he is eligible for membership in the Local Union established to represent persons in his craft—and that's that!

Indeed, it is necessary for me to declare in the plainest possible terms that I will have no choice, whenever such situations are brought to my attention, but to place the guilty local union under trusteeship, wherever it persists in flaunting our constitution on this point.

II. EMPLOYER EXPERIENCE

The views of employers who have sought to carry out a policy of non-discrimination, on how best to implement such a policy, largely agree, we believe, with the unions' conclusions on this subject. We wish particularly to call attention to the testimony on this subject of Ivan L. Willis, Vice President in Charge of Industrial Relations, International Harvester Company, given at Hearings on "Discrimination and Full Utilization of Manpower Resources", before the Subcommittee on Labor and Labor-Management Relations of the Senate Committee on Labor and Public Welfare . . . The quotation is long, but, we believe, well worth the Court's consideration:

In carrying out our nondiscrimination policy, our approach is about this.

"First, we do something about the problem, rather than just talk about it.

Second, we take our actions at as rapid a pace as circumstances permit, and, once taken, we do not retreat.

Third, we try to keep everyone involved as well informed as possible, all the time.

To illustrate this approach, let me take the example of a new factory located in a Southern city. In this particular city there are state laws in effect which require separate drinking fountains, separate toilet facilities, separate eating facilities, and so forth. Obviously, we have to comply with state laws, and we do.

But, beyond that, many questions arise. The first question is, of course, "Are we going to hire Negroes at all?" Our answer is "Yes."

The second question then may be: "If we do hire Negroes, are we going to segregate them, in the sense that we will simply have all-Negro departments?"

Our answer is "No." We do not favor all-Negro or all-white departments.

The third question is: "Shall we start out that way, or shall we start in conformity with local customs and try to make a change later?"

Our answer was: "We are going to start on an unsegregated basis".

The next question is: "How can we do that?"

Our answer—for now we are coming to the root of the problem—was more complicated. We said: "First, we will have to make sure that our managerial people, our foremen, and supervisors thoroughly understand our policy and the reasons behind it, so that they will be able and willing to do a good job in its application."

Second, we said, "Everybody must know our policy". So, as men came to the hiring office to apply for work in the new plant, they were all told what our policy was.

I might insert there, Senator, when we first started employing people at that plant, we permitted all applicants regardless of their race or color to come into a common waiting room. That was our first departure perhaps from the customary practice in that area where it was normally the practice to have white employees come into one room for interviews and the Negroes be either hired at the gate or to come into a separate room.

They were told that they might find themselves working next to a Negro employee and were given the opportunity at that time to decide whether that would be distasteful to them. Surprisingly few withdrew at that point. Next, in the orientation classes for new employees, all employees were taken together, with no segregation. Finally, their job assignments were made on the same basis. As time has passed and they have gained experience, their promotion and upgrading to better jobs have been carried out on the basis of seniority and ability.

We have had very few evidences of resentment or bad feeling as a result of our policy. A few times, in this southern plant, there have been incidents, principally arising in cases where a Negro employee was being upgraded. These have not been too serious in nature and have been met successfully, through the joint efforts of the company and the labor union involved, which was the UAW–CIO.

As a consequence of our experience, we feel perfectly sure that progress can be made, with proper planning and execution of policy. We know that more progress will be made in the future. We have every reason to be quite satisfied with the development of our Negro employees, in productivity and in other ways.

In the introduction of Negro employees into some of our offices, as distinguished from the manufacturing shops, we have followed essentially the same procedures. First, we have thoroughly discussed all phases of the change with supervisory people. Next, we have had similar discussions with the employees already on the rolls. In practice, we have not met any difficulty which I would consider to be a real problem. In general, things have gone smoothly, and the Negro men and women have fitted in quite well with the rest of the group.

As a result of our total experience, I think all of us are convinced that there is nothing insuperable about the problem of integrating minority groups into industry, in any area of the United States. We recognize that progress may be faster in some places than in others, but we do see progress all along the line.

If the views set forth in this testimony are compared with those of Brendan Sexton, UAW Educational Director, quoted *supra*, . . . it will be seen that here is one subject on which the views of the company and the union coincide to a remarkable degree. They are in full agreement that the best way to effectuate a policy against racial discrimination or segregation is to announce it firmly and carry it out unequivocally, instead of attempting to depart gradually from local customs.

These views likewise find support in the conclusions of the New York State War Council Committee on Discrimination in Employment. In a pamphlet issued in 1942, entitled "How Management Can Integrate Negroes in War Industries", the Council stated:

> *Introduction of the Negro Worker. Necessity for Firmness and a Real Desire to Integrate Negroes.*
>
> *All persons who have dealt with the problem, including the personnel managers and government officials interviewed, agree that nothing is so important as a firm position on the part of management. Once this position has been stated in terms of Executive Order 8802 and the laws of the State of New York and a recalcitrant white worker still refuses to work with colored persons, management can only transfer the worker or ask for his resignation. This will seldom or never be necessary if the situation is clearly explained. Of all the companies interviewed only one found it necessary to allow a person to resign.*

Finally, we respectfully call attention to certain conclusions which resulted from a study conducted by the New York State School of Industrial and Labor Relations, at Cornell University. Its Research Bulletin No. 6, February 1950, on "Negroes in the Work Group", states:

> *Certain conclusions may be reasonably inferred from the data obtained from this study. Again it must be noted that this is a selected study of a few firms, all of which had a good record for employing Negroes.*
>
> *(1) A Firm and Unequivocal Stand*
>
> *Employers who decide to hire Negroes for the first time or to hire additional Negroes in new capacities should adopt a firm attitude in this matter. The employer must be resolute in his intentions to enforce this policy regardless of any real or illusory objections that may be raised by people in the organization.*
>
> *By adhering to a determined attitude to make the program work, any obstacles that may be raised will be smoothed over or adjusted. Employers earnest in their determination to integrate the Negro will soon find their subordinates as well as their employees following their views.*

CONCLUSION

For the reasons stated, we respectfully suggest to the Court, that if it concludes, as we think it should, that segregation in public schools violates the Fourteenth Amendment, it would be preferable for it to implement this conclusion by directing the cessation of segregation "forthwith" rather than by "gradual adjustment".

Respectfully submitted,

ARTHUR J. GOLDBERG
General Counsel

THOMAS E. HARRIS
Assistant General Counsel

DAVID E. FELLER
Assistant General Counsel

4. Brown *v*. Board of Education: *the Implementing Decision**

MR. CHIEF JUSTICE WARREN DELIVERED THE OPINION OF THE COURT

These cases were decided on May 17, 1954. The opinions of that date, declaring the fundamental principle that racial discrimination in public education is unconstitutional, are incorporated herein by reference. All provisions of federal, state, or local law requiring or permitting such discrimination must yield to this principle. There remains for consideration the manner in which relief is to be accorded.

Because these cases arose under different local conditions and their disposition will involve a variety of local problems, we requested further argument on the question of relief. In view of the nationwide importance of the decision, we invited the Attorney General of the United States and the Attorneys General of all states requiring or permitting racial discrimination in public education to present their views on that question. The parties, the United States, and the States of Florida, North Carolina, Arkansas, Oklahoma, Maryland, and Texas filed briefs and participated in the oral argument.

These presentations were informative and helpful to the Court in its consideration of the complexities arising from the transition to a system of public education freed of racial discrimination. The presentations also demonstrated that substantial steps to eliminate racial discrimination in public schools have already been taken, not only in some of the communities in which these cases arose, but in some of the states appearing as *amici curiae,* and in other states, as well. Substantial progress has been made in the District of Columbia and in the communities in Kansas and Delaware involved in this litigation. The defendants in the cases coming to us from South Carolina and Virginia are awaiting the decision of this Court concerning relief.

Full implementation of these constitutional principles may require solution of varied local school problems. School authorities have the primary responsibility for elucidating, assessing, and solving these problems; courts will have to consider whether the action of school authorities constitutes good faith implementation of the governing constitutional principles. Because of their proximity to local conditions and the possible need for further hearings, the courts which originally heard these cases can best perform this judicial appraisal. Accordingly, we believe it appropriate to remand the cases to those courts.

In fashioning and effectuating the decrees, the courts will be guided by equitable principles. Traditionally, equity has been characterized by a practical flexibility in shaping its remedies and by a facility for adjusting and reconciling public and private needs. These cases call for the exercise of these traditional attributes of equity power. At stake is the personal interest of the plaintiffs in admission to public schools as soon as practicable on a nondiscriminatory basis. To effectuate this interest may call for elimination of a variety of obstacles in making the transition to school systems operated in accordance with the constitutional principles set forth in our May 17, 1954, decision. Courts of equity may properly take into account the public interest in the elimination

*349 U.S. 294–301 (1955). [Footnotes omitted.]

of such obstacles in a systematic and effective manner. But it should go without saying that the vitality of these constitutional principles cannot be allowed to yield simply because of disagreement with them.

While giving weight to these public and private considerations, the courts will require that the defendants make a prompt and reasonable start toward full compliance with our May 17, 1954, ruling. Once such a start has been made, the courts may find that additional time is necessary to carry out the ruling in an effective manner. The burden rests upon the defendants to establish that such time is necessary in the public interest and is consistent with good faith compliance at the earliest practicable date. To that end, the courts may consider problems related to administration, arising from the physical condition of the school plant, the school transportation system, personnel, revision of school districts and attendance areas into compact units to achieve a system of determining admission to the public schools on a nonracial basis, and revision of local laws and regulations which may be necessary in solving the foregoing problems. They will also consider the adequacy of any plans the defendants may propose to meet these problems and to effectuate a transition to a racially nondiscriminatory school system. During this period of transition, the courts will retain jurisdiction of these cases.

The judgments below, except that in the Delaware case, are accordingly reversed and the cases are remanded to the District Courts to take such proceedings and enter such orders and decrees consistent with this opinion as are necessary and proper to admit to public schools on a racially nondiscriminatory basis with all deliberate speed the parties to these cases. The judgment in the Delaware case—ordering the immediate admission of the plaintiffs to schools previously attended only by white children—is affirmed on the basis of the principles stated in our May 17, 1954, opinion, but the case is remanded to the Supreme Court of Delaware for such further proceedings as that Court may deem necessary in light of this opinion.

It is so ordered.

[The success of the Supreme Court's ruling on segregation in the public schools depends ultimately upon the vigor and persistence of the federal district judges who must implement it. Some of the strains and problems attendant on this dependence are underscored by Professor Paul Sanders. His treatment provides an excellent analysis of general problems of federal court relationships as well as specific problems relating to the segregation decision.]

5. The Warren Court and the Lower Federal Courts: Problems of Implementation*

Within recent days it has made news that the House of Delegates of the American Bar Association received a report of the Association's Committee on the Bill of Rights

*Paul H. Sanders, "The Warren Court and the Lower Federal Courts," Unpublished paper delivered at the 1959 Annual Meeting of the American Political Science Association, Washington, D.C., September, 1959, pp. 1–13. Reproduced with permission of the author.

which indicated that the Supreme Court of the United States was acting courageously and in the best judicial tradition in the field of civil liberty. That the acceptance of such a report should have occurred only after considerable protest might seem rather odd if one looked merely at the wording of the Federal Bill of Rights and the first of the Canons of Professional Ethics of the American Bar Association. Canon One declares it to be the duty of the lawyer to maintain toward the courts (presumably all courts) a respectful attitude, not for the sake of the temporary incumbent of the judicial office, but for the maintenance of its supreme importance. The Canon goes on to declare: "Judges, not being wholly free to defend themselves, are peculiarly entitled to receive the support of the Bar against unjust criticism and clamor."

This relatively minor movement in the opposite direction merely underlines the overwhelming criticism that has been heaped (frequently with the help of lawyers and judges) upon the Supreme Court of the United States, its Chief Justice, and many of the individual Justices in the last few years. This criticism, fomented and sustained by those protesting the School Segregation Decisions, has even proceeded in some degree from the ranks of the federal judiciary itself. A national news magazine saw fit to circularize judges of the United States Courts of Appeals and United States District Courts, asking whether they agreed or disagreed with certain critical comments approved by the conference of chief justices of the various state courts. Although many of the judges refused to reply, it is reported that of the 128 federal judges who did reply, 39% disagreed with the criticism of the state chief justices, while 15% preferred not to express any view, leaving 46% who expressed agreement with the adverse criticism. . . . This percentage of disagreement, perhaps not too significant when the total number of federal judges is considered, brings us to the special topic of this discussion, which has reference to the interaction between the Supreme Court and the lower federal courts in the period since the beginning of Chief Justice Warren's term of service. The reported decisions of the Supreme Court reveal the deep divisions that at times exist within that body itself. It should occasion no particular surprise to find that presently there are varying viewpoints within the ranks of the total federal judiciary in their acceptance and implementation of Supreme Court pronouncements. We can safely assume that this situation has always existed to some degree and will continue with varying degrees of intensity. It is more remarkable, perhaps, that there has not been more during this period of crisis.

Article III of the Constitution of the United States speaks of vesting the judicial power of the United States in the Supreme and "inferior" courts as if it were some unitary or indivisible substance, but the article specifies no method of achieving or maintaining any such unitary character in the exercise of the power. The Founding Fathers foresaw pressures operating upon the courts exercising this judicial power of the United States and sought to relieve against it, so far as it was possible to do so by giving the judges security of tenure and compensation. These constitutional provisions which make for independence in the federal judiciary as against pressures from other branches of government and the general public will, undoubtedly, also generate in a member of the lower federal judiciary a belief that he is something more than a mere reflection of the High Tribunal—a mere spokesman for applying its decisions. He will sense that his judicial independence includes to a degree, independence as against the higher courts in his own system.

The received tradition for a judge of the United States District Court is that he is obliged to follow, as binding precedent, the decisions of the Supreme Court of the United States and of the Court of Appeals of his own circuit. In turn, of course, the judges of the Federal Courts of Appeals are bound, under the accepted doctrine, by the decisions of the Supreme Court of the United States. This doctrine is not a matter of mere lip service. It is believed that, if one were to poll the individual district judges, almost unanimously the response would be that this obligation is controlling in the approach to a particular decision. If he discussed the matter further and candidly he would probably reveal his great distaste for being reversed by a higher court and perhaps some of the techniques he may utilize to minimize this hazard. It is a real deterrent in forces shaping his action.

In contrast to the point just made and speaking generally, without regard to relationships during the last five-year period, it is quite obvious that the general doctrine as to the binding character of Supreme Court decisions has never been fully adhered to nor could one reasonably expect that it would be followed with unvarying consistency. This is another way of stating the obvious fact that the application of federal judicial power is not unitary or indivisible on any particular legal topic— never has been, and never will be. The Supreme Court of the United States, the Courts of Appeals of the various circuits, the district courts, and indeed, each individual federal district judge, constitute separate centers of power. These centers of power exert forces in opposite directions at times, rather than in harmony, even after a presumably binding precedent has been established at the highest level. In serving as an attorney for a federal department, I found that I could become accustomed to speaking of "the law in the Fourth Circuit" as one distinct thing and "the law in the Sixth Circuit" as something entirely different, even under the same statute. It was a little more difficult to adjust to the idea that "the law" under a single federal statute, extensively interpreted by the Supreme Court of the United States and within a single circuit, could vary rather remarkably in its actual result from one federal district court (or judge) in a state to another in the same state. Furthermore, it can be assumed that each of the judges being compared under the above circumstances would be seeking to do what he thought was "right" and would subscribe in full to the binding character of the decisions of the Supreme Court and of his own particular Court of Appeals,

Narrowing the matter to the relationships between the centers of power represented by the District Courts and the Courts of Appeals as opposed to the Supreme Court, several reasons will indicate why divergency and difference to some degree can be expected, even though full weight is given to intellectual honesty and good intention on the part of the lower court judge. First of all, divergency is furthered by the sheer number of cases that are being disposed of at the various judicial levels. During the fiscal year 1958, more than 95,000 civil and criminal cases were commenced in the United States District Courts. The figure has been in this vicinity at least since 1955. . . . During the fiscal years 1954 through 1958, the appeals and original proceedings commenced in the United States Courts of Appeals varied from approximately 3500 to 3700 per year. . . . The Supreme Court of the United States has received from the federal district courts and the Courts of Appeals the following number of cases between the 1954 and 1957 terms inclusive: 618 (1954); 811 (1955); 835 (1956); 930 (1957); Of these, in 1954, the decision below was left undisturbed (certiorari denied) in 491 cases out of 618. The corresponding figure left undisturbed for the other years was 655 (1955), 664 (1956), and 724 (1957). . . . These figures suggest that the Supreme Court could not maintain any rigid uniformity of adherence to its announced principles in the federal judicial system. Chief Justice Vinson indicated in 1949 that the Court was not even particularly concerned to achieve this identity of result in the federal courts. He said:

> *The Supreme Court is not, and never has been, primarily concerned with the correction of errors in lower court decisions. . . . The function of the Supreme Court is, therefore, to resolve conflicts of opinion on federal questions that have arisen among lower courts, to pass upon questions of wide import under the Constitution, laws and treaties of the United States and to exercise supervisory power over lower federal courts. If we took every case in which an interesting legal question is raised, or our prima facie impression is that the decision below is erroneous, we could not fulfill the constitutional and statutory responsibilities placed upon the Court. To remain effective, the Supreme Court must continue to decide only those cases which present questions whose resolution will have an immediate importance far beyond the particular facts and parties involved. . . . Lawyers might be well advised, in preparing petitions for certiorari, to spend a little less time discussing the merits of their cases and a little more time demonstrating why it is important that the court should hear them. . . .*

The inevitability of variation within the federal system resulting from such an approach would seem to be obvious.

Variation in the administration of justice in the federal courts and a degree of freedom in the lower federal courts to act as independent centers of power is furthered by the extensive statutory arrangements provided by Congress for the exercise of federal judicial power. We do not have the Supreme Court of the United States acting in some generalized supervisory capacity over the lower federal courts, something in the manner of a schoolmaster and his pupils. Rather, the whole matter of what may be taken into each of the various courts and from one to another is to a high degree specified, regulated and controlled by the Judicial Code. . . . Federal judicial power is not unitary or indivisible because it has been in fact divided and allocated and limited at the various judicial levels by congressional enactment. Some bills introduced into Congress, you will recall, have sought to utilize this approach to curtail rather drastically the authority of the Supreme Court to exercise appellate jurisdiction in some of the areas covered by its more controversial decisions.

Divergency between the lower court and the Supreme Court is furthered also by the uncertainty or "fuzziness" of the high court precedent and, perhaps most of all, by doubts as to whether it will remain a precedent. If the edict itself is uncertain, or if there is a question as to whether the high court would itself now follow it, the possibility of variation and flexibility in lower court action is multiplied tremendously. Will the high court itself stand firm, or will it overrule or distinguish the precedent? As Charles P. Curtis has pithily remarked: "It is a little difficult for the lower court to have to follow the Supreme Court of the next succeeding year." . . .

Leaving aside the specific pressures that may be generated by particular issues before the court, one can observe certain circumstances normally surrounding the appointment of a federal district judge, which to a varying and immeasurable degree cannot help but be reflected in the functioning of the several courts. A federal district judge is usually (but not always) a resident of the district where he is named to serve. He cannot fail to be aware of and to be responsive in some degree to the forces and the social, economic and political values which are dominant in that area. If he is named by the political party which is in the majority in that area, he will have been the recipient of what is normally regarded from the political point of view as the one bit of patronage that has no superior. Even when an individual is given full credit for a desire to be a "good judge" and to be unswayed by political pressures and to be "fair to friend and foe" alike he remains the product of forces which it will be at times extremely difficult to ignore. These interests, to which would be added the social and economic interests of the individual judge, set up generalized tensions within which he carries out his basic accepted obligation to conform to the controlling precedent established by the Supreme Court and by the Court of Appeals of his circuit. These generalized pressures may or may not work against this basic obligation but it is obvious that the product of these pressures, plus much more specific pressure that may be generated in a case deeply involving the emotions of the area, may strain to the uttermost the normal idea of conformity to Supreme Court edict and may in fact displace any such sense of obligation.

The foregoing divisive factors which can be regarded as more or less inherent in the federal system can obviously be greatly aggravated when other and larger forces move into the arena where a choice must be made by the court between implementing or refusing to implement a particular Supreme Court pronouncement. Perhaps a particular pronouncement will stir the dominant social, economic, or political structure to its depth and result in a marshaling of forces of resistance in an extraordinary manner. In other words, major fears are aroused, and major efforts at containing and combating the feared pronouncement will result. Furthermore, aggravated divisive factors are operative when Congress or influential members of Congress must be counted as a force against the implementation of a particular pronouncement and a force toward the minimizing, if not overriding, of the precedent. Further, it is obvious that the pressures on the lower court will be very great if some part of the Executive branch of the government (such as the FBI) or even the office of the President itself participates in the pressure to minimize or avoid implementation of the Supreme Court pronouncement. An example of these aggravated forms of pressure might be taken from another era. It will be recalled that Circuit Judge John J. Parker, in the case of *UMWA* v. *Red Jacket Consolidated Coal & Coke Co.* . . . . , approved an injunction against union organizational activities directed against employees under a "yellow dog" contract. In so holding, he was following the pronouncement of the Supreme Court of the United States in *Hitchman Coal Co.* v. *Mitchell* . .

which had not been overruled. The United States Senate apparently took this as a sufficient basis for refusing to confirm him as a Justice of the Supreme Court of the United States.

If we turn from these general considerations and think specifically of the Supreme Court as we have known it in the last few years and its relationship with the lower federal courts, it is necessary to peg a point of beginning and that in itself would be most difficult if much precision is required. The Warren court succeeded the Vinson court, which in turn had succeeded the Stone court and the Hughes court which in 1937 began a constitutional revolution which is still in process. It is still in process because we have not yet reached that degree of equilibrium which gives at least a relative sense of stability in constitutional pronouncement. Law, it has been said, is always in the process of becoming, and presumably constitutional law is even more so. The lower federal court judge, attempting in good faith to carry out his basic obligation, has been faced with something of a frustrating process over much of this entire period. The unstable basis upon which the Warren court initiated its relationship in terms of lower court adherence to Supreme Court pronouncement is indicated by the following quotation from Professor Ralph E. Bischoff in 1953:

> *If laymen, and often the scholars, are confused by the revolutionary decade [i.e., 1937–1947] in which precedents fell to the left and to the right, they are hardly enlightened by the recent emphasis on prolixity, the frequent concurring opinions and the mass of dissents.*

The interaction between the Supreme Court and the lower federal courts is set out statistically for the five years of the Warren Court in the November 1958 issue of the *Harvard Law Review* . . . The statistics for the five preceding years (that is, 1948 through 1952) are set out in Volume 67 of the *Harvard Law Review* . . . These tables show the following number of reversals out of the total number of cases coming from the federal courts of appeals for the particular year:

> 1948: *58 reversals out of 607 cases;* 1949: *42 reversals out of 645 cases;* 1950: *40 out of 566;* 1951: *19 out of 582;* 1952: *40 out of 606;* 1953: *23 out of 558;* 1954: *57 out of 595;* 1955: *54 out of 773;* 1956: *60 out of 791;* 1957: *69 out of 876.*

While these figures indicate something of a sustained higher percentage of reversals in the last four years, there is no figure as high as the percentage of reversals for 1948 within the "Warren Court." On the whole, the percentage variation does not appear to be too significant and this generalization is not affected even if the figures relating to cases "vacated and remanded" and "dismissed" are added to the compilation.

In order to fully cover the topic of this discussion it would be necessary to take in each field of the law the decisions of the Supreme Court since the accession of Chief Justice Warren and see how those decisions have been received by the lower federal courts. Have they been accepted as binding and controlling? Have they been received hospitably and perhaps given even larger scope? Has there been an obvious refusal to follow them? Have they been distinguished, and has the distinguishing process been logically sound, or on a forced basis, eating into the vitality of the precedent? If this were done, it is believed that the picture would be far from uniform. In other words, the degree of acceptance and compliance would vary widely, depending upon the subject matter and the types of pressures operating in the local area and in the country when its application was called for in a particular case. There is no apparent revolt by the lower federal courts comparable to that engaged in by the Fifth Circuit in N.L.R.B. cases under the Wagner Act. There is nothing to indicate that the tensions between the Supreme Court and the lower federal judiciary is any more aggravated on the whole than has been true over the last quarter century.

While detail will deal with the interaction between the Supreme Court and the lower federal courts in the area of race relations, the foregoing generalities have been tested by checking lower court use of certain precedents developed during the Warren court term. One sensitive area in which there would be obvious local pressures upon a federal district judge and in turn, to some degree upon the judges of the courts of appeals, is in the matter of the administration of criminal law in the federal courts. There is always a conflict in this area between the matter of efficient and effective law enforcement and the protection accorded the accused or prospective accused under the Constitution or under the rules developed by the Supreme Court in its supervisory capacity.

In *Mallory v. United States* . . . the Supreme Court reversed and remanded in a case in which a person had been convicted of rape at a trial where his signed confession was introduced in evidence. The confession was obtained during a period of interrogation by the police after arrest and before arraignment of approximately 10 hours duration. The court ruled that Rule 5A of the Federal Rules of Criminal Procedure had been violated in that the arrested person had not been taken "without unnecessary delay" before the nearest available Commissioner. The Court declared,

> *We cannot sanction this extended delay, resulting in confession without subordinating the general rule of prompt arraignment to the discretion of arresting officers finding exceptional circumstances for its disregard. In every case where the police resort to interrogation of an arrested person and secure a confession, they may well claim, and quite sincerely, that they were merely trying to check on the information given by him. Against such a claim and the evil potentialities of the practice for which it is urged stands Rule 5A as a barrier.*

In the Shepherd Citator for the United States Reports (through August 1959) 58 citations have been found where a federal district court or a federal court of appeals discussed the above 1957 decision of the Court. Using the symbols in Shepherd's Citator, in 23 instances out of the 58 the lower federal court distinguished the *Mallory* case as being different in fact or law from the case before it. In three instances, the court followed the *Mallory* case and followed it as controlling authority. In eight instances, the *Mallory* case was cited in the dissenting opinion. In four instances out of the 58 the symbol indicates that the court explained the *Mallory* opinion and its importance in some detail. In one instance the court harmonized the decision in the

Mallory case to show that its apparent inconsistency with other decisions did not exist. The other cases carry no special symbol and in no instance did the editor of the Citator say that the lower federal court had "limited" or "questioned" the *Mallory* decision of the Supreme Court. It must be judged that on the whole in this instance the lower federal courts have not received favorably the *Mallory* precedent.

Something of the negative tone in the lower court decisions is indicated by the following quotation from the majority opinion in *Starr* v. *United States.* . .

> *Thus the Mallory opinion excludes only "incriminating statements elicited from the defendants." It follows that none of the three Supreme Court opinions mentioned applies to the present situation where the statement given by Starr was not incriminating but was clearly exculpatory.*
>
> *But, if the Mallory opinion be construed to hold inadmissible an exculpatory statement taken during unnecessary delay in arraignment, the question arises whether that decision changes the law concerning non-prejudicial error in the reception or rejection of evidence.*
>
> *Under the law as it existed before the Mallory case was decided, the harmless error rule required that if, upon an examination of the entire record, substantial prejudice does not appear, any error must be disregarded as harmless. This is commanded by the salutary statute which Congress passed to correct the abuses that had grown up because, as one trial judge put it, the courts of review had come to "tower above the trials of criminal cases as impregnable citadels of technicality."* . . .

Another decision in the field of criminal law administration is found in *Rea* v. *United States* . . . In this case, the Supreme Court held that it was error for the federal court not to enjoin the use of illegally obtained evidence by a federal official in a state criminal proceeding. The court said in this instance that the federal agent had violated the federal rules governing searches and seizures and that the power of the federal courts extends to policing those requirements and making certain that they are observed. . . ." The Shepherd Citator through August 1959 shows 16 citations for this precedent by federal courts of appeals and federal district courts. In no instance does the symbol indicate that the case was followed. In one case the importance of the decision was explained in some detail. In four instances the precedent was distinguished as different in law or in fact from the case before the court. There were no other symbols, but actually it appears that in other instances the case might very well be listed as among those distinguishing the *Rea* precedent. Again, in the era of administration of criminal law, the record indicates an unfavorable reaction by the lower federal courts to a recent Supreme Court precedent.

Two other cases might be similarly examined. In the case of *Yates* v. *United States* . . . an important part of the decision was a holding that the charge to the jury was in error in failing to indicate the proximity of the danger in the advocacy of violent overthrow of the government. The language of the Court in this respect is generally considered as an important modification of the doctrine of the *Dennis* case (decided during the term of Chief Justice Vinson) which had seemed to establish what is sometimes called the "clear and probable" danger test in this regard. The Shepherd Citator shows ten references in lower federal courts to the *Yates* decision. The result seems on the whole favorable to the vitality of the precedent. Two instances are listed as following the precedent; two are listed as accepting it as controlling and explaining it in some detail. There are no instances listed of the precedent being distinguished nor of it being relied upon by a dissenting judge.

In the case of *Watkins* v. *United States* . . . a check of the citations in the lower federal courts reveals no particular pattern of response to this somewhat controversial decision. The portion of the decision which denied a power in Congress to engage in exposure of individuals for the sake of exposure, as opposed to some legislative purpose, and the portion which required that the legislative purpose be shown with some particularity in respect to a question before the refusal to answer the question could be deemed the basis of contempt—these portions together have three references in lower federal courts; once by a dissenting judge, once the precedent is distinguished, and in one instance it is shown to have been followed. The result is therefore inconclusive.

The race relations area is the one which of course is primarily responsible for our even being interested in this topic at this time. The School Segregation Decision in 1954 is perhaps unprecedented in the extent to which it has shaken the social values of an entire region of the country. The writer believes, however, that the overall judgment as to the functioning of the lower federal courts in relationship to the Supreme Court has been favorable in terms of the implementation of the Supreme Court's pronouncement. It is decidedly more favorable, it would appear, than the response to a precedent such as that involved in the *Mallory* case. The fact of normal acceptance of the principle and the normal absence of a grudging approach to its implementation brings into even greater prominence the two or three instances in which federal district courts have seemed to engage in undue delaying tactics in the implementation of the Supreme Court's pronouncement.

The rather generous acceptance of the principle of the *School Segregation Cases* by the lower federal courts, at least in the period prior to 1958, is best evidenced perhaps by the applications made of the principle in areas other than education. The Court of Appeals for the Fourth Circuit, in *Dawson* v. *Mayor and City Council of Baltimore* . . . held that the principle announced by the United States Supreme Court applied also to state and local activity in recreational facilities. The Supreme Court affirmed without opinion. . . . Again, in *Fleming* v. *South Carolina Electric & Gas Co.* . . . the United States Court of Appeals for the Fourth Circuit applied the principle of the *School Segregation Cases* to transportation on a local bus and held that the federal district court had jurisdiction of a damage suit against a bus driver who was enforcing segregation under the Federal Civil Rights Act. A premature appeal to the Supreme Court of the United States prevented this decision from becoming the basis of acceptance of the doctrine by the Supreme Court itself. Instead, the first authoritative decision was made by a three-judge district court, sitting in the Middle District of Alabama. . . . In this case too, the lower federal court held that segregation on local buses in Montgomery, Alabama violated the equal protection and due process clauses of the Fourteenth Amendment because the separate-but-equal rule of *Plessy* v. *Ferguson* had been impliedly overruled in the *School Segregation Cases.* The Supreme Court of the United States affirmed, again without opinion, on November 13, 1956. . . . The Court of Appeals for the Fifth Circuit, in *Derrington* v. *Plummer,* . . . held that the action of a lessee in operating a restaurant on a segregated basis in a county courthouse was unconstitutional state action. This result was clearly not absolutely established in all of its detail in the state of Supreme Court precedent existing at the time of its announcement. The same general pattern can be observed in the action of the Court of Appeals for the Sixth Circuit in *Detroit Housing Commission* v. *Lewis.* . . . In this instance, the United States District Court had issued a permanent injunction at the request of Negro plaintiffs who sought to enjoin segregation practices in the allocation of public housing units. The Sixth Circuit Court of Appeals affirmed the District Court's decision and remanded the case for further proceedings if necessary, in conformity with the decision of the United States Supreme Court in the *School Segregation Cases.*

The two outstanding examples of the apparent efforts of federal district judges to delay the implementation of the Supreme Court pronouncement with respect to schools are observable in the various opinions of Judge Hutcheson with respect to the Prince Edward County case and the decisions of one or more federal district judges at Dallas, Texas, with regard to the desegregation suit against school officials in that city.

The course of events in Prince Edward County is set out in this latest summary in 4 *Race Relations Law Reporter* . . . :

> *"One of the original* School Segregation Cases *(1 Race Rel. L. Rep. 5, 11) was returned with the mandate of the United States Supreme Court to the federal district court in Virginia. On the remand, the three-judge district court entered a decree requiring the admission of Negro children to schools in Prince Edward County, Virginia, without discrimination on the basis of race, and with all deliberate speed.* Davis v. School Board of Prince Edward County, 1 *Race Rel. L. Rep. 82 (E.D. Va. 1955). The plaintiffs then moved for the fixing of a definite time for desegregation of the county schools. Prior to action on these motions, the original three-judge court dissolved itself and turned over the supervision of the case to a single judge. 142 F. Supp. 616, 1 Race Rel. L. Rep. 1055 (1956). The defendants then filed a motion for dismissal of the case on the ground that recently enacted Virginia legislation had provided an adequate state remedy for the plaintiffs. After hearings, the district court held that the plaintiffs would not be required to exhaust the state remedies but that present conditions in the county, including public opinion unfavorable to desegregation, required that it defer an order requiring desegregation. 149 F. Supp. 431, 2 Race Rel. L. Rep. 341 (1957). The Court of Appeals for the Fourth Circuit reversed and remanded the case with directions to the district court to enter a decree requiring the abolition of racial discrimination in school admission policies "without further delay." After a hearing at which evidence of the deteriorations of race relations in the county was submitted, and plans to conduct a survey of the county's school problems were disclosed, the district court fixed ten years*

432

following the 1955 decision in the Brown *case as the time for compliance. The court ordered preliminary steps toward the formulation of a plan of compliance, meanwhile; directed defendants to report their progress on or before January 1, 1959, and reserved the power to accelerate or extend the date of compliance should the interest of the parties or the public call for it. 164 F. Supp. 786, 3 Race Rel. L. Rep. 964 (E.D. Va. 1958). On appeal, the Fourth Circuit again reversed and remanded on the ground that plaintiffs' constitutional rights were not to be yielded because of race relations deterioration nor the probability of violence if precipitate action were taken. It was observed that recognition of the particular problems of a rural county where the races are practically equal in number had already been given effect in this case, but that defendants had taken no action during the four years since the* School Segregation Cases *were decided and were contemplating none. In order to give effect to the Supreme Court's mandate, the district judge was directed to issue an order enjoining defendants from any action regulating on the basis of color the admission, enrollment, or education of Negro children in county high schools; requiring them to consider applications of Negro children for admission to the "white" high school on a non-racial basis so as to permit entrance therein in September, 1959; and requiring them to make plans for admitting pupils to elementary schools on a non-racial basis and to receive and consider applications to that end "at the earliest practical day." The order also directed that state pupil assignment laws are to be observed so long as they do not cause racial discrimination, that administrative remedies therein specified must be exhausted by plaintiffs before applying for judicial relief on the ground of an alleged injunction violation, and that jurisdiction be retained for such further action as may be necessary."*

The latest Dallas summary reads:

In a class action, Negro school children in Dallas County, Texas, sought a declaration of rights and injunctive relief in a federal district court with respect to their admission to public schools in that county on a nonsegregated basis. The district court refused a motion to convene a three-judge district court, found that the public school facilities furnished for white children and Negroes were substantially equal, and held that the United States Supreme Court's implementation decision in the School Segregation Cases *required that integration be accomplished on the basis of planning to be done by the school officials and the lower courts. The district court further found that no such plan then existed and dismissed the suit without prejudice. Bell v. Rippy, 133 F. Supp. 811, 1 Race Rel. L. Rep. 318 (N.D. Tex. 1955). On appeal, the Court of Appeals, Fifth Circuit, one judge dissenting, held that there was no basis in the evidence nor in law for the action taken by the district court and vacated, reversed and remanded the case. Brown v. Rippy, 233 F. 2d 796, 1 Race Rel. L. Rep. 649 (1956). On the remand the district court, indicating that it would be a "civil wrong" to white pupils to admit Negroes to already crowded white schools, declined to issue an injunction and dismissed the case "in order that the school board may*

433

have ample time . . . to work out this problem." Bell v. Rippy, 146 F. Supp. 485, 2 Race Rel. L. Rep. 32 (N.D. Tex. 1956). The plaintiffs again appealed to the Court of Appeals for the Fifth Circuit from this dismissal. The Court of Appeals reversed the dismissal and remanded the case to the district court with directions to enter a decree requiring the school officials to desegregate the schools "with all deliberate speed." The court stated that administrative remedies available to the plaintiffs had, in effect, been exhausted by the refusal of the school officials to admit them to the requested schools and they were not required to pursue further a futile remedy. 247 F. 2d 268, 2 Race Rel. Rep. 805 (1957). On petition to the Court of Appeals for rehearing it was contended that recent Texas legislation (2 Race Rel. L. Rep. 695), which would debar a school district from receiving state funds if it was integrated without first obtaining an affirmative vote in an election held for that purpose, would result in large losses to the district if it complied with the court order. The Court of Appeals denied the petition for rehearing, stating that the legislation could not operate to relieve either federal or state officials of their duty to uphold the United States Constitution. 2 Race Rel. L. Rep. 984 (1957). On the remand order of the Court of Appeals, the district court issued the order requiring the integration of the Dallas schools to be commenced at the mid-winter term (January, 1958). 2 Race Rel. L. Rep. 985 (1957). The defendants then appealed this order to the Court of Appeals for the Fifth Circuit. The Court of Appeals reversed the judgment and remanded the case with directions to the district court to enter an order in compliance with its prior opinion and to retain jurisdiction of the case to supervise the carrying out of the order. The court observed that, under the prior mandate, school authorities should be accorded a reasonable further opportunity promptly to meet their primary responsibility.

In the latest development in Dallas, United States District Judge T. Whitfield Davidson declined on July 30 to order immediate desegregation. He said at that time that further hearings would be granted in the spring of 1960 if either side requested it, and indicated that September 1960 might be time enough for the district to complete its preparations. He declared. "I will postpone a final ruling on this hearing until a future date to be set by the court closer to the fall of 1960." . . . Judge Davidson is quoted further as having said that the school board "should perhaps take some definite action maybe toward holding an election next spring."

These last two instances have been set out to demonstrate the possibilities of delay. If we can imagine the action of a United States District Court judge in a state where the pressures would be even greater to delay, we can begin to visualize some of the problems ahead in the matter of implementation of the Supreme Court's desegregation pronouncement.

Each of the other affected federal Courts of Appeals has taken action similar to that of the Fourth and Fifth Circuits to bring into line a district court which is deemed to have accorded too much value to the "good reasons" for delay in the particular locality. The Sixth Circuit early overruled the federal district judge in the Hillsboro, Ohio case. . . . More importantly, the Court of Appeals for the Eighth

Circuit set aside Judge Lemley's 1958 decision permitting postponement in carrying out the previously approved Little Rock plan. . . . You will note that the several Courts of Appeals have not yet sustained a district court action with respect to school desegregation which patently gives aid and comfort to those denying the basic validity of the principles announced by the Supreme Court. In the action of the Fourth Circuit in establishing the requirement of exhausting administrative remedies . . . and that of the three-judge district court which found no invalidity on the face of the Alabama Pupil Placement Law . . . both were careful to uphold the principle of the *School Segregation Cases* even while giving approval to doctrines that can be utilized for delay purposes. But the doctrines so announced were already well established. The Supreme Court itself has indicated its approval of these two lower federal court decisions, thus signifying in some degree a relaxation of any idea of rigid and hurried implementation. The most important indication of the working of the federal judiciary may be found in the fact that the Supreme Court has not yet overturned a single Court of Appeals decision in this area of law. It seems to me that the functioning of the federal judiciary in this emotional area has evidenced on the whole a high degree of cooperation and sense of institutional protection. Obvious disaffection is a luxury that most of the lower court judges may feel they cannot afford. Of course we have not yet reached the cases in the "hard core" areas of the deep South which will generate the greatest pressures to avoid the Supreme Court pronouncement.

[Sanders' remarks about the strong pressures upon federal judges who vigorously fulfill their judicial obligations in the face of local or regional political opposition were given particular emphasis in 1961 by the storm of political opposition to the possible promotion of federal district judge J. Skelly Wright to the federal Court of Appeals for the Fifth Circuit.]

6. Local Pressure on Federal Judges: Louisiana House Fights Promotion of Judge Wright*

BATON ROUGE, La., May 19 (AP)—A resolution calling upon Louisiana's congressional delegation to oppose any promotion offered United States District Judge J. Skelly Wright has been approved by the Louisiana House of Representatives.

The New Orleans Federal Judge blocked the Legislature's fight against New Orleans school desegregation.

Rep. Wellborn Jack, Caddo Parish segregationist, offered the resolution which urged opposition to any move to promote Wright to the U.S. 5th Circuit Court of Appeals or any higher bench.

Wright has been mentioned as a potential appointee to one of the two judgeships in the 5th Circuit included in 73 Federal judgeships recently created by Congress.

Washington Post, May 19, 1961, p. 2.

"He had utter disregard for the sovereignty of the state of Louisiana," Jack charged. "He is directly responsible for the ruining of the health" of State Education Supt. Shelby M. Jackson.

Jackson is recovering from a long attack of asthma, which came after a Federal contempt citation against him was postponed indefinitely.

7. Louisiana's Senator Long Blocks Appointment of Judge Who Ordered Integration*

WASHINGTON, D.C.—Senator Russell Long (Dem., La.) has asked the Kennedy administration not to promote the federal district judge who ordered the integration of the New Orleans schools.

Long is believed to have told the administration that he would fight the appointment of Judge J. Skelly Wright of New Orleans to the fifth circuit court of appeals, and would declare the appointment personally obnoxious on the floor of the Senate.

Judge Wright has been considered the logical choice for the vacancy. He is known to want the appointment. He is the choice of many in the justice department.

But Senator Long faces re-election next year. He is known to feel that the elevation of Judge Wright would become a major campaign issue against him—and would make him vulnerable to segregationist attacks.

Long's opposition thus appears to have stopped Judge Wright's chance for appointment. The post was established by the recent bill creating new federal judgeships.

"I campaigned very hard in my state and the South for this administration, and if the administration appointed a man without consulting me, I'd take it very unkindly," Long said.

"I am not supporting Skelly Wright," he said.

The fifth circuit court of appeals has the states of Louisiana, Texas, Mississippi, Alabama, Georgia and Florida in its jurisdiction.

[The unexpected sequel to this development came on December 16, 1961. President Kennedy, in an obvious move to outflank regional opponents of Judge Wright, nominated him to succeed Judge E. Barrett Prettyman on the federal Court of Appeals for the District of Columbia.[1]]

8. The Aftermath of the Desegregation Decision— Implementation by the Lower Courts†

The decree in *Brown* v. *Board of Educ.* was the implementation of the Supreme Court's decision of a year before, which had held, in suits brought to enjoin en-

*David Halberstam, "Louisiana's Long Blocks Judge Who Mixed Schools," *Des Moines Register*, June 1, 1961, p. 1.
[1] *Washington Post,* December 16, 1961, p. 1.
†Note, "Implementation of Desegregation by the Lower Courts," *Howard Law Review*, LXXI (1957–58), 486–502. [Footnotes omitted.] Reproduced with permission of the publisher. Copyright © 1957 by the Harvard Law Review Association.

forcement of laws requiring regregation or to enjoin the state from practicing segregation, that racial segregation by the state in its public school facilities was such a denial of the equal protection of the laws as is prohibited by the fourteenth amendment to the Constitution. The decree, which remanded the cases for enforcement, instructed the lower courts that the local school boards retain primary responsibility for "elucidating, assessing, and solving" the varied local school problems of the period of transition. But in framing their mandates the lower courts are "to consider whether the action of school authorities constitutes good-faith implementation of the governing constitutional principles." Though "it should go without saying that the vitality of these constitutional principles cannot be allowed to yield simply because of disagreement with them," the public interest in overcoming a variety of obstacles in an orderly manner may permit delay in granting a remedy. Such delay, which has been upheld in other types of equitable actions when circumstances of the public interest so demanded, is thus applied to suits for enforcement of the equal-protection guarantee. However, in every case, the school boards are to be required to make "a prompt and reasonable start" toward compliance. The burden of proof of the extent of the delay necessary is on the school board, and in determining what delay should be granted the courts should consider problems related to "administration, arising from the physical condition of the school plant, the school transportation system, personnel, revision of school districts and attendance areas into compact units to achieve a system of determining admission to schools on a nonracial basis, and revision of local laws and regulations which may be necessary in solving the foregoing problems." During the transitional period the courts are to retain jurisdiction of the cases.

An important question is whether the delay permitted by the Brown decree is based upon factors cognizable only in equity, so that a sucessful action for damages at law for denial of equal protection could be prosecuted despite delayed enforcement, or whether the delay permitted is a recognition that there is no denial of equal protection until the delay has become, under all the circumstances, unreasonable. Since in the original cases the plantiffs sought only equitable relief, the decree does not deal with this question. However, the recovery of damages at law by a large number of plantiffs when equity would not decree immediate desegregation would seem to be an anomalous result.

I. DELAYS IN IMPLEMENTATION

A. PROCEDURAL DELAYS

Suits brought pursuant to the Brown decision are usually initiated by a Negro plantiff on behalf of himself or of a class of similarly situated Negroes within an administrative area. The class action avoids procedural delay by permitting a final determination in a single lawsuit of the school board's responsibility to desegregate. However, some states have attempted in two ways to delay enforcement by procedural devices. First, they have enacted statutes requiring elaborate administrative appeals from decisions of local school boards affecting pupil assignments. Second, they have required that such remedies be pursued by individual plaintiffs, not by representatives of a class. When the administrative appeals provided by the statute cannot provide relief, as when the passage of time required for the appeals would in every case render the initial complaint moot, the statute may be held unconstitutional on its face as an attempt to create prolonged delays. And, when it is evident from the conduct or avowed policy of the appeals boards that even though relief could be afforded under the statute it will not be, the administrative procedures may be avoided by invocation of the maxim that "equity does not require the doing of a vain thing as a condition of its relief." If the statute on its face and in the light of administrative policy could provide adequate relief, the remedies it provides must be exhausted. But one court minimized potential delay by finding that the administrative procedure would not provide adequate relief if the final decision were delayed an unreasonable time. Having determined that a delay of more than four months would be unreasonable, the court required the plaintiff to seek administrative relief, with the proviso that if the administrative decision were not final by the designated date, he could reapply to the court for further relief. However, if the state's requirement of individual proceedings were held to limit a class, for purposes of a federal class action, to those plantiffs who have exhausted the remedy, the value of the class action as an expediting device to avoid multiple litigation would be destroyed At least one court has indicated that it might avoid this result be requiring that only some representatives of the class need exhaust the statutory remedy in order to maintain a representative suit for declaratory and injunctive relief.

B. DELAYS IN FORMULATING A PLAN

The courts, in reviewing local school boards, have exhibited great diversity in according weight to the administrative factors enumerated in the *Brown* decree, and in the scope of review accorded the boards' actions. The cause of this diversity appears to be the response of the courts and the school boards to the factors of community hostility. Although this factor is not expressly considered in the *Brown* decree beyond the statement that "disagreement" cannot alone prevent ultimate enforcement, since the Court ordered retention of jusisdiction of the cases by the lower courts it seems probable that in some instances the Court contemplated a protracted period of transition. Some courts and commentators have found that the *Brown* decree forecloses consideration of actual or potential local hostility in determining the need for delay, and that only the enumerated elements of administrative difficulty may be weighed in determining the need for delay in plans for desegregation. On the other hand, several courts have placed direct reliance on hostile community attitudes in order to justify delay. Even when the courts have not expressly relied on this ground, three types of decisions manifest *sub silentio* consideration of hostile community attitudes. First, some courts have decided that the administrative difficulties put forward by the board justify extensions of time, but the delays granted seem too great to be supported on administrative grounds alone. For example, in *Aaron* v. *Cooper,* the Eighth Circuit affirmed a plan of desegregation not expected to be completed for seven years. The school board's stated reasons for delay were the size and complexity of the job, the need for planned new facilities whose creation should be awaited, the need in order to begin where fewer teachers and students are involved to desegregate by descending grades, and the value of gaining experience gradually to avoid "mistakes." None of these difficulties, treated as administrative problems, appears to present a reasonable basis for requiring a seven-year transitional period. Therefore, it seems that the court must have allowed some weight to be given to the factor of community hostility which is latent in the reasons given by the school board. Although such administrative matters as overcrowding might justify a short period for a determination of the optimum manner of redistributing the existing load on existing facilities, since the school system has the same physical facilities and, at most, the same total number of pupils if the schools are desegregated, this ground alone does not justify prolonged delay. Because such difficulties as overcrowding provide equal reason for excluding some qualified white students from a facility, when they are not so excluded this ground for delay has been expressly rejected by some courts. This result is obviously correct, if only administrative difficulty is considered, when newly resident white children continue to be admitted to the segregated facility.

Second, several courts, upon finding that a prompt and reasonable start towards compliance has been made by the school board, have deferred to the board's exercise of discretion in formulating the plan unless the plan appeared "unreasonable." Through this procedure the court defers to a judgment based upon the school board's often unstated recognition of community hostility, although it confines that judgment within a stated standard of reasonableness. Finally, several courts have framed decrees that either enjoin segregation without designating an effective date for the operation of the restraint, or simply order the defendant to proceed without issuing an injunction. In this case, since no plan is required by the court, total discretion is left in the school board. It may base unlimited delays upon its judgment of community hostility subject only to a latter determination, on the renewed application of the plantiff, that further delay is unreasonable. This procedure seems improper, in so far as it may merely delay the formulation of any plan. When delay is likely, the court, as a condition of withholding an injunction, should require the school board to make a prompt and reasonable start, including formulation of the plan by which ultimate desegregation is to be achieved.

The question of hostility arises at two separate stages of desegregation litigation. It occurs at the planning stage, when the plan itself is formulated and adopted as the present mode of enforcement of the plaintiff's right under a desegregation decree. At that stage every consideration of local public and private interest, including hostility, would appear to be relevant to the court's review of the proposal. It occurs again at the enforcement stage, when hostility may be directed at frustrating the benefits afforded plaintiffs by the earlier decree. At this later time the recognition of violence as a factor causing new delay would be an invitation to lawlessness. But this fact should not obscure the potential effectiveness of the initial decree in anticipating and avoiding resorts to violence. The conscientious school-board defendant can represent to the court a sober judgment of the limits of what is peacefully possible at a particular place and time. The court may find that recognition of the plaintiff's right requires greater speed, and disapprove the plan in whole or in part; but by refusal to consider hostility the court will cut itself off from a valuable source of relevant information. The mandate of the *Brown* decree that "the vitality of these constitutional principles cannot yield simply because of disagreement with them," seems consistent with this view. The decree's clear requirement of a prompt and reasonable start ensures that the constitutional right will not yield. A beginning must be made, and it is plain that hostility cannot be the basis of a refusal. Delay per se is not acceptable. But progress may be made in terms of a plan adapted to local needs and capable of achieving the requisite final result.

A similar problem arises when the board relies upon a state statute designed to obstruct the implementation of the *Brown* decree. Although the Virginia legislature enacted a law effectively closing desegregated school facilities, the court in *Beckett* v. *School Bd.* held that the failure of the defendant to make a prompt and reasonable start towards desegregation was sufficient reason to issue an injunction against any further segregation of school facilities despite the board's reliance on the statute as a ground for further delays. A contrary decision involving the same statute was reached in *Davis* v. *County School Bd.* In that case, the injunction of a three-judge district court required the termination of segregation "with all deliberate speed," but set no date for the accomplishment of the purpose. Plaintiffs later moved, in a single-judge district court, to fix a date because the defendant had taken no action whatever. The court found, however, that in the light of public hostility and of the statute which would effectively close the schools, defendant's inaction did not constitute a lack of "good faith," and therefore no date was set. It seems clear that the reversal of this result by the Fourth Circuit was proper, since if such legislative action could justify a federal court in delaying a decree, the *Brown* mandate would be illusory.

When the court is convinced that local officials are refusing to cooperate the problem of desegregation becomes more complex. Since the *Brown* decree makes delay a matter of equity discretion and places on the defendant school board the burden of showing the need for delay and of formulating plans for overcoming obstacles, in the absence of the board's co-operation the court has no means of formulating a plan of its own. Several courts have met school-board inaction by issuing affirmative orders to compel the presentation of a plan. If such an order is construed as a decree delaying plaintiff's remedy on condition that the defendant take the required action, the defendant's default would have no other consequence than the issuance of the injunction that could have been issued at the outset upon a finding of a failure to make a prompt and reasonable start. The disadvantage of this construction is that it limits the court to a blanket injunction or none at all, even though the court might have reason to believe that gradual desegregation was preferable in the light of local conditions. Since an object of the system of enforcement must be to minimize disruption of educational processes during the transition period, a blanket injunction that is not adapted to local needs, though it be enforced by judicial or police action, is undesirable. A remedy, other than a blanket injunction against all segregation, is needed to compel action by the administrative unit primarily responsible for the solution of local problems. Although the obvious solution is the enforcement of an affirmative order to compel the formulation of a plan by the application of appropriate sanctions against the school board itself for disobedience, the eleventh amendment to the Constitution may bar such a procedure.

The eleventh amendment, which incorporates the doctrine of sovereign immunity, protects a state from suits by citizens of another state in the federal courts. In *Hans* v. *Louisiana,* similar protection based upon the immunity of the sovereign was construed to extend to suits by a citizen against his own state. The state's immunity may apply whenever it is the real party in interest, although nominally the suit is against individual officers. The state can waive sovereign immunity by statute or by voluntary appearance, and municipal corporations and counties do not automatically receive shelter from the immunity of the state. However, when the state constitution or laws declare the agency or subdivision to be a part of the state for immunity purposes, the immunity is usually effective, and waiver must be by statute. Therefore, in the absence of an authorized waiver by participation in a suit, or the statutory consent of the state, state officials normally may not be subjected in their official capacity to the affirmative commands of a federal court.

However, judicially developed exceptions to immunity may provide a basis for the issuance of a mandatory injunction to compel the formulation of a plan. An action will lie in a federal court against an officer of the state who threatens to act under color of unconstitutional state law. This exception is made on the theory that such action by officials, being unlawful, is taken in their private capacities. Several segregation cases in suits for prohibitory injunctions have relied on this exception to reject defenses based upon the doctrine of the eleventh amendment. An additional exception to sovereign immunity has been created for cases in which mandatory injunctions are used to aid in effectuating prohibitory orders. In *Lester* v. *Parker* the court issued a mandatory injunction to require the issuance of a seaman's security pass in aid of a prohibitory order enjoining the defendants from interfering with the employment of the plaintiffs, and further enjoining them from refusal to take steps to advise shipping companies that the plaintiffs were entitled to employment. In reply to a defense of sovereign immunity, the court said that it had "done no more than to follow the recognized power of courts of equity in issuing injunctions, to make those injunctions effective by ancillary provisions, in aid of the injunction, which may require the defendant to do something." Such ancillary power should provide a ground for similar jurisdiction over local school boards. Thus, if an injunction prohibiting further segregation were issued to be effective from and after the passage of a reasonable time, then the mandatory requirement that the steps be planned, presented to the court, and carried out would be in aid of the prohibition. If the mandatory injunction is employed, then the public interest in an orderly transition is served by compelling the production of information concerning relevant local questions to the court, or, failing production, by sanctions directed against the school board. The objection that the court may not control the discretion vested in an administrative official would be inapposite because it is the exercise of discretion that is commanded, not a particular act.

Although modification of a plan that is submitted borders on judicial creation of a plan, such modification does not seem to be prohibited by the *Brown* decree. The placing of an already formulated plan before the court provides the court with evidence upon which to grant a delay. The purpose of making the grounds for delay a matter of defense apparently is to assure that this evidence of the local situation will be presented to the court. Once such a presentation has been made, and the plaintiff has had an opportunity to contest it, partial judicial disapproval of the plan seems indistinguishable from the review of any proposed equity decree.

When the parties are able to reach agreement upon a desirable course of desegregation, they may embody their agreement in a consent decree. A party who varies from the detailed terms of such a decree without the approval of the court would be subject to citation for contempt. Thus the plaintiff would achieve enforcement of the agreement, as by an affirmative order, while the defendant would be protected from further litigation as long as he abides by the decree. Even if it were found that a local school board is a state agency for purposes of sovereign immunity, and that it does not have power to consent to initial jurisdiction on behalf of the state, its consent to an affirmative order in the course of proceedings that are based upon a jurisdiction already established should be effective. It would be anomalous if the board were subject to a total prohibition but could not consent to a lesser restraint.

II. REMEDIES TO COMPEL OBEDIENCE TO DECREES AND TO PREVENT INTERFERENCE WITH DESEGREGATION

A. CONTEMPT PROCEEDINGS

Once an enforceable decree has been issued against a school board, violations are subject to the contempt powers of the federal courts. Proceedings in civil contempt are to coerce obedience to the decree, and may be used to subject the members of the school board to remedial fines or imprisonment for disobedience. Similarly, those with actual knowledge of the decree, who act in concert or participation with the board, as well as its agents, officers, servants, employees, and attorneys, may be subject to contempt remedies for disobedience of the decree. Liability in civil contempt does not require proof of willfulness, and the defendants have no right to jury trial. When the remedy is considered a vindication of the authority of the court, the proceedings are in criminal contempt and any fines or imprisonment imposed are punitive. Under rule 42 (b) of the Federal Rules of Criminal Procedure, criminal-contempt actions must be initiated by the court or the United States Attorney, but may not be initiated by the plaintiff. In certain cases, in which the act to be punished is otherwise a crime, the defendant may have a right to a trial by jury.

Whether private persons who act to prevent desegregation but who are not in privity with a party to the decree are liable in contempt is doubtful. The hostile acts of such individuals in response to segregation orders take two recognizable forms. They are either directed at coercing into disobedience the officials who seek to implement the order or at intimidating the Negroes themselves so as to prevent them from taking advantage of the decree. The extent of the power to bring acts of coercion directed at school officials within contempt proceedings is governed by statute. Subsection 3 of the statute applies the contempt power to resistance or disobedience of the court's lawful order, but the scope of the power conferred is unclear. In *In re Reese,* the court punished a defendant who had performed acts which were prohibited by a prior injunction, although he was neither a party nor in privity with a party to the injunctive decree. However, this broad construction of the criminal-contempt power as applied to orders of the court was expressly rejected by the Second Circuit in *Alemite Mfg. Corp.* v. *Staff.* The court held that a person could not be found guilty of contempt unless he was either a party to the injunction or in privity with such a party. The court reasoned that since the accomplishment of the pro-scribed acts by nonparties and those not in privity with parties is an assertion of an independent right which has not been adjudicated, contempt proceedings should not lie. In *Chase Nat'l. Bank* v. *City of Norwalk,* the Supreme Court rejected the proposal that "conduct of persons who act independently and whose rights have not been adjudged according to law" could be controlled by an injunction. The Court thus indicated that privity with a party was required to make conduct in frustration of the decree actionable as contempt. Although only the scope of the injunction was in question, and not the scope of the contempt power, the Court supported its view by citation of the *Alemite* decision. However, the *Reese* case has not been expressly dis-approved by the Supreme Court, and may still have vitality.

When private persons seek to coerce a school board into violation of an injunction against segregation, the privity required by the *Alemite* decision should not be a bar to the use of contempt power. Although the concept of privity advanced in that case appears to incorporate traditional agency and conspiracy principles in order to bring a defendant into privity with named parties and thus make him amenable to the contempt power, it essentially rests on the fact that the defendant is not asserting a right to act which has been left unadjudicated in the action in which the original decree was formulated. When the defendant has sought to act through a party to a prior decree, even though that action does not rest on an agency or conspiratorial relation but is based on coercion, he cannot reasonably be said to assert an unadjudi-cated right, and his actions seem sufficient to allow the invocation of the contempt power against him. However, in those cases in which the school board does not yield to the defendant's coercion, it is difficult to find that he has "resisted" the decree within the meaning of the *Reese* decision, since the act enjoined has not been committed.

When acts of hostility by private individuals are directed not at the school board but at coercing the Negro plaintiffs into foregoing the benefit of the state's compliance with the decree, even if there were no other bar, the restriction of the *Alemite* decision would prevent the application of the contempt power. In such a case the defendant is neither a party to the original proceeding nor in privity with a party. Although the doctrine of the *Reese* case, if still applicable, would not bar a contempt conviction for such acts, the restrictions on the scope of the federal power to imple-ment the equal-protection guarantee of the fourteenth amendment would prevent such a conviction. The guarantee of section I of the fourteenth amendment protects any person subject to the jurisdiction of a state against a denial by the state of the equal protection of the laws. The power of a federal court in implementing this guarantee is limited to forbidding an act under authority or color of authority of the state. Therefore, private acts of violence directed at Negroes, or at the parents of students, or at private persons generally who favor desegregation, do not fall within the lawful limits of the decree, and cannot constitute contempts of the court's "lawful order," whether under the *Reese* or *Alemite* doctrines. Once the state assigns pupils to schools without regard to race and refrains from discrimination in the operation of the facility, the full purpose of the decree originally sought by the plaintiff has been accomplished. The decree enjoins segregation enforced by the state. Acts of violence by private individuals, though they may be torts or even crimes, are nevertheless still private acts of segregation. When the right protected by the court is an affirmative constitutional guarantee, such as the right to vote in a federal election, interference with it by private individuals is both possible and redressable. But there is nothing in the *Brown* opinions to indicate that the Constitution is now interpreted to guarantee a right to nonsegregated education protected from interference by private individuals as well as by the state. However, if punishment through contempt proceedings of *attempts* to coerce school officials is within the contempt power, the fourteenth amendment does not appear to impose a limitation on the power. Protection of the plaintiff's adjudicated right by prevention of an immediate threat to it would seem to be an appropriate exercise of the legislative power delegated by the amendment. However, it remains doubtful whether such attempts should be reached by the contempt power without statutory authority.

Subsection I of the contempt statute makes punishable acts of misbehavior in the presence of the court, or "so near thereto as to obstruct the administration of justice." Although this section was for a time construed to include contempts not involving a prior decree, and not in the physical presence of the court, the Supreme Court in *Nye* v. *United States* held that the words "so near thereto" imposed a geographical limitation. Since the *Nye* decision, this subsection applies only to contempt by obstructive acts committed in the presence of the court or in areas immediately adjoining it physically. Furthermore, it seems doubtful that threats directed at Negro plaintiffs or at a school board could be construed as acts of contumacy directed at the court. It thus appears that federal statutory contempt powers cannot often be applied to hold in contempt private persons not otherwise enjoined, who seek to oppose desegregation orders.

B. SUPPLEMENTARY INJUNCTIVE PROCEEDINGS

Although it seems clear that no federal jurisdiction exists over private activity directed at private individuals in opposition to desegregation, there are several grounds for the exertion of federal judicial control over hostile private conduct directed at state officials. First, in lieu of the direct use of the contempt power, the plaintiff in the proceeding for a prohibitory injunction against segregation may petition the court to issue an additional injunction against interference with the decree by private parties. Even if the private action has not been sufficiently completed to be subject to contempt, when the plaintiff's adjudicated right to secure nondiscriminatory action from a school board is imperiled, equity can extend its power to prevent impending frustration of its decree. The issuance of such an injunction should depend upon a finding of an intentional threat to plaintiff's rights under the decree. The determination of hostile intent directed at the school board will in many cases involve difficult findings of fact, since mere private opposition to desegregation can create sufficient local tension to cause an incidental danger to those persons who favor and implement desegregation. An injunction should not issue under such circumstances unless named defendants are found to have threatened or otherwise coerced the school board itself, since it would otherwise result in a blanket prohibition of permissible private activity. The use of supplementary injunctive procedure ensures that the named defendants will have their day in court to question the propriety of the plaintiff's claim of intentional interference with his rights under the decree. The selection of the acts to be enjoined presents a similar factual problem. Rule 65 (d) of the Federal Rules of Civil Procedure requires that the order must be clear and specific. If the defendant has shown a proclivity for the proscribed action, however, the order may be general enough to prevent experimentation with disobedience of the law. Since a defendant who is in doubt can apply to the court for modification or dissolution of the injunction before taking any action, the defense of vagueness may be precluded by failure to do so. When the injunction is vague, however, the defense may be available to persons not parties who could not reasonably be expected to petition for modification. In enforcement proceedings it must further appear that the party named in the injunction was a principal actor, and that those who participated with him actually knew of the injunction.

A second ground for assertion of judicial control over private action may arise if the school board applies for an injunction against coercive interference with its voluntary program of desegregation. In *Brewer* v. *Hoxie School Dist. No. 46,* the absence of a prior court decree enjoining segregation by the board prevented reliance upon the ancillary equity power. The court instead found that the school officials were under a constitutional duty to desist from segregation and therefore had a right to federal protection in the performance of their functions. The court relied on cases which had found a federal right to protection in the performance of duties essential to the functioning of the federal government. The result of such a construction, however, is to make interference with state officials who are observing constitutional prohibitions a matter of federal concern creating equity jurisdiction to enjoin the disruptive activity. Since, however, the constitutionally imposed duty in such a case is to refrain from certain state action, the recognition of a correlative "right" to be free from private interference should be made in the light of the limitations on the application of the fourteenth amendment which is restricted to the correction of state action.

A third ground for the assertion of jurisdiction exists when resistance to desegregation becomes so institutionalized through the formation of white-citizens councils and similar organizations as to exert a controlling power over government. In such a situation the organizations themselves may be directly subject to the proscriptions of the fourteenth amendment, and their discriminatory activity may then be enjoined.

C. REMEDIES UNDER THE CIVIL RIGHTS ACTS

Several civil-rights statutes provide remedies that may be effective in securing the equal protection of the laws in public education to Negro plaintiffs. Section 242 of the Criminal Code provides sanctions for the denial of the equal protection of the laws. Under this section willful action or inaction under color of law to deprive another of the equal protection of the laws is a misdemeanor. To secure a conviction a specific intent to deprive the party injured of a constitutional right must be shown. Section 241 of the Criminal Code probably applies only to conspiracies to deprive an individual of rights which arise from the relationship of citizens to the federal government, and not to the deprivation of fourteenth-amendment rights. But if Negroes are deprived by an act of conspiracy of the right to institute contempt proceedings or even to initiate suits for initial injunctions, the conspirators may be indictable thereunder. A section of the Civil Rights Acts, now section 1983, provides a civil action for deprivation under color of law of rights secured by the fourteenth amendment, and provides a remedy in damages at law, or equitable relief. The section is also applicable to private individuals who conspire with state officials to a similar end. Section 1985 (3) provides, *inter alia,* a civil action for damages for a conspiracy to deprive a person of the equal protection of the laws. The constitutionality of such a provision if construed to allow recovery against private persons is extremely doubtful. The Supreme Court has not ruled on the constitutional question. Instead, it has construed the statute as only extending to such conspiracies as amount to the organized control of government by the defendants. Section 1985 (3) also provides a civil action against any of the conspirators for injuries sustained as a result of acts in furtherance of a conspiracy to coerce state officials to deny any person within the state the equal protection of the laws. Thus, all those persons injured in the course of a conspiracy to coerce state officers may have an action under this section. Although the Court has never considered this provision, it seems to be an appropriate exercise of the delegation of legislative power in the fourteenth amendment.

There is some doubt whether section 1985 (3) can be made the basis of an injunction against interference with state officials, since in terms it applies only to an action for damages. Although it has been argued that the lack of an express grant of equity jurisdiction in a federal statute is not fatal to equitable jurisdiction, this statute requires as a condition of relief an act which is in furtherance of the conspiracy and which either injures the plaintiff in person or property or actually deprives him of a constitutional "right or privilege." At least one court has held that damage must be shown to secure an equitable remedy under this subsection. On this reasoning, if a denial of equal protection occurs as a result of acts in furtherance of the conspiracy, then the class of persons so injured has suffered damage and may seek an injunction against all further acts in pursuance of the conspiracy, as well as damages for past injury. Similarly, if the school board is considered to be entitled to federal protection in its efforts to observe federal constitutional prohibitions, then, if the conspiracy actually causes it to default, it too may invoke this section to enjoin all acts in furtherance of the conspiracy. But when the conspiracy has not achieved such a denial or deprivation, only suits based upon injury to the plaintiffs, resulting from acts in furtherance of the conspiracy can be based on this section. In such a case the plaintiff's claim to relief at law runs only against such injury as he has sustained, and he therefore seems entitled under the statute to an injunction only against the repetition of such injury. If, however, the exercise of federal equity jurisdiction is proper over intentional private interference with state officials which threatens but has not yet produced a deprivation of rights, the assertion of the inherent equity power to protect its decrees is not impeded by the absence of statute.

There are no significant statutory limitations on the scope of the equity power to frame its remedies. And even if section 1985 (3) were construed to apply, it would encounter the same problems of the proper scope of the injunction as does the inherent ancillary equity jurisdiction. However, one anomaly is produced by the absence of statutory jurisdiction, since a school board which desegregates only after a decree is issued against it would receive federal protection under the ancillary equity power and one which voluntarily desegregates would not. This problem would be removed if the statute were construed to confer jurisdiction in equity without a prior denial of equal protection.

[What factors make for vigorous implementation or footdragging delay in problem areas such as desegregation? Judicial selection, as the foregoing items on Judge J. Skelly Wright indicate, is often a fierce arena of political combat because of generally held assumptions about the relationship of a potential judge's social, economic, and political background to his subsequent decision-making. The next section of *Constitutional Law in the Political Process* is devoted to some exploratory studies on this relationship.]

9 The Roots of Judicial Behavior

A. THE IMPORTANCE OF THE JUDGE HIMSELF

[I saw where justice lay, and the moral sense decided the court half the time; I then sat down to search the authorities . . . I might once in a while be embarrassed by a technical rule, but I almost always found principles suited to my view of the case. . . .

This frank description of the scope of judicial discretion in the legal process was presented by Chancellor James Kent, today considered one of the great common law judges of the nineteenth century. The common law is, of course, judge-made law. But constitutional interpretation and statutory interpretation similarly permit considerable judicial leeway. One of the finest early analyses of this conception of the legal process was by Thomas Reed Powell in 1923.]

1. Judicial Discretion in Constitutional Interpretation*

Minimum-Wage legislation has been of two main kinds. One is the Massachusetts variety which vests a commission with power to make inquiries and publish results. Employers are exposed to public censure or public praise. Sentiments of decency or

*Thomas Reed Powell, "The Judiciality of Minimum Wage Legislation," *Harvard Law Review*, XXXVII (1923–1924), 545–53. [Footnotes omitted.] Reproduced with permission of the publisher. Copyright (1923) by the Harvard Law Review Association.

of vanity may move the niggardly to mend their ways, but the recalcitrant are left free to bargain as they can and will. The other type of legislation adds physical to moral force. A commission is authorized to discover and to declare the minimum cost of decent subsistence and on this basis to prescribe the minimum wage that may be paid to women and minors. Employment at less than the prescribed wage subjects the employer to punishment. While the variations in the wages fixed by various boards for various employments indicate that the cost of living is not always the sole criterion of the boards' determinations, there has been no judicial adjudication that their prescriptions have exceeded the cost of decent living. The constitutional issue raised by such compulsory legislation is therefore whether an employer may be compelled to pay the cost of maintaining the employee whose full services he voluntarily uses in the conduct of his enterprise.

This constitutional question finds no answer in the Constitution. While the legislation, like substantially all legislation and all law, involves a deprivation of liberty or property, such deprivation is constitutionally innocuous unless it is "without due process of law." The Constitution does not define due process of law. The task of definition is committed to the judges. They have recognized that definition is impossible. They have told us that instead of definition they will employ a process of "judicial inclusion and exclusion," and give us the reasons. These reasons can not come from the Constitution. They come from the judges. The law of constitutional due process is therefore as much judge-made law as any common law is judge-made law. Until some due-process issue is authoritatively settled, one who would make a constitutional prophecy or a constitutional argument should be familiar with the outlook and the temper of the judges by whom the issue is to be decided. In cases of any considerable novelty, few reasons can be so compelling as to meet with universal acceptation. The determination of closely-controverted constitutional issues depends, therefore, in large part upon the composition of the court of last resort at the particular time when the issue comes before it.

Nowhere does this analysis find firmer confirmation than in the history of judicial decisions on the constitutionality of minimum-wage legislation. The question first came before the Oregon court in 1914, and in two decisions seven judges declared themselves in favor of the legislation and none was opposed. The Oregon case went to the Supreme Court of the United States, and in 1917 the decree of the state court was sustained by a vote of four to four. Mr. Justice Brandeis, having been of counsel, did not sit. His general outlook on what is called social legislation is so well known that there can be no doubt that, had he not been of counsel, he would have voted in favor of the law. In that event, the consequent five-to-four vote almost certainly would have established the constitutionality of such legislation against subsequent attack in the federal courts. Though conceivably a favorable decision might later have been overruled by a differently composed Supreme Court, the experience is that police issues of this general character are finally settled by such favorable decision. A four-to-four vote, however, settles nothing, except that the particular decision below is not reversed. After this tie vote, the constitutional issue still remained an open one. A prophet would be confident that if the same Supreme Court bench had the question to decide in a case in which Mr. Justice Brandeis should sit, the answer would be in favor of the legislation. By reason of this confidence, he might add to it the further confidence that the objectors to the legislation would not again bring the issue to the Supreme Court until its personnel had changed. Such turned out to be the fact. Four changes in the Supreme Court had taken place before the issue again came before it.

In the meantime four other courts had passed upon the question. Two decisions of the Minnesota Supreme Court in 1917 and 1920 record six judges in favor of the legislation and none opposed. An Arkansas decision of 1917 sustained the legislation by a vote of four to one, though one of the majority refrained from dissent only because he thought that the legislation was entitled to the benefit of the Supreme Court tie until it was broken. Two decisions of the Supreme Court of Washington in 1918 and 1920 add eleven judges to those in favor of the legislation and none to those opposed. Thus the compulsory minimum-wage legislation of the states of Oregon, Minnesota, Arkansas, and Washington was thought constitutional by twenty-seven judges of the courts of those states and unconstitutional by only two judges, three of the four courts being unanimously in favor of the statutes.

Then came the anomalous somersault in the case before the Court of Appeals of the District of Columbia. This involved the act of Congress applicable to the District. On the first hearing Mr. Justice Robb was unable to sit because of illness. Under statutory authority the other two Justices designated Mr. Justice Stafford of the Supreme Court of the District to sit in his place. The decision, on June 6, 1921, was two to one in favor of the statute. Chief Justice Smyth and Mr. Justice Stafford were in favor; Mr. Justice Van Orsdel was opposed. Motions for a rehearing were denied on June 22 of the same year. Three days later, Mr. Justice Robb, who had now recovered, wrote the Chief Justice that he was considering an application for a rehearing. On July 1 he wrote that he had decided to vote for a rehearing and had so notified counsel and Mr. Justice Van Orsdel. Later Justices Robb and Van Orsdel instructed the clerk to enter an order granting a rehearing. The Chief Justice dissented. The case was reargued on February 14, 1921, and decided on November 6, 1922. The vote was two to one against the statute. Chief Justice Smyth in dissenting severely scored the method by which a rehearing was obtained. Thus those who sat in the two hearings in the District Court of Appeals were divided two to two. Summarizing the votes outside of the United States Supreme Court, we have twenty-nine judges thinking compulsory minimum-wage legislation not wanting in due process as against four judges thinking the contrary.

The District of Columbia adverse decision was appealed to the United States Supreme Court where it was argued on March 14, 1923, and decided on April 9, 1923, in *Adkins* v. *Children's Hospital*. The dates of the several proceedings in the District of Columbia case from its initiation to its final disposition in the Supreme Court are significant, for, as will later appear, the unconstitutionality of minimum-wage legislation has been dictated by the calendar rather than by the Constitution. The Supreme Court decision annulled the act of Congress by a vote of five to three. Mr. Justice Brandeis, *ex majore cautela,* from which Mr. Justice Robb was immune, did not sit, notwithstanding the fact that technically he was eligible since his disqualification was confined to the Oregon litigation in which he had been of counsel. The opinion of the Court was written by Mr. Justice Sutherland and concurred in by Justices McKenna, Van Devanter, McReynolds and Butler. Chief Justice Taft wrote a dissenting opinion in which Mr. Justice Sanford concurred. Mr. Justice Holmes wrote an additional dissenting opinion. Adding these Supreme Court votes to the votes in the lower courts, we have a total of thirty-two judges voting in favor of the constitutionality of minimum-wage legislation and nine judges voting against it.

Now for the importance of the time when the question reached the Supreme Court. Three of the five Justices who voted against the legislation in 1923 were on the bench in 1917 when the Supreme Court was divided four to four. These were Justices McKenna, Van Devanter, and McReynolds. We may be confident, therefore, that they gave three of the four votes against the law in 1917. The other Justices sitting in 1917 were Chief Justice White and Justices Holmes, Day, Pitney, and Clarke. Since Mr. Justice Holmes dissented in 1923, we know that he voted for the law in 1917. Followers of Supreme Court divisions can be certain also that Mr. Justice Clarke was on the same side. This confines the surmise as to the fourth Justice against the law in 1917 to Chief Justice White and Justices Day and Pitney. The evidence of other divisions of opinion points almost conclusively to Chief Justice White as the fourth in opposition. He had been more consistently with Justices Van Devanter and McReynolds against extensions of the police power than had either Mr. Justice Day or Mr. Justice Pitney. In writing the opinion sustaining the constitutionality of the Adamson Law, he made a distinction between prescribing wages after the parties have failed to agree and prescribing wages in conjunction with forbidding or restricting an agreement, thus carefully differentiating minimum-wage legislation from the Adamson Law. Mr. Rome G. Brown, one of the counsel before the Supreme Court in the first minimum-wage case, picks Chief Justice White as one of the four opposed to the legislation. It seems, therefore, as safe a guess as any guess can be, that in 1917 Chief Justice White voted against minimum-wage legislation and Justices Day and Pitney voted in favor of it. Certainly three of these four Justices were in favor of the legislation and only one opposed, so that these votes added to the others already counted make a judicial majority of thirty-five to ten in favor, with the participating Supreme Court Justices divided six to six and a non-participating Justice known to be in favor.

The bench sitting in 1917 continued until the end of the October term of 1920. During the October term of 1921 the only change was that of Chief Justice Taft in place of Chief Justice White. If our guess as to Chief Justice White is correct, the Supreme Court from October, 1921, to June, 1922, contained six Justices who thought minimum-wage legislation constitutional. One of these was Mr. Justice Brandeis who doubtless would have refrained from sitting then as he did in 1923. The others were Chief Justice Taft and Justices Holmes, Day, Pitney and Clarke. If, therefore, any state case or the District of Columbia case had been argued before and decided by the Supreme Court between November, 1921, and June, 1922, the decision would, in all probability, have been five to three in favor of minimum-wage legislation. Even if the surmise as to Chief Justice White were incorrect, and either Mr. Justice Day or Mr. Justice Pitney were opposed to the legislation, the vote would have been four to four, with Chief Justice Taft, Justices Holmes and Clarke, and either Mr.

Justice Day or Mr. Justice Pitney in favor. This would have sustained the state decisions and the first District of Columbia decision had Mr. Justice Robb not intervened to bring about a rehearing. That intervention, be it noted, set aside a decision rendered on June 6, 1921, and postponed the ultimate decision in the District of Columbia Court of Appeals until November 6, 1922. The appeal from this decision reached the Supreme Court for argument in March, 1923, and was decided less than a month later. Thus the earlier 1921 District of Columbia decision might have reached the Supreme Court for adjudication some time before June, 1922. If, therefore, Mr. Justice Robb had sat at the first hearing and the decision had then been against the act of Congress, the appeal might have been decided by the Supreme Court before June, 1922, when there were certainly only four Justices of the Supreme Court opposed to the legislation and, in all probability, only three opposed to it. Thus the state laws would surely have been saved for the time from annulment, and almost certainly both state and national legislation would have been sustained by a decision that would have been accepted as settling the issue forever. So, for a second time, the course of constitutional principles was changed by circumstances peculiar to an individual judge: first, because Mr. Justice Brandeis chanced to have been of counsel at an earlier stage of the Oregon case; and, secondly, because Mr. Justice Robb of the District of Columbia Court of Appeals was indisposed when the act of Congress first came before that court for consideration.

Before the District of Columbia case came on for argument before the Supreme Court, there had intervened three further changes in the composition of that body, all due to resignations of sitting justices. Mr. Justice Clarke was succeeded by Mr. Justice Sutherland; Mr. Justice Day, by Mr. Justice Butler; and Mr. Justice Pitney, by Mr. Justice Sanford. By these changes either a possible tie vote of four to four or, more probably, a five-to-three vote in favor of minimum-wage legislation was turned into a five-to-three vote against it. It would, of course, be idle to speculate as to whether the new appointees to the bench would have been the same had the resigning Justices been different or had their resignations been in a different order. It can, however, hardly be attributed to anything but chance that the resignations after June, 1922, were of two or three Justices favoring minimum-wage legislation and that the new appointments added two Justices opposing it. It can not well be attributed to any assumed leanings of the appointing authority, since the four new Justices appointed by President Harding were evenly divided on the issue. The political complexion of the bench at the time is of no significance. It is doubtless idle, too, to speculate as to whether Justices Sutherland and Butler might have voted differently had the question not come before them until they were further away from their days of legislation and of advocacy, and therefore perhaps more impregnated with the professed traditions of judicial tolerance in passing upon the constitutionality of legislation under the amorphous caution of the due-process clauses. Suffice it to say that minimum-wage legislation is now unconstitutional, not because the Constitution makes it so, not because its economic results or its economic prospensities would move a majority of judges to think it so, but because it chanced not to come before a particular Supreme Court bench which could not muster a majority against it and chanced to be presented at the succeeding term when the requisite, but no more than requisite, majority was sitting. In the words of the poet, it was not the Constitution but "a measureless malfeasance which obscurely willed it thus."—the malfeasance of chance and of the calendar.

Such is the only possible realistic account of the reason why minimum-wage legislation is unconstitutional. Literary interpretation of the Constitution has nothing whatever to do with it. Neither legal learning nor economic exposition can explain it. Arguments *pro* and arguments *contra* have no compelling inherent power. The issue was determined not by the arguments but by the arbiters. The majority of the arbiters on the state courts favored the legislation, but under our constitutional system the majority of the arbiters on the Supreme Court have the determining voice. The unanimous vote of the electors of a state through solemn amendment of the constitution of the state could not reverse the vote of five members of the Supreme Court of the United States. This can be done only by the Supreme Court itself or by amendment of the Constitution of the United States.

While the decision under review was confined to the act of Congress for the District of Columbia, the interpretation of the due-process clause of the Fifth Amendment, is a precedent for the interpretation of the same words in the Fourteenth Amendment, and the judicial aversion to the federal law would necessarily invalidate similar laws. There would, it is true, be a possible distinction by reason of the decisions of the state courts sustaining the state laws. The Supreme Court often professes to give weight to the sanction given by state judges to state laws. Such professions of respect are, however, honored in the breach as well as in the observance. In all substance there was as much reason to respect the state decisions in passing upon the issue which was the same as that presented by the state laws, as there would have been if a state law had been directly involved in the litigation. If, at some later time, a state law is sustained by the Supreme Court it will be either because one or more of the annulling five Justices has repented of his action in the *Adkins* case or because he has yielded his place on the bench to a successor of different temper or outlook. When the personnel of the Supreme Court changes sufficiently, the constitutionality *vel non* of minimum-wage legislation will again be an open question. Practitioners who take seriously the saying of Mr. Justice Holmes that law is a prophecy of what courts will do in fact will then have to consider the attitudes and dispositions of the new members of the Court, for those attitudes and dispositions will be the determining factors in the resolution of the constitutional issue.

This perhaps may make it worth while to seek for the attitude and the disposition which underlay the action of the majority in the present case. It makes us eager to know why ten judges had this attitude and disposition when thirty-five judges did not, but such a quest would be too baffling to undertake. We should be fortunate if we could have any confidence in our estimate of what attitude and what disposition animated the five Justices whose action invites our inquiry. The published opinion of one of them cannot be taken as, in all details, the exact embodiment of the major and minor elements in the thought and the outlook of the others. Indeed the reasons which any individual gives for his own decisions may not be the reasons which moved him to make them. Many passages in judicial opinions are quite patently argumentative justifications rather than inducing reasons. The talk in the consultation chamber must often be very different from the talk in the published opinion. Yet to these arcana the uninitiated are not admitted. We must take the opinion as it is given to us and do our best with this imperfect explanation of the judgment.

[Despite the widespread contemporary acceptance of the notion that judges *make* rather than merely *find* law, there is considerable disagreement about the manner in which they make law. Perhaps the clearest analysis of the problem was contributed by Oliver Wendell Holmes in 1879.]

2. Law and Public Policy: How Judges Make Law*

. . . The little piece of history above [Holmes's previous topic], very well illustrates the paradox of form and substance in the development of law. In form its growth is logical. The official theory is that each new decision follows syllogistically from existing precedents. But as precedents survive like the clavicle in the cat, long after the use they once served is at an end, and the reason for them has been forgotten, the result of following them must often be failure and confusion from the merely logical point of view. It is easy for the scholar to show that reasons have been misapprehended and precedents misapplied.

On the other hand, in substance the growth of the law is legislative. And this in a deeper sense than that which the courts declare to have always been the law is in fact new. It is legislative in its grounds. The very considerations which the courts most rarely mention, and always with an apology, are the secret root from which the law draws all the juices of life. We mean, of course, considerations of what is expedient for the community concerned. Every important principle which is developed by litigation is in fact and at bottom the result of more or less definitely understood views of public policy; most generally, to be sure, under our practice and traditions, the unconscious result of instinctive preferences and inarticulate convictions, but none the less traceable to public policy in the last analysis. And as the law is administered by able and experienced men, who know too much to sacrifice good sense to a syllogism, it will be found that when ancient rules maintain themselves in this way, new reasons more fitted to the time have been found for them, and that they gradually receive a new content and at last a new form from the grounds to which they have been transplanted. The importance of tracing the process lies in the fact that it is unconscious, and involves the attempt to follow precedents, as well as to give a good reason for them, and that hence, if it can be shown that one half of the effort has failed, we are at liberty to consider the question of policy with a freedom that was not possible before.

What has been said will explain the failure of all theories which consider the law only from its formal side, whether they attempt to deduce the corpus from a priori

*Oliver Wendell Holmes, Jr., "Common Carriers and the Common Law," *American Law Review*, XIII (1879), 630–31.

postulates, or fall into the humbler error of supposing the science of the law to reside in the *elegantia juris,* or logical cohesion of part with part. The truth is, that law hitherto has been, and it would seem by the necessity of its being is always approaching and never reaching consistency. It is for ever adopting new principles from life at one end, and it always retains old ones from history at the other which have not yet been absorbed or sloughed off. It will become entirely consistent only when it ceases to grow. . . .

[The validity of Holmes' analysis has been established both by the excellent conventional case studies of Powell, Fellman, Corwin, Cushman, and Mendelson, to mention a few, and by the application of behavioral techniques in judicial studies by Rodney Mott in the 1930's; by Herman Pritchett in the 1940's; and by Joseph Tanenhaus, Glendon Schubert, and Sidney Ulmer in the 1950's. By the late 1950's, the application of such methods as Guttman scalogram analysis became as conventional in public law studies as traditional case analysis. In fact the traditional and the new methodological approaches have served concomitantly as tools of analysis. Professor Ulmer's study, reproduced below, is a fine example of the application of scalogram analysis and represents one of a growing number of systematic verifications of Holmes' basic hypothesis about judicial behavior.]

3. *Supreme Court Behavior and Civil Rights**

The highlight of the 1956 term of the United States Supreme Court was the expanded protection given civil liberties. Court holdings considerably weakened the restrictive provisions of the Smith Act, opened FBI files to defendants in certain cases, and established safeguards around the exercise of congressional investigatory powers. The term was also notable for the fact that voting statistics identified the operation of a new libertarian bloc of Douglas, Black, Warren, and Brennan. While the 1957 term continued the same general patterns, analysis reveals several highly suggestive deviations. The purpose of this paper is to explore the patterns of judicial behavior in civil liberties cases decided by the Court in the 1957 term. A focus on this particular area of decision-making is justified by the heavy emphasis in American Public Law on civil liberties problems. Selection of such a focus is buttressed further by the suspicion abroad that attitude on the part of the Court has had too much and the law too little to do with deciding such cases in recent years. One should recognize, of course, that diagnosis of the motives underlying positions taken by Supreme Court justices is fraught with peril. But one cannot ignore phenomena which appear from the record. Nor should one close one's ears to confessions of garrulous

*S. Sidney Ulmer, "Supreme Court Behavior and Civil Rights," *Western Political Quarterly,* XIII (June, 1960), 288–311. [Footnotes omitted.] Reproduced with permission of the author and the publisher. Copyright © 1960 by the *Western Political Quarterly.*

judges that it is now popular on the Court "to regard every so-called civil liberties question as constitutionally self-answering."

The identification of civil liberties cases presents some difficulty. But since this discussion is not to explore semantical problems a simple definition is adopted. In this paper a civil liberties case is one involving a claimed right of the type covered by the Bill of Rights and Civil War Amendments to the Constitution. On this definition it makes no difference whether the claim calls for constitutional or statutory interpretation as long as the right involved is primarily a personal rather than a property right.

Within the framework of this definition the Supreme Court decided forty-six civil liberties cases in the 1957 term. This is an increase of twelve over the previous term. While 71 per cent of the 1956 cases involved claims against the federal government or its officers, only 43 per cent are so classified in the 1957 term. Claims against the state or its officers increased from 29 to 50 per cent. It is unlikely that the number of claims against either state or federal government varied significantly from one year to the next. The figures suggest, therefore, that the Court was less disposed to hear claims against the states. One reason for this might be that the Court was less inclined to decide civil liberties claims against the federal government in the 1957 term. On the same basis one should suppose that the Court was more willing to decide against the state. These expectations flow from the fact that the Court has virtually complete control of its docket. Access to this docket, for all practical purposes, is at the discretion of the Court or of four of its justices where the case comes up on certiorari. The first inference is supported by the evidence since only 65 per cent of the cases were decided against the federal government in the 1957 term as against 75 per cent in the preceding term. The inference respecting state cases, however, is not supported by the relevant data. The Court held against the state in 70 per cent of the 1956 cases but in only 52 per cent of those decided in the following term. This points to probable differentiation among blocs of justices on the question of access to the Court. Investigation would likely reveal a higher compositional correlation between blocs bringing up and deciding federal cases than between blocs bringing up and deciding state cases. It is reasonable to surmise that the percentage of state cases gaining access to the Court through permission of minimal four-justice blocs increased from 1956 to 1957. The justices are not likely to bring up cases involving claims against a state for the purpose of affirming the denial of the claim at a lower level. Thus it appears that in a number of instances the four-justice blocs responsible for bringing up the state cases were not able to pick up the fifth vote needed to hold for the claimant. The blocs responsible for bringing up the federal cases do not seem to have had this particular difficulty. A failure of the type indicated should, of course, be reflected in a less favorable disposition of the Court as a whole toward civil liberties claims. Analysis verifies that over-all the Court was more sympathetic to such claims in the 1956 term than in the term following. Thus while 26 per cent of the claims were denied in the 1956 term, the following term featured denials in 41 per cent of the cases. The foregoing data strongly suggest a greater differentiation in the attitudes of Supreme Court justices toward claims against the state than toward claims against the federal government. In short, the present balance of power on the Court seems more permissive toward state activity than toward federal and, overall, more permissive toward governmental activity in general in the civil liberties field.

II

TABLE I. *Civil Rights Most Frequently in Contention in the 1957 Term*

Subject Matter	Number of Cases
Former Jeopardy*	6
Free Speech†	6
Rights of Citizenship‡	5
Search and Seizure§	5**
Jury Trial††	4
Coerced Confessions‡‡	4
Right to Counsel§§	3

* *Yates* v. *U.S.* (1), *Eubanks* v. *Louisiana, Ciucci* v. *Illinois, Hoag* v. *New Jersey, Gore* v. *U.S., Green* v. *U.S.* (1).
† *Staub* v. *City of Baxley, Youngdahl* v. *Rainfair, First Unitarian Church* v. *Los Angeles, Valley Unitarian Church* v. *Los Angeles, Prince* v. *San Francisco, Speiser* v. *Randall.*
‡ *Trop* v. *Dulles, Perez* v. *Brownell, Nishikawa* v. *Dulles, Kent* v. *Dulles, Dayton* v. *Dulles.*
§ *Benanti* v. *U.S. Rathbun* v. *U.S., Jones* v. *U.S., Miller* v. *U.S., Giordenello* v. *U.S.*
** Includes two wiretap cases: *Benanti* v. *U.S.*, 355 U.S. 107 (1957) and *Rathbun* v. *U.S.*, 355 U.S. 96 (1957).
†† *Green* v. *U.S.* (2), *Eubanks* v. *Louisiana, Harmon* v. *Brucker, Abramowitz* v. *Brucker.*
‡‡ *Ashdown* v. *Utah, Payne* v. *Arkansas. Thomas* v. *Arizona, Crooker* v. *California.*
§§ *Crooker* v. *California. Cicenia* v. *La Gay, Moore* v. *Michigan.*

The substantive rights most frequently in contention before the Court in the 1957 term were the traditional ones pertaining to speech, counsel, search and seizure, etc. But not quite so traditional was the fact that five of the forty-six civil liberties cases involved claimed rights of citizenship. Table I shows that only cases concerning free speech and former jeopardy exceeded in number the citizenship cases.

While constitutional and statutory requirements were certainly important factors in civil liberties decisions in the 1957 term, they were by no means the only factors involved. Indeed in some instances they were perhaps less significant than other so-called nonlegal factors. This seems incontestably clear in several of the citizenship cases. The opinions in *Perez* v. *Brownell* and *Trop* v. *Dulles* show rather vividly that the attitudes of the decision-makers can be of prime importance. One can ignore the importance of the man in the judge only at a serious loss to scholarship. This point has been well stated by Frankfurter, who expresses it this way:

> *We speak of the Court as though it were an abstraction. To be sure, the Court is an institution, but individuals, with all their diversities of endowment, experience and outlook, determine its actions. The history of the Supreme Court is not the history of an abstraction, but the analysis of individuals acting as a Court who make decisions and lay down doctrines, and of other individuals, their successors, who refine, modify, and sometimes even overrule the decisions of their predecessors, reinterpreting and transmuting their doctrines. In law, also, men make a difference. It would deny all meaning to history to believe that the course*

of events would have been the same if Thomas Jefferson had had the naming of Spencer Roane to the place to which John Adams called John Marshall, or if Roscoe Conkling rather than Morrison R. Waite had headed the Court before which came the Granger legislation. . . . There is no inevitability in history except as men make it.

Thus we shift here to individual action. Although leading ultimately to comparative evaluation, attitude analysis must concentrate upon the behavior of individual justices. The men who occupy seats on the United States Supreme Court have available to them alternative choices in each specific case situation. The choice configurations sometimes reveal significant relationships which tend to be overlooked in straight legal analysis. For example, we find that in the 1957 term the justices differed appreciably in the extent to which each chose to express himself in written opinions in civil liberties cases. During the term a total of seventy-five opinions were written in such cases. This represented approximately 34 per cent of all opinions written during the term. Justice Clark wrote the largest number, thirteen, followed by Douglas with twelve and Frankfurter with eleven. Clark also had the largest percentage of his total opinions in civil liberties cases. Exactly one half of Clark's opinions are so classified. He was followed in this respect by Brennan and Warren with 40 per cent and by Frankfurter with 34 per cent.

Table II gives the opinion record in civil liberties cases of all the justices for the 1957 term. The table also indicates the percentage variance of such opinions from that expected from the fact that these cases constituted approximately 31 per cent of the term total. The variance runs from +19 in the case of Clark to —8.8 in the case of Harlan. This scale might be taken as one indication of the strength of each justice's feeling about civil liberties problems. It would seem from this that Clark had rather intense feelings and perhaps a definite "position" on personal rights issues that came before the Court during the term. Harlan and Whittaker, on the other hand,

TABLE II. *Written Opinions of Individual Justices in Civil Liberties Cases—1957 Term*

Justice	Opinions of Court	Dissenting	Total	Civil Liberties Opinions (% of Total Opinions)	Variance from Expectation*
Douglas	3	9	12	34.2	+3.2
Black	3	4	7	31.8	+ .8
Warren	4	4	8	40	+9
Brennan	4	4	8	40	+9
Frankfurter	4	7	11	34.3	+3.3
Harlan	6	2	8	22.2	—8.8
Whittaker	3	1	4	23.5	—7.5
Burton	3	1	4	33.3	+2.3
Clark	3	10	13	50	+19

*Expected percentage of civil liberties opinions for each justice would be approximately 31 per cent since the civil liberties cases constituted 31 per cent of the opinion cases decided during the term.

appear to have been relatively disinterested. Warren and Brennan apparently identified closely with the values represented by the personal claims. It is also possible to interpret the scale as showing the extent to which a particular justice had a unique position. If Justice A can adequately express a point of view it may not be necessary for Justice B to write an opinion. But the more intensely interested one is in a specific problem or problem area, the less likely it is that another's expression will be adequate. Thus the broader interpretation encompasses the more narrow explanation.

The opinion table suggests several additional questions which are directly related to attitude study. For example, one type of power on the Supreme Court is that possessed by the chief justice, or the senior justice in the majority, to assign the writing of the Court's opinion. The choices made in the exercise of this power may reveal something about the attitudinal relationship of one judge to another and about the makeup of dispositional blocs. Analysis of the 1957 term reveals that opinions in all forty-six cases were assigned by Warren or by Frankfurter. This is to say, of course, that Warren and Frankfurter never dissented together. Each time that Warren was in the minority, Frankfurter was in the majority. Moreover, each time Warren was in the dissent he was joined by Black. Otherwise, Black, being senior to Frankfurter, would have assigned the opinions of the Court.

Table III shows that Warren assigned twenty-one opinions while Frankfurter assigned twelve. One might generally expect these opinions to be assigned almost automatically in such a way as to equalize work load. While this is plausible in respect to total opinions it is not necessarily reasonable in a selected subject-matter area. Thus one could not easily predict assignment patterns in civil liberties cases. Table III reveals the number of times each justice was available for assignment, the number of assignments made and the ratio of the latter to the former.

An assigning justice has a number of alternatives open to him in selecting opinion-writers. He may, for instance, make assignments to members of the Court on the basis of the interagreement rate between himself and each other justice. Tables III a and b list the names of the justices in order of times available for assignment.

TABLE IIIa.   *Warren Opinion Assignments in Civil Liberties Cases— 1957 Term*

Justices	Times Available	Opinions Assigned	Percentage
Warren	21	4 (1)*	19
Brennan	20	4	20
Black	20	3	15
Douglas	19	3	15.7
Whittaker	18	3 (1)*	16.6
Frankfurter	14	0	0
Harlan	13	3	23
Burton	11	1*	9
Clark	7	0	0

*Decided against the civil liberties claim.

TABLE IIIb. *Frankfurter Opinion Assignments in Civil Liberties Cases —1957 Term*

Justices	Times Available	Opinions Assigned	Percentage
Frankfurter	12	4*	33.3
Harlan	12	3*	25
Burton	11	2*	18.1
Clark	10	2*	20
Whittaker	8	1*	12.5
Brennan	4	0	0
Warren	0	0	0
Black	0	0	0
Douglas	0	0	0

*Decided against the civil liberties claim.

If the interagreement rates constitute the basic factor underlying assignment the number of opinions assigned each justice should correlate at a high level with the number of opportunities. This turns out to be the case since the coefficient of correlation (r) is .84 for Table III a and .90 for Table III b. The coefficient of determination (r^2) is 70 per cent for the Warren assignments and 81 per cent for those by Frankfurter. Thus 70 per cent of the variance in the Warren assignments and 81 per cent of the variance in the Frankfurter assignments can be accounted for by the variance in the number of times the members of the Court were available for opinion assignment.

Delineation of the other factors operating in this choice-making situation must, at this stage, be somewhat speculative. Certain discrepancies in the assignments, however, are noticeable. One of these is that Warren never assigned a civil liberties opinion to Frankfurter even though Frankfurter was available in fourteen instances. This can be explained, of course, in terms of equalizing the work load. Frankfurter and Warren both wrote four opinions of the Court in civil liberties cases in the 1957 term. The tables, in other words, must be read in conjunction. When this is done the equalization-of-work theory seems to explain adequately every case except that of Harlan. It is seen that Harlan wrote six opinions of the Court, two more than any other justice. And his average rate of assignment was approximately 25 per cent in both the Warren and Frankfurter camps. This is by no means surprising in respect to the Frankfurter assignments. Harlan agreed with Frankfurter in every civil liberties case in which Frankfurter was the senior justice. Moreover, he is so often in agreement with Frankfurter in all types of cases that he is sometimes referred to as one of Frankfurter's "little hot dogs." The over-all rate of agreement between Harlan and Frankfurter in the 1957 term was the highest of each with any justice. These two justices joined in opinion in 95 of the 117 cases in which both participated. Interaction process analysis for the 1957 term indicates that the interaction was predominantly from Harlan to Frankfurter. Thus the opinion data from Table III b is in line with the normal expectation. The Warren assignments are a little more difficult to explain. Since Harlan wrote three opinions assigned by Frankfurter, it would have been consistent with the equalization-of-work theory for Warren to omit assignments to Harlan as he did to Frankfurter. Other factors appear to be operating in the Harlan case. One possible explanation might be that the figures merely reflect the fact that Harlan occupied a center position on the Court in the civil liberties cases in the 1957 term. This would suggest that his acceptance in both camps merely delineates his role as "swing justice" during the term. The difficulty with this is that Frankfurter and Whittaker occupied essentially the same position. These three were the "swing justices" in civil liberties cases during the term. This is evidenced by the fact that they were in the majority more often than any of the others. But of the three, Whittaker was more often in the majority. Thus, if any one justice is to be characterized as "swing justice" it would have to be Whittaker, not Harlan. We are left with the inference that of the three justices occupying the middle ground in the 1957 term Harlan for some reason was more acceptable to Warren (and probably the libertarian bloc) than Frankfurter or Whittaker. It should be noted that Harlan's role as number one opinion writer for the Court in civil liberties cases is entirely consistent with his indicated disinterested attitude.

III

It has been suggested that the number of opinions that a justice chooses to write in a selected subject-matter area has some significance. It may reveal something about the extent to which he identifies himself with the values encountered in the area. In the civil liberties opinions of the 1957 term we pointed to Clark, Warren, and Brennan as identifying most closely with the allocation of the values in contention. But our opinion evidence did not indicate the direction of the identification. This direction can be clearly portrayed through analysis of voting statistics.

In examining the voting statistics in civil liberties cases in the 1957 term one is immediately struck by discrepancies in individual reactions to certain fact-law situations. One cannot, of course, expect a collegial court of nine justices to decide all cases unanimously. Differences in interpretation of Constitution and statute there most assuredly will be. But when the reactions of the justices are markedly different over a long series of cases one is led to suspect that individual characteristics are important decision-shaping factors. Analysis reveals that in twenty-two non-unanimous civil liberties cases decided in the 1956 term, Douglas and Black voted *for the civil liberty claim twenty-one times*. Clark, on the other hand, voted for the civil liberty claim in one case and *against the claim in twenty-one*. In the 1957 term out of forty-one non-unanimous civil liberties cases Douglas voted *for the claim in forty instances*. Clark, with the same number of opportunities voted *against the claim in thirty-nine cases*.

Certainly discrepancies of this nature are not alone due to mere differences as to the meaning of Constitution or statute. Indeed it is reasonable in this context to suggest that the *attitude* of the judge toward civil liberty claims was the factor shaping the individual decisions. Llewellyn and the legal realists have often noted that the important factor in judicial decision-making is the reaction of the judge to the fact-stimuli of life around him. This observation would seem pertinent in the area of civil liberties decisions if anywhere.

We shall hypothesize, therefore, that the responses of the justices in civil liberties cases are in terms of *one dominant variable: deprivation of a claimed civil liberty.* This hypothesis assumes that the justice will make his decision not by asking "What does the law require?" but by asking himself such questions as: "Shall I allow any deprivation of a claimed civil liberty? Shall I allow deprivation to the extent of X? to the extent of Y? to the extent of Z?" Since the civil liberties cases have been selected in terms of one common factor: *deprivation of a claimed civil liberty,* verification of response to *one dominant variable* will constitute strong support for the hypothesis. Failure to verify *one dominant operative variable* will nullify the hypothesis.

Identification of the operative variable may be attempted through the use of Guttman Scalogram Analysis. This research tool was developed by Louis Guttman in the early 1940's to cope with a basic problem in opinion research. The problem is to determine if questions asked on a single issue have a single meaning for the respondents. Only if such a single meaning is present can respondents be ranked along an attitude continuum in order of favorableness. Scalogram analysis is designed to detect the presence or absence of this single meaning or dominant variable in terms of which responses are made and respondents may be ranked. Such a variable is identified if a "scale" exists. A perfect scale is said to exist if the questions and responses can be arranged in such a way that "persons who answer a given question favorably all have higher ranks than persons who answer the same question unfavorably." From the rank or scale score of the respondent we know exactly which questions he favored and can therefore say that a response to any question defines the respondent's attitude. Perfect scales, however, are not expected in practice. The difference between a perfect scale and a given scale pattern is measured by a coefficient of reproducibility (CR). Guttman has arbitrarily classified any pattern with a CR of less than .90 as non-scale type.

The attitude of a respondent toward a primary operating variable is measured relatively by his rank order. It is denoted numerically by his scale score. Thus, the complete behavior of a respondent to a series of questions can be indicated by a numerical score within the margin of error denoted by the CR.

As applied to Supreme Court cases, certain slight modifications in Guttman's techniques are necessary. The cases are conceptualized as less deprivational than the one preceding it. The non-unanimous civil liberties cases for the 1956 term, when analyzed, form a scale with properties well within the requirements of scale theory. The existence of the scale indicates: (1) a structured attitude continuum along which response is highly consistent, and (2) the presence of one dominant operating variable. The variable hypothesized is the one in terms of which the cases were originally selected: *deprivation of a claimed civil liberty.* Thus, the data for the 1956 term supports the general hypothesis. The scalogram in Figure I ranks the justices in order of favorableness toward civil liberty claims. Douglas and Black turn out to be most favorable toward such claims with Burton and Clark least favorable. Reed's ranking is of little significance due to his large number of nonparticipations. Consistency of the justices in these cases is measured by the coefficient of reproducibility of .973. This indicates that 97.3 per cent of the over-all response can be accounted for by one operating variable.

FIGURE I. Scalogram Analysis: Civil Liberty Cases—United States Supreme Court—1956 Term

	Douglas	Black	Warren	Brennan	Frankfurter	Harlan	Whittaker	Burton	Clark	Reed	Vote
Scale Score	22	22	20	19	14	12	11	5	0	0	
As Percentage of First Rank	100	100	90.9	81.7	63.6	54.5	50	22.7	0	0	
Jencks v. United States	+	+	+	+	+	+	n	+	−	n	7–1
Yates v. United States	+	+	+	n	+	+	n	+	−	n	6–1
Schneiderman v. United States	+	+	+	n	+	+	n	+	−	n	6–1
Richmond v. United States	+	n	+	n	+	+	n	+	−	n	6–1
Boviaro v. United States	+	+	+	+	+	+	n	n	−	n	6–1
Watkins v. United States	+	+	+	+	+	+	n	−	−	n	6–1
Kremen v. United States	+	+	+	+	+	+	n	−	−	n	6–2
Kinsella v. Krueger	+	+	+	+	+	+	n	−	−	n	6–2
Reid v. Covert	+	+	+	+	+	+	n	−	−	n	6–2
Sweezy v. New Hampshire	+	+	+	+	+	+	n	−	−	n	6–2
Chessman v. Teets	−	+	+	+	+	+	+	−	−	−	6–3
Gold v. United States	+	+	+	+	+	+	n	−	+	−	6–3
Fikes v. Alabama	+	+	+	+	+	+	n	−	−	n	6–3
Paoli v. United States	+	+	−	+	−	−	n	−	−	−	4–5
Konigsberg v. State Bar	+	+	+	+	−	−	n	+	−	n	5–3
Petition of Groban	+	+	+	+	−	−	−	−	−	−	4–5
Kingsley Books v. Brown	+	+	+	−	−	−	n	−	+	n	4–5
Nilva v. United States	+	+	+	−	−	−	n	−	−	−	4–5
Pollard v. United States	+	+	+	−	−	−	n	−	−	n	4–5
Breithaupt v. Abrams	+	+	+	+	−	+	−	−	−	−	3–6
Roth v. United States	+	+	−	−	−	+	−	−	−	n	3–6
Alberts v. United States	+	+	−	−	−	−	−	−	−	n	2–7
Number of Participations	22	21	22	19	22	22	5	21	22	6	182
Inconsistencies	1	1	1	0	0	1	1	1	1	0	5

Coefficient of Reproducibility $= 1 - \dfrac{5}{182} = .973$

Legend: + for the civil liberty claim
− against the civil liberty claim
n nonparticipation

Note: Case titles have been shortened in some instances.

FIGURE 2. *Scalogram Analysis: Civil Liberty Cases—United States Supreme Court—1957 Term*

	Douglas	Black	Warren	Brennan	Frankfurter	Harlan	Whitaker	Burton	Clark	Vote
Scale Score	40	36	35	31	16	14	11	8	0	
As Percentage of First Rank	100	90	87.5	77.5	40	35	27.5	20	0	
First Church v. Los Angeles	+	+	+	+	+	+	+	+	−	8–1
Valley Church v. Los Angeles	+	+	+	+	+	+	+	+	−	8–1
Speiser v. Randall	+	+	+	+	+	+	+	+	−	8–1
Prince v. San Francisco	+	+	+	+	+	+	+	+	−	8–1
Nishikawa v. Dulles	+	+	+	+	+	−	+	+	−	7–2
Harmon v. Brucker	+	+	+	+	+	+	+	+	−	8–1
Abramowitz v. Brucker	+	+	+	+	+	+	+	+	−	8–1
Staub v. City of Baxley	+	+	+	+	−	+	+	+	−	7–2
Jones v. United States	+	+	+	+	+	+	+	−	−	7–2
Miller v. United States	+	+	+	+	+	+	+	−	−	7–2
Payne v. Arkansas	+	+	+	+	+	+	+	−	−	7–2
Sacher v. United States	+	+	+	+	+	+	−	n	−	6–2
Giordenello v. United States	+	+	+	+	+	+	−	−	−	6–3
Yates v. United States (2)	+	+	+	+	+	+	−	−	−	6–3
Kent v. Dulles	+	+	+	+	+	−	−	−	−	5–4
Dayton v. Dulles	+	+	+	+	+	−	−	−	−	5–4
Lerner v. Casey	+	+	+	+	−	−	−	−	−	4–5
Beilan v. Board of Ed.	+	+	+	+	−	−	−	−	−	4–5
Cicenia v. La Gay	+	+	+	n	−	−	−	−	−	3–5

Case										Vote
Thomas v. Arizona	+	+	+	+	−	−	−	−	−	4–5
Ciucci v. Illinois	+	+	+	+	−	−	−	−	−	4–5
Hoag v. New Jersey	+	+	n	+	−	−	−	−	−	3–5
Green v. United States (2)	+	+	+	+	−	−	−	−	−	4–5
Brown v. United States	+	+	+	+	−	−	−	−	−	4–5
Trop v. Dulles	+	+	+	+	n	−	−	−	−	5–4
Eskridge v. Washington	+	+	+	+	−	−	+	+	+	6–2
Green v. United States (1)	+	+	+	+	−	+	−	−	−	5–4
Moore v. Michigan	+	+	+	+	−	−	−	−	−	5–4
Lambert v. California	+	+	+	+	−	+	−	−	+	5–4
Gore v. United States	+	+	+	+	−	−	−	−	−	4–5
Crooker v. California	+	+	+	+	−	−	−	−	−	4–5
Perez v. Brownell	+	+	+	+	−	+	−	−	−	4–5
Knapp v. Schweitzer	+	+	+	−	−	−	−	−	−	3–6
Yates v. United States (1)	+	+	+	−	−	−	−	−	−	3–6
Youngdahl v. Rainfair	+	+	+	−	−	−	−	−	−	3–6
Ashdown v. Utah	+	+	+	−	−	−	−	−	−	2–7
Wilson v. Leow's	+	+	+	−	−	−	−	−	−	1–8
Rathbun v. United States	+	+	+	+	−	−	−	−	−	2–7
Caritativo v. California	+	+	+	+	+	−	−	−	−	3–6
Rupp v. Dickson	+	+	+	+	+	−	−	−	−	3–6
Lawn v. United States	−	+	+	+	+	+	+	−	−	3–6
Number of Participations	41	41	41	39	40	41	41	40	41	365
Inconsistencies				3	5	2	4	1	2	17

Coefficient of Reproducibility $= 1 - \dfrac{17}{365} = .953$

Legend: + for the civil liberty claim
− against the civil liberty claim
n nonparticipation

Note: Case titles have been shortened in some instances.

There were only five inconsistent votes out of 182 cast. Frankfurter and Harlan had two each for half of the total. Detailed analysis of the data for the 1956 term is omitted here since the material is included for the purpose of comparison with the following term. But before leaving the 1956 scalogram it should be noted that this scale can be used as a predictive device. As long as the same justices sit and the same types of questions are raised, one can predict from the 1956 scale that the relative ranking in terms of favorableness toward civil liberty claims will be maintained. Thus, from the 1956 data, one could have predicted the same relative ranking for the 1957 term.

The analysis of non-unanimous civil liberties cases in the 1957 term produces a scale with a CR of .953 which is slightly less than that of the preceding term. True to prediction, the relative ranking of the justices is unchanged. Douglas remains most favorable toward civil liberty claims and Clark remains least inclined to support them. Out of 365 responses there were only seventeen inconsistent votes. Frankfurter had the largest number—five, followed by Whittaker with four, and Brennan with three. Warren, Black, and Douglas had a perfectly consistent voting record in the civil liberties cases in the 1957 term. Black also showed perfect consistency in the 1956 term. This suggests that his attitude is perhaps the most rigidly structured in the civil liberties field of any justice on the Court. Frankfurer, on the other hand, would appear to have the least rigid outlook in this area.

Seven of the inconsistent votes were cast by Frankfurter, Harlan, and Brennan in the three cases of *Caritativo* v. *California, Rupp* v. *Dickson* and *Lawn* v. *United States.* Frankfurter and Brennan were both inconsistent in *Caritativo, Rupp,* and *Lawn.* The first two cases were consolidated for judgment which, *per curiam,* held against the civil liberty claim. The cases concerned the treatment of insane criminals who have become insane after conviction. They raised questions of due process rights under the Fourteenth Amendment.

The due process clause of the Fourteenth Amendment requires a fair hearing in the states. But the Court has never held that the clause applies against the states all the procedural requirements of the Bill of Rights. The Court has been selective and has insisted that those procedural rights which are "essential to justice" are protected at the state level. The list of procedural rights "essential to justice" has been greatly expanded since 1923. But this has been done with caution. And the Court has not seen fit to require the federal procedure at the state level, nor the wisest or best conceivable procedure. As a result the requirements of federal due process at the state level are minimal.

Under the California Penal Code, an insane criminal who has become insane after conviction may not be executed. Wardens in the state prisons are obligated to initiate legal proceedings to determine sanity when there appears "good reason" for so doing. Caritativo and Rupp had been sentenced to death upon conviction for first degree murder. They sought suspension of the execution under the statute. *Ex parte,* the warden of San Quenton, refused to initiate the proceedings. His primary reason was that on several occasions psychiatrists had examined the petitioners and advised that they were sane. In the case of Rupp, the warden refused to hear evidence from petitioner and his counsel even though Rupp had a long history of mental illness.

The Supreme Court majority held that the warden's denial did not constitute a violation of due process. The majority reached this conclusion on the authority of *Solesbee* v. *Balkcom,* a case upholding a Georgia statute granting power to determine insanity to the Governor. Frankfurter's dissent (in which Brennan and Douglas joined) in *Caritativo* reiterated in part his dissent in *Solesbee.* The dissent stressed the common-law rule against executing the insane. And it is generally recognized that the Fourteenth Amendment protects against such execution. His complaint, however, was not substantive but procedural. He does not suggest that a person in the place of Caritativo has a right to have his claim tested in a judicial proceeding or in a formal adversary hearing before the warden. He does insist, however, that the warden should be required to hear the claim of the party. What kind of a constitutional right is it, he asks, "the vindication of which rests wholly in the hands of an administrative official whose actions cannot be inquired into, and who need not consider the claims of the person most vitally affected, the person in whom the constitutional right is said to inhere?" The Frankfurter argument is particularly cogent in view of Rupp's long history of mental illness. The inconvenience to penal administration which would result from a change in the procedure is recognized by Frankfurter. But he declares this better than that California "should have on its conscience a single execution that would be barbaric because the victim was . . . mentally unfit to meet his destiny."

In *Lawn* v. *United States,* the Court upheld a conviction for income tax evasion over contentions that tainted evidence had been used to obtain it. This evidence had been secured by a Grand Jury in 1952. But the indictments voted at the time were later dismissed by the District Court on the ground that the petitioner had not been notified of his constitutional privilege against self-incrimination. The indictment at issue in the instant case was voted in 1953. Lawn contended that conviction on the later indictment was based on evidence obtained in the 1952 investigation thereby violating the Fifth Amendment. The Court found that Lawn's counsel had waived any objection to the introduction of the evidence. Lawn contended that due process of law was denied him by a failure of the District Court to grant him a full hearing to determine the extent to which the 1952 evidence was used in the subsequent proceeding. No merit was found in this contention. Finally, the majority rejected, on the record, petitioner's argument that he was denied an opportunity to examine and cross-examine witnesses at the trial to determine use of the tainted evidence. Harlan, Frankfurter, and Brennan dissented in part.

The three cases here are significant for splitting the libertarian and less-libertarian blocs on the Court. Douglas and Brennan from the libertarian bloc and Frankfurter from the Court's less-libertarian bloc joined in holding for the claim in *Caritativo* and *Rupp.* In *Lawn,* Harlan and Frankfurter from the right and Brennan from the left joined in supporting the claim. The remainder of the Court opposed. The seven inconsistent votes in these three cases can be explained in part by the peculiar nature of the questions raised. All three presented extraordinary problems. In general, the responses indicate the extent to which the justices disagree as to the nature of the "hearing" required by due process of law in criminal proceedings.

The only other case in which there were as many as two inconsistent votes was

Eskridge v. *Washington,* another case involving a state criminal proceeding. In this, two justices from the right wing of the Court, Burton and Clark, joined the libertarian bloc of Warren, Douglas, Black, and Brennan to hold for the civil liberty claim. *Eskridge* was decided *per curiam* as were *Caritativo* and *Rupp.* The similarities between the three cases do not stop there. All three concerned persons convicted of murder. All three were actions brought by inmates of state penal institutions. In the instant case the petitioner sought and was denied a free transcript of his trial proceedings in order to appeal his murder conviction. Washington law authorized a trial judge to furnish such a stenographic transcript to an indigent defendant at public expense if in the judge's opinion "justice will be done." The judge here opined negatively and the Washington Supreme Court dismissed the appeal.

The majority of the United States Supreme Court found a violation of the Fourteenth Amendment. The opinion pointed out that while the Amendment does not require a state to furnish a transcript in every case involving an indigent defendant, a state denies a constitutional right if it allows all convicted defendants to have appellate review except those who cannot afford to pay for the records of their trial.

This holding was first made in *Griffin* v. *Illinois.* Since *Eskridge* concerned a 1935 conviction Harlan and Whittaker felt that *Griffin* should not control. The point made by Harlan and Whittaker is important since it involved retrospective lawmaking. Judge-made law is often distinguished from that of legislatures. It is said that legislative law operates prospectively only while judge-made law has retrospective as well as prospective force. But, the restrospective [*sic*] element is usually considered to be restricted to the case in which the law is made. This appears to be acceptable to Harlan and Whittaker. The burden of their objection seems to be that the retrospective operations of the Court's decisions should be so restricted. Otherwise there would be no objection to applying *Griffin* to a 1935 trial.

The break-point case for Warren was *Ashdown* v. *Utah.* This case concerned a of deprivation of the civil liberty involved became acceptable to the respective justices. For Douglas, only the case of *Lawn* v. *U.S.* accomplishes this. Black breaks in *Wilson* v. *Loew's* where he rejected the claim of a "right to work." Petitioner had been blacklisted in the movie industry for invoking the Fifth Amendment before the Congressional Committee on Un-American activities. After granting the writ of certiorari the Supreme Court dismissed the writ as improvident. Douglas dissenting, said he saw no difference between the "right to work" being denied because of race and where, as here, because the witness had exercised a Fifth Amendment right. Both cases, Douglas urged, violated equal protection.

The break-point case for Warren was *Ashdown* v. *Utah.* This case concerned a claim by Milda Ashdown that she had been coerced by Utah authorities into making a murder confession. Miss Ashdown had conversed with the authorities prior to requesting an attorney as well as after making the request. The oral confession was given prior to the first request. The Utah court excluded all testimony of what was said subsequent to the request for counsel but admitted all that was said before the request. The United States Supreme Court on a complete review of the facts found that the confession was admissable and that it had been obtained under constitutional conditions. Douglas dissented, along with Black, on the ground that a request for counsel made by the father and brother of the accused almost immediately after arrest should have been honored.

Ashdown was one of four cases in which the central issue was the claim of a coerced confession. But, it was the only one of the four in which Warren thought the confession admissible.

In *Thomas* v. *Arizona,* the petitioner, a Negro, was convicted of murder and sentenced to death. He asked the Supreme Court to reverse on the ground that his confession, introduced as evidence in the trial, had been coerced by fear of lynching. Such fear was allegedly induced by the fact that when arrested by a sheriff and posse, Thomas had been lassoed around the neck by a local rancher and jerked toward the nearest trees. Writing for the Court, Clark held that the confession, made some twenty hours after the incident, was not induced by fear of lynching. Warren, Black, Douglas, and Brennan in dissent thought otherwise.

In *Payne* v. *Arkansas,* a nineteen-year-old mentally dull Negro was convicted of murder in Jefferson County and sentenced to death by electrocution. The Supreme Court of Arkansas affirmed. The United States Supreme Court granted certiorari to examine the charge that the petitioner's confession was coerced. Payne alleged that the chief of police had threatened that thirty or forty people were trying to "get him" but that a confession would enable the chief to prevent it.

The chief of police admitted the substance of the statement. Whittaker for the Court found that in addition, the petitioner was (1) arrested without a warrant; (2) denied a hearing before a magistrate at which time he would have been advised of his right to counsel; (3) not advised of his right to remain silent or of his right to counsel; (4) held incommunicado for three days without counsel, advisor, or friend; and (5) denied food for twenty-five hours and then after two sandwiches for fifteen additional hours. The totality of this conduct created such fear, the Court held, as to taint the confession in violation of the Fourteenth Amendment. Burton and Clark in dissent thought that the confession was voluntary.

In *Crooker* v. *California,* the petitioner's claim of coercion was based on a denial of his request to contact counsel. But, in view of the fact that Crooker was educated, intelligent, and informed of his rights, the Court found the confession voluntary.

It is notable that *Thomas* and *Payne* involved Negroes while *Ashdown* did not. Thus, *Ashdown* is distinguishable on that basis. This is not, however, to suggest that such a factor explains Warren's reaction in the three cases. But it is worth noting that two members of the libertarian bloc thought the confessions coerced in all three cases. And of the three members of the Court most favorable to civil liberty claims in the 1957 term only Warren voted against the claim in *Ashdown.*

Perez v. *Brownell* was the first case on the list which found Brennan opposed to the civil liberty claim. *Perez* was one of several important citizenship cases decided during the term. The role of Brennan in two of these deserves some comment. These two, *Perez* and *Trop* v. *Dulles,* concerned expatriation and the rights of the natural-born citizen.

In deciding them, the whole question of the role of the Supreme Court became involved in the differing views of the justices. Remarks from the bench became unusually bitter and waspish, and the philosophic diversity on the Court was clearly revealed. The cases tested the constitutionality of a federal statute depriving native-born Americans of citizenship for certain proscribed acts. In *Perez* v. *Brownell,* petitioner had been deprived of citizenship for voting in a political election in a foreign state in violation of Section 401 of the Nationality Act of 1940. Frankfurter, for the Court, found that Congress was merely exercising its power to regulate foreign affairs. The basic restriction upon this power is that its exercise must be reasonable or have its basis in rationality. It is recognized that voting in foreign elections might well embroil the United States in embarrassing situations to the jeopardy of successful conduct of foreign relations. Frankfurter thought it reasonable, therefore, to discourage the practice. He found nothing unreasonable about the particular means of discouragement chosen by Congress. For, as he put it, "The termination of citizenship terminates the problem." The majority failed to reach the constitutional issue.

In dissent, Chief Justice Warren, joined by Black and Douglas, argued that Congress lacked the power to deprive the native born or the lawfully naturalized citizen of American citizenship. Responding to the Court opinion he asserted that "a government of the people cannot take away their citizenship simply because one branch of that government can be said to have a conceivably rational basis for wanting to do so." The Warren opinion recognized that a citizen may voluntarily relinquish citizenship by renouncing it expressly or by acting in such a manner as to compromise his allegiance. In the latter category he felt that voting in a foreign election might be an act of voluntary relinquishment under appropriate circumstances. But the Nationality statute does not limit the challenged section to "those situations that may rationally be said to constitute an abandonment of citizenship." Pointing out that of eighty-four nations, the United States is the only one specifically to designate foreign voting as an expatriating act, Warren concluded that "the mere act of voting in a foreign election . . . without regard to the circumstances attending the participation, is not sufficient to show a voluntary abandonment of citizenship."

Thus in *Perez,* we find Frankfurter speaking for one view of the Supreme Court's role in its relationship with Congress. The Court, in his view, should defer to Congress on all doubtful questions. The elected branches of the government should have broad power in a democratic system. Congressional statutes should be upheld if Congress has a rational basis for adopting them. This philosophy is anathema to Warren, Black, and Douglas. These justices stand for a more assertive role of the Supreme Court in its relations with Congress. For example, Douglas, in a separate opinion in which he was joined by Black, took sharp issue with the Frankfurter philosophy. He described it as "foreign to our constitutional system . . . this philosophy has no place here." "It gives," he declared, "supremacy to the legislature in a way that is incompatible with the scheme of our written Constitution."

Following Frankfurter's more restrained approach in *Perez* were Clark, Harlan, Burton, and Brennan. The first three of these are often grouped with Frankfurter in such cases. Brennan and Whittaker have said that they subscribe to the philosophy of self-restraint. But in *Perez* and the companion case of *Trop* v. *Dulles* they voted independently and decided the issue in each instance. In *Trop* a native-born American was deprived of citizenship by reason of a court martial conviction for wartime desertion. As in *Perez,* the issue was whether the forfeiture was in violation of the Constitution. The Court, speaking through Warren, decided that the statute providing for loss of citizenship for one dishonorably discharged after conviction for desertion was unconstitutional. Warren attempted to distinguish the instant case from *Perez* on the ground that Section 401 (g) of the 1940 Nationality Act was involved here, while 401 (j) was involved in *Perez*. The Court saw the question posed by 401 (g) as whether or not denationalization may be inflicted as a punishment, even assuming that citizenship may be divested pursuant to some governmental power. (This assumption is specifically rejected by Warren in his *Perez* dissent.) Holding 401 (g) to be a penal statute, the Court found that the Constitution did not permit Congress to take away citizenship as a punishment for a crime. Denationalization as a punishment for crime, Warren declared, is barred by the Eighth Amendment. For while there may be no physical mistreatment and no primitive torture, "there is instead the total destruction of the individual's status in organized society." This, the Court felt, was cruel and unusual.

The distinction between *Perez* and *Trop* is indeed tenuous at most. The fact is that the vote of eight of the justices reflected the same attitude in both cases. But Brennan switched from the majority position in *Perez* to the majority position in *Trop* constituting the fifth vote in each case. In making this switch Brennan conceded that "It is . . . paradoxical to justify as constitutional the expatriation of the citizen who has committed no crime by voting in a Mexican political election, yet find unconstitutional a statute which provides for the expatriation of a soldier guilty of the very serious crime of desertion in time of war." But, he explained, in *Perez* expatriation was a means reasonably calculated to prevent evils which might obstruct or embarrass our diplomatic interests. In *Trop,* Brennan held, expatriation for desertion in time of war was not a means reasonably calculated to aid in the successful waging of war.

Thus the decision in the case turned upon Brennan's conception of "reasonableness" between ends and means. Clearly, the *Trop* case overturning a federal statute has at most a tenuous rationale. It is not likely to have much use as precedent. It is precisely the kind of situation in which Frankfurter would say that the legislature should prevail. The Brennan position, which was crucial in the pair of cases, is not easily explainable unless one accepts his comments on "reasonableness" at face value. Refuge in such terminology has too often in the past been taken by judges interested in the manipulation of legal symbols to accomplish desired ends. As a result there is much to be said for the Frankfurter position. Moreover, if "reasonableness" of the relationship between means and ends is to be a vital factor one would expect the Court to consider more than one or two factors in a given situation. It may be reasonable for Congress to ban participation of American citizens in foreign elections where such participation interferes with effective conduct of foreign affairs. But conceivably there are elections where these considerations do not apply. The election of the head of state in the Vatican is a case in point. Certainly, American Cardinals cannot be constitutionally barred from taking part in the selection. Likewise, there may be instances where the foreign state permits voting by resident aliens. Would this interfere with effective conduct of foreign relations? Clearly the nature of the election and the policies of the nation involved are factors that should be considered in determining the "reasonableness" of congressional restrictions.

The break-point case for Justice Frankfurter was *Lerner* v. *Casey,* one of two cases during the term involving the applications of the due process clause of the Fourteenth Amendment to the discharge of public employees. *Lerner* tested the constitutionality of the New York Security Risk Law enacted in 1951. This statute gives the State Civil Service Commission the authority to classify any bureau or agency within the state as a "security agency." The appointing authority of each such agency is then given powers of suspension and dismissal as to any employee whose continued employment would "endanger the security or defense of the nation and the state." Findings may be made upon the employee's past conduct. Legal rules of evidence do not apply in such cases but the evidence is not to be "limited" to evidence of membership in organizations found by the state Civil Service Commission to be "subversive."

In 1953, the Commission found the New York City Transit Authority to be a "security agency." In March 1954, it found the Communist party to be "subversive." In November, 1954, the appellant was summoned to the office of the Commissioner of Investigations of the city of New York in the course of an investigation being conducted under the Security Risk Law. Being sworn he was asked whether he was then a member of the Communist party. A refusal to answer was based on the Fifth Amendment privilege. The Transit Authority suspended the appellant without pay and advised him that he could appeal within thirty days. Instead of appeal Lerner brought process in the state courts for reinstatement. The state courts refusing relief, the United States Supreme Court reviewed on appeal papers treated as application for Writ of Certiorari. While several claims were advanced the major contention took the line that the administrative finding of reasonable grounds for the belief that the appellant was "of doubtful trust and reliability" and therefore a security risk, offended due process. The finding, Lerner argued, rested on an inference that he was a member of the Communist party. This inference, it was suggested, was drawn from Lerner's invocation of the Fifth Amendment privilege. He asked the Court to recognize that there was no rational connection between the inference and his refusal to answer. This the Court refused to do. Harlan, for the majority, found that Lerner had not been discharged because of any inference about Communist party membership nor for invoking the Fifth Amendment. The discharge, the Court said, came about because of "doubt created as to his 'reliability' by his refusal to answer a relevant question put by his employer." The discharge rested solely, therefore, on the refusal to respond. The inference as to reliability was based upon lack of frankness in answering relevant questions. Thus, it now appears that federal or state government may ask employees questions relevant to job fitness and fire them for refusing to answer. The fact that the refusal may be accompanied by the assertion of the Fifth Amendment privilege does not taint the constitutionality of the discharge.

Harlan, the man with whom Frankfurter is most often in agreement, split from his mentor in the now famous passport case of *Kent* v. *Dulles* decided June 16, 1958. The Harlan break-point case was one concerning two applications for passports by Rockwell Kent and Walter Briehl, both of which were denied by the Secretary of State. In both instances, the denials were based in general on the failure of the applicants to furnish certain information regarding their alleged participation in Communist activity—specifically the failure to submit an affidavit as to whether the applicants were or had been members of the Communist party. Both applicants defended on the ground that matters unrelated to the question of citizenship were irrelevant to the right of passport. Briehl, in addition, maintained that every American citizen has a right to travel regardless of politics and that the burden was on the Secretary of State to prove illegal activities on the part of the applicant. The District Court upheld the Department of State. The Court of Appeals affirmed *en banc* by a divided vote.

The majority of the United States Supreme Court, per Douglas, noted that for most of our history the passport was not, as presently, a condition of entry and exit. While recognizing that the right to travel is a part of the liberty of which the citizen cannot be deprived without due process, the Court avoided the constitutional issue, deciding the case on statutory construction. Congress had not, Douglas declared, delegated to the Secretary of State the authority to deny passports because of beliefs or associations.

Clark wrote a dissenting opinion in which Burton, Harlan, and Whittaker joined. The dissenters thought that Congress had intended that the Secretary should deny passport to those whose travel abroad would be adverse to national security. They would have reached the constitutional issue but declined comment on the constitutional question in view of the majority decision.

Finally, Whittaker and Burton broke respectively in *Sacher* v. *United States* and *Jones* v. *United States*. In *Sacher* the petitioner contested a conviction in the District Court (D.C.) for failure to answer three questions put to him by a sub-committee of the Senate Committee on the Judiciary. The Court of Appeals affirmed. The Supreme Court granted certiorari, and remanded for reconsideration in light of the decision in *Watkins* v. *United States,* decided in the 1956 term. On reargument the Court of Appeals for the District of Columbia sitting *en banc* affirmed by a divided bench. The Supreme Court again granted certiorari. In a *per curiam* opinion the Court held that where the subject matter of inquiry was "recantation of prior testimony by a witness named Matusow" questions concerning "proposed legislation barring Communists from practice at the federal bar" were not pertinent to the authorized subject of investigation. Clark and Whittaker dissenting, objected to the reversal urging upon the Court that "pertinency is clearly established."

In *Jones* v. *United States,* the petitioner was convicted of various violations of federal liquor laws including possession of an illegal still. The District Court entered adverse judgment. The Court of Appeals affirmed. The Supreme Court granted certiorari. Jones made the claim that some of the evidence used against him in the trial should have been suppressed because it was obtained by an unlawful search and seizure. The evidence in question consisted of a boiler, a fuel burner, and fifteen barrels seized in rear rooms and the attic of the house occupied by Jones. Entry into the house had been over the protests of the wife of the accused. Moreover, it had been made at night without a nighttime warrant. The state argued that the question was simply whether the search was reasonable under the circumstances. The officers had reason to suspect that a crime was being committed for they had previously detected mash in a hollow behind the house, the odor of hot mash from the direction of the house, a hose from which mash emerged running in the direction of the house, and the sound of a blower burner from the same direction. It was admitted that the officers had plenty of time in which to obtain a warrant.

The majority noted that it is settled doctrine that probable cause for belief that certain articles subject to seizure are in a dwelling, cannot of itself justify a search without a warrant. The government's answer to this was that entry had been made for the purpose of arrest. While looking for the accused the government claimed a right to seize all contraband in sight. The Court did not speak to the merits of this theory but merely observed that the record failed to support the argument.

Black concurred without opinion. Clark wrote a dissenting opinion with which Burton concurred. Clark argued that "although there are many ways to kill a cat, drowning remains the most favored. The Court applies that method to this conviction —drowning it by watering down the findings of fact and conclusions of law." Clark would have accepted the judgment of the lower courts and the government that "the officers had authority to enter the house, arrest any persons engaged in the illicit operation, and, not finding petitioner, arrest him upon his return to the scene. . . . Since the entry . . . was lawful," Clark thought the officers had a right to seize the contraband property.

When we look at Clark's position on the scalogram, we find that he has no break point. His voting record reflects a consistent attitude against civil liberty claims. He finds only two of the forty-one non-unanimous cases deprivational enough to justify support for the claim. One of these, *Eskridge* v. *Washington* has already been noted. The other case was *Lambert* v. *California* which raised general considerations of "fairness" under due process requirements.

In *Lambert,* the Court considered the constitutionality of a Los Angeles Felon Registration Ordinance as applied to a person who had no actual knowledge of a duty to register. Douglas, speaking for the majority, held the statute as applied unconstitutional since notice is required in circumstances of this type. The Douglas opinion distinguished the ordinance here from registration laws in general in that violation of the Los Angeles ordinance is unaccompanied by any activity whatever.

In dissenting, Burton declared that no constitutional rights were violated. Frankfurter, joined by Harlan and Whittaker, in a biting dissent charged the majority with (1) drawing a constitutional line between a state's requirement of doing and not doing; (2) quoting Holmes out of context (which Frankfurter remedied by repeating the quotation and including its context); and (3) making a decision that will turn out to be an isolated deviation from the strong current of precedent—"a derelict on the waters of the law."

Justice Clark was one of two justices casting a lone dissent in a non-unanimous civil liberty case during the 1957 term. Douglas cast such a vote in favor of the claim in *Wilson* v. *Loew's,* the "right to work" case. But Clark is the only justice to cast a lone dissent during the term in a case decided for the claim. He does this not once but on six different occasions. There seems little question that his attitude toward civil liberty claims differs in degree from that of the other justices. Indeed, the magnitude of the disparity almost suggests a difference in kind.

If one compares the scales for the two terms of 1956 and 1957, several important facts quickly emerge. First, it is quite clear that the ranking of the justices in the former term is the same as the ranking in the latter. While these two terms constitute too short a period from which to make overly confident predictions, a tentative statement might be made. That is: the ranking of the justices in civil liberties cases during the 1958 term will be identical with that of the two preceding terms in respect to those justices participating in all three periods.

While the relative ranking of the justices did not change in the two terms the relative positions in the latter period reflect some degree of spatial movement. We may consider the Douglas position in 1956 and 1957 as the "most favorable" toward civil liberty claims. All other ranks may be interpreted in relation to the Douglas pole. The relative positions may then be compared from one term to the next. The data for the 1956 and 1957 terms are suggestive. Obviously, the four justices most favorable to civil liberties claims in the 1956 term may be viewed as a libertarian bloc. The existence of a bloc can be more precisely established by the use of a cohesion index derived by the formula $\frac{Ai}{Ai+Aj}$ x 100 where Ai is the number of times Justice A agrees with another and Aj is the number of disagreements between the same two justices. Thus, the index furnishes a percentage rate of agreement between each two justices on a descending scale. We may consider a justice "linked" to a bloc if his percentage rate of agreement with the justice preceding him on the scalogram is 75+. In the 1956 term we identify the existence of two blocs. Douglas and Black link at 95 per cent; Black and Warren at 85 per cent; and Warren and Brennan at 89 per cent. But Brennan and Frankfurter link at the rate of 73 per cent. Thus, Frankfurter is not a member of the first bloc composed of those most favorable to civil liberty claims in the 1956 term. Frankfurter and Harlan form the second bloc since they link at 82. Whittaker and Reed are eliminated from consideration as a result of their large number of non-participations. Since Burton and Harlan link at 62, and Clark and Burton link at 67 we identify only two blocs and two unaffiliated justices.

In the following term we again identify two blocs but these include collectively all nine justices. The four-member bloc of Douglas, Black, Warren, and Brennan occupies the position most favorable to civil liberties claims. The linkage rates within this bloc run from 82 to 98 per cent. Frankfurter's linkage rate with Brennan is 63 per cent and thus he again constitutes the break-point between blocs. But Frankfurter and the remaining justices on the descending scale all link with scores of 77 per cent and above. Thus we identify two blocs at either end of the Court. We fail to identify a center group although obviously Frankfurter and Harlan and Whittaker are closer to center than other members of the Court. The dispositional status of the two blocs is revealed by the end of the attitude continuum toward which they tend. The justices most favorable to civil liberty claims compose a libertarian bloc which may be called left. Those least favorable to such claims compose a less-libertarian bloc which may be called right.

In terms of relative spatial position, the following may be said. In the libertarian bloc, Black, Brennan, and Warren are not as closely identified with Douglas as in the 1956 term. Clark is so negative that he has a scale score of zero in both terms. All the justices with scale scores above that level, are further divorced from the Douglas pole in the 1957 term than in the preceding one. Three possible inferences may be drawn from this. It might be suggested that Douglas stood still spatially with the movement of the remaining justices tending toward a less libertarian position. Or it may be thought that the Court stood still, and Douglas became even more favorable to civil liberty claims. Finally there may have been movement by Douglas on the one hand and the remainder of the Court on the other, but in opposite directions. The first inference seems to be more consistent with other data,

The break between the blocs is much more conspicuous in the 1957 term. The Court as a whole was less favorable to civil liberty claims in the period. The Douglas position is consistent and equivalent in both terms. Douglas and Black could find not a single non-deserving claim in a non-unanimous civil liberty case in the 1956 term. In the following term Douglas found one such claim but Black found five. The most tenable inference seems to be that the Court cooled toward civil liberty claims with the exception of Douglas during the most recent term. In addition, the evidence on balance suggests that the 1956 term represents the zenith of favorable Court attitudes toward civil liberty claims as a reaction to the "McCarthy period." The pendulum appears to be tending in the opposite direction; a development consistent with the so-called conservative thinking in the country as a whole in recent times. But it also reflects the impact of the Whittaker appointment to the Court as well as a more conservative outlook on the part of Frankfurter and Harlan.

IV

In conclusion, the analysis of the behavior of the United States Supreme Court in civil liberties cases for the 1957 term produces concrete as well as inferential findings. These may be summarized as follows: (1) The Court was less favorable as a whole toward civil liberty claims in the 1957 term than in the term preceding it. (2) Two distinct cohesion blocs operated on the Court in civil liberty cases in both terms but in the 1957 term these two blocs encompassed collectively all nine justices. (3) The blocs cohered in terms of disposition toward civil liberty claims and can be designated on this basis as libertarian and less libertarian. (4) The relative ranking of the justices in terms of attitude toward civil liberty claims remained the same in both terms. (5) The positions of the justices relative to the Douglas polar position showed movement toward a less libertarian role for all justices except Clark. (6) In both the 1956 and 1957 terms the Court decided civil liberty claims in terms of one dominant variable: deprivation of a claimed civil liberty. (7) The evidence is that the Guttman scalogram techniques can be used successfully to predict the relative rank of each justice in terms of attitude toward civil liberty deprivations. Thus in the 1958 term, Douglas will be expected to be most favorable toward civil liberty claims with his colleagues ranked behind him in the order of: Black, Warren, Brennan, Frankfurter, Harlan, Whittaker, and Clark.

[Holmes never intimated, of course, that public policy-making by judges resembled the kind of policy-making engaged in by legislators or top executive decision-makers. Indeed, a good deal of the academic and professional con-

troversy about contemporary conceptions of the judicial process concerns fundamental differences over the significance of the institutional factor in judicial
behavior. One of the most striking statements supporting the notion that
judicial behavior must be sharply distinguished from legislative and executive
behavior was that of Felix Frankfurter in *Public Utilities Commission* v. *Pollak*.]

4. Does the Judicial Robe Change the Man?*

The judicial process demands that a judge move within the framework of
relevant legal rules and the covenanted modes of thought for ascertaining them.
He must think dispassionately and submerge private feeling on every aspect of a
case. There is a good deal of shallow talk that the judicial robe does not change the
man within it. It does. The fact is that on the whole judges do lay aside private
views in discharging their judicial functions. This is achieved through training,
professional habits, self-discipline and that fortunate alchemy by which men are
loyal to the obligation with which they are entrusted. But it is also true that reason
cannot control the subconscious influence of feelings of which it is unaware. When
there is ground for believing that such unconscious feelings may operate in the
ultimate judgment, or may not unfairly lead others to believe they are operating,
judges recuse themselves. They do not sit in judgment. They do this for a variety
of reasons. The guiding consideration is that the administration of justice should
reasonably appear to be disinterested as well as be so in fact.

This case for me presents such a situation. My feelings are so strongly engaged
as a victim of the practice in controversy that I had better not participate in judicial
judgment upon it. I am explicit as to the reason for my non-participation in this
case because I have for some time been of the view that it is desirable to state why
one takes himself out of a case.

[Justice Frankfurter's statement raises both a methodological question and a
public policy issue. Most discussions of the question of whether the assumption
of the role of judge changes the behavior of the man have been conducted at a
rather dogmatic level. Justice Frankfurter cited no supporting evidence for his
cryptic assertion. On rare occasions "inside information" may become available
to an able judicial biographer. Alpheus Mason's biography of Stone contained
an illuminating section which serves to highlight the public policy issues inherent
in the very act of judicial disqualification. If a justice accepts the position of
Frankfurter that judges should not sit because "the administration of justice
should reasonably appear to be disinterested," the judicial process would become
vulnerable to the aggressive attacks of militant private interests.]

* Mr. Justice Frankfurter in *Public Utilities Commission* v. *Pollak*, 343 U.S. 466–467 (1959).

5. Discretion and Policy in Disqualification*

During most of the term no public event so dramatic as the Burlingham letter of the previous year disturbed the judicial atmosphere, yet the course of justice was far from smooth. The Court surpassed its own record for disagreement. In the 162 majority opinions announced, it cast a total of 231 dissenting votes. The Chief Justice himself dissented 29 times, more than anyone else, except for Roberts' unparalleled 53. Schismatic factors produced a veritable stream of split decisions, of which 27 were 5 to 4 rulings, almost doubling the previous year's total. By a one-vote margin the judges held Western Union messengers exempt from child labor provisions of the wages and hours law; invalidated a Texas statute requiring a license before a union agent could address a meeting; ruled that conscientious objectors could be barred from law practice; forbade revision of a National Labor Relations Board order after Court review, even though the Board had erred; and permitted a patentee to obtain a sub-patent on an integral part of his invention with the avowed intention of suppressing use of that part so as to protect his broader claim.

"The work has been heavy and the gyrations of my brethren have not made it any lighter," Stone commented gloomily. In addition to routine work, petitions *in forma pauperis,* the brunt of which fell primarily on the Chief, rose phenomenally. The Court disposed of over 107 such pleas directed against the Warden of the Illinois State Penitentiary alone. As to reports of his resignation, he blandly retorted that he hadn't given it any thought. "I am too busy," he remarked. When rumors began to circulate about his "being tired," he snorted: "I am only tired of some of the unfortunate stuff I see in the newspapers. No doubt they are inspired by thoughts of who will get my place."

The deep personal rivalries of his colleagues were muffled, confined to conference, provoking no repetition of the outspoken denunciations of the 1943 term. Then, at the very end, the bench was rocked from within by a rancorous quarrel over the most delicate of all judicatory subjects—judicial disqualification.

Since the reconstitution of the Court in 1941 the Justices had been increasingly touchy on this matter. With three former Attorneys General and a former Solicitor General on the bench, the Court was constantly in danger that important government litigation could not be heard for lack of the statutory quorum of six Justices. The situation had come to a head in the North American Company case of 1943, a constitutional appeal from an SEC ruling under the so-called "death penalty" clause of the Public Utility Holding Company Act. Stone announced his disqualification at the time certiorari was granted, "on the assumption that we had a full court to deal with the case." Douglas, as onetime SEC chairman, was also ineligible. After the case came up for oral argument Reed and Jackson made known their disqualification. At this juncture the quorum question came forcibly to the attention of Congress. The legislature made no provision for the North American case,

---

*Alpheus T. Mason, *Harlan Fiske Stone: Pillar of the Law* (New York: Viking Press, 1956), pp. 639–45. [Footnotes omitted.] Reproduced with permission of the publisher. Copyright © 1956 by Alpheus Thomas Mason.

but passed a bill that enabled the Justices to transfer the earlier Alcoa case to the Circuit Court of Appeals for the Second Circuit for final review. The Chief Justice was much disturbed that litigants, otherwise entitled to it, could not have their day in Court. His concern grew as more cases involving features of the holding company law were filed. Should not this consideration, he wondered, overbalance those that moved him initially to announce disqualification? As no former law partner or client was present in these cases, he now saw no reason to disqualify himself. When he broached the matter in conference, however, Justice Roberts objected to his sitting on the ground that similar issues were raised in all the cases, and that if he were disqualified in the one, he ought not to sit in judgment on a related case. Roberts' suggestion, apparently querying the Chief Justice's honor and implying that he would discuss in an opinion the propriety of Stone's sitting, brought on a heated debate. The accusation so angered the Chief that he had his clerk prepare a memorandum of cases on which Roberts had sat although his old firm or former clients were involved.

Roberts' attack, especially its accusative tone, also annoyed certain of Stone's colleagues. "Apropos the discussion in conference Saturday," Justice Rutledge wrote, "I want to add to you personally what I thought it as well for me not to say under the circumstances of that discussion, namely: I think it is outrageous for anyone to suggest that there is any valid reason, or semblance of one, why you should not sit in either of the cases, or both, according to your own preference and decision. It is even more outrageous," he continued, "to suggest writing to discuss your action, whether the decision is one way or some other. And I, for one, think that if any member of the Court should assume to do this, all other members—again including yourself or not, solely as you might wish and decide— should reply in an opinion which would leave no doubt about the matter." Rutledge said he "ordinarily would venture no suggestion" as he thought "the whole business is purely one of taste, not of law or morals," but "since the circumstances have made it necessary for you to have counsel, I want you to have no doubt as to my views or position."

"Thank you for your kind note about the troublesome holding company cases," Stone replied warmly. "They have annoyed us so long that I think we may have all lost a little sense of proportion, but I am greatly troubled by the fact that suitors who have come to our Court who are entitled to be heard cannot be heard. It would seem to me that the simplest solution would have been to have heard the case which I am free in every possible aspect to hear, and leave the other alone." Roberts' remarks seem to have brought Stone's stubborn streak to the fore. As there was objection to his proposed course, he concluded, "I think I shall be willing to be the goat and sit in them both, although it is a very embarrassing situation for me."

Action on these cases was deferred while tempers cooled, and certiorari was ultimately granted on June 5, 1944. Though Stone had determined his course, the disputed cases stood in abeyance another year. On May 28, 1945, the Court ordered them set for argument on October 8, 1945. "Chief Justice Stone made it known," the *New York Times* reported, May 29, "that he had decided that he was eligible to sit." Just as Stone announced his recantation the bench was confronted by a brash petition for a rehearing of the inflammatory coal miners' portal-to-portal pay case, which the Court, affirming the Circuit Court of Appeals, had decided 5 to 4 in the union's favor. The coal company's petition for rehearing alleged that Justice Black, one of the majority judges, should have stayed out of the case because the mine union's claim was presented by Crampton Harris, the Justice's law partner in a short-lived practice twenty years before.

The original Jewell Ridge case had been bitterly contested within the confines of the conference room. Legally and economically the issues had been troublesome. Tempers, frayed by the vexing term, had been at the breaking point. The first untoward development had found Justice Reed first agreeing with, and then turning away from the judges, including Stone, who were opposed to travel-time pay. The consequent change in the result had required reassignment of the case by Justice Black. Loss of victory by such a turn may have nettled the dissenters. Stone, convinced that coal miners' contracts fixed a "high wage" that included compensation for travel, had thought the new majority's conclusion an "injustice." Justice Jackson, in his dissent, quoting Senator Black by name, had sought to prove that Congress had not contemplated use of the Fair Labor Standards Act to alter collective bargaining agreements where the hours worked were less than forty and the wages set were above the minimum. In effect accusing Black of abandoning the position he had taken as a legislative sponsor of the wage-hour law, the dissenter had thrust an intolerable burr under Black's saddle. "The very page from which the dissent quotes," the outraged former Senator had protested, "negatives the inference which the dissent draws from my single sentence which the dissent does quote. If the dissent does go down as now printed, it will be a fair representation of the true facts." The minority, unperturbed, had retained the disputed quotation.

In this atmosphere of acid disagreement the Jewell Ridge Coal Corporation's petition for a rehearing precipitated what has been called the "greatest fight in the nation's highest and most secret judicial conference room." In presenting a *per curiam* opinion to the conference denying the Jewell Ridge petition, the Chief Justice, to the surprise of the brethren, suggested that a statement be included to the effect that no question of disqualification is ever open for consideration by the Court. Such a proposal Justice Frankfurter said, raised a "brand-new matter," and Black insisted on denial of the petition without any explanation.

The question was a delicate one. Since disqualification was a matter of personal decision, with no specific rule to cover the matter, the petition had to be denied. The difficulty arose in the phrasing of the denial. A flat refusal of the petition, as Black desired, would have implied approval by the whole Court of his having sat, a position inconsistent with the absence of any rule on the subject and one to which none of the dissenting Justices in the original case were willing to give "blind and unqualified approval." The most feasible way out of the predicament, Stone surmised, would be a colorless explanation of the absence of any Court rule on the subject. By such a method no approval or disapproval of Black's action, either implied or expressed, would be given.

The depth of feeling, heightened to fever pitch by the unrelenting tensions of an arduous term, could not be placated by compromise. Black suspected that behind the maneuvers of the dissenters lay a desire to put his actions in an unfavorable light. The disposition of the petition thus took on for him overtones of a fight for personal vindication. At conference on June 9 argument grew so heated that the Chief Justice accepted Murphy's suggestion that final decision be postponed one week. Several days later Stone proposed a compromise *per curiam* he thought "all could join without embarrassment." "This Court," his brief opinion read, "is without the authority and does not undertake to pass upon the propriety of the participation, by its members, in the decision of cases brought here for review." Such an announcement would, of course, at the very least imply neutrality on Black's conduct in the Jewell Ridge case. But Black still preferred ambiguous silence. "If the *per curiam* goes down in this case, as you have today suggested," he responded to the Chief's memorandum, "please put the names of the Justices who agree to it, and leave mine out." Those who sided with Black on the merits of portal-to-portal pay also lined up with him against the *per curiam.*

Although Stone now must have perceived that any such opinion would arouse Black's ire, he continued to press for a statement. Taking advantage of a technicality in Court rules, by which a petition for rehearing is addressed only to judges adhering to the protested decision, he redrafted his *per curiam* so that it would require the assent only of the dissenters in the original Jewell Ridge case. "If our brethren are unwilling to declare that this Court is without authority to pass upon the propriety of Justice Black's sitting" in the Jewel [*sic*] Ridge case, he wrote, "the least we can do is say something like the following: "The Chief Justice, Justice Roberts, Justice Frankfurter, and Justice Jackson, who dissented from the opinion of the Court in this case, do not pass on the petition for rehearing, and they do not pass upon the propriety of the participation by any Justice of the Court in the decision of this case." The Justices named promptly accepted.

At a final conference on June 16 Jackson made it evident that he was in no way willing to imply approval of Black's role. "Mr. Justice Black became very angry," Jackson declared later, "and said that any opinion which discussed the subject at all would mean a declaration of war." The flames had swept beyond control, and Jackson decided then and there "that I would not stand for any more of his bullying and that, whatever I would otherwise do, I would now have to write my opinion to keep self-respect in the face of his threats." Frankfurter agreed and joined in Jackson's brief concurrence annexed to the simple denial of the petition, handed down on June 18.

"Since announcement of a mere denial of this petition for rehearing might be interpreted to rest upon any one of several grounds," Jackson wrote in part, "I consider it appropriate to disclose the limited grounds on which I concur.

"The unusual feature of the petition in this case is that it suggests to the Court a question as to the qualification of one of the Justices to take part in the decision of the cause. This petition is addressed to all of the Court and must either be granted or denied in the name of the Court and on the responsibility of all of the Justices. In my opinion the complaint is one which cannot properly be addressed to the Court as a whole and for that reason I concur in denying it.

"No statute prescribes grounds upon which a Justice of this Court may be disqualified in any case. The Court itself has never undertaken by rule of Court or decision to formulate any uniform practice on the subject. . . . It appears always to have been considered the responsibility of each Justice to determine for himself the propriety of withdrawing in any particular circumstances. . . . There is no authority known to me under which a majority of this Court has power under any circumstances to exclude one of its duly commissioned Justices from sitting or voting in any case."

In this showdown Stone backtracked. "The Chief Justice told me," Jackson stated later, "that at his age he did not want to be in the war which was threatened and withdrew his proposed opinion and kept silent."

Afterward, when commentators pointed out that the Chief Justice himself had sat in cases involving the interests of persons as close to him as Crampton Harris to Black, Stone, repeating earlier explanations, carefully distinguished his own situation from that of his colleague. In the Jewell Ridge case a petition for rehearing had been entered, premised upon the failure of Black to disqualify himself. Some explanation of the inability of the Court to act on such a motion was obviously necessary. It was the Chief Justice's attempt to achieve an impartial handling of the problem that had run headlong into a most explosive situation.

The Chief Justice recognized that such disputes as the one involved in the Jewell Ridge case more often than not were grounded in real difficulties. Without posing as oracles of the Constitution, without ceremonial, the Justices attempted to work out a new alignment and distribution of powers within the federal structure and among the Departments of the Government itself. "Congressional legislation of the past ten years," Stone wrote, "has entered new constitutional fields and created new problems, the nature of which is not always fully understood by the bar and is altogether mysterious to the public. All this has put a great strain on the Court as an institution."

Stone attributed much of his difficulty to a "bad press." Popular journals were given to overplaying divisions among the judges, evaluating and explaining them in personal terms.

B. BACKGROUNDS AND DECISIONS

[The opportunities for reconstructing the internal setting of the Supreme Court are ordinarily so limited as to prohibit the kind of analysis undertaken by Professor Mason in his excellent biography of Stone. However, careful use of publicly available materials, such as the written opinions of the justices, may provide evidence of significant uniformities in decision-making tendencies. Doctrinal choice may be significantly related to certain background attributes of the justices. The subsequent portion of *Constitutional Law in the Political Process* is based upon two previously published articles on judicial behavior by the present editor. The section is co-authored by Professor David Gold and emphasizes the methodological problems inherent in such research as well as the promising prospects for further advances in the field.]

1. The Influence of Background Factors on Decision-making in the Supreme Court*

The notion that judicial decision-making may be influenced in some manner by the social, educational, economic, or political backgrounds of the judges or justices has had strong support in many eras of American history. On a number of occasions, dramatic political debates were engaged in over the question whether certain background factors predispose a potential judge or justice to decide cases in a particular way. In comparatively recent times, the nomination of Charles Evans Hughes to the Chief Justiceship was opposed on the ground that his conditioning as a corporation lawyer would render him insensitive to the constitutional claims of the under-privileged. A few years later, the nomination of Senator Hugo L. Black to an associate justiceship was vigorously opposed because his earlier membership in the Ku Klux Klan would allegedly predispose him to deny the litigatory claims of racial minorities.

At a somewhat broader level, the strong and continuing debates over the comparative merits or demerits of the elective or appointive methods of judicial selection often reflect deep-seated convictions that the pre-judicial career patterns of judicial candidates may be prime determinants of the manner in which these individuals may behave after achieving a seat on the bench. Another closely related argument which has had serious contemporary federal executive and legislative consideration is that appointees to higher appellate benches should have prior judicial experience because such experience generates judicial self-restraint and recognition of the need for stability in decision-making. In 1956, Senator Stennis, speaking in support of a legislative proposal providing that appointees to the federal Supreme Court be persons with at least five years prior judicial experience on the inferior federal bench or on the highest appellate court of a state, argued that:

> . . . a majority of [the present members of the Supreme Court] should have gone through the process of judicial seasoning and judicial experience, which is almost the only way to make an outstanding jurist who is wedded to the system of precedents. . . .

The range of assumptions about the kinds of factors that purportedly are of significance to judicial behavior and decision-making is, to say the least, very broad. In addition to the factors mentioned above—occupational background, individual career pattern, and group associations—emphasis has often been placed upon party affiliation, religion, economic circumstances in early life, and educational training and influences. Similarly, the uses to which background data have been put have varied considerably in accordance with the purposes, and, perhaps as importantly, the intellectual sensitivity of the users. At the public policy level, the background attributes

*Adapted by John R. Schmidhauser and David Gold from John R. Schmidhauser, "Stare Decisis, Dissent, and the Background of the Justices of the Supreme Court of the United States," *University of Toronto Law Journal*, XIV (May, 1962), 194–95. [Footnotes omitted.] Reproduced with the permission of the publisher. Copyright © 1962 by the *University of Toronto Law Journal*.

of candidates for elective or appointive judicial offices have provided real or ostensible arguments for selection or rejection. For example, the Eisenhower Administration has, for several years, included prior judicial experience as one of its criteria for selection to federal appellate courts.

Academicians frequently invoke various background factors as "causes" or explanations for certain decision-making tendencies. Thus, Professor Fred Rodell made the following reference to Roger Brook Taney: "There is not one of his decisions as Chief Justice . . . but can be traced, directly or indirectly, to his big-plantation birth and background." Interestingly enough, even those academicians who support the position that judges discover rather than make law have often assumed that the proper judge becomes "proper" through environmental conditioning before ascension to the bench. Thus, in the following excerpt, an anonymous writer, in denying that the background factor of political attachment provides a safe guide to a potential judge's decision-making tendencies, impliedly assumed that educational training did provide such a guide with respect to adherence to the doctrine of *stare decisis:*

> . . . *There is certainly no evidence that any Justice of the Supreme Court of the United States ever deliberately decided the cases before him on any other basis than on the theory of stare decisis. Certain Presidents have found that the political doctrines held by a Justice before his appointment were not necessarily a safe guide to his reasoning after ascending to the bench. The lawyer is trained to follow precedent, and certainly, the lawyer who becomes a judge, decides a case by asking himself what the law is on this point rather than consider his personal predilections.*

Conversely, Cortez A. M. Ewing, in an interesting early test of the Turner thesis, argued that "To bring men of [diverse sectional] origins to the same unprejudiced and impersonal interpretation of rights, duties and even of the Constitution of the United States would, it seems, require more common experiences than are to be found in mere preparation for the legal profession."

Members of the legal profession have concerned themselves for a number of years with judicial selection at the local and state as well as federal levels of government. The background attributes considered desirable by leaders of the bar often differ considerably from those considered significant by academicians. Contrast, for example, the view expressed by Professor Robert Carr that selection of law professors for the Supreme Court represented an attempt to secure justices with broader sociological, economic, and philosophical training and outlook than professional, and frequently, corporation lawyers with the position taken by Clarence M. Botts, a professional lawyer and a member of the Board of Editors of the *American Bar Association Journal.* Botts suggested:

> . . . *that, in addition to the general qualifications of ability, temperament and integrity, there may be peculiar additional qualifications essential to the particular* [*judicial*] *post to be filled. This would seem to be especially true with respect to courts consisting of more than one judge. It might not be too difficult to imagine*

such a court overloaded with law professors or specialists in one line, to an extent that it would appear to be desirable, as opportunity is presented, to give the court, and the public, the assistance of one or more good common sense country lawyers.

Not that a country lawyer is more learned than his city brother, but he is likely to be more wise. His experience will have been wider and more varied, and he will have absorbed and developed a feel for the law, to an extent not possible to the teacher or specialist, except in a very narrow field. A lawyer with his roots in the soil knows a "heap" of law that is not written in books.

Walter P. Armstrong, former president of the American Bar Association, stressed a somewhat different viewpoint when, in analyzing Justice William O. Douglas' conception of the role of *stare decisis* in constitutional law, he argued that "it is to be noted that the Justices who in their private practice had to advise clients with large property interests have been the strongest adherents to *stare decisis* and former legislators and schoolmen are least influenced by it." Presumably, one would choose corporation lawyers rather than politicians or law professors if one desired greater stability in constitutional interpretation.

Some of these assertions can, of course, be dismissed as erroneous on the basis of general observation. For example, all members of the Supreme Court have been lawyers. Consequently, if legal training conditions individuals to adherence to precedent, it seems clear that the impact of such conditioning has varied considerably among the 92 lawyers who, since 1789, have served on the Court. More importantly, the conception of *stare decisis* implicit in several of these discussions suggests that it imparts to the judicial process an essentially static quality—which is, in fact, illusory. Despite the fact that serious questions may be raised about the validity of the sweeping generalizations concerning the significance of background factors, many of their assumptions have provided an ostensible basis for public policy recommendations, and, in some instances, for the nomination and selection of judges and justices.

Although assumptions about the significance of background factors have often been acted upon, very few systematic investigations of the actual impact, if any, of these factors upon decision-making have been undertaken. The exceptional few are, however, worthy of note. In the early 1930's, Cortez A. M. Ewing contributed a pioneering article on the relationship of the regional origin of justices to their positions on due process clause issues in the period 1880–1925. Glendon Schubert recently completed a study of the relationship of party affiliation to decision-making tendency in Workmen's Compensation cases decided by the Supreme Court of Michigan. And Stuart Nagel has undertaken a comprehensive analysis of the relationship of background factors to decision-making by justices of several of the highest appellate courts of the states.

Most early discussions of the possible relationship of background to decision-making tended to stress the ideological orientation of the judges or justices and the alleged impact of such orientation upon the doctrinal content of relevant opinions. Critics of the behavioral approach soon revived the old argument that the legal process in general, and appellate decision-making in particular, are so complex as to defy attempts at systematic analysis through quantification. Like Fortescue's ancient plea that the law is a professional mystery, the argument that appellate decision-making is so complex as to defy comprehension by the laity is a partial truth that remains self-generating because it is self-serving. Those who urge that decision-making is complex often assert that they themselves really understand the process. Thus Frankfurter may on one hand argue that "inferences from opinions to the distinctive characteristics of individual justices are treacherous. . ." ; yet this sharp admonition is in contrast with his positive assertion in *Public Utilities Commission* v. *Pollak* that:

> *There is a good deal of shallow talk that the judicial robe does not change the man within it. It does. The fact is that on the whole judges do lay aside private views in discharging their judicial functions. This is achieved through training, professional habits, self-discipline and that fortunate alchemy by which men are loyal to the obligation with which they are entrusted.*

Though such contrasting statements smack of intellectual "inside dopesterism," the insistance by Frankfurter and others upon the significance of institutional factors did broaden the scope of contemporary investigations of the influence of background factors. The works of Karl Llewellyn proved particularly important in providing a frame of reference for study of the relative impact of relevant background factors upon public policy issue orientation and institutional tradition. The first of two exploratory investigations by the present writers concerned the Taney Court in the period 1837–1860. [See the following selection.]

2. Judicial Behavior and the Sectional Crisis, 1837–1860*

The central thesis of this study is that the voting responses of the members of the Supreme Court of the United States to issues arising in periods of national stress may provide significant evidence concerning the relative influence upon the decision-making process of factors as disparate as the background of the justices and the traditions of the venerable institution of which these individuals had become a part. In addition, the responses of the Court as an institution to issues related to such crises can provide data for the systematic comparison of these judicial responses with the responses of the President and the Congress to similar or identical issues. And, finally, intensive analysis of the roles played by the justices acting as individuals or in groups may provide insight concerning their behavior as participants in a highly institutionalized small group process. Initial emphasis in the study will be given to the problem of the significance of background factors.

*Adapted by John R. Schmidhauser and David Gold from John R. Schmidhauser, "Judicial Behavior and the Sectional Crisis of 1837–1860," *Journal of Politics*, IV (November, 1961), 615–40. [Footnotes omitted.] Reproduced with permission of the publisher. Copyright © 1961 by the Southern Political Science Association.

SECTIONAL BACKGROUND, PARTY AFFILIATION, AND
JUDICIAL BEHAVIOR

Before the Civil War the institution of slavery divided the nation on sectional lines in a manner never equalled since. If the cultural heritage of historic regions conditions judicial decision-making, presumably the impact of this factor would be manifest in the ante-bellum decisions of the Supreme Court.

Conversely, the fundamental issues which divided Whig from Jacksonian Democrat occasionally blunted purely regional differences. Moreover, a considerable number of academicians have seriously argued that the influence of background factors such as sectional conditioning and party affiliation is considerably diluted, if not dissipated, by the countervailing influence of certain institutional factors. Professor Karl Llewellyn, in a general discussion of the traditions of higher appellate courts, provided an excellent description of these factors:

> . . . in the craft-tradition of the appellate courts, we find a number of attributes . . . which are seldom phrased . . . [These are] effort at "impartiality"; effort to keep the mind open till both sides have been heard; effort to dissociate the "true essence" of the controversy from accidents of person, personality or the like; avoidance of a case in which a judge is or may be thought personally interested. . . .
>
> . . . Some portion of this is institutionalized. "Independence of the judiciary" . . . and non-reduceability of salary, seek both to make much "judicial" conduct possible and to further it. Rules of law against bribery, practices set against "influence," loose but useful practices of self-disqualification, even looser but still recognizable practices about judicial manners, the disciplinary pressure of phrasing an explanation of a decision in a published opinion, the policing power of possible open dissent by any member of the court who may see or feel outrage—these form a gap-filled hedge to mark and to half-police the tradition.

Stated differently, the institutional traditions of the Supreme Court may condition the behavior of justices so that, presumably, they do not feel that they should render decisions on perhaps the same sort of considerations that might be appropriate for a member of Congress or a policy-maker in the executive branch. Unlike the politically responsible officials, the Supreme Court justice need not feel that his voting record should reflect loyalty to party or reverence for the traditions or economic and political interests of the region from which he was chosen. This is not to argue that the justice may feel free of any responsibility. Rather it is to emphasize that his responsibility may be essentially different in character. Indeed, this purported difference is basic to Justice Frankfurter's statement that "by the very nature of the functions of the Supreme Court, each member of it is subject only to his own sense of trusteeship of what are perhaps the most revered traditions in our national system."

Whether so sharp a distinction between judicial and other forms of political behavior is warranted has, of course, long been a subject for intense debate. If such a distinction is sound, one may validly assume that the voting responses of the justices would not coincide with the legislative divisions by party and/or section on approximately comparable issues which were dealt with by the members of Congress. The first step in an investigation of this assumption is the classification of those opinions of the Supreme Court which were acknowledged by contemporaries and by historians to be of importance in the growing cleavage between North and South in the period 1837–1860.

CLASSIFICATION OF THE VOTING RESPONSES OF THE JUSTICES

Three categories of cases comprising a total of fifty-two decisions were considered appropriate for the analysis because they embraced issues frequently mentioned by historians as fundamental to the historic division between North and South. These were slavery, the commerce clause, and the status of corporations. As a preliminary step, the institutional responses of the Supreme Court to these issues were contrasted with the Court's mode of response to ordinary issues. In this respect, in aggregate terms, the Taney Court produced a much higher percentage of separate opinions in the cases which allegedly reflected sharp regional antagonisms than was usual in that era. From 1837 to 1860, the Taney Court recorded 1,856 separate voting responses to the legal issues which it took under consideration (a total of 1,493 issues). Of the voting responses, 1,491 (80 per cent) were majority opinions, 293 (16 per cent) were recorded dissents, and 72 (4 per cent) were concurring opinions. By contrast, 160 voting responses were recorded in the group of fifty-two cases purportedly involving sectional issues. Only 49 (31 per cent) were majority opinions, 61 (38 per cent) were recorded dissents, and 50 (31 per cent) were concurring opinions. Despite this exceptionally high tendency to write separate opinions, it should be noted that twenty-three of the fifty-two cases were unanimous decisions of the Taney Court. Further, a number of these unanimous decisions, notably *Jones* v. *Van Zandt, Ableman* v. *Booth,* and *Kentucky* v. *Dennison,* involved public policy issues which were among the most combustible to arise during this period. In short, the Taney Court was subjected to the same severe stresses that affected the Congress and the public at large. In the face of these stresses, the Court still contrived to maintain a semblance of institutional unity, but the extremely divisive nature of the issues raised considerably weakened the tendencies making for such unity. The fact that the Court tended to divide much more often than was usual did not, of course, prove that such frequent division reflected regional or party attitudes.

What then was the rationale for characterizing fifty-two decisions as potentially indicative of the influence of regional and/or party background? The first group of cases comprised decisions directly related to slavery. Decisions weakening the position of slavery were designated pro-northern; those enhancing or defending the position of slavery, pro-southern.

The second category consisted of cases which involved the interpretation of the commerce clause. Commerce clause interpretations upholding the internal police power of the states were related, in southern thinking, to the southern desire to regulate the ingress and egress of Negroes, whether slave or free, in order to safeguard the social structure of the region. Furthermore, since virtually the only public regulation of business during this period was by the governments of the states, advocacy of exclusive federal control of interstate and foreign commerce became associated, in the thinking of some of the southern plantation aristocracy, with the goals of an antagonistic northern capitalism. Consequently, judicial responses asserting exclusive federal control of interstate commerce were designated pro-northern, and the converse, pro-southern.

Third, judicial interpretations of the status of corporations, whether in contract clause or diversity of citizenship cases, similarly reflected regional economic and cultural antagonisms. For purposes of classification, decisions enhancing or defending the position of corporations were categorized as pro-northern, while those which were antithetical were dubbed pro-southern.

The use of this method of classification in no sense implies that differences in judicial interpretation may be attributed only to the public policy positions of the justices or that the Court's decisions in those cases were solely the products of regional antagonisms. In many of the cases analyzed in this study, individual justices expressed reasons for their decisions which were often at odds with a purely regional dichotomy. For some, national supremacy or states' rights was stressed as a major consideration; for others, the integrity of the Court as a judicial institution demanded neutrality on regionally divisive questions; and for still others, positions rather close to contemporary Whig or Jacksonian Democratic Party policy stands were decisive. Conversely, contemporary and historical evaluations of the Supreme Court were often made on the basis of the anticipated consequences of these decisions for the North or the South. Indeed, such evaluations were often integral parts of the opinions of members of the Supreme Court themselves. For example, Justice John Archibald Campbell, in his dissent in *Marshall* v. *Baltimore and Ohio Railroad Company,* stated that:

> *It may be safely assumed that no offering could be made to the wealthy, powerful and ambitious corporations of the populous and commercial states of the Union so valuable, and none which would so serve to enlarge the influence of those states, as the adoption, to its full import, of the conclusion, "that to all intents and purposes, for the objects of their incorporation, these artificial persons are capable of being treated as a citizen as much as a natural person."*

However, in many decisions it is often difficult to identify with certainty the true basis for a justice's voting response. *Prigg* v. *Pennsylvania* provides an excellent illustration. The majority opinion, written by Justice Story, held that a Pennsylvania law interfered with the proper enforcement of the federal Fugitive Slave Law of 1793. All the members of the Court concurred in this ruling. However, Story went further by asserting that federal power over the rendition of fugitive slaves was exclusive and that as a consequence state laws obstructing *or* aiding the federal government were invalid. His stated doctrinal rationale was national supremacy. Taney, Thompson, and Daniel each wrote opinions concurring in the result but disagreeing with Story's doctrine of exclusive federal control. Story's opinion encouraged northern state officials who were opposed to aiding in the enforcement of the Fugitive Slave Law to refrain from doing so, thus ultimately forcing southern congressmen to press for stronger federal legislation. As Story himself recognized, the very fact that the South had to seek legislative action served to defeat hitherto successful southern efforts to prevent congressional debate on the institution of slavery. Why did Story decide the *Prigg* case in the manner that he did? Does his publicly stated reason, national supremacy, suffice? Or was his privately stated antagonism to the South the decisive factor? Was Story a consistent supporter of the doctrine or a consistent opponent of the South in most politically relevant cases?

Consistency in judicial voting responses may well reflect basic attitudes toward broad public policy controversies which do not coincide with the doctrinal positions expressed in written opinions. Through the use of Guttman scale analysis, it is possible to determine whether the pattern of voting responses is consistent with the inference that such basic underlying attitudes do exist. The key question to be explored is whether the justices participating in the fifty-two cases consistently split in terms of being more and less pro-North or pro-South despite other possibly compelling factors such as attitudes toward national supremacy, the integrity of the judicial institution, or the position of their political parties. Having characterized the vote on each of these cases as representing a North-South position, we look for a very special pattern of voting. If Justice A is more pro-North than Justice B, it means not simply that A has taken a North position on more cases than B, but that A has taken a North position on all the *same* cases on which B has taken a North position, *and in addition* A has taken a North position on one or more other cases on which B has taken a South position. Only this kind of cumulative pattern over all the votes by all the justices justifies the inference that a single ordering variable can account for the differences between the justices on this set of issues. Guttman scale analysis determines the degree to which the given data approximate this special pattern.[1]

Sixteen justices participated in one or more of the cases. In Table 1 they are classified by party affiliation and by regional background. Party designation was determined on the basis of expressed preferences or identification during the period under study (1837–1860) rather than by the affiliation of the President originally making the appointment. Story, who was a National Republican at the time of his appointment, was an avowed neo-Federalist or Whig during most of his years on the Bench. Although Presidents have rather consistently chosen only the ideologically and politically sound for Supreme Court posts, historical periods when the correspondence between ideology and party orientation has been distorted have often produced appointments which, from the vantage point of hindsight, appear to be striking exceptions to the general rule. Story, McLean, and Wayne were obviously not Whigs at

---

[1] In attempting a Guttman scaling analysis, Schubert has suggested a more or less invariant ordering of *cases* in terms of the division of votes. We have not followed this practice in setting up our scales. *Justices* are ordered without regard to the actual division of their total votes in order to achieve the closest approximation to a perfect unidimensional scale pattern under the assumption that departures from the perfect scale pattern, if they are not too numerous, simply serve to obscure the basic over-all unidimensional pattern. By the same token, it seems to us that *cases* may also be ordered to achieve the closest approximation to a perfect scale. Departures from the perfect scale pattern in the votes of an individual justice are no different than departures in the votes on a single case. For a thorough discussion of the technique of Guttman scale analysis, see Glendon A. Schubert, *Quantitative Analysis of Judicial Behavior* (Glencoe, Ill.: The Free Press, 1959), pp. 269–376.

TABLE 1. *Participating Justices* (1837–1860) *Classified by Party and by Regional Background*

Name	Years Served	Section	Party
Joseph Story	1811–1845	North (Mass.)	Whig
Smith Thompson	1823–1843	North (N.Y.)	Democrat
John McLean	1829–1861	North (Ohio)	Whig
Henry Baldwin	1830–1844	North (Penna.)	Democrat
James M. Wayne	1835–1867	South (Ga.)	Whig
Roger B. Taney	1836–1864	South (Md.)	Democrat
Philip P. Barbour	1836–1841	South (Va.)	Democrat
John Catron	1837–1865	South (Tenn.)	Democrat
John McKinley	1837–1852	South (Ala.)	Democrat
Peter V. Daniel	1841–1860	South (Va.)	Democrat
Samuel Nelson	1845–1872	North (N.Y.)	Democrat
Levi Woodbury	1845–1851	North (N.H.)	Democrat
Robert C. Grier	1846–1870	North (Penna.)	Democrat
Benjamin R. Curtis	1851–1857	North (Mass.)	Whig
John A. Campbell	1853–1861	South (Ala.)	Democrat
Nathan Clifford	1858–1881	North (Maine)	Democrat

the time they were appointed. All were chosen in periods of rapid party reorientation. After 1837, however, they rather clearly aligned themselves with the Whigs although Wayne maintained personal ties with the Jacksonians.

The scalogram of cases deemed regionally divisive (Table 2) did indicate a significant scale pattern of voting responses, i.e., a coefficient of reproducibility of .935 further tested by Menzel's measure of scalability (coefficient of scalability = .765). Thus it can reasonably be inferred that the justices participating in cases deemed regionally divisive by historians were voting in terms of a basic underlying attitude toward the positions of the North and South. In responding to such underlying attitudes, did the justices tend to divide in accordance with their sectional and/or party backgrounds? In Table 3 the justices were ranked in accordance with their scale scores and classified in terms of "regional" voting tendencies. As the classification stands three of the five attitudinal subdivisions are both politically and regionally homogeneous. Furthermore, if the six justices (marked with asterisk) who participated in less than ten of the cases scaled in Table 2 are removed, *all* of the attitudinal groupings are composed of justices with similar party and sectional backgrounds.

The most extreme advocates of both North and South represented two groups of justices each of which was homogeneous with respect to both party and regional background. The justices compiling a strong pro-southern score were southern in regional background and Jacksonian Democrats by party. Three—Daniel, Barbour, and Campbell—were the sons of plantation owners who had been prominent in politics and, in Campbell's case, law. Catron's father had been a poor farmer. At the opposite end of the voting spectrum, the three justices comprising the strong pro-northern voting group were all northern in sectional background and were all closely identified with the Whig political party. Story was a member of a family long

TABLE 2. *Scalogram Analysis of Cases Deemed Regionally Divisive*

Scale Scores	29	28	22	22	20	16
Cases / Justices	Story	McLean	Curtis	Baldwin	Wayne	McKinley
Commissioners of Knox County v. Aspinwall (1858)	*	(+)	*	*	(+)	*
Covington Drawbridge Co. v. Shepard (1857)	*	(+)	*	*	(+)	*
Planters' Bank v. Sharp (1848)	*	('+'	*	*	(+)	*
The Armistad (1841)	('+')	(+)	*	n)	(+)	(+)
Rundle v. Delaware & Raritan Canal Company (1852)	*	(+)	(+)	*	(+)	*
Dodge v. Woolsey (1855)	*	(+)	(+)	*	('+')	*
Mechanics' & Traders' Bank v. Debolt (1855)	*	(+)	(+)	*	('+')	*
Mechanics' & Traders' Bank v. Thomas (1855)	*	(+)	(+)	*	('+')	*
Piqua Branch Bk. v. Knoop (1853)	*	('+')	(+)	*	(+)	*
Marshall v. B & O R. R. (1853)	*	(+)	(+)	*	(+)	*
Curran v. Arkansas (1853)	*	(+)	(+)	*	(+)	*
Vincennes U. v. Indiana (1852)	*	('+')	(+)	*	(+)	*
Woodruff v. Trapnell (1850)	*	('+')	*	*	(+)	(+)
Paup v. Drew (1850)	*	('+')	*	*	(+)	(+)
Ohio Life Insur. & Trust Co. v. Debolt (1853)	*	'+')	'+')	*	+)	*
Prigg v. Pennsylvania (1842)	('+')	('+'	*	(+)	('+'	(+)
Bank of Augusta v. Earle (1839)	(n)	(n)	*	('+'	(n)	'—')
The Passenger Cases (1849)	*	('+'	*	*	('+'	('n'
Richmond, F. & P. R. R. Co. v. Louisa R. R. Co. (1851)	*	+)	'+')	*	+)	(—)
Cooley v. Board of Port Wardens of Philadelphia (1851)	*	'+')	('n')	*	+)	(n)
Dred Scott v. Sanford (1857)	*	'+')	'+')	*	('—'	*
Groves v. Slaughter (1841)	n)	('+'	*	('+'	(n)	n)
Perrine v. Chesapeake & Delaware Canal Co. (1850)	*	'+')	*	*	(—	*
West River Bridge Co. v. Dix (1848)	*	'+')	*	*	+)	*
Moore v. Illinois (1852)	*	'+')	(—)	*	(—)	*
Mills v. St. Clair County (1850)	*	+)	*	*	(—)	*
Charles River Bridge (1837)	'+')	'+')	*	('—'	(—)	*
The License Cases (1847)	*	('+'	*	*	(n	(n
Mayor of N.Y. v. Miln (1837)	'+')	(—)	*	('—'	(—)	*
Participations	6	29	13	6	29	10
Inconsistencies	2	1	1	1	2	0

Legend:
+ = a pro-northern vote
— = a pro-southern vote
n = a neutral vote
* = not participating in the decision

' ' = wrote opinion
( ) = joined in the majority opinion
(= joined in a concurring opinion
) = joined in a dissenting opinion

(*1837–1860*)

Woodbury	Clifford	Taney	Grier	Nelson	Thompson	Catron	Campbell	Daniel	Barbour	Votes
14	14	14	12	10	10	4	1	0	0	
*	(+)	(+)	(+)	('+')	*	(+)	(+)	'—')	*	8–1
*	(+)	('+')	(+)	(+)	*	(+)	(—	'—')	*	7–2
('+')	*	—)	(+)	(+)	*	(+)	*	'—')	*	6–2
*	*	(+)	*	*	(+)	(+)	*	*	*	7–1
*	*	(+)	('+')	(+)	*	('—'	*	'—')	*	6–2
*	*	(+)	(+)	(+)	*	—)	'—')	—)	*	6–3
*	*	(+)	(+)	(+)	*	—)	'—')	—)	*	6–3
*	*	(+)	(+)	(+)	*	—)	'—')	—)	*	6–3
*	*	(+	(+)	(+)	*	'—')	'—')	'—')	*	6–3
*	*	(+)	('+')	(+)	*	'—')	'—')	'—')	*	6–3
*	*	(+)	(+)	—)	*	'—')	(+)	'—')	*	**6–3**
*	*	'—')	+	(+)	*	—)	*	—)	*	5–3
(+)	*	(+)	'—')	—)	*	—)	*	—)	*	5–4
(+)	*	(+)	(—	('—'	*	(—	*	('—'	*	5–4
*	*	('—'	(—	+)	*	('—'	('—'	('—'	*	4–5
*	*	('—'	*	*	('—'	('—'	*	(+)	*	6–3
*	*	('n')	*	*	(n)	(n)	*	*	(n)	**1–(7–1)8**
'n')	*	'—')	('—'	—)	*	('—'	*	'—')	*	**2–(2–5)7**
*	*	(—)	('—')	(—)	*	(—)	*	*	*	**3–5**
*	*	(n)	(n)	(n)	*	(n)	*	('—'	*	**2–(5–1)6**
*	*	('—')	('—'	('n'	*	('—'	('—'	('—'	*	**2–(1–6)7**
*	*	('—'	*	*	('n')	*	*	*	*	**2–(4–1)5**
+)	*	('—')	(—)	+)	*	(—)	*	(—)	*	3–5
('—'	*	(—)	(—)	(—)	*	(—)	*	('—')	*	2–6
*	*	(—)	('—')	(—)	*	(—)	*	(—)	*	1–7
(—)	*	(—)	(—)	(—)	*	('—')	*	(—)	*	1–7
*	*	('—')	*	*	(+)	*	*	*	(—)	3–4
('n')	*	('—'	('—'	(—	*	('—'	*	('—'	*	**1–(3–5)8**
*	*	(—)	*	*	('—'	*	*	*	'—')	1–6
8	2	29	23	23	6	26	10	23	3	246
1	0	2	0	3	1	0	1	1	0	16

$$\text{Coefficient of Reproducibility} = 1 - \frac{16}{246} = .935$$

$$\text{Coefficient of Scalability} = 1 - \frac{16}{68} = .765$$

TABLE 3. *The Relationship of Scale Score to Regional and Party Background*

Category*	Scale Score	Name	Judicial Experience	Section and Party
Strong Pro-Northern				
Score	29	Story*	No	Northern
	28	McLean	Yes	Whigs
Moderate Pro-Northern	22	Curtis	No	Northern Whig
Score	22	Baldwin*	No	Northern Democrat
	20	Wayne	Yes	Southern Whig
Neutral Score	16	McKinley	No	Southern Democrat
	14	Woodbury*	Yes	Northern Democrat
	14	Clifford*	No	Northern Democrat
	14	Taney	No	Southern Democrat
Moderate Pro-Southern	12	Grier	Yes	Northern
Score	10	Nelson	Yes	Democrats
	10	Thompson*	Yes	
Strong Pro-Southern	4	Catron	Yes	Southern
	1	Campbell	No	Democrats
	0	Daniel	No	
	0	Barbour*	Yes	

*It should be noted that a simple Guttman scale as used here does not provide categorical designations such as "moderate pro-Northern" or "neutral." The scale allows only statements that one justice is more or less pro-North or pro-South than another. These labels have been arbitrarily attached to what appeared to be five more or less "natural" clusterings of scale scores, but in no sense do we wish to suggest, for example, that justices in our "neutral" category were *truly* neutral.

prominent in New England social, political, and professional life. McLean was the son of a skilled laborer who had become a relatively poor midwestern farmer. Even though Story participated in only six of the possible twenty-nine cases, the position of his pro-northern votes viz. with relation to McLean strongly suggests that he is quite appropriately classified in the strongest pro-northern category. Barbour's position, on the other hand, cannot be established on the basis of the scalogram. There is no question about his categorization as a pro-southern justice, but it is impossible to determine the intensity of his pro-southern attitude. It should be noted, however, that his omission or a shift to a moderate pro-southern category would not weaken the conclusions drawn with respect to the basic relationship between background and voting response.

When one turns to the moderate categories, it may be concluded that for Whigs, party was stronger than regional background while for Democrats, party was only slightly less influential. Justice Wayne, the lone southern Whig on the Court, voted a consistent moderate pro-northern position. Northern Democrats, conversely, were split, Baldwin compiling a moderate pro-northern score; Clifford and Woodbury, neutral scores; and Grier, Nelson, and Thompson, moderate pro-southern scores. However, northern Democrats had two strong voting characteristics: They avoided the extreme positions on either end of the spectrum; and, with the exception of Baldwin, they did not compile pro-northern scores.

Of the four justices in the moderate and neutral categories whose participations in cases utilized in Table 2 totaled less than ten, the relative positions of the voting responses of Baldwin and Woodbury suggest that their scale scores are accurate. For Clifford and Thompson, conversely, there is far less assurance. As was indicated in earlier situations, the omission of these two (or all four) low participants would strengthen rather than weaken the conclusions drawn about the moderate and neutral justices. Two southern Democrats compiled neutral scores, Chief Justice Taney and Justice John McKinley.

Given the possible variation in the placement of those justices upon whom the data are insufficient along the North-South scale, the following general inferences do seem warranted. The Whigs definitely tended to be more pro-North (or less pro-South) than the Democrats, with the one southern Whig tending to be somewhat less pro-North than the other Whigs. Among the Democrats, those from the North tended to be more pro-North (less pro-South) than those from the South. The combination of party and regional background tends quite clearly to result in northern Whigs at the north end of the scale and southern Democrats at the south end of the scale, with northern Democrats generally in between.

Did the combination of three kinds of legal issues tend to obscure the basic attitudes of some justices on particular issues such as slavery? Because of the very small number of divided opinions arising under the commerce clause, sub-scalograms were constructed only for the slavery cases and for the cases involving the status of corporations. In Table 4 and 5, voting patterns on slavery and corporation issues produced sub-scalograms indicating that the positions of justices relative to each other with respect to scale scores remained similar. The difference between the coefficients of reproducibility of .927 in slavery cases and of .957 in corporation cases suggests that the justices divided more consistently over corporation issues than over slavery questions. A comparison of scores for all three scalograms is provided in Table 6. The slavery cases did tend to produce a slightly sharper regional alignment. But the strength of the division over corporation cases supports the notion that party was the stronger factor influencing the justices. Many of the status-of-corporation issues concerned matters in basic dispute between Whigs and Jacksonian Democrats in the federal and state legislatures. Wayne, the only southern Whig on the Court, did shift to a relatively neutral voting position on slave issues and to a strong pro-northern position on corporation questions, shifts paralleling the public policy positions of southern Whig congressmen on similar issues.

Two general hypotheses are suggested by the material in Tables 3, 4, and 5. First, among the extreme justices, party background and sectional background both strengthened underlying attitudes toward regionally divisive cases. Second, among moderate and neutral justices, party frequently proved stronger than regional background. Baldwin, Taney, and McKinley were exceptions to these generalizations. Scalogram analysis could not provide explanations concerning such exceptions. Its chief value lay in establishing general attitudinal patterns. Deviations from such patterns often present challenging problems for orthodox research, particularly in judicial biography.

Unfortunately, the existing historical accounts of this era and the biographical accounts of Justices Baldwin and McKinley shed little light on their judicial behavior. Baldwin had very distinct ideas about the relationship of property rights to the prob-

TABLE 4. Sub-Scalogram of Slavery Cases (1837–1860)

Scale Scores	5	5	4	4	2	2	1	1	1	1	1	0	0	0
Cases / Justices	Story	McLean	Curtis	Baldwin	Wayne	McKinley	Taney	Grier	Nelson	Thompson	Catron	Campbell	Daniel	Vote
United States v. The Armistad	('+')	(+)	*	n)	(+)	(+)	(+)	*	*	(+)	(+)	*	*	7–1
Prigg v. Pennsylvania	('+')	('+'	*	(+	('+'	(+)	('–'	*	*	('–'	('–'	*	(+)	6–3
Dred Scott v. Sanford	*	'+')	'+')	*	('–'	*	('–'	('–'	('n'	*	('–'	('–'	('–'	2–(1–6)7
Groves v. Slaughter	n)	('+'	*	('+'	(n)	n)	('–'	*	*	('n')	*	*	('–'	2–(4–1)5
Moore v. Illinois	*	('+')	(–)	*	(–)	*	(–)	('–')	(–)	*	(–)	*	(–)	1–7
Participations	3	5	2	3	5	3	5	2	2	3	4	1	3	41
Inconsistencies	1	0	0	1	0	0	0	0	0	0	0	0	1	3

$$\text{Coefficient of Reproducibility} = 1 - \frac{3}{41} = .927$$

$$\text{Coefficient of Scalability} = 1 - \frac{3}{9} = .667$$

Legend:
+ = a pro-northern vote
— = a pro-southern vote
n = a neutral vote
* = not participating in the decision
'; = wrote opinion
( ) = joined in the majority opinion
( ) = joined in a concurring opinion
) = joined in a dissenting opinion

lems arising out of slavery. He was essentially a maverick during his entire judicial career. His eccentricity and alleged insanity in later life emphasized by his biographers may perhaps explain his seemingly deviant behavior, but in the view of this writer the final verdict on the role of Henry Baldwin must await fuller biographical exploration and analysis.

With respect to Justice McKinley, it seems clear that there is a discrepancy between his actual voting record as a member of the Supreme Court and his persistent biographical image as a pro-slavery justice. For example, in writing of the congressional criticisms of the Supreme Court which occurred in 1856, Charles Warren contended that:

> *The falseness of the charge that the Court was controlled by the slavery interests was palpable. For since 1840, when the slavery question first became a heated issue, the only appointments to the Bench had been those of Judges Grier, Nelson, Curtis and Campbell, of whom only one—Campbell—was from the south of pro-slavery views, and that one simply succeeded Judge McKinley,* who held like opinions on the subject. [*Emphasis added.*]

McKinley, like Wayne, actually compiled a relatively neutral voting record on slavery issues and unlike Wayne maintained a fairly consistent position as a "middle" justice on all issues. The existing biographical materials on McKinley stress that he was a pro-southern justice, but this conclusion is not supported by McKinley's voting record on the Supreme Court.

The data not only suggest the necessity for a thorough reappraisal of the biographical materials relating to Baldwin and McKinley, they serve to repudiate Fred Rodell's sweeping assertion that "there is not one of his [Taney's] decisions as Chief Justice . . . but can be traced, directly or indirectly, to his big plantation birth and background." Several justices in addition to Taney had a "big plantation" southern background: McKinley, Wayne, Campbell, Daniel, and Barbour. Three of these, indeed, did vote a strong pro-southern position. But Taney and McKinley were neutrals; while Wayne was a moderate pro-northern voter. Taney's neutral position was shared not only by McKinley, but by two northerners who did not have a plantation and slave-holding background.

Taney was, of course, a rather complex figure. His private letters often reflected *personal* sentiments which were identical to those implied or expressed in the judicial opinions of the strong pro-southern justices—Catron, Campbell, Daniel, and Barbour. Did Taney's deep sense of institutional responsibility temper and moderate his judicial opinions and his administration of the post of Chief Justice? His voting record suggests that it did. Further, his exercise of the case assignment power reinforces that conclusion.

THE CASE ASSIGNMENT PROCESS UNDER ROGER B. TANEY

Alpheus T. Mason's judicial biography of Harlan Fiske Stone underscored in unmistakable fashion the significance of the case assignment policies of the Chief

TABLE 5. *Scalogram of Status of Corporation Cases* (1837–1860)

Scale Scores		18	18	16	16	16	12
Cases	Justices	Story	McLean	Curtis	Baldwin	Wayne	McKinley
Commissioners of Knox County v. *Aspinwall* (1858)		*	(+)	*	*	(+)	*
Covington Drawbridge Co. v. *Shepard* (1857)		*	(+)	*	*	(+)	*
Dodge v. Woolsey (1855)		*	(+)	(+)	*	('+')	*
Mechanics' & Traders' Bank v. *Debolt* (1855)		*	(+)	(+)	*	('+')	*
Mechanics' & Traders' Bank v. *Thomas* (1855)		*	(+)	(+)	*	('+')	*
Planters' Bank v. Sharp (1848)		*	('+'	*	*	(+)	*
Rundle v. Delaware & Raritan Canal Company (1852)		*	+)	+)	*	(+)	*
Marshall v. B & O R. R. (1853)		*	(+)	(+)	*	(+)	*
Piqua Branch Bk. v. Knoop (1853)		*	('+')	(+)	*	(+)	*
Curran v. Arkansas (1853)		*	(+)	('+')	*	(+)	*
Woodruff v. Trapnell (1850)		*	(+)	*	*	(+)	(+)
Paup v. Drew (1850)		*	('+')	*	*	(+)	(+)
Vincennes U. v. Indiana (1852)		*	('+')	(+)	*	(+)	*
Ohio Life Insur. & Trust Co. v. Debolt (1853)		*	'+')	'+')		+)	
Richmond, F. & P. R.R. Co. v. Louisa R. R. Co. (1851)		*	+)	'+')	*	+)	(−)
West River Bridge Co. v. Dix (1848)		*	'+')	*	*	+)	*
Charles River Bridge (1837)		'+')	'+')	*	('—'	(−)	*
Mills v. St. Clair County (1850)		*	+)	*	*	(−)	*
Bank of Augusta v. Earle (1839)		(n)	(n)	*	('+'	(n)	('—')
Participations		2	19	10	2	19	4
Inconsistencies		0	0	0	1	0	0

Legend: + = a pro-northern vote
        − = a pro-southern vote
        n = a neutral vote
        * = not participating in the decision
        ' ' = wrote opinion
        ( ) = joined in the majority opinion
        (= joined in a concurring opinion
) = joined in a dissenting opinion

12	12	12	10	9	9	2	1	0	0	
Woodbury	Clifford	Taney	Grier	Nelson	Thompson	Catron	Campbell	Daniel	Barbour	Vote
*	(+)	(+)	(+)	('+')	*	(+)	(+)	'—')	*	8–1
*	(+)	('+')	(+)	(+)	*	(+)	(—	'—')	*	7–2
*	*	(+)	(+)	(+)	*	—)	'—')	—)	*	6–3
*	*	(+)	(+)	(+)	*	—)	'—')	—)	*	6–3
*	*	(+)	(+)	(+)	*	—)	'—')	—)	*	6–3
('+')	*	—)	(+)	(+)	*	(+)	*	'—')	*	6–2
*	*	(+)	('+')	(+)	*	('—'	*	'—')	*	6–2
*	*	(+)	('+')	(+)	*	'—')	'—')	'—')	*	6–3
*	*	(+	(+)	(+)	*	'—')	'—')	'—')	*	6–3
*	*	(+)	(+)	—)	*	'—')	(+)	'—')	*	6–3
(+)	*	(+)	'—')	—)	*	—)	*	—)	*	5–4
(+)	*	(+)	(—	('—'	*	(—	*	—)	*	5–4
*	*	'—')	(+)	(+)	*	—)	*	—)	*	5–3
		('—'	(—	(+)		('—'	('—'	('—'		4–5
*	*	(—)	('—')	(—)	*	(—)	*	*	*	3–5
('—'	*	(—)	(—)	(—)	*	(—)	*	('—')	*	2–6
*	*	('—')	*	*	+)	*	*	*	(—)	3–4
(—)	*	(—)	(—)	(—)	*	('—')	*	(—)	*	1–7
*	*	('n')	*	*	(n)	(n)	*	*	(n)	1–7
5	2	19	17	17	2	18	9	16	2	163
0	0	1	1	2	1	1	1	0	0	8

$$\text{Coefficient of Reproducibility} = 1 - \frac{8}{163} = .9571$$

$$\text{Coefficient of Scalability} = 1 - \frac{8}{34} = .765$$

TABLE 6. *Ranking of Justices Under Separate Issue Classifications (Derived from Scalograms in Tables 2, 4, 5)*

Category	Combined Issues		Slavery Issues		Corporation Issues	
	Name	Scale Score	Name	Scale Score	Name	Scale Score
Strong Pro-Northern Score	Story	29	Story*	5	Story*	18
	McLean	28	McLean	5	McLean	18
			Curtis	4	Curtis	16
			Baldwin*	4	Baldwin*	16
					Wayne	16
Moderate Pro-Northern Score	Curtiss	22				
	Baldwin*	22				
	Wayne	22				
Neutral Score			Wayne	2		
	McKinley	16	McKinley	2	McKinley	12
	Woodbury*	14			Woodbury*	12
	Clifford*	14			Clifford*	12
	Taney	14			Taney	12
Moderate Pro-Southern Score			Taney	1		
	Grier	12	Grier	1	Grier	10
	Nelson	10	Nelson	1	Nelson	9
	Thompson*	10	Thompson*	1	Thompson*	9
			Catron	1		
Strong Pro-Southern Score	Catron	4			Catron	2
	Campbell	1	Campbell	0	Campbell	
	Daniel	0	Daniel	0	Daniel	0
	Barbour*	0			Barbour*	0

Justices. A strong Chief Justice such as Charles Evans Hughes may virtually guide the direction of constitutional interpretation through deft but firm direction of the case assignment process. Of necessity, a Chief Justice must vote with the majority in order consistently to exercise the case assignment prerogative.

It should be acknowledged that the case assignment policies of a Chief Justice may reflect considerations other than the desire to influence the ideological development of particular courses of judicial interpretation. As Danelski perceptively indicated, the ability and special competence of certain justices as well as a normal desire to achieve an equitable distribution of case assignments may underlie the choices of a particular Chief Justice. Another strong consideration is maintaining the institutional integrity of the Supreme Court. As was indicated, Taney's voting record suggests that he was impelled by such considerations to the point of submerging his strong personal pro-southern feelings.

The criteria for determining whether or not a justice is strongly motivated by a sense of institutional responsibility are difficult to establish. Many modern critics of the Court, for example, extoll as institutionally responsible those justices who refrain from writing too many separate opinions and who rigoriously adhere to *stare decisis*. The problem is more complex. For if unity and consistency in decision-making are the only criteria for institutional responsibility, justices like Woodbury (who fashioned the novel commerce clause doctrine of "selective exclusiveness") and Nelson (who chose to write a separate opinion in Dred Scott) would appear to be weakening the integrity of the Court. Yet both were probably seeking "middle" ground ideologically in order to maintain public confidence in the Court. In the context of the developing sectional crisis prior to the Civil War, the seeking of "middle ground" was very likely the most important manifestation of such institutional responsibility.

If this assumption is correct, those justices who were categorized as moderates or neutrals in Table 3 (and like Nelson had a high number of inconsistent scores) were more highly motivated by a sense of institutional responsibility than the justices in the extreme categories. Did Taney's opinion-writing assignments tend to favor such justices?

TABLE 7. *Chief Justice Taney's Opinion-Writing Assignments*

	To Pro-Northern Justices			To Neutral Justices			To Pro-Southern Justices	
	Num-ber	Per Cent		Num-ber	Per Cent		Num-ber	Per Cent
Strong	8	18	Himself	12	27	Strong	8	18
Moderate	6	14	Others	1	2	Moderate	9	20
Total	14	32	Total	13	29	Total	17	39
			Total Moderate and *Neutral*	28	63			

Note: 44 Cases = 100 per cent.

Taney's ability to influence decision-making rested, in large part, upon his willingness to accept the majority view expressed in conference. The assignment of five cases among the fifty-two was beyond Taney's control. Two in 1844 occurred during Taney's absence because of illness; the remaining three, in 1847, 1849, and 1853, were cases in which the justices could not agree upon a majority opinion. In three additional cases, Taney forfeited his assignment prerogative by choosing to vote with the minority. Thus in 13 per cent of the fifty-two cases Taney was not in a position to control the opinion-writing assignments. How did he exercise this power in the remaining forty-four cases? In twelve of the remaining forty-four cases, Taney wrote the majority opinion himself. The remaining three-quarters of the assignments were distributed among thirteen of the justices. Two justices were never assigned a majority opinion in this group of cases. Clifford's omission is probably explicable on the basis of the short time which he served on the Court during the period under study. But McKinley's omission invites further investigation, for he served for over a decade (1839–1851). His was the circuit most remote from Washington. Consequently, he failed to attend during substantial portions of the 1840 and 1848 terms of the Supreme Court because of the burdens of the circuit and illness. Despite these absences, McKinley was present during the Court sessions during ten of his twelve years on the bench. Yet Taney never assigned the writing of a majority opinion in one of the crucial sectional cases to him. Was the omission predicated on Taney's estimate of McKinley's opinion-writing abilities or lack of them?

No single justice was assigned as many of these crucial opinion-writing assignments as Taney assigned to himself. Interestingly enough, the justice to whom Taney assigned the most opinions next to himself was McLean, a strong pro-northerner and a Whig. McLean was the most disdainful of the institutional traditions of the Supreme Court. In two fateful situations, McLean's insistence upon the consideration of issues which were not necessary to resolution of the litigatory questions before the Court projected the Supreme Court into bitter public controversies. In the first, *Groves* v. *Slaughter,* McLean violated the institutional proprieties by whipping out a prepared dissenting opinion without warning during the formal announcement of the Court's decision. His surprised associates delivered oral replies. The episode made for short tempers on the Court and for confusion and uncertainty in legal circles. It was McLean (with Curtis) who first insisted upon considering the validity of the Missouri Compromise in the Dred Scott case. Originally, Taney had assigned the opinion to Justice Nelson who intended to limit the decision to the narrowest possible ground. Later Taney undertook to write the majority opinion himself. Nelson alone adhered to the original objective of avoiding consideration of the constitutionality of the Missouri Compromise. McLean probably was the most troublesome member of the Court throughout Taney's Chief Justiceship. One suspects that Taney's apparent graciousness may well have reflected a desire to placate and neutralize an ideological opponent and, perhaps more importantly, to maintain institutional integrity. These assumptions are supported by the fact that Taney's assignments to strong pro-northern and strong pro-southern justices were largely confined to situations in which such justices were willing to take moderate positions.

Taney's failure to assign any opinions to McKinley may, ironically, be accounted for in part by the fact that McKinley usually took a neutral position. Taney apparently did not trust the writing of "middle" ground opinions to anyone but himself (one assignment to Woodbury proved to be the exception). The fact that he assigned 63 per cent of the total opinions available to him to moderate or neutral justices would bear out the interpretation of his voting record. For Taney, institutional responsibility generally overrode personal viewpoints on the regional crisis.

PRIOR JUDICIAL EXPERIENCE AND INSTITUTIONAL RESPONSIBILITY

In 1956, the Smathers bill, providing that appointees to the federal Supreme Court be persons with at least five years prior judicial experience on the inferior federal bench or on the highest appellate court of a state, was proposed on the ground that prior judicial experience provided the kind of conditioning that insured "proper" institutional behavior. If the ante-bellum justices had been chosen on the basis of a modified version of the Smathers bill, eight of the sixteen would have been qualified to sit on the Supreme Court. Since a strong sense of institutional responsibility is a *sina qua non* of "proper" judicial behavior, how did the justices with prior judicial experience compare with the eight who would not have been qualified to sit on the Court? Of the eight with prior judicial experience (designated "yes" in Table 3), three were in the most extreme voting categories, four in the moderate categories, and one in the neutral category. Conversly, three of the other justices (designated "no" in Table 3) were in the extreme categories, two in the moderate categories, and three in the neutral category. If taking a "middle" position is accepted as the strongest evidence of a sense of institutional responsibility, the advocates of the Smathers bill might have fulfilled their ostensible objective by disqualifying persons with prior judicial experience for the Supreme Court. More appropriately, however, the general conclusion which may be drawn from this limited evidence is that prior judicial experience in and of itself has little bearing on institutional responsibility.

A final evaluation of the Taney Court's responses to the sectional issues of its era necessitates a shift from the behavior of individual Court members to the manner in which the Court as an institution dealt with these issues.

INSTITUTIONAL RESPONSES: A COMPARISON OF THE CONGRESS AND THE COURT

How did the patterns of Supreme Court voting responses contrast to regional and party voting patterns in the Congress? During the period 1837–1860, the national legislature acted upon issues essentially similar to those faced by the Taney Court. Were the congressional divisions on slavery, the status of corporations, and the scope of the commerce clause markedly different from the judicial responses? And if so, do such differences suggest that the Taney Court was restrained because of the institutional factors which purportedly differentiate judicial from political functions?

The definitive historical analysis by Allan Nevins and Arthur C. Cole provided essential data on regional and party divisions in key congressional actions during the period 1837–1860. In addition, Charles O. Paullin's *Atlas of the Historical Geography of the United States* included four plates indicating key congressional divisions along regional lines. It is quite clear that the sharpest regional divisions in Congress arose over controversies related to slavery. However, Congress, through the medium of party discipline, was capable of effectively muting the issue during the initial stages of the period under study. Conversely, the Taney Court, in accordance with the tradition of dissent firmly established through the persistent efforts of Justice William Johnson, could not mute the issue if even one of its members felt impelled to broaden the scope of Court consideration to include the topic. Thus a determined critic of the moderate pro-southern position of Taney such as Justice McLean could, and frequently did, force the majority to consider issues which were capable of arousing fierce sectional antagonisms.

The pattern of Supreme Court voting divisions did not, however, follow the congressional voting divisions. In fact, after the Dred Scott decision, the Taney Court generally maintained institutional unity, while Congress tended to divide more sharply on regional lines. Furthermore, the members of the Court actually divided more intensely over the issues which traditionally divided the Whig and Democratic parties than they did over the sectional issue of slavery. Thus the most striking divisions occurred with respect to the status of corporations; while slavery was of secondary and the scope of the commerce clause of tertiary significance. This pattern of division on the Court was similar to congressional voting divisions in the 1830's and 1840's when, in Sellers' description, major differences were not sectional in character. The fact that the Supreme Court tended to respond in a manner different from the sectional emphasis which became paramount in Congress after 1850 very probably reflected two influences—the felt need to preserve the integrity of the Court as an institution and the generational effect produced by the constitutional guarantee to the justices of life tenure on good behavior.

Limiting the generalizations to the historic era encompassed in this investigation, the data suggest that while party affiliation and regional background are significant factors, the public policy choices of the justices are to some extent inhibited by a sense of institutional obligation acquired after ascension to the Supreme Court.

SUMMARY AND CONCLUSIONS

The findings in this exploratory study are subject to several qualifications. First, to the extent that party and regional background influenced decision-making, such influence may have been limited to the particular historic era under study. Second, the phrase "influence of background factors" connotes an association between pertinent background factors and the relevant decision-making tendencies. It is obviously impossible to establish irrefutably any so-called cause and effect relationships.

With these important qualifications in mind, the results of the study may be summarized as follows:

(a) Scalogram analysis has indicated that despite a variety of doctrinal rationales, the pattern of votes by the justices participating in the fifty-two cases deemed regionally divisive by several historians is consistent with the notion that a single basic underlying attitude involving the anticipated public policy consequences of the decisions ordered the votes.

(b) Although the voting divisions were designed in terms of anticipated regional consequences, the grouping of the justices in relation to their scalogram scores and the later institutional comparison with congressional responses to similar issues suggest that the fundamental division more closely approximated the public policy differences of Whigs and Jacksonian Democrats rather than those of northerners and southerners.

(c) The data on Justices Baldwin and McKinley suggest that existing biographical accounts of them are seriously deficient.

(d) The data on Chief Justice Taney lend support to those judicial biographers who evaluate him as a genuine respecter of the integrity of the institution over which he presided.

(e) The limited evidence refutes the notion that justices who fulfilled the requirements of a modified Smathers bill have a stronger sense of institutional responsibility than those who did not.

(f) Last, the data suggest that judicial responses to the developing crisis were different from legislative responses partly because of apparent generational differences in issue orientation, and partly because of basic differences in perceptions of institutional role.

[The foregoing investigation indicated that judicial perceptions of institutional role tended to mitigate to some extent the impact of sectional and party background upon decision-making. This supported Frankfurter's broad assertion that the judicial robe changes the man within it. However, subsequent investigation indicates that a justice's conception of his institutional role may, in turn, be influenced by certain background factors.]

3. Stare Decisis, *Dissent and the Background of the Justices**

This study is an effort to investigate the degree to which a series of background factors are associated with the propensity of justices of the Supreme Court to adhere to precedent and to dissent from majority opinions. An empirical analysis of the Supreme Court's tendency to overrule precedents which was recently completed by Professor Sidney Ulmer provided a carefully classified group of those cases which in direct fashion had presented clear-cut choices between change and stability to the justices. The sample included all the decisions (81 in number) in which precedents were overruled in the period 1790–1957. It is, of course, acknowledged that the overruling of precedents is not the only manifestation of change in Supreme Court decision-making. Indeed the less dramatic processes of modification of doctrines and careful distinguishing of fact situations may well be the more decisive instrumentalities of change. Moreover, Justice Brandeis pointed out that "movement in constitutional interpretation and application—often involving no less striking departures from doctrines previously established—takes place also without specific overruling or qualification of earlier cases."

Granting that movement and change in judicial decision-making may take a variety of forms, it is important to stress that the overruling decisions represent the single group of cases that can be objectively identified as deliberate judicial vehicles of change. Conversely, while many cases in which precedents are distinguished may represent sophisticated judicial efforts at achieving change while maintaining the outward form of continuity, it is equally true that the act of distinguishing may simply represent what it purports to represent—the recognition of a new factual situation to which no precedent is directly applicable. The observations of an exceptionally keen observer of judicial behavior, Professor Karl Llewellyn, are pertinent. "The doctrine of precedent is two-headed . . . Janus-faced . . . There is one doctrine for

* Adapted by John R. Schmidhauser and David Gold from John R. Schmidhauser, *"Stare Decisis,* Dissent, and the Background of the Justices of the Supreme Court of the United States," *University of Toronto Law Journal,* XIV (May, 1962), 196–212. [Footnotes omitted.] Reproduced with permission of the publisher. Copyright © 1962 by the *University of Toronto Law Journal.*

TABLE 8. *Strength of 103 Precedents Overruled in 81 Decisions*

Chief Justices in Chronological Order	Unanimous		Strong		Close		Weak		Combined Unanimous and Strong Votes		Combined Close and Weak Votes		Totals	
	N	%	N	%	N	%	N	%	N	%	N	%	N	%
Marshall (1801–1835)	(2)	67	(1)	33		0		0	(3)	100		0	(3)	100
Taney (1836–1864)	(4)	80		0	(1)	20		0	(4)	80	(1)	20	(5)	100
Chase (1864–1873)	(3)	38	(5)	63		0		0	(8)	100		0	(8)	100
Waite (1874–1888)	(8)	67	(2)	17	(1)	8	(1)	8	(10)	83	(2)	17	(12)	100
Fuller (1888–1910)	(4)	67		0		0	(2)	33	(4)	67	(2)	33	(6)	100
White (1910–1921)	(2)	33	(3)	50		0	(1)	17	(5)	83	(1)	17	(6)	100
Taft (1921–1930)	(2)	33	(3)	50	(1)	17		0	(5)	83	(1)	17	(6)	100
Hughes (1930–1941)	(7)	25	(13)	46	(2)	7	(6)	22	(20)	71	(8)	29	(28)	100
Stone (1941–1946)	(6)	38	(5)	31	(1)	6	(4)	25	(11)	69	(5)	31	(16)	100
Vinson (1946–1953)	(8)	62	(1)	8	(1)	8	(3)	23	(9)	69	(4)	31	(13)	100
Warren (1953 through 1957)		0		0		0		0		0		0		0
Total	(45)	44	(34)	33	(7)	7	(17)	17	(79)	77	(24)	23	(103)	100

getting rid of precedents deemed troublesome and one doctrine for making use of precedents that seem helpful." Therefore, while the overruling cases are not the only vehicles of change, they do represent the most important unambiguous manifestations of it.

Before relating pertinent background factors to the voting responses of the justices in the overruling decisions, it was necessary to determine whether these decisions actually presented the participating justices with bona fide choices between adherence to *stare decisis* or its repudiation. Conceivably, justices with a sense of genuine respect for this norm of institutional behavior might vote without compunction to overrule a precedent which they considered to be of very dubious influence because the decision establishing the precedent had been close and sharply divided. Conversely, if the original decisions comprised strong majorities, it may be assumed that the decision to overrule these precedents involved a serious choice between the institutional norm and a deliberate departure from that norm.

In order to establish a consistent measure of the strength or weakness of a precedent-setting decision, four categories of voting strength or weakness were employed. Since the size of the Supreme Court varied considerably in different historical periods as a result of congressional changes, the deaths or resignations of members, and the absences ocasioned by circuit duty or illnesses, an absolute numerical measure of the strength of the original decision could not be developed. Instead, criteria which consistently measured the size of the precedent-establishing vote relative to the size of the Court were employed. Thus, the strongest precedent-setting vote was a *unanimous* one. A *strong* vote was defined as one in which there was a two to one majority or better for the establishment of a precedent (but non-unanimous); and a *weak* precedent-setting vote was defined as one in which a change in a single vote would have altered the position of the Court. A *close* vote represented a situation in which the vote for establishment of a precedent was less than two to one but more than a single vote margin.

The 81 overruling cases repudiated a total of 103 established precedents. The classification of 103 precedent-establishing decisions in Table 8 indicates that slightly over three-fourths of these decisions were supported by majority votes which were either unanimous (44 per cent) or strong (33 per cent). Consequently, a large proportion of the overruling decisions embody cases which represent fairly clear choices between stability or deliberate change in judicial interpretation.

THE CHARACTERISTICS OF THE JUSTICES

If it can be assumed that the overruling cases comprise a series of relatively unambiguous judicial choices between change and stability in interpretation, can it also be validly assumed that the voting responses of the justices in these cases provide a reliable clue to the general attitude of each participating justice toward *stare decisis*? In one important respect the answer is negative. The 81 overruling cases are unique in the sense that each represents a *successful* attempt at repudiation of precedent. Consequently, a study of voting responses relating to change or stability which is limited to these cases necessarily fails to take into account the *unsuccessful* attempts at abandonment of precedent. For example, the vain effort of Justice Hugo L. Black to persuade the Court to reject the Santa Clara doctrine, that under certain circumstances a corporation could be considered a "person" within the meaning of the Fourteenth Amendment, would not be taken into account because his attempt to effectuate change failed. Aside from this limitation, the overruling cases do provide a clear, if limited, basis for testing the validity of the above-mentioned assumptions about the relationship of background factors to decision-making tendencies.

It should be noted that not every manifestation of disapproval of or unwillingness to support the repudiation of a precedent took the form of a dissent. In several instances, justices concurred in the result for the litigants but indicated in separate opinions their disapproval of the majority's deliberate abandonment of precedent. In a few instances, concurring opinions indicated complete neutrality on such issues.

In addition to testing the validity of the relationship of the above background factors to stability or change in judicial voting responses, several other background attributes were similarly investigated. These are party affiliation, family background, regional background, and general reputation with respect to the writing of dissents.

Seventy-one justices participated in one or more of the eighty-one overruling decisions. In Table 9 these justices are listed in the order of their appointments to the Supreme Court. Beside each name is a fraction. The numerator is the total of voting responses for repudiation of precedents. The denominator is the total number of overruling cases in which the justice participated. Each fraction is transposed into a percentage score for each justice (e.g., ½ = 50 per cent). These percentage scores were grouped according to size and translated into an index of the intensity of voting responses for change and stability.

Of the total of 71 justices, 40 fall inside category 1 and 14 in category 2. Thus 54 justices are in the categories indicating relatively strong propensity for change. Of the remaining 17 justices, 6 were in category 3, 7 in category 4, and 4 in category 5. The categories indicating strongest propensity for abandonment of *stare decisis* (1 and 2) were combined, while the three categories comprising the justices most reluctant to abandon *stare decisis* (3, 4, and 5) were similarly combined. It should be clearly understood that our use of labels "strong" and "weak" is arbitrary. The differences between the categories are ones of degree, moving from strongest propensity for change to least strong propensity for change or from weakest tendency to least weak. It is simply the awkwardness of talking in terms of one modifier that suggests using "strong" and "weak." One might reasonably conclude, for example, that the term "weak" should not be applied, as we have done, to a justice who has voted 75 per cent on the side of change.

Each justice was then classified as having either significant prior judicial experience, or not. Justices were classified as leaving such experience if they met the requirements of a modified version of the proposed Smathers bill. As indicated above, the Smathers proposal would limit appointments to the Supreme Court to persons who had at least five years' prior judicial experience on either an inferior federal court or on the highest appellate court of a state. The modified version here applied kept the time requirement intact but broadened the concept of court experience to include any court that is (or was at the time of a justice's appointment) within the American

TABLE 9. *Index of Intensity of Voting Responses—For Change or Stability*

Justices	Fraction	Percentage for Change
Category 1		
Bushrod Washington	1/1	100
William Johnson	3/3	100
Brockholst Livingston	1/1	100
Thomas Todd	1/1	100
Gabriel Duvall	2/2	100
Joseph Story	3/3	100
Smith Thompson	2/2	100
John McLean	6/6	100
Henry Baldwin	2/2	100
James M. Wayne	4/4	100
Roger B. Taney	3/3	100
John Catron	4/4	100
John McKinley	2/2	100
Robert C. Grier	4/4	100
Benjamin R. Curtis	2/2	100
John A. Campbell	2/2	100
Noah H. Swayne	10/10	100
Stephen J. Field	19/21	90
Ward Hunt	4/4	100
William B. Woods	4/4	100
Stanley Matthews	7/7	100
Samuel Blatchford	9/9	100
Lucius Q. C. Lamar	3/3	100
Melville W. Fuller	5/5	100
George Shiras, Jr.	3/3	100
Rufus Peckham	1/1	100
Joseph R. Lamar	1/1	100
Mahlon Pitney	7/7	100
William H. Taft	4/4	100
George Sutherland	9/10	90
Edward T. Sanford	3/3	100
Benjamin N. Cardozo	4/4	100
Hugo L. Black (through 1957)	32/35	91
William O. Douglas (through 1957)	29/30	96.6
James F. Byrnes	3/3	100
Harold Burton	9/10	90
Fred M. Vinson	9/9	100
Tom C. Clark (through 1957)	3/3	100
Sherman Minton	3/3	100
Category 2		
Samuel Nelson	4/5	80
Samuel F. Miller	15/18	83
David Davis	5/6	83
William Strong	7/8	87.5
Joseph P. Bradley	14/17	82
Horace Gray	10/12	83
William R. Day	5/6	83

TABLE 9. *Index of Intensity of Voting Responses—For Change
or Stability* (Cont.)

Justices	Fraction	Percentage for Change
Category 2 (Cont.)		
Charles E. Hughes	17/20	85
Willis Van Devanter	14/17	82
Louis D. Brandeis	14/17	82
John H. Clarke	4/5	80
Harlan F. Stone	31/35	88.7
Frank Murphy	21/25	84
Wiley Rutledge	12/14	85.7
Category 3		
Peter V. Daniel	3/4	75
Nathan Clifford	7/9	78
Edward D. White	7/9	78
Joseph McKenna	7/9	78
Oliver W. Holmes	10/13	77
Stanley F. Reed	26/33	77.7
Category 4		
John Marshall	2/3	66.6
Salmon P. Chase	2/3	66.6
John M. Harlan (1st)	10/15	66.6
David J. Brewer	3/5	60
Owen J. Roberts	20/29	69
Felix Frankfurter (through 1957)	22/33	66.6
Robert H. Jackson	12/20	60
Category 5		
Henry B. Brown	2/4	50
Howell E. Jackson	1/2	50
James C. McReynolds	12/23	52
Pierce Butler	8/15	53.5

Legend:

Percentage	Category Designation	Category Number
90–100% of votes for change =	Strongest Propensity for Change =	1
80–89% of votes for change =	Strong Propensity for Change =	2
70–79% of votes for change =	Moderate Resistance to Change =	3
60–69% of votes for change =	Strong Resistance to Change =	4
Below 60% of votes for change =	Strongest Resistance to Change =	5

common law judicial tradition. A substantial number of justices (29) fall into this group. However, 42 justices either lacked judicial experience, had not fulfilled the time requirement of five years service, or had not served on a court properly within the American common law judicial tradition.

It should be noted that the seventy-one justices participating in the overruling decisions were also classified on the basis of their primary legal careers. Thus a justice might well have achieved classification as a possessor of significant judicial experience and yet be also properly classified as a lawyer who was primarily a politician. As a matter of fact, only four of the total of twenty-nine possessors of significant judicial experience were qualified for the designation as lawyers who were primarily judicial administrators—Thomas Todd, Horace Gray, Oliver Wendell Holmes, and Benjamin N. Cardozo. The biographical sources indicated that the remaining twenty-five justices largely comprised individuals who were primarily politicians. In a word, the greater portion of the justices who would have qualified for the Supreme Court under a modified version of the Smathers bill were men who combined extensive judicial careers with intensive political activity. The roster includes, among others, John McLean, John Catron, Stephen J. Field, David Davis, Ward Hunt, William H. Taft, William Strong, Willis Van Devanter, David J. Brewer, and Henry Billings Brown.

Given that a John McLean might balance his significant service on the Ohio Supreme Court with decades of effort to secure nomination to the Presidency, that a John Catron might combine high talent as a justice of the Tennessee Supreme Court with even greater talent as a party manager for Andrew Jackson and Martin Van Buren—the question remains, does significant judicial service prior to ascension to the federal Supreme Court condition a potential justice's attitude toward *stare decisis?*

Senator Stennis assumed that prior experience is virtually the only way to develop a jurist wedded to precedent. If his assumption is correct, a higher proportion of the justices possessing significant prior judicial experience would resist abandonment of precedent than those justices who lacked such prior experience. Actually, the data indicate that a higher proportion (86 per cent of 29) of the justices possessing significant prior judicial experience showed a strong propensity to abandon *stare decisis* than did the justices lacking such experience (69 per cent of 42). Similarly, the justices chosen from families which had a tradition of judicial service were more prone (83 per cent of 18) to abandon *stare decisis* than the justices who were not chosen from such families (73 per cent of 53). The evidence furnished by these data definitely do not indicate that any one of these variables can be considered as *the* important variable which accounts for the variation among these justices in the propensity to abandon *stare decisis*. However, these data do indicate quite conclusively that no case for prior judicial experience as a factor which increases tendency to adhere to *stare decisis* can be empirically supported by the behavior of the Supreme Court justices. If prior judicial experience has any effect at all upon this tendency, it is precisely opposite that believed to exist by those who have advocated prior judicial experience as a criterion for appointment to the Supreme Court.

The relationship between prior judicial experience and propensity to dissent was similarly investigated. *It should be emphasized that propensity to dissent is measured not simply on voting responses in the overruling decisions, but on the basis of the over-all record of each justice in dissenting from majority opinions throughout his entire judicial career.* The fact that some justices dissented in the overruling decisions had little bearing on their general reputation in this regard.

Although the propensity to dissent has been subjected to severe criticism since the era of John Marshall, certain justices have strongly asserted their independence and insisted upon recording the grounds for their disagreement with the majority. Two types of dissenters were of historic importance. The "great" dissenter was notable because of the persuasiveness of his opinions; the inveterate dissenter achieved fame (or notoriety) on the basis of his persistent defense of lost causes. Both types comprise the justices herein referred to as indicating a strong propensity to dissent. The data indicate that the justices who had significant prior judicial experience were somewhat more parsimonious (72 per cent of 29) in the use of dissent than the justices lacking such experience (55 per cent of 42). The same tendency, though less strong, is apparent in the relationship of family tradition of judicial service to propensity to dissent. Justices chosen from families with a tradition of judicial service were more reluctant to dissent (72 per cent of 18) than justices who were not chosen from such families (62 per cent of 53).

Since the Age of Jackson, the members of the Supreme Court have been drawn, for the great part, from the professionalized upper middle class in American society. Members of this class tended to maintain traditions of civic responsibility and intellectual open-mindedness which were distinctive. The justices who, on the basis of paternal occupation, were chosen from families sharing these traditions were contrasted, with respect to attitudes toward *stare decisis* and dissent, with justices chosen from relatively humble family beginnings. The justices from families in the professionalized upper middle class and justices of humble background responded in virtually identical fashion with respect to adherence to *stare decisis*. However, they differed very substantially where propensity to dissent was concerned. Justices of humble background had a very strong propensity to dissent (78 per cent of 9), while the justices of upper middle class background tended almost equally strongly not to become "great" or frequent dissenters (only 32 per cent of 62 were "great" or frequent dissenters). Since, however, there were only 9 among the 71 justices who came from humble family background, this factor cannot be considered as an important one which would explain the actual differences in propensity to dissent which did occur.

Realistic identification of political party background with a recognizable body of ideological assumptions has, throughout American history, required something more precise than haphazard designation of Republicans and Democrats. The historic changes in party names and organizational objectives have created serious problems in situations where a degree of continuity in basic ideological objective is of primary analytical importance. The work of Professor Seymour M. Lipset provided a viable method for classifying members of the Supreme Court. Federalists, National Republicans, Whigs, Native Americans and Republicans were classified as conservative while Jeffersonian Republicans, Jacksonians, and Modern Democrats were categorized as liberal. Since Lipset's classification is based, in terms of ideology, on differences in attitudes toward economic and non-economic freedom, it is necessary to identify the bases for the factional splits within major parties which actually reflect fundamental ideological differences. Thus in classifying justices, William H. Moody, a Republican of the Progressive wing of Theodore Roosevelt, would be classified as liberal, while William Howard Taft's appointee, Horace Lurton, a conservative Southern Democrat, would be properly classified as a conservative.

The data indicate that justices chosen from a liberal party background were somewhat more prone to abandon *stare decisis* (82 per cent of 33) than their conservative counterparts (71 per cent of 38). The materials show that they were also a bit more inclined to become identified as dissenters (42 per cent of 33) than were justices chosen from a conservative party background (34 per cent of 38).

The basic assumption of former ABA President Walter Armstrong that corporation lawyers tend to adhere to precedent to a significantly greater degree than lawyers who were primarily politicians or academicians was scarcely supported by the evidence. The percentage of justices with careers primarily in corporation law (26 per cent of 23) was virtually identical with the percentage of the justices who had been politicians or academicians (23 per cent of 44). With respect to propensity to dissent the percentage relationships were, in fact, identical. In both categories 39 per cent were "great" or frequent dissenters.

Modern critics of the Supreme Court frequently equate abandonment of *stare decisis* and the propensity to dissent as behavior typical of those justices who were not properly conditioned for high judicial office. The data available in this study were investigated to test the validity of this assumption. Although a majority of justices in each classification favored change over stability within the context of the overruling decisions, the justices with career reputations as dissenters tended to resist abandonment of *stare decisis* (41 per cent of 27) to a far greater extent than the justices who were generally known as non-dissenters (14 per cent of 44). This is a statistically significant association at beyond the .01 level of confidence. Thus, among all the background factors investigated, this is the one factor that does account for some substantial amount of the variation in propensity to adhere or to abandon *stare decisis*. Whatever may account for the development of this propensity to dissent among the justices, such justices are definitely more likely to favor adherence to *stare decisis*. Thus, the justices who have a general reputation as dissenters are also dissenters from the majority who have favored abandonment of *stare decisis* in the 81 cases involved in this analysis. It should be noted that this behavior is contrary to the notions of many contemporary critics of the Supreme Court . . .

Regional background was similarly cross-tabulated with judicial behavior. The justices from two of the oldest regions, the South and the Northeast, indicated the greatest reluctance to abandon *stare decisis*. 33 per cent of the 9 northeasterners and 32 per cent of 22 southerners strongly adhered to precedent while only 12 per cent of the 17 justices from the Middle Atlantic region, 21 per cent of the 19 midwesterners, and 25 per cent of the 4 justices from remaining regions did so. The justices from the Northeast comprised the only regional group which was composed of a relatively large number of dissenters—78 per cent of 9 as compared to 18 per cent of 17 (Middle Atlantic), 32 per cent of 22 (South), 47 per cent of 19 (Midwest), and 25 per cent of 4 (West Coast and Mountain Region). It is noteworthy in relation to this finding that New England has had a reputation as one of two regions in which the quality of legal education, the distinguished character of the bar, and a venerable tradition of distinctive selection have operated to produce exceptionally able jurists at the state appellate level as well as in the hierarchy of federal courts.

MULTIVARIATE ANALYSIS

A crucial question which must be raised about these findings is whether these two-fold relationships would continue to stand up, and in the same fashion, with the introduction of additional factors. For example, it might well be that any association noted between dissent and propensity to abandon is a result of the association of each with ideology, and when ideology is held constant, the association between dissent and propensity to abandon tends to disappear. The first of these multivariate analyses is reported in Table 10, in which it is clear that the original relationships do not tend to disappear. The results in Table 10 may be summed up as follows:

TABLE 10. *Per Cent Showing Strong Propensity to Abandon* Stare Decisis *by Prior Judicial Experience, Party Background, and Propensity to Dissent*

Justices with Strong Propensity to Abandon *Stare Decisis*	Significant Prior Judicial Experience			
	Liberal		Conservative	
	Dissenter	Was Not	Dissenter	Was Not
Per Cent	80	100	33	91
Total Number	(5)	(10)	(3)	(11)
	No Significant Prior Judicial Experience			
Per Cent	67	78	50	79
Total Number	(9)	(9)	(10)	(14)

(1) Holding prior judicial experience and ideology constant, the originally noted relationship between dissent and propensity to abandon continues to stand up. In each of the four possible comparisons in which the judges have the same ideology and the same prior judicial experience, a greater proportion of the non-dissenters tended to abandon *stare decisis* than did the dissenters. It might also be worth noting that the difference between dissenters and non-dissenters tended to be somewhat greater among the conservatives.

(2) The associations between prior judicial experience and adherence to *stare decisis* and between liberal-conservative ideology and adherence to *stare decisis* do not consistently stand up when the other two variables are held constant. In three of the four possible comparisons, a slightly greater proportion of the liberals than the conservatives show the stronger propensity to abandon *stare decisis;* and among non-dissenters with no prior judicial experience, there is no difference at all. In three of the four possible comparisons, a slightly greater proportion of those with prior judicial experience than those without showed a stronger propensity to abandon *stare decisis;* among conservative non-dissenters, the opposite was true. Clearly, our previous suggestion that a great deal of importance in accounting for adherence to *stare decisis* cannot be attached to prior experience and to ideology is reinforced.

(3) However, it is perhaps noteworthy that these three factors in combination do show some tendency toward an increased effect. Those non-dissenters who were additionally liberals with prior judicial experience were without a single exception among

those with the stronger propensity to abandon *stare decisis;* while only half of the dissenters who were conservatives without prior judicial experience showed stronger propensity to abandon *stare decisis.*

(4) Considering only prior judicial experience and ideology (party affiliation) in relation to adherence to *stare decisis,* it can be noted that there is virtually no difference at all between liberals and conservatives, i.e., whatever slight association exists between ideology and propensity to abandon *stare decisis* virtually disappears with prior judicial experience held constant. Thus, it would appear that if any effect at all upon adherence to *stare decisis* can be attributed to either of these two variables, prior judicial experience is the more important. The reason that any relationship may be noted between ideology and propensity to abandon precedent is that a greater proportion of liberals seem to have had prior judicial experience and this in turn is associated with a stronger propensity to abandon *stare decisis.*

The results indicated earlier suggest that it makes little difference whether a judicial appointee had been a corporation lawyer or not. Holding constant prior judicial experience and liberalism-conservatism, there are four comparisons that can be made between "matched" corporation lawyers and those who were not corporation lawyers in Table 11. No consistent pattern emerges among these four comparisons.

TABLE 11. *Per Cent Showing Strong Propensity to Abandon* Stare Decisis *by Prior Judicial Experience, Corporation Law Background, and Party Affiliation*

Justices with Strong Propensity to Abandon *Stare Decisis*	Significant Prior Judicial Experience			
	Corporation Lawyer		Was Not	
	Liberal	Conservative	Liberal	Conservative
Per Cent	100	75	92	80
Total Number	(1)	(4)	(14)	(10)
	No Significant Prior Judicial Experience			
Per Cent	75	72	76	50
Total Number	(8)	(11)	(13)	(10)

There is hardly any difference at all in two of the comparisons; and one of the comparisons is rendered quite meaningless by the existence of only one member in the subgroup. Though in this instance the differences between liberals and conservatives and between those with prior judicial experience and those without are consistent, they are quite small. (In some comparisons a change of one member would change the direction of the difference.)

In Table 12 party affiliation, class origin, and legal career prior to judicial service are simultaneously cross-tabulated with propensity to dissent. The earlier conclusion that the corporation lawyer per se did not behave differently than the non-corporation lawyer is upheld; no consistent differences emerge. Despite the very small number of judges with humble class backgrounds, the previously noted tendency for those from humble backgrounds to show strong propensity to dissent remains clearcut. The data

TABLE 12. *Per Cent Showing Strong Propensity to Dissent by Corporation Law Background, Party Affiliation and Family Class Origins*

Justices with Strong Propensity to Dissent	Corporation Lawyer			
	Liberal		Conservative	
	Middle Class	Humble	Middle Class	Humble
Per Cent	43	0	29	100
Total Number	(7)	(0)	(14)	(2)
	Was Not			
Per Cent	38	60	25	100
Total Number	(21)	(5)	(20)	(2)

would seem to warrant further investigation of the relationship of class origins to propensity to dissent, perhaps among the much larger number of judges of inferior federal courts.

Perhaps one of the more interesting results may be obtained by putting together prior judicial experience, party affiliation, and family traditions of judicial service, each of which separately has shown some relationship, small though it may be, to propensity to adhere to *stare decisis*. Prior judicial experience is associated with an increased tendency to abandon precedent. Liberal affiliation is somewhat associated with an increased tendency to abandon precedent; and a family tradition of judicial service is somewhat associated with an increased tendency to abandon. Therefore, if these three factors in combination serve simply to reinforce the effects of each other, we would expect that those who were liberal, came from a family tradition of judicial service, and had prior judicial experience, would show the greatest tendency to abandon precedent. And conversely, those who were conservative, came from a family lacking the judicial tradition, and lacked prior judicial experience, would be least likely to show a strong propensity to abandon. The latter is indeed true, but the former expectation is not upheld (Table 13). Thus, no simple reinforcing effect can be posited for these three variables. As further evidence of the complexity of the

TABLE 13. *Per Cent Showing Strong Propensity to Abandon* Stare Decisis *by Prior Judicial Experience, Family Tradition of Judicial Service, and Party Affiliation*

Justices with Strong Propensity to Abandon *Stare Decisis*	Significant Prior Judicial Experience			
	Family Tradition of Judicial Service		Lacked Family Tradition of Judicial Service	
	Liberal	Conservative	Liberal	Conservative
Per Cent	75	75	100	80
Total Number	(4)	(4)	(12)	(10)
	Lacked Significant Experience			
Per Cent	100	88	72	56
Total Number	(2)	(9)	(14)	(16)

interaction of these three variables, it may be noted that no simple pattern of differences in the same direction emerges (as was the case in Table 11) for any one set of possible comparisons with two of these three variables constant.

Finally, the interaction of prior judicial service, ideology, and regional background with propensity to dissent is reported in Table 14. Just as was the case in Table 12 with humble backgrounds, so in this table the small number of judges from the Northeast may render the findings open to serious question. Nevertheless, it is worth noting that the tendency for northeastern judges to be dissenters does hold up with prior judicial experience and ideology constant. The data are sufficiently consistent to warrant further investigation of these factors in future studies involving a larger number of cases (e.g., several hundred past and present members of the inferior federal courts).

TABLE 14. *Per Cent Showing Strong Propensity to Dissent by Regional Background, Prior Judicial Experience and Party Affiliation*

Justices with Strong Propensity to Dissent	Significant Prior Judicial Experience				Lacked Such Experience			
	Liberal		Conservative		Liberal		Conservative	
	NE	NonNE	NE	NonNE	NE	NonNE	NE	NonNE
Per Cent	50	31	0	21	100	36	66	38
Total Number	(2)	(13)	(0)	(14)	(4)	(14)	(3)	(21)

INTERPRETATION OF THE RESULTS

On the basis of the relationships indicated in Tables 8–14, many fundamental assumptions about the conditioning effects of certain background factors are patently invalid. The notion that significant prior judicial experience predisposes justices to adhere to *stare decisis* is clearly without foundation. Indeed, to the extent that significant prior judicial experience conditions attitudes toward *stare decisis* at all, those members of the Supreme Court who were thoroughly integrated within the American common law judicial tradition prior to their appointments to the high court were actually more prone to deviate from the institutional norm of adherence to *stare decisis* than were the justices who were not so integrated.

More important, the data contribute interesting insights with respect to the realities of internal Court operation. Propensity to dissent and tendency to repudiate precedents are often equated in contemporary criticisms because of an underlying assumption that both facets of judicial behavior are symptomatic of the innovating justice. Thus, it is often assumed that Holmes was a highly successful doctrinal innovator and that his career was typical of other frequent dissenters. Leaving aside the question whether Holmes was actually a doctrinal innovator, the evidence suggests that the typical dissenter has been a tenacious advocate of traditional legal doctrines which were being abandoned during his tenure; consequently he adhered to precedent with far greater regularity than his non-dissenting colleagues, and his persistent attempts at turning back the doctrinal tides of his era usually met with failure.

In terms of background attributes, the typical dissenter more often than not lacked thorough integration in the American common law judicial tradition prior to his appointment to the Supreme Court. He was more likely than most other justices to be among the handful of Court members chosen from families of essentially humble social status.

Only if he were chosen from a humble background or from a liberal political party would his propensity to dissent be equated to a slight extent with a propensity to depart from, rather than adhere to, precedent. In fact, significant prior judicial experience (or lack of it) and party affiliation, emerged as the only consistently (somewhat) influential of the background factors which were investigated. Of these the first was the more important.

Significant prior judicial experience was consistently though not greatly associated with a propensity to abandon precedent and with a tendency not to dissent. The data cannot provide evidence as to why such associations developed. However, the following tentative hypothesis is suggested. This factor apparently provided a degree of psychic security to the justices who were thoroughly integrated in the American common law judicial tradition prior to ascension to the Supreme Court. In particular the justices lacking such thorough integration prior to their Supreme Court appointments may tend to over-compensate by more rigid adherence to what they conceive to be an important institutional norm. Conversely, the justices with significant prior experience tend to be more flexible with respect to adherence to this norm.

The tendency toward greater inflexibility with respect to *stare decisis* exhibited by justices who came to the Supreme Court relatively uninitiated in the norms of judicial behavior becomes more striking with respect to the propensity to dissent. Since the inveterate dissenter was typically a defender of old legal traditions rather than an innovator, strong propensity to dissent may be considered as symptomatic of doctrinal rigidity. Perceptive studies of the internal operation of the court, such as Alexander Bickel's *The Unpublished Opinions of Mr. Justice Brandeis,* have indicated that doctrinal inflexibility is inversely related to success in influencing judicial colleagues. This suggests a concomitant hypothesis. The justices who were institutionally integrated before their appointments to the Supreme Court not only enjoy a measure of psychic security with respect to institutional norms, but their resultant doctrinal flexibility permits them to play a more influential role in intracourt affairs than their inflexible colleagues.

Of particular interest is the fact that the underlying attitudes of justices toward the norms of institutional behavior differ so consistently with respect to certain background attributes. This is noteworthy because no attempt has been made in this study to relate such differences to the kinds of dichotomies conventionally employed in studies of judicial attitudes (e.g., "liberal" or "conservative" doctrinal positions on questions relating to the economic or non-economic freedoms). Justices as disparate doctrinally as Pierce Butler and Robert H. Jackson or James McReynolds and Felix Frankfurter, shared not only the common characteristic of lack of thorough integration in the American common law judicial tradition prior to their Supreme Court appointments, but responded in very similar fashion with respect to propensity to dissent and adherence to precedent. Ironically, Justice Frankfurter's self-appointed role as guardian of the institutional norms of the Supreme Court may well reflect the tendency to overcompensate for lack of prior experience rather than the alleged transferal of the habits of the seminar in the judicial conference so often alluded to by his contemporary critics.

With respect to the initial question, do background attributes condition decision-making behavior, the results justify a very qualified affirmative. Determination of the extent of such conditioning in the areas of public law concerned with substantive doctrine rather than underlying attitudes toward the norms of institutional behavior awaits subsequent investigation.

10 *Conclusion*

A. THE AMERICAN JUDICIAL PROCESS

[If the foregoing collection of essays, decisions, and empirical studies captured the essential richness and diversity of the American judicial processes, the editorial and writing efforts made were perhaps worthwhile. But the student of American constitutional law should indeed understand clearly the tentativeness of the effort. Because so much of the legal literature of the past half century has been primarily exhortive rather than empirical, firm answers to many questions about the nature of the judicial process are still lacking.

The contributions to be derived from behavioral research give promise that we may be on the threshold of an empirically rigorous and intellectually rewarding era with respect to studies of the judicial process. Yet many fear that overemphasis upon the sometimes grim realities may dull sensibilities and destroy hope for the attainability of the ideal objectives. Solicitor General Archibald Cox's remarks successfully convey the crucial conception that in order to make progress toward goals considered desirable, intelligent understanding of the true nature of our system of justice is essential. In short, his plea for understanding of the nature of Supreme Court litigation has implications for the whole complex of judicial systems which comprise the American judicial process.]

1. The Nature of Supreme Court Litigation*

One following the Supreme Court intimately cannot avoid being struck by the very special nature of its work. There are many cases which might arise in any court and which are not unusual except in their difficulty, but more than half the docket,

---

* Archibald Cox, Solicitor General of the United States, "The Nature of Supreme Court Litigation," *Journal of the American Judicature Society,* XLV (October, 1961), 93–96. [Footnotes omitted.] Reproduced with permission of the author and the publisher. Copyright © 1961 by the American Judicature Society.

I estimate—and much the most important half—is quite different from normal judicial business and quite unlike the usual flow of litigation through state and inferior federal courts. Too often we tend to forget the difference and its consequences.

For one thing the size and quality of the interests affected is quite extraordinary. I do not mean merely that there are suits between the United States and du Pont and General Motors, or that even the case against a small taxpayer may establish a rule affecting millions of dollars. The point is that in many cases the real contest is not so much between individuals and business corporations as between institutions and ways of life; and in reaching decisions this fact is explicitly recognized. Throughout American history the prime examples have been the contests between state and federal authority and the definitions of the powers of the executive and legislative branches, but familiarity does not lessen the intensity of the contest and new aspects are always arising. Consider, for example, the recent work of the Court in defining the investigatory powers of Congress.

PROFOUNDLY INFLUENTIAL DECISIONS

Less familiar examples also abound. Next term the Court will hear *Arizona* v. *California,* an original suit to determine the rights of six states and the United States in the waters of the Colorado River. The decision will profoundly influence the relative growth and prosperity of Southern California, most of Arizona, and perhaps parts of Nevada and New Mexico. It may also affect whether the trend of our water law is national or local.

The school segregation cases, the appeals from the conviction of "sit-ins," and the inevitable litigation over the "freedom riders" grow out of the conflict between the ideal of liberty and equality expressed in the Declaration of Independence, on the one hand, and, on the other, a way of life rooted in the customs of many of our people since before the signing of the Declaration. The cases cannot be decided wisely without facing the underlying issue.

FUNDAMENTAL ISSUES OF OUR TIME ARE HEARD BY THE COURT

Indeed, an extraordinarily large proportion of the most fundamental issues of our times ultimately go before the Supreme Court for judicial determination. They are the issues upon which the community, consciously or unconsciously, is most deeply divided. They arouse the deepest emotions. Their resolution—one way or the other— often writes our future history. I have already mentioned race relations and the conflict between pressures for conformity and individual freedom. A newer example is the tightening contest for political power between rural areas which are now grossly overrepresented in the state legislatures and growing metropolitan districts whose problems, because of malapportionment, are too often neglected. This October the Court will hear reargument in the Tennessee reapportionment case upon whether the claim that gross malapportionment in both houses of a state legislature violates the Fourteenth Amendment, presents a justiciable question.

Perhaps it is an exaggeration to suggest that in the United States we have developed an extraordinary facility for casting social, economic, philosophical and political questions in the form of actions at law and suits in equity, and then turning around and having the courts decide them upon social, economic, and philosophical grounds. It is plainly true that we put upon the Supreme Court the burden of deciding cases which would never come before the judicial branch in any other country.

THE COURT MUST OFTEN WRITE UPON A CLEAN SLATE

The unique nature of the Court's work, more than any other characteristic, places its stamp upon the institution, creates the Court's own peculiar problems, and shapes its role in our national life.

The criteria and materials relevant in reaching decisions are unlike those in other cases. Neither precedent nor the words of the First or Fourteenth Amendments would even point to a decision, one way or the other, in the Sunday law cases. There are few instances in which *Farrand* or the *Annals of Congress* contribute anything useful to constitutional exegesis. All too often the Court must write upon a clean slate. During the past two decades, for example, it has created a completely new body of law dealing with the substantive relation and procedures which should obtain between public employees and the government.

DIVISIONS ARE INEVITABLE

It is the special quality of the litigation which explains the sharp divisions within the Court. The character of the issues would make divisions inevitable even if the self-restraint practiced by some earlier justices in withholding dissent still prevailed. I submit, however, that the divisions and disagreements are not only desirable, but essential. Unanimity could be achieved only by appointing to the Court nine justices with one cast of mind and one set of experiences. Then we would have unanimous decisions and a clear cut line of authority, all one way or all the other. This might seem desirable to those who know that they know all the right answers to all questions —provided, of course, that the Court's unanimous answers were the same as theirs. In truth, the most fundamental and divisive issues that face the community should not be decided over-night, nor should they be decided in clean-cut fashion, all one way or all the other, until time and events have matured the analysis. One makes safer and quicker progress through an unfamiliar swamp by proceeding hummock to hummock, island to island, sometimes taking two steps forward and one step back, or even two steps back for one step forward.

It is also the character of the Court's business which catches it up in public debate and makes the justices the subjects of bitter controversies. Anyone who reads its history knows that this is nothing new. The stupid attacks upon Chief Justice Warren and his associates, however shocking, are hardly as virulent as the shafts which were loosed against John Marshall. Nor is proper criticism to be regretted. Our law is the richer and the wiser because academic criticism is part of the stream of development. And laymen have much to add, even though one may wish at times that they had greater awareness of the nature and limits of the judicial function. It is essential, just because the public questions which the Court faces are pressing and divisive, that they be thoroughly canvassed in public each step at a time while the Court is pragmatically evolving new principles. The ultimate resolution of questions funda- mental to the whole community must be based in a common consensus of opinion.

Let me make it plain that in emphasizing the unique quality of the Supreme Court's work, I do not mean to imply that it should be otherwise or that the Court should exercise more care not to deal with cases which would not be justiciable under other political systems. The process is an integral part of our constitutional system. It has worked remarkably well.

THE PROCESS OF DECISION ACCORDING TO LAW

The reasons for the Court's success are less evident and a good deal more compli- cated. If someone were to propose that we establish a Council of Nine Wise Men, appointed for life, to whom we would refer all the country's most difficult questions, all those which divided the community most sharply, which aroused the strongest feelings, and which would have the greatest future in importance, the country would unanimously reject the suggestion. What works—and what the country accepts—is the process of decision *according to law*.

It would be interesting to press on and inquire into the meaning of "decision according to law" in the very field from which many conventional legal guide posts are lacking. One would have to inquire into the advantages of the adversary system and reasoned presentation and into such precepts as that the Court will decide only a "case or controversy" and then only such questions as are necessarily presented; to indicate the irrelevance of partisan political considerations and the existence of a limiting, albeit undefined framework of discourse; and to note that the Court is bound by law even as it makes it—and even though the system would fail if new law were evolved too slowly.

It is our common devotion to the process of decision according to law that binds together the legal profession. And it is the community's deep and common devotion to the rule of law that supports our process of constitutional decision. More than anything else it binds all of us together.

There is nothing very new in what I am trying to say. Others have said it far more effectively. I dwell upon these reflections partly because they are the deepest impressions of my six months in office, but also for two other reasons.

First, because the Supreme Court does play so large a part in our national develop- ment, because we call upon it to resolve issues which embroil it in controversy, it is important to have the country understand the Court's true nature.

Second, if my reflections hit anywhere near the mark, they suggest an important distinction. It is one thing to criticize a particular decision—or even to criticize every decision—and to seek to have the law changed by statute or later decisions. Such criticism, as I have said, is not only proper but essential. But criticism of decisions in the effort to produce a change is one thing. Encouragement to disobedience, to stalling and deliberate evasion are quite another. The essential difference between the western world and the Communist dictatorships is expressed in the ancient words of Bracton —"*Non sub homine sed sub Deo et lege*"—"Not under man but under God and Law." The rule of law depends upon voluntary acceptance. Those who disregard— or stall-off by obvious evasion—the decisions of the Court, are endangering the rule of law scarcely less than those who invite mob violence; and this is true, I think, whether the decisions be flouted by private citizens or public officials.

Similarly, one must mark the line between criticism of decisions and attacks upon the integrity of the justices and the processes of constitutional adjudication. To disregard this line, however fine it sometimes seems, and thereby to attack the rule of law, is a gross disservice to the nation.

THE BAR'S OBLIGATION

At a time when the rule of law is challenged not only all over the world but sometimes at home, surely the bar has an obligation to speak out in explanation of the process, and to bespeak compliance with law as one of the foundations of civilization. Some voices are loud and clear. Erwin Griswold has brought distinction to the Harvard Law School and Eugene Rostow to Yale by their public speeches in defense of the Court. The country would gain if the voices of the American Bar Association and individual practicing lawyers were heard more often—not simply in the glittering generalities of Law Day but in the defense of the specific application of the rule of law to controversial decisions. Surely it is the duty of lawyers to plead publicly and in their own communities for observance of the rule of law even in the case of unpopular decisions.

One who argues cases from time to time and sits in the Supreme Court day by day during both oral arguments and the delivery of opinions soon acquires both admiration and affection for the Court and all the justices. The problems with which they deal are so difficult, the number and variety of cases are so overwhelming, the implications are so far-reaching that one sits humbled by the demands upon them. That the judges are human—that some opinions seem inadequate and some decisions may be wrong—makes the experience more moving because the whole attests to the sincerity and capacities of man.

Appendix

Constitution of the United States

WE THE PEOPLE of the United States, in order to form a more perfect union, establish justice, insure domestic tranquillity, provide for the common defense, promote the general welfare, and secure the blessings of liberty to ourselves and our posterity, do ordain and establish this Constitution for the United States of America.

ARTICLE I

SECTION 1. All legislative powers herein granted shall be vested in a Congress of the United States, which shall consist of a Senate and House of Representatives.

SECTION 2. (1). The House of Representatives shall be composed of members chosen every second year by the people of the several States, and the electors in each State shall have the qualifications requisite for electors of the most numerous branch of the State legislature.

(2). No person shall be a Representative who shall not have attained to the age of twenty-five years, and been seven years a citizen of the United States, and who shall not, when elected, be an inhabitant of that State in which he shall be chosen.

(3). Representatives and direct taxes[1] shall be apportioned among the several States which may be included within this Union, according to their respective numbers, which shall be determined by adding to the whole number of free persons, including those bound to service for a term of years, and excluding Indians not taxed, three fifths of all other persons.[2] The actual enumeration shall be made within three

[1] Modified as to income taxes by the 16th Amendment.
[2] Replaced by the 14th Amendment.

years after the first meeting of the Congress of the United States, and within every
subsequent term of ten years, in such manner as they shall by law direct. The number
of Representatives shall not exceed one for every thirty thousand, but each State shall
have at least one Representative; and until such enumeration shall be made, the State
of New Hampshire shall be entitled to choose three, Massachusetts eight, Rhode Island
and Providence Plantations one, Connecticut five, New York six, New Jersey four,
Pennsylvania eight, Delaware one, Maryland six, Virginia ten, North Carolina five,
South Carolina five, and Georgia three.

(4). When vacancies happen in the representation from any State, the executive
authority thereof shall issue writs of election to fill such vacancies.

(5). The House of Representatives shall choose their Speaker and other officers;
and shall have the sole power of impeachment.

SECTION 3. (1). The Senate of the United States shall be composed of two Senators
from each State, chosen by the legislature thereof,[3] for six years; and each Senator
shall have one vote.

(2). Immediately after they shall be assembled in consequence of the first election,
they shall be divided as equally as may be into three classes. The seats of the Senators
of the first class shall be vacated at the expiration of the second year, of the second
class at the expiration of the fourth year, and of the third class at the expiration of
the sixth year, so that one third may be chosen every second year; and if vacancies
happen by resignation, or otherwise, during the recess of the legislature of any State,
the executive thereof may make temporary appointments until the next meeting of
the legislature, which[3] shall then fill such vacancies.

(3). No person shall be a Senator who shall not have attained to the age of thirty
years, and been nine years a citizen of the United States, and who shall not, when
elected, be an inhabitant of that State for which he shall be chosen.

(4). The Vice President of the United States shall be president of the Senate, but
shall have no vote, unless they be equally divided.

(5). The Senate shall choose their other officers, and also a president pro tempore,
in the absence of the Vice President, or when he shall exercise the office of President
of the United States.

(6). The Senate shall have the sole power to try all impeachments. When sitting
for that purpose, they shall be on oath or affirmation. When the President of the
United States is tried, the Chief Justice shall preside: and no person shall be convicted
without the concurrence of two thirds of the members present.

(7). Judgment in cases of impeachment shall not extend further than to removal
from office, and disqualification to hold and enjoy any office of honor, trust or profit
under the United States: but the party convicted shall nevertheless be liable and subject to indictment, trial, judgment and punishment, according to law.

SECTION 4. (1). The times, places and manner of holding elections for Senators
and Representatives, shall be prescribed in each State by the legislature thereof; but
the Congress may at any time by law make or alter such regulations, except as to the
places of choosing Senators.

[3] Modified by the 17th Amendment.

(2). The Congress shall assemble at least once in every year, and such meeting shall be on the first Monday in December, unless they shall by law appoint a different day.

SECTION 5. (1). Each House shall be the judge of the elections, returns and qualifications of its own members, and a majority of each shall constitute a quorum to do business; but a smaller number may adjourn from day to day, and may be authorized to compel the attendance of absent members, in such manner, and under such penalties as each House may provide.

(2). Each House may determine the rules of its proceedings, punish its members for disorderly behavior, and, with the concurrence of two thirds, expel a member.

(3). Each House shall keep a journal of its proceedings, and from time to time publish the same, excepting such parts as may in their judgment require secrecy; and the yeas and nays of the members of either House on any question shall, at the desire of one fifth of those present, be entered on the journal.

(4). Neither House, during the session of Congress, shall, without the consent of the other, adjourn for more than three days, nor to any other place than that in which the two Houses shall be sitting.

SECTION 6. (1). The Senators and Representatives shall receive a compensation for their services, to be ascertained by law, and paid out of the Treasury of the United States. They shall in all cases, except treason, felony and breach of the peace, be privileged from arrest during their attendance at the session of their respective Houses, and in going to and returning from the same; and for any speech of debate in either House, they shall not be questioned in any other place.

(2). No Senator or Representative shall, during the time for which he was elected, be appointed to any civil office under the authority of the United States, which shall have been created, or the emoluments whereof shall have been increased during such time; and no person holding any office under the United States, shall be a member of either House during his continuance in office.

SECTION 7. (1). All bills for raising revenue shall originate in the House of Representatives; but the Senate may propose or concur with amendments as on other bills.

(2). Every bill which shall have passed the House of Representatives and the Senate, shall, before it become a law, be presented to the President of the United States; if he approve he shall sign it, but if not he shall return it, with his objections to that House in which it shall have originated, who shall enter the objections at large on their journal, and proceed to reconsider it. If after such reconsideration two thirds of that House shall agree to pass the bill, it shall be sent, together with the objections, to the other House, by which it shall likewise be reconsidered, and if approved by two thirds of that House, it shall become a law. But in all such cases the votes of both Houses shall be determined by yeas and nays, and the names of the persons voting for and against the bill shall be entered on the journal of each House respectively. If any bill shall not be returned by the President within ten days (Sundays excepted) after it shall have been presented to him, the same shall be a law, in like manner as if he had signed it, unless the Congress by their adjournment prevent its return, in which case it shall not be a law.

(3). Every order, resolution, or vote to which the concurrence of the Senate and

House of Representatives may be necessary (except on a question of adjournment) shall be presented to the President of the United States; and before the same shall take effect, shall be approved by him, or being disapproved by him, shall be repassed by two thirds of the Senate and House of Representatives, according to the rules and limitations prescribed in the case of a bill.

SECTION 8. (1). The Congress shall have power to lay and collect taxes, duties, imposts and excises, to pay the debts and provide for the common defense and general welfare of the United States; but all duties, imposts and excises shall be uniform throughout the United States;

(2). To borrow money on the credit of the United States;

(3). To regulate commerce with foreign nations, and among the several States, and with the Indian tribes;

(4). To establish an uniform rule of naturalization, and uniform laws on the subject of bankruptcies throughout the United States;

(5). To coin money, regulate the value thereof, and of foreign coin, and fix the standard of weights and measures;

(6). To provide for the punishment of counterfeiting the securities and current coin of the United States;

(7). To establish post offices and post roads;

(8). To promote the progress of science and useful arts, by securing for limited times to authors and inventors the exclusive right to their respective writings and discoveries;

(9). To constitute tribunals inferior to the Supreme Court;

(10). To define and punish piracies and felonies committed on the high seas, and offenses against the law of nations;

(11). To declare war, grant letters of marque and reprisal, and make rules concerning captures on land and water;

(12). To raise and support armies, but no appropriation of money to that use shall be for a longer term than two years;

(13). To provide and maintain a navy;

(14). To make rules for the government and regulation of the land and naval forces;

(15). To provide for calling forth the militia to execute the laws of the Union, suppress insurrections and repel invasions;

(16). To provide for organizing, arming, and disciplining the militia, and for governing such part of them as may be employed in the service of the United States, reserving to the States respectively, the appointment of the officers, and the authority of training the militia according to the discipline prescribed by Congress;

(17). To exercise exclusive legislation in all cases whatsoever, over such district (not exceeding ten miles square) as may, by cession of particular States, and the acceptance of Congress, become the seat of the government of the United States, and to exercise like authority over all places purchased by the consent of the legislature of the State in which the same shall be, for the erection of forts, magazines, arsenals, dockyards, and other needful buildings; and

(18). To make all laws which shall be necessary and proper for carrying into execution the foregoing powers, and all other powers vested by this Constitution in the government of the United States, or in any department or officer thereof.

SECTION 9. (1). The migration or importation of such persons as any of the States now existing shall think proper to admit, shall not be prohibited by the Congress prior to the year one thousand eight hundred and eight, but a tax or duty may be imposed on such importation, not exceeding ten dollars for each person.

(2). The privilege of the writ of habeas corpus shall not be suspended, unless when in cases of rebellion or invasion the public safety may require it.

(3). No bill of attainder or ex post facto law shall be passed.

(4). No capitation, or other direct, tax shall be laid, unless in proportion to the census or enumeration herein before directed to be taken.[4]

(5). No tax or duty shall be laid on articles exported from any State.

(6). No preference shall be given by any regulation of commerce or revenue to the ports of one State over those of another: nor shall vessels bound to, or from, one State, be obliged to enter, clear, or pay duties in another.

(7). No money shall be drawn from the Treasury, but in consequence of appropriations made by law; and a regular statement and account of the receipts and expenditures of all public money shall be published from time to time.

(8). No title of nobility shall be granted by the United States: and no person holding any office of profit or trust under them, shall, without the consent of the Congress, accept of any present, emolument, office, or title, of any kind whatever, from any kind, prince, or foreign State.

SECTION 10. (1). No State shall enter into any treaty, alliance, or confederation; grant letters of marque and reprisal; coin money; emit bills of credit; make anything but gold and silver coin a tender in payment of debts; pass any bill of attainder, ex post facto law, or law impairing the obligation of contracts, or grant any title of nobility.

(2). No State shall, without the consent of the Congress, lay any imposts or duties on imports or exports, except what may be absolutely necessary for executing its inspection laws; and the net produce of all duties and imposts, laid by any State on imports or exports, shall be for the use of the Treasury of the United States; and all laws be subject to the revision and control of the Congress.

(3). No State shall, without the consent of Congress, lay any duty of tonnage, keep troops, or ships of war in time of peace, enter into any agreement or compact with another State, or with a foreign power, or engage in war, unless actually invaded, or in such imminent danger as will not admit of delay.

ARTICLE II

SECTION 1. (1). The executive power shall be vested in a President of the United States of America. He shall hold his office during the term of four years, and, together with the Vice President, chosen for the same term, be elected, as follows:

(2). Each State shall appoint, in such manner as the legislature thereof may direct,

[4] Modified by the 16th Amendment.

a number of electors, equal to the whole number of Senators and Representatives to which the State may be entitled in the Congress: but no Senator or Representative, or person holding an office of trust or profit under the United States, shall be appointed an elector.

The electors[5] shall meet in their respective States, and vote by ballot for two persons, of whom one at least shall not be an inhabitant of the same State with themselves. And they shall make a list of all the persons voted for, and of the number of votes for each; which list they shall sign and certify, and transmit sealed to the seat of the government of the United States, directed to the president of the Senate. The president of the Senate shall, in the presence of the Senate and House of Representatives, open all the certificates, and the votes shall then be counted. The person having the greatest number of votes shall be the President, if such number be a majority of the whole number of electors appointed; and if there be more than one who have such majority, and have an equal number of votes, then the House of Representatives shall immediately choose by ballot one of them for President; and if no person have a majority, then from the five highest on the list the said House shall in like manner choose the President. But in choosing the President, the votes shall be taken by States, the representation from each State having one vote; a quorum for this purpose shall consist of a member or members from two thirds of the States, and a majority of all the States shall be necessary to a choice. In every case, after the choice of the President, the person having the greatest number of votes of the electors shall be the Vice President. But if there should remain two or more who have equal votes, the Senate shall choose from them by ballot the Vice President.

(3). The Congress may determine the time of choosing the electors, and the day on which they shall give their votes; which day shall be the same throughout the United States.

(4). No person except a natural born citizen, or a citizen of the United States, at the time of the adoption of this Constitution, shall be eligible to the office of President; neither shall any person be eligible to that office who shall not have attained to the age of thirty five years, and been fourteen years a resident within the United States.

(5). In the case of the removal of the President from office, or of his death, resignation, or inability to discharge the powers and duties of the said office, the same shall devolve on the Vice President, and the Congress may by law provide for the case of removal, death, resignation, or inability, both of the President and Vice President, declaring what officer shall then act as President, and such officer shall act accordingly, until the disability be removed, or a President shall be elected.

(6). The President shall, at stated times, receive for his services, a compensation, which shall neither be increased nor diminished during the period for which he shall have been elected, and he shall not receive within that period any other emolument from the United States, or any of them.

(7). Before he enter on the execution of his office, he shall take the following oath

[5] This paragraph was replaced in 1804 by the 12th Amendment.

or affirmation:—"I do solemnly swear (or affirm) that I will faithfully execute the office of President of the United States, and will to the best of my ability, preserve, protect and defend the Constitution of the United States."

SECTION 2. (1). The President shall be commander in chief of the army and navy of the United States, and of the militia of the several States, when called into the actual service of the United States; he may require the opinion, in writing, of the principal officer in each of the executive departments, upon any subject relating to the duties of their respective offices, and he shall have power to grant reprieves and pardons for offenses against the United States, except in cases of impeachment.

(2). He shall have power, by and with the advice and consent of the Senate, to make treaties, provided two thirds of the Senators present concur; and he shall nominate, and by and with the advice and consent of the Senate, shall appoint ambassadors, other public ministers and consuls, judges of the Supreme Court, and all other officers of the United States, whose appointments are not herein otherwise provided for, and which shall be established by law: but the Congress may by law vest the appointment of such inferior officers, as they think proper, in the President alone, in the courts of law, or in the heads of departments.

(3). The President shall have power to fill up all vacancies that may happen during the recess of the Senate, by granting commissions which shall expire at the end of their next session.

SECTION 3. He shall from time to time give to the Congress information of the state of the Union, and recommend to their consideration such measures as he shall judge necessary and expedient; he may, on extraordinary occasions, convene both Houses, or either of them, and in case of disagreement between them, with respect to the time of adjournment, he may adjourn them to such time as he shall think proper; he shall receive ambassadors and other public ministers; he shall take care that the laws be faithfully executed, and shall commission all the officers of the United States.

SECTION 4. The President, Vice President and all civil officers of the United States, shall be removed from office on impeachment for, and conviction of, treason, bribery, or other high crimes and misdemeanors.

ARTICLE III

SECTION 1. The judicial power of the United States, shall be vested in one Supreme Court, and in such inferior courts as the Congress may from time to time ordain and establish. The judges, both of the Supreme and inferior courts, shall hold their offices during good behavior, and shall, at stated times, receive for their services, a compensation, which shall not be diminished during their continuance in office.

SECTION 2. (1). The judicial power shall extend to all cases, in law and equity, arising under this Constitution, the laws of the United States, and treaties made, or which shall be made, under their authority—to all cases affecting ambassadors, other public ministers and consuls;—to all cases of admiralty and maritime jurisdiction;—to controversies to which the United States shall be a party;—to controversies between two or more States;—between a State and citizens of another State;[6]—between citizens

[6] Restricted by the 11th Amendment.

of different States,—between citizens of the same State claiming lands under grants of different States, and between a State, or the citizens thereof, and foreign States, citizens or subjects.

(2). In all cases affecting ambassadors, other public ministers and consuls, and those in which a State shall be party, the Supreme Court shall have original jurisdiction. In all the other cases before mentioned, the Supreme Court shall have appellate jurisdiction, both as to law and fact, with such exceptions, and under such regulations as the Congress shall make.

(3). The trial of all crimes, except in cases of impeachment, shall be by jury; and such trial shall be held in the State where the said crimes shall have been committed; but when not committed within any State, the trial shall be at such place or places as the Congress may by law have directed.

SECTION 3. (1). Treason against the United States, shall consist only in levying war against them, or in adhering to their enemies, giving them aid and comfort. No person shall be convicted of treason unless on the testimony of two witnesses to the same overt act, or on confession in open court.

(2). The Congress shall have power to declare the punishment of treason, but no attainder of treason shall work corruption of blood, or forfeiture except during the life of the person attainted.

ARTICLE IV

SECTION 1. Full faith and credit shall be given in each State to the public acts, records, and judicial proceedings of every other State. And the Congress may by general laws prescribe the manner in which such acts, records and proceedings shall be proved, and the effect thereof.

SECTION 2. (1). The citizens of each State shall be entitled to all privileges and immunities of citizens in the several States.

(2). A person charged in any State with treason, felony, or other crime, who shall flee from justice, and be found in another State, shall on demand of the executive authority of the State from which he fled, be delivered up, to be removed to the State having jurisdiction of the crime.

(3). No person held to service or labor in one State, under the laws thereof, escaping into another, shall, in consequence of any law or regulation therein, be discharged from such service or labor, but shall be delivered up on claim of the party to whom such service or labor may be due.

SECTION 3. (1). New States may be admitted by the Congress into this Union; but no new State shall be formed or erected within the jurisdiction of any other State; nor any State be formed by the junction of two or more States, or parts of States, without the consent of the legislatures of the States concerned as well as of the Congress.

(2). The Congress shall have power to dispose of and make all needful rules and regulations respecting the territory or other property belonging to the United States; and nothing in this Constitution shall be so construed as to prejudice any claims of the United States, or of any particular State.

SECTION 4. The United States shall guarantee to every State in this Union a republican form of government, and shall protect each of them against invasion; and on application of the legislature, or of the executive (when the legislature cannot be convened) against domestic violence.

ARTICLE V

The Congress, whenever two thirds of both Houses shall deem it necessary, shall propose amendments to this Constitution, or, on the application of the legislatures of two thirds of the several States, shall call a convention for proposing amendments, which, in either case, shall be valid to all intents and purposes, as part of this Constitution, when ratified by the legislatures of three fourths of the several States, or by conventions in three fourths thereof, as the one or the other mode of ratification may be proposed by the Congress; Provided that no amendment which may be made prior to the year one thousand eight hundred and eight shall in any manner affect the first and fourth clauses in the ninth section of the first article; and that no State, without its consent, shall be deprived of its equal suffrage in the Senate.

ARTICLE VI

SECTION 1. All debts contracted and engagements entered into, before the adoption of this Constitution, shall be as valid against the United States under this Constitution, as under the Confederation.

SECTION 2. This Constitution, and the laws of the United States which shall be made in pursuance thereof; and all treaties made, or which shall be made, under the authority of the United States, shall be the supreme law of the land; and the judges in every State shall be bound thereby, anything in the constitution or laws of any State to the contrary notwithstanding.

SECTION 3. The Senators and Representatives before mentioned, and the members of the several State legislatures, and all executive and judicial officers, both of the United States and of the several States, shall be bound by oath or affirmation to support this Constitution; but no religious test shall ever be required as a qualification to any office or public trust under the United States.

ARTICLE VII

The ratification of the conventions of nine States, shall be sufficient for the establishment of this Constitution between the States so ratifying the same.

Done in Convention by the unanimous consent of the States present the seventeenth day of September in the year of our Lord one thousand seven hundred and eighty-seven, and of the independence of the United States of America the twelfth. In witness whereof we have hereunto subscribed our names.

Go WASHINGTON—

Presidt. and Deputy from Virginia

Articles in addition to and amendment of the Constitution of the United States of America, proposed by Congress, and ratified by the legislatures of the several States, pursuant to the fifth article of the original Constitution.

ARTICLE I[7]

Congress shall make no law respecting an establishment of religion, or prohibiting the free exercise thereof; or abridging the freedom of speech, or of the press; or the right of the people peaceably to assemble, and to petition the government for a redress of grievances.

ARTICLE II

A well regulated militia, being necessary to the security of a free State, the right of the people to keep and bear arms, shall not be infringed.

ARTICLE III

No soldier shall, in time of peace be quartered in any house, without the consent of the owner, nor in time of war, but in a manner to be prescribed by law.

ARTICLE IV

The right of the people to be secure in their persons, houses, papers, and effects, against unreasonable searches and seizures, shall not be violated, and no warrants shall issue, but upon probable cause, supported by oath or affirmation, and particularly describing the place to be searched, and the persons or things to be seized.

ARTICLE V

No person shall be held to answer for a capital, or otherwise infamous crime, unless on a presentment or indictment of a grand jury, except in cases arising in the land or naval forces, or in the militia, when in actual service in time of war or public danger; nor shall any person be subject for the same offense to be twice put in jeopardy of life or limb; nor shall be compelled in any criminal case to be a witness against himself, nor be deprived of life, liberty, or property, without due process of law; nor shall private property be taken for public use, without just compensation.

ARTICLE VI

In all criminal prosecutions the accused shall enjoy the right to a speedy and public trial, by an impartial jury of the State and district wherein the crime shall have been committed, which district shall have been previously ascertained by law, and to be

[7] The first ten Amendments were adopted in 1791.

informed of the nature and cause of the accusation; to be confronted with the witnesses against him; to have compulsory process for obtaining witnesses in his favor, and to have the assistance of counsel for his defense.

ARTICLE VII

In suits at common law, where the value in controversy shall exceed twenty dollars, the right of trial by jury shall be preserved, and no fact tried by a jury shall be otherwise reexamined in any court of the United States, than according to the rules of the common law.

ARTICLE VIII

Excessive bail shall not be required, nor excessive fines imposed, nor cruel and unusual punishments inflicted.

ARTICLE IX

The enumeration in the Constitution, of certain rights, shall not be construed to deny or disparage others retained by the people.

ARTICLE X

The powers not delegated to the United States by the Constitution, nor prohibited by it to the States, are reserved to the States respectively, or to the people.

ARTICLE XI[8]

The judicial power of the United States shall not be construed to extend to any suit in law or equity, commenced or prosecuted against one of the United States by citizens of another State, or by citizens or subjects of any foreign State.

ARTICLE XII[9]

The electors shall meet in their respective States and vote by ballot for President and Vice-President, one of whom, at least, shall not be an inhabitant of the same State with themselves; they shall name in their ballots the person voted for as President, and in distinct ballots the person voted for as Vice-President, and they shall make distinct lists of all persons voted for as President, and of all persons voted for as Vice-President, and of the number of votes for each, which lists they shall sign and certify, and transmit sealed to the seat of the government of the United States, directed to the president of the Senate;—The president of the Senate shall, in the presence of the Senate and House of Representatives, open all the certificates and the votes shall then be counted;—The person having the greatest number of votes for

[8] Adopted in 1798.
[9] Adopted in 1804.

President, shall be the President, if such number be a majority of the whole number of electors appointed; and if no person have such majority, then from the persons having the highest numbers not exceeding three on the list of those voted for as President, the House of Representatives shall choose immediately, by ballot, the President. But in choosing the President, the votes shall be taken by States, the representation from each State having one vote; a quorum for this purpose shall consist of a member or members from two thirds of the States, and a majority of all the States shall be necessary to a choice. And if the House of Representatives shall not choose a President whenever the right of choice shall devolve upon them, before the fourth day of March next following, then the Vice-President shall act as President, as in the case of death or other constitutional disability of the President.—The person having the greatest number of votes as Vice-President, shall be the Vice-President, if such number be a majority of the whole number of electors appointed, and if no person have a majority, then from the two highest numbers on the list, the Senate shall choose the Vice-President; a quorum for the purpose shall consist of two thirds of the whole number of Senators, and a majority of the whole number shall be necessary to a choice. But no person constitutionally ineligible to the office of President shall be eligible to that of Vice-President of the United States.

ARTICLE XIII[10]

SECTION 1. Neither slavery nor involuntary servitude, except as a punishment for crime whereof the party shall have been duly convicted, shall exist within the United States, or any place subject to their jurisdiction.

SECTION 2. Congress shall have power to enforce this article by appropriate legislation.

ARTICLE XIV[11]

SECTION 1. All persons born or naturalized in the United States, and subject to the jurisdiction thereof, are citizens of the United States and of the State wherein they reside. No State shall make or enforce any law which shall abridge the privileges or immunities of citizens of the United States; nor shall any State deprive any person of life, liberty, or property, without due process of law; nor deny to any person within its jurisdiction the equal protection of the laws.

SECTION 2. Representatives shall be apportioned among the several States according to their respective numbers, counting the whole number of persons in each State, excluding Indians not taxed. But when the right to vote at any election for the choice of electors for President and Vice President of the United States, Representatives in Congress, the executive and judicial offices of a State, or the members of the legislature thereof, is denied to any of the male inhabitants of such State, being twenty-one years of age, and citizens of the United States, or in any way abridged, except for participation in rebellion, or other crime, the basis of representation therein shall be reduced in the proportion which the number of such male citizens shall bear to the

[10] Adopted in 1865.
[11] Adopted in 1868.

whole number of male citizens twenty-one years of age in such State.

SECTION 3. No person shall be a Senator or Representative in Congress, or elector of President and Vice President, or hold any office, civil or military, under the United States, or under any State, who, having previously taken an oath, as a member of Congress, or as an officer of the United States, or as a member of any State legislature, or as an executive or judicial officer of any State, to support the Constitution of the United States, shall have engaged in insurrection or rebellion against the same, or given aid or comfort to the enemies thereof. But Congress may by a vote of two thirds of each House, remove such disability.

SECTION 4. The validity of the public debt of the United States, authorized by law, including debts incurred for payment of pensions and bounties for services in suppressing insurrection or rebellion, shall not be questioned. But neither the United States nor any State shall assume or pay any debt or obligation incurred in aid of insurrection or rebellion against the United States, or any claim for the loss or emancipation of any slave; but all such debts, obligations and claims shall be held illegal and void.

SECTION 5. The Congress shall have power to enforce, by appropriate legislation, the provisions of this article.

ARTICLE XV[12]

SECTION 1. The right of citizens of the United States to vote shall not be denied or abridged by the United States or by any State on account of race, color, or previous condition of servitude.

SECTION 2. The Congress shall have power to enforce this article by appropriate legislation.

ARTICLE XVI[13]

The Congress shall have power to lay and collect taxes on incomes, from whatever source derived, without apportionment among the several States and without regard to any census or enumeration.

ARTICLE XVII[13]

The Senate of the United States shall be composed of two Senators from each State, elected by the people thereof, for six years; and each Senator shall have one vote. The electors in each State shall have the qualifications requisite for electors of the most numerous branch of the State legislatures.

When vacancies happen in the representation of any State in the Senate, the executive authority of such State shall issue writs of election to fill such vacancies: *Provided,* That the legislature of any State may empower the executive thereof to make temporary appointments until the people fill the vacancies by election as the legislature may direct.

This amendment shall not be so construed as to affect the election or term of any Senator chosen before it becomes valid as part of the Constitution.

[12] Adopted in 1870.
[13] Adopted in 1913.

ARTICLE XVIII[14]

SECTION 1. After one year from the ratification of this article the manufacture, sale, or transportation of intoxicating liquors within, the importation thereof into, or the exportation thereof from the United States and all territory subject to the jurisdiction thereof for beverage purposes is hereby prohibited.

SECTION 2. The Congress and the several States shall have concurrent power to enforce this article by appropriate legislation.

SECTION 3. This article shall be inoperative unless it shall have been ratified as an amendment to the Constitution by the legislatures of the several States, as provided in the Constitution, within seven years from the date of the submission hereof to the States by the Congress.

ARTICLE XIX[15]

The right of citizens of the United States to vote shall not be denied or abridged by the United States or by any State on account of sex.

The Congress shall have power to enforce this article by appropriate legislation.

ARTICLE XX[16]

SECTION 1. The terms of the President and Vice President shall end at noon on the 20th day of January, and the terms of Senators and Representatives at noon on the 3rd day of January, of the years in which such terms would have ended if this article had not been ratified; and the terms of their successors shall then begin.

SECTION 2. The Congress shall assemble at least once in every year, and such meeting shall begin at noon on the 3rd day of January, unless they shall by law appoint a different day.

SECTION 3. If, at the time fixed for the beginning of the term of the President, the President elect shall have died, the Vice President elect shall become President. If a President shall not have been chosen before the time fixed for the beginning of his term, or if the President elect shall have failed to qualify, then the Vice President elect shall act as President until a President shall have qualified; and the Congress may by law provide for the case wherein neither a President elect nor a Vice President elect shall have qualified, declaring who shall then act as President, or the manner in which one who is to act shall be selected, and such person shall act accordingly until a President or Vice President shall have qualified.

SECTION 4. The Congress may by law provide for the case of the death of any of the persons from whom the House of Representatives may choose a President whenever the right of choice shall have devolved upon them, and for the case of the death of any of the persons from whom the Senate may choose a Vice President whenever the right of choice shall have devolved upon them.

SECTION 5. Sections 1 and 2 shall take effect on the 15th day of October following the ratification of this article.

[14] Adopted in 1919. Repealed by Article XXI.
[15] Adopted in 1920.
[16] Adopted in 1933.

section 6. This article shall be inoperative unless it shall have been ratified as an amendment to the Constitution by the legislatures of three fourths of the several States within seven years from the date of its submission.

ARTICLE XXI[17]

section 1. The Eighteenth Article of Amendment to the Constitution of the United States is hereby repealed.

section 2. The transportation or importation into any State, Territory or Possession of the United States for delivery or use therein of intoxicating liquors in violation of the laws thereof is hereby prohibited.

section 3. This article shall be inoperative unless it shall have been ratified as an amendment to the Constitution by conventions in the several States, as provided in the Constitution, within seven years from the date of submission hereof to the States by the Congress.

ARTICLE XXII[18]

section 1. No person shall be elected to the office of the President more than twice, and no person who has held the office of President, or acted as President, for more than two years of a term to which some other person was elected President shall be elected to the office of the President more than once. But this Article shall not apply to any person holding the office of President when this Article was proposed by the Congress, and shall not prevent any person who may be holding the office of President, or acting as President, during the term within which this Article becomes operative from holding the office of President or acting as President during the remainder of such term.

section 2. This article shall be inoperative unless it shall have been ratified as an amendment to the Constitution by the legislatures of three-fourths of the several States within seven years from the date of its submission to the States by the Congress.

[17] Adopted in 1933.
[18] Adopted in 1951.

Index

Printed in U.S.A.